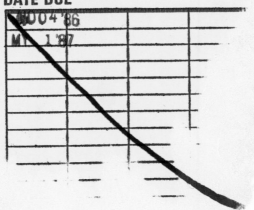

Controversies of State and Local Political Systems

MAVIS MANN REEVES
PARRIS N. GLENDENING
University of Maryland

Boston: Allyn and Bacon, Inc.

Library of Congress catalog card number: 75–171939

Contents

Preface

The 1960s were years of growing controversy, conflict, and fear about the future of the American nation. As one reflects on the turbulent sixties, one becomes aware that students today have relatively little interest in the formal study of state and local political systems. One reason is the approach that is generally employed in such study—structural, formalistic, and dry. However, the study of the interaction currently taking place at the state and local level can be exciting, interesting, and meaningful. This gives a tripartite foundation for this book: controversy, relevance, and recency.

Controversy

Rather than parallel the organization of the typical state and local government text—i.e., a chapter on the legislature, a chapter on the executive, a chapter on the courts, and so on—this collection concentrates on the *controversies* of state and local political systems. Each chapter presents opposing views of the major issues facing state and local governments. The following questions, then, become the focal points: Is the American system of intergovernmental relations basically one of conflict or cooperation? Is revenue sharing the answer to the financial problems of state and local governments? Should the Supreme Court's reapportionment decisions be reversed by constitutional amendment? Do we need metropolitan government? Why have the voters consistently opposed the establishment of metropolitan governments? What are the causes of urban violence? How do the states and localities deal with such violence?

No final answers are given. Juxtaposition of different answers and perspectives provides the basis for discussion, analysis, and individual decision-making.

Relevance

Concentration on major issues of the 1960s and 1970s should make the study of state and local government much more relevant than the traditional focus. It has become increasingly clear that the traditional subjects of constitutional revision, judicial reform, council-manager systems have only limited importance for today's college students. The topics of equal representation, politics of metropolitan reorganization, urban riots, decentralization, urban redevelopment, governmental responsiveness, and so forth, will be obviously and immediately relevant to students.

Recency

More than half of the selections were written after 1967. This is particularly important when one considers the tremendous advances made in the study of state and local political systems in recent years, such as the research of Ira Sharkansky, to name only one. In addition, many of the subjects of study are of recent origin—riots, for example.

The editors did not, of course, discard material merely because of publication dates. We have included, for example, Harold Laski's classic critique of the federal system (1939), the excellent debate by Roger Baldwin and Eliot Kaplan on collective bargaining by public employees (1941), and Edward C. Banfield's pertinent comments on the politics of metropolitan reorganization (1957).

We are grateful to authors and publishers who granted us permission to reprint their material. Further, we owe a very deep note of thanks to Louise R. Jung who performed so brilliantly and untiredly in assisting in the preparation of this manuscript, and to Ben F. Reeves and Conley H. Dillon who provided much useful editorial assistance. We also thank John C. Bollens of the University of California at Los Angeles,

David Booth of the University of Massachusetts, Harvey
Boulay of Boston University, Daniel R. Grant of Ouachita
Baptist University, and Henry J. Schmandt of the University
of Wisconsin–Milwaukee for their helpful comments and
suggestions during the preparation of this anthology which
notably improved its quality.

It is traditional to note that the editors accept the full
responsibility and blame for the book. We do so readily; this
is as much because no one else wished to share the
responsibility or blame as for any other reason.

M.M.R.
P.N.G.

Introduction

State and local political systems are the primary arenas for resolution of political conflict. Because they do more, spend more, and regulate more in the domestic realm than does the federal government, they are the centers of most political controversies in the United States. By controversies we mean the clashes of opinions in the realm of public policy—disputes over what should be done, if anything, and how.

Controversy results from differences among individuals. Variations in occupation, social status, education, religion, ethnic background, experience, age, life styles, and other things are the basis of disagreements. These contribute to different perspectives from which individuals view a public issue and to varying concepts of the "public interest." Opposing ideas and diverse interests exist in almost every phase of public policy. Consensus is rare. As long as human beings differ, controversy will be with us. And so will politics, for politics consists in the activities by which people try to further their points of view on public issues. These activities run the gamut from reasoned discussion and voting to riot and bombings, but the intended result is the same.

The articles in this book emphasize the controversies important to state and local governments, rather than the administration of programs. It is not that administration is unimportant; rather, it cannot be separated from politics. The forces operating to determine public policy questions before the legislature also influence administrative actions. And administrative decisions may have grave political consequences.

None of the controversies presented in this anthology exist in isolation. In the heterogeneous society of the United States, many conflicts interrelate with other conflicts and these interrelationships generate important political activity.

Sometimes, in studying political interactions, it is useful to isolate one issue in order to understand its ramifications, and that is how controversies are presented in this book. Each has its own arena, its actors, and its supporting interests. For example, apportionment conflicts are centered in the state legislatures and the courts. The state legislature determines the districts from which its own members and those of the United States House of Representatives are selected, and it may have a determining voice in setting the basis of selection for local councils or boards. The courts have final authority over the fairness of representation arrangements. Occasionally, in recent years, courts have set district lines.

The actors involved in an apportionment controversy are citizens and public officials of cities and suburbs trying to increase their legislative membership. Or they could be people from areas that might suffer a loss if urban representation is increased. Supporting interests include those who would gain or lose if the political balance changes. Some of the interests involved in a state representation dispute might be:

1. A chamber of commerce concerned with business interests of the city;
2. Urban communications media and other urban-oriented interest groups;
3. The Farm Bureau Federation seeking to prevent loss of rural power and to preserve a climate favorable to agriculture;
4. County officials and their organizations, who may be divided in the dispute depending upon the effect of the proposed reapportionment on one or more counties;
5. Public-advocacy groups, such as the League of Women Voters, concerned with fair representation of every citizen.

As complicated as this one controversy may be in isolation, it is simple compared to the complex interactions created when it is placed in the context of other conflicts occurring at the same time. A plethora of controversies stimulates competition among various disputants for public attention and resources and, consequently, dilutes attention and divides resources. At any given time, the political system may focus on one conflict. When this happens, participants in other controversies strive to regain public attention.

Each conflict and its resolution affect all other conflicts. Thus, apportionment affects state tax levies and how the taxes are spent. This may set up pressures which increase or decrease the likelihood of urban violence, which affects urban renewal, and so on. But more than a chain reaction is established; the apportionment controversy's effect is one of radiation. Impulses move in several directions simultaneously, then feed back to the original dispute.

Controversies selected for this anthology are intricately woven into the entire political system. They are not the only disputes engaging the attention of state and local political systems, but they are basic ones and representative of the clashes taking place in public arenas. The choice of controversies for inclusion here centered on finding disputes which manifest enduring conflicts, those which succinctly express opposing theoretical viewpoints, those which provide insight into the political process, and those which emphasize both state and local aspects of the disputes, as they are interrelated. Where possible, the conflicts presented reflect disagreements within the political science profession about these issues.

Space does not permit inclusion of all controversies that meet these standards. The editors did not include those on which people substantially agree as to problem and solution, where the controversy raged around who will pay or make the rules, as in ecology. Also omitted were conflicts whose solutions are so technical that the layman cannot be expected to master them. In this category are the technical aspects of transportation, education, housing, and pollution control alternatives. The editors tried to avoid arguments which have occupied attention for so long that their major components are in most political science textbooks: unicameral or bicameral legislatures, district or at-large representation in city councils, election or appointment of judges, for example. Nor does space permit the inclusion of the problems of racial antagonisms, control of police discretion, and other important issues.

The articles included are only a few of the many fine writings on state and local government. It is hoped they will help to stimulate better understanding of state and local political systems. To encourage the reader to explore other sources of information, five or six additional readings are suggested at the end of each section.

The readings in Part 1 deal with settings where controversies occur. The writings selected for this section were not chosen to reflect controversy themselves but to provide some background for the conflicts selected.

Basic to any discussion of American government is the place of the states in the federal system. Part 2 deals with what the federal system is and whether or not states are obsolete. Then the question of how tax monies are to be allocated between the federal government and the states is debated.

Part 3 concerns apportionment and the various arguments connected with it. Part 4 presents disagreements over metropolitan reorganization and the political implications involved. Part 5 points up the continuing controversy over where to get the money for public activities, particularly in urban areas.

Problems of urban violence are discussed in Part 6 and the question is raised whether we are going to live in a community or in the jungle that will exist if conditions provoking urban riots are not alleviated. Arguments over urban renewal in Part 7 tie into the preceding controversy on urban violence. On every urban renewal project are arguments over demolition, relocation of residents, provision of facilities to replace those eliminated, and so on. A more basic argument has developed over whether we should have urban renewal at all. While this conflict is primarily one for the central city, it has ramifications that affect other governments as well. Some of the proposed solutions necessitate state action, and many require federal funds.

Any discussion of democratic government must consider how well government operations correspond to public desires. In almost every area, the citizen's ability to control the bureaucracy is a primary question. Does the government hear? Three areas were chosen for presentation in Part 8: control of administrative discretion through an ombudsman, government decentralization to ensure more citizen control, and collective bargaining by public employees, which raises the question of whether the government can hear voices from within. In Part 9, the editors present some thoughts on the future of state and local government in the United States.

1/Controversy
in the Political-
Cultural Environment

To understand the policies and problems of a particular
political system, one must understand the environment in which
it operates. Just as environment helps determine the way
a child develops and behaves, so environmental factors help
shape the structure, behavior, and preferences of political
systems.

For individuals, environmental components make
distinctive experiences possible and give rise to political
preferences. Often one person's preferences conflict with those
of another. We select among them when we make public
policy. Life in an ethnic ghetto may produce favorable
attitudes toward welfare programs, while a suburban
"self-made" man may resent welfare, feeling that if others
worked as hard as he, they would not need assistance.
Property ownership and tenancy engender diverse attitudes on
enforcement of building codes. Religious differences lead
to conflicting opinions on abortion laws and on public support
for parochial schools. Income levels affect attitudes on the
types of taxes that should be levied.

Any state or community also has unique experiences and
attributes that set it apart from other areas. These affect
political behavior and preferences, thus are determinants of its
public policies. While the United States as a whole has a
common political culture, each state and even each local unit
is individualized by the context in which it operates. The
broad differences between North and South, East and West
come easily to mind. One does not expect government in
Texas to be the same as that in New York or Hawaii. The
progressivism of Wisconsin certainly is not reflected in
Indiana. The Mormon influence on Utah sets it apart from all

other states in some respects. The South is perhaps the most cohesive region of the country and the most distinguishable from the rest, but there are variations within it, too. In some states, such as California, political culture remains in a state of flux because of constant immigration of people from other sections of the country. And within that state, northern California's viewpoints often differ from those of the Los Angeles area.

Students of elections know that nonpartisan elections vary from city to city and, in some localities, are actually converted to partisan elections in all but name. A sheriff in one county may be a crusading law enforcement official; in an adjacent county, he may simply serve as bailiff of the court and tax collector and make no effort to enforce the law. It is easier in some states to sell whiskey, get a divorce, obtain an abortion. A few states have "right-to-work" laws, while others adopt legislation favoring labor. These differences reflect the unique political culture of each jurisdiction. The most important variables here are demographic or population characteristics, economic factors, and history and tradition.

Demographic characteristics are obvious. The distinctive life styles produced by population distribution among urban, suburban, and rural areas often result in distinctive political preferences. Composition of the population in terms of national origin, education, and age, among other things, may fashion variations. For example, ethnic background will probably bear on political participation and choice. Ethnic groups sometimes vote as blocs consistently enough to suggest that their experiences created similar preferences and values. Various components of the "new immigration"—those coming to the United States from southern and eastern Europe around the turn of the century—vote significantly less often than the Anglo-Saxon "core" society. Sometimes groups within a state or community are sufficiently heterogeneous that the friction generated by their conflicting demands molds the political system. Economic factors figure prominently in the political culture. How people make a living and what their economic level is influence their feelings and actions. Whether the predominant occupation in an area is farming, industrial labor, or government service affects the political attitudes of its population. At the same time, there is a significant correlation between income levels and voting turnout on a national basis. In general, a person with a high income is more likely to vote than one with a low income.

Historic events and traditions sometimes determine political patterns to a greater extent than demographic and economic characteristics. The Civil War set a pattern of political party preference from 1865 until at least 1932. It inspired a tradition of Democratic voting among southern states while establishing a Republican heritage in some small-farm low-income counties of the border states and upper South that exists to this day. As the result of the Russian Sputnik, national embarrassment moved education in the United States to the forefront of priorities, a position it retained until the urban riots of 1968 brought on other demands. Not all political heritage results from such explosive events. The tradition of "machine politics" in some states sustains an environment of political favoritism; in other places with a different legacy, the model is closer to that of "good government."

Because of rich variations in the makeup of population, economic bases, and historical experiences and traditions, distinctive political environments are created. From these arise state and local political systems fed by differing demands and preferences, staffed by individuals whose ideas deviate from those of their neighbors, and operating on a unique set of demographic and economic factors. Within each area, conflicting individual and group preferences ensure controversy over the proper course for public policy to take.

The readings in Part 1 are intended to provide some understanding of the factors affecting government decisions and to furnish a setting for the controversies included elsewhere in this book. James S. Coleman analyzes the setting and initiation of controversy and considers some general patterns of conflict. His article highlights the impact of such environmental factors as differences in economic structure, population shifts and heterogeneous values, and existing cleavages as the residuum of past controversy. Samuel G. Patterson is concerned with interstate variations in political culture. Mavis Mann Reeves and Parris N. Glendening discuss some recent trends and developments in state and local government that provide a background for controversy.

JAMES S. COLEMAN

The Setting and Initiation
of Controversy

Community Involvement and Controversy

Everybody knows that there are no controversies where there is
nothing to quarrel about. Yet it is often overlooked that community
disagreements are also a measure of community life. If communities
held only the physical things of existence for their members, there
would be no disagreement.

Communities differ widely in the degree to which community
life is important enough to argue about. Within large cities, for example, there is usually considerably less to involve the residents in
civic affairs than there is in a small, self-sufficient town. In a large
city, a man's work is outside his neighborhood; often his children go
to school outside that neighborhood; and in the extreme case, the
neighborhood itself is hardly distinguishable as a unit. Thus, in the
large cities, involvement in controversy is usually least widespread,[1]
often confined to a few activists.

This relationship between the degree of involvement of the
members of the community and the frequency of controversy is not
confined to communities and cities. Other organizations exhibit the
same tendencies. For example, when trade unions play an important
part in their members' lives, one finds active internal politics, with
lively factional fights, internal disputes, and challenges from the
ranks. "Business unions," on the other hand, which do no more than
carry out wage negotiations, and whose members are little involved,
are quiet, stable bureaucracies with little internal discord.[2]

Even more extreme in their bureaucracy and mass apathy are
such voluntary organizations as consumer co-operatives, automobile
clubs, professional societies, business associations, and veterans'
groups. Such organizations, of only segmental importance to their
members, seldom have membership opposition to administrative
policies or to a proposed slate of officers. Opposition, if it comes at all,
is usually from within the ranks of leaders; there is no controversy on
the membership level, merely a "circulation of elites."[3]

Because controversy goes hand-in-hand with membership participation, the recent increase in community disputes should be not

only a cause for concern about democratic processes, but at the same time an indication of a continued and perhaps reawakening interest in the local community. It may be that the movement to the suburbs, the increase in leisure time, and the consequent refocusing of life around the home and the neighborhood, have brought people back into community life, both psychologically and physically.

Kinds of events and the crises they create. Not every kind of event which deeply affects people in a community will create a conflict. Communities are beset by many kinds of crises—floods, storms, factory shutdowns, school controversies, vigilantism, political disputes, religious contention, crime waves, etc.,—which may result in many kinds of responses, including conflict.

Floods, for example, most often generate united action within a community. An extended drought, on the other hand, might well throw a community into despair; far from uniting, drought defeats, as the dust storms of the thirties defeated the most energetic families and communities of the southwest plains. Economic depression can have a similar effect. The shutdown of a steel plant in Marienthal, a small city in Austria, reduced a lively and active town to an apathetic one whose members were listless and hardly interested in the life of their community (Lazarsfeld-Jahoda and Zeisel, p. 36 ff.).

In contrast, such crises as the Supreme Court desegregation edict, for example, or the floating of a school bond, or the charge "Communist" leveled at a public official, may create real controversy and conflict.

As these examples suggest, the *type of event* helps determine whether a crisis will unite a community, defeat it, or cause controversy. A flood, as we have said, seldom divides a community; it affects all men much the same, pits them all against a common enemy. A school desegregation pronouncement, however, has diverse effects: it affects Negroes differently from whites, parents differently from people without children, prosegregationists differently from those who condemn segregation. Yet the crises are alike in that both permit action. In contrast, there arise problems for which communities have no solutions, such as the Okies' plight in the midst of drought or the Marienthalers' insoluble unemployment problem.[4]

Not only the type of event shapes the nature of the crisis; the kind of community in which it happens is equally important. The charge "subversive" against a schoolteacher will divide some communities into opposing camps, other communities will unite to protect the teacher, while still others will unite against the teacher.[5] Communities have widely different "styles of life" with which they approach problems, and these are important determinants of the course of conflict. One author (Walker, 1950, p. 26) reports that a town faced with the removal of its major plant responded actively and in a unified way, in part because "the people are self-sufficient and self-reliant, supplying most of their own needs and standing on their own feet in the face of emergencies."

Yet the response cannot be wholly explained by a "self-sufficient and self-reliant" people. Two other towns, equipped with similar independence of spirit, responded with bitter internal strife when faced with a seemingly simpler problem: the arrival of industrialization (Pope, 1942: Cressey, 1949). There are other factors, some psychological, others a matter of social organization. (In the city which successfully met a threatened plant removal the well-organized and active Chamber of Commerce was ready to meet the challenge.) In any case, numerous studies make evident that it is neither the kind of problem facing a community nor the community's characteristics which alone determines the pattern of conflict, but rather a conjunction of the two.

Events and Incidents
Which Lead to Dispute

Criteria. If the differences in events and in communities which lead toward unification, division, or defeat are closely examined, the following three criteria become evident in the development of controversy out of an event: (a) The event must touch upon an important aspect of the community members' lives[6]—education of their children, their means of livelihood, religion, taxes, or something similar. Obviously, *different* areas of life are important to different communities, to different people within a single community, and at different periods of time. Some of these differences, and their effects on community conflict, are discussed [later]. (b) The event must affect the lives of different community members differently. A tax proposal, for example, affects property-owners one way and non-property-owners another. (c) Finally, the event must be one on which the community members feel that action can be taken—not one which leaves the community helpless.

Given these three criteria, then, it is possible to say something about the events which will lead a given community to conflict, to unified action, or to demoralization. But what are some examples of conflict-producing events? A few are listed below:

1. In Northampton, Massachusetts, a controversy over fluoridation of the water supply began after the mayor appointed a commission and, following its recommendation, initiated a plan for carrying out fluoridation. Here the event which set off the controversy was the publication of a complete plan for fluorida-

tion without prior public discussion of the proposal (B. and J. Mausner, 1955).

2. In other cities (e.g., Cincinnati, Seattle, Williamstown [Massachusetts]) a similar pattern appears: controversy began *after* machinery had been set up to carry out fluoridation (Mausner, 1955, p. 39).

3. In Norwalk, Connecticut, a controversy arose over the announcement by a community organization (the VFW post) of a plan to report to the FBI the names of those persons in the community whose activities were "not related to a strong America" (Groh, 1954).

4. In Athens, Tennessee, a group of World War II veterans attempted, as a reform group, to wrest political control from the entrenched regime (White, 1947). In other southern towns similar uprisings occurred in the early postwar years (Key, 1950, pp. 201–204).

5. In a number of southern towns which underwent rapid change from rural to industrialized areas, intense industrial conflict occurred. Although the precipitating incidents differ in different cases, the event which really presaged conflict in all cases was the advent of industrialization (Cressey, 1949; Pope, 1942).

6. In Scarsdale, New York, conflict over books in the public schools began when a local citizen became disturbed over what he felt to be the domestic menace of communism, and besieged the school board with complaints against books in the school library (Shaplen, 1950).

7. The Pasadena, California conflict, which resulted in the ouster of the superintendent of schools, began ostensibly as a fight over a budget and tax assessment for the new school year. It had its real beginnings, however, soon after the superintendent arrived, in a number of small dissatisfactions with his administrative procedure, above all his inaccessibility to powerful persons in the community (Hurlburd, 1950).

8. Other school controversies are precipitated by varied kinds of incidents. Some began by accusations from local citizens that a superintendent, principal, librarian, teacher, board member, or even P.T.A. member was subversive or suspect, or that "progressive education" was being practiced. In some of these cases, the initial information came from sources outside the community, that is, from one of the right-wing organizations which keep files on persons who have been members of left-wing groups, or from the files of a state or national investigating committee. But in most cases, it appears that the initial charges arose locally and only later, if at all, did material from the outside play a part.[7]

9. Other school controversies began when a speaker with right-

wing or left-wing affiliations was invited to the community. Characteristically, heckling occurred during the speech, and the speaker's past associations were revealed in the discussion periods after the speech.[8]

10. A study of community conflict published in 1929 cited several examples of conflict arising when church-building and other activities by one church group in the community offended members of other churches (The Inquiry, 1929, p. 25, 31, 70, 81).

11. A study of abandonment of the city manager plan in four cities indicates that in each of the four, opposition to the plan was organized by a man on the fringe of the local business community who had been rebuffed in dealing with the city council. But this can hardly be called the sole precipitating incident; in all four cities, dissatisfaction had developed over the years, principally among the working class (Stene and Floro, 1953, pp. 21–39).[9]

12. In one New York town, the Republican city fathers selected the location of new water wells without going through the forms of democracy. Incensed community members held firmly to their democratic rights and an extended controversy ensued (The Inquiry, 1929, p. 60, 73).

13. In Milford, Delaware, Bryant Bowles made inflammatory speeches against desegregation and led the parents, children, and other townspeople into mass picketing. In Clinton, Tennessee, John Kaspar and Asa Carter delivered speeches which provoked a wave of violence against the integration of twelve Negro children into the Clinton high school. All three were outsiders to the communities involved (*Life*, 1954; *Southern School News*, 1956).

Internal and external sources. These and the other conflicts studied allow some generalizations about the kinds of incidents and events which set off disputes. In the first place, there is a clear distinction between disputes which arise *internally* and those which are a consequence of some *external* incident. The most completely internal include: the fluoridation controversies[10] (1, 2); the political uprising in southern towns (4); the church conflicts (10); abandonment of the city-manager plans (11); and location of the water wells (12). Not only were these incidents set off by community members themselves; the issues involved were purely local. A second group of conflicts were local in origin but fed on national issues: the Norwalk vigilantism (3); the Scarsdale and Pasadena school conflicts, and other school conflicts which centered around local school figures (6, 7, and 8). The incendiary incidents here came from sources within the community, though they did involve nationwide issues. Finally, a group of controversies must be laid primarily to external sources: industrialization in southern communities (5); conflicts resulting from the

Supreme Court desegregation ruling implemented by state policies (13); and a few of the school controversies in which persons and propaganda from the outside began the controversy (9, 13).

This, then, is one important difference in the origin of community conflicts. Some need no external issue or incident to set them off, but are generated by processes internal to the community itself. In other cases, the community is more or less at the mercy of the world outside: a national climate of opinion like the recent fear of Communist subversion, industrial expansion or depression, a national law which contravenes the community's mores such as the Supreme Court ruling. This is not to say that a community can do nothing to affect the course of such controversies once they have begun. To be sure, it is a major premise of this report that much *can* be done, whether the conflict arises internally or externally. But when the problem arises from external sources, it is, in a sense, dumped on the community's doorstep.

As one might expect, community conflicts are now more often related to national affairs than they once were. In the 1929 book on community conflict mentioned above, about four out of forty community conflicts described could be said to be externally produced. In contrast, a great many present-day community conflicts—some of those cited above are indicative—have their sources outside the community. Whether we like it or not, the community is less often the locus of important social decisions than it once was. Even though school and church policy are still local matters, and community taxes remain important, the economic fate of a community often rests in the hands of men who have never passed through town.[11] Similarly, there is a continual shrinkage of the jurisdictional areas of community-level laws by state and federal governments which find it necessary to have a consistent policy. Thus, the prospect for the future is toward an increase in the proportion of externally caused community controversies—although there are, and always will be, certain areas of social decision-making which are the province of the community or neighborhood.

The content of the issue and the area of life it affects. A second difference among the incidents which set off community disputes is in the area of life they affect. Three general areas can be roughly distinguished.

One is *economic*. Many communities have been split down the middle by economic issues. Whether a matter of livelihood (e.g., the movement of a factory to town), or the payment of taxes, or still a different issue, economic issues are likely to produce strong response.

Power or *authority* in the community constitutes a second important area of life. In the four city-manager disputes which led to abandonment of the city-manager plan, the increasing dissatisfaction with the plan had its origin in certain groups (primarily the working class) which felt in effect disenfranchised. Similarly, in the rebellion of southern veteran groups, the possibility of taking political power away from the machine led the veterans to initiate conflict. The cases are many, but the motives appear to be the same.

Nevertheless, in the struggle for power, often only a few are affected: those who stand to gain office, and those who stand to lose it. The structure of political authority often remains the same, and only those who have something at stake feel their pulses quicken as events lead to a dispute. How the rest of the community becomes involved—and, to be sure, it often does—is another matter, and one which will be treated later.

The third "area of life" is less easily defined, but may be thought of quite generally as *cultural values* or *beliefs*. The current school controversies are most often disputes between conflicting values or philosophies of education; the desegregation disputes are conflicts between two deeply felt beliefs—ingrained attitudes toward Negroes and equally ingrained attitudes toward equality of opportunity. The fluoridation plans which have generated controversy in so many towns apparently touched on values of individualism and anti-scientism in provoking the resistance which has occurred.[12] Differing values and doctrines may also be touched off by religious incidents, though these often include elements of community power and group hostility as well.

Besides these three major "areas of life," there is a fourth important basis on which people respond, deriving from attitudes toward particular *persons or groups* in the community, rather than from attitudes toward an incident, event, or policy. Existing antagonism between individuals, between clans, between ethnic groups, or between other groups in the community can lead people to take sides quickly—to say, "I'm against it because *he's* for it."

Many conflicts which appear to be centered around other issues are in fact a result of the existing hostility between two groups in the community. In such disputes, the particular issue involved can hardly be considered a unit in itself—it is only part of a continuing conflict, periodically active, the rest of the time languishing. These antagonisms are vestiges of previous disputes which often leave the community divided, and thus "load the dice" against peaceful resolution of future problems. The antagonism seems to keep the community alerted, open at any time to new dispute. Robin Williams (1947), in an excellent monograph on intergroup conflicts, shows some of the ways in which such antagonism opens the way to disruptive conflicts.

There is no suggestion intended that any given community conflict feeds on a single basis of response. On the contrary, often a conflict widens to include many bases of response. Nor is it true that a single incident which sets off a community conflict—say, a school bond proposal—receives all its response from the same source. One side may be largely involved through its economic interests in keeping taxes low; its opponents may be motivated by a particular philosophy of education. Even on the same side, there may be different bases of response for different men: some may be motivated by economic interests, some by a philosophy of education, and still others by a chance for power in the community.

Thus far our implicit approach has been something like this: an incident, event, or problem requiring solution faces a community, and meets differing responses among the members as it touches upon areas of life which act as *bases of response* to the event. These bases of response, primarily economic interests, power, and values, provide the initial dynamics for the controversy. They drive a nucleus of adherents to carry forward the dispute, to expand and intensify it until perhaps the whole community is involved. The dynamics by which this intensification occurs—or fails to occur—will be discussed in Chapter II. At this point, however, it is useful to examine variations in communities, that is, the social conditions underlying the response to one or another kind of incident.

Conditions for Controversy

Differences in economic structure. Communities differ widely in their economic systems. Some are self-contained in the sense that men both live and work there. These include towns with small and diversified industry, agricultural towns (which form an economic unit with the surrounding farmland), and one-industry towns. Others are towns in which most men (with the exception of the few merchants and others who provide the necessary community services) live but do not work. Suburban communities provide the best example. (Westchester County communities, for instance, have been called the "bedrooms of New York City.") Finally, there are towns which are largely economic service organs for nonresident groups, e.g., resort towns whose primary industries exist to serve vacationers.

Naturally, different kinds of economically related incidents arise in different kinds of towns and evoke different kinds of response. In economically self-contained towns it is economic disputes which are most common and most intense, for here economic disputes often concern men's livelihoods, not only their taxes or some other ancillary economic issue. Such disputes ordinarily begin within the plant— between workers and management—though they may be initiated by all sorts of incidents.

The diverse and often inconsequential nature of incidents which set off economic disputes suggests that the incident itself is hardly important, that there has already been a strong predisposition to controversy. As students of labor relations well know, the strength of the response is only partly based on economic interests. Often it is compounded by the antagonism generated through the day-to-day relationships of labor and management in the plant.[13] This labor-management antagonism is a special and frequent case of the inter-personal and intergroup hostility which can arise between any two groups in the community. In some agricultural towns, farmer-merchant disputes similar to the quarrels of labor and management have broken out over similarly minor precipitating incidents. The farmers' distrust of merchants, particularly of banks and bankers, parallels the workers' distrust of management. The farmers' response, based both on economic interests and personal hostility, may help a trivial incident blossom into full-fledged conflict.[14]

Thus, towns with a self-contained economy can generate a most intense response to economically related incidents, a response based in part on economic interests, and in part on the antagonism created between different parts of an economic system. Farmers and workers, neither of whom have much control over their economic destinies, are the groups in which this antagonism is most often generated. (Not all controversies originating in economically self-contained towns concern economic matters, of course. Cleavages over values—religion or "subversion"—can split such towns just as they split the suburbs.)

In towns which do not constitute an economic unit, towns where men live but do not work, this kind of division is not generated; controversies set off by economically related incidents seem to be less frequent and less intense. A man who lives in Long Island and com-mutes to work in New York will not take as the object of his economic frustrations the local merchant, businessman, or his next-door neigh-bor who works in another industry. It will be his employers, or perhaps "Wall Street financiers," but hardly others within his own community. It is true, however, that *tax* issues can be an important source of controversy in any community. It seems to be particularly important, in fact, in suburban communities where a high proportion of residents own their own homes.

The lack of economic class cleavage in many suburban towns does not imply that these towns are free from dispute. On the con-trary, a high proportion of the community conflicts receiving national publicity in recent years have arisen in suburbs of large cities. But the incidents which have provoked these controversies, and the bases of responses which have drawn men into them, have often been quite different from those which divide economic classes. These controversies have centered around differing values: educational values, political beliefs, and patriotic concerns. There are several reasons why men who live side by side in suburban communities should hold such different values. One is the great mobility these people have; another is the fact that the communities have often been settled in two or more "waves," creating "old residents" and "newcomers" who are frequently of different age groups, different ethnic groups, and live in different sections of town. Finally, if men commute to work at diverse tasks in a large city, their values may wander apart, with nothing to pull them back within a "range of tolerance." Suburbanites may live for years next door to someone with radically different views; they mind their own business until some important community decision must be made, or until someone attempts to impose his views on a community institution like the school system.

The third general economic type mentioned—service towns, particularly resort towns—are composed of "natives," a permanent, old-time group, and "outsiders," who are sometimes summer residents, sometimes year-rounders, but who in any case have come to town to rest or play, not to make a living. The responses which are touched off in these towns when an incident arises seem partly a consequence of economic resentments (for the "outsiders" are the primary customers of the "natives"), and partly a consequence of the extreme social barriers which isolate the two groups. Reports of the Peekskill riots (Rorty and Rauschenbush, 1950) show a good example of conflict in this kind of town. They indicate how isolation was in part responsible for the hostility of the town to the resort colony.

Finally, another variation in economic structure must be mentioned—the variation between towns dominated by business interests and those dominated by political authority (through control of patronage, road contracts, and other local governmental contracting). In the latter, found most often in the nonindustrialized south, the absence of industry and the dominance of politics makes concern with politics much greater, and increases the likelihood that politically related incidents will set off controversy.

Thus, towns with different economic structures differ widely in the kinds of economic controversy they generate. At the same time, it can hardly be said that one kind of controversy is specific to a particular kind of community.

Changes in time. Certain bases of responses are more important at one time than another. In the 1929 book on community conflict, nine out of forty conflicts were directly related to church matters. In the contemporary conflicts reviewed, none appears to be centered around the church (though there are, to be sure, such controversies still continuing—controversies, for example, over relocation of churches in residential areas populated largely by people of different faiths). Religion seems to be a less important value and a less frequent basis of community conflict than it once was. Few communities today, for example, are so split religiously that Baptists and Methodists feel compelled to organize separate banks in a town which can hardly support one bank! The 1929 study reports such a case (The Inquiry, p. 70).

On the other hand, certain institutions, and the values which surround them, are just as strong today as they were thirty years ago. School controversies seem just as frequent (they contributed eleven of forty community controversies in the 1929 study), if not more so.

Besides long-run value changes, which affect the frequency of certain kinds of controversies, there is perhaps an even more important time effect—short-term changes in the social climate. A national climate of fear and distrust can provide a basis of response for numerous kinds of conflicts. After World War II, fear of Communist subversion acted as a kind of exposed "nerve"; when touched by an incident involving the schools, public health, and a host of other matters, it unleashed intense response. Of the conditions which tend to generate community conflict, such temporary climates of feeling seem to be among the most important. They appear to equip people with a kind of sensitivity to things which would leave them ordinarily unmoved. Often their greatest effect is on people who have been inactive in the community; that is, they bring into the controversy those community members who customarily remain on the sidelines.

Population shifts and heterogeneous values. At some time or another, mass migration may deposit a whole new group of people into an existing community. Often, these newcomers differ from the natives in their "styles of life"; they may have different religions, different cultural backgrounds, different occupations. The resulting "community" consists of two very dissimilar parts, and unless extraordinary measures are taken to integrate them, they can remain distinct groups for as long as a hundred years. Probably the two most outstanding examples of this phenomenon are the New England villages of the nineteenth century whose native Americans faced immigrants of quite different backgrounds, and, in our time, the small, quiet, suburban villages outside large cities which are suddenly mushrooming with migrants from the city. Dissimilar as these two groups of communities are in other respects, they are alike in this; and this similarity alone means that some of the same kinds of incidents divide the towns: school appropriations, churches, taxes. Whenever a difference in values and in interests is created by the influx of new residents, it becomes a potential basis of conflicting response and sets the stage for precipitating incidents. An excellent study by Elin Anderson (1938) shows the effects of waves of immigration on one New England town; a series of articles in the New York *Times* by Harrison Salisbury

(1955) on Yonkers, New York, shows the similar effects of migration on a suburb.

Existing cleavages: the residuum of past controversy. A final difference which leads some communities to respond to an incident with conflict and allows others to pass it by is the past history of controversy in the community, which may have created mutual antagonisms or fostered unity. We repeat this because of its extreme importance in predisposing a community to respond to *any* kind of precipitating event, be it one of economic interests, of values, or of political power.

General Patterns in the Initiation of Controversy

When a well-developed theory of community conflict is constructed, it will be possible to say much more about the initiation and early stages of controversy. In particular, it will be possible to show how several elements combine to set off a controversy, just as a boy, a match, and a firecracker combine to set off an explosion. Such a theory will show the specific role that each element plays and will make explicit the *different* kinds of elements which help initiate controversy.

One crude example may indicate how valuable this could be for reducing controversy. In a number of recent school controversies (not all, by any means, but the Pasadena and Houston controversies at least), three elements seem to have been crucial in the initiation of the dispute:

(1) the existence in the community of a few extreme activists, who gain moral support, and sometimes information, leaflets, etc., from national sources; (2) the existence of a national climate of fear and suspicion concerning internal subversion; (3) the lack of close and continued relations between school administration and community organizations representing conservative as well as liberal segments of the population.

Evidence (discussed more fully later) suggests that if any one of these elements had been absent, controversy would never have begun. Thus, such controversies, in theory at least, could have been prevented in three ways, that is, through eliminating any one of the three elements.[15] Though the example is crude, it illustrates the potential value of such an approach.

Revolts against an administration: the pattern of initiation. There is one large class of conflicts which can be thought of as revolts against an administration. These disputes, which include some of the fluoridation controversies, the school disputes cited in the example above, the disputes over continuation of the city-manager plan, and many industrial disputes, are characterized by the following:

(1) *The administration in power becomes the defendant in the controversy which ensues.*

In the fluoridation controversies, this has been the town officials; in school controversies, the school administration (either the school board or the superintendent); in the disputes which led to abandonment of the city-manager plans, it has been the city-manager and usually the council as well; and in industrial disputes, the plant management.

(2) *A few active oppositionists, men who are continually in opposition, oppose the administration. These men are sometimes motivated by the hope of power, but often they are ideologically committed to a "cause."*

In the recent school controversies, these have often been men who are sincerely convinced the schools are subversive, men who are against all modern trends in education, or whose whole political philosophy is far to the right of present-day parties. Though their "causes" may differ, the men are fully dedicated.[16] In labor-management disputes, the "oppositionists" are the active and ideologically-committed union leaders who never relax in their opposition to management. Like the dedicated right-wingers in the school controversies, their opposition to the "regime" is often based on a commitment to a cause which goes far beyond the immediate content of any dispute (Pope, 1942). In the four city-manager plan abandonments (Stene and Floro, 1953), the opposition leaders were evidently frustrated men on the fringes of the power elite. Their opposition appears to have been based completely on personal hostility and a desire for power. In the fluoridation controversies, the leader seems sometimes to have been a man with a desire for power; nevertheless, the leaders often included men who had little to gain personally but whose political philosophy moved them to oppose fluoridation as an infringement of individual rights.

(3) *A large group exists—often the majority of the people—who are ordinarily inactive, acquiescent to the administration, but not actively supporting it.*

In many school controversies, this is that large segment of the community, neither very liberal nor very conservative, which take little interest or active part in school affairs. In the fluoridation episodes, the situation has been quite similar; the majority of the population is often apathetic, participating very little in community affairs. In the city-manager disputes leading to abandonment of the plans, voting statistics show that the working-class sections of town, constituting the majority of the population, were ordinarily quite apathetic, content to let the city government be elected without voting. (It was the large increase in the *number* of these working-class votes, not in their *distribution*, which accounted for the final abandonment [Stene and Floro, 1953, Chap. 6].) In labor-management disputes which became community conflicts, the workers as a whole, in contrast to their leaders, were usually apathetic.[17]

(4) *An active group exists, usually a minority of the population, who continually support administration policies, and who were responsible for putting the administration in office in the first place.*

In school controversies, this includes the P.T.A., the school board, and other laymen who take part in school-community activities. In the fluoridation and city-manager controversies, these are usually the business and professional groups in town, organized and generally active in support of administration policies. In labor-management disputes, this is anyone from foremen on up who supports management within the company, and the community organizations which usually provide support for management from the community as a whole.

(5) *The large passive group, or a part of it,* [(3) *above*] *becomes active in one of two ways:* (a) a change in the general climate of opinion, reinforced by national mass media and by current events, mobilizes certain basic values and dispositions (e.g., patriotism and resulting fear of subversion) which the passive majority has held continuously, but which have been dormant. The current events and attendant publicity act, in effect, to create a completely new atmosphere of suspicion, where values which were well accepted only a short time ago are liable to attack. In this atmosphere, the administration needs to commit only one tiny misstep and the suspicion will be directed against it; it is operating under a set of values antagonistic to those who brought it into power. (b) The administration commits a series of blunders in matters which are of considerable importance to the members of this passive majority, e.g., circumvention of democratic procedures by a city administration in setting up fluoridation plans or arbitrary exercise of power by management in industry.

Be it changes in a national climate of opinion or changes in the local climate of opinion brought on by specific acts of the administration, the effect is the same: the inactive majority is made ready for action.

(6) *The ideologically-committed, active oppositionist is now able to use this new hostile atmosphere to gain his ends.* He can now lead the large, mobilized group against the administration and its supporting minority. Seldom are his objectives and values those of the majority, but he uses them for his own purposes while they are active and in opposition to his adversary.[18]

In school controversies, for example, the majority seldom agrees with the educational or political philosophy·of the right-wing leader even when it follows him. In the fluoridation controversies, the leaders are often chiropractors and others on the fringes of the medical profession who have private grudges. In labor-management disputes, the active, ideological union leaders have left-wing political goals quite different from the immediate economic gains of their followers.

This process of initiation of controversy seems to be a very general one, accounting for many of the controversies examined in the literature. The general pattern is revolt against the group in power; the mechanisms through which the revolt occurs seem to be those above. Unfortunately, perhaps, these mechanisms suggest manipulation of the masses by "evil" opposition. But a sophisticated administration often manipulates just as effectively to prevent conflict. For example: In many southern border states, school boards, school superintendents, and city governments co-operated to bring about school integration without incidents and without community conflict. During the period of integration, residents of these communities were asked, in conjunction with a national survey of attitudes toward Negroes, whether they favored integration. Two-thirds of the white population in these areas which had quietly integrated said that they opposed integration (Hyman and Sheatsley, 1956, p. 39). Thus the school and community administration had skillfully initiated a policy—often with apparent widespread public support— which was at variance with the privately expressed attitudes of a majority of the people.

Cases which lack one of the elements. Some incipient controversies, which never really became true controversies or in which the administration was never seriously threatened, demonstrate why *each* initiating element must be present. In Scarsdale, New York, for example, dispute began when one citizen, sincerely convinced that books in the school libraries by Communists and leftists were aiding the cause of communism, attempted, first by himself, and then with the aid of a few fellow-citizens (a minister, a psychologist, a college professor, and others), to set up a watchdog committee to advise the Board of Education about books in the school library (Shaplen, 1950). After some controversy, during which the major governing organization and other organizations in town stood firmly against this committee, the Board of Education and the school superintendent repudiated all its efforts. At the next school board election, the incumbent members of the board were overwhelmingly reelected by the community. Although the attacks continued, the opposition was never able to gain concessions from the school board, and the right-wing supporters never constituted more than a tiny minority of the community. At no time was there a divided community; the administration never lost community support.

In Scarsdale, two important elements were present: a national climate of opinion and a dedicated opposition leader. But a third, the passive majority aroused against the school, was not. Scarsdale, an upper- and upper-middle-class community, has probably a higher proportion of community members active in its organizations than other towns throughout the country.[19] A close relationship existed between the community and its schools, as measured both in individual interest and in community-school organizations. Thus the formula lacked one major ingredient, the passively acquiescent majority which could be mobilized against the administration. The actively-supporting group [(4) in the schema above] was not a minority but the great majority of townspeople.

Similarly, in Denver, Colorado, two of the ingredients which created full-scale controversy in Pasadena and Houston were missing. The climate of opinion existed, but there was no avid right-wing leader to take advantage of it, though there were less radical and less dedicated oppositionists. Also, relations between the school system and the community, though not as close as those in Scarsdale, were close enough that the school's active supporters [(4) in the schema above] constituted a large segment of the Denver population.

These cases of controversy which never blossomed into successful revolt indicate the importance of each element in the genesis of controversy.

Patterns of initiation in other types of controversy. Not all community controversies develop along these lines. Port Washington, Long Island, for example, has been the scene of continual controversy between two factions—one favoring a traditional educational policy, the other a progressive one.

Desegregation controversies do not fit this pattern either; here the central issue is the conflict of *new* policy with established community beliefs. Riots like those in Cicero and Peekskill do not constitute revolt against an administration. Many other controversies, e.g., the continued disputes between new and old residents in Yonkers and other fast-growing suburbs, or the ethnic-related controversies in New England towns, are also quite different. It is clear that the pattern of initiation we have discussed holds only for a certain class of controversy; other controversies follow other patterns. It is one task of a theory of community controversy to make these patterns explicit, to show (much more precisely than we have done) how they *combine* to initiate a conflict. Such a theory would be of considerable value for the practical problems of community decision-making.

Notes

1. Controversies surrounding desegregation of schools provide a good example of this. The greatest controversies have been in small towns, such as Milford, Delaware, and Clinton, Tennessee, in which a large part of the populace has risen in arms. In contrast, Baltimore and Washington, both with a higher proportion of Negroes than Milford, accomplished desegregation with only a small amount of picketing and other opposition by parents.

See James Rorty (1954). Also, in controversies precipitated by right-wing attacks on the schools, it has been in the largest cities (Houston and Pasadena) that the critics, who constituted a minority, have succeeded in ousting the controversial person before most of the public was aroused and fought back. See David Hurlburd (1950), and the report on Houston by the National Defense Commission of the National Educational Association.

2. A recent case study of a union with an active democratic system discusses this point in detail, presenting much evidence to show that democracy in a union can hardly exist unless the occupational associations surrounding it fulfill a wide range of functions for the members. (See Lipset, Trow, and Coleman, 1956).

3. For a comprehensive study of the development of bureaucracies within organizations which were once active democracies, see Michels (1949).

4. It may be, however, that problems insoluble *within* the community can be solved by recourse to some external power. Primitives turned to magic; some Marienthalers turned to radical political movements.

5. Among the school controversies studied, all three of these responses could be detected, although neither of the extremes was met precisely. Port Washington, Long Island, where the liberal and conservative groups have often shifted control, each time by a tiny majority, is the best example of a community evenly split over school issues. The recent Scarsdale conflict comes close to being unified support of the school administration, for almost all the community organizations and leaders supported the administration, and as a climax to the conflict, a school board election drew the largest vote of confidence an incumbent board had ever received. The Houston school controversy is most nearly the other extreme of those examined. All these incidents are discussed more fully in later pages.

6. The event, of course, need not be important to all persons in the community; some controversies are carried on by only a minority of the community.

7. Controversies in Houston, Denver, and Eugene, Oregon, among others are in this class. See the report of the National Defense Commission of the National Educational Association on the Houston controversy (1953); also on Houston, "The Ebey Story," *The Nation* (1953). For Denver, see Martin (1951); for Eugene, Oregon, see Tugman (1951).

8. The Englewood, New Jersey, controversy began this way, as did at least one of the several eruptions which have marked a long period of dispute in Port Washington, Long Island. See August J. Weisner, Jr., (1951) and Louis Engel (1951).

9. This phenomenon—tensions building up through lack of daily means of redress rather than dissipating through contact and controversy— has often been presented as a cause of radicalism of labor in large plants, taking the place of the feeling of friendliness to the employer which exists in the small shops where channels to management are both informal and open.

10. In a few cases, the opponents of fluoridation utilized material distributed nationally as anti-fluoridation propaganda (see Vic Reinemer, 1955), but undoubtedly this has occurred on both sides in all fluoridation disputes, the proponents citing medical and dental authorities concerning its effectiveness, and the opponents citing evidence of its harmful effects.

11. The Depression in the thirties was the first awakening of many formerly self-sufficient communities to the fact that their economic fate was firmly tied to that of the nation as a whole. Lynd's *Middletown in Transition* (1937) portrays well the inability of the community to comprehend this, and the attendant frustrations and despair it produced.

12. This is well documented for Northampton, Massachusetts, in one of the few opinion surveys carried out on cases of community conflict. The less educated, older, more individualistic, more science-resistant citizens voted against (and defeated) the fluoridation plan. (Bernard and Judith Mausner, 1955).

13. There has been a considerable amount of work done in this area by students of industrial relations. Beginning with the Hawthorne studies in the nineteen thirties (see F. J. Roethlisberger and W. J. Dickson, 1939), and continuing to the present (see, for example, Kornhauser, Dubin, and Ross, 1954). This work has developed some fruitful insights which will be useful at various points in this study of community conflict.

14. The collection of examples of community conflict published in 1929 contains two excellent cases of this. In one case, farmers were incensed over a town decision to remove the watering trough in the center of town, although most of the farmers came to town in cars. The conflict resulted probably not over the content of the decision but because it was made without consulting the farmers. In another case, farmers rebelled when the local creamery and bank invited them to a dinner in co-operation with an agricultural expert who had been working with the farmers. The farmers' reasons went like this: "If the bank and creamery are setting us up to a dinner, they're going to get it back out of us somehow." Such statements show clearly the latent hostility of the farmers to the merchants. The Inquiry, 1929, pp. 21, 22, 28, 29.

15. Whether in actual fact any one of the three ways could be used to prevent conflict depends on what elements one controls in the situation. Since those wishing to prevent conflict in such situations are usually persons in the school administration or sympathetic to the administration, the only one of these three elements which is even partly under their control is the third—the school-community relationship. It may be, of course, that the cost, in terms of an emasculated school policy, of placating certain community interests is greater than the administration would care to pay.

16. The Scarsdale, Pasadena, Englewood, and Houston controversies best illustrate this among the school controversies examined here.

17. Exceptions to this occur when management policies are continually overbearing and provocative, or when social conditions particularly favor workers' action, e.g., among miners and longshoremen.

18. There is a parallel to this in internal union politics. In the 1930's, a small, radical, left-wing party, the Amalgamation Party, existed in the New York City printers' union. Until the printers felt the Depression, in the late 1930's, this party was composed of only a few activists, Communists or Communist sympathizers. When the economic pinch came, this party was able to use the existing climate of opinion to ride to power— upon the backs of the unemployed, so to speak. After 1940, the party again lost its following, and combined with one of the two major parties in the union. (See Lipset, Trow, and Coleman, 1956, p. 301-306.)

More generally, this seems to be the history of many small ideological parties in civil politics: to languish until the right climate of opinion arrives. This climate of opinion brings with it issues by which the small group of activists can attract a large and often heterogeneous group whose values are quite different from those of the "hard core." There are indications of this among Senator [Joseph] McCarthy's following: dispositions among the mass following were far removed from the ideological beliefs of the inner core.

19. It is a town of 14,000; the Town Club, which is the major governing body in town (as it "taps" men in the community to serve on the village board and school board) has a membership of 900.

SAMUEL C. PATTERSON

The Political Cultures
of the American States

The term "Political Culture" is not one of unambiguous content. For many social scientists *culture* remains in the exclusive and esoteric province of anthropology, where internecine warfare continues over its definition. For others, *political culture* suggests the more unfortunate qualities of national character analyses. Happily, we can extract what is useful for political analysis from both traditions without resolving the well-known definitional and analytical difficulties they present. In somewhat the same vein, certain dangers attend the comparative analysis of state politics when one departs from the usual emphasis upon parties and elections. It is possible, nonetheless, to make the case that research in state politics ought to be comparative, and that it can in important ways fruitfully be guided by the organizing notion of political culture.

I. *The Concept of Political Culture*

Political culture is a somewhat open-ended, multi-faceted, sensitizing concept. It is open-ended in the sense that a rather wide variety of cognitions, values, and emotional commitments might be included in an analysis. It is multi-faceted, or multi-dimensional, in the sense that it consists of several analytically distinct though presumably inter-related factors. Finally, it is a sensitizing concept in the sense that it directs attention to potential, or largely unexploited, political data for the purpose of enhancing knowledge about subjective orientations to politics. The concept is not a theory about politics, nor does it invoke new political phenomena. It does focus attention on the symbolic, evaluative, and cognitive responses people have to the political system, and on the relationships of these orientations to other aspects of politics.

The concept had its genesis in the seminal formulation of Almond a decade ago, and has been applied mainly in the cross-national research nurtured by the Committee on Comparative Politics of the Social Science Research Council.[1] Verba gives the most lucid

Samuel C. Patterson, "The Political Cultures of the American States," *The Journal of Politics*, vol. 30 (February 1968), 187–209. Reprinted by permission.

and thorough treatment of the concept in his essay on "Comparative Political Culture."[2] He defines it as "the system of empirical beliefs, expressive symbols, and values which defines the situation in which political action takes place."[3] By *empirical beliefs* he means the ways people perceive and interpret the nature of a political relationship. By *expressive symbols* he means the ways people feel toward political institutions and leaders; patterns of political loyalty, identification, and commitment in the political system. By *values* he means the standards used to set the general goals of the political system; standards used to evaluate political demands, processes, and products. A political culture can be characterized by relative, empirically determinable levels of consensus in the sharing among people of these beliefs, symbols, and values.

Political culture and political system. Following Easton, we suggest that subjective political orientations may be directed toward three distinctive levels of the political system: the government, the regime, and the political community. *Government* refers to those who occupy official positions, the authorities who make the binding decisions for the society. *Regime* denotes the constitutional order, the norms, and basic form of the system. *Political community* refers to the group of persons who are bound or drawn together to solve common problems, participating in a common division of labor.[4] These levels of the political system are closely interlaced, but it is possible for changes to occur at one level without corresponding changes at others.

Table 1.   Paradigm of political culture

Levels of a Political System	Elements of Political Culture		
	Empirical beliefs	Expressive symbols	Values
Government			
Regime			
Community			

Each level of the political system may be regarded as an object of orientation for elements of the political culture. Borrowing from Easton's familiar diagram, it is useful to draw a simple paradigm of political culture in terms of its major objects of orientation. Evaluations, commitments, interpretations, identifications, and loyalties may vary between government, regime, and community. These analytical distinctions have utility if for no other reason than to avoid neglect. Research on political orientations in the United States has, for instance, much more frequently focused on responses to government than on support for the regime. Even now our knowledge about empirical beliefs supportive of the regime is fragmentary.[5]

Dimensions of political culture. The integration and maintenance of political systems is heavily dependent upon adequate resolution of the problem of conflict and consensus over "basic political orientations."[6] Political culture may be said to regulate—provide limits and opportunities for—the want conversion process in a political system, and thus affect the frequency, intensity, and quality of demand input. As Easton suggests, "the values and biases of political culture will prevent many demands from ever arising."[7] By inhibiting demand input, political culture may reduce elapsed time in demand processing, and thus contribute to the effectiveness or capability of the political system in managing demand overload.

Since the input of demands on a political system is often directly related to the degree of political participation, and the political culture regulates the extent to which, and in what ways, individuals become politically involved, the importance of political culture is manifest. If the political culture facilitates wide political participation, demands for want conversion are relatively numerous and the pressures on the political leaders are great to respond to, anticipate, and represent the demands of followers. On the other hand, where participation is constricted, demands on the political elite for want conversion may be minimal, and followers may be willing to leave wide areas of otherwise public concern to the authorities.

In addition to affecting the demand input of political systems, the political culture lies across the feedback channels of the system, responding to system outputs. Orientations to system outputs—to decisions, policies, services, events, and images—may have important effects on political cohesion and stability, and on future demand inputs. Thus, the consequences of political culture are dynamic, regulating not only input demands and the system of political interactions but also influencing the conversion of system outputs into new or modified inputs.

Political integration and performance capability are partly dependent upon the supportive dimension of political identification. As Verba points out, "It is the sense of identity with the nation that legitimizes the activities of national elites and makes it possible for them to mobilize the commitment and support of their followers."[8] System identification, pride, commitment, and loyalty may be associated with political sub-systems as well as with the national entity, and a sequence or matrix of identifications may be either cleavage-tending or consensus-building. A high degree of pride, loyalty, and identification with Indiana may contribute to national unity in the particular circumstances of the United States, but identification with Quebec contributes to cleavage and system-periling disunity in Canada. Uncertainties about political identity are related to individual attributes of self-confidence and self-esteem, as well as to conflicts between parochial and national loyalties. Again, a political culture can be characterized "by the extent to which individuals identify with each other as members of the same system."[9] Ego identity and self-other attachments probably work together with system identification to constitute a cluster of intertwined dimensions of political identity. Faith in self, faith in people, and faith in the system are qualities of a political culture that enhance stability, and, in all probability, provide the best support for democratic policy.

Political style and learning. Political style is an important aspect of political culture. The term refers to the ways in which political beliefs are held and applied.[10] Verba makes an important distinction between ideological and pragmatic political styles. The ideological style "involves a deeply affective commitment to a comprehensive and explicit set of political values which covers not merely political affairs but all of life, a set of values which is hierarchical in form and often deduced from a more general set of 'first principles'."[11] The pragmatic political style "consists of an evaluation of problems in terms of their individual merits rather than in terms of some preexisting comprehensive view of reality."[12] Verba then identifies three distinctive dimensions of political belief, which can be summarized in a simple diagram (see Table 2). Both ideological and pragmatic political styles can be analyzed in terms of the receptivity, specificity, and symbolic formulation of beliefs. Thus, political beliefs may be

Table 2. Paradigm of political style*

Types of Political Style	Dimensions of Political Beliefs					
	Receptivity		Specificity		Symbolic Formulation	
	Open	Closed	Implicit	Explicit	Instrumental	Expressive
Ideological		X		X		X
Pragmatic	X		X		X	

*An X in the cells indicates the most obvious combination of style and belief.

held or expressed tentatively or rigidly, explicitly or implicitly, instrumentally or expressively. Edelman has explored political language and ritual along the expressive-instrumental dimension of political acts, identifying four distinctive styles of language: hortatory, legal, administrative, and bargaining.[13] While in the American setting a pragmatic political style reflecting open, implicit, and instrumental political beliefs is doubtless common, differences among states and regions in pragmatic-ideological styles, and in political symbolism and civility, may be very important.

Political values, beliefs, and commitments are learned from experiences with the political process or from a host of non-political experiences. Political socialization is continuous over the lifespan, although the available research indicates the great importance of childhood experiences and the impact of the political values of primary groups. Where the socialization process results in disparities between what is learned in childhood and the experiences of adult contact with the political process, the political system suffers some strain. In a society, variations in political socialization may occur in terms of the content—the politico-cultural values—learned, and in terms of the relative gaps between pre-adult and adult experiences when, for example, the nature of political processes vary.

II.   American Political Culture

The American political culture has been characterized as allegiant, participant, and civic.[14] Americans are relatively highly exposed to and involved in politics, have a relatively potent sense of civic competence, and tend to have a high degree of pride in and attachment to the political system. Substantial proportions of the population exhibit positive orientations to the national government, and attitudes toward the national government show little change across ethnic, racial, or other group boundaries.[15]

Basic American political beliefs are homogeneous, and can be characterized in a general way as liberal in the Lockian sense.[16] Following Mitchell, we can summarize the major theme associated with the American political belief system:[17]

—Political action should be minimized, and allocations of values should be dependent chiefly on private action.
—Political power is tangible and limited in quantity, and tends to be evil.
—To be legitimate, political authority and power must be rational and legal.
—The duties of citizenship are distinct from the more general duties of social life.
—Americans exhibit ambivalent attitudes toward compromise.
—Public office is a public trust, and political action should be taken only in the public interest.
—Politics tends to be thought of as a game.
—Political interpretations and assessments tend to be moralistic.
—Political problems can be resolved by intelligence, good will, and hard work.

If these attributes roughly characterize the basic American belief system, it must be noted that they are not universally accepted. Under the stress of national crisis, civic obligation in America has often been converted into extreme insecurity about the political loyalty of others, as can best be illustrated by McCarthyism.[18] When distrust of politics and ambivalence about compromise get converted into conspiratorial interpretations of the most extreme sort, we observe the "paranoid style" in American politics.[19] As Hofstadter and others have pointed out, these elements of the American belief system are not new, extending from the domestic panic over the allegedly subversive activities of Weishaupt's Illuminati in the late eighteenth century to the contemporary political style of Robert Welsh and his followers. Finally, particularistic intolerance with respect to race and denials of political equality, most notable in the Southern states, has for over a hundred years constituted an important source of stress in the political system.

III. Interstate Variations in Political Culture

The notion of interstate variations in political culture within the American political system is intuitively attractive. The states are political sub-systems which, in all probability, crucially affect the persistence of the national political system. Obviously, the states are highly influenced by national policy, and politics in the United States has become increasingly nationalized. Yet, the states can be treated for analytical purposes as relatively independent political systems with political cultures at least somewhat distinctive to themselves.

We have very little empirical data on the characteristics of political culture within American states. That there are differences seems obvious, and these have been noted by a number of observers of American politics. A variety of differences were noted by John Gunther from his rich impressionistic experience with the practice of politics across the country. He thought "Oregon and Washington are twins except as to character," but "nowhere else in the country can the extraordinary tenacity of state characteristics be better observed, the deep-rooted instinct of a state to grow its own way without regard to its neighbor."[20] Key found significant differences between two Southern states.[21]

> The political distance from Virginia to Alabama must be measured in light years. Virginian deference to the upper orders and the Byrd machine's restraint of popular aberrations give Virginia politics a tone and a reality radically different from the tumult of Alabama. There a wholesome contempt for authority and a spirit of rebellion akin to that of the Populist days resist the efforts of the

big farmers and "big mules"—the local term for Birmingham in-
dustrialists and financiers—to control the state. Alabamians retain
a sort of frontier independence, with an inclination to defend liberty
and to bait the interests.

The generality of these kinds of differences is unknown. No one
would expect the American political culture to be uniformly distributed spatially; our evidence is adequate enough to show that the
political culture of Mississippi is not the same as that of Iowa. Some
states may stand out more distinctively than others, and some group
themselves in sections or regions that are distinctive. Barring these
potential complications, at least for the moment, it may be useful
to set forth some of the kinds of interstate variability in political
culture and refer to the fragmentary data, some of it in the form of
inter-regional comparisons.

Basic attitudes vary. Attitudes of tolerance of nonconformity vary
on an areal basis; North-South differences have been shown to be
independent of differences in urbanism or education. After a very
shrewd analysis of his survey data, Stouffer concluded:[22]

> Southerners are more rural than Northerners. Southerners also
> tend to have less education. But neither of these facts alone will
> explain the North-South differences in tolerance of nonconformists.
> There is something in Southern culture that tends to differentiate
> Southerners, in cities as well as rural areas, at all educational levels,
> from all other regional groups.

Stouffer's research dealt mainly with the threat of communism and
intolerance of nonconformity. Prothro and Grigg drew samples from

Table 3. Percentage of "democratic" responses to basic
principles of democracy among selected population groups (1960)

	Democratic Response*	Michigan (Ann Arbor)	Florida (Talla-hassee)
Majority Rule			
Only informed vote	—	56	38
Only tax-payers vote	—	21	21
Bar Negro from office	—	89	67
Bar Communist from office	—	41	46
AMA right to bloc voting	+	45	46
Minority Rights			
Allow anti-religious speech	+	67	57
Allow socialist speech	+	81	77
Allow Communist speech	+	51	33
Bar Negro from candidacy	—	86	58
Bar Communist from candidacy	—	44	38

*agreement = +; disagreement = −.

Source: James W. Prothro and Charles M. Grigg, "Fundamental Principles
of Democracy: Bases of Agreement and Disagreement," *Journal of Politics*,
XXII (1960), 285.

Michigan (Ann Arbor) and Florida (Tallahassee), and interviewed respondents about their basic attitudes toward majority rule and minority rights.[23] They found that education had the greatest effect on inter-community differences over democratic values, but that inter-regional differences remained intact. As Table 3 shows, the Michigan sample exhibited considerably more democratic beliefs than the Florida sample; especially in the area of minority rights. A Harris Survey in late 1965 underscored the difference in tolerance of nonconformity levels between the South and the rest of the country: 68 percent of Southerners were scored as intolerant of nonconformist political or professional behavior, while the East was at 56 percent, the Midwest at 58 percent, and the West at 56 percent. The Harris Survey included questions about toleration of American Communists, people who do not believe in God, anti-Vietnam war pickets and other demonstrators, members of the Birch Society, lawyers who defend notorious criminals, and so forth, and the relatively high intolerance levels are the result of the rather wide sweep of the questions asked.[24]

A Harris Survey in 1964 makes it possible to view one aspect of the political culture of Mississippi, perhaps the most traditional, ascriptive, particularistic, and underdeveloped state in the country.[25] Senator Goldwater received 87 percent of the 1964 presidential election vote in Mississippi. After the election, the Harris Survey asked Mississippians to rate the performance of Lyndon Johnson on a variety of criteria, and these ratings were compared with the South and the nation as a whole. Mississippians generally gave the President very much lower ratings on his handling of a whole range of foreign and domestic policy issues than all Southerners. The same survey revealed that more than three times as many Mississippians as Americans generally saw Communist infiltration of the government as the major problem the nation faced, and 96 percent of those in the Mississippi sample opposed the Civil Rights Acts (compared to 54 percent of Southerners). Further, while most Americans viewed Lyndon Johnson as a conservative or middle-of-the-roader, more than half of the Mississippians viewed him as a liberal and an additional quarter classified him as a "radical." While most Americans saw Barry Goldwater as a "radical," nearly three-fourths of the Mississippians saw him as a conservative. Finally, while 64 percent of the national sample and 58 percent of the Southern sample classified themselves as liberal or middle-of-the-road, 88 percent of the Mississippians classed themselves as conservative.

V. O. Key described the substantial interstate variations of political structure and practice in the South, which suggest differences of political culture in the region. Mississippi certainly differs in important ways from the rest of the South. The South has, for obvious reasons, attracted the most attention in terms of its cultural peculiarities. To what extent the scope and content of basic political orientations vary between states generally we do not know.

Political identification varies. Almond and Verba found pride in governmental and political institutions more prevalent in the United States than in the United Kingdom, Germany, Italy, or Mexico; 85 percent of the Americans interviewed volunteered that they were proud of their government.[26] Van Dyke has underscored the importance of national pride in the policy-making process, with special reference to the space program.[27] We can assume that Americans feel identified with, and proud of, their nation *and their states*. In a federal structure, the states are likely to constitute important focuses for identification, loyalty, and pride. National integration will be influenced by some mix of national and state loyalties.

Unfortunately, political scientists have not given the integrating factor of national identification much attention, perhaps especially in research on the American political system. The importance of this factor is suggested by the speculation of Almond and Verba:[28]

> The attitude most relevant to long-term political stability may not be the individual's level of satisfaction with governmental out-put or with his role as participant. Rather, long-run political stability may be more dependent on a more diffuse sense of attachment or loyalty to the political system—a loyalty not based specifically on system performance.

But, if we really know very little about the effects of national identification for the United States, we know almost nothing about the effects of state identifications on the stability of state political systems, nor do we know much from empirical data about the unifying-divisive functions of the intermingling of national and state loyalties. The example of the American Civil War is temporally distant, and not likely to recur, though it undoubtedly provides instructive lessons on this point. In all, de Tocqueville may have been right that "every citizen of the United States transfuses his attachment to his little republic in the common store of American patriotism."[29]

We are all, presumably, aware of the phenomenon of state pride. We suspect Americans are generally proud to be Iowans, Texans, Wisconsinites, or Michiganders. Gunther found the phenomenon of state pride ("Maine has great pride. Almost all its people are proud, from the marmoreally entrenched aristocracy of Bar Harbor to the lonely professor living in a shack on a deserted beach."),[30] and believed it to be stronger in some states than others. He identified Maine, Texas, Kansas, and Indiana as the states where pride and loyalty were most notable. The pride of Texans is notorious, and it surely seems to have had political consequences there. Pappy O'Daniel, politician and poet laureate of the Texas flour industry, once wrote a local hit song called "Beautiful Texas."[31]

Yet, pride in a state may sometimes be largely an artifact of history, tradition, or sentiment. It may not always be converted into pride in the state political system, especially where state political institutions and issues have low cognitive salience. Intervening identifications may wash out state identification; those who live in New York City are likely to identify with the City, and only much less to the state. Finally, state pride may under some circumstances be manifested by its counterpart, humiliation or mortification. It may be that many in the South accept racial integration not so much because they believe that integration is desirable, but because they want to avoid stigma in the eyes of those who live elsewhere in the country. They want to be proud, but cannot when they know that most people in the United States (and in other parts of the world) look at their states with reproof. Interstate comparisons as referents for pride are probably fairly generally made, and the rank of a state on one criteria or another may have a bearing on the extent to which citizens are proud or mortified.

Participant-subject orientations vary. The extent of political participation varies from state-to-state, and so does the extent to which individuals submit apathetically to decisions participated in by others. As Milbrath puts it, "the political cultures of some states such as Idaho and Utah facilitate the involvement of citizens in political activity," while "the political cultures of other states, especially those in the deep South, place barriers to participation in politics."[32] Milbrath deals with a variety of correlates of participation. The illustrations here will be confined to fragments of data at the level of basic political attitudes.

Since levels of educational attainment vary among the states, and political participation is highly related to education, interstate differences in participation (other than merely in voting) may be expected. Americans are characterized by relatively high degrees of subjective civic competence.[33] Are attitudes supportive of political participation variables among states? That is a plausible expectation. Inter-regional variations in the degree of political efficacy and citizen duty are suggestive, though again the South is the main vil-

**Table 4.   Regional differences
in political efficacy and citizen duty (1952) (in percentages)**

Region	Political Efficacy		Citizen Duty		Number of Cases
	High	Low	High	Low	
Northeast	30	15	50	7	390
Midwest	30	19	49	6	580
South	18	32	28	20	440
Far West	30	12	45	2	204

Source: Angus Campbell, Gerald Gurin, and Warren E. Miller, *The Voter Decides* (Evanston, Illinois, 1956), 192 and 197.

lain. In Table 4 are reproduced the regional comparisons for the 1952 Survey Research Center (Michigan) study, showing the High and Low political efficacy and civic duty scores. South–Non-South differences in the sense of political efficacy and the sense of citizen duty are sustained after control for differences in education, though of course highly educated individuals tend to feel much more politically potent and civically competent than those with limited educations.[34]

It ought to be possible to array the states on a continuum from highly participant to highly subject (non-participant). This is easy to do simply in terms of voter turnout in state elections, but it would also be desirable to include other indicators of participation such as subjective competence, civic obligation, working in campaigns, contributing money, or letter writing.[35] For example, Idaho, Connecticut, and Indiana might be considered highly participant political cultures, while South Carolina, Georgia, and Mississippi might be considered highly subject political cultures. This kind of analysis might seem quite conventional; it is commonplace, for instance, to talk of the effects of party systems and partisan conflict on voter turnout. What is being suggested is that we now also ask what are the differential bases of support for political systems in political cultures that vary in participant-subject orientations. To put it another way, do the more participant political culture of Idaho and the less participant political culture of South Carolina contribute in different ways to the stability and performance of the political systems involved?

Political styles vary. If there are interstate variations in basic political orientations, we would expect political styles to vary. Even where political cultures are quite similar, ways of holding and applying beliefs may differ. Some state political cultures are manifestly more homogeneous than those in other states, and a relatively diverse state political culture may lead to distinctively different political styles within a state.

Where states have highly homogeneous political cultures (perhaps most of the states of the South, the Midwest, the Great Plains, and the Rocky Mountains), it may be possible to characterize them in terms of dominant political styles. The dominant Iowa political style can be described as highly pragmatic, non-programmatic, cautious, and moderate. The Virginia political style may be distinctive in its sense of honor and gentility.[36] Though the demagogic-hortatory political style is by no means limited to them, Louisiana and Mississippi political cultures seem to be dominated by this style.[37] In states with mixed political cultures, differential styles arise. The ethnically and religiously diverse, relatively cynical, alien and hostile political environment of Massachusetts produces a variety of response styles.[38] Pennsylvania provides an example of the consequences of sharply differing rural and urban political subcultures, and the styles associated with them.[39] The ethnic bifurcation of New Mexico (and of Texas) produces stylistic differences, where the distinctive political style of the Spanish-American sector is that of "patronism" or "bossism."[40] California's political culture is divided geographically, separated by the Tehachapi mountains. The distinctive political style of Southern California is extremist, paranoid, and hortatory.[41] Though surveys have indicated that Californians support the geographical integrity of the state, numerous attempts have been made to divide the state in two, the most recent by Senator Richard J. Dolwig of San Francisco. The distinctiveness of Southern California arises mainly from the torrential inflow of population (Gunther said, "Los Angeles is Iowa with palms.").[42] Lipset has tried to account for the strength of the Birchite style of politics in Southern California in terms of tensions in population growth and community integration.[43] The political styles of Massachusetts, Pennsylvania, and California appear to be relatively more ideological in character than those of other states for which we have explicit evidence.

Political socialization varies. We have no systematic evidence of the interstate variability in political socialization, and the subject itself is only beginning to be studied. Children do learn to become Iowans, Hoosiers, Oregonians, or South Carolinians, even though images of the national government and its authority figures are more prominent in their socialization.[44] Strength of identity with the state political systems probably varies, as may comparative positive or negative affect toward the political system and participation in it.[45] Evidence does not exist of substantial differences in most of the basic democratic values that children learn in different states or regions, although of course children in the South learn different attitudes toward racial equality than children in other regions of the country.[46]

   In terms of adult political socialization, variability is to be expected as a function both of politico-cultural support for participation and of political institutions available and operating as socializing agents. The data now available, limited to state legislators in California, New Jersey, Ohio, and Tennessee, indicate variations in socializing agents among these states.[47] For instance, Eulau argues that, since more than half the legislators in New Jersey and a fifth in Ohio referred to party work as initiating their interest in politics, "this is likely to be due to the more solid institutionalization of party politics in these two states, and in New Jersey to the highly politicized atmosphere characteristic of that state's metropolitan areas. In other words, party politics seems to operate as its own socializing agent."[48] Furthermore, adults generally seem to be differently socialized to partisan loyalties and attachments when Northern states are grouped into those whose election laws maximize partisanship and those whose laws minimize it.[49]

IV.   Correlates of
Politico-Cultural Variability

If there are significant variations in the elements of political culture among American states, then why do these variations occur? What seem to be some of the correlates of interstate variance in political culture?

One obvious set of variables is that of *group differences* in education, ethnicity, race, religion, sex, and social class. Almond and Verba found from cross-national comparisons that education had the greatest impact on political culture.[50]

> That higher education tends to reduce national differences suggests that the nature of political culture is greatly determined by the distribution of education . . . the more highly educated segments of all five nations show a cross-national uniformity in political orientation . . . To say that education replaces national differences is of course an exaggeration; national differences persist . . . even among the highly educated; moreover, the generalization being made here applies only to specific political orientations. Nevertheless, the highly educated participate in politics, no matter what their nation; participation by the less educated depends more heavily upon nation.

Since education is unevenly distributed across the American states we would expect variants in political culture to be in part, a function of variation in educational attainments. Variations in the ethnic mix of state populations and "ethnic salience" make a contribution to differences in political cultures; thus, "it appears that concern with national origins is much greater in the Northeast than in some other parts of the country."[51] Ethnicity and religious differences work closely together, though religious differences seem to have independent consequences on politico-cultural variations.[52] Differences in racial composition have a substantial impact on state political cultures, suggested by North-South and Negro-White differences in political socialization.[53] Sex differences in acculturation are plainly of importance, especially between the regions of the North and South.[54] Differences in social class composition, and especially differences in status polarization and mobility, have significant political effects which vary among states and regions.[55]

Another set of correlates of variations in political cultures among American states is that of *social and economic forces*. Urbanization, industrialization, population movement, affluence and economic growth probably have substantial consequences in terms of interstate politico-cultural differences. The metropolitan-industrial milieu fosters tech-nocratic political styles and expectations which Litt has aptly characterized as "managerial progressivism."[56] Population in-migration and out-migration not only provides a source of demand stress for political systems, but affects basic political orientations as well. Differential economic development can affect political cultures in the sense that abundance and economic growth are more likely to support a civic culture than poverty and immiseration. As affluence increases, inter-personal trust increases, political partisanship takes on a different meaning, class awareness relaxes and class voting diminishes in importance, the openness of the political system of par-ticipation by racial minorities is facilitated, and political alienation declines.[57]

Interstate variations in political culture have fairly often been explained in terms of *historical patterns of settlement*. In-migrants are shown to bring to a state particular political beliefs and attachments which persist over time. Munger and Key argued that "the long persistence of county patterns of party affiliation despite changes in 'interest' and the disappearance of issues that created the pattern, and the existence of contrasting partisan patterns in essentially similar counties, point toward a 'political' grouping at least to some extent independent of other social groupings," and "their persistence suggests that they may represent, no mere derivatives from other social groupings, but political groups with a life of their own."[58]

A final set of variables which seem to be related to variations in state political cultures is that of *institutional impact*. The authors of *The American Voter* have suggested, for example, that "quite apart from differences in the level of partisanship from state to state we find that identifiers in some communities behave differently from their counterparts elsewhere."[59] Differences in meanings given to electoral institutions are indicated as having a causal linkage to variations in political responses. Again, where political parties are highly organized they not only are available as socializing agents, as Eldersveld's study of Detroit politics suggests, they also are impor-tant contributors to public confidence in the political system.[60] Further, the structure and beliefs of the elite in the political system have an impact on the political culture. In this regard, Virginia has been a comparatively closed system. "Of all the American states," Key said, "Virginia can lay claim to the most thorough control by an oligarchy." There "political power has been closely held by a small group of leaders who, themselves and their predecessors, have subverted democratic institutions and deprived most Virginians of a voice in their government."[61] The contrast is marked between Virginia and, to take one illustration, Washington, where cultural traditions and political institutions support a high degree of political independence and participation.[62]

Another kind of institutional impact that is felt on state political cultures comes from the federal structure and the federal government. States affect each other, and some of these manifest institutional effects are obvious. For instance, interstate comparisons are often made by citizens and political leaders as referents for political behavior (goals) or as sources for the articulation of state pride. The federal impact is also obvious, though its more subtle forms have scarcely been examined. For example, Key pointed out that:[63]

> In the organization and spirit of their politics the states vary markedly. Their oddities and variations may be accounted for in part by the fact that they are members of a federal system. The impact of national policies and parties powerfully influences the form and behavior of state political systems. The manner in which that impact strikes different states, differently constituted and situated, contributes to the variations in organization and conduct of state politics.

The national welfare state, with economic policies reaching into every state and almost every life, seems to have a rather fundamental impact on state political cultures. Litt points out, for instance, that in Massachusetts political corruption, rather than issues of substantive policy, provides the focus of major public attention. He argues that attention to political corruption is a characteristic of a political system in a state of flux, especially "when the causes of transition are largely outside the state political system and seriously threaten values within the system." He contends further that "the national political economy has altered the power position of many local interests in industrial states such as Massachusetts," and "that corruption itself is an attempt to compensate for values that are dysfunctional to the official norms of the system."[64]

V.   Conclusion

This essay has attempted to suggest and illustrate some focuses for research in comparative state politics which, while not novel in principle, are presently severely limited in application. Such research will greatly improve our understanding of the maintenance of state political systems, and contribute to knowledge about national integration. In the past political scientists have tended to view the states as sources of national diversity and political conflict. That is important, but now we probably need to give more attention to the states in terms of their contribution to national cohesion and stability, where conflicts can be managed without disintegration.

To those whose principal focus is on the formulation and administration of public policy, one can say that components of state political cultures are often considered as determinants of policy processes and output, or they are simply assumed to be in the field. For an enlightening illustration of the explanation of a particular policy issue in terms of politico-cultural factors, read Rogow's description of the outcome of the loyalty oath issue in Iowa:[65]

> The Senate's refusal to support Doud [major proponent of the loyalty oath bill] also owes much to the general character of Iowa political and social life. Thus far, Iowa has experienced few of the tensions that elsewhere have generated major controversies about loyalty and subversion. Political, economic, and social homogeneity have been more characteristic of Iowa than of a large number of other states. The agricultural section of the population, which is heavily represented in the legislature, enjoys a substantial measure of economic security, social influence, and political dominance. The urban-rural division, while it is increasing, has not yet become a major factor in Iowa politics. The AFL-CIO is relatively insignificant compared with the Iowa Farm Bureau Federation, or even the Iowa Manufacturers Association. Even the usual rich man-poor man distinctions are more difficult to make; the extremes of wealth and poverty are not as visible in Iowa as elsewhere in the nation. There are no large numbers of recent immigrants to assimilate, and the state's non-white population has remained small. Political differences exist, but they exist less between the parties than within the parties, and within the parties they tend more to be personal or factional than ideological. At any given moment, therefore, the political mood of the state is likely to be conservative, cautious, and "standpat."

The political cultures of American states ought to be a major focus of study, in terms of systemic analysis, in terms of inhibitions or restrictions on the scope and substance of policy issues, and in terms of policy processes and application. Such research will open a significant area for comparative study.

Notes

1. Gabriel A. Almond, "Comparative Political Systems," *Journal of Politics*, XVIII (1956) 391–409; Gabriel A. Almond and James Coleman (eds.), *The Politics of the Developing Areas* (Princeton, 1960); Gabriel A. Almond and Sidney Verba, *The Civic Culture* (Princeton, 1963); and Lucian W. Pye and Sidney Verba (eds.), *Political Culture and Political Development* (Princeton, 1965).

2. Pye and Verba, *op. cit.*, pp. 512–60.

3. *Ibid.*, p. 513. Easton uses the term "basic political orientations" to characterize these elements. See David Easton and Robert D. Hess, "Youth and the Political System," in Lipset and Lowenthal, *op. cit.*, pp. 226–51, and "The Child's Political World," *Midwest Journal of Political Science*, VI (1962), pp. 229–46. Verba's basic framework is undoubtedly adapted from Parsons and Shils. See Talcott Parsons, Edward A. Shils, and James Olds, "Systems of Value Orientation," in Parsons and Shils (eds.), *Toward a General Theory of Action* (Cambridge, Mass., 1954), pp. 159–89.

4. See David Easton, *A Systems Analysis of Political Life* (New York, 1965), pp. 171–219. The concept of regime is used in a somewhat different

sense in Robert E. Agger, Daniel Goldrich, and Bert E. Swanson, *The Rulers and the Ruled* (New York, 1964), pp. 82–93.

5. James W. Prothro and Charles M. Grigg, "Fundamental Principles of Democracy: Bases of Agreement and Disagreement," *Journal of Politics*, XXII (1960), pp. 276–94; Herbert McClosky, "Consensus and Ideology in American Politics," *American Political Science Review*, LVIII (1964), pp. 361–82; Robert A. Dahl, *Who Governs?* (New Haven, 1961), pp. 311–25.

6. Easton speaks of cultural "inhibitors" and "releasers" in *A Systems Analysis of Political Life*, pp. 100–116.

7. *Ibid.*, p. 103.

8. Pye and Verba, *op. cit.*, p. 529. See also Gabriel A. Almond, "A Developmental Approach to Political Systems," *World Politics*, XVII (1964), pp. 204–5.

9. Pye and Verba, *op. cit.*, p. 535.

10. *Ibid.*, pp. 544–50.

11. *Ibid.*, p. 545.

12. *Ibid.*

13. Murray Edelman, *The Symbolic Uses of Politics* (Urbana, 1964), pp. 130–51.

14. Almond and Verba, *op. cit.*, pp. 440–55. Value orientations in American society have been treated by Robin Williams, *American Society* (New York, 1951); Seymour Martin Lipset, *The First New Nation* (New York, 1963); Gabriel A. Almond, *The American People and Foreign Policy* (New York, 1950), pp. 29–68; David M. Potter, *People of Plenty* (Chicago, 1954); John Gillin, "National and Regional Cultural Values in the United States," *Social Forces*, XXXIV (1955), pp. 107–13; Lee Coleman, "What is American? A Study of Alleged American Traits," *Social Forces*, XIX (1941), pp. 492–99; Geoffrey Gorer, *The American People* (New York, 1964).

15. Donald E. Stokes, "Popular Evaluations of Government: An Empirical Assessment," in Harlan Cleveland and Harold D. Lasswell (eds.), *Ethics and Bigness* (New York, 1962), pp. 61–72.

16. Louis Hartz, *The Liberal Tradition in America* (New York, 1955).

17. William C. Mitchell, *The American Polity* (New York, 1962), pp. 104–21.

18. Edward A. Shils, *The Torment of Secrecy* (Glencoe, Ill., 1956).

19. Richard Hofstadter, *The Paranoid Style in American Politics* (New York, 1965).

20. John Gunther, *Inside U.S.A.*, rev. ed. (New York, 1961), pp. 89 and 93.

21. V. O. Key, Jr., *Southern Politics* (New York, 1950), p. 36.

22. Samuel A. Stouffer, *Communism, Conformity, and Civil Liberties* (Garden City, N. Y., 1955), pp. 109–30. For an extensive analysis of the foreign policy attitudes of Southerners, and voluminous material on the Southern subculture, see Alfred O. Hero, Jr., *The Southerner and World Affairs* (Baton Rouge, La., 1965).

23. Prothro and Grigg, "Fundamental Principles of Democracy: Bases of Agreement and Disagreement," *loc. cit.*

24. Harris Survey, September 27, 1965; see also, Allen W. Moger, "Virginia's Conservative Political Heritage," *South Atlantic Quarterly*, L (1951), pp. 318–29.

25. Harris Survey, November 23, 1964; see also James W. Silver, *Mississippi: The Closed Society* (New York, 1963).

26. Almond and Verba, *op. cit.*, p. 102.

27. Vernon Van Dyke, *Pride and Power* (Urbana, Ill., 1964), pp. 136–62.

28. Almond and Verba, *op. cit.*, p. 246.

29. Alexis de Tocqueville, *Democracy in America* (London, 1946), pp. 107–8. Converse comments that "even in the modern United States,

there are scattered pockets of the population that are rather vague about national identity." We encounter respondents, for example, who when asked if they were born in the United States, answer "No, I was born in Georgia." See Phillip E. Converse, "The Nature of Belief Systems in Mass Publics," in David E. Apter (ed.), *Ideology and Discontent* (New York, 1964), p. 258.

30. Gunther, *op. cit.*, p. 498. For an interesting treatment of the distinctiveness of Indiana Hoosiers, see John R. Seeley *et al.*, *Community Chest* (Toronto, 1957), pp. 48–55.

31. W. Eugene Hollon, *The Southwest: Old and New* (New York, 1961), p. 372.

32. Lester W. Milbrath, "Political Participation in the States," in Jacob and Vines, *op. cit.*, pp. 25–60.

33. Almond and Verba, *op. cit.*, p. 186.

34. Angus Campbell, Phillip E. Converse, Warren E. Miller and Donald E. Stokes, *The American Voter* (New York, 1960), pp. 479–80.

35. Data might be gathered for the states along the lines of Julian L. Woodward and Elmo Roper, "The Political Activity of American Citizens," *American Political Science Review*, XLIV (1950), pp. 872–85.

36. Key, *Southern Politics*, p. 19.

37. See Allan P. Sindler, *Huey Long's Louisiana* (Baltimore, 1956); and, A. J. Liebling, *The Earl of Louisiana* (New York, 1961).

38. Edgar Litt, *The Political Cultures of Massachusetts* (Cambridge, Mass., 1965); Murray B. Levin with George Blackwood, *The Compleat Politician* (Indianapolis, 1962); and, Lawrence H. Fuchs, *The Political Behavior of American Jews* (Glencoe, Ill., 1956).

39. Frank J. Sorauf, *Party and Representation* (New York, 1963), p. 149.

40. John C. Russell, "State Regionalism in New Mexico," *Social Forces*, XVI (1937), pp. 268–71; and Key, *Southern Politics*, pp. 271–76.

41. Paul Seabury, "The Antic Politics of California," *Harper's Magazine* (June, 1965), pp. 82–93; and, James Q. Wilson, "A Guide to Reagan Country: The Political Culture of Southern California," *Commentary*, XLIII (May, 1967), pp. 37–45.

42. Gunther, *op. cit.*, p. 50.

43. Seymour Martin Lipset, "Three Decades of the Radical Right: Coughlinites, McCarthyites, and Birchers," in Daniel Bell (ed.), *The Radical Right* (Garden City, New York, 1963), pp. 436–7.

44. At least in Chicago, Illinois, and New Haven, Connecticut. See David Easton and Jack Dennis, "The Child's Image of Government," *Annals of the American Academy of Political and Social Science*, CCCLXI (1965), p. 51; and, Fred I. Greenstein, "The Benevolent Leader: Children's Images of Political Authority," *American Political Science Review*, LIV (1960), p. 937–9.

45. A comparative analysis of socialization effects is Edgar Litt, "Civic Education, Community Norms, and Political Indoctrination," *American Sociological Review*, XXVIII (1963), pp. 69–75.

46. For inter-regional comparisons of the attitudes of teenagers toward political involvement and the Bill of Rights, see H. H. Remmers and D. H. Radler, *The American Teenager* (Indianapolis, 1957), pp. 178–221.

47. John C. Wahlke, Heinz Eulau, William Buchanan, and LeRoy C. Ferguson, *The Legislative System* (New York, 1962), pp. 77–94.

48. *Ibid.*, p. 86.

49. Campbell, Converse, Miller and Stokes, *op. cit.*, pp. 270–1.

50. Almond and Verba, *op. cit.*, p. 383.

51. Raymond E. Wolfinger, "The Development and Persistence of Ethnic Voting," *American Political Science Review*, LIX (1965), pp. 896–908;

Litt, *The Political Cultures of Massachusetts*, pp. 64–67, 159–62; Lockard, *op. cit.*, pp. 305–19.

52. See Gerhard Lenski, *The Religious Factor* (Garden City, N. Y., 1961), pp. 134–211; Arnold M. Rose, "The Mormon Church and Utah Politics; An Abstract of a Statistical Study," *American Sociological Review,* VII (1942), pp. 853–4.

53. Dwaine Marvick, "The Political Socialization of the American Negro," *Annals of the American Academy of Political and Social Science,* CCCLXI (1965), pp. 112–27.

54. Campbell, Converse, Miller, and Stokes, *op. cit.*, pp. 483–93.

55. *Ibid.*, pp. 367–8.

56. Litt, *The Political Cultures of Massachusetts*, pp. 87–90.

57. Robert E. Lane, "The Politics of Consensus in an Age of Affluence," *American Political Science Review,* LIX (1965), pp. 874–95.

58. V. O. Key, Jr., and Frank Munger, "Social Determinism and Electoral Decision: The Case of Indiana," in Eugene Burdick and Arthur J. Brodbeck (eds.), *American Voting Behavior* (Glencoe, Ill., 1959), p. 287.

59. Campbell, Converse, Miller, and Stokes, *op. cit.*, p. 272.

60. Samuel J. Eldersveld, *Political Parties: A Behavioral Analysis* (Chicago, 1964), pp. 492–501.

61. Key, *Southern Politics*, p. 19.

62. Morris Showel, "Political Independence in Washington State," *Public Opinion Quarterly,* XVI (1952), pp. 399–409.

63. Key, *American State Politics*, pp. 19–20.

64. Both quotations above are from Litt, *The Political Cultures of Massachusetts,* p. 87.

65. Arnold A. Rogow, "The Loyalty Oath Issue in Iowa, 1951," *American Political Science Review,* LV (1961), pp. 861–69. Quote is on p. 869.

MAVIS MANN REEVES
PARRIS N. GLENDENING

Background for Controversy

State and local governments, as other American institutions, emerged from the turbulence of the 1960s with their integrity under attack, with the desirability of their continuance in present forms questioned. What changes account for this situation? What trends can be identified as the 1960s are left behind? These empirical questions cannot be entirely answered because complete information is never available. But they are more susceptible to response than the normative questions requiring value judgments: Do we like where we are going? If not, what changes do we want? Are there other alternatives we have not considered? Questions such as these require a reexamination of values and provoke controversies among groups seeking different ends. This essay attempts to identify some of the changes that have occurred, along with those still under way; to highlight trends in state and local government; and to point to some of the questions around which the controversies of the 1970s will probably rage.

Demographic Change

Demographic trends already begun in previous decades continued during the 1960s and added new dimensions. The tremendous population growth of the United States continued, adding to the burden of state and local governments. Population growth was not uniform, which accounts for many problems plaguing governmental machinery. Some states in the interior of the country lost population, and peripheral states gained. This peripheral movement created difficulties for those who lost manpower as well as for those who gained.

Urbanism became more completely the way of life as the migration of Negroes, Spanish-speaking Americans, and rural residents into cities continued. Despite this incursion, the suburbs grew faster than the central cities. Some older cities of the East and Middle Atlantic regions declined in population.[1] The middle-class move to the suburbs, counter-balanced only slightly by a return to some cities by the elderly, left the central cities with a diminished economic base from which to provide services for an increasingly dependent population. A trickle of blacks to the suburbs was discernible, but on balance, the central cities became blacker. This is more the result of declining death rate and high birth rate among blacks than of increased migration. The tendency of the population to concentrate in large metropolitan areas accelerated. The population of the United States, already metropolitan as well as urban by 1960, was even more concentrated in metropolitan areas by the end of the decade.

Governmental Changes

State and local governments expanded in interests and activities during the 1960s. As the 1970s dawned, they were spending more, employing more, and doing more. This increase in activities was not only absolute but relative. The aggregate of state and local activities accounted for a significant portion of the total range and volume of government services in the United States. They spent more than two-thirds of the outlay for domestic programs in the country and employed about 12 percent of all nonagricultural wage and salary workers.[2]

State and local interests and activities changed in scope and emphasis as well as in volume, and important breakthroughs were made in areas previously ignored. One significant area of growth and new concern was *planning*. State planning activities and agencies mushroomed, largely as the result of federal grant-in-aid requirements. At the same time, federal funds were used to launch hundreds of new local planning activities, many of them multi-jurisdictional.

Regional planning districts developed to coordinate rural and metropolitan areas. The emphasis of planning shifted in many instances from the purely local and physical to a comprehensive, state-wide, socio-economic approach. The new technologies of electronic data processing and systems analysis and the program-planning-budgeting technique were employed for more effective planning operations. States, particularly, began to reclaim and develop physical resources and to control and eliminate environmental pollution. The state of New Jersey redeveloped its marshlands and pooled taxes from the redeveloped land for distribution to the localities where the land is located on the basis of acreage. New York established an Urban Development Corporation whose powers include housing construction, urban renewal, commercial and industrial development, and authority to develop entirely new communities.[3] "New towns" with advance planning for total development were established in many parts of the country, especially in warm states, such as California; however, these are private rather than public developments. Other new towns are projected throughout the nation. The New York agency is planning the development of Lysander as a completely planned community. Maryland adopted a pioneering statute on environmental pollution and took steps to protect the wetlands along its coast. Four states entered the Delaware River Basin Compact for the control of water resources, and the governors of seventeen southern states, Puerto Rico, and the Virgin Islands set up a Southern Regional Environment Council to make recommendations for controlling pollution and preserving natural resources.

States and localities became more concerned with the physical well-being of their citizens and, in addition to planning environmental control, undertook new and enlarged programs of health care and food and drug regulation. Broadened consumer protection was added to the list of services included in the police power of the states.

A significant decrease in at least one state activity occurred during the decade: regulation of morals. Marriage and divorce laws were substantially liberalized. Hawaii pioneered legislation permitting abortions, followed by New York, and other states were considering repealing existing legislation prohibiting abortions when the 1960s ended. "Blue laws" were abandoned or modified in some states, alcoholic beverage legislation became more permissive, and prohibitions against marijuana were attacked in others. Maryland is the only state still retaining a motion picture censorship board.

The 1960s saw the development of new relationships among levels of government. The increase in direct federal–city relations was the most significant of the intergovernmental changes. This period saw substantial allocations of federal funds directly to the cities without routing through state governments. This relieved the cities of some state control and juxtaposed majors and governors in the competition for federal funds. In other areas there were important alterations. Several federal–state regional commissions were created: Appalachian, Coastal Plains, Four Corners, New England, Ozarkia, and Upper Great Lakes. These organizations represented an innovative development in federalism. State departments of local affairs were established by many states. While some states had departments of similar name for many years, they were primarily agencies for control of local finances or for supplying information to local units. The new ones, first developed in Pennsylvania in 1966, are comprehensive departments of cabinet level that include such functions as technical assistance to local governments, planning aid, and help with a wide variety of operational programs including urban renewal, Model Cities, recreation, antipoverty, and mass transit.

Councils of government, which draw into voluntary cooperation a variety of local units within a metropolitan area, multiplied substantially under the impetus of federal planning requirements.[4] Both they and the regional planning districts are potential vehicles for later types of regional authority, perhaps even regional governments.

Attempts to revitalize state and local governments gained new momentum in the 1960s, but the results did not produce organizations competent to deal with the urban crisis.[5] As a result of court decisions or threatened court action, legislatures were finally reapportioned, some in time for only one election before the 1970 census. The rewards of increased representation went not to the cities, who long had sought them, but chiefly to the suburbs. Several states undertook constitutional revision and executive reorganization. Those who failed in the complete revision process began the task piecemeal. Adoption of metropolitan-wide government continued to meet voter resistance everywhere except in a few places, largely in the South.

Nontraditional responses to some of the demands on governments developed in a few places. There was an effort to break away from the single-line approach and to make a more comprehensive and pragmatic attack on problems. This kind of response was limited primarily to urban problems and included such devices as the Urban Redevelopment Corporation.[6] In other innovative programs, Hawaii was the first state to adopt the Scandinavian ombudsman for protecting citizens against the misuse of administrative discretion. State intern programs for recruiting and training professionals grew, and states moved toward closer interstate cooperation with new compacts, the establishment of the Institute of State Programming for the Seventies,[7] and new vitality for existing state and local associations, including the Council of State Governments, the Conference of State Legislatures, the National Association of Counties, the National Conference of Mayors, the National League of Cities, and others.

More attention was paid to finance during the 1960s than at any other time since the 1930s. The staggering increase in federal grants-in-aid created problems of coordination and red tape and resulted in insistence on simplification or consolidation of grant-in-aid programs. Differing proposals ranged from block grants to shared revenues, but it became apparent that revenue sharing in some form would be the result once agreement of the distribution formulas could be reached. Removal of certain functions to the next higher level of government gained momentum during the decade. Michigan prepared to take over financing of its entire school system; the Nixon administration sent to Congress proposals for a family assistance plan to replace aid to dependent children. Such transfers of financing for major programs would free funds on the lower level for other uses, while assuring some minimum standards of welfare and education over a wider area. Local controls over the programs would be weakened at the same time.

During the 1960s, both the form and the content of demands on state and local government were altered. Violence reasserted itself as a political weapon. The 1950s were marked by bus boycotts, marches, picketing, and peaceful sit-ins, largely in support of the civil rights movement. Rising expectations and militancy of blacks, impatient at the slow pace of progress in achieving goals, and the precedent of selective observance of law under the doctrine of civil disobedience produced violence in the next decade.

Harsh demands on the political system whetted the appetites of other minorities for a larger share of political power. They demanded more than equality; they wanted reparations for previous deprivations. Values of the past were critically examined and sometimes found wanting. Migrant workers, Indians, government employees, teachers, women, the poor, and those long regarded as having the best of all possible worlds—college students—began to reassess their positions and demand to be heard.

The United States Supreme Court played a major role in this turbulence. In civil rights cases and in apportionment, its decisions succored those seeking to reallocate power and resources in American society. The Presidents and Congresses of the decade intervened from time to time to tip the scales toward the challengers. But it was largely state and local governments on whom the demands were made.

The most emotional controversy revolved around individual freedom and equality. While most states and localities complied with court edicts, a few governors defied court orders that schools desegregate, amassed state police, and stood in the schoolhouse door to prevent integration. Presidents sent in federal troops and marshals and used the powers of the federal government to force compliance.

Parents and citizens' groups exerted maximum pressure, pro and con, on the issue of busing children to integrate schools. State legislatures found themselves at the center of conflict over equality in public accommodations, open housing, and decentralization of school control. States, cities, counties, and school districts were besieged by demands for reallocation of school resources on the one hand and maintenance of the status quo on the other.

In other areas, controversies raged. "Law and order" became a major issue as crime against persons increased and riots erupted. Efforts to establish civilian review boards for police produced heated conflict. Strikes by public employees increased. Rising militancy of the poor against welfare inadequacies produced mothers' strikes, property destruction, and demands for a voice in matters affecting their lives. College students' rioting against university establishments or protesting the Vietnam War generated arguments over control of police discretion, the role of the university, academic freedom, and a student voice in college affairs. This, predictably, produced a reaction against students, faculties, and universities. The use in court of advocacy proceedings for consumer protection and to force public agencies' compliance with legal requirements in the public interest developed to embryonic stage. The lack of government response to citizen complaints was attacked. All in all, the 1960s constituted one of the country's most turbulent decades, and the effects of this turbulence were felt at every level of government.

Future Trends

Discernible trends involving state and local governments can be identified as the country moves into the 1970s. These trends raise normative questions as governments struggle to decide public policy. Sometimes this decision-making stirs little interest when old values are reinforced and resources distributed in much the way they always were. But when the environment where governments operate changes, and additional groups seek to be recognized as participants in the decision-making process, a reexamination of values must occur. Political scientists are concerned with the effects of these controversies and solutions on governmental systems.

State and local government activities will continue to expand as society becomes more urbanized and complex. This is especially true of housing, redevelopment, health services, environmental control, and consumer protection. Has the increasing need for government services in our urban society made the federal system obsolete? Have states a useful and vital role? Should they be abolished? *Could* they be abolished? If we did not have states, would we have to invent them? Are they the hope of the future in solving metro-

politan problems? Can direct federal–city relations be reversed?
Should they be?

Shifts of functions among levels of government are imminent.
The trend of the 1970s will likely be toward centralization, with the
federal government assuming almost complete responsibility for welfare and taking a stronger role in health services and pollution
control. States may duplicate the trends of the 1930s and take on
the burden of providing all education and public transportation
programs and participate to a greater extent in provision of housing.
What standards can be established for determining whether the
federal, state, or local level should perform a function? As centralization increases, how can we maintain local initiative? How can we
solve the dilemma of turning to centralization to achieve the solution
of area-wide problems and to decentralization to give citizens a
greater voice?

Regional organizations on an interstate and local basis are
increasing and are beginning to work with greater effectiveness.
Regional organizations might be created throughout the country.
Will regional authorities be more effective in solving problems than
traditional government units have been? Or will they remove government just one step farther from control of the people?

There is no indication that peripheralization of population on
a national basis is abating. This raises a question of whether national
or regional population growth policy is desirable. If so, what kinds
of inducements or restraints should be used to locate people in
selected areas?

Great population movements will continue to promote greater
metropolitanization, although some affluent Americans are beginning
to abandon the suburb for the city. Because of some minorities'
moving to the suburbs, and because of general population growth,
the suburbs will increasingly find themselves faced with problems
like those of the central city. Are these the types of suburban-city
patterns we want? Should the state assume extraordinary powers
to overcome local zoning so that housing for families with low and
moderate incomes can be built in the suburbs? What will happen if
the courts outlaw zoning as some civil rights groups advocate?

The 1960s was the most violent decade of this century. After
the 1968 riots, raw violence abated, but it continued as a political
weapon. Are the long hot summers of the late 1960s over? Do riots
constitute lawlessness, or is the political system so closed that riots
are the only way minorities can influence public policy? Will the
1970s see a real attempt to get at the roots of ghetto problems, or will
the new decade produce more control and repression? Or will we
have a tyranny of the minority?

Demands will heighten for responsive government and for
citizen participation in decision-making. Carried to the extreme,

and coupled with advocacy actions now beginning, these demands could impede government action to the point where very little can be accomplished. Are we immobilizing government? Are obstructionists allowed to impose delay after delay upon government programs? Will police review boards alleviate the misuse of police discretion, or will they portend over-cautious policemen afraid to enforce the law? Will community control of schools raise or lower standards of education?

Militancy will increase on the part of blacks, students, women, ethnic minorities, and others who feel the government is not responsive to their needs. Since militancy often produces reaction, maintenance of public order will continue to be a major problem. In addition, state and city governments may find their own employees adding to their difficulties during the next decade unless employee discontent is ameliorated. As public employees become militant, the question of whether to permit strikes by state and local employees must be answered. If they are permitted, does this change state and locality into just another bargainer on the market? Particularly in health and police and fire protection, does the public have an interest the state should protect through strike prohibitions? What about the rights of public employees? Should an unresponsive government be able to prohibit their collective action?

Financial problems at all levels of government will increase. Demands for federal revenue sharing are expected to grow louder. In all likelihood, some agreement will be reached on the method of transfer and amount of funds to states. But what about the central cities? Should federal funds for cities pass through the states? Should suburbanites who draw their subsistence from cities help solve city financial problems? If so, how? Metropolitan government? Shared revenues? Tax credits? Grants-in-aid? Commuter taxes? How should tax systems be reformed to meet public goals?

State legislatures will become more urban-oriented, but this may have no salubrious effect on central city problems. If reapportionment produces changes in legislative output, it should occur now that the incremental period is passing.

The critical evaluation of urban renewal inherited from the 1960s will probably continue. Fundamental questions will be raised: What is the effect of urban renewal on neighborhoods? Should we stop "gilding the ghetto" and seek voluntary dispersal of its residents? Should states intervene and force some form of metropolitan government? Should some ghetto residents be moved to "new towns" on a voluntary basis?

New towns will develop at an accelerated pace, using both private and public capital. Prospects are that such completely planned communities will alleviate some central city problems by dispersing population. Already, conflicts have developed in planned communities between the developers and residents over management of local affairs. How can the dichotomy between the need for overall control of new town development and the desirability of citizen participation be reconciled?

What should be done about the District of Columbia? Home rule? Voting representation in Congress? Statehood? Reduce its size and prohibit its use as a residential area? Give it back to Maryland?

Concern with environmental and land use policies will intensify. Large, urban states are likely to follow a trend begun by Massachusetts and attempt to break through local zoning barriers against low-income housing. Pressure groups concerned with minority rights are already challenging local zoning ordinances in court.

Education will continue to account for a significant portion of our energies, resources, and controversies. What is equality of education? Despite efforts to provide equal and even compensatory education for ghetto children, how will we alleviate inequities caused by residence patterns? If, as some studies indicate, the most important factor in a child's education is the background of his classmates, how can we give each child an equal chance? Should we attempt to redress the intensifying financial plight of parochial schools, or should we absorb most of these children into the public school system? What would be the effect of giving each child a voucher for educational costs and allowing him to use it in public or private schools? If parochial and private schools are aided, will the public school system be seriously weakened or become a black school system? Battles over these questions currently rage in state and federal courts, in state legislatures, and in popular referenda. A clear, decisive victory is unlikely to occur in this decade; such a victory would require an extraordinary concurrence of judicial and political decisions at the state and federal level.

All these questions indicate a controversial decade ahead in which new forces attempt to push their way into the political system. Difficult decisions will have to be made on the allocation of scarce resources and on methods of problem solution. State and local units will be the arenas for resolving most of the conflicts of the 1970s.

Notes

1. Advisory Commission on Intergovernmental Relations, *Urban America and the Federal System*, prepared by Allen D. Manvel (Washington, D.C.: U. S. Government Printing Office, 1969), pp. 4–5.

2. For a fuller discussion of these points see Daniel R. Grant and H. C. Nixon, *State and Local Government in America* (Boston: Allyn and Bacon, Inc., 1968), pp. 2–6.

3. John N. Kolesar, "The States and Urban Planning and Development," in *The States and the Urban Crisis*, ed. Alan K. Campbell (Englewood

Cliffs: Published for the American Assembly by Prentice-Hall, Inc., 1970), pp. 124–126.

4. Parris N. Glendening, "The Federal Role in Regional Planning Councils: Trends and Implications," paper presented to the Southeastern Regional Science Association, New Orleans, April 9, 1970.

5. Alan K. Campbell, "Breakthrough or Stalemate? State Politics," in *The States and the Urban Crisis, op. cit.*, pp. 196–203.

6. Kolesar, *op. cit.*, p. 115.

7. Terry Sanford, *Storm over the States* (New York: McGraw-Hill Book Company, 1967), p. 120.

Suggested Readings: Political Culture

ALMOND, GABRIEL A., and SIDNEY VERBA. *The Civic Culture*. Princeton: Princeton University Press, 1963. The landmark study of political culture, a multinational analysis.

DEVINE, DONALD J. *The Political Culture of the United States*. Boston: Little, Brown and Company, 1971. The latest major contribution to the study of political culture in the United States.

ELAZAR, DANIEL J. *American Federalism: A View from the States*. New York: Thomas Y. Crowell Company, 1966. Note especially Chapter 4, "The States and The Political Setting," which discusses various types of political cultures and their spread throughout the United States.

KEY, V. O., JR. *American State Politics: An Introduction*. New York: Alfred A. Knopf, Inc., 1956. The classic study of American state politics which set the pattern for much of the later work in this field.

————. *Southern Politics in State and Nation*. New York: Alfred A. Knopf, Inc., 1949. Although somewhat outdated, this leading study contains much useful information.

LOCKARD, DUANE. *New England State Politics*. Princeton: Princeton University Press, 1959. This valuable sectional study stresses inter-party competition and legislative politics.

MATTHEWS, DONALD R., and JAMES W. PROTHRO. *The New Southern Politics*. New York: Harcourt, Brace and World, 1967. Emphasizes the blacks' role and importance in the South.

2/Intergovernmental Relations: Competitive? Cooperative? Creative?

Nothing has engendered more controversy in the United States than the relationships among various levels of government, particularly relations between the federal government and the states. This conflict came close to dissolving the Union at its very outset and later embroiled the country in civil war. While the Union has not been seriously threatened since, relations have been strained on more than one occasion, notably as the result of the Supreme Court's apportionment and school desegregation decisions.

The framers of the Constitution were practical men. They labored to create a central government strong enough to operate effectively while leaving the states enough powers so as not to jeopardize ratification of the Constitution. Their product established a set of constitutional, administrative, and political relationships among governments that determined what government was to be in the United States. Complexities introduced by the federal system have sometimes appeared to impede action. But they have permitted people of diverse views to live as one nation.

The dynamism of the federal system produces a constantly changing set of relationships as well as divergent opinions as to what these relationships are. In this section, the late Morton Grodzins gives his view of the federal system as one of shared functions that run together like a "marble cake," rather than as one of separate functions for each level of government as in the "layer cake" theory predominant for many years. Harry N. Scheiber, in a study prepared for the Intergovernmental Relations Subcommittee of the Senate Committee on Government Operations, disagrees with Grodzins's view of the condition of federalism. Not only do these two scholars disagree as to how federal and state powers and functions intertwine, but they present a contrast in approaches to the study of a question: Grodzins uses a political science approach and Scheiber an historical one.

Recently, scholars have been concerned with the viability of states as units of government. Proposals have been made for their abolition. In his classic essay, Harold Laski points out what he believes to be the obsolescence of the federal system. Former governor of North Carolina Terry Sanford counters with a ringing defense of states.

The issue of how to pay for public services is currently the center of intergovernmental discussions. It has been aptly said that cities have the problems, states have the power, and the federal government has the money. Increasing demands for, and costs of, public services hit the cities hardest because that is where most services are dispensed. States, too, are hard pressed for revenue. The federal government, supported by prime borrowing power and the tremendous yield of income tax, is in a superior financial position to the state and local governments. Currently, the federal government gives money to the states through a multitude of grants-in-aid. Restricted to particular purposes, these grants are allocated on the basis of predetermined formulas and are subject to conditions which vary with each grant. The controversies now debated revolve around new methods for making federal resources available to states and local units and whether money should be given directly to cities by the federal government without passing through the states. In the articles that follow, Deil S. Wright discusses alternatives in the federal grant-in-aid system; William Anderson and Roger A. Freeman take opposite sides on the question of revenue sharing.

MORTON GRODZINS

The American System
as a Single Mechanism

I. *The Chaos of American Governments*

Democratic government, in the abstract at least, should be simple
government, if not simple in process at least structured simply enough
to be easily comprehended by the citizenry. For simplicity maximizes
fulfillment of an important democratic ideal: that citizens understand
public institutions. Without this understanding the public cannot
make intelligent judgments, especially cannot know how to reward
at the polls those who have done well and penalize those who have
done poorly. But government in the United States is not simple,
either in structure or process.

The structure of the United States government is chaotic. In
addition to the federal government and the 50 states, there are
something like 18,000 general-purpose municipalities, slightly fewer
general-purpose townships, more than 3,000 counties, and so many
special-purpose governments that no one can claim even to have
counted them accurately. At an educated guess, there are at present
some 92,000 tax-levying governments in the country. A given citizen
may be buried under a whole pyramid of governments. A resident
of Park Forest, Illinois, for example, though he may know very
little else about them, knows that he pays taxes to the following
governments:

> The United States of America
> The State of Illinois
> Cook (or Will) County
> Cook County Forest Preserve District
> Suburban Tuberculosis Sanitary District
> Rich (or Bloom) Township
> Bloom Township Sanitary District
> Non-High School District 216 (or 213)
> Rich Township High School District
> Elementary School District, 163
> South Cook County Mosquito Abatement District

Morton Grodzins, "The American System as a Single Mechanism," in
Morton Grodzins, *The American System: A New View of Government in the
United States*, ed. Daniel J. Elazar (Chicago: Rand McNally & Company,
1966), pp. 3–10. Reprinted by permission.

The Park Forest citizen enjoys more governments than most people in the United States. But he is by no means unique, and although no one has made the exact calculation, it is not unlikely that a majority of citizens are within the jurisdiction of four or more governments, not counting the state and national ones.

The multitude of governments does not mask any simplicity of activity. There is no neat division of functions among them. If one looks closely, it appears that virtually all governments are involved in virtually all functions. More precisely, there is hardly an activity that does not involve the federal, state, and some local government in important responsibilities. Functions of the American governments are shared functions. Consider a case that seems least likely to demonstrate this point: the function of providing education. It is widely believed that education is uniquely, even exclusively, a local responsibility. Almost half of all governments in the United States are school districts. Is this a great simplifying fact? Does it indicate a focusing of educational responsibilities in the hands of single-purpose local governments?

The answer to both questions is a clear "no." That there exist something like 37,000 school districts in the United States does not indicate that the educational function, even in the grade and high schools, is in any sense an exclusive function of those districts. In several states local districts are largely administrative arms of state departments of education, and the educational function is principally a state responsibility. In all states, to a greater or lesser degree—and the degree tends to be greater not lesser—local districts are dependent upon state financial aid, state teacher certification, state prescription of textbooks, and state inspection of performance in areas as diverse as building maintenance and the caliber of Latin instruction. School districts also have intricate and diverse relationships with county and city governments: the latter, for example, often act as tax-levying and tax-collecting agencies for the districts; they are responsible for certifying that standards of health and safety are maintained on school property; they must provide special police protection to students.

Nor is the federal government's finger out of the pie. The United States Office of Education provides technical aids of all sorts. Throughout the 1950's a federal milk and school lunch program contributed more than $250 million annually in cash and produce to supply food and milk at low cost to 11 million children in all 50 states. Federal surplus property supplies many essentials of school equipment. Federal aid to vocational education programs makes possible the employment of special teachers. In many areas "affected by" national government installations, federal funds build and maintain school buildings and contribute to general school support. Federal aid trains high school teachers of science, mathematics, and foreign languages; contributes equipment and books for instruction in these fields; makes possible testing and guidance programs for the identification of superior students; and may be used generally to strengthen state departments of education. All of these were initiated before the passage of recent legislation to enlarge further the national government's participation in education.

All this barely hints at the diverse ways in which all planes of governments in the United States participate in the function of education. It does not consider the political relationships among leaders of city, county, state, nation, and school district that basically establish the level of support that schools receive. Nor does it take into account the informal professional ties among teachers, administrators, and other specialists, ties that criss-cross governmental boundaries and from which a good fraction of new ideas and new programs emerge. A complete description of intergovernmental sharing in education would also have to consider how the school district's job is affected by the *mélange* of private, quasi-private, municipal, state, and federally financed programs and institutions that provide education beyond the high school in the United States. Nevertheless, the larger point is clear: grade and high school education is not simply a function of local school districts. It is not neatly a responsibility of one sort or one "level" of government. Rather, education is provided through the joint efforts of many governments. What is true of the "hard case" of education is also true of virtually all functions performed by the governments of the United States.

Many overlapping governments involved in many overlapping functions produce other attributes of the chaotic American system. Areas of government do not often correspond with problems of government. In order to provide adequate facilities for, and control of, automobile transportation, a given large city will have to deal with literally hundreds of other governments. This lack of congruence between area and function complicates the official's problem; it complicates the citizen's even more so. Where does he go and whom does he blame if super-highways become clogged with cars and the air polluted with their exhaust? What does he do if his water tastes foul? It is purchased from one city, runs in open lines through six others, is filtered and chlorinated by his own municipality, and is affected by the drainage systems of several dozen governments as well as by the septic tanks of several thousand homes in unincorporated areas. How does the citizen begin if he wishes to do something about his deteriorating neighborhood? Slum clearance involves three sets of law—local, state, and federal—and perhaps half a dozen separate administrative agencies, each with its own body of regulations. Points of influence and centers of decision are diffuse and obscure. More often than not the citizen cannot name most of the officers he elects, or describe the responsibilities of the governments that serve him. How can he hope to make them responsive to his wishes?

The chaos of structure and function is matched by a chaos of political process. The political parties play a key role, as later discussion will show, but it is a role different in almost every respect from what political parties are classically supposed to perform. Nominating procedures more often than not deprive the voter of genuine choices. Party platforms are election slogans, not statements of program. Legislative procedures are complex and unpublicized. If it is difficult on the administrative plane to discover what government does what, it is frequently impossible in the legislative halls—of locality, state, and nation—to discover who initiates, who obstructs, who is for or against what. Leadership functions, even in the national government, are typically splintered. Legislation and administration proceed through a system of pushing, hauling, bargaining, and cajoling. Legislative committee and economic interest group compete for influence with the administration, which often speaks through several opposing voices, with party leaders in and out of office, with local and state political chiefs, and with professional associations of all varieties. The two houses of the Congress, unlike any other major legislature in the world, vie with each other for power, the leaders of those houses, even when of the same party, often taking opposite sides on a given issue.

To penetrate this jungle and to bring his influence to bear, the citizen votes, writes to his congressman, joins forces with others in order to promote what he wishes to promote and, more typically, oppose what he wishes to oppose. As a businessman he pays dues to the National Association of Manufacturers; as a father of school-age children he contributes to the National Citizen's Council for Better Schools; as a churchgoer he supports the National Association of Churches of Christ. Frequently when these organizations speak they express the citizen's own views. But not always. He is enraged, because he is a humanitarian, when "his" manufacturer's group opposes a bill before Congress to extend social security. He feels betrayed, because he believes in the local control of education, when "his" committee on education favors federal aid for school construction. He is frightened, because he is opposed to all totalitarian government, when a high officer of "his" church group is accused by a senator of being tinged with Communism. The citizen's interest groups may not represent his interests just as his congressman may seem to represent no interest at all except that of his own re-election.

This view of chaos in government is not one of despair. The system of American government flaunts virtually all tenets of legislative responsibility and administrative effectiveness. It appears always to be wasteful of manpower and money. At times it threatens the very democracy it is established to maintain. But it works, it works—and sometimes with beauty.

II. Government by Chaos and Cooperation

Lord Bryce commented on the "working relations" of the national and state governments in the following words:

> The characteristic feature and special interest of the American Union is that it shows us two governments covering the same ground, yet distinct and separate in their action. It is like a great factory wherein two sets of machinery are at work, their revolving wheels apparently intermixed, their bands crossing one another, yet each set doing its own work without touching or hampering the other.[1]

Classic works are sometimes responsible for classic errors. Lord Bryce was wrong, even for the period of his own observations, in describing the federal government and the states as "each . . . doing its own work without touching or hampering the other." Subsequent chapters will demonstrate how fallacious this description is for the contemporary American scene. Yet it cannot be said that the error has been, or is, widely recognized. During the very years that Bryce was in the United States the Supreme Court announced:

> There are within the territorial limits of each state two governments, restricted in their sphere of action, but independent of each other, and supreme within their respective spheres. Each has its separate departments, each has its distinct laws, and each has its own tribunals for their enforcement. Neither government can intrude within the jurisdiction of the other or authorize any interference therein by its judicial officers with the action of the other.[2]

The misunderstanding persists today. Lip service is frequently paid to the high degree of collaboration between the units of government in the American system. And there are a few scholars who have explicated some aspects of the collaborative pattern. But the general view is the view of the three-layer cake of government, the institutions and functions of each "level" being considered separately.

In fact, the American system of government as it operates is not a layer cake at all. It is not three layers of government, separated by a sticky substance or anything else. Operationally, it is a marble cake, or what the British call a rainbow cake. No important activity of government in the United States is the exclusive province of one of the levels, not even what may be regarded as the most national of national functions, such as foreign relations; not even the most local of local functions, such as police protection and park maintenance.

If you ask the question "Who does what?" the answer is in two parts. One is that officials of all "levels" do everything together. The second is that where one level is preponderant in a given activity, the other makes its influence felt *politically* (here the voice of the peripheral power units are heard most strongly) or through *money* (here the central view is most influential) or through *professional associations*.

The actual joint sharing of functions is easily illustrated in the field of public welfare. Here the national, state, and local governments together administer public assistance programs; the national government alone administers the old age insurance program commonly known as "social security"; the national government and the states (without the local governments but with the assistance of local business groups) administer employment security; the states and the local governments (without the national government) handle general assistance; and, to complete the circle of possible combinations, all three branches of government together administer child welfare services.

This is only the formal view. The informal aspects of welfare administration illustrate the second part of the answer. Even in general assistance programs, where the states and localities formally have exclusive jurisdiction, the national government's standards of professional conduct are greatly influential and becoming more so all the time. Even in a welfare field of so-called exclusive federal concern —hospital care for military veterans, for example—the states and localities exercise controlling power over many fundamental decisions. They can, for example, make it difficult, in some cases impossible, for the national government to close a hospital or to move it from one site to another.

That one set of officials is paid out of the national treasury, one out of state funds, and a third from local budgets is the least important aspect of the matter. If one looks closely at the route of payments, the fact of common concern becomes clear again. All levels collect taxes from the same people. And the government that collects the tax frequently does not pay the officer; intergovernmental transfers, for example, account for a very large fraction of both state and local welfare expenditures. Consider the health officer, styled "sanitarian," of a rural county in a border state. He embodies the whole idea of the marble cake of government. The sanitarian is appointed by the state under merit standards established by the federal government. His base salary comes jointly from state and federal funds, the county provides him with an office and office amenities and pays a portion of his expenses, and the largest city in the county also contributes to his salary and office by virtue of his appointment as a city plumbing inspector. It is impossible from moment to moment to tell under which governmental hat the sanitarian operates. His work of inspecting the purity of food is carried out under federal standards; but he is enforcing state laws when inspecting commodities that have not been in interstate commerce; and somewhat perversely, he also acts under state authority when inspecting milk coming into the county from producing areas across the state border. He is a federal officer when impounding impure drugs shipped from a neighboring state; a federal-state officer when distributing typhoid immunization serum; a state officer when enforcing standards of industrial hygiene; a state-local officer when inspecting the city's water supply; and (to complete the circle) a local officer when insisting that the city butchers adopt more hygienic methods of handling their garbage. But he cannot and does not think of himself as acting in these separate capacities. All business in the county that concerns public health and sanitation he considers his business. Paid largely from federal funds, he does not find it strange to attend meetings of the city council to give expert advice on matters ranging from rotten apples to rabies control. He is even deputized as a member of both the city and county police forces.

The sanitarian is an extreme case, but he accurately represents an important aspect of the whole range of governmental activities in the United States. Functions are not neatly parceled out among the many governments. They are shared functions. It is difficult to find any governmental activity which does not involve all three of the so-called "levels" of the federal system. In the most local of local functions—law enforcement or education, for example—the federal and state governments play important roles. In what, *a priori*, may be considered the purest central government activities—the conduct of foreign affairs, for example—the state and local governments have considerable responsibilities, directly and indirectly.

The federal grant programs are only the most obvious example of shared functions. They also most clearly exhibit how sharing serves to disperse governmental powers. The grants utilize the greater wealth-gathering abilities of the central government and establish nationwide standards, yet they are "in aid" of functions carried out under state law, with considerable state and local discretion. The national super-vision of such programs is largely a process of mutual accommodation. Leading state and local officials, acting through their professional organizations, are in considerable part responsible for the very stand-ards that national officers try to persuade all state and local officers to accept.

Even in the absence of joint financing, federal-state-local col-laboration is the characteristic mode of action. Federal expertise is available to aid in the building of a local jail (which may later be used to house federal prisoners), to improve a local water purification system, to step up building inspections, to provide standards for state and local personnel in protecting housewives against dishonest butchers' scales, to prevent gas explosions, or to produce a land use plan. States and localities, on the other hand, take important formal responsibilities in the development of national programs for atomic energy, civil defense, the regulation of commerce, and the protection of purity in food and drugs; local political weight is always a factor in the operation of even a post office or a military establishment. From abattoirs and accounting through zoning and zoo administration, any governmental activity is almost certain to involve the influence, if not the formal administration, of all three planes of the federal system.

So the functions of government are not in neat layers. Rather, they are all mixed up: marbled, to use the baker's term. And in no neat order: chaotic, to use the reformer's term. Unless one sees the American federal system from this perspective, he misses the most important fact of all: the system is, in effect, one government serving a common people for a common end.

Notes

1. James Bryce, *The American Commonwealth* (New York: The Macmillan Company, 1916), Vol. I, p. 318.
2. *Tarble's Case*, 13 Wall. 397 (1871).

HARRY N. SCHEIBER

The Condition of American Federalism: An Historian's View

Introduction

The Great Society programs, the reapportionment of State legislatures, and the activities of the Advisory Commission on Intergovernmental Relations, all have generated rising interest in the condition of the American federal system. Assessments of the capacity of State and local governments to cope with today's complex social and economic problems, and of their proper role in the federal system, vary widely indeed. Some authorities, including Lyndon Baines Johnson, call for a new "creative federalism" and perceive "a new era of resurgence and vitality" among the State and local governments. Others assert flatly that the States are "sick, sick, sick," and despair of their revitalization short of a major ideological and political transformation. Some deplore what they see as a centralizing tendency in

Harry N. Scheiber, *The Condition of American Federalism: An Historian's View.* A Study Submitted by the Subcommittee on Intergovernmental Operations, United States Senate, 89th Congress, 2nd Session, 1966.

American government; others welcome what California's Governor Brown terms "jet-age federalism," which would bring the States into a more distinctly subordinate position in the Republic.[1] Although it is widely admitted the spatial limits of State and local jurisdictions hamper their efforts to meet problems which are national in scope, the long-standing difference continues, in American political dialogue, as to what costs democracy must pay if Federal powers are further enlarged.

This debate has been colored lately by differences of opinion concerning the actual historic tradition of American federalism. The long-standard view was that throughout the 19th century, and in most respects until the New Deal, "dual federalism"—in which the functions of the three levels of government were well delineated and in which their administrative activities were kept separate and autonomous—was the prevailing system. Only in the 20th century did there emerge a new order, termed "cooperative federalism," in which all the levels of government became "mutually complementary parts of a *single* governmental mechanism all of whose powers are intended to realize the current purposes of government according to the applicability of the problem at hand."[2]

Now there has become popular a new historical view, associated mainly with the late Morton Grodzins, that dual federalism never characterized the American political system. From the beginning, it is asserted, there was a high degree of intergovernmental activity, involving shared functions and responsibilities; indeed, there was "as much sharing" in the period 1790–1860 as there is today.[3] Surprising as it may seem, this historical construct has gained wide currency among political scientists and bids fair to become the new conventional wisdom about American federalism.

In this essay, I shall argue that American federalism has undergone a series of major transformations from 1790 to the present, with fairly distinct stages that can be identified in terms of how power was progressively redistributed between the Federal and State-local governments. Analysis of these stages of evolution will provide the historical context for a reappraisal of the Great Society programs now operative or recently proposed by President Johnson. The direction of recent changes in power distribution among levels of government will be explored, with a view towards suggesting portents of further change in the near future.

I.   *The Fallacy of Continuity*

The model of "cooperative federalism" portrays the present-day federal system as one in which most of the important functions of government are shared. Professor Grodzins argued that the system does not resemble a layer cake "of three distinct and separate planes" so much as a marble cake: "there is no neat horizontal stratification," for both policy-making and administrative functions are shared by Federal, State, and local governments. Grodzins went further, declaring that the marble-cake analogy was applicable no less to American federalism in the 19th century than it is today. "There has in fact never been a time," he wrote, "when Federal, State, and local functions were separate and distinct. Government does more things in 1963 than it did in 1790 or 1861; but in terms of what government did, there was as much sharing then as today."[4]

This historical construct has enormous potential in terms of its political impact. For it lends the weight of historical authority and precedent to the *status quo*, or indeed to any centralization of power that is accompanied by arrangements for the sharing of administrative functions. It has the further advantage of discrediting those who might fear centralization because they attribute the historic strength of representative government in America to the tradition of dual federalism. "One cannot hark back to the good old days of State and local independence," Grodzins declared, "because those days never existed." This refrain was echoed, with good political effect, by Lyndon Johnson during his 1964 Presidential campaign, and surely it will be heard frequently as the Great Society programs are debated hereafter.[5]

Grodzins himself provided little evidence on which to judge his version of historic federalism. He asserted, *ex cathedra*, that "whatever was at the focus of State attention in the 19th century became the recipient of national grants" in the form of cash aid, land grants, or loans of technical personnel. To support such contentions, Grodzins relied heavily on the historical research of his student Daniel Elazar. Elazar in turn has asserted (1) that when government assumed responsibility in specific functional fields, government at all levels "acted in concert"; and (2) that "Federal funds provided the stimulus for new programs throughout the nineteenth century." In his research, he has found that "virtually every domestic governmental program involved intergovernmental cooperation in some form."[6]

There are three main flaws in the Grodzins-Elazar construct. First, it does not cover systematically the whole spectrum of State policy concerns and administrative activities to prove the contention that "whatever was at the focus of State attention" received Federal aid. The Grodzins-Elazar argument can be upheld, in short, only if one accepts a tautological definition of "the focus of State attention"; those programs which *did* receive Federal aid must be viewed as at "the focus."

Second, Grodzins and Elazar do not establish plausible criteria as to what was trivial and what important in the field of "intergovernmental cooperation." Thus they treat the most superficial administrative contacts (for example, State libraries' exchange of legal volumes with Federal agencies, or loan of surveying instruments to the States by the U.S. Coast Survey) as evidence of viable cooperation.[7]

Finally, and most centrally, they do not consider the basic issue of power as it was distributed relatively among levels of government. Indeed, they do not even consider power as it was exercised at different levels in the few State programs that *were* aided with Federal grants of cash, personnel, or land.

The question of Federal cash grants in the 19th century can be disposed of readily: they were of negligible importance by any quantitative measure.[8] The first cash-grant program on a continuing basis, aside from cash aid for maintaining pensioned Civil War veterans in State homes, came in 1887, when the Hatch Act provided $15,000 per year to the States in aid of agricultural research. As late as 1902, less than one percent of all State and local revenues came from the central government, by contrast with perhaps 20 percent in 1934 and 14 percent in 1963. Obviously there was *not* "as much sharing then as today," measured either by the relative magnitude of Federal grants in total State-local financing or by the proportion of State-local policy concerns affected by Federal cash aid. Loans of Federal technical personnel were even less important, comprising mainly the services of the Army Engineers for the brief period 1824 to 1838.[9]

The Federal land grants to the States comprise the only substantial evidence for the Grodzins-Elazar historical construct. These grants were mainly for two purposes: education and transportation.[10] In the field of education, there were two land-grant programs of importance, the cession of portions of the Federal land in public-land States of the West for support of common schools; and the Morrill Act cessions of 1862, granting scrip receivable for public lands to all States in proportion to their population, for support of agricultural and mechanical colleges.

Neither program, however, comprised genuine sharing comparable to that which characterizes the modern grant-in-aid programs— for neither significantly narrowed the range of policy-making discretion enjoyed by the States. In common education, the States continued to have exclusive control over professional and certification standards, over determination of levels of total support, over curriculum structure and content, and the like. There was no matching formula operative; there were no administrative contacts with agencies of the Federal government charged with policy or administrative functions (the U.S. Office of Education was not even established until 1867); and there was no auditing nor inspection by Federal officials.[11]

Federal land grants for transportation offer somewhat more persuasive evidence of genuine "sharing" of 19th century policy-making functions. The grants to the States and to private railroad companies did affect vitally the pace and location of new transport construction. However, supportive and subsidy activity was only one aspect of policy-making in this field. Equally important was regulation of rates and operating practices on the lines of transport. One cannot find government at all levels "acting in concert" (Elazar's phrase) in this policy area. It was the States alone that established basic corporation, property, taxation, and eminent-domain law under which transportation facilities were built, financed, and operated. From the 1830's on, the States had control over railroad charges; and the Granger laws of the 1870's had ample precedent in State regulatory legislation of the preceding decades. Not until 1887, when it established the Interstate Commerce Commission, did Congress first assert its power in the regulatory field. The relative distribution of power over transport costs in the national economy cannot, moreover, be judged alone by reference to statutes and court decisions. For in their administrative operations, the States exercised real control over the ostensibly free internal-transport market. As owners and operators of basic lines of internal transport in the canal era, 1825-1850, the States blatantly evaded Constitutional limitations on their power to regulate interstate commerce. In every major canal State, the public authorities levied discriminatory tolls that favored their own producers at the expense of those located out of State. As a result, the State canal tolls until 1850 constituted a web of effective barriers to free internal trade.[12]

In sum, even if one takes into account the cash value of Federal land ceded to the States, the 19th-century Federal grants did not involve pervasive sharing of policy-making powers. Intergovernmental administrative contracts were casual at best: even in the major land-grant programs, the Federal administrative role was limited mainly to the bookkeeping operations of the General Land Office. It requires tortured semantics and neglect of the critical issue—relative power— to argue basic continuity in the history of the 19th and 20th century federalism on evidence such as Grodzins and Elazar have adduced. If this historical construct of cooperative federalism is fallacious, what, then, is the record?

The federal system may be rather understood as having gone through four major stages of power distribution. The basic pattern of intergovernmental relations has been redefined and reformulated in each of these stages—and the "creative federalism" advocated by President Johnson must be comprehended in a context of successive transformations rather than as a mere variant of a timeless theme.

II.   The Stages of Historic Federalism, 1790-1966

Two basic features of the 19th century federal system must be noted at the outset if we are to recognize the structure of power in that period. In the first place, the issues of Constitutional principle were deeply embedded in the American political consciousness; and a manifest bias favoring decentralization was evident in the policy choices no less than in the political rhetoric of that era. Although pragmatic attitudes often overcame such scruples, when Americans considered matters of public policy,

> the question was never simply: should the most suitable agency of government undertake collective action to solve the problem? Always there was the second question: according to the Constitution, should the national government, or State or local governments, undertake the action?[13]

Not until well after the Civil War was this Constitutional issue subordinated as Federal power became enlarged in response to nationalization of the economy and the emergence of urgent social, economic problems national in their dimensions.

In the second place, the power of State and local governments in the 19th century, especially considering the degree of control they could effectively exercise prior to consolidation of national business corporations whose activities transcended State lines, was impressive in scope and significance. Thus, William Anderson reminds us that the States exercised nearly exclusive jurisdiction in many crucial fields of policys in some of which even today they play the dominant role: "property rights (including eminent domain law), business organization, family life, social relations, criminal and civil law; and provisions for law enforcement and courts, local government, elections, education, civil rights, [and] conservation."[14] In short, the evidence for genuine dual federalism is sound, and the areas of autonomous State-local functions were hardly unimportant.

(A) Rivalistic state mercantilism, 1790-1860:

The initial period from 1790 to 1860 was one in which dual federalism, involving effective separation of powers, became the framework for a pervasive rivalism among the individual States and among local communities within the States.

In national politics the spirit of rivalry, as it was manifested in "sectionalism," often rendered Congress impotent in crucial areas of policy. But rivalry was no less intense when the focus of power passed to the States. In the case of transportation, for example, proponents of the great State canal programs of 1817–1837 argued for active government enterprise on essentially mercantilistic grounds: they regarded each State as a community of interest, transcending local differences within the State, and operating in a hostile universe of rival State communities acting on similar premises. As Louis

Hartz has noted, however, the idea of transcendent community self-interest "had no area around which it could effectively come to a focus. If it could be used on the State level, it could also be used on the sectional level, and if it could be used there it could also be invoked to rationalize the ambitions of one hamlet as against another within a section."[15]

Thus in most of the States, regional power groupings blocked State action temporarily and then paradoxically forced governments into transport-investment programs that were comprehensive enough to satisfy the ambitions of a majority coalition. Often the result was action beyond the resources of the State, and a wave of defaults and debt repudiations bespoke this fact in the depression of the early 1840's. In the same manner, regional and functional interest groups struggled over the vital issue of State canal tolls, which governed terms of trade in many areas of the country in the forties. And when State regulation of private railroad rates emerged as the more important instrument of transport policy, substate interest groups formed to support strong regulation, if they were being victimized by rate discrimination; or else to oppose it, if they benefited from discriminatory policies or if they feared that regulation would discourage new investment when they lacked adequate facilities.[16]

State mercantilistic rivalries were no less striking in the areas of taxation, corporation law, and land policy. Governments discriminated against out-of-State interests, curbed investment by outsiders or participation by nonresidents in corporation directorates, and regulated closely the activities of what they termed (characteristically) "foreign corporations." There was occasionally telling intervention by the Federal courts while John Marshall was Chief Justice, and yet many such practices persisted without effective challenge well into the 20th century. As the result of rivalistic mercantilism the American market remained "Balkanized" in essential respects—despite the Constitution's obvious intent otherwise—long past the period of initial industrialization and national economic integration.[17]

This Balkanization was possible because of the viability of dual federalism, which permitted the States to exercise so wide a range of powers, and to do so without obstruction by way of Federal preemption of critical policy areas and functions. If, as David Fellman asserts, State-local powers "must necessarily be significant in the aggregate" if "federalism is to be a reality," then the American federal system before 1860 fully met this sensible standard.[18]

Aside from the wide range of functions on which the States operated nearly free of significant interference from the National government, noted earlier, they exercised a high degree of control over banking and monetary policy, virtually exclusive control over conditions of labor, and nearly complete autonomy in the field of civil rights as well.

(B) Centralizing federalism, 1860-1933:

Gradually the power center shifted, marking a second historical era in American federalism, in which the central government gradually preempted functions and policy-making powers formerly lodged in the lower levels of government. This was accomplished partly as a result of the Civil War, when with the Southern agrarian element absent the ascendant Republicans—however divided as to specific programs—acted on a consensus that Congress ought to provide a uniform national legal framework that would stimulate economic development. In part, too, it was accomplished out of negative motives: to forestall State or local exercise of powers that hampered industrial growth—especially as the judiciary struck down State regulatory legislation inimical to business interests. It was also a natural, if not altogether inevitable, response to the new national dimensions of business enterprises and labor organizations, and to the consumer problems of an increasingly urbanized society.[19]

The flowering of judicial review after 1865, although at first used for conservative and negative purposes, did have the effect of asserting superior Federal powers. As to the legislative record, Congress dominated banking and monetary policy after 1862, when the National Banking Law was enacted. In 1887, Federal regulation of railroads in interstate commerce was inaugurated, and three years later the Sherman Act ended exclusive State control over corporate consolidations and operational practices. At first (in the 1890's) through court injunctions and later by way of positive legislation affecting railroad labor, maritime workers and the status of labor unions under Sherman Act provisions, a Federal policy in the field of labor-industrial relations emerged. Meanwhile, the period 1891–1908 brought active Federal policy in resource conservation; in quality and disease control in food, drug, and livestock marketing; and in the elaboration of railroad, banking, and monetary regulation.[20]

All these measures manifested the most obvious centralizing tendencies in the federal system. But late in the 19th century, there was also a move toward genuine sharing of functions in the system: closer intergovernmental cooperation and sharing of policy-making powers and their implementation. The Carey Act of 1894, which authorized Federal grants to the States of arid land needing irrigation, differed from earlier programs of Federal aid in land by requiring that the States submit comprehensive reclamation plans for prior approval by Federal authorities. In 1900, the Lacey Act banned interstate shipment of birds and wild animals taken in violation of State laws—a move toward enlarged Federal-State cooperation in exercise of police powers, long an exclusive State responsibility. Similar congressional legislation during 1895–1919 supported State police statutes regulating lotteries, "white slave" traffic, and stolen motor vehicles.[21]

Meanwhile, the programs of cash grants by Congress to the States became more important. In 1902 there were still only five such programs, involving aid to the State colleges and experiment stations, to veterans, and to the blind, together contributing $3 million to State and local governments. But the principles which mark the modern cash grant programs, distinguishing them from their 19th century counterparts, began to appear at this time. In 1911, regular inspection of State operations by Federal officials was instituted in the forestry program, and the requirement for matching of Federal grant funds by the States was inaugurated. With enactment of the first highway-aid grants in 1916, the Federal Government penetrated the borders of State administration even more massively. Each recipient State was required to submit advance plans, to make progress reports, and to establish a department of highways (only 17 had such an agency at the time) with power deemed sufficient to administer the grants effectively.[22]

Gradual growth of the modern grant programs was paralleled by another development, lying outside the formal political structure of power distribution but nonetheless integral to the operative federal system: the emergence of functional bureaucracies. Government officials with similar functions developed a sense of professional community that cut across intergovernmental lines and even bridged the private and public sectors. Their professional standards and assumptions about policy and programs began to affect policy formulation as well as administration, as legislative bodies became increasingly reliant upon experts in a complex industrialized society. The most important manifestation was in the Agricultural Extension Service, founded in 1914. Under the Smith-Lever Act agricultural agents were named in every rural county, and their activities were financed with Federal money channeled through the land-grant colleges. The agents reported both to the colleges and, in a much looser way, to the U.S. Department of Agriculture. The Extension Service personnel became emblematic of bureaucracy's political potential in cooperative intergovernmental programs, for the agents gave a class bias to agricultural extension by working mainly with the more substantial farmers, giving little attention to poor tenants or migrants. At the same time, they formed an alliance with the quasi-private American Farm Bureau Federation—a self-reinforcing alliance, since the AFBF threw its political support to the county agents whenever they were subjected to political attack.[23]

As of 1920, there were eleven intergovernmental programs in operation, involving over $30 million of Federal grants per year. As late as 1922, however, Federal grants provided only 2.5 percent of State and local revenues, and in 1927 they provided only 1.7 percent. No new programs were instituted in the 1920's, a period of what Elazar aptly terms "normalized retrenchment" during which there was some "expansion of existing programs and refinements of their cooperative administration."[24] But there was nothing either gradual or refined about what followed in the New Deal years.

(C) The New Deal and a new federalism, 1933-1941:

The New Deal was crucial in shaping modern cooperative federalism. In the first place, it brought dramatic centralization of power, as the Federal Government responded to a depression crisis with sweeping labor, agricultural, public works and welfare programs. These were in addition to the experiments with regional planning and development (notably T.V.A.), the short-lived but radical National Recovery Act program for control of industrial production and prices, and the expansion of Federal regulatory activity, both in new fields such as stockmarket operations and in established fields such as communications and transportation. At the same time, vigorous application of the Federal income taxing power sealed with finality the central government's effective preemption of this type of revenue source; and the exercise of compensatory fiscal powers, on Keynesian lines, had an overarching effect on volume of business activity and the pattern of economic changes.[25]

While the Supreme Court reversed its traditional position on the basic issues of power distribution in the federal system, it also overturned landmark due-process decisions which had long curbed State and local efforts at social and economic regulation; and so it paved the way for enlarged power of regulation of all three levels of government. The commerce clause was revitalized in the broad terms originally set out by John Marshall, and the Court wrote a sweeping new construction of Federal tax power. In the 1940's, the Supreme Court moved decisively to strike down vestigial State powers that were the heritage of rivalistic mercantilism. Opinions of the Court celebrated the "federal free trade unit" and inveighed against State laws which discriminated against other States and threatened to set off "fantastic rivalries and dislocations and reprisals."[26]

As the scope of Federal activity grew broader and the locus of power in the political order moved toward Washington, a second basic change affected the new cooperative Federal order. This was the proliferation of intergovernmental programs, with a sharp increase in commitment of public funds to them. During 1933–35 alone, new intergovernmental programs were established for distribution of surplus farm products to the needy, free school lunches, child welfare, maternal and children's health, and crippled children's services; old-age assistance, aid to dependent children, aid to the blind, general health services, emergency highway expenditures, and emergency work relief; and aid in support of general local-government costs, general relief, and administration of Social Security insurance. Between 1935 and 1938, Congress added new programs for fish and wildlife conservation, public housing, emergency road and bridge construction, and venereal disease and tuberculosis control.[27]

Measured in terms of cash expended for Federal grants to State and local government, the New Deal programs dwarfed anything that had been undertaken before. The "revised" statistics of Federal grants, usually cited today, show a rise in Federal payments to State and local government from $232 million in 1932 to a pre-World War II peak of $976 million in 1934, with the level of payments never falling below $762 million (1938) thereafter until the war.[28] These "revised" data have produced an ironical distortion in interpretation of the New Deal's impact on cooperative federalism, for they exclude all programs labeled as "emergency" measures. In table I, the "revised" data are compared to "actual" data, which do incorporate emergency-program funds channeled through State and local governments.

The more comprehensive "actual" data demonstrate that the magnitude of the New Deal's grant programs was far greater than is usually recognized. The dollar amount of payments for 1939 was not equalled again until the 1950's, when gross national product was about three times as large as in 1939. Moreover, the role of welfare-type programs in intergovernmental relations was much greater in the 1930's than the "revised" data indicate. The proportion of total Federal intergovernmental aid representing payments for welfare purposes is usually quoted for example as 30 percent for 1938, whereas the actual data indicate that welfare comprised some 80 percent of the total.[29]

Table 1.   Federal grants-in-aid
to state and local governments (In millions of dollars)

Year	Officially "revised"	Actual total:[1]
1933	([2])	$ 193
1934	$976	1,842
1936	908	2,313
1938	762	2,175
1939	([2])	2,904
1940	884	2,395
1942	887	1,820

[1]Includes emergency programs.
[2]Not available.

Sources: "Revised" data are from *Historical Statistics of U.S. Colonial Times to 1957* (Bureau of the Census, 1960), p. 724. "Actual" data, including emergency programs, are from Advisory Commission on Intergovernmental Relations, *Periodical Congressional Reassessment of Federal Grants-in-aid to State and Local Governments,* June 1961 (Report A-8), p. 12.

The shift toward welfare aid (including aid for public housing) represented a major break from the earlier functional emphases on Federal aid. From 1916, when Federal highway aid began, until 1932, highway and education programs had comprised 75 percent or more of grant-in-aid payments. The dominant role of welfare after 1933 was even more significant because these programs were administered with a high degree of discretion vested in national officials. The Federal Emergency Relief Agency, for example, had authority to allocate funds, State by State, on whatever basis it chose. Under Harry Hopkins, FERA distributed its largesse "without strings" to local agencies in some States; in other States, Hopkins required Governors to institute changes in organization or administration of relief; and where local relief agencies appeared to him "hopelessly incompetent" FERA moved in directly and set up its own organization.[30]

Enlargement of Federal administrators' discretionary authority was only one side of centralization. For there were also important initiatives in this direction by Congress itself. As the scope and number of grant programs was enlarged, Congress mandated new detailed formulae for determination of State eligibility for aid: States and local governments were required to match funds and to undertake administrative reforms (including institution of Civil Service Merit Systems) to qualify; and the principle of equalization, designed to adjust payments according to States' needs and resources, was instituted. Finally, recipient governments were sometimes required to submit regional, local, or State planning reports in order to qualify for aid.[31]

Other important features of the new federalism, manifest in the 1930's, although sometimes regarded as more recent in origin, were as follows:

A bypassing tendency.—The emergency relief agencies pioneered in making grants-of-aid directly to local agencies of government, bypassing the States—a tendency which culminated in the post-World War II years when new programs for airport aid, urban renewal, housing, and education provided for direct grants of Federal money to local governments. Other New Deal programs cut across the traditional political jurisdictions, either by creating special-district governmental units (e.g., soil conservancy districts) or by establishing regional administrative offices that supervised activities in several States (e.g., the Tennessee Valley Authority). Such new units forced the States and local governments—and also political pressure groups— to operate within a new system of power relationships.[32]

A skewing effect.—The infusion of massive grant-in-aid funding also caused a skewing of State and local government financing. Especially in the poorer States, legislators tended to allocate revenues to programs that commanded matching Federal funds, so as to maximize the local impact of State dollar expenditures. Often this was at the expense of meeting other needs—especially given the crisis condition of State and local revenues in this period. The 1934 Highway Act, for example, favored States that earmarked user revenues for their road programs. This diminished State-local discretion in the use of their total revenues, although the option of refusing Federal aid did remain open. As a result, the highway aid program discouraged expenditures on secondary roads that commanded no Federal matching funds; and it also intensified already-scandalous neglect of urban mass transit needs and intraurban roads—an unfortunate aspect of the Federal transportation policy until the 1960's.

The skewing effect also carried over into State and local debt structure. Federal program administrators encouraged State-local issues of non-guaranteed bonds as a means of obtaining matching funds. This lent an element of additional instability to governmental finance, and it often meant that States or localities committed themselves to servicing a debt not incurred on the basis of rational overall planning for long-term needs.[33]

Fractionalizing of responsibility.—The rising importance of intergovernmental programs resulted in a serious fractionalization of responsibility and power. Program planning and specific decisions to allocate funds (matching and otherwise) became dependent upon action at two or more levels of government; and decisions at one level were often made contingent on policies of another. Within the context of multi-level and multi-agency fractionalization, there operated growing "functional communities of specialist civil servants" whose common professional attitudes were often more important than their loyalty to the level of government or the agency which employed them. In the familiar manner, these bureaucratic communities, like some government agencies with well-delineated jurisdictions, developed a "clientele" relationship with special interest groups. Multilevel and multi-agency fractionalization made it difficult to fasten clearcut responsibility on a single unit of government. They also opened new routes of political "access" for pressure groups seeking to influence policy or administrative decisions; and they created many basic points of tension between the "area-based claims of government" (the communities of interest that the traditional political units represented) and the bureaucracies and private interest groups organized on functional lines.[34]

Use of "action" and "demonstration" programs.—The disruptive potential—for good or ill—of intergovernmental programs as they affected the existing power structure was nowhere more evident than in "action" and "demonstration" projects fostered by the Federal Government in the New Deal years. In the agricultural programs of the 1930's, for example, working farmers and private citizens were brought into special district and county, state, and regional committees or demonstration projects that eventually involved over

900,000 participants. Just as the poverty agencies' action programs threaten the regular local political organizations in the cities today, the farmer-citizens' committees of the 1930's were a counterweight to the entrenched agricultural "Establishment": the land-grant colleges, the Extension Service, and the Farm Bureau Federation. The New Deal also used the demonstration approach, at first with relatively tame local land-use and crop experiments, but later with Farm Security Administration-organized programs of aid to selected depressed rural communities. Some agencies, including T.V.A., shied away from direct confrontation with such local political institutions as Negro segregation or with functional-bureaucratic interests like the Forest Service; but others, notably F.S.A., assaulted the local power structure, especially in the South, and to no less a degree threatened the more conservative Federal and State-local agencies. Like the demonstration projects recently proposed or instituted in transportation and urban renewal, however, the demonstration programs of the thirties did a great deal for only a few communities, and nothing at all for most.[35]

Intensified emphasis on planning.—There was, finally, a concern in the New Deal years to support planning efforts by State and local authorities with Federal funds. The National Resources Board gave financial and technical assistance to States which established planning authorities; but there was also new Federal support for narrower types of planning efforts. Federal administrators in agricultural extension, forest-fire prevention, employment services, and public-health services required plans relating to administrative organizations and proposed procedures before approving funds. The FERA went further and required of the States what the Administrator deemed "adequate and sound relief policies," not merely adequate organizational structure and personnel quality. Similarly, grants for vocational education were predicated on adoption of sound State policies governing the local agencies which ultimately administered Federal funds; and highway aid was made dependent on long-term, comprehensive plans by the States. In the case of Federal grants for administration of the Social Security program, the States were not required to make matching contributions; yet the Federal authorities in effect passed judgment on State budgets and set broad guidelines for administrative organization and procedures.[36]

(D) Since the New Deal, 1941–1966:

None of the features of the New Deal's brand of cooperative federalism, as outlined above, had characterized intergovernmental relations in a significant way prior to 1933. And all have persisted to the present day. There have been some major departures, however since the coming of World War II.

The war itself was significant for involving State and local officials in administration of Federal programs, notably the draft conscription and the various rationing and priority programs. But the war years also witnessed a sharp curtailment of State and local governmental services, as some were no longer needed because the depression had ended, others being cut back in order to conserve resources. As State-local revenues increased with prosperity conditions at home, debt was retired rapidly; and so many viewed the "buoyancy of the State finances" and the concurrent increase in the Federal debt as a portent of resurgent State-local power. But at least one contemporary analyst, James A. Maxwell, viewed the vast increase in the Federal establishment, its enlarged financial resources, and the massive nationalization of power in the wartime emergency, as a potent long-term force for centralization rather than for State-local resurgence. His insight proved well founded. In the postwar period, as the role of a Federal government committed to growing welfare functions was enlarged, the States found it difficult to sustain even their traditional level of services. Together with growth of Federal programs, however, came renewal of emphasis upon intergovernmental efforts.[37]

Despite a temporary retardation in the first Eisenhower Administration, there has been a long-term proliferation of programs and expansion of funds involved. Much of the increase has come since 1963. Federal payments to State and local governments increased from $2.4 billion in 1950 to $14.7 billion estimated for fiscal 1967. Constituting 11 percent of State-local revenues a decade ago, Federal payments now comprise about 15 percent.[38] (See table 2.)

Table 2.   Federal financial assistance
to state and local governments, selected years 1944–67

	Total aid *(millions)*	*Per capita* *aid*	*Federal aid as percent of State-local general revenues (percent)*
1944	1,072	7.75	9.8
1948	1,771	12.08	10.3
1952	2,585	16.47	10.3
1957	3,873	22.73	10.1
1960	6,994	38.86	13.8
1962	7,735	41.63	13.3
1963	8,507	45.10	13.9
1965	10,900	(1)	(1)
1966 estimate	12,800	(1)	(1)
1967 estimate	14,700	(1)	(1)

[1]Not available.

Sources: 1944–63: Alan K. Campbell, in *Annals*, Vol. 359, p. 96. 1965–67: *Budget of the U.S. Government, Fiscal Year ending June 30, 1967* (Washington, 1966), p. 440.

There have been significant shifts also in the purposes for which the grants are distributed. Welfare programs declined from the levels reached in the Depression, stabilizing at about 30 percent of total payments in recent years, whereas highway aid has assumed renewed importance as the result of the Interstate Highway program. New urban-oriented programs, mainly instituted in the Kennedy and Johnson administrations, have assumed a large place; and in the last year education aid has begun to take on much greater importance. (See table 3.)

Table 3.   Federal grants[1] to state and local
governments by function, selected years, 1950-67 (In millions of dollars)

Function	1950	1953	1956	1959	1962	1964	1967[2]
Veterans benefits and services	15	6	8	8	8	8	9
International affairs	—	—	—	—	7	4	5
Agriculture and agricultural resources	106	97	389	322	524	656	428
Natural resources	17	23	27	34	35	45	193
Commerce and transportation	465	528	746	2,671	2,842	3,979	4,308
Housing and community development	10	68	128	207	354	452	878
Health, labor, and welfare[3]	1,563	1,810	2,080	2,800	3,554	4,259	6,615
Education	39	231	238	281	405	479	2,033
National defense[4]	—	—	—	—	35	35	39
Total grants-in-aid	2,226	2,781	3,642	6,356	7,785	9,969	14,550
Total Federal aid to State-local government[5]	2,269	2,857	3,753	6,813	8,190	10,314	14,647

[1]Includes trust funds.
[2]Estimated, 1967 Budget.
[3]Includes School Lunch Program.
[4]Small items for community defense facilities under "Housing and Community Development," to 1960. Range = $1 million to $15 million.
[5]Includes shared revenues, loans, and repayable advances.

Sources: 1950-64, *Statistical Abstract;* 1967, *Special Analyses, 1967 Budget,* p. 137. Payments for "General Government" (range = $15 million to $52 million) not itemized, but included in Total.

There is heavier emphasis also upon planning by States and localities as a requirement of eligibility for grants. Especially in programs affecting metropolitan areas, these requirements have encouraged communities to break with tradition and to plan—even if only nominally—for large areal units embracing numerous political jurisdictions. In addition, Federal grants have gone to State and local planning agencies, and contracts have been awarded to non-governmental agencies (especially research organizations and universities) to produce what are essentially plans for various grant programs. Meanwhile, procedures and criteria for Federal supervision of grants and their uses have been tightened. The line between auditing and supervision is often hazy, and at what point inspection verges into coercion has become a subject of frequent dispute between agencies at different governmental levels.

Another important characteristic of postwar programs is the rising institutionalized concern with the formal constitutional and operational aspects of intergovernmental relations. Aside from research projects, conferences, and position statements endorsed by the Conference of Governors and similar groups, the Federal Government itself has established an agency with specific responsibility in this area: the Advisory Commission on Intergovernmental Relations, organized in 1959. The Commission has brought unusual energy to a task fraught with political perils. It has proposed—indeed boldly, given the delicacy of its position—constitutional, statutory, and administrative changes both to the States and to Congress; and it also has conducted staff research of high caliber. In effect, the ACIR has become a "third force" in its own right.

Finally, the post-1945 programs have increased the bypassing tendency in two ways. First, direct Federal grants directly to local units of government have become larger, especially with the growth of three major programs (airports, housing, and urban renewal) geared to aid to urban centers. This will no doubt be further intensified as educational grants to local school districts grow. Second, more recently, bypassing has taken a new turn with growth of community-action projects under the Poverty programs. In effect, new political power centers have been nurtured at the expense of both local party organizations and established political or administrative units. The infusion of Federal money into Poverty agencies has set off bitter power struggles between local party machines and the community organizations suddenly raised in their bailiwicks. In the same way, school districts which have long maintained the P.T.A. as their only concession to community participation are suddenly drawn into programs that must change their established professional orientation, to say nothing of their cherished insulation from the political storms that rage outside school walls. The new programs have bypassed established functional bureaucracies as well—witness the conflict between social workers and activist elements in local contests for control of community action agencies.

Whatever direction President Johnson's emergent "creative federalism" may take, it is clear that the power distribution in American federalism, as it has emerged since the New Deal, bears little resemblance to earlier days.

III. "Creative Federalism": A Departure?

In his proposals for Great Society programs and his political speeches, President Johnson has denied that he seeks aggrandizement of centralized Federal power: rather he seeks to design programs of intergovernmental action, thereby assuring continued vitality of State

and local units, in what he has called a framework of "creative federalism" involving "new federal partnerships." Occasionally he defends
this approach as a new departure, necessary because of the urgency
of current problems. More often, however, he emphasizes that his
proposals are an extension of historic American federalism, with
ample precedent in the 19th-century history of land grants and in the
more recent history of cooperative federalism.[39]

"Creative federalism," as Johnson has formulated it, has received little careful analysis as yet. At first blush, its main feature
appears to be a willingness to establish direct Federal-local programs,
bypassing the States. This is the feature that Johnson emphasized in
his May 1964 University of Michigan address on urban problems,
when he first introduced creative federalism as a formal concept.[40]
But when he elaborated his views during 1964, Johnson asserted more
than this. For he declared that urban problems would require not
only Federal action but also "the cooperation of the State and the
city, and of business and of labor, and of private institutions and of
private individuals."[41] The new partnership, in short, is to be a much
broader one than that which has marked cooperative federalism
since the 1930's: for creative federalism would mobilize private
interests as well as public agencies in intergovernmental programs.

This vital element in the Johnson concept became manifest in the
1964 Presidential campaign. Each time he discussed creative federalism, Johnson underscored also that "for our entire history we
have worked with local government and private enterprise."[42] Political
rhetoric yielded to more concrete programmatic aims without loss
of this element. Thus the Appalachia program's cabinet-level coordinating committee was directed to collaborate with the region's
Governors, T.V.A., and all Federal agencies, to assure "optimum
benefits from the expenditure of Federal, State, and local funds, and to
facilitate and promote private investment in the development of
Appalachia."[43] In his 1966 Transportation Message, Johnson invoked "enlightened Government serving as a full partner with private
enterprise." In the Conservation Message of 1966, he called for
combining "all the means at our disposal—Federal, State, local,
and private," in the assault upon river pollution. And in administering
the Poverty program, the Johnson administration has contracted with
private business firms to operate job retraining centers; and it has
financed separate institutes to train labor leaders and businessmen
for involvement in community action programs.[44]

Private interests have been quick to perceive that creative
federalism promises to be operational consensus politics: it broadens
the intergovernmental partnership to include elements of the private
sector, even encouraging the involvement of rival private-interest
groups eager to obtain a share of the influence and funds such programs offer. The Nationwide Insurance Company no doubt reflects a

common business attitude in urging its employees in Appalachia to become involved in action programs, "on the assumption that any economic improvements will create more customers for insurance and improve the company's image." The business press has responded favorably to what the *Wall Street Journal* terms "a growing, and reciprocal, rapprochement between business and the Federal Government." *Fortune*, even more exuberantly, hails creative federalism as "a fundamental break with the welfare-state trend."[45]

Second, the concept of creative federalism is based upon a sense that the ultimate objective is overall growth in the economy, and in government at all levels, too, as a means of enlarging the problem-solving capacity of the society. Thus one of the principal architects of the urban programs in Congress asserts that the "unifying thought" behind expanded Federal activity in the cities is "the effort to shore up local tax bases." Similarly, the President has declared that enlarged Federal grant-in-aid programs will increase "the tempo of effort at all levels of government." And the Budget Director has cited sustained overall economic growth as the most important single component of "the framework around which the Great Society is built." In the manner of John Kenneth Galbraith, then, the Johnson administration is stressing the possibilities of affluence. It regards the revenue "pie" as one that is growing, and that must be helped to grow; and not as one that is static, so that slicing it in different proportions diminishes governmental power at one level while it enhances power at another.

Third, creative federalism embraces a new administrative and planning method. This method entered Federal operations by way of systems analysis, the Pentagon, and program-budgeting in the McNamara manner. It is the "Planning-Program-Budgeting System"—"finding the least cost alternatives" of meeting carefully defined (and when possible, quantified) objectives, as Budget Director Charles Schultze has described it. Under PPBS, programs will be "project oriented"; and if the old political units or established administrative agencies are found irrelevant or obsolete, they will be disregarded. Program objectives, and budgeting of funds as well, will not be tied to the operations of specific Federal agencies or allocated to levels of government by formulae. Instead, the ideological imperatives that produced the formula concept in the first place will be discarded; the constitutional scruples and administrative inertia that channeled funds in established ways will be cast aside. Now the large social problems will be evaluated through careful cost-benefit analysis. Their solution will be pursued pragmatically through whatever combination of public and private interests seems appropriate. According to Schultze, PPBS is a process of (1) defining objectives, (2) measuring the anticipated "output" of alternative programs to attain those objectives, (3) determining the "total system costs of our programs on a multi-year basis"; (4) reviewing frequently the alternative programs possible; and (5) providing "a systematic flow of information on outputs and costs for department heads and under them their bureau chiefs." Finally, there must be intensive coordination both of planning and of programs in operation. The old concerns about "jurisdiction," by agency or by level of government, will give way to a much more urgent concern for coordination.[46]

IV. Prospects and Portents

Although appraisal of the Great Society and its potential impact upon American federalism must be tentative, nonetheless certain problems are already manifest and tendencies are perceivable which may well be "pressure points" that will channel the course of future changes in the political system.

The most obvious problems flow out of the "expanded partnership" which has drawn elements of the private sector into intergovernmental programs. Until the Johnson years, cooperative federalism had meant indirect private benefits from Federally aided programs; in some programs, such as urban renewal, profits (often handsome) were realized directly from investment opportunities opened by dint of public action. But now the pattern of derived private benefits may give way to a clash of interests within the framework of cooperative federalism. Private interest-group conflicts may become as prominent *within* shared-program administration as they have been, traditionally, in the legislative process.

The private interests which become involved in shared programs cannot be expected to put aside lightly their private goals: witness the already deep conflict between educators and private contracting firms over the proper nature of job retraining activities. Business firms will not neglect profit considerations any more than, say, the universities will cease to pursue large overhead allowances in administering Federal research grants, or than former consumer-cooperative professionals will desist from educating the poor in consumer economy when they become officials in community-action programs. For example, alarmed by bus boycotts, Poverty Board-directed clean-up drives against the unsanitary shops of local food merchants, and the like, some businessmen have allegedly determined to "get in there and make sure the job gets done right"—that is, assert their own interests and their opposition to such activities by participating in the action programs themselves.[47]

By welcoming manifold special-interest groups into the administration of shared programs, the Great Society scheme will probably intensify also the classic conflict between policy-makers and the functional bureaucracies which have interests and viewpoints of their own. Again the job-retraining centers portend the future. To the business firms which contract to run centers, the program offers entry into "the huge growth market of education" and provides an opportunity to subsidize experimentation with teaching equipment and techniques.[48] To the teachers and universities that become involved, the program represents something quite different. In the Poverty agency's programs, paid and volunteer workers comprise a corps of "irregulars" amidst a cadre of entrenched professionals—what Saul Alinsky contemptuously terms the Poverty Establishment, consisting of a social worker hierarchy that is, on the whole, deferential to the political establishment. In New York City, efforts by Federal workers and local action groups to inaugurate pre-school programs for the poor have run up against the city health inspectors' refusal—no doubt with good cause—to license facilities whose improvement will involve high capital costs and delay initiation of the programs.[49]

One must ask too what the expanded partnership promises for the continued vigor of leadership in private institutions or groups. The Negro rights organizations and activists among the poor already face this issue; and they are split between those who would take government posts, or hitch their organizational activities to the Poverty program's star, and those who prefer to continue operations independently of the government. In short, it is the timeless issue of "joining or licking 'em."

Another set of issues flow's from the Planning-Programming-Budgeting System and its approach to solution of urgent problems. In the first place, it involves an emphasis on rationalization and integration of agency responsibilities. But ironically there are signs already, as Republican spokesmen charge, of "increased complexity, regulation, and awkwardness" in the intergovernmental programs. Democratic Senator Muskie, one of Congress' best informed members on the question of intergovernmental relations, has charged that administrative bottlenecks and gaps, "empire building" in the Federal agencies, and unreasonably complex organization of departments (notably Housing and Urban Development) that were created specifically to break through complexities, now threaten to cripple grant programs.[50]

The drive to integrate Federal agency efforts often has taken the surprisingly prosaic form of reorganizing existing agencies. In the long run, this may, as hoped, permit more effective program budgeting and implementation. In the short run, however, it can create confusion and paralyze the bureaucracy. Not least, it can render it impossible for local or State officials to expedite programs or obtain commitments of funds. In the case of the environmental-pollution program, reorganization has led to mass resignations of the very men whose expertise the reorganization was designed to use more efficiently. The exodus of some Federal pollution experts into private industry suggests, moreover, that involvement of private firms in shared programs may sometimes result in hiring away of the government personnel best qualified to coordinate such programs and to assure the primacy of the public interest in their execution.

The PPBS promises also to give creative federalism a uniquely technocratic tone. Proponents of the system argue that it will help undermine logrolling and other special-interest techniques by putting hard data before Congress on the costs and benefits of alternatives to proposals that are ground out of the legislative mill. "In allocation of health dollars," *The Wall Street Journal* explains,

> PPBS budgeting will influence such choices as whether $20 million of Federal money would do most against cancer through research for a cure, training of doctors and other programs to secure early detection, or building of new treatment facilities . . . .[51]

Major difficulties inhere in cost-benefit analysis of such social-welfare programs. For example, one of the important factors in estimation of social benefits from control of a specific disease will be dollar value of workers' job time saved through its control. This may build in a bias against public investment in control of diseases which have their highest incidence among low-income workers. "The obvious but important point," one economist has asserted in his review of a similar problem, urban-renewal investment, "is that public investment can seldom be justified solely on the basis of market considerations." In comparing costs and benefits, "the balance sheet will be a statement in a number of different currencies without specification of exchange rates."[52] Perhaps Selma Mushkin of the Council of State Governments and Housing and Urban Development Secretary Robert C. Weaver are correct in warning that basic research is needed on the proper basis for comparing alternative programs designed to strengthen human resources before we abdicate to PPBS in governmental fields that touch human lives so closely as public health or city planning. Yet even they in effect thereby call for "operations research" (or PPBS) no less than do proponents of cash-benefit analysis of specific programs; their concerns are larger, but their proposed solution is no less technocratic than, say, Secretary McNamara's.[53]

A broader political problem raised by creative federalism involves the emerging political response to the emphasis on economic growth, with more activity by all levels of government, which marks the Great Society proposals. As a fiscal concept, the stress on the need for growth is sound enough. When confounded with issues of power, however, it can be intoxicating. Thus *Fortune* extols the demise of the enslaving notion that "the total amount of power (is) constant."

> * * * it is possible to think of vast increases of federal government power that do not encroach upon or diminish any other power.

Simultaneously, the power of states and local governments will increase; the power of private organizations, including business, will increase; and the power of individuals will increase.[54]

This unofficial manifesto suggests the perils of assuming that rapid economic growth renders obsolete the classic questions of how power is distributed. According to *Fortune*, "the overall degree of centralization or decentralization is seldom an interesting or even useful question." This kind of cavalier assertion may be reassuring, but it will prevent us from examining one vital dimension of program proposals. The desirability of centralization or decentralization continues to be a useful question indeed—particularly so when evaluating the chances of a program for success requires a further estimate of how the involvement of private interests may impede or aid its effective implementation. If it is desirable to force new changes in the federal system, to enhance or diminish the initiatory role of the central government, or to accept skewing of State resource allocations—and it may well be desirable—still it aids us little to make the blithe assumption that power at all levels will increase.

Any judgment of how the relative power of State-local governments may be affected by creative federalism must rest, moreover, upon assessment of fiscal realities. Here again we find that the statistics in common use often obscure the facts. For example, President Johnson has sometimes cited the swift growth since 1945 in State-local expenditures and indebtedness as evidence of vigorous, healthy expansion of real power in those levels of government. As he computes it, Federal spending rose 168 percent and Federal debt 21 percent during 1948–64, while State-local spending increased 268 percent and debt 365 percent in the same period.[55] This is difficult to square with the actual evidence, that Federal spending was $35 billion in fiscal 1948 and $118 billion in 1964. Federal "civilian expenditures" (excluding national defense and interest payments) rose from $13.8 billion to $54.6 billion, or more rapidly than State-local spending.

Professor Alan K. Campbell, prominent analyst of intergovernmental finance, has made a similar evaluation, asserting in 1964 that State and local governments were "the most dynamic part of the American economy today." He computed Federal expenditures as rising during 1952–62 only 25 percent (actually the increase was 44 percent), which he compared to a rise of 128 percent in State-local spending during the same period.[56]

However we compute them, the trends registered during 1952–62 should not dictate our interpretation of the entire postwar era. Even prior to 1962, there was a slowing in the growth rate in State-local governments' expenditures of their own funds, from 7.6 percent annual increase (constant dollars) during 1948–56 to 6.3 percent during 1956–62. The Federal Government's civilian expenditures registered no increase in terms of constant dollars, during 1948–56. But they rose at a 9.7 percent rate during 1956–62.[57] When we consider the more recent data, the emergent differences are even more striking, as shown in table 4. This table indicates that "the most dynamic sector" comprises the civilian programs of the Federal Government. Students of American federalism who treat growth of State-local expenditures as firm evidence of unique "vitality" in that sector will need to reconsider the data, especially in light of Great Society domestic programs and their prospects.

Moreover, the recent growth of State-local spending has not come effortlessly.

Table 4. Total federal, federal-civilian, and
state-local expenditures, 1956–64 (fiscal years) (dollars in billions, current)

	1956	1964	Increase 1956–64	Percent of increase 1956–64
General Federal expenditures	$69.8	$117.1	$47.3	+ 68
Federal-civilian expenditures[1]	24.6	54.6	30.0	+122
State-local (total) expenditures[2]	36.7	69.3	32.6	+ 89
State-local expenditures (own funds)	33.4	59.3	25.9	+ 78

[1]Excludes national defense and interest.
[2]Includes Federal grants expended.

Sources: *Economic Report of the President,* January 1966, pp. 281, 283; Federal civilian expenditures computed as Federal expenditures in the National Income Accounts, less National Defense and Interest, from *Budget of the United States Government, 1967* (Washington, 1966), pp. 439–440.

Prospects for improving the equitability or the revenue-increasing effects of property and sales taxes, which are still the main props of State-local fiscal strength, appear dim at best. This suggests that the States and local governments will become far more, rather than less, reliant upon Federal funds if they are to enlarge their range of services or increase their relative importance in administration of domestic programs. With Federal funding presumably will come the panoply of controls, centralized initiatives, and skewing effects—for better or worse—according to how one assesses the prospects of centralization—which has so disturbed champions of "grass roots democracy" and States rights.*

Furthermore, the debts of State-local government have more than doubled during 1955–1965, and increased five-fold during 1947–65. To be sure, forty-two of the fifty States still devoted 4 percent of

*This presumes that unrestricted grants (the Heller plan) will not be politically feasible in the near future.

revenues or less to servicing their debts in 1963. This does not suggest intolerable budgetary strains. Still, some local governments are already encountering grave debt problems (witness the case of New York City). Furthermore, as James Maxwell has noted, the sustained market for municipal and State bonds is supported by a Federal tax exemption that has retrogressive effects; State constitutional debt limitations often hamper borrowing operations at both the State and local levels; and an alarming proportion of recent bond issues has been in the form of nonguaranteed securities, which were 12.4 percent of State-local debt in 1949 but some 30 percent in 1963 (and 53 percent of State debt alone in 1963).[58] In sum, the growth of State-local debt appears to denote growing burdens rather than dynamic strength.

The questionable fiscal capacity of the States and localities underlines a more fundamental problem in federalism: the objective relevance of State and local units to solution of problems which transcend, in terms of origins and scope, their restricted areal jurisdictions. Critics of decentralized government have condemned the States and localities for many reasons. Some emphasize the allegedly undemocratic power structure that prevails at the "grass roots." Others condemn the States as characteristically reactionary and parochial, pointing especially to their resistance to welfare legislation (at least since the Progressive era), the notorious anti-urban bias of many legislatures, and the record in the South on civil rights and in the North on open occupancy. Critics also question the quality of State and local bureaucratic personnel; and they point to the dramatic scandals and corruption in the State legislatures and the county courthouses. But even in the best of all possible worlds—with clean, efficient, well-financed "progressive" State-local government—now there is still doubt whether their areal jurisdictions are genuinely relevant to the solution of such social and economic problems as poverty, unemployment, environmental pollution, and the like.

The Great Society proposals would attack precisely those problems whose dimensions transcend small-unit jurisdictions. Hence the possibility of meaningful policy initiatives and exercise of effective problem-solving power at the State or local level becomes increasingly remote. To be sure, the established procedures of cooperative federalism will permit sharing of administrative functions. Indeed, they might also permit frustration of national programs where State or local officials wish to accomplish it. But if pressure increases for effective assaults upon poverty, deterioration in the American cities, or environmental pollution, within the framework of creative federalism —with private interests involved, with PPBS influencing policy decisions and administration, and with the States probably increasingly reliant on Federal funds—will the procedures of cooperative federalism need to be discarded? And even if they can be preserved, can the present balance of power be preserved too, assuming that it can be justified? Can we maintain a federal system that meets the definitional requirement that "matters entrusted to the constituent units must be substantial and not merely trivial"?[59]

The American political system has undergone a revolution since 1933, and another major departure appears in process now. This retrospective view suggests, first, a warning that behind us is no homogeneous history of cooperative federalism, and that the Great Society may bring changes no less pervasive than those produced by the New Deal. It may be comforting to assume that cooperative federalism dates from 1790, just as it is comforting to assume that the real power of State-local government has recently grown more rapidly than the Federal Government's, or that issues of relative power are now irrelevant. But such assumptions will foreclose meaningful discussion of how shifts in power distribution (which are not automatically negated by mere administrative sharing) will in the future affect the federal system and the welfare of the Nation. If cooperative federalism from 1933 to the 1960's differs from the projected creative federalism of Lyndon B. Johnson, either in style or specific functional arrangements, the historical record suggests the perils of performance falling short of promise. It also indicates the importance of understanding what changes in power distribution we are prepared to accept—as matters of necessity or matters of choice.

James Madison wrote in 1787:

> Conceiving that an individual independence of the States is utterly irreconcilable with their aggregate sovereignty, and that a consolidation of the whole into one simple republic would be as inexpedient as it is unattainable, I have sought for a middle ground which may at once support a due supremacy of the national authority, and not exclude the local authorities wherever they can be subordinately useful.[60]

We might do well to recall that purpose; for now that creative federalism is focusing on the problems basic to the quality of American life, the stakes are high and the possibility of either failure or stifling uniformity is appalling.

Notes

1. Press Conference, Aug. 18, 1964, in Lyndon B. Johnson, *Public Papers, 1963–64* (2 vols., Washington, 1964), p. 976; Charles Press and Charles R. Adrian, "Why Our State Governments are Sick," *Antioch Review*, 24:165 (1964); Governor Edmund Brown, "How to Put the States Back in Business," *Harper*, 229:100 (Sept. 1964).

2. Edward S. Corwin, "The Passing of Dual Federalism," in R. G. McCloskey, ed., *Essays in Constitutional Law* (New York, 1957), p. 205.

3. Morton Grodzins, "Centralization and Decentralization," in R. A. Goldwin, ed., *A Nation of States* (Chicago, 1963), p. 7.

4. Grodzins in *Nation of States*, pp. 3–4, 7.

5. Grodzins' preface to Daniel Elazar, *The American Partnership* (Chicago, 1962), p. ix; Johnson, *Public Papers*, p. 1096.

6. Grodzins, "The Federal System," *Goals for Americans* (President's Commission on National Goals, New York, 1960), p. 270; Elazar in *Annals*, Vol. 359, p. 11; Elazar, *Amer. Part.*, p. 338.

7. Elazar, *Amer. Part.*, *passim*.

8. Up to 1860, only $42 million in cash was granted by the Federal Government to the States and localities, of which two-thirds comprised the 1837 distribution of the Treasury surplus, a one-time, unique effort. (This was in addition to Federal assumption of State debts in 1790). Paul B. Trescott, "The U.S. Government and National Income, 1790–1860," in National Bureau of Economic Research, *Trends in the American Economy in the 19th Century* (Princeton, 1960), pp. 337–61. Elazar's own analysis of Minnesota State finance, 1860–1900, supports my contentions. Federal cash payments constituted one-third total State receipts in 1863, a unique instance; all other years computed show Federal payments as 1 to 2 percent of receipts at most (*Amer. Part.*, p. 280.)

9. Forest Hill, *Roads, Rails, and Waterways: The Army Engineers and Early Transportation* (Norman, Okla., 1957).

10. Minor programs of aid—measured in terms of personnel and/or funds involved—many of them dating only from the 1890's, are given in Elazar, *Amer. Part.*, pp. 302–303n. Both Grodzins and Elazar treat "19th century origins" of intergovernmental programs in a loose temporal framework, often emphasizing the significance of Federal grants that originated only in the nineties. This, together with their emphases on trivial data (measured in terms of policy-making powers actually shared or in terms of cash magnitudes involved), is distortive, I think, of the actual evolution of techniques and principles at issue.

11. Harry Kursh, *The U.S. Office of Education* (Phila., 1965).

12. H. Scheiber, "Rate-Making Power of the State in the Canal Era," *Political Sci. Quar.*, 77:397–413 (1962).

13. Currin V. Shields, "The American Tradition of Empirical Collectivism," *Amer. Poli. Sci. Rev.*, 46: 109–110 (1952). See also Carter Goodrich, *Government Promotion of American Canals and Railroads* (N.Y., 1960).

14. William Anderson, *Intergovernmental Relations in Review* (Minneapolis, 1960), p. 142.

15. Hartz, *Economic Policy and Democratic Thought: Pennsylvania, 1776–1860* (Cambridge, 1948), p. 9. On the broader issue of State mercantilism, see also Gerlad D. Nash, *State Government and Economic Development: . . . California* (Berkeley, 1964); and, more generally, Oscar and Mary Handlin, *The Dimensions of Liberty* (Cambridge, 1961), and James Willard Hurst, *Law and the Conditions of Freedom in the 19th Century U.S.* (Madison, Wisc., 1964).

16. H. Scheiber, "Urban Rivalry and Internal Improvements in the Old Northwest," *Ohio Hist.*, 71:227–39 (1962).

17. Felix Frankfurter, *The Commerce Clause* (Quadrangle ed., Chicago, 1964), pp. 60 ff.

18. David Fellman, "The Future of the States," in R. B. Dishman, ed., *State of the Union* (New York, 1965), p. 68.

19. Scheiber, "Economic Change in the Civil War Era," *Civil War Hist.*, 11:396–411 (1965); Richard Hofstadter, *Age of Reform* (N.Y., 1956); Samuel P. Hays, *Response to Industrialism* (Chicago, 1957).

20. Hurst, pp. 71–108; Sidney Fine, *Laissez-Faire and the General-Welfare State* (Ann Arbor, 1956).

21. Fine, p. 365; W. Brooke Graves, *American Intergovernmental Relations* (N.Y., 1964), pp. 325–27; Roy Robbins, *Our Landed Heritage* (Bison ed., Lincoln, Nebr., 1962), p. 328.

22. Graves, p. 517; *Annals*, Vol. 359, p. 17; Jane Perry Clark, *Rise of a New Federalism* (N.Y., 1938), pp. 142–43; James A. Maxwell, *Fiscal Impact of Federalism in the U.S.* (Cambridge, 1946), p. 187. Statistical data on Federal grants, here and subsequently, exclude aid for government of the District of Columbia.

23. Gladys Baker, *The County Agent* (Chicago, 1939); Russell Lord, *The Agrarian Revival* (New York, 1939); Philip Selznick, *TVA and the Grass Roots* (Torchbook edn., 1966), 117ff., 169ff.

24. *Annals*, Vol. 359, pp. 18, 96.

25. Thomas C. Cochran, *The American Business System* (Cambridge, 1957), pp. 140–63; Corwin in McCloskey, *Essays*, pp. 201–10.

26. R. G. McCloskey, "Economic Due Process and the Supreme Court," in P. B. Kurland, *The Supreme Court and the Constitution* (Chicago, 1965), pp. 158–186; Robert L. Stern, "The Problems of Yesteryear—Commerce and Due Process," in McCloskey, *Essays*, pp. 150ff.; quotations from Jackson, J., in Duckworth *v.* Arkansas, 314 U.S. at 400–401, and from *id.*, in Hood & Sons *v.* DuMond, 336 U.S. at 538–39.

27. Advisory Commn. on Intergovernmental Relations, *Periodic Congressional Reassessment of Federal Grants-in-Aid* (Report A–8, 1961), pp. 44–67; Graves, pp. 526–36; Maxwell, *Fiscal Impact*, chs. 6–11.

28. The revised data are now official as issued by the Census Bureau.

29. ACIR, *Periodic Congressional Reassessment*, p. 46.

30. Arthur M. Schlesinger Jr., *Coming of the New Deal* (*The Age of Roosevelt*, Vol. II, Boston, 1959), p. 267. Hopkins' administration of welfare funds is treated fully in Maxwell, *Fiscal Impact*, pp. 141ff.; see also Clark, p. 174.

31. Clark, p. 178ff.; Graves, p. 532; V. O. Key Jr., *Administration of Federal Grants to the States* (Chicago, 1937), pp. 266ff., on varieties of Federal controls over quality and organization of State personnel.

32. Roscoe C. Martin, *The Cities and the Federal System* (New York, 1965), pp. 111–12; R. H. Connery and R. H. Leach, *The Federal Government and Metropolitan Areas* (Cambridge, 1960), chs. 1–2; Graves, pp. 857–63; Robert J. Morgan, *Governing Soil Conservation* (Baltimore, 1966), pp. 50ff.

33. James A. Maxwell, *Financing State and Local Governments* (Washington, 1965), pp. 72, 199; Graves p. 519; Maxwell, *Fiscal Impact*, pp. 88, 390; David Davies, "Financing Urban Functions and Services," *Law and Contemp. Prob.*, 30:145 (1965).

34. James Fesler, "Understanding of Decentralization," *Journal of Politics*, 27:556–58 (1965). See also Key, p. 244; T. J. Anderson in *Annals*, Vol. 359, pp. 120–21; and, on a conflict of the 1930's between bureaucracies and experts in the field of planning, Henry Fagin, "Planning for Future Urban Growth," *Law & Contemp. Prob.*, 30:12–13 (1965).

35. Roscoe Martin, *Grass Roots* (Harper edn., N.Y., 1964), p. 16; Gaus and Wolcott, pp. 104–107, 240–246, 463–468; Selznick, chs. 3–5; Rexford G. Tugwell, "The Resettlement Idea," *Agric. Hist.*, 33: 159–63 (1959); Richard S. Kirkendall, "Howard Tolley and Agricultural Planning," *ibid.*, 39: 32–33 (1965).

36. Key, pp. 33ff.; Maxwell, *Fiscal Impact*, p. 142 *et passim;* Graves, 532–34.

37. *Fiscal Impact*, p. 38.

38. *Economic Report of the President*, Jan. 1966, p. 281; *Budget of the U.S. Government*, 1966, p. 466.

39. Johnson, *Public Papers*, 706, 958, 1094–96, 1131.

40. *Ibid.*, 706.
41. Speech to N.Y. Liberal Party, Oct. 15, 1964, *ibid.*, pp. 1350–51.
42. *Ibid.*, p. 1131; also, pp. 1096, 1158.
43. Exec. Order #11, 186 (Oct. 25, 1964), *ibid.*, 1433–34.
44. Messages of 23 Feb. 1966, 2 March 1966; "Great Society Corp." in *Wall St. Journal*, Apr. 7, 1966, p. 1.
45. *Ibid.*; Max Ways, "Creative Federalism and the Great Society," *Fortune*, Jan. 1966, p. 121.
46. Charles L. Schultze, "The Great Society and Its Implications for Urban Management," *1965 Conference Proceedings*, International City Managers Association, Quebec, Sept. 10–22, (1965), pp. 33–37.
47. *Nation's Business*, March 1966, p. 61.
48. *Wall St. Journal*, April 7, 1966.
49. "A Professional Radical Moves in on Rochester," *Harper's*, 231: 52ff. (1965); *New York Times*, Feb. 23, 1966, p. 46 ("Dismissed VISTA Volunteers"); and March–April 1966 *Times* coverage of N.Y.C. pre-school program.
50. Republican minority statement, "Report of the Joint Economic Committee . . . on the Jan. 1966 Economic Report of the President," (Jt. Comm. Print, U.S. Cong., 1966), p. 67; Muskie, speech in Senate, March 25, 1966.
51. April 28, 1966.
52. Frederick O'R. Hayes in Brookings Institution, *Measuring Benefits of Government Investments* (Washington, 1963), p. 352.
53. *Ibid.*, p. 414; Weaver, *Urban Complex*, p. 183.
54. Ways, "Creative Federalism," pp. 121–22.
55. *Public Papers*, p. 950.
56. Campbell, "Most Dynamic Sector," *National Civic Review*, 53: 1–12 (1964). Repeated in *Annals*, Vol. 359, p. 98. My 1952–62 data from *Historical Statistics of the United States* (1960) and its *Continuation*.
57. Alvin H. Hansen, *The Postwar American Economy* (New York, 1964), p. 27; given in constant (1962) dollars.
58. Maxwell, *Financing*, pp. 200–204, 236, 247–48.
59. A. W. Macmahon, "The Problems of Federalism," in Macmahon, ed., *Federalism, Mature and Emergent* (N.Y., 1955, 1962), p. 4.
60. James Madison, *The Forging of American Federalism*, ed. S. K. Padover (Torchbook edn., N.Y., 1965), p. 184 (letter to Geo. Washington, April 16, 1787).

HAROLD J. LASKI

The Obsolescence of Federalism

No one can travel the length and breadth of the United States without the conviction of its inexpugnable variety. East and West, South and

Harold J. Laski, "The Obsolescence of Federalism," *The New Republic*, vol. 98 (May 3, 1939), 367–369. Reprinted by permission.

North, its regions are real and different, and each has problems real and different too. The temptation is profound to insist that here, if ever, is the classic place for a federal experiment. Union without unity —except in the Soviet Union and China, has variety ever so fully invited the implications of the famous definition? Geography, climate, culture, all of them seem to have joined their forces to insist that, wherever centralization is appropriate, here, at least, it has no meaning. Tradition demands its absence; history has prohibited its coming. The large unit, as in Lamennais' phrase, would result in apoplexy at the center and anemia at the extremities. Imposed solutions from a distant Washington, blind, as it must be blind, to the subtle minutiae of local realities, cannot solve the ultimate problems that are in dispute. A creative America must be a federal America. The wider the powers exercised from Washington, the more ineffective will be the capacity for creative administration. Regional wisdom is the clue to the American future. The power to govern must go where that regional wisdom resides. So restrained, men learn by the exercise of responsibility the art of progress. They convince themselves by experiment from below. To fasten a uniformity that is not in nature upon an America destined to variety is to destroy the prospect of an ultimate salvation.

This kind of argument is familiar in a hundred forms. I believe that, more than any other philosophic pattern, it is responsible for the malaise of American democracy. My plea here is for the recognition that the federal form of state is unsuitable to the stage of economic and social development that America has reached. I infer from this postulate two conclusions: first, that the present division of powers, however liberal be the Supreme Court in its technique of interpretation, is inadequate to the needs America confronts; and, second, that any revision of those powers is one which must place in Washington, and Washington only, the power to amend that revision as circumstances change. I infer, in a word, that the epoch of federalism is over, and that only a decentralized system can effectively confront the problems of a new time.

To continue with the old pattern, in the age of giant capitalism, is to strike into impotence that volume of governmental power which is necessary to deal with the issues giant capitalism has raised. Federalism, I suggest, is the appropriate governmental technique for an expanding capitalism, in which the price of local habit—which means, also, local delay—admits of compensation in the total outcome. But a contracting capitalism cannot afford the luxury of federalism. It is insufficiently positive in character; it does not provide for sufficient rapidity of action; it inhibits the emergence of necessary standards of uniformity; it relies upon compacts and compromises which take insufficient account of the urgent category of time; it leaves the backward areas a restraint, at once parasitic and poisonous, on those which seek to move forward; not least, its psychological results, especially in an age of crisis, are depressing to a democracy that needs the drama of positive achievement to retain its faith.

Before I turn to the case for this view, it is worth while to dwell for a moment upon the lessons of non-American experience. It is not, I think, accident that the heavy weather encountered by the federal system in the United States has been experienced also by the three major experiments elsewhere—by Germany, by Canada and by Australia. In the first, significantly, both federalism and democracy have gone. In the others the need for constitutional revision, the sense that the historic division of powers hampers the need for social and economic reconstruction at every turn, is one of the major themes of debate. Commissions seek to discover desirable terms of effective revision in both of them. Their literature speaks of "breakdown" and "collapse." In each, also, the federal government lacks, by its bondage to a past shaped in the faith of unlimited expansion, the power effectively to cope with its outstanding problems. In each, too, the political parties are geared psychologically to that past; and their inability to escape from the framework in which it has imprisoned them, leads to emergence of new political orientations which threaten alike their unity and their democratic foundation. Proportionately, I suspect, their problems are less susceptible of direct solution than those of the United States. But it is, I think, an expression, not of local circumstance, but of world-historical causes, which has made federalism everywhere in the world today a handicap and not a help to governmental progress.

Giant capitalism has, in effect, concentrated the control of economic power in a small proportion of the American people. It has built a growing contrast between the distribution of that economic power and the capacity of the political democracy effectively to control the results of its exercise. It has transcended the political boundaries of the units in the American federation so as to make them largely ineffective as areas of independent government. Whether we take the conditions of labor, the level of taxation, the standards of education, public health, or the supply of amenities like housing and recreation, it has become clear that the true source of decision is no longer at the circumference, but at the center, of the state. For forty-eight separate units to seek to compete with the integrated power of giant capitalism is to invite defeat in every element of social life where approximate uniformity of condition is the test of the good life.

The poor state is parasitic on the body politic. It offers privileges to giant capitalism to obtain its taxable capacity, offers escape from the impositions of rich states, in order to wrest from the wealthy some poor meed of compensation for its backwardness. It dare not risk offending the great industrial empires—cotton, coal, iron and steel, tobacco—lest it lose the benefits of their patronage. Their vested interests thus begin to define the limits within which the units of the federation may venture to move. And since the division of powers limits, in its turn, the authority of the federal government to intervene—the latter being a government of limited powers—it follows that the great industrial empires can, in fact, prevent the legislation necessary to implement the purposes of a democratic society. The situation may, briefly, be summarized by saying that the Constitution inhibits the federal government from exercising the authority inherent in the idea of a democracy; while the risk to a state government of attack upon the conditions exacted by those industrial empires for their patronage is too great to permit the states to jeopardize what they have by issuing challenge. Whether, therefore, it be the hours of labor, the standards of health and housing, the effective organization of the trade unions, at every point the formal powers of the states are rarely commensurate with the actual authority they may venture to exercise. And it is the common citizen of the United States who pays the price of that margin between formal and effective power.

Political systems live by the results they can obtain for the great mass of their citizens. A democracy is not likely to survive on formal grounds merely; it will survive as it is able to convince its citizens that it adequately protects their powers to satisfy the expectations they deem their experience to warrant. In the present phase of American capitalist democracy, the central government largely lacks the power to implement the ends it is essential it should serve if its democratic context is to be maintained. It cannot obtain adequate standards of government in many of the major fields it seeks to enter. It is hamstrung, partly by the division of powers from which it derives its authority; partly because the Constitution has not enabled it to develop the instrumentalities essential to the purposes it must seek to fulfill. Its effort to obtain the proper recognition of collective bargaining may be stricken into impotence by a state law against picketing. Its effort to produce proper control of public utilities may be rendered vain by local franchises granted in a period when the recognition of the need for uniformity in this field had not dawned upon the public consciousness. So, also, with conservation; with the provision of adequate educational opportunity; with the effective prohibition (a commonplace of any well ordered state) of child labor; with the coordination of relief for unemployment; with public works, especially in the utilization of the possible sources of electric power; with public-health legislation, not least in the field of maternity and child hygiene; with a proper policy of public roads—witness the breakdown of federal-state cooperation in Arkansas in 1923, in Kansas in 1926 and Maine in 1929; with a proper policy in housing. I take examples only. The central point of my argument is the simple one that in every major field of social regulation, the authority of which the federal government can dispose is utterly inadequate to the issues it is expected to solve.

I do not think this argument is invalidated by the rise of co-operation between the federal government and the states, or between groups of states. That use has been carefully investigated in detail by Professor Jane Clark in an admirable and exhaustive monograph ("The Rise of a New Federalism," 1938). When all is made that can be made of the pattern she there reveals, I think it is true to say that, compared to the dimension of the problem, it amounts to very little. And set in the background of the urgent problems of time, it is, I think, clear from her account that in no fundamental matters will the pressure of political interests (behind which can be seen at every turn the hand of giant capitalism) permit the necessary uniformities to be attained by consent within the next fifty years. Not even the resiljency of American democracy can afford to wait so long. Professor Clark demonstrates admirably the inescapable interest of the federal government in a hundred subjects at every turn of which it encounters the power of the states; but she also demonstrates that the problems of dual occupancy of the same ground hinders at every turn the creative solution of the problems involved unless we conceive of those solutions in terms of geological time.

I am not arguing that the administration of government services ought to be centralized in Washington. It is true, as Professor Clark says, that "there is a line beyond which centralized administration cannot go without falling because of its own weight." My argument is the very different one: that (a) there are certain objects of administrative control now left to the states for which they are no longer suitable units of regulation. Economic centralization makes necessary at least minimum standards of uniform performance in these objects, *e.g.*, health, education, unemployment relief; and in others, *e.g.*, labor conditions, railroad rates, electric power, complete federal control without interference by the states; and (b) that the proper objects of federal supervision cannot any longer be dependent upon state consent. Where this dependency exists, state consent will be, in its turn, largely controlled by giant capitalism. That is why Delaware is merely a pseudonym of the du Ponts, and Montana little more than a symbol of the Anaconda Copper Corporation. That is why the people of the state of Washington, who ought long ago to have been permitted to have the advantage of the municipal electric-power plant of Seattle, still suffer from the division of its potential benefits through the survival of the Puget Sound Light and Power Company.

Nor would the problem be met if, instead of the states, America were divided, as writers like Professor Howard Odum suggest, into regions more correspondent with the economic realities of the situation. If America were to consist of seven or nine regions, instead of forty-eight states, that would still leave unsolved the main issues if they operated upon the basis of the present division of powers, and if their consent were necessary to any fundamental change in that division. Once again, it must be emphasized that the unity which giant capitalism postulates in the economic sphere postulates a correspond-ing unity in the conference of political powers upon the federal government. There is no other way, up to a required minimum, in which the questions of taxation, labor relations and conditions, conservation, public utilities (in the widest sense), to take examples only, can be met.

At this point, of course, the relation of a federal system to the power of judicial review becomes fundamental. No one now believes Marshall's famous assertion that "courts are the mere instruments of the law, and can will nothing"; it has been obvious, above all since the Civil War, that the Supreme Court is the effective master of federal legislation. And it is clear, further, that this mastery is exercised in the main not on objective tests of constitutionality (which do not exist), but upon the accident of a temporary majority's view of what it is "reasonable" for the federal government to under-take. The Court has become a non-elective third chamber of the government which may, as in the income-tax cases, defeat for many years purposes of which its members do not happen to approve. In an epoch of rapid change, it is a grave danger to any society that the will of a federal legislature should be subject to judicial control, and more especially when, as Marshall said, the amending process is "cumbrous and unwieldy." In a phase of liberal construction the difficulties of judicial review are obscured from the public. But the years before the controversy over the President's Court plan should be a sufficient reminder of the immense dangers lurking within it.

The view here urged, of course, looks toward a fundamental recon-struction of traditional American institutions. It is not impressed by the view, associated with the great name of Mr. Justice Brandeis, that the "curse of bigness" will descend upon any serious departure from the historic contours of federalism. The small unit of government is impotent against the big unit of giant capitalism. It may be that the very power of giant capitalism is no longer of itself compatible with the maintenance of a democratic political structure in society; there is much evidence to support this view. What, at least, is certain is this: that a government the powers of which are not commensurate with its problems will not be able to cope with them. Either, there-fore, it must obtain those powers, or it must yield to a form of state more able to satisfy the demands that it encounters. That is the supreme issue before the United States today; and the more closely it is scrutinized the more obviously does its resolution seem to be bound up with the obsolescence of the federal system.

For that system presents the spectacle of forty-nine governments seeking to deal with issues for many of which they are inappropriate as instrumentalities whether in the area they cover or in the authority they may invoke. They are checked and balanced upon a theory of the state completely outmoded in the traditional ends upon which its postulates are based. Giant industry requires a positive state; federalism, in its American form, is geared to vital negations which contradict the implications of positivism. Giant industry requires uniformities in the field of its major influence; American federalism is the inherent foe, both in time and space, of those necessary uniformities. Giant industry, not least, requires the opposition of a unified public will to counteract its tendency to undemocratic procedure through the abuse of power; a federal system of the American kind dissipates the unity of public opinion in those fields where it is most urgently required. And, above all, it is urgent to note that giant industry, in an age of economic contraction, is able to exploit the diversities of a federal scheme, through the delays they permit in the attainment of uniformity, to reactionary ends. Thereby, they discredit the democratic process at a time when it is least able to afford that discredit. For, thereby, the confidence of the citizen body in its power to work out democratic solutions of its problems is gravely undermined.

Men who are deprived of faith by inability to attain results they greatly desire do not long remain content with the institutions under which they live. The price of democracy is the power to satisfy living demands. American federalism, in its traditional form, cannot keep pace with the tempo of the life giant capitalism has evolved. To judge it in terms of its historic success is to misconceive the criteria by which it becomes valid for the present and the future. No political system has the privilege of immortality; and there is no moment so fitting for the consideration of its remaking as that which permits of reconstruction with the prospect of a new era of creative achievement.

TERRY SANFORD

Creative Tensions

The states are indecisive.
The states are antiquated.
The states are timid and ineffective.
The states are not willing to face their problems.
The states are not responsive.
The states are not interested in cities.

These half-dozen charges are true about all of the states some of the time and some of the states all of the time. On the other hand, at points in history, most of these charges have been applicable to both the national and local governments.

Admitting, for the sake of improvement, that there is validity to the charges, what can be done? If nothing much can be done, then indeed the states will soon be finished. And the federal system, the great compromise that brought together a wide and diverse land, will have collapsed.

Of course, something would evolve to replace the present system. It would surely be some form of unitary government. It would be a *national* government as distinguished from a *federal* government. On the face of it, as it now appears to be forming, it does not look bad. In fact, it looks more efficient. The regional offices of a completely national government would have dividing lines which make "sense." The lines of administrative authority could be drawn with more clarity. The bottlenecks, which some contend states are, would be broken. Policies and programs could be carried out with dispatch. No state could stubbornly slow down or stop a program that Congress had started.

We would have a clean-cut, efficient, neat governmental structure, capable of solving its problems, serving its people, and functioning without the confusion, muddle, and clutter of overlapping, competing levels of government that indeed were born out of compromise.

But this structure might not be what it seems. Although it might be shocking to admit, we should not try to have a neat government. Part of the genius of the American system of government is that it has been a bit untidy. More than we may realize, this has given us a flexibility, has permitted change, and has made innovation possible. If a proposal did not work in one place, it could be tried out in another. If an idea is turned down at one point, there is always another point where it might find acceptance. If something cannot be started or stopped in a state legislature, the advocates of doing something or stopping something can try city hall or their congressman. Neither the states nor Washington is the only port of entry for ideas, the single route to action, or the one blockade to mistakes.

The President rarely has his unrestrained way with the Congress. The troubles of John F. Kennedy, after his narrow victory in 1960, are much more typical than the legislative successes of Lyndon B. Johnson. It is far easier in Congress to beat something than to get it passed. Kennedy's problems were dramatized in a book by James MacGregor Burns, in which he pointed out that congressional deadlock was a common characteristic in American history, spotted as it has been with spurts of furious legislative activity.[1]

English politics rarely countenance disloyalty to the party

line. The member of Parliament follows his prime minister or his leader of the loyal opposition. The English fail to appreciate the flexibility of our situation where a vote on any substantive matter is seldom without dissenters and line crossing from both sides of the aisle. Our broadly based parties have differences within their ranks, and the coalition shifts from vote to vote and subject to subject. Our freewheeling system, for all its apparent disorganization, is much more democratic and more creative than the English.

When some naturalists wanted forestry practices controlled but some insisted that control would destroy nature's balance in the wilderness, our untidy response was to have both. The U.S. Forest Service follows the first alternative, the U.S. Park Service the other, and the future has been better served.

Thus we can rejoice in a competitive, combative, contentious system that brawls its way to resolution and is provided with many openings for a fair hearing as well as ample safeguards against precipitate action. Some states permit liquor bottles on the table, some allow only mixed drinks, others insist that the bottle be under the table, and still others allow neither bottle nor glass. Not neat, but apparently it satisfies a lot more people than the uniform national approach once tried. When some states were enacting laws against closed-shop clauses in union contracts, others were either declining to do so or repealing such laws already on the books. There are strong arguments being made that this contract provision should be dealt with by one national law; there are also arguments being made against a single approach. Ours is a government with alternatives.

If the nation had a single divorce law, it would be much more restrictive than that of the most lenient state and more lenient than that of the most puritanical state. Who is wise enough to formulate for one and all the proper grounds for divorce in a nation as large and varied as this one? Twenty-three states this year considered changes in their abortion laws. That changes in a subject so delicate can even be discussed without a nationwide controversy over a federal law is a tribute to our diverse structure and a credit to the system. The very fact that in the enactment of such legislation some states may seem too lax to others is of value to society. The states are the outriders who test the limitations and restrictiveness of our accepted doctrines.

Capital punishment is another debated subject in which the cause of justice is well served by the options the states offer. If some contend that doing away with the death penalty will result in more murders, this opinion doesn't lead to an endless argument. Some state can try it. Michael V. DiSalle, a former governor of Ohio, makes the point that[2]

     . . . In the capital punishment states, a law enforcement officer's chance of being shot down in the performance of his duty is 1.3 per 100,000. In the abolitionist states, the rate is 1.2.

At the present time, thirteen states have abolished the death penalty altogether. Some states have not abolished it by statute, but have done so in practice. Vermont, which has executed two men in twenty-eight years, abolished capital punishment except for repeaters and killers of policemen and prison guards. New York passed a limited bill, retaining it only for killers of policemen and prison guards. Tennessee developed its own technique. When the abolition of capital punishment failed in the Tennessee senate by one vote after overwhelmingly passing in the house, the governor commuted the sentences of everyone on death row.

The states test whether the opinions by which we live our lives and run our governments are myths or facts. This is federalism at its best—always probing, always testing, always seeking a better way. The states allow experimentation, change, and local leadership, especially in controversial subjects involving deep societal values in which feelings run high and attitudes vary all across the nation.

Neat conformity in government is found only in dictatorships. This price is too great. The fact that we have somehow understood this all along, that we have permitted and indeed encouraged a certain amount of flexibility and local adjustment has given added vitality to our development, and has brought many benefits over the past two hundred years.

The tension in our system stimulates competition, and the colliding loyalties encourage improvement. New ideas can surface close to home where local leadership can put them into practice with the confidence of the people. To smooth out this creative tension, then, is to waste resources. In every section of the country there are talented people who are devoted to their states and care about their cities. They are not apathetic, not selfishly protective, and they want to do what must be done.

No one locus of government has a monopoly on brains and creativity. Men with these traits follow leadership whenever leaders want to do the job. Mayor John Lindsay in New York City has assembled a first-rate group of men to pick up the reins of the toughest city anywhere. When Richard Hughes began to lead New Jersey and make its people conscious that they lived in a state, good men were attracted to his call. And in the national government, John Gardner took over a depressed and confused department and made of it the most creative place to work in Washington.

The challenge to the leadership on every level is to harness the bureaucracy to its goals. The governors and mayors share the goals of Washington's top leadership. They want to do all they can to improve education, help the poor, and find better jobs and opportunities for their people. Dismissing their suggestions, excluding their views, or disregarding their potential service undercuts the achievement of all the goals.

It is often the fashion to refer to state lines as obsolete, and therefore to treat state officials as provincial leaders of outmoded territories. But would neat and "sensible" state boundaries add anything useful to our system? Long before the New Deal, even in the nineteenth century, some political scientists were advocating regional governments to replace the illogical lines of the states. Admittedly the lines were not originally drawn with an awareness of developments to come in communications, transportation, and living patterns. But is the solution today to sit down together the best brains and computers for the purpose of redrawing them with calculated accuracy? Who has that wisdom and vision, even in tandem with computers?

Nobody can really believe that state lines will be redrawn. The Constitution stands in the way of that. Instead, new lines will come, if they do, as the invention of the technocrats after the atrophy and neglect of the present states. Then in disregard of the states and the old lines, the new administrative units of the national government could be shaped with some purpose in mind. The New York harbor would be neatly wrapped into one subdivision by some of New Jersey, Connecticut and New York State. Newark and Atlantic City would not be together; neither, for that matter, would Los Angeles and San Francisco. Each subdivision would be designed to carry out the national objectives.

No such fantasy will be started deliberately on a draftsman's board. But it might develop if the states and the cities, giving up self-reliance, lean too much upon national aid, complaining only that they must go to too many different regional headquarters to get what is coming to them and to find out what to do. If this fantasy did come true, it would probably start with the consolidation of all regional offices, according to logical lines, but as compromised out by the various agencies that already had field offices. For a while state boundaries would be generally followed in the groupings. Later it would make more sense, be more workable, to draw the lines according to terrain and population groupings.

The whole thing would turn out to be easier to teach in school. The lines dividing the country neatly into sixteen national administrative subdivisions or units (NATS) could be flashed on the wall-high television screen. Hawaii might cause some difficulty, but it could be tucked in a corner with an arrow indicating that it belonged to to the Los Angeles NAT.

It would all seem so orderly and efficient. The governors and state legislatures would not have anything substantial to do. Many critical political scientists would write that it was good that congressmen still had to come from districts drawn within the old state lines. This, they would contend, had almost eliminated logrolling. The U.S. senators would be almost irrelevant, not that the administrative personnel would not pay attention to them. They would have to; they would still vote the appropriations. But since they came from states, they would not have much meaning as far as the administrators of the NATS were concerned. Since the unit boundaries would have to be drawn with population as well as distances in mind, it would have turned out that four of the NATS had only one senator, one had nine, and the New York NAT didn't have any. But this kind of drift could only follow an abandonment of self-reliance by the states and cities.

The ultimate aim of our political structure is not orderliness and efficiency, and it is not simply to break bottlenecks or avoid blockage by state action. The chief need of the federal system is not compactness and straight lines of authority. Instead, the citizens of the United States need diversified political strengths. Diversity, such as we have in our country, necessitates a federal system. Diverse political strength develops varied answers to assorted problems. It establishes the tensions for improvement. The power centers of the states protect our liberty from the possible tyranny of the national government, just as the power of the national government protects each citizen from the tyranny of the states.

The states are not merely subdivisions for administrative purposes. They may frequently act in that capacity, but they are more. They are, fundamentally, political units within a federal system, wherein both the parts and the whole rest on constitutional bases. No administrative subdivision could attain such a position.

Can we afford to let our present governmental relationships change substantially? We are moving into the era of joint responsibilities, the marble cake and the matrix, the partnership for seeking and solving problems, and the shared taxes. But can we allow one part of our federalism to become feeble, to lose position as a political force? The Articles of Confederation provided no power for the Congress, no way for it to withstand the political power of the individual state, no way for it to act for all the states combined into one nation. Consequently, the new nation was falling apart. The adoption of the U.S. Constitution eliminated that weakness. It created the power and authority needed for the states to act in unison. Now the question is, do we go to the other extreme?

The question can be posed very simply. Do we want a single national government, or a federal government which combines a national government with governments of the several states? The answer depends on our willingness to look for the faults and find the cures for the illnesses of state government. It is not possible to detail the disabilities of each state; some have one, and some have others, and some have too many to count. There is medicine to cure the illness and to put the states back on their feet. There remains the difficulty, however, of whether the people, the voters, want to take it.

Notes

1. James MacGregor Burns, *The Deadlock of Democracy*, (Englewood Cliffs, New Jersey: Prentice-Hall, Inc., 1963).
2. Michael V. DiSalle, *The Power of Life or Death*, (New York: Random House, 1965), p. 9.

DEIL S. WRIGHT
Grant Alternatives

Grant Alternatives

Grants are an institutionalized part of our federal system backed by a half-century of solid precedent. This in itself is a practical reason for settling for the minimum change required to ease the strain that grants are imposing on federal-state-local relations. Yet, entirely different financial techniques for aiding state-local governments might serve the nation far better. The underlying case for alternative techniques is the hard fact that prosperity produces both fiscal benefits and fiscal burdens—and the benefits tend to be national, the burdens state and local. In short, economic growth swells federal revenues while the problems and demands for services tend to pile up at the state-local level. The question is: How, other than by the much-used grant device, can we bridge this revenue/responsibility gap?

Direct federal expenditures

One approach would be for the national government to assume *direct* and *full* responsibility for more public programs. Medical assistance for the aged, for example, was ultimately resolved in this fashion after an unsuccessful attempt to work through the grant technique. However, while appealing to political liberals, this approach

Deil S. Wright, "Grant Alternatives," in *Federal Grants-in-Aid: Perspectives and Alternatives* (Washington, D. C.: American Enterprise Institute for Public Policy Research, 1968), 138–153. Reprinted by permission.

contradicts America's tradition of channeling most civilian functions of government through state and local units—of nourishing opportunities for local diversity and experimentation. Moreover, if the snail's pace at which medicare moved through Congress is a reliable measure, states and local units would be inundated with problems and/or tied in fiscal knots before federal "relief" was forthcoming.

Federal tax reduction

In what way is tax reduction an alternative to grants-in-aid? First, federal tax cuts may stimulate economic expansion. Second, in those 19 states that treat federal income taxes as a deductible item against the state income tax, federal tax cuts increase the tax base and thus tax revenues. Discussing these two effects, Professor Walter Heller estimates that "$3 billion extra a year is flowing into state-local coffers from the 1964 tax cut alone, a 7 percent increase for both state and local tax revenues."[1] If his estimate is correct then the federal tax cut was responsible for nearly 90 percent of the $3.5 billion in added tax revenue obtained by the state-local sector in fiscal 1965 over 1964![2] This is an unusually high proportion. However, since most state legislatures were not in session in 1964 to enact tax increases effective in fiscal 1965, the percentage is not as unreasonable as it might seem.

Thirdly, lower federal taxes provide the opportunity for states and localities to take up the "slack" by increasing their tax rates. For example, Senator Jacob Javits (R., N.Y.) has estimated that "in 1964, state-local tax increases siphoned off one-third of the $6.5 billion Federal tax cut."[3] Given the number of new and increased taxes enacted by state legislatures since 1965, the proportion must be considerably higher by now.

The tax reduction approach to bridging the revenue/responsibility gap has the advantage of allowing states and localities maximum discretion to make their *own* choices about increasing service levels and taxes. But, in the eyes of some observers, it reduces the federal role without providing any guarantee that states and localities will increase their taxes and services. Others point out that it contains no element of interstate equalization of fiscal burdens. For all its merits, therefore, federal tax reduction does not appear—at least, at this time—to be a realistic solution to state-local revenue problems.

Tax credits

A tax credit, in contrast to a tax deduction, is a decrease in tax liability to the full extent of the allowable credit. Two long-standing examples are the federal tax credits for state death tax and unemployment insurance tax payments.[4] In addition, seven states have experimented with this device, primarily to afford tax relief to economically disadvantaged groups. Colorado, Hawaii, and Indiana allow per person tax credits (both positive and *negative*) against a taxpayer's state income tax liability as a means of softening the regressivity of sales taxes. Wisconsin adopted the device to give property tax relief to senior citizens. Massachusetts, Minnesota, and Nebraska also adopted tax credit legislation in 1966 or 1967. These new ventures at the state level have much to commend them, especially on economic and administrative grounds.

An ingenious proposal of the Advisory Commission on Intergovernmental Relations is generating interest in wider use of tax credits on the federal-state scene. The commission recommended that taxpayers be given the option of either (a) continuing to itemize state and local income tax payments as deductions on their federal returns or (b) claiming a substantial amount (from 25 to 50 percent) of such payments as a direct credit against their federal income tax liability. The commission suggested a 40 percent credit which would, at 1965 tax rates, put about $700 million at the disposal of state and local units levying income taxes. The amount would, of course, be larger if more states enacted income taxes. Under the commission's most liberal assumption about new and increased income taxes, the states would gain an anticipated $2.7 billion while the federal revenue loss would approach only $2 billion.[5]

This proposal has three major advantages. The first is its ease, simplicity, and high degree of taxpayer visibility. The taxpayer would simply specify all state-local income taxes paid, take 40 percent of that amount and then *subtract* the result from his previously calculated federal tax bill. The second is the incentive bias of the proposal. In contrast to the traditional form of tax credit as a ceiling percentage of the *federal* tax liability, this idea ties the credited percentage to the state-local income tax liability. Thus, no matter how high state and local income taxes rise, 40 percent of that amount could be subtracted from the federal tax. This approach would stimulate state-local effort in the income tax field. The third advantage of the plan is its income base. Since the income tax is highly responsive to economic growth, the proposal contains a built-in growth factor. States could more assuredly hitch their tax revenue wagons to the rising star of national economic growth.

Against these advantages must be weighed at least three limitations. First, 15 states do not currently have income taxes, a few because of constitutional barriers and others because of policy, ideological, or other reasons. Adoption of the Advisory Commission's otherwise excellent proposal would, in practice, induce or coerce these states to adopt the income tax in order not to "lose" revenues to the federal treasury. Such a "shotgun marriage" between the tax credit and state income taxes produced a dissent from four of the commission's 26 members: "It is up to each state to determine the degree to which, if any, it wishes to use the income tax as a source of revenue," and it is inappropriate "to presume upon the independence of state governments in suggesting the types of taxes which they employ."[6]

Two other limits on the tax credits may be quickly noted. Like federal tax reduction, it does not allow for interstate income redistribution. It does allow for some interpersonal equalization because of the greater marginal value of the credit to low-income taxpayers but this is relatively modest for most and nonexistent for those who pay no federal (or state) income taxes. Finally, the device would provide an initial windfall benefit to taxpayers, rather than to state-local governments, in those 35 states already taxing income.

On balance, while this novel proposal deserves further study, it appears to fall short chiefly on the practical ground of state autonomy in tax as opposed to expediture policy.

Tax sharing

Revenue sharing is not a novel concept. As early as 1887, William H. Jones proposed a system of centrally-collected revenues shared on a per capita basis among the states.[7] In Australia, about three-fourths of all federal fiscal aids to the states are in the form of unrestricted general revenue payments based on income tax collections.[8] Canada, too, relies heavily on a type of revenue sharing, moving only recently toward the more conditional grants.[9] In contrast, there are only nine revenue sharing programs in the United States, all in the natural resources field and amounting to less than $200 million in 1968. But the idea is gaining favor. Here we will describe major proposals for federal-state tax sharing, examine the pros and cons, and discuss briefly how the idea fits the criteria for making federalism more effective in the United States.

The Plan

In the last few years, revenue sharing has been most closely associated with Professor Walter Heller, economist and chairman of the Council of Economic Advisers from 1961–64. Heller calls it "per capita revenue sharing."[10] The proposal, however, has gone by a number of different names: block, general, unconditional, unrestricted, non-tied, no-strings, and unencumbered grants. Whatever the name, the essential idea is the same—to return to the states a "substantial" amount of federal revenues with minimal restrictions on the use of the funds. The immediate purpose is to relieve state-local fiscal pressures; secondary purposes—depending on the particular plan—often involve fiscal equalization, improved income distribution, and greater state autonomy.

A revenue sharing plan entails five major factors: form, revenue base, amount, distribution formula, and limiting conditions.

As to the first, there seems to be considerable agreement that revenue sharing funds should be placed in a trust fund from which distributions to the states would be made. This arrangement would represent a type of contractual understanding on the part of the federal government that the funds were due the states as a matter of right, free from the vagaries of the annual appropriation process. It would also give the states a prior claim, a fractional tithe, upon federal funds in advance of general expenditures, tax reduction, debt retirement, etc.

As to the base to be used for calculating revenue sharing funds, three alternatives have been proposed: (1) all federal revenues, (2) federal personal income tax revenues, and (3) the federal personal income tax *base*. Walter Heller—as well as Senator Javits in his 1965 Federal Tax Sharing Bill—recommended the last, on the grounds that it offered a more constantly growing and less variable base than the other two.[11] On the other hand, the Republican Coordinating Committee's plan used total personal and corporate income tax revenues as its base,[12] and the plan proposed by Representative Charles Goodell (R., N.Y.) used personal income tax collections.[13] The last two proposals contain provisions protecting the trust fund (and the state-pledged revenues) against shrinkage in the event of economic downturns and/or federal tax reductions.

The amount of revenue to be returned to the states is obviously the product of a specified rate applied to a given base. Heller judged that a 1 percent rate applied to the federal individual income tax base would have yielded $2.8 billion in 1966. The Republican Coordinating Committee estimated that a 2 percent rate applied to all income tax collections would have provided about $2 billion in fiscal 1967. The committee also proposed that the rate be advanced two percentage points each two years, to a ceiling of 10 percent in fiscal 1975. Heller's proposal also contemplates an escalating rate,[14] while Senator Javits' bill does not.

A gradually increasing rate during the first few years of revenue sharing has merit. It would provide a predictable build-up capacity that the states could rely on over and above economic growth. It would also permit orderly rather than sudden fiscal management and allocation choices at the state level. What support levels should be targeted? Most thinking centers on a beginning annual figure in the neighborhood of $2 billion, or about $10 per capita. Escalating rates plus economic growth might legitimately put the annual amount around $6 billion, or $30 per capita, in six to eight years.

The distribution formula is perhaps the most difficult question because it determines the proportion each state would receive. Tax sharing funds could be distributed according to (1) federal personal income taxes paid within a state, (2) state population (per capita), or (3) various combinations of population, personal income, and tax effort. The federal income tax formula would produce reverse geographic equalization, that is higher rewards for the richer states. Very few seriously discussed proposals for revenue sharing urge the primary use of this formula.[15] The most widely accepted formula is population, which produces a moderate degree of equalizing. This is Heller's formula and it gives rise to the title of his plan, "per capita revenue sharing." Its greatest virtue is its simplicity. State officials and citizens alike can quickly grasp the concept of (x) dollars per person coming to the state from the revenue trust fund.

Varying the straight per capita formula slightly, Senator Javits and Representative Goodell would set aside, respectively, 20 percent and 10 percent of the trust fund to be allocated separately to either one-fourth or one-third of the states with lowest per capita personal incomes. The purpose of the extra "bonus" for low income states is to introduce a greater degree of equalization than that resulting from the simple per capita formula.

TABLE.   Percentage of 1963 state personal income obtained by states from a hypothetical $1 billion revenue sharing program based on four distributional criteria

States Ranked by Per Capita Personal Income	Federal Personal Income Taxes	Population	Population & Personal Income	Population, Personal Income & Tax Effort
	(average percentage of personal income from revenue sharing)			
1st Quintile	.2375	.1756	.1355	.1270
2nd Quintile	.2143	.2152	.2039	.2053
3rd Quintile	.1949	.2366	.2445	.2738
4th Quintile	.1801	.2656	.3114	.3518
5th Quintile	.1714	.3124	.4376	.4552

Source: Adapted from George F. Break, *Intergovernmental Fiscal Relations in the United States* (Washington: The Brookings Institution, 1966), p. 259.

The extent of equalization produced by the different distribution formulas is shown in the table. It is clear that the federal personal income tax formula produces reverse equalization. The ten states with highest per capita incomes would receive .2375 percent of total personal income in those states, while the ten states with lowest incomes would receive only .1714 percent. The population formula sharply shifts the balance in favor of equalization, with the ten highest income states receiving .1756 percent and the ten lowest .3124. The greatest equalization is achieved by a combination of population, personal income, and tax effort—because the lower income states are also exerting, on the average, greater tax effort.

The final factor in a revenue sharing plan is the conditions to be attached to the use of the funds by the states. The rationale of the plan dictates that conditions be held to the absolute minimum. But what is the "absolute minimum"? There is general agreement about the advisability of requesting reports (*not* detailed audits) on how the money was spent, of requiring compliance with Title VI of the Civil Rights Act of 1964, and of preventing use of the funds for highway purposes (since a federal trust fund already exists for that purpose). Beyond this point, however, there is a wide variety of suggested conditions.

Senator Javits would restrict funds to health, welfare, and education uses. This seems neither feasible nor desirable. Representative Goodell would earmark 45 percent of each state's share for redistribution to local governments, a proviso designed to meet the demands from cities for their "share of the pie." This may be practical politically, but it is probably unnecessary. About one-third of all state expenditures currently go to local units and it is highly probable, should revenue sharing come into being, that local units would obtain a significant share. In addition, it would be unwise to restrict such a large proportion of the revenues to any particular use.

The Goodell proposal further required that 5 percent of each state's share be earmarked for state "executive staff and management purposes as a means of improving the central staffing and management functions of state government."[16] This would be a unique way of strengthening the governing capabilities of the states. But it would seem equally desirable to provide a smaller percentage for the state executive branch, say 3 percent, and a similar percentage for the *legislative* branch. State legislatures deserve and could use improved staffing and better research in most if not all states. A 5 or 6 percent restriction appears minor enough to leave intact the underlying concept of a "pure" unrestricted aid to the states.

Public opinion appears to be on the side of confidence in the states' abilities to use funds wisely. According to a 1967 Gallup Poll, when asked whether state or federal government spent the taxpayer's money more wisely, 49 percent responded state and only 18 percent said federal (17 percent said "neither").[17] The same poll also asked this question about tax sharing: "It has been suggested that three percent of the money which Washington collects in federal income taxes be returned to the states and local governments to be used by these state and local governments as they see fit. Do you favor or oppose this idea?" The response was a solid 70 percent in favor of the plan and only 18 percent against it. These general public endorsements of state government, together with our evaluation of the capabilities of the states, argue for very few restraints on revenue sharing funds. Reporting requirements, nothing for highways, the application of Title VI, and perhaps state executive-legislative staffing come close to the upper limit of such restraints.

Pros and Cons of the Plan

We repeat below, with minimal comment, the major arguments drawn from the revenue sharing debate.

For revenue sharing:

1. Simplicity. The plan is straightforward, clear, and direct in its conception and operation.
2. State discretion. It allows the states more discretion and greater fiscal autonomy in meeting their particular needs as their state (and local) officials see them.
3. Major needs. It would be a continuing rather than a stop-gap measure for providing substantial funds to those governments that carry the major responsibilities for civilian services. A healthy fiscal shot-in-the-arm, it would enhance public confidence in state and local governments by enabling them to meet public demands more effectively.
4. Revenue growth. Not only would revenue sharing furnish major sums but those sums, hitched closely to economic growth, would automatically increase at a pace greater than the growth rate.
5. Flexibility. As we have seen, the base, rate, and distribution criteria governing the funds can be employed to achieve desired policy goals—for example, more or less stability and growth, more or less interstate equalization.
6. Progressivity-regressivity. The plan would have the effect of financing a greater share of state and local services from the progressive federal income tax rather than regressive sales, consumer, and property taxes.
7. Grant relief. Enactment of revenue sharing is likely to forestall further major grant-in-aid programs and therefore prevent more proliferation, complexity, and problems in the grant field. Whether revenue sharing would eventually replace existing grants is an open question.
8. Economic stabilization. By tying a greater portion of state-local receipts and outlays to the business cycle, revenue sharing would act as an additional built-in compensator. It would also reduce

"fiscal drag" brought on by surplus federal revenues, a development that some economists anticipate with foreboding when Vietnam costs can be reduced.

9. Less distortion. By providing relatively unrestricted funds to the states, revenue sharing would constitute a major step in reducing (or compensating for) the distortion in state budgets brought about by federal grants-in-aid.

10. Administrative economies. One study has estimated the overhead costs on ten grant programs at about 1.6 percent.[18] Assuming this percentage holds across the board, then about $300 million is consumed annually in collecting and administering grant-in-aid funds. This conservative estimate does not count compliance costs at the state level. Because of its basic simplicity, the revenue sharing device would hold federal-state overhead costs to the bare minimum.

11. Income redistribution. The net budget of the state-local sector —the combined effect of taxes and expenditures—is estimated to be more beneficial to lower income groups than is the federal budget.[19] Given the nature of state-local responsibilities, revenue sharing could be expected to reinforce this effect.

12. Attitudinally acceptable. Revenue sharing not only is acceptable to the public at large but fits well with the views of state and local officials connected with existing grant programs. Moreover, it does not directly threaten any power bloc in the sense of reducing benefits being received under current grant programs. Yet it is opposed in varying degrees by such status quo groups as organized labor, the NEA, big city mayors (who are demanding "pass through formulas" as a condition of their support), and federal aid administrators. What it needs is support from a solid pro-state lobby. Only the governors can furnish such support and there is some indication that they are moving in this direction. Other than the governors, who lobbies for the states in Washington? The answer seems to be—nobody!

13. Ample precedent. Experience with tax sharing in other countries, at the state-local level in this country, and in an infinitesimal form at the federal-state level provides a wealth of material upon which to draw in undertaking full-fledged consideration of the proposal, in both academic and public circles.

Against revenue sharing:

1. National drain. Revenue sharing would absorb funds that could be put to better use at the federal level. In its extreme form, this argument holds that "If the federal government spends it, it must be good!"

2. Leaky purses. On the other side of the coin, revenue sharing with

the states would put money in hands that do not exercise proper care, responsibility, and foresight. In a stinging expression of this view, Christopher Jencks attacked the Heller plan because the states were "unfit to govern" and represented "a kind of cancer."[20]

3. Reduced effort. More money to the states under revenue sharing would cause them to reduce their tax efforts just when those efforts should be stepped up.

4. Local needs. By giving money directly to the states, tax sharing fails to recognize the pressing fiscal needs of the cities, who traditionally have gotten short shrift from state legislatures. Reapportionment, it is argued, will not help much because it favors suburbia, not central cities.

5. Rat hole theory. Even if significant amounts of money trickle down to the local level, much of it will disappear in the rat hole of local government overlapping, duplication, mismanagement, and just plain waste.

6. Tax reform. Revenue sharing would greatly reduce the pressure to bring about much-needed state (and local) tax reform. The only way to get these reforms is to keep the pressure on, even if it means precipitating fiscal crisis and occasionally near-bankruptcy.

7. Grant cuts. Increased state revenues via tax sharing might generate skepticism regarding old as well as new grants, perhaps to the point of undermining existing grant programs.

8. Responsibility. Under tax sharing, the responsibility for raising revenues is divorced from spending authority, a situation that could produce ill-advised expenditures and less responsiveness to the electorate.

9. Tax reduction. One version of this argument says that revenue sharing is just a way of plucking the goose with the least amount of squawking. All taxes are too high and should be reduced. A second version, as we saw above, holds that federal tax reduction is a preferable (though indirect) alternative for expanding state-local fiscal resources.

10. Debt reduction. Similar to the first version of the tax reduction argument, this view gives top priority to debt reduction.

11. Prosperity assumed. Tax sharing rests heavily on the assumption of continuous prosperity tied in with a federal surplus. But prosperity is by no means assured, there has been only one balanced budget (either administrative or cash) in the past decade, and it is spurious to talk about sharing a nonexistent "surplus" with the states.

These appear to be the major arguments for and against revenue sharing. In this writer's opinion, revenue sharing comes off best of all the possible alternatives to grants-in-aid, with the unique tax credit proposal of the Advisory Commission running second. Revenue sharing is simple. It is consistent with a body of attitudinal perspectives broadly distributed among officials and the public. It recognizes the interrelatedness of our federal-state-local fiscal system and seeks to deal with that system in a manner calculated to broaden the autonomy of the states. It holds out the prospect of a better federal system by enhancing the existing strengths of the states. The basic question, as Walter Heller has put it, is this: "Do you want stronger states?" One vote here is cast in the affirmative.

Concluding Observations

The theoretical base for fiscal equity within a federal system has been adequately argued by James Buchanan. He demonstrates that the policy objective of equality formulated in interpersonal terms can be served through interstate fiscal equalization and discusses tax sharing on a per capita basis as a means to this end.[21] There is strong justification on equity grounds for unconditional equalizing grants to the states. With state-local tax effort built into the distribution formula, unconditional grants would become a vehicle for achieving a degree of equalization that is not now even approximated by categorical and conditional grants.

The contrasting equalization impact between current grants and proposed unconditional grants was recently identified by James Plummer. As of 1964, he found a positive correlation of only .09 between per capita personal income and per capita federal grants but a positive correlation of .274 between per capita personal income and revenue sharing based on a population/tax effort formula. If 10 percent of the funds were distributed among the 17 poorest states and the remainder allocated on the population/effort formula, the correlation rose to .708.[22] Only slight adjustments are necessary, then, to produce powerful equalizing effects in unconditional grants.

Furthermore, the inclusion of tax effort as a factor in the distribution formula would produce a modest reactivity effect—that is, it would reduce the possibility that states would use the unrestricted funds to decrease taxes or forego tax increases.[23] In other words, the tax effort factor would induce states to increase their tax levels in relation to personal income at a rate at least equal to the national average or else incur the penalty of receiving a smaller proportion of available shared revenues.

Perhaps the greatest obstacle to revenue sharing stems from doubts about the adequacy and responsibility of state governments. We have observed that states possess more strengths than weaknesses from the standpoints of political tradition, fiscal effort, administrative capability, and institutional position. Their one important weakness remains their structural disabilities.

But the states can do little more than demonstrate that they are ready for more responsibility. The power to solve the major fiscal and non-fiscal problems of federalism rests not with the states, but with the President and the Congress. They are the basic arbiters of the federal system and, unfortunately, the forces of functionalism make it difficult for these institutions to bring about the needed reforms. The organization of the Congress, as we have seen, is such that the "intergovernmental interest" tends to be ignored in the legislative decision process. To take this point further, the House and Senate Subcommittees on Intergovernmental Relations, units that have contributed significantly to understanding federal problems, are subsidiaries of their respective parent Committees on Government Operations. And these parent committees can only review problems and legislation *after* substantive programs have been in operation for varying lengths of time. Moreover, the fate of revenue sharing will rest with the House Ways and Means Committee and the Senate Finance Committee, both of whom are wrestling with the problems of an overcommitted budget.

When we look past the Congress to the executive branch, we also find little institutional evidence of concern for the complexities of intergovernmental relations. The White House staff, the Bureau of the Budget, and most major agencies are not equipped to deal effectively with the increasing complexity of multi-system government. Senator Muskie's proposal for "staffing up" to the task of program coordination deserves serious consideration.

The one voice that has made an articulate case for intergovernmental relations is the Advisory Commission on Intergovernmental Relations. Its accomplishments, and there are several, arise from solid research and mature recommendations. Yet it does not possess, nor can it marshal, the necessary power to achieve more than marginal adjustments in intergovernmental conflicts.

However, in the author's opinion, major rather than marginal reforms are needed in our federal fiscal system. The commission's tax credit recommendation was an effort to grapple with the need. In spite of its merits, however, the tax credit approach lacks appeal on the same three counts that favor the eventual adoption of some form of revenue sharing: (1) simplicity, (2) attractiveness to the public at large and to state-local elected officials, and (3) party sponsorship. Only the last needs a brief concluding comment. Republicans in the Congress have been vocal and active in behalf of revenue sharing and some leading Democrats are beginning to come around. A subcommittee of the Joint Economic Committee has held brief although relatively unnoticed hearings. What will happen in the future is anyone's guess. But certainly the problems to which revenue sharing is addressed can no longer be ignored.

Notes

1. Walter W. Heller, *New Dimensions of Political Economy* (Cambridge: Harvard University Press, 1966), p. 140.

2. U.S. Bureau of the Census, *Governmental Finances in 1964-1965*, Series GF-No. 6 (Revised, Washington, February, 1967), p. 18.

3. *Congressional Record*, October 11, 1965, p. 25618.

4. James A. Maxwell, *Tax Credits and Intergovernmental Fiscal Relations* (Washington: The Brookings Institution, 1962).

5. Advisory Commission on Intergovernmental Relations, *Federal-State Coordination of Personal Income Taxes* (Washington: Government Printing Office, October, 1965).

6. *Ibid.*, p. 14.

7. James M. Buchanan, "Federalism and Fiscal Equality," in *Fiscal Theory and Political Economy* (Chapel Hill: University of North Carolina Press, 1960), p. 178.

8. Albert J. Robinson, "Implementing Policies of Growth and Stability in a Federation," *National Tax Journal*, March, 1965, p. 63.

9. R. M. Burns, "Inter-governmental Relations in Canada: Further Developments," *National Tax Journal*, March, 1965, pp. 15–24.

10. Heller, *op. cit.*, pp. 144–72. A recent description and discussion of revenue sharing proposals is Legislative Analysis, No. 7, *Federal Revenue Sharing Proposals: General Grants to the States with "No Strings Attached"* (Washington: American Enterprise Institute, July 31, 1967).

11. Heller, *op. cit.*, pp. 145–46; and Javits, *Congressional Record*, daily ed., October 11, 1965, pp. 25608–19.

12. Republican Coordinating Committee, *Financing the Future of Federalism: The Case For Revenue Sharing* (Washington: Republican National Committee, March, 1966).

13. Charles E. Goodell, "A Proposal for General Aid to State and Local Governments Through Sharing of Federal Taxes," press release, November 27, 1966.

14. Heller, *op. cit.*, p. 149.

15. The Republican Coordinating Committee recommended that one-half of the shared revenues be distributed on the basis of income taxes and the other half on a combination of population and personal income.

16. Goodell, *op. cit.*, p. 4.

17. *Des Moines Register*, January 1, 1967, p. 6G.

18. *Federal-State-Local Relations . . ., op. cit.*, p. 60.

19. W. Irwin Gillespie, "Effect of Public Expenditures on the Distribution of Income," in Richard A. Musgrave (ed.), *Essays in Fiscal Federalism* (Washington: The Brookings Institution, 1965), pp. 122–86.

20. Christopher Jencks, "Why Bail Out the States?" *The New Republic*, December 12, 1964, pp. 8–10. Jencks' attack was a rejoinder to an article favorable to revenue sharing by Edwin L. Dale, Jr., "Subsidizing the States," *The New Republic*, November 28, 1964, pp. 11–12.

21. James Buchanan, *op. cit.*, pp. 170–89.

22. James L. Plummer, "Federal-State Revenue Sharing," *Southern Economic Journal*, July, 1966, pp. 120–26.

23. See Charles J. Goetz, "Federal Block Grants and the Reactivity Problem," and James L. Plummer, "Federal-State Revenue Sharing: Further Comment," *Southern Economic Journal*, July, 1967, pp. 160–65 and 166–68.

WILLIAM ANDERSON

The Perils of "Sharing"

DEAR SENATOR BAKER:

Thank you for sending me the pages from the *Congressional Record* of March 9, 1967, relating to and including the text of your bill, S. 1236, for the proposed tax sharing act of 1967. I had heard of various proposals for such an act of Congress, but this is the first text of a bill that has come to my attention. It prompts me to put down on paper and to send to you, and to others who are interested in such a proposal, the following thoughts and questions about your plan.

I am writing this letter as a means of putting myself on record with respect to your bill, and, at the same time, of considering the related though different proposal of Walter W. Heller, as set forth in his book, *New Dimensions of Political Economy* (Cambridge, Harvard University Press, 1966). Indeed, I am writing my thoughts not only for you two, but also to transmit them to others who are interested in what is now called "tax sharing." Having done this much, I will excuse myself from participating in any hearings that may be held on your bill and/or other similar proposals.

Under any act of Congress such as you propose, it seems to me that whatever formula is used to guide the annual distribution of funds among the several states, the actual distribution will result in either (1) giving each state almost exactly that portion of the United States tax revenue involved that has been paid in by the taxpayers of that state, or (2) in giving some states less than their taxpayers paid and other states, more.

The first is, I think, most unlikely; but if it should happen, it would simply mean that each state might just as well have levied and collected its own tax in order to bring in the amount actually received. In this case, the national government would simply have been a collecting agency for the states.

William Anderson, "The Perils of 'Sharing,'" *National Civic Review*, vol. 56 (June 1967), 329–334. Reprinted by permission.

This idea is not the same as, but is in line with, a proposal now being made in some states to the effect that the United States Treasury annually pay over to each state a certain percentage (as high as 5 percent in some proposals) of the federal income tax collected within the state. Instead of having the national government collect and turn over to the state such a tax, why not have the state, each state, simply levy an income tax figured as a certain percentage of the federal income tax, but collected as a state tax? In this sort of setup, there would be no question of one state getting a share of the money paid by taxpayers in other states, or of the taxpayers in some states having paid into the federal treasury more than their own states received in revenue. Each state could, of course, set its own rate according to its own needs.

The more likely result is that of the second case above, whether under your proposal or that of Professor Heller, which is tied to the federal income tax. That is to say, no matter how the national formula for distribution among the states is worked out and interpreted in practice, some states will get back in any year less than their income taxpayers or general taxpayers contributed to the fund, while other states will get more of the total fund than their taxpayers contributed to it. Furthermore, because the economies of the states are generally slow to change, the same states are likely to remain in the same over-paid or under-paid class for a long time. The drain of funds from state to state could be considerable.

Professor Heller, whose book has contributed much to the current discussion of tax sharing, that is, of state sharing in the tax revenues of the national government, frankly admits that this sort of result—the funnelling of nationally collected tax funds from some states into others for expenditure—would take place under his proposal to distribute 2 percent of the federal income tax revenue each year among the states, if it is made into law.

* * *

Your own distribution formula clearly takes into account the factor of "state revenue effort," but this is modified by other factors like population and per capita income; and nothing that I have found in your bill suggests that no state shall get more or less than its own taxpayers contributed. It seems to me, therefore, that both you and Professor Heller are under some obligation to defend, as a permanent policy of the national government, an annual partial redistribution of income and wealth among the states by action of the national government, without providing any directives to the states as to how those who are the gainers shall use the funds they receive.

Your proposal, like that of Professor Heller, is, of course, entirely different from the existing grants-in-aid laws. Those laws are not based on any sharing of the national government tax revenues by the states, nor on the idea of redistributing any wealth or income between the more well-to-do and the less well-do-to states. They are based on the recognized national interest in the people of the whole nation and in the provision of the particular public services to be aided. In important instances, the national government cannot honestly ignore or neglect this national interest. In a nation with a highly mobile population, and one imbued with the high purpose of advancing the level of its civilization, it is necessary that all children and young adults be educated up to at least a minimum standard. In the national interest, the function of public education cannot be left solely to the many states, with their different levels of ability to provide that education and diverse ideals in the field. For similar reasons, and some additional ones, public health in all parts of the country is a national interest. So is social welfare—for the children, for the aged, indeed, for all ages and conditions of the people. In a different category, national transportation, nationwide travel and interstate commerce interests similarly justify the provision of national aid for highways. And so on through the categories of federally aided functions of government.

In the bill you have drawn, however, the expenditure of the funds to be turned over to the states may be made by them for any purposes they choose, without any regard for the national interest. To take an extreme case, a state might even use some of its share of the revenues to subsidize industries to move from other states into its area.

It seems to me that a sum comparable to what you propose, appropriated by Congress to increase the grants-in-aid now in effect, would do just as much for the economy of each state. This would not provide unrestricted funds, but it would release moneys now used by the states to match the federal grants. While the proportion paid by the national government would be increased, the states could reduce their contributions to the aided functions by similar amounts and, thus, have more unrestricted funds to spend. And the states would continue to control and administer the aided functions, only reporting to Congress and the national Administration as in the past.

In back of some of the arguments I have read and heard for "tax sharing" lie, I think, at least two myths. One is the myth of the national government's rolling in unneeded wealth. The facts are, of course, (a) that there have been fifteen federal deficits in the last twenty years, through fiscal 1966; (b) there has been a large increase in the federal debt in the same period; and (c) the current high costs of the military operations in Vietnam are piling up another deficit and bringing a further large increase in the national debt.

* * *

Another myth, as it seems to me, is the idea that "tax sharing" is going to pump new public funds into the states and the national economy. While there will obviously be some differences regionally and by states in the pattern of national government spending (and that of the states if they get some unrestricted federal funds), aside from the priority items of national defense and foreign affairs, that spending is practically all within the confines of the 50 states. The only real difference is that it is the national government that is doing the spending. Neither your bill nor the various proposals for passing some of the income tax revenue on to the states will increase the total amount of the public moneys to be spent. There is, of course, the possibility that some of the states that get funds from the proposed tax-sharing will actually reduce their own taxes and spend less from their own resources. In this case, there will be less to be spent on public services in these states.

* * *

I am almost inclined to add a third myth to the list. In fact, I think I will. This is the myth that all the states have reached the absolute limit of their ability to find and raise additional revenues for the support of their own public services. It seems to me that this cannot be demonstrated. The economic forces that are at work increasing the incomes and jobs of the people, and making it possible for the national government to increase its revenues, are also at work in the states. In fact, they are based in the states, so that most, if not all, of them are getting larger returns from their existing revenue sources and laws and are capable of increasing their tax rates and even imposing new taxes from time to time, without great, if any, harm to their economies or their competitive positions among the states as a group. Any comparison of the efforts of the states will reveal that some with great economic capacity are not putting forth nearly a total effort to support state and local services. Others are undoubtedly near their potential limits, although no one can state exactly what their potentials are.

A clear omission from your bill, and one that reflects to some extent the attitudes of the state governments, is that you make no distinct provision for meeting the needs of the local governments within the states, and especially not for the needs of the cities and the rising metropolitan areas. Much of the brunt of the new load of providing for the people's public needs, as they move from the declining rural areas into the centers of population, falls upon the large cities and the emerging metropolitan areas. The malapportioned legislatures of earlier days set the state pattern almost everywhere, and that pattern was to make the cities dependent almost entirely on the local property tax. Now that that tax has taken such a beating due to a number of factors like the taking of much property off the tax rolls through public acquisition, the growth and multiplication of tax-exempt churches and other factors, it is to be hoped that the recently reapportioned legislatures will take a new look at their responsibilities to the urban places, and for the essential urban services of education, fire and police protection, streets that double as state highways, and health and welfare services to mention only some of the most important ones. But that time has not yet come, and there is much that needs to be done for the urban places.

I realize, of course, what men say—that we must have confidence in the states. I think this is true, but my confidence is not that which many others seem to be thinking about. I believe in combining confidence with a measure of caution and a bit of foresight checked against a good deal of history and hindsight. You will recall the distribution among the states in 1837, under President Andrew Jackson, of the considerable surplus of revenues from federal land sales and customs duties. Historians do not seem to have been able to find out what happened to that money. With 50 states now in the Union, it is going to be harder than ever to know what goes on in the handling of the states' public moneys. If your bill should pass, it will be comforting to know that at least the reporting of the use of shared funds will be expected.

* * *

My confidence in the governments of the states is based on a fairly long and careful study of them, and it is my judgment that many, if not, indeed, most of them, are doing very well. I think that today the state governments, by and large, are better organized, better administered, more public-service minded and more conscientious about "doing a good job" than ever before. They are also better and more amply financed than in the past. There are, of course, some exceptions, but Professor Heller himself, a strong advocate of the new "tax sharing" idea, applauds what the states have done and are doing. He says: "In the 1955–65 decade, states and localities increased revenues from their own sources from $28 to $63 billion, or by an average of 8.6 percent a year. Meanwhile, Federal grants-in-aid grew from $3 billion to $11 billion."

The states have also greatly increased their borrowings in this period, as he shows, but not, I think, to a dangerously high level. I think this is a remarkable showing, of which the peoples, leaders and officials of the states may well be proud. I believe also that, with economic growth and production increasing as they are, the states can continue to improve their financial strength by their own efforts, and that they will be the stronger for doing it in that way. The less they have to depend on the national treasury for their funds, the better for them, and the more proud they can justifiably be of their achievements.

Your proposal starts, of course, with a modest sum, or at least one that is modest in terms of present day national budgets. Yours is a sort of "foot-in-the-door" approach, but, clearly, the proponents of such tax-sharing measures do not intend to stop with such relatively small sums, as the suggestions of Professor Heller reveal. A little stimulant, it can be argued, will be a good thing, and, if it whets the appetite for more, that "more" will be even better.

It seems to me, Senator Baker, that if your bill is enacted into law, several things will begin to happen. Before Congress and the national administration, official and unofficial groups and individual lobbyists from different states will begin trying to get changes in the distribution formula that will be more favorable to their own states and interests. They also will likely try to get the entire appropriation increased at once. A number of complaints about the distribution formula and about the smallness of the amounts appropriated will come from various sources, including pressure groups, newspapers and periodical editors.

In the meantime, in the several states, various interest groups will begin to try to get some of the "free money" for their own projects and purposes. It is not necessary to try to list the types of interest that will be heard from. These will begin to communicate with others in various states and to organize new pressure groups on a regional and even national level. And so your proposed law, with its promise of new funds not raised specially and locally, will help to raise up new pressure groups to lobby before both state legislatures and Congress.

And what will the pressure groups and the lobbying be for? Money, and more money and money without strings. Once the money is there and available, there will be drives to find what to do with it. Is this not a sort of Alice in Wonderland procedure?

You call your bill a "tax sharing" measure, and other proponents of similar ideas are using the same term. This is probably as good a term as can be found, so I will not go into that. This proposed unconditional granting of money by the national government to the states is advocated by Professor Heller and other experts as a fiscal measure to preserve the American federal system of government ("our federalism" in Professor Heller's terminology). My contention is that the more the states permit themselves to become dependent upon the national government for their financial support, the less independence, strength and weight they will have in the long run within the federal system. They may have trouble today (indeed, they do) in satisfying all the demands put upon them for money for this and that, but they are in a healthy condition and they are in a stronger position than they would be if supported increasingly by federal largesse.

I realize that Professor Heller does not look upon it in this way. He argues "that the Federal commitment to share income tax revenues with the states should be a contractual one, good through thick and thin, through surplus and deficit in the Federal budget." But he does not tell us how that can be done constitutionally, or how it is practically feasible. Congress and the national executive would have to be completely bypassed in some way. How? By a constitutional amendment? However it is proposed to be done, it could be the beginning of the complete erosion of national leadership and control in the American federal system.

* * *

I realize fully, Senator Baker, that your bill does not propose any such change in the constitutional system of the United States, and that nothing in your bill suggests that you espouse Professor Heller's "contractual" idea about tax sharing. But he is a noted economist and fiscal policy authority, and many may become interested in his suggestion as to how to make it possible for tax sharing to be binding on the national government permanently, "through thick and thin."

Although your proposal is a more modest and limited one than that which Professor Heller seems to be putting forth, for other reasons that I have set out in this letter, I think that your bill should not be enacted.

ROGER A. FREEMAN

Perils of Not Sharing

DEAR SIR:

In "The Perils of Sharing" William Anderson raises some telling points against the proposition that the national government ought to return part of its revenue collections to the states. He reminds us that there have been fifteen deficits in the federal budget in the past twenty years, that the federal debt has risen sharply, that current and prospective costs of national defense (including the Vietnam action) are high. He calls the assertion that the states have reached an absolute limit of their tax-raising ability a myth and similarly discards the idea that tax sharing would pump new funds into the states and the economy. Last, but not least, Dr. Anderson warns that the states should not be made increasingly dependent on the national treasury for their financial support and that they will be better off and stronger in the long run if they raise their funds under their own powers. He also cautions against the danger of pressure groups lobbying for more money once such an "Alice in Wonderland" procedure as tax sharing has been established.

These arguments have some validity and cannot easily be shrugged off. But all of them can be used with equal if not more justi-

Roger A. Freeman, "Perils of Not Sharing," *National Civic Review*, vol. 56 (September 1967), 453–455, 469. Reprinted by permission.

fication against all forms of channeling federal funds to states, including programmatic grants-in-aid which now total $17 billion a year. But Dr. Anderson does not attempt or intend to make a case against categorical grants. Nor does he mention the specific charges which are being brought against such grants: the confusion and often near chaotic conditions produced by more than 400 sometimes duplicating and overlapping, often uncoordinated and even conflicting programs of numerous competing agencies. He does not mention the decisive change those grants have brought about in our federal system by shifting decision-making power over most domestic activities of government to the national level, to the President, Congress and an ever-expanding federal bureaucracy.

Support for tax sharing has multiplied in recent years in Congress, among state and local officials, and among the public,˙ as a growing number of Americans come to realize that the present system of categorical grants, and its rapid expansion, are destroying state and local government in this country and are converting our federal system into a unitary system of government with centralized control being assumed by Washington. State governments are not losing because their leaders "seemed more intent on keeping down state taxes than promoting the revitalization of state government" (see the *Review*, July 1967, page 376). In the current century—between 1902 and 1965—federal tax collections multiplied 193 times and state tax collections 210 times, and when we eliminate war periods (when national concentration was, of course, essential) we find that states have been boosting their tax revenues at least three times faster than the national government. State governments are losing because the major decisions over their activities are no longer being made in the state capitols, but in Washington.

The enactment in recent years of well over 400 authorizations for grants-in-aid to state and local governments, each with its accompanying control and supervision by an ever-expanding federal bureaucracy, has, for all practical purposes, vested power over almost all domestic services in the national government and its administrative departments. The course "toward gradual transformation of state and local governments into administrative units commanded and directed from the seat of the national government in Washington," to repeat a quote from the recent Committee for Economic Development report *Modernizing State Government*, cited editorially in the *Review* for July (page 376), has, for all practical purposes, achieved its aim. When Roscoe Drummond said some years ago, "The federal system no longer exists," he was probably right. The means by which the federal system was abolished—in fact though not in name—leaving all power concentrated in the national government and all other governments reduced to carrying out orders, was the categorical grant-in-aid.

The damage is being wrought not by the flow of funds from the national treasury to state and local treasuries but by the controls that accompany it. It can be avoided—and the centralized trend reversed—by changing over from categorical grants to revenue sharing and tax credits. It is for this reason that a recent report on the subject, prepared by the study group on revenue sharing of the (National) Republican Coordinating Committee, of which I am chairman, is titled *The Restoration of Federalism in America*.

* * *

The reader might conclude from Dr. Anderson's letter to Senator Howard H. Baker, Jr., that revenue sharing is a brand-new and untried idea in the United States. As a matter of fact, it has long been widely used by the states, most of which allocate to counties, cities and other units part of their collections from sales, income, liquor, motor vehicle and numerous other taxes. This works exceedingly well and the practice is expanding. Just within the past few months, Nevada and Texas adopted legislation, as other states did earlier, which allocates part of state-collected sales taxes to counties and cities. If we regard the states as laboratories to carry on experiments, why should we not use on a national scale a method that has proven eminently beneficial in the state-local relationship?

In a previous article (see the *Review*, June 1959, page 298), I described the changeover from categorical grants to unconditional fiscal (block) grants to local authorities which had then just been enacted in Great Britain. Several years earlier, while serving on the staff of the Commission on Intergovernmental Relations (Kestnbaum Commission), I had proposed that the commission, by recommending a replacement of categorical grants with tax sharing, could best carry out the mandate it had received from the President and the Congress "because the activity of the federal government has been extended into many fields which, under our constitutional system, may be the primary interest and obligation of the several states . . . ." Dr. Anderson, a member of the commission, opposed the plan then, as he does now.

* * *

Along with others, I testified for tax sharing before the Joint Economic Committee of Congress in 1957, but the idea has gained broad support only in the past few years in both political parties, in and out of Congress.

The crucial question is: Who should make the decisions on the multitude of public services in education, public assistance, hospitals, police, streets, etc.? Should it be the national government or should it be state and local governments (and the communities themselves through votes on bonds, taxes or other ballot propositions)?

The main argument for centralization is the provision of more nearly uniform public services throughout the country, regardless of location. The main arguments for a wide dispersal of power and local autonomy are that in a free country such as ours the people themselves are able to judge what they want from government; that views differ from place to place and that communities are entitled to live according to their own concepts; that, at this time, problems of defense, international relations and space are of transcending importance and require more study and attention than the President and Congress can give them as long as they devote most of their time to deliberating on and deciding domestic issues which state and local officials can judge at least as well, if not better. Last, but not least, is the proposition that freedom is indivisible. When home rule is permitted to erode and vanish, so will individual liberty.

I mentioned above that support for federal revenue sharing has been growing rapidly in both political parties. This summer, a congressional committee held hearings on the subject for the first but probably not the last time. Following is a short outline of a particular plan drawn up by the Republican Coordinating Committee's study group. Several details are still in the process of formulation, but the main characteristics are:

1. The more than 400 present authorizations for grants-in-aid are to be merged into fewer than a dozen functional block grants. Most of the funds are allocated among states on a per capita basis, with a small percentage reserved to increase aid to low-income states on an equalizing basis. Other factors such as density of population, migration, extent of territory and road mileage may also be considered. A substantial share of each state's allocation (specified in the federal legislation) must be passed on to the cities, possibly also to other local units.
2. A revenue sharing fund will be allocated to the states without earmarking on a basis similar to the functional block grants.
3. Federal income tax credits will be granted for the payment of state and local taxes.
4. Federal income tax credits will be considered for tuition and other expenses, and donations to educational institutions.

In its basic features, this plan has been approved and adopted by the top council of one of our two major parties. It is hoped that the other party will—as many of its members in and out of Congress already do—recognize the merits of the plan and help to enact it before very long.

To sum this up: Dr. Anderson is correct in saying that there are "perils in sharing." But there are far greater perils in continuing our present system. With the necessary safeguards, tax sharing and tax credits offer an avenue to a rational solution and to "a restoration of federalism in America."

Suggested Readings:
Intergovernmental Relations

ADVISORY COMMISSION ON INTERGOVERNMENTAL RELATIONS. *Reports.*
Washington, D.C.: U.S. Government Printing Office. This permanent body, which includes representatives of all levels of
government and which has a permanent staff, issues reports on
many aspects of federal-state-local and inter-local problems.
Some of the best publications in the intergovernmental field are
issued by the Commission.

BREAK, GEORGE F. *Intergovernmental Fiscal Relations in the United
States.* Washington, D.C.: The Brookings Institution, 1967.
This report explains why states and cities find it difficult to
raise adequate tax revenues and suggests alternative solutions
to the revenue problem including improved tax coordinating
systems, revised federal grants, and ways of apportioning unconditional grants.

GRAVES, W. BROOKE. *American Intergovernmental Relations.* New
York: Charles Scribner's Sons, 1964. Dated in a few places, this
is still the comprehensive text in this area.

MACMAHON, A. W. (ed.) *Federalism: Mature and Emergent.* New
York: Russell and Russell Publishers, 1962. This is one of the
best collections of essays on various aspects of federalism. See
especially Edward W. Weidner, "Decision-Making in a Federal
System."

SUNDQUIST, JAMES L., with DAVID W. DAVIS. *Making Federalism
Work: A Study of Program Coordination at the Community Level.*
Washington, D.C.: The Brookings Institution, 1969. Detailed
analysis of the problems and politics of coordinating intergovernmental programs in the area of housing and community
development.

WRIGHT, DEIL S. *Federal Grants-in-Aid: Perspectives and Alternatives.* Washington, D.C.: American Enterprise Institute for
Public Policy Research, 1968. One of the best analyses of the
alternatives available in the field of federal grants-in-aid.

3/Apportionment:
One Man, One Vote?

By 1962 more than three-fourths of the states had severely malapportioned legislatures. The consequences of this had significance for democratic theory of representation, for the viability of the federal system, and for problems of citizens in large urban areas.

The equity of the system of representation is of direct importance for democratic theory. Then Chief Justice Earl Warren, writing for the majority in *Reynolds* v. *Sims* (1964), noted that

> State legislatures are, historically, the fountain head of representative government in this country. . . . Representative government is the essence of self-government through the medium of elected representatives of the people, and each and every citizen has an inalienable right to full and effective participation in the political processes of his State's legislative bodies. Most citizens can achieve this participation only as qualified voters through the election of legislators to represent them. Full and effective participation by all citizens in state government requires, therefore, that each citizen has an equally effective voice in the election of members of his state legislature.

In addition to concern about democratic theory, there was a very real and practical concern about the effect of continued long-term malapportionment on public policy in the federal system, and on the citizens of the larger urban areas. The states were perceived to be increasingly less viable, and the cities turned to the federal government for aid rather than to unrepresentative, unresponsive state governments. Of prime importance was the observation by many citizens and professionals that the "urban crisis" and the rising sense of alienation of urban blacks and poor was

due, in large part, to decades of unresponsive state
governments. As the U. S. Department of Justice argued
before the Supreme Court in *Baker* v. *Carr*,

> In Tennessee, as in many other states, the under-representation of
> urban voters has been a dominant factor in the refusal of state
> legislatures to meet the growing problems of our urban areas.
> Urban governments now tend to by-pass the states and to enter
> directly into cooperative arrangements with the national
> government in such areas as housing, urban development, airports
> and defense community facilities.

The first selection in Part 3 summarizes the major
reapportionment cases since the 1962 *Baker* v. *Carr* decision.

The movement of the Supreme Court into the area of
reapportionment opened a major area of controversy that
has not been completely settled. Does the Court have power
in the area of reapportionment? Should the apportionment
decisions be overturned? If so, how? Should it be by
constitutional amendment, which would permit one house
of the state legislatures to be apportioned on a basis other
than population, as proposed by the late Senator Dirksen?

After several defeats in Congress for the proposed
Dirksen Amendment, efforts were undertaken to call a
constitutional convention for the purpose of reversing the
Supreme Court's reapportionment decisions, particularly
that of *Reynolds* v. *Sims*. The call for such a convention
was almost successful in 1968 when the thirty-third state,
of a needed thirty-four, petitioned Congress for a convention.
As of this writing, twenty-eight states have valid petitions
before Congress.

Support for the proposed amendment came from
sources as varied as the far-right Liberty Lobby to the
pinnacle of respectability, the American Bar Association.
In February 1965, the House of Delegates of the American
Bar Association approved a resolution supporting a
constitutional amendment whereby one house of a
bicameral state legislature could be apportioned, in part, on
the basis of other factors in addition to population. The
resolution was based on a report by the ABA's Standing
Committee on Jurisprudence and Law Reform in favor of
such an amendment and, further, calling for removal of the
state apportionment question from the jurisdiction of the
United States Supreme Court.

These events provide the background for two of the articles that follow. The editors of *State Government* invited leading constitutional experts to respond to the ABA's actions. Responses, reprinted here from the resulting symposium, came from Alfred de Grazia, who favors the proposal and would even bar all federal intervention in apportionment, and from Robert B. McKay, who warns that the Constitution should be left alone.

Two versions of the Dirksen Amendment follow these articles. Additionally, a biting condemnation of the Court's position is presented in the selection by A. Spencer Hill.

In addition to the myriad of constitutional-legal controversies surrounding the Supreme Court's action, there is the question of what public policy changes, if any, have resulted from reapportionment. Previously, fair urban representation was viewed as a panacea for most problems of the states and especially of big cities. Statements such as the following were typical:

> When one reflects on all that would have been done about slum clearance, urban renewal, juvenile delinquency, mass transportation, and similar problems in the last twenty years if Congress had devoted the same attention to urban problems, the imagination is staggered. The feedback from these historic court decisions can be expected to become inputs of the greatest importance for other decision-making agencies.[1]

Recent studies, however, suggest that public policy changes resulting from the increased urban representation will be neither as immediate nor as sweeping as was originally hoped. Conclusions such as, "On the whole, the policy choices of malapportioned legislatures are not noticeably different from the policy choices of well apportioned legislatures,"[2] or "In general malapportionment is not as significant a factor as has been posited,"[3] or "Reapportionment has had little effect on the urban legislative product,"[4] are now commonplace.

Reasons for the limited change are complex. Two major explanations are the incremental nature of the budgetary process and the realization that urban membership in a legislative chamber is not necessarily the same as urban influence or power. The former is elaborated upon in Part 5. The second explanation is illustrated by the last reading in Part 3, by Brett W. Hawkins and Cheryl Whelchel.

Notes

1. Marian D. Irish and James W. Prothro, *The Politics of American Democracy* (3rd ed.; Englewood Cliffs: Prentice-Hall, Inc., 1965), p. 333.

2. Thomas R. Dye, "Malapportionment and Public Policy in the States," *Journal of Politics*, vol. 27 (August 1965), p. 599.

3. David Brady and Douglas Edmonds, *The Effects of Malapportionment on Policy Output in the American States* (Iowa City: Department of Political Science, The University of Iowa, 1966), p. 18.

4. Samuel K. Gove, *Reapportionment and the Cities* (Chicago: Center for Research in Urban Government, Loyola University, 1968), p. 33.

ROSS E. ROBSON
PARRIS N. GLENDENING

Apportionment: Judicial Intervention

With the 1962 decision of *Baker* v. *Carr* the Supreme Court began a period of judicial involvement in the area of apportionment. Prior to 1962 the Court had maintained on the basis of the *Colegrove* v. *Green* decision that apportionment was a political matter and beyond the jurisdiction of the judicial system. The Court has, however, maintained an unaltering position since the 1962 decision. Namely, in a representative democracy one man's vote must be equal to another man's vote regardless of place of residence.

The Colegrove case arose when three qualified voters in Illinois sought a declarative judgment to invalidate the districting act of 1901 and an injunction to stop the congressional elections of 1946 due to larger populations in their districts than in others. In 1946, the 7th district had 914,053 people compared to 112,116 for the 5th district. Although the majority opinion acknowledged that great disparities in apportionment existed throughout the United States, the Court by a four to three decision noted that

> To sustain this action would cut very deeply into the very being of Congress. Courts ought not to enter this *political thicket*. The remedy for unfairness in districting is to secure State legislatures that will apportion properly, or to invoke the ample powers of Congress.[1]

In a dissenting opinion Justice Black argued that

> While the Constitution contains no express provision requiring that congressional election districts established by the States must contain approximately equal populations, the constitutionally guaranteed right to vote and the right to have one's vote counted clearly imply

the policy that state election systems, no matter what their form, should be designed to give approximately equal weight to each vote cast.[2]

Justice Black's opinion proved to be predictive. The Colegrove case actually had a majority of the justices in favor of judicial intervention. However, one justice, while concurring with the minority sentiments about justiciability, declined to rule in favor of the appellant on the grounds that there was not enough time between the decision and the elections to offer effective relief. This "hidden majority" would not reemerge until the *Baker* v. *Carr* decision sixteen years later.[3]

Involved in the Baker case was a constitutional requirement that both houses of the Tennessee general assembly shall ". . . be apportioned among the several counties or districts, according to the number of qualified electors in each." The Tennessee Constitution also required decenial reapportionment;[4] however, since 1901 no major change in reapportionment had been adopted. The Supreme Court, after concluding that the District Court had jurisdiction, that the appellants had standing and that Baker had presented justiciable arguments subject to adjudication in the courts, said:

> We conclude that the complaint's allegations of a denial of equal protection present a justiciable constitutional cause of action upon which the appellants are entitled to a trial and a decision. The right asserted is within the reach of judicial protection under the Fourteenth Amendment.[5]

Thus, the door for additional reapportionment challenges was open. One year later the Supreme Court in *Gray* v. *Sanders* said:

> The conception of political equality from the Declaration of Independence, to Lincoln's Gettysburg Address, to the Fifteenth, Seventeenth, and Nineteenth Amendments can only mean one thing—*one person, one vote.*[6]

In question was Georgia's county-unit system as a basis for counting votes in a Democratic primary election for the nomination of a United States Senator and statewide officers. The system weighed heavily in favor of less populated counties. The Court added that ". . . once the class of voters is chosen and their qualifications specified, we can see no constitutional way by which equality of voting may be evaded."[7]

Less than one later year in *Wesberry* v. *Sanders* the Supreme Court applied the principle of "one man, one vote" to Congressional districting.[8] The appellants claimed that the population of their district was from two to three times larger than that of some other Georgia congressional districts. The Court noted that "it may not be possible to draw congressional districts with mathematical precision."[9] However, "the command of Art. 1, 2, that Representatives be chosen 'by the People of the several states' means that as nearly as is practicable one man's vote in a congressional election is to be worth as much as another's."[10] Thus, the standard of "as nearly as is practicable" was established as the guideline for the principle of "one man, one vote." The meaning of this vague standard was left for several years virtually undefined.

Within months after the Wesberry case the Court handed down six decisions dealing with apportionment of state legislative districts. The leading case was *Reynolds* v. *Sims* involving the state of Alabama.[11] Although each of the cases involved somewhat different situations, the primary issue was similar to the Baker, Gray and Wesberry cases discussed above. In *Reynolds* v. *Sims*, the appellants argued that their rights under the Alabama Constitution and under the "Equal Protection Clause" of the Fourteenth Amendment were being deprived due to a malapportioned state legislature. The majority opinion noted that "population-variance ratios of up to about 41-to-1 existed in the Senate, and up to 16-to-1 in the House."[12] It was concluded that the

> Equal Protection Clause requires that a State make an honest and good faith effort to construct districts, *in both houses of its legislature*, as nearly of equal population as is practicable. We realize that it is a practical impossibility to arrange legislative districts so that each one has an identical number of residents, or citizens, or voters. Mathematical exactness or precision is hardly a workable constitutional requirement.[13]

The opinion further suggested that what may be permissible in one state may not be acceptable in another due to differing circumstances. With regard to the drawing of district boundaries, "a state may legitimately desire to maintain the integrity of various political subdivisions, in so far as possible, and provide for compact districts of contiguous territory in designing a legislative apportionment scheme," however, "the overriding objective must be substantial equality of population."[14]

It was not until four years later that the Supreme Court in *Avery* v. *Midland County, Texas* applied the "one man, one vote" principle to local governmental units which have general governmental powers over an entire geographical area.[15] Justice White in writing the majority opinion quoted a 1958 case which said that ". . . the prohibitions of the Fourteenth Amendment extend to all action of the State denying equal protection of the laws; whatever the agency of the State taking the action."[16] Thus, it was concluded:

> We therefore see little difference, in terms of the application of the Equal Protection Clause and of the principles of *Reynolds* v. *Sims*,

between the exercise of state power through legislatures and its exercise by elected officials in the cities, towns, and counties.[17]

One general exception was made concerning the application of this ruling to local governmental units:

> Were the Commissioners Court a special purpose unit of government assigned the performance of functions affecting definable groups of constituents more than other constituents, we would have to confront the question whether such bodies may be apportioned in ways which give greater influence to the citizens most affected by the organizations' functions.[18]

Between 1962 and 1968, the Supreme Court applied the principle of "one man, one vote" in the apportioning and districting of our national, state and local governmental units. However, there were many disparities found from state to state in the application of the "as nearly as is practicable" standard. In the Reynolds case, it will be recalled, Chief Justice Warren wrote that "mathematical exactness or precision is hardly a workable constitutional requirement."[19] In an attempt to clarify the issue, the Court accepted a case from Missouri during the October term, 1968.

Involved in the *Kirkpatrick* v. *Preisler* case was the apportioning and drawing of congressional districts.[20] It was concluded that "we can see no nonarbitrary way to pick a cutoff point at which population variances suddenly become de minimis."[21] The "as nearly as is practicable" standard became ". . . absolute equality, or for which justification is shown."[22] Rejected was the use of a certain percent disparity from one district to another as a guideline. The Court reiterated that "citizens, not history or economic interests, cast votes."[23]

On February 25, 1970, the Supreme Court rendered what would appear to be the final blow to any who had hoped for some flexibility at some levels of government. In *Hadley* v. *Junior College District*, another Missouri case, the Court has said:

> We . . . hold today that as a general rule, whenever a state or local government decides to select persons by popular election to perform governmental functions, the Equal Protection Clause of the Fourteenth Amendment requires that each qualified voter must be given an equal opportunity to participate in that election, and when members of an elected body are chosen from separate districts, each district must be established on a basis which will insure, as far as is practicable, that equal numbers of voters vote for proportionally equal numbers of officials.[24]

In summary, the Supreme Court has required that representation from the U. S. House of Representatives down to limited purpose units of local government be apportioned on the basis of one man, one vote. The Court's rigid adherence to this principle has led one student of judicial behavior to condemn the Court for its "dogmatic conceptions of equality" and total lack of "judicial self-restraint."[25] Further, the decisions may be based on what Justice Stewart has called "the uncritical simplistic and heavy-handed application of sixth-grade arithmetic."[26]

The net effect of the reviewed cases on public policy is yet undetermined. The implications of the decisions for democratic theory are not yet thought through. The wisdom of the Court's lack of judicial restraint is debatable. Yet one point stands out clearly: in the United States, except for elections for the President and Vice President and for the U. S. Senate, one man means one vote.

Notes

1. *Colegrove* v. *Green*, 328 U.S. 549, 556 (1946). Emphasis added. For a more extensive discussion of the cases mentioned herein, as well as a review of other relevant cases, see Robert G. Dixon, Jr., *Democratic Representation: Reapportionment in Law and Politics* (New York: Oxford University Press, 1968); and Calvin B. T. Lee, *One Man, One Vote* (New York: Charles Scribner's Sons, 1967).

2. *Ibid.*, 570.

3. 369 U. S. 186 (1962).

4. Tennessee, *Constitution*, Article II, Sections 4, 5, 6.

5. 369 U. S. 237 (1962).

6. 372 U. S. 368, 381 (1963). Emphasis added.

7. *Ibid.*, 381.

8. 376 U. S. 1 (1964).

9. *Ibid.*, 18.

10. *Ibid.*, 7–8. Emphasis added.

11. 377 U. S. 533 (1964).

12. *Ibid.*, 545.

13. *Ibid.*, 577. Emphasis added.

14. *Ibid.*, 578–579.

15. 390 U. S. 474 (1968).

16. Quoting *Cooper* v. *Aaron*, 358 U. S. 1, 17 (1958).

17. *Avery* v. *Midland County, Texas*, 390 U. S. 481 (1968).

18. *Ibid.*, 483–484.

19. 377 U. S. 533, 577 (1964).

20. 394 U. S. 526 (1969).

21. *Ibid.*, 531.

22. *Ibid.*

23. *Ibid.*, 533.

24. U. S. (1970).

25. A. Spencer Hill, "The Reapportionment Decisions: A Return to Dogma," *The Journal of Politics*, vol. 31 (February 1969), p. 186. See pp. 151–168 in this book.

26. *Lucas* v. *Colorado*, 377 U.S. 715, 746–750 (1964).

ALFRED DE GRAZIA

Righting the Wrongs
of Representation

When a mistaken policy is adopted by some one branch of government, the whole wrong, wherever possible, should be righted. The
Supreme Court has insisted in a series of cases that each chamber of a
state legislature be apportioned so that its members will come from
districts of equal population. The two questions then must be: Is the
Supreme Court right or wrong? If wrong, can the wrong be corrected?

The Wrong

It is rare for the Supreme Court to be so mistaken and so consistently
mistaken as in the decisions that began with *Baker* v. *Carr*, extended
through *Gray* v. *Sanders* and ended temporarily with *Reynolds* v. *Sims*
and several associated cases. The errors of the Court and its supporters
are several, each of which must be understood, if a proper reform is to
be planned.

The prevailing opinions rewrite history grotesquely. They deny
the widescale sentiment that has throughout American history insisted upon the analogy between the federal government and the
state government structures. They create bodies of public opinion
where opinion did not exist and inflate the extent of popular support
for certain doctrines, making majority beliefs out of minority ones
to suit their convenience.

The Court decisions grossly distort the Constitution. Only if
it is good law now to disregard utterly the intentions of those who
framed constitutional language, and to coin meanings freely, can the
theories of the several opinions be defended on constitutional grounds.
The Fourteenth Amendment was *not* intended, despite its importance
in other regards, to reconstruct the legislatures of the states.

Damages done

The judges have damaged the federal system. National law can now
penetrate a large and vital area of state government on the flimsiest
pretext. American federalism, unique in its strength and durability

Alfred de Grazia, "Righting the Wrongs of Representation," *State Government*, vol. 38 (Spring 1965), 113–117. Reprinted by permission.

in world history, depends upon the autonomy of the states, which in turn depends upon the independence of four state institutions— the elective system, the police system, the court system, and the legislative system with its powers to tax and spend. Intervention and disruption of any one of these must be considered to have serious import for the whole federal structure. The apportionment decisions have weakened the general role of the states in the government of Americans.

The Court has also invaded the legislative branch, in violation of the formal and widely accepted principle of the separation of powers. It has taken upon itself the reconstituting of the basis of power in the state governments. It has set itself above the law, above the state constitutions, and above the people, wherever the people, as in Colorado and other states, can be said to have expressed themselves on the question in opposition to the Court.

The Justices have imposed upon themselves and the state and lower federal courts the quixotic task of making countless political decisions on detailed matters of the organization of state government. Congress had shown no interest in this task, the people had shown no interest either, but the states were now adjudged incompetent for the purpose, while the courts, with their infrequent sessions, popular unaccountability, disgraceful backlogs of cases, and a structural incompetence to formulate, organize, integrate, and promulgate legislation, have opted for the task.

The principle proposed

In all of this, the dimensions of which must sometimes astonish its creators, some end is sought. And one point should be admitted: History, the Constitution, the federal system, the separation of powers, and the efficient performance of judicial tasks—all of these can be dismissed in the face of some great and pressing need, some emergency, something larger than all of these principles and institutions. Only in order that some one great principle, some one great need, be served, can it be granted that these should be shunted aside, temporarily or permanently.

What is this principle or need? It is buried in a mass of double-talk and verbiage, but it is there. It turns out to be a point of view, a sentiment, a sympathy, which is philosophically disputable, to say the least, and which, though it be even conceded, is without the consequences that are intended to follow its victory.

The principle rests behind the doctrine of equal-population districts (which for propaganda purposes is often termed the "one-man one-vote" doctrine). The doctrine of equal-population districts (which could, expecting a number of different consequences, be called also the doctrine of "equal voter-population districts" and other related terms) is one part of one major stream of democratic thought that seeks to equalize power among individuals regardless of their different abilities, contributions, background, knowledge, civic interest, or promises to perform services.

In a hundred different institutions of the government of the American republic, this idea is contradicted and even discriminated against, whether for the sake of differing democratic principles or for practical reasons. American government—national, state, and local— is simply not intended to operate, nor does it operate, according to this idea.

If that is so, then this principle, in all of its vagueness, must take its place along with many another principle that can be employed in the philosophical underpinnings of government. The Supreme Court has never been charged with creating the political philosophy of Americans. It has been entitled only to take the opportunities afforded it, within the limits set by the governmental process and the Constitution, to lend its voice to the concert of voices setting the philosophical tone of American politics.

Nonexistent justification

The illegitimacy of the Supreme Court as authoritarian philosopher in the apportionment cases might be again overlooked, as might all the highly dangerous conditions it has additionally created as defined above, provided that, philosophy and principles aside, some real emergency of the people is shown to exist. Such is not the case.

The courts of the land, beginning even before the decision in *Baker* v. *Carr*, have tested the doctrine of equal population districts by every imaginable justification:

They have sought proof by history and tradition and have failed.

They have said the doctrine possessed intrinsic rationality, and thereupon found "rationality" wherever they wished and "non-rationality" in the same way.

They have sought to apply the test of racial discrimination. Yet they have not found it generally in opposition to their general principle of equal population districts. Even the opposite was discovered in New York City and elsewhere.

They have looked for some over-arching partisan favoritism to be attacked by the doctrine, and found now one party and now another contented or discontented.

They have sought invidious discrimination and have not found it, except by calling whatever they disliked "invidious."

They have searched for discrimination against urban areas, and have found correlations without proven consequences.

They have applied the test of "fairness" only to become "unfair" to other equally good Americans.

They have sought to unblock certain avenues of opinion in state government, and in doing so have obstructed other channels.

In seeking for simplicity they have compounded confusion.

The final judgment in this regard can only be that the Supreme Court has been moved, by a blind faith in "numbers-magic," to unreasonable and arbitrary opinions. A kind of black magic has driven the Court into every state of the land, to the desolation of its institutions.

No one should, of course, attempt to fend off the attacks of the Court by a senseless defense of state government as it exists, and especially of the system of representation and apportionment. The states do not stand right and well as they are. Very little constructive imagination has been employed to adapt the representative governments of the states and localities to the problems of large cities, mass education, and performance of local functions independently of national executive direction.

But the solution of these problems and the part that the reform of representative government can play in their solution are irrelevant to the present discussion. Suffice to say that much, and to add that the Supreme Court decisions lend no direction to their solution. A regime by judiciary cannot substitute for a forthright assault upon these problems by the constitutional authorities and forces of opinion in the states and localities themselves.

The Remedy

If the Court is wrong, then what is the remedy?

The remedy that has been most prominently proposed and which has achieved an admirably concerted response is an amendment to the Constitution. This amendment, which may originate in the legislatures of the states, or in the Congress, would reintroduce something other than the so-called population principle into one branch of the legislature, provided the people of the state approve the modification of that principle.

This proposed remedy, it is fair to say, has been put forward by men who would, under other circumstances, agree with the position generally contained in this paper.

However, they would assert that "half a loaf is better than none." Therefore, three questions arise: Is the proposed amendment likely to do good? Is another proposal superior? Is any other proposal more likely to be adopted?

Current proposal found wanting

The proposed amendment has one substantive merit and several substantive defects:

The merit lies in permitting, under restricted conditions, the experimentation or continuation in one house of a legislature of devices other than equal population groupings to compose the basis for seats. Thus if society, for the purposes of representative government, is felt to consist of something other than numbers, which thing would not be reflected well by sheer nose-counting, then some means is provided for expressing that feeling.

A defect of the proposed amendment is that its application is too limited and constraining. It shuts off avenues of reform excepting the narrow one opened up. It prevents the full planning of representation in the modern state government, and forecloses many potential moves of the future.

By defining the population principle as such it admits it as a concrete enforceable principle, which it is not. By stating it, so necessarily vague in language, the amendment may be inviting almost as much litigation and political controversy as the present opinions of the Court allow.

The apportionment scene is further complicated by the amendment when it constrains the states to adopt a principle other than population only by prescribed means; that is, by popular vote. The amendment practically demands that the popular vote be the only way of providing for apportionment plans. Providing such means furthermore lends an implication that any deviation from the population principle is suspect and has to be approved by the popular referendum.

Finally the amendment is negative in spirit and language. It improves nothing about state government, save that it resists some element of the law, which by its resistance, it accepts as a whole. It only apparently blocks the trend. It may be little more than a disdainful flick of the cat's tail as it marches out of the forbidden room.

Proposed solution:
Strengthen the Tenth Amendment

The proper remedy for the decisions of the Supreme Court is a constitutional amendment that would begin to reconstruct the Tenth Amendment to the Constitution. That amendment, as is well known, was one of the most popular ever to be adopted. It holds that "the powers not delegated to the United States by the Constitution, nor prohibited by it to the States, are reserved to the States respectively, or to the people."

To it should be appended the rule that among the powers reserved to the states is that of determining the character, construction, and disposition of the constituencies that compose their legislatures, and of all other constituencies that compose the conciliar bodies of all units of government created by the states.

An amendment of this nature would be true to the philosophy that is only partially expressed in the amendment under consideration. It would permit flexible and full reforms of representative government in the states. It would be positive in spirit. It would restore the initiative for self-governing institutions to the states themselves. It would relieve the courts of the burdens they have unreasonably and arbitrarily brought upon themselves. It would wipe out completely the unfortunate record of the apportionment cases.

Furthermore, such a proposed amendment would have no less chance of becoming law. The "one-house" amendment would not muster as strong support because it is too readily identified as mildly ameliorative and more than mildly illusive in its effect. The same public arguments will have to be made in the controversies over both proposals. People will have to be persuaded and mobilized for action on the same philosophical and practical grounds.

Yet the full force of the argument against the Court position will not be available under the one-house amendment, because so much of the Court's case is conceded. All the underpinnings of the Court case, which have been here shown to be dangerously unbalanced, would be approved in fact and the superstructure changed only somewhat.

It is possible that neither amendment will be approved. The large and scattered mass of sentiment around the country which favors our being governed as a republic has once again shown that it is incapable of coming together for constructive purposes, and neither can it act effectively for constitutional defense. A supreme effort of organization would be required in any case to put through an amendment. The amendment adopted—or failed—then should be the best and truest mirror of the ideal.

Apportionment, like representation as a whole, should be conceived as one way to achieve a better form of society. Federalism, which has much at stake in this same controversy, has a similar goal. If the institutions of the state and the federal system are to be weakened, the states will finally be only haunted houses whose shutters bang to recall another age. Then, as many supporters of the Court in these matters more or less secretly hope, the structures may be completely demolished to make way for a fine new building.

No signs indicate that this fine new institution is to be, or is even imagined. It is difficult to see what the alternative to federalism can be except a *reformed* federalism, still based on the principles of an independent, representative government, having independent powers of taxing, spending, police and courts. If the states were gutted or destroyed, they would have to be reinvented. But the invention would have to be designed and adopted in the face of a centralized, bureaucratized government. Chances for success under the circumstances would be small.

It is much more reasonable and sure of success to seek now those reforms which, while always difficult to enact, will become increasingly so later on. Unity in diversity, efficiency amid liberty, friendship within the great society—these goals bespeak a federal republic whose internal constitution is founded upon federated and representative communities, a congeries of smaller and smaller territorial and functional republics existing in fact and guarded by law. To gain such ends it is well to decide upon full measures.

ROBERT B. McKAY

Don't Amend the Constitution

Amending the Constitution of the United States is serious business. The Council of State Governments, the General Assembly of the States, and the American Bar Association ask no less than repudiation of the decisions in the *Reapportionment Cases* in which the Supreme Court of the United States held that substantial equality of population among election districts is constitutionally required for each house of a bicameral legislature. In addition, the Council of State Governments and the General Assembly of the States would include in the proposed amendment a provision freeing the apportionment of subordinate units of state government from the imposition of any federal standards that might otherwise be found in the Constitution of the United States.

The General Assembly of the States, in its resolution adopted December 3, 1964, set forth the text of a proposed joint resolution submitted for action by state legislatures, applying to Congress for a constitutional convention to propose such an amendment. Although the call for a convention would be superseded by intervening congressional proposal of an amendment identical to that in the resolution, the novelty of the proposal calls for comment.

Difficulties in the Convention Approach

Article V of the Constitution provides that "on the Application of the Legislatures of two thirds of the several States, [Congress] shall call

Robert B. McKay, "Don't Amend the Constitution," *State Government*, vol. 38 (Spring 1965), 121–125. Reprinted by permission.

a Convention for proposing Amendments. . . ." The Constitution has never been amended in this fashion, all amendments having gone instead the route of proposal by two-thirds vote of both Houses of Congress. Analysis of the unresolved problems that lie in the path of proposing amendment to the Constitution by convention convened by Congress on the application of the states suggests that novelty may be the only thing to be said in its favor. Professor Arthur Earl Bonfield has detailed these problems in his article, *Proposing Constitutional Amendments by Convention: Some Problems.*[1] The difficulties may be summarized as follows:

(1)   It is by no means certain that the resolution proposed for adoption by the state legislatures satisfies the constitutional requirement for an "application" to Congress. The Constitution specifies that Congress is to "call a Convention for *proposing* amendments." If, as has been assumed, the "Convention" contemplated by Article V was intended to be a fully deliberative body for the consideration of various alternatives, a resolution which offers no alternative choices may not satisfy the "application" requirement. Moreover, the amendment proposed for uniform state adoption specifies that, if approved by Congress, it shall be ratified by "the state legislatures." Since Article V gives to Congress the power to determine the method of ratification, the proposed "application" form seems defective in this respect, too, as an intrusion upon authority conferred exclusively on Congress.

(2)   It is by no means clear how nearly contemporaneous with each other the state legislative applications must be. Is it essential that each state have acted within that most recent period during which all state legislatures had an opportunity to consider the question during a full regular session? Would a five-year period be too long? Ten years? Have the federal courts authority to prescribe a limitation period?

(3)   May states withdraw applications once tendered? The question, which probably should be answered in the affirmative, may have special relevance in the context of apportionment. It is not inconceivable that an application for constitutional amendment approved by a malapportioned legislature might be withdrawn by a later-elected legislature constituted in accordance with the equal-population principle.

(4)   If requisite "applications" are submitted to Congress within a "reasonable" time, presumably Congress is obligated to call a convention; but there is probably no way to force a reluctant Congress to take the necessary action. Indeed, Congress alone has the authority to prescribe the terms on which a convention would be constituted, how it would operate, and what would be

its authority. Congress would have to decide such important matters as whether the vote in convention should be by states (which seems undesirable and unlikely) or in accordance with populations, as well as the majority necessary for approval.

Admittedly, however, the foregoing problems are not the central objections to the proposed amendment. After all, similar proposals have been introduced in Congress, where they are free of any problems arising under Article V. The balance of this discussion will deal with the objections to any of the various amendments proposed to date.

Basic Objections

The proposed constitutional amendments, in any of their suggested forms, would not only allow retention or restoration of formulas that have produced malapportionment in the past, but would go so far as to permit representation by interest groups, in stark contrast with the majoritarian principle that has previously been thought controlling in this nation. If these proposals should be adopted, there would be nothing to prevent a transient (or permanent) political majority in a state, upon "approval" by a majority of its adherents among the electorate, from imposing its own political stamp in virtually irreversible fashion upon one house of the legislature. The political minority of the moment could be rendered permanently impotent, with its pockets of strength isolated in political 'ghettos denied full representation; and the gerrymander could be used to its full bizarre potential.

The only seeming protection, approval by the electorate, is a perilously frail reed on which to rely for vindication of the democratic impulse. The political majority might well be persuaded to approve a plan which might forever bar other political groups from control of one legislative house. Worse is the fact that there is no provision for reversal by a repentant electorate or by an electorate of a different political persuasion. Fewer than half the states have the constitutional initiative by which a plan once "approved" could be reviewed in the absence of legislative consent. Even where the initiative is available, it has not proved entirely reliable in such matters. One difficulty with the initiative, which is also a problem of majority vote on apportionment plans generally, is the fact that voters are not always presented with clear choices. If the voters are presented with two alternatives, both of which they consider unsatisfactory, it can scarcely be said that "approval" of either choice should be read as an approval of that formula for all time.

Proponents of any plan to amend the Constitution to achieve such anti-democratic results necessarily bear a heavy burden of persuasion, which has not been satisfactorily met. The difficulty is compounded by the almost unseemly haste to secure approval of a constitutional amendment, in fact or in principle, before the decisions in the *Reapportionment Cases* can be further implemented. It is apparently desired to seek approval of an amendment from the unreconstituted legislatures, as far as possible *before* reapportionment. If this proposal has real merit and genuine popular support among the voters (as opposed to support among the legislators whose self-interest cannot be discounted), there should be no reason to avoid the extended debate that an issue of this importance merits, and no reason to avoid presentation of the question to legislatures apportioned in accordance with population.

The Role of Interest Groups

The central feature of the proposal is the reliance on interest groups as units of representation. However disguised by reference to history, geography, or political subdivisions, the bare fact is that the proponents of constitutional amendment advocate restraint of majority rule by allowing the retention of a veto power in the hands of minority interest groups. The principle of retained minority control is not diminished by the fact that presumably only one house would be based on nonpopulation factors. The power of the veto is the significant restraint. An additional danger is that, where the basis for representation is radically different in the two houses, legislative stalemate might be the result.

It is not a sufficient answer to say that we have always accorded minorities special protections against majorities and that majority rule is thus not an important part of our political tradition. The obvious answer is that there are some values which we have ranked as fundamental in our society and thus assured to all regardless of the momentary heedlessness of the majority. Thus, by constitutional command we protect freedom of speech, press, and religion from conformity that might otherwise be required by an unthinking majority. Similarly, we require certain minimum standards of fairness in criminal proceedings, however unpopular or even guilty the defendant may be. And we make sure that racial discrimination may not be dictated by majority vote.

To urge, on the other hand, that the popular majority should in *all* matters be restrained from fulfilling its goals because of the objections of economic or social interest minority groups is to confuse high principle with cynical expediency. Yet that is exactly what those dissatisfied with the equal population principle have urged. Mr. Justice Harlan, dissenting in *Reynolds* v. *Sims* argued that "legislators can represent their electors only by speaking for their interests—

economic, social, political. . . ."[2] In like spirit Professor Alexander Bickel has offered a frank justification for ethnic-group constituencies as follows: "I believe the Silk Stockings should be represented by a man specially responsive and congenial to them, . . . I think the same of Negroes, Puerto Ricans, farmers, and other distinguishable groups of reasonable size."[3]

There are, however, at least two important reasons why businessmen cannot always be represented by a businessman, dairy farmers by one of their own, Negroes by a Negro, and Lutherans by a member of that denomination. In the first place, no individual is just a businessman, dairy farmer, Negro, or Lutheran. He may be all of those or none of those; but surely no one of those groups as such, simply because it is less than a majority, is entitled to exercise a veto over decisions made by representatives of the majority. Moreover, members of these alleged interest groups ordinarily do not isolate themselves in particular geographical areas around which election district lines can be drawn. The heterogeneous community is the genius of the American political system in which businessmen, dairy farmers, Negroes, and Lutherans can all live together and somehow come to a viable consensus through their elected representatives.[4]

Congress' Model Does Not Apply

The only other justification that is commonly advanced as a basis for rejecting majority rule in favor of interest-group representation depends on a misconceived reliance on history. The argument is that population has customarily been subordinated in one house of most state legislatures, on the model of Congress and that the principle must accordingly be justifiable. That view of history is not sound, and in any event the conclusion does not follow.

The notion of interest-group representation is entirely foreign to the American system of legislative representation, with the single exception that separate representation has sometimes been given to the political subdivisions of a state. But certainly the states have not adopted systems of representation based on economic status, ethnic groupings, or historical considerations. Indeed, to have done so would have been to defy American tradition. But all these would be possible under the proposed amendments.

A word should be said about representation based on political subdivisions, allegedly on the congressional model. The differences between Congress and the state legislatures are greater than the similarities. The formula for representation in the United States Senate is specified in the Constitution as the result of a compromise that recognized the sovereign identity of the several states. The local political subdivisions of the states, on the other hand—the counties, towns, cities, and villages—are not sovereign but are creatures of the state legislatures, subject to enlargement, contraction, or elimination; and they have no guaranteed residual authority as have the states. Moreover, the state districting and apportionment processes are subject to the equal protection clause of the Fourteenth Amendment, which does seem to ordain equality.

Since the Fourteenth Amendment was added to the Constitution only in 1868, it is relevant to observe practice before that date. The story revealed by that investigation is very interesting. Although several of the original thirteen states adopted apportionment formulas which today produce substantial inequality among election districts, it is clear that they did not act on the model of Congress. In fact, the original state constitutions predated the Federal Constitution, which in turn was not copied from their example. Moreover, the population at the time these formulas were approved was much more evenly spread among the counties that were given equal representation (as in Delaware and New Jersey) and among the towns that were given equal representation (as in Connecticut and Rhode Island) than today when the situation has been vastly altered by the shift of population to the great urban centers.

Even more significant is the fact that between 1790, when Vermont was admitted, and 1889, when Montana was admitted almost 100 years later, every state admitted to the Union entered with a constitution providing for representation based principally on population in both houses of the legislature. Indeed, the original constitutions in thirty-six of the fifty states provided for representation largely in accordance with population in both houses of the legislature.[5] It was not until late in the nineteenth century that the states began the movement away from representation in accordance with population, sometimes by a change in formula and sometimes simply by failing to live up to their own constitutional requirements. By the time *Baker* v. *Carr*[6] was decided in 1962, the movement was virtually complete. Malapportionment was king nearly everywhere. But even by that date no more than ten states had formulas even roughly comparable to the alleged congressional model, and even those differed somewhat from Congress and from each other. In short, as the Court noted in rejecting the so-called federal analogy, reliance on it was an "after-the-fact rationalization offered in defense of maladjusted state apportionment arrangements."[7]

Flexibility for Majority Rule

Unquestionably, implementation of the *Reapportionment Cases* requires substantial adjustment of apportionment formulas in many states. But the Supreme Court made it clear in the original decisions that there is considerable room for variation of formula depending, for example, on the governmental role played by local political subdivisions in the various states. Clearly, mathematical precision is not required. The recent decision in *Fortson* v. *Dorsey*[8] reinforces that conclusion, for there the Court upheld the Georgia formula calling for multi-member election districts in the populous areas and single-member districts elsewhere.

It is especially significant to note that individual states have found in the rule the flexibility that the Court said was there. Thus, in both Oklahoma and Wisconsin the reapportionment has been accomplished without crossing county lines, while other states have replaced their old schemes altogether with new formulas designed to achieve more effective representation. The point here is simply that it is too soon to call a halt to a noble experiment in application of majority rule, an experiment which I believe is now in the process of being proved eminently workable.

Notes

1. 39 *Notre Dame Lawyer* 659 (1964).
2. 377 U.S. 533, 623–24.
3. Letter to Editor, 36 *Commentary* 344 (1963).
4. See Auerbach, *The Reapportionment Cases: One Vote, One Value,* 1964 Supreme Court Review 1, 30–61.
5. *Advisory Commission on Intergovernmental Relations, Report on Apportionment of State Legislatures,* 10–11, 35, 69 (1962).
6. 369 U.S. 186.
7. *Reynolds* v. *Sims,* 377 U.S. 533, 573 (1964).
8. 379 U.S. 433 (1965).

Dirksen Amendment Texts: 1965 and 1966

*1965 Dirksen Amendment**

That the following article is proposed as an amendment to the Constitution of the United States, which shall be valid to all intents and purposes as part of the Constitution when ratified by the legislatures of three-fourths of the several states within seven years from the date of its submission by the Congress:

*Source: S.J. Res. 66, 89th Cong. 1st session (1965).

Section 1. The people of a state may apportion one house of a bicameral legislature using population, geography, and political subdivisions as factors, giving each factor such weight as they deem appropriate, or giving reasonable weight to the same factors in apportioning a unicameral legislature, if in either case such plan of apportionment has been submitted to a vote of the people in accordance with law and with the provisions of this Constitution and has been approved by a majority of those voting on that issue. When a plan of apportionment based on factors of population, geography, and political subdivisions is submitted to a vote of the people under this Section there shall also be submitted, at the same election, an alternative plan of apportionment based upon substantial equality of population.

Section 2. Any plan of apportionment which has been approved under this article shall be resubmitted to a vote of the people, or, another plan may be submitted under the provisions of Section 1, at the November general election held two years following each year in which there is commenced any enumeration provided for in Section 2 of Article I, and upon approval by a majority of those voting thereon, such plan of apportionment shall continue in effect until changed in accordance with law. and with the provisions of this Constitution.

*1966 Dirksen Amendment***

That the following article is proposed as an amendment to the Constitution of the United States, which shall be valid to all intents and purposes as part of the Constitution when ratified by the legislatures of three-fourths of the several states within seven years of its submission to the states by the Congress, provided that each such legislature shall include one house apportioned on the basis of substantial equality of population in accordance with the most recent enumeration provided for in Section 2 of Article I:

Section 1. The legislature of each state shall be apportioned by the people of that state at each general election for Representatives to the Congress held next following the year in which there is commenced each enumeration provided for in Section 2 of Article I. In the case of a bicameral legislature, the members of one house shall be apportioned among the people on the basis of their numbers and the members of the other house may be apportioned among the people on the basis of population, geography, and political subdivisions in order to insure effective representation in the state's legislature of the various groups and interests making up the electorate. In the case of a unicameral

**Source: S.J. Res. 103, 89th Cong., 2nd session (1966).

legislature, the house may be apportioned among the people on the basis of substantial equality of population with such weight given to geography and political subdivisions as will insure effective representation in the state's legislature of the various groups and interests making up the electorate.

Section 2. A plan of apportionment shall become effective only after it has been submitted to a vote of the people of the state and approved by a majority of those voting on that issue at a statewide election held in accordance with law and the provisions of this Constitution. If submitted by a bicameral legislature the plan of apportionment shall have been approved prior to such election by both houses, one of which shall be apportioned on the basis of substantial equality of population; if otherwise submitted it shall have been found by the courts prior to such election to be consistent with the provisions of this Constitution, including this Article. In addition to any other plans of apportionment which may be submitted at such election, there shall be submitted to a vote of the people an alternative plan of apportionment based solely on substantial equality of population. The plan of apportionment approved by a majority of those voting on that issue shall be promptly placed in effect.

A. SPENCER HILL

The Reapportionment Decisions: A Return to Dogma?

The more the author has reflected upon the reapportionment decisions, the more they appear to him to resemble the decisions delivered by the Supreme Court at the turn of the century relative to the constitutionality of laws regulating wages and hours. Though there are differences between the wages and hours decisions and the reapportionment decisions, both types were based on dogmatic conceptions of equality, both assumed the fundamental soundness of opposite social theories without attempting to prove them, and both rejected judicial self-restraint and the pragmatic examination of inter-institutional relationships.

In the later wage and hour cases, the Court followed suggestions made by Justice Holmes in his earlier dissent, moving from its

A. Spencer Hill, "The Reapportionment Decisions: A Return to Dogma?" *Journal of Politics*, vol. 31 (February 1969), 186–213. Reprinted by permission.

reliance primarily upon dogmatic theory to dependence upon a realistic pragmatic examination. Instead of assuming, as did Spencerian theory, that bargaining was a private relation between an individual employee and an individual employer, and that wage and hour legislation was by definition an arbitrary interference in the personal liberty of employer and employee, the Judges examined the *real world* of bargaining relationships and found it so fraught with public consequences that they decided the federal and state legislation in these areas did not violate personal rights. Whether or not legislation was arbitrary in terms of the factual social conditions, was to be determined by careful examination of the real social world—not by mere reference to abstract theory.

The recent reapportionment decisions mark a foreboding about-face. The Court has moved from its original position, that apportionment laws dealt with subjects so intertwined with group socio-economic content that they constituted political questions better decided by elected officials in contact with political reality, to the position that whenever apportionment laws departed from per-capita equality in representation, individuals in the under-represented areas were denied their constitutional rights.

It is the author's contention that the Court's move from dogma to pragmatism in the wage and hours cases was more consistent with the Constitution and its philosophy, more in accord with the legal power of the Court, better adapted to the difficult role the Court must play, and better related to the economic and social necessities of our time than was the earlier dependence upon dogma. He fears that the Court has unwisely reversed its position relative to pragmatism and dogmatism in the reapportionment cases and sees no compelling reason for the reversal. He feels that the Court has falsely assumed (reminiscent of the early wage and hour decisions) that reapportionment is a simple matter of individual rights—rather than the very complex socio-economic problem with individual rights implications that it really is. The very complexity of the problem of reapportionment makes the author seriously question this departure from pragmatism in the attempts to solve the problem. As Justice Abe Fortas said in condemnation of the most recent application of dogma to local government, reapportionment demands "a reasoned, conservative, empirical approach to the intricate problem of applying constitutional principle to the complexities of local government" and not "the hatchet of one man-one vote." "In the circumstances of this case equal protection of the laws may be achieved—and perhaps can only be achieved—by a system which takes into account a complex of values and factors, and not merely the arithmetic simplicity of one equals one."[1] The author would only add that the same reasoning logically applies to reapportioning state legislatures as well.

The Absolute Right of Contract Dogma

Those who insisted that wages and hours laws were unconstitutional argued that the Judges could not concern themselves with any question other than whether or not legal equality existed between contracting parties. Any interference with the contractual relationship between private individuals was an interference in their individual rights. To be justified it had to be proven necessary in the interest of the health, welfare, and morals of the people. Hours of clearly unhealthy occupations like mining could be regulated on the basis of health, and the hours of minors might be regulated because it was presumed that they lacked the requisite maturity to enter into a contract. But when Congress sought to regulate the wages of women in the District of Columbia, the regulation was regarded by Justice George Sutherland as strictly arbitrary on two grounds. First, these were "adult women who were legally as capable of contracting for themselves as men." Government, then, unlawfully interfered in a purely private affair advantageous to both parties without a clear showing that it was necessary in the interest of the health or welfare of either.[2] Secondly, it discriminated against the employer since it forced upon him the unpalatable choice "of abandoning his business" or paying the minimum wage and "going on at a loss."[3]

In a similar vein, Justice Rufus W. Peckham argued in the *Lochner* case that the "general right to make a contract . . . is a part of the liberty of the individual protected by the Fourteenth Amendment. . . ."[4] Regulation of the hours of bakers was unconstitutional because it interfered arbitrarily between equals in a private bargaining agreement. The only possible justification that the state might give for interfering in this private contractual arrangement would be its overwhelming necessity in the protection either of the health of the bakers or of the public.[5] Since no direct connection could be proved between the regulation in question and the health of either the bakers or the public, the regulation was regarded as an arbitrary interference in personal rights of contracting individuals.

Several assumptions underlay the reasoning of the Justices quoted above: (1) Wage and hour contracts are contracts involving the private wills of individuals and not contracts involving the fundamental interests of the state. (2) Since the relationship is private, voluntary, and relatively untinged with social consequences, interference by the state is an interference in the personal rights of individuals. (3) Workers, no matter what their economic or social status—whether isolated, unskilled women or well-protected, unionized, *skilled* craftsmen—are both factually and legally the equal of the organized businesses with which they enter into contractual relations. (4) Disastrous consequences will follow if states are allowed by the courts—the bulwark of individual liberty—to interfere by wage and hour laws with the economic laws postulated by Herbert Spencer and other economists of the laissez-faire school.

So committed were the Justices to the notion that the economic and social health of the nation was tied to preserving unregulated contractual relations in private business that they never questioned one of the assumptions above. They never sought to determine if in the real world partners in the contracting relationship were in fact as well as in theory equals. They never sought to determine the extent of social injury from sub-standard wages or excessive hours of labor, merely assuming the validity of the social darwinian–laissez-faire theories. Justice Oliver Wendell Holmes Jr. alone pleaded for the self-restraint and pragmatism that came to characterize the court of a later day.

> The Fourteenth Amendment does not enact Mr. Herbert Spencer's Social Statics . . . a constitution is not intended to embody *a particular economic theory, whether of paternalism and the organic relation of the citizen to the State or of laissez-faire* . . .
> General propositions do not decide concrete cases . . . I think that the word "liberty" in the Fourteenth Amendment is perverted when it is held to prevent the *natural outcome of a dominant opinion, unless it can be said that a rational and fair man necessarily would admit that the statute proposed would infringe fundamental principles as they have been understood by the traditions of our law.*[6]

Abandonment of Dogma for Empirical Observation

When the decisions outlawing wage and hour laws were reversed, they were reversed because the Court refused to negate legislation unless empirical observation confirmed that the discrimination alleged to exist in theory existed also in fact. Thus, Chief Justice William Howard Taft, dissenting in the *Adkins* Case, alluded to the absence of equality between employers and employees in the real world alleged by Spencer and Justice Sutherland to exist in theory.

> Legislatures, in limiting freedom of contract . . . proceed on the assumption that employees in the class receiving least pay are not upon a full level of equality . . . with their employer, and in their necessitous circumstances are prone to accept . . . anything that is offered. They are particularly subject to the over-reaching of the harsh and greedy employer.[7]

Whether minimum wage laws remedied the situation was irrelevant, for it was "not the function of this Court to hold congressional acts invalid simply because they were passed to carry out economic views which the Court believed to be unwise or unsound."[8] Similarly, the Court held wage and hours laws of the State of Washington constitutional despite the obvious theoretical interference in the right of contract, since pragmatic review of economic conditions convinced the Judges that "reasonable legislators" might conclude that equality did not exist between employers and employees, regardless of the contrary dictates of legal theory. This same pragmatic, realistic examination convinced the Justices also that the question was not one simply of the private right to contract, but one in which certain workers were at such a disadvantage that the state was faced with the choice of setting minimum wages or taxing the whole community for their support.[9]

Thus, what appeared to Justices considering only Spencerian theory to be a private bargaining situation into which the state could not enter without violating contract rights turned out, upon pragmatic examination of the real world, to be a social situation which involved the health and welfare of the community—a legitimate legislative concern.

Clearly the Court moved in wage and hour decisions from the "absolute right of contract" dogma to the pragmatic acceptance of governmental regulations which did not appear, in the light of the examination of the real world, to be grossly unreasonable. The history of reapportionment decisions seems to move in exactly the opposite direction—from the pragmatic treatment of apportionment statutes as political questions to the position that arithmetical equality in representation is an individual right regardless of social, political, or economic considerations that might indicate that another representative scheme might be more appropriate.

The Case for Judicial Restraint

Considerations both of expedience and constitutional law compel the Supreme Court to exercise relative restraint in deciding cases in the long-run. The Supreme Court must assume a role which makes a strict adherence to a mere social theory, meritorious or otherwise, impractical if not impossible. The Court must make decisions that harmonize a number of variables which are often very difficult to reconcile: decisions must simultaneously comply relatively strictly with a provision of the Constitution, render substantial justice in the individual case, comply with the statutes of the United States, and remain consistent with its other decisions directly or indirectly applicable to the case at hand. The task is difficult enough when the Court acts only in cases where examination reveals that severe injustice will be done if the act of the legislature or governmental agency is not reversed. The task becomes a near impossibility when the Court dogmatically asserts that every act of the legislature must be reversed which does not conform to justice as defined by abstract social theory. For this reason, whether it be a Court dissatisfied with politics because that Court is reactionary, as it was in the wage and hour cases, or because the Court is revolutionary, as it has been in the reapportionment cases, the impossible "political thicket" into which the Court is driven by its dogma tends sooner or later to drive the court back to safer, more pragmatic grounds.[10]

Considerations of constitutional law seem to require judicial restraint in both the wage and hour cases and the reapportionment cases. Though the Constitution did not precisely define either the power or the role of the Supreme Court, the Court was required by its own rules and by the nature of the federal system within which it operates, to exercise self-restraint. A prodigious student of federalism, K. C. Wheare, has insisted that the nature of American federalism requires that the "States be *co-equally supreme* within their sphere," and "in no legal sense . . . *subordinate corporations*" to the national government.[11]

If the states are to remain "co-ordinate" governments and not become "subordinate" federal agencies, then it follows that the Supreme Court, which is itself a branch of the central government, should give the state the benefit of the doubt when trying to decide whether or not a state law is constitutional. Justice John M. Harlan in his *Lochner* dissent alluded to this necessity by contending that the "State is not amenable to the judiciary in respect of its legislative enactments unless such enactments are *plainly palpable, beyond all question, inconsistent with the Constitution* . . ."[12]

This mandate was particularly binding in the case of reapportionment, for in these cases the Supreme Court was holding legislation invalid which determined the basic structure of state government. If the states cannot even determine the nature of one of their most important branches of government, they have lost the requisite independence to be regarded as a partner in a federal system and have moved a long distance toward the vassalage more appropriate to the unitary system of government. The Court recognized this fact and acted accordingly in the first case on apportionment coming before it. It refused to take jurisdiction on the grounds that the "basis for the suit is not a private wrong, but a wrong suffered by Illinois as a polity."[13] In judging a state, the Court implied it must give it the benefit of the doubt.

There are two other rules of procedure traditionally accepted by the Supreme Court which have been seriously violated in *Reynolds* v. *Sims* and *Lucas* v. *Colorado*. These rules are: (1) That those challenging a state statute have the burden of proof and must show that it is a clearly arbitrary statute which "no rational man" could claim was related to the powers granted the state by the Constitution of the United States; (2) That a person seeking a remedy in equity from the courts of the United States must establish that he is personally and substantially—and not generally or superficially—harmed.

Nothing occurs more frequently in the literature supporting the "one man–one vote" dogma than the assertion that the opponents of judicial intervention have not shown that court-ordered reapportionment will harm rural groups or other minorities apt to lose representation as a result. Since the state legislatures have not proved that their apportionment laws are not arbitrary, the laws must as a consequence fall.[14] The point conveniently ignored by Carl A. Auerbach and others who have argued this way is that when state statutes are challenged, it is the petitioner who bears the burden of proof.

If Chief Justice Warren had applied his own words in the *McGowan* case to the *Sims* case, he could never have concluded that the little federal system of reapportionment was unconstitutional. In the McGowan case he claimed that the Fourteenth Amendment permitted states to enact laws which affect citizens differently.

> The constitutional safeguard is offended only if the classification rests on grounds *wholly irrelevant to the achievement of the State's objective*. State legislatures are presumed to have acted within their constitutional power despite the fact that, in practice, their laws result in some *inequality. A statutory discrimination will not be set aside if any state of facts reasonably may be conceived to justify it.*[15]

In the reapportionment cases "the Court refused to examine the state's reapportionment to see if any state of facts reasonably may be conceived to justify it."[16]

What the Court has done in the reapportionment cases is to assume what its own rules required it to prove. In the words of Robert G. Dixon Jr.:

> The Court accepts mathematical proof in the nature of arithmetic abstractions which shows major numerical disparities in size of districts and allocation of representatives, and it states in conclusionary fashion that "invidious discrimination" exists. Next, and this is a very critical point, the Court *shifts the burden of proof to the defenders* to show a *"rational plan."* By *"rational plan"* is meant a plan which is internally consistent and proceeds logically from a set of identifiable and clear principles. *But how can there be a rational plan from a highly political process of compromise and adjustment regarding apportionment and districting, or indeed, regarding legislation generally? Judicial insistence on rational plans of apportionment confuses the reasoned process of adjudication with the intricate process of multi-laterally negotiated settlements which characterize the political legislative arena.* By thus shifting the burden of proof after finding that population disparities alone make out a prima facie case of invidious discrimination, the courts are really skirting the basic constitutional issue of what constitutes a fair apportionment.[17]

The retort often given by proponents of court-ordered reapportionment when they are confronted with the evidence that they have shifted the burden of proof to the defendants is that this is the usual practice in cases involving personal rights and is within the tradition and rules of the courts. The first assumption requiring proof is that malapportionment results in a loss of an individual right to those demanding redress.

To begin with, malapportionment denies no one the right to vote in the traditional sense. As Justice Stewart said in his dissent in the *Lucas* Case:

> Nobody's right to vote has been denied. Nobody's right to vote has been restricted. The voting right cases . . . are, therefore, completely wide of the mark. Secondly, these cases have nothing to do with "weighting" or "diluting" of votes cast within any electoral unit. The rule of *Gray* v. *Sanders* . . . is, therefore, completely without relevance here . . .[18]

It is questionable, therefore, the extent to which malapportionment deprives anyone of a personal right. Paul C. Kauper is convinced that the Court was wrong to focus upon "a specious conception of personal right rather than upon the institutional aspect of the problem."[19] Dixon, while not going so far, believes that the Court had falsely assumed that reapportionment cases were purely and simply cases involving individual rights. He contends that at best, reapportionment cases involve cases in which the *"personal civil right of the voter is intertwined with . . . political philosophies and practices of representation . . . in which groups and parties are as relevant as individuals."*[20]

But even if we do assume that their personal rights are involved in the reapportionment cases, the decisions do not comply with those reached in other cases involving similar types of personal rights. Dixon argues that the burden of proof is not always shifted to the defendant in all civil rights cases. Where the burden of proof has been shifted, this shift occurred in cases "where a distinctly and uniquely personal impact of state policy is at issue, rather than the dilution of the mixed personal-political exercise of the franchise."[21] The burden of proof has been shifted in cases where the "basic constitutional right . . . was already established . . . In contrast in the apportionment cases, the basic constitutional right is not yet established, i.e., the question of a right to numerical equality in one or both houses. . . ."[22]

McGowan v. *Maryland* is a case in point. It involved personal rights much more directly than apportionment did. The statute in *McGowan* subjected Jews and Seventh-Day Adventists to loss of two of the best days of the week for business or a denial of their consciences. Ostensibly, the Court ignored the fact that the day in question in *McGowan*, Sunday, is a sacred day to the majority, and it based its decision upon the police power to regulate health. But the personal impact of *McGowan* upon Jews and Seventh-Day Adventists is far more "invidiously discriminatory" than the impact upon urban dwellers from the existence of one house in the state legislature apportioned partly on factors other than population. Yet Chief Justice Warren upheld the state statute closing all business on Sunday and commented as follows:

> The applicable principles are that a state statute may not be struck down as offensive of *equal protection* in its scheme of classification unless it is *obviously arbitrary*, and that except in the case of a statute whose discriminations are so *patently without reason that no conceivable situation of fact could be found to justify them, the claimant who challenges the statute bears the affirmative demonstration that in the actual state of facts which surround its operation, its classifications lack rationality.*[23]

Not only did the Court fail to prove that reapportionment statutes in question were arbitrary, irrational, and "invidiously discriminatory" in their personal impact upon those suing the state, but it did not bother to examine a *single issue* other than whether or not there were disparities in per-capita representation between legislative districts.

True to its consistent tradition, the Warren Court allowed less time to the states to reapportion than to effect desegregation. In the segregation cases a careful examination of the effect of segregation was ordered, and absence of equal protection of the laws was determined only after examination of the social environment proved conclusively that harm was done by legal segregation. When the Court conclusion was drawn, the Court allotted the state time to comply according to circumstances faced by the particular state.

Such was not the case with reapportionment decisions. Considering the co-ordinate status of state governments, the Justices should have taken pains to examine the intricate reapportionment schemes weighing and considering thoroughly their consequences. Certainly state apportionment laws deserved as much attention as had been accorded state segregation laws, but the Court seemed disinclined to give it. The Court's hasty action in considering reapportionment, and its disregard for the mitigating circumstances existing in different states caused Kauper to exclaim that "never before has the country witnessed such a spectacle of judicial power run riot."[24]

Dixon reached the same conclusion and elaborated further:

> Desegregation is conceptually far more simple than legislative apportionment and unlike reapportionment, is almost exclusively a matter of vindicating a personalized civil right. And yet in desegregation we

have had "all deliberate speed" over a ten year period, whereas in reapportionment we have been treated to a spectacle of courts pressuring and threatening legislators and fixing exact deadlines measured in months, or even weeks.[25]

The nation has paid for the Court's haste: numerous (and expensive!) special sessions were convened in statehouses from Alabama to Colorado, and one state had to finance an at-large election of the legislature totally confusing to the voters. The result at least makes questionable whether or not the newly developed judicial activism relative to reapportionment has been valuable to the nation.

Had the Justices in the reapportionment cases followed their own rules, they would have declared unconstitutional reapportionment statutes only after weighing the situation in each state to determine whether the effect of the apportionment statute was such as to put the petitioner to such a disadvantage that he could be said to be personally harmed by legislative districts (classifications) established. If the Court had to choose between political philosophies, (as Auerbach, the most effective defender of the decisions, cheerfully admits that they did)[26] then the philosophy chosen should have been one clearly preferred by the Constitution of the United States, the constitutions of the states, the history of states, and their actual practices.

If the Court is going to follow the pattern established when wage and hour statutes were finally held constitutional, it must not conclude with blinders on that if certain districts have a per-capita disadvantage in the representation, they are victims of discrimination. The Court must examine the position of these groups in other elections and in the total institutional picture, including economic institutions, to see if the aggrieved groups do not have compensating advantages elsewhere. This the Court did not do.

It seems to the author that, like the Justices in the wage and hour cases, the Justices in the apportionment cases were so certain of the soundness of the social theories which they felt were threatened by the legislation in question that they abandoned judicial self-restraint in favor of judicial activism. Liberals have been loud in their condemnation of the absence of judicial self-restraint in the wage and hour legislation. They are, however, lavish in their praise of the abandonment of self-restraint by the Court in reapportionment cases, since the Court is now intervening in support of a social theory of which they approve.

Logic of Democracy
and Reapportionment Decisions

How well does court-ordered reapportionment stand up in terms of democratic theory?

It is on these grounds that defenders of reapportionment are usually most willing to defend the action of the courts. They argue that the Constitution is a living document. They argue that whatever limitations the Constitutional Fathers might have meant to put on majority rule due to their concepts of separation of powers or federalism has been removed by the logic of democracy as conceived in the Twentieth Century: the trend of constitutional interpretation and the evolving Constitution have led to a new conception of federalism which holds that both the national and state governments share rather indefinite powers, and that the powers exercised by each will depend at any moment on which responds best to the will and needs of the majority. Thus, it is assumed—as granted—that any restriction placed upon the majority, except where the majority infringes on a clearly established individual right, must of necessity be an informal rather than a formal restriction. They have come to accept the conclusion of Robert A. Dahl: formal constitutional checks on a majority are unnecessary because informal social checks are built into the system.[27] Consequently, they easily and specifically reject Chancellor Kent's suggestion as quoted in *Colegrove* v. *Green*, that one of the legitimate purposes of apportionment statutes was to prevent "the aggregate minority of the people in the state . . . from being wholly overpowered by the combined action of the numerical majority."[28] Few political scientists seem to realize that a concept like democracy, as Professor Dahl suggests in another article, is a "giant glob of oily ambiguity . . ." which often leads the unwary into confusion rather than light.[29] Should a mere "headcount" suffice to determine a majority whose will must be legally respected? Does such a majority exist when it has but a vague preference of some sort exposed by an election or preference poll, or does such a majority exist only when it feels deeply enough about an issue to organize and campaign to effect its ends? How and when does one give effect to majority preferences? To what extent can the Court practically give effect to majority preference whichever way it chooses to define it? And finally, add to the problems of majority rule raised above the additional problem of determining "a majority of what?" In such confusion, how does the court arrive at the principles it espoused in the *Reynolds* and *Lucas* cases?

In the *Reynolds* and *Lucas* cases the Court was driven to the conclusion that the "equal protection" clause requires "that each citizen have an equally effective voice in the election of members of his state legislature."[30] Thus, any apportionment scheme which gave any person a vote less effective than any other person would be constitutionally suspect. If one means by democracy the rule of the national majority over the national minority, then it seems to the author such reasoning vindicates those who charge that the principle logically requires that all officers—federal, state, and local—be elected at large and by proportional representation.[31] If the justification for equal representation of the states in the Senate rests on the sovereignty of those states, then the U.S. Senate must also be reapportioned: the states lost their sovereignty at least as long ago as the Civil War!

Obviously the person who casts his vote for a minority party has less representation in a state than the person who casts his vote for one of the two major parties. Consequently, if apportionment schemes demand that each person be given an equally effective vote, then some scheme of at-large election and/or cumulative voting is demanded by that principle, for in the case cited above the individual as well as the minority party is hurt.

If the effects of gerrymandering[32] upon majorities in subgroups are to be considered, then multi-member districts are just as subject to constitutional criticism under the principle of an "equally effective vote." Dixon stated the matter when he noted:

> And if the Court ordered sub-districting for an impacted and unrepresented racial minority, I do not see why they should refuse to do so for an impacted political party minority. The basic democratic interest in each case would be the same—to achieve at least some representation of a particular view-point in a multi-membered deliberative body.[33]

The Court, trying to operate on such an impossibly difficult abstract principle as an "equally effective vote," is bound to be inconsistent and contradictory. While holding, in a dictum in *Lucas*, that multi-member districts were undesirable, it refused to overturn a multi-member district in which Negro voters were reduced from *forty-two percent* of the total population of the original single member district to *twenty-nine percent* of the newly established multi-member district.[34] This was done in spite of the fact that "Henrico County plaintiffs claimed that since the county was not much more than half the size of the city, the city would elect all eight representatives although having the population for *only five*."[35]

The fact that the principle of an "equally effective vote" results in such contradictory unpredictable results has caused Dixon to remark that "apparently the one man–one vote principle is better than a mere neutral principle; it is a chameleon principle which can yield opposite conclusions."[36]

Clearly it is impossible for the government, let alone the Court, to guarantee each citizen in every situation even approximately "an equally effective vote." The standard set for reapportionment was impractical and has not been adhered to in practice. The Court should have ordered reapportionment only where examination of the position of the groups involved indicated that the total effect of the plan in question was "so arbitrary or capricious that it [could] not fit into any rational scheme of representation."[37]

Factors Mitigating
the Effect of Unreapportioned Legislatures

If we examine the total institutional arrangement rather than confining ourselves to measures of per-capita representation, we shall
find that those claiming hardship under pre-Warren apportionment
schemes may well have received compensation via special advantages
in other areas. If rural areas had an advantage in one election, urban
areas had advantages in others. To use David Truman's terms, rural
minorities had special access to the legislature, while urban majorities
had special access to the executive. This was Justice Harlan's argument in *Gray* v. *Sanders* which Pritchett quoted with such contempt.[38]

That urban representatives were not concerned only for majority
rule when they sought reapportionment, but also were interested
in power, was evidenced by the fact that they inconsistently rejected
majority-adopted amendments in Colorado and opposed amendments
apportioning electoral college votes to popular votes.[39]

Until recently the rural districts of the country had greater
than their per-capita representation in state legislatures and in the
U. S. House of Representatives. If in the United States Senate, small
rural states had the advantage over the large urban states, it is most
probable that the urban areas within the small rural states had more
than their share of influence over the Senators from those states, for
the urban areas largely determine whether or not the Senator will be
elected.[40] The large urban centers have the overwhelming advantage
in the election of the President, certainly the most powerful officer in
the country.

Political science literature is filled with the assertion that the
over-represented rural majorities prevented the cities from obtaining
progressive legislation. There is little or no scientific evidence to
support this position. David Derge established that in Illinois and
Missouri when urban legislators had a cohesion of sixty-seven percent
or better, they were on the prevailing side of the question eighty to
ninety percent of the time.[41] Furthermore, when urban legislators were
opposed, opposition came not largely from the rural areas, which
would be reduced in numbers through reapportionment, but from
urban legislators of the opposite party, urban legislators not wishing
to increase the political power of city officials in the party and/or
suburban legislators whose representation would be increased by
reapportionment.[42]

Other studies demonstrate that progressive legislation desired by
city administrators has not been simply blocked by rural legislators.
Referenda on such legislation excluding rural voters and rural legislators have fared little better, if not worse, than they did when presented to the state legislature.[43] When the vote of congressmen from
urban areas has been weighted to accord with the population of their

respective districts, the recomputed results suggest that the "liberals" benefited from congressional maldistricting.[44] Richard K. Hofferbert finds no positive correlation between a state's relative malapportionment and its lack of "liberal" or welfare-oriented policies beneficial to urban groups, or its lack of inter-party competitiveness or divided party control over the executive and legislative branches—all the evils which some political scientists have laid to rurally-dominated state legislatures.[45]

An examination of the economic institutions of the country does not support the notion that people living in rural America have excessive protection from the legislatures of the country. Though the United States has twice the number of farmers per-capita than does Britain, the British farmer receives a higher subsidy.[46] While the U. S. farmer increased his productivity 7.7 percent in the 1950's as opposed to a 2.8 percent rise for industrial workers, he received only 37¢ on the dollar of the products marketed in 1964.

> The grower receives 2.5¢ for the corn in a 29¢ box of cornflakes, 2.5¢ for the wheat in a 21¢ loaf of white bread, 25¢ for the cotton in in a $4 shirt. The farmer's share of the take has declined *15% in 20 years*, and it is still going down.[47]

It seems strange that the share of the food dollar going to the farmer should decline in the very years he was allegedly the most efficient and most over-represented!

It is possible that the farmer has never been over-represented. Though in per-capita terms the bulk of representatives have come from areas of small population, the percentage of representatives residing in the smallest size towns may never have been much greater than the population of these cities warranted. When the author classified New Mexico's legislators in terms of the size of city in which they resided, he found that only 2 percent more came from the smallest size cities—even before reapportionment—than their population warranted. Consequently, with reapportionment it may be that the rural areas are or shortly will be under-represented, applying this standard.[48]

In the light of empirical evidence, is reliance upon the formula "one man—one vote" a return to a dogma reminiscent of the "absolute right of contract" of an earlier day? Justice Stewart seems to think so and this author tends to agree. Justice Stewart condemns the dogmatic assumption that the vote is debased because there is a difference in per-capita representation between districts.

> As the Court explains it, "to the extent that a citizen's right to vote is debased, he is that much less a citizen." We are not told how or

why the vote of a person in a more populated legislative district is debased, or how or why he is less a citizen, nor is this proposition self-evident. I find it impossible to understand how or why a voter in California, for instance, either feels or is less a citizen than a voter in Nevada, simply because, despite their population disparities, each of these States is represented by two United States Senators . . .

With all respect, I am convinced these decisions mark a long step backward into that unhappy era when a *majority of the members of this Court were thought by many to have convinced themselves and each other that the demands of the Constitution were to be measured not by what it says, but their own notions of wise political theory.* The rule announced today is at odds with long established principles of adjudication under the Equal Protection Clause, and it stifles values of local individuality and initiative vital to the character of the Federal Union which it was the genius of our Constitution to create. . .

I do not pretend to any specialized knowledge of the myriad of individual characteristics of the several states . . . I do know enough to realize that Montana with its vast distances is not Rhode Island with its heavy concentrations of people . . . The Court today declines to give any recognition to these considerations and countless others . . . *Instead the Court says that the requirements of the Equal Protection Clause can be met . . . only by the uncritical simplistic and heavy-handed application of sixth-grade arithmetic.*[49]

Clearly, a case can be made that the Court is just as dogmatic today as was the conservative Court of "wages and hours" fame. Certainly, it appears to the author that the justices who insisted upon declaring wage and hour laws unconstitutional, and justices who outlawed state apportionment schemes were both motivated by their intense convictions relative to a social theory. Both sets of justices were convinced that individual rights were abridged by the laws they found unconstitutional. One real difference separates the history of early wage and hour decisions from that of recent reapportionment decisions: while political scientists either derided the Court for its wage and hour dogma or remained aloof, they have supported as propagandists, not scientists, this most recent dogma.

The author does not oppose reapportionment as such. He merely argues that facts presented by the Court do not seem to justify actions taken by the Court. We cannot be certain that careful examination of legislation and other factors relevant to the balance of interests would not disclose injustices of sufficient extent that judicial cognizance could be made of it *under the Equal Protection Clause.* Admittedly, like many past changes which have appeared to have little constitutional justification, reapportionment may not lead to drastic change for good or for ill. What is of much more concern to the author than the effects of reapportionment is the disturbing trend he thinks he sees in the Court to make decisions not on the basis of empiricism or pragmatism but on rigid and dogmatic social theory.

Notes

1. *Avery* v. *Midland County, Texas,* 88 S.Ct. 1114, 1126 (1968) (dissenting opinion).

2. *Adkins* v. *Children's Hospital,* 261 U.S. 525, 554 (1923).

3. *Ibid.,* at 557.

4. *Lochner* v. *New York,* 198 U.S. 45, 53 (1905).

5. *Ibid.,* at 58.

6. *Ibid.,* at 75, 76. Emphasis supplied.

7. *Adkins* v. *Children's Hospital,* at 562.

8. *Ibid.*

9. *West Coast Hotel Co.* v. *Parrish,* 300 U.S. 379, 394, 398–399 (1937).

10. There seems already to be evidence that the Court is having afterthoughts relative to one man–one vote. The Court seemed to ignore its implications in the election of Governor Maddox by the state legislature. [*Fortson* v. *Morris,* 385 U.S. 231 (1966)]. It tolerated election districts of greatly different population sizes in the local government cases of *Dusch* v. *Davis,* 387 U.S. 112 (1967) and *Sailors* v. *Board of Education,* 387 U.S. 105 (1967). (In these cases the Court did insist that these units might be more properly regarded as administrative units than as political units). But what is most interesting is that Justice Fortas, who eloquently dissented in *Fortson* v. *Morris,* denouncing it as a step backward (385 U.S. 231, 246–251), joined traditional dissenters in reapportionment cases—Justices John Marshall Harlan and Potter Stewart—when the Court returned to one man–one vote dogma in *Avery* v. *Midland County* (see ftn. 1 *supra*). All three were concerned by the addition of 88,000 local governments to the apportionment burden borne by the Court and deplored the lack of flexibility that dogma imposed on the Court in local government cases.

11. K. C. Wheare, *Federal Government,* 4th ed., (New York: Oxford University Press, 1964), p. 2. Emphasis added.

12. *Lochner* v. *New York,* at 73. Emphasis added.

13. *Colegrove* v. *Green,* at 552.

14. See Carl A. Auerbach, *op. cit.,* pp. 49–53.

15. *McGowan* v. *Maryland,* 366 U.S. 420, 425–426 (1961).

16. "Notes on Reapportionment," 79 *Harvard Law Review* 1243 (1966).

17. Robert Dixon, "Apportionment Standards and Judicial Power," *op. cit.,* 379. Emphasis added.

18. *Lucas* v. *Colorado,* at 744.

19. Paul C. Kauper, "Some Comments on the Reapportionment Cases," 63 *Michigan Law Review,* 243–244 (1964).

20. Dixon, "Reapportionment in the Supreme Court and Congress: Constitutional Struggle for Fair Representation," 63 *Michigan Law Review* 218 (1964). Emphasis supplied.

21. Dixon, "Apportionment Standards and Judicial Power," *op. cit.,* 380.

22. *Ibid.*

23. 366 U.S. 420, 532–535 (1961). Emphasis supplied.

24. Paul C. Kauper, "Some Comments on the Reapportionment Cases," *op. cit.,* 252.

25. Robert Dixon, "Reapportionment in the Supreme Court and Congress," *op. cit.,* 229.

26. Auerbach, *op. cit.,* p. 22.

27. Robert A. Dahl, *A Preface to Democratic Theory* (Chicago: University of Chicago Press, 1956), p. 137.

28. *Colegrove* v. *Green*, 328 U.S. 523 (1946).

29. Robert A. Dahl, "A Rejoinder," *American Political Science Review*, Vol. LI (December, 1957), p. 1056.

30. *Reynolds* v. *Sims*, 377 U.S. 533, 565 (1964).

31. The following persons have argued that the Court's principle demanding an equally effective vote for each person implies at large elections and proportional representation:

1. Justice Stewart, *Lucas* v. *Colorado* (Chicago: U. Chicago Press), 377 U.S. 715, 750 n. 2.
2. Philip Neal, "Baker vs. Carr: Politics in Search of Law," *Supreme Court Review* 1962 (Chicago: U. Chicago Press), pp. 252, 282.
3. Jo Desha Lucas, "Legislative Apportionment and Representative Government," 61 *Michigan Law Review*, 711, 767 (1963).
4. Gerold Israel, "Non-Population Factors Relevant to an Acceptable Standard of Apportionment," 38 *Notre Dame Lawyer*. 510–511, 799 (1963).

32. Dixon notes relative to equal population districts and gerrymandering that shortly after being ordered to reapportion "Maryland's old-line legislators, acting under judicial pressure provoked howls of shock and anguish by unveiling a plan for new, arithmetically equal districts that actually would have worsened the position of the under-represented suburbs that had brought the redistricting suit." "Reapportionment in the Supreme Court and Congress," *op. cit.*, 216.

33. "Notes on Reapportionment," 1259.

34. *Ibid.*, emphasis added.

35. *Ibid.*, emphasis added.

36. Dixon, "Reapportionment in the Supreme Court and Congress," *op. cit.*, 221.

37. Kauper, *op. cit.*, 248.

38. Pritchett, *op. cit.*, p. 874.

39. "Senator Kennedy argued that the urban interests ought to have this power (of dominating the Presidency)—that it has been built into our political system as a compensation for other ways in which these interests are at a disadvantage," *The Reporter*, December 8, 1960, as quoted in Howard D. Hamilton, *Political Institutions* (New York: Houghton-Mifflin, 1962), p. 135.

40. Republicans often have a two-to-one lead in all parts of the state but the major city or cities and lose the election because of majorities in these cities for Democrats.

41. David Derge, "Metropolitan and Outstate Alignments in Illinois and Missouri Legislative Delegations," *American Political Science Review*, vol. LII (December, 1958), pp. 1058–1059.

42. *Ibid.*, p. 1065.

43. U.S. Advisory Commission on Intergovernmental Relations, *Factors Affecting Voter Reactions to Governmental Reorganization in Metropolitan Areas* (publisher, 1962), p. 27, note 35.

44. Andrew Hacker, *Congressional Districting* (Washington D.C.: Brookings Institution, 1963), p. 90.

45. Richard J. Hofferbert, "The Relation Between Public Policy and Some Structural and Environmental Variables in the American States," *American Political Science Review*, vol. LX (March, 1966), pp. 73–83.

46. J. R. Pennock, " 'Responsible Government,' Separated Powers and Special Interests: Agricultural Subsidies in Britain and America," *American Political Science Review*, vol. LVI (September, 1962), pp. 621–633, especially 622–623.

47. *Time*, September 3, 1965, p. 23. Emphasis added.

48. A. S. Hill, "Major Sessions of the New Mexico Legislature, 1958–63," unpublished manuscript, Summary in *Western Political Quarterly*, September 1964, Supplement, pp. 77–78.

49. *Lucas* v. *Colorado*, 377 U.S. 715, 746–750 (1964).

BRETT W. HAWKINS
CHERYL WHELCHEL

Reapportionment and Urban Representation in Legislative Influence Positions: The Case of Georgia

Because of its county unit, "rule of the rustics," past, Georgia is one state in which reapportionment might be expected to have a real impact. Georgia's court-ordered reapportionment was hailed by its supporters as the beginning of the end of rural domination of the General Assembly. They argued that rapid urbanization and reapportionment would combine to produce an urban-run Legislature and, eventually, more urban-directed policies. Others suggested, however, that reapportionment would not change the operation and decisions of the Georgia Legislature because (1) urban legislators are too diverse a group to act as a bloc, (2) no distinct urban-rural split ever existed in the Legislature, and (3) more experienced rural legislators, representing less socially diverse and politically competitive districts, would continue to dominate in positions of influence. Thus one rural Senator told a University of Georgia interviewer, in substance if not in words, that it takes ten years just to find out where to go to the toilet around the General Assembly.

This paper focuses on post-reapportionment changes in influence positions in the General Assembly of Georgia. It also examines the effect on urban position-holding of the passage of time after reapportionment. While political scientists and others have made many assumptions about these kinds of change, there are few if any systematic, empirical studies that attempt to specify their nature and direction. This study attempts to do so. It is designed to help answer these and other questions about the effect of reapportionment—questions that seem newly troublesome in the light of recent research.

"Reapportionment and Urban Representation in Legislative Influence Positions: The Case of Georgia" by Brett W. Hawkins and Cheryl Whelchel is reprinted from *Urban Affairs Quarterly*, volume 3, no. 3 (March 1969) pp. 69–80, by permission of the Publisher, Sage Publications, Inc.

Methods

The statistics analyzed here are indices of proportionate urban and metropolitan representation in each chamber of the Georgia Legislature, and especially in the following influence positions:

1. Key committee[1] memberships.
2. Key committee chairmanships and vice-chairmanships.
3. Major legislative leaders (Speaker of the House, Speaker Pro Tempore of the House, Administration Floor Leader of the House, President Pro Tempore of the Senate, and Administration Floor Leader of the Senate)[2]

These positions are considered to have potential for the exercise of disproportionate influence. The present analysis therefore focuses on the potential for influence inherent in key committee and leadership positions, and not on the direct exercise of influence. Such a positional study, however, provides a basis for inferences about the exercise of influence. Category 3 seems especially important in a positional study of the Georgia Legislature, because in Georgia committee members and officers are picked by the presiding officers of each house.[3] Nevertheless, key committee chairmen are powers in their own right; and some committees remain more influential on the legislative end product than others.

The indices used here are similar to those used by Matthews in his study of the United States Senate.[4] They are measures of proportionate position-holding, or the degree to which urban representation is higher or lower than one would expect from the operation of chance. For instance, if all Georgia legislators were selected by chance, and without regard to their residence, urban representation could be expected to be the same as the urban composition of the universe from which they were selected; that is, the population of the state. And if influence positions within the Legislature were selected by chance, urban representation in such positions would be expected to be the same as the urban composition of the universe from which they were chosen; here the total membership in each house.

Population indices, as used in this study, are based on the percentage of Georgia's population that is urban, according to the 1960 census:

Membership population index

$$\frac{\text{Percentage of house membership that is urban}}{\text{Percentage of urban population of the state}}$$

Position population index

$$\frac{\text{Percentage of influence positions held by urban legislators}}{\text{Percentage of urban population of the state}}$$

The *legislative index*, in contrast, refers to index numbers based on the percentage of each house's membership that is urban:

$$\frac{\text{Percentage of influence positions held by urban legislators}}{\text{Percentage of urban members in house}}$$

The authors began with the expectation that urban position-holding after reapportionment would lag behind somewhat, because of the lack of seniority of the new urban members. Such a lag would be reflected in the legislative index. A disproportionate number of the veterans could be expected to be rural in the immediate post-reapportionment sessions. However, our investigations showed that this is less a problem than expected. In fact, it is no problem at all in the Senate, because (1) before reapportionment a rotational system (by county) operated within the 52 three-county districts, causing virtually 100 percent turnover after each session, and (2) in the first session after reapportionment only four veterans returned, two urban and two rural. Since the first session, Senate turnover has declined; but it has been greater for rural legislators than for urban.

In the House, one is justified in expecting some lag, because after reapportionment almost two-thirds of the members were veterans, and two-thirds of those were rural. In the second post-reapportionment House session, however, about three-fourths were veterans and exactly half of those were urban. Thus legislative index numbers made up of averages of the two post-reapportionment sessions reflect a declining problem of lag. In addition, legislative indices that drop from *above 1.0* (more than proportionate representation) to below it are important in their own right. An index number of 1.0 indicates perfectly proportionate representation.

The adjective "urban" as used here refers to those legislators representing districts in which more than 50 percent of the people live in urban places. "Metropolitan" is treated as a subcategory of "urban," and describes legislators from districts in which 75 percent of the people live in urban places.[5]

House of Representatives

The Georgia House was reapportioned in 1965. Indices describing urban and metropolitan representation before reapportionment are averages from the 1961–62, 1963–64, and 1965 sessions. Indices describing representation after reapportionment are averages from the 1966 and 1967–68 sessions.

The most obvious effect of reapportionment was to boost total urban membership from 24.88 percent of the seats to 48.29 percent. The urban membership population index almost doubled and the same index for metropolitan legislators more than tripled. Interestingly, however, urban gains along an absolute scale, and in terms of the state's population, were accompanied by drops in proportionate position-holding. In relation to their numbers in the House, urban legislators before reapportionment enjoyed disproportionate representation in influence positions, with a legislative index of 1.44 for all positions taken together. Metropolitan representatives were similarly overrepresented, with a legislative index of 1.17. With reapportionment, however, both urban and metropolitan legislative indices dropped from well above 1.0 to well below 1.0 (see Table 1B). On the other hand, rural legislative indices (Tables 1B, 1C, 1D, and 1E) all rose after reapportionment. In proportion to their numbers, therefore, there were fewer urban/metropolitan-held positions after than before reapportionment; and most legislative indices dropped from above to below the 1.0 mark. Positional gains were evident in terms of the composition of the state's population, however; but all position population indices remain well below the 1.0 level.

Turning to specific House positions, urban representatives have managed to acquire 50 percent of the key committee chairmanships and vice-chairmanships—as compared with 35.42 percent before reapportionment. Accompanying this absolute gain, however, was a large drop in the legislative index (see Table 1D). For metropolitan representatives, the 67-point drop represents a fall to an index of .82.[6]

The Speaker of the House was drawn from rural districts in all sessions studied here: there was no change. In other House leadership positions (category 3), substantial changes have accompanied reapportionment, although the numbers involved are necessarily small. The urban legislative and position population indices both dropped after reapportionment—the former by 144 points. At the same time, the rural legislative index increased by 87 points.

Senate

Urban Senators, when compared with urban Representatives, are in no better circumstances, despite an additional post-reapportionment session. The Senate was reapportioned in 1962. Indices representing the situation before reapportionment are averages from the 1959–60 and 1961–62 sessions. Indices representing the situation after reapportionment are averages from the 1963–64, 1965–66, and 1967–68 sessions. Urban Senators held 25.93 percent of all Senate seats before reapportionment, and 40.74 percent after. Metropolitan membership jumped even more—from 7.41 percent to 37.04 percent. The latter figure represents a membership population index close to equality (.94).

In all Senate influence positions taken together (Table 2B), however, urban representation as measured by the legislative index fell off 45 points. More surprising, in view of the general pattern, is the fact that the urban population index for all influence positions

Table 1. Legislative indices, population indices, and seats: Georgia House of Representatives before and after reapportionment

	Rural				Urban				Metropolitan			
	Leg. Index	Pop. Index	Seats No.	%	Leg. Index	Pop. Index	Seats No.	%	Leg. Index	Pop. Index	Seats No.	%
State's population in percentages (1960):		44.71				55.29				39.49		
1A				*ALL HOUSE MEMBERS*								
Before reapportionment	—	1.68	154	75.12	—	.45	51	24.88	—	.28	23	11.22
After reapportionment	—	1.16	106	51.71	—	.87	99	48.29	—	.87	70	34.15
1B				*ALL INFLUENCE POSITION INDICES COMBINED*								
Before reapportionment	.86	1.44			1.44	.64			1.17	.33		
After reapportionment	1.21	1.07			.78	.68			.72	.76		
Net Change	+.35	-.37			-.66	+.04			-.45	+.43		

Table 1. (Continued)

KEY COMMITTEE MEMBERS

	Rural				Urban				Metropolitan			
	Leg. Index	Pop. Index	Seats No.	Seats %	Leg. Index	Pop. Index	Seats No.	Seats %	Leg. Index	Pop. Index	Seats No.	Seats %
Before reapportionment	.97	1.63	566	72.75	1.10	.49	212	27.25	1.03	.29	90	11.57
After reapportionment	1.06	1.22	311	54.56	.94	.82	259	45.44	.85	.74	166	29.12

KEY COMMITTEE CHAIRMAN AND VICE-CHAIRMEN

1D	Rural				Urban				Metropolitan			
	Leg. Index	Pop. Index	Seats No.	Seats %	Leg. Index	Pop. Index	Seats No.	Seats %	Leg. Index	Pop. Index	Seats No.	Seats %
Before reapportionment	.86	1.44	31	64.58	1.42	.64	17	35.42	1.49	.42	8	16.67
After reapportionment	.97	1.12	16	50.00	1.04	.90	16	50.00	.82	.71	9	28.13

HOUSE LEADERS

1E	Rural				Urban				Metropolitan			
	Leg. Index	Pop. Index	Seats No.	Seats %	Leg. Index	Pop. Index	Seats No.	Seats %	Leg. Index	Pop. Index	Seats No.	Seats %
Before reapportionment	.74	1.24	5	55.56	1.79	.80	4	44.44	.99	.28	1	11.11
After reapportionment	1.61	1.86	5	83.33	.35	.31	1	16.67	.49	.42	1	16.67

Table 2. Legislative indices, population indices, and seats: Georgia Senate before and after reapportionment

	Rural				Urban				Metropolitan			
	Leg. Index	Pop. Index	Seats No.	Seats %	Leg. Index	Pop. Index	Seats No.	Seats %	Leg. Index	Pop. Index	Seats No.	Seats %
State's population in percentages (1960):		44.71				55.29				39.49		

ALL SENATE MEMBERS

2A	Leg. Index	Pop. Index	Seats No.	Seats %	Leg. Index	Pop. Index	Seats No.	Seats %	Leg. Index	Pop. Index	Seats No.	Seats %
Before reapportionment	—	1.66	40	74.07	—	.47	14	25.93	—	.19	4	7.41
After reapportionment	—	1.10	32	59.26	—	.74	22	40.74	—	.94	20	37.04

ALL INFLUENCE POSITION INDICES COMBINED

2B	Leg. Index	Pop. Index			Leg. Index	Pop. Index			Leg. Index	Pop. Index		
Before reapportionment	.78	1.30			1.36	.76			.72	.13		
After reapportionment	1.06	1.41			.91	.67			.75	.70		
Net Change	+.28	+.11			−.45	−.09			+.03	+.57		

(Table 2. Continued)

KEY COMMITTEE MEMBERS

2C

	Rural				Urban				Metropolitan		
	Leg. Index	Pop. Index	Seats No.	%	Leg. Index	Pop. Index	Seats No.	%	Leg. Index	Pop. Index	Seats No.	%
Before reapportionment	.97	1.61	140	72.16	1.07	.50	54	27.84	1.11	.21	16	8.25
After reapportionment	1.05	1.39	230	62.33	.92	.68	139	37.67	.86	.81	118	31.98

KEY COMMITTEE CHAIRMEN AND VICE-CHAIRMEN

2D

	Rural				Urban				Metropolitan		
	Leg. Index	Pop. Index	Seats No.	%	Leg. Index	Pop. Index	Seats No.	%	Leg. Index	Pop. Index	Seats No.	%
Before reapportionment	1.04	1.72	20	76.92	.89	.42	6	23.08	1.04	.19	2	7.69
After reapportionment	1.30	1.72	30	76.92	.57	.42	9	23.08	.48	.45	7	17.95

SENATE LEADERS

2E

	Rural				Urban				Metropolitan		
	Leg. Index	Pop. Index	Seats No.	%	Leg. Index	Pop. Index	Seats No.	%	Leg. Index	Pop. Index	Seats No.	%
Before reapportionment	.34	.56	1	25.00	2.12	1.36	3	75.00	—	—	—	—
After reapportionment	.84	1.112	3	50.00	1.23	.90	3	50.00	.90	.84	2	33.33

also fell off, by 9 points. Metropolitan Senators enjoyed a 57-point gain in the position population index, but both groups remain greatly underrepresented in relation to the state's population. All rural legislative indices (Tables 2B, 2C, 2D, and 2E) increased after reapportionment.

As for committee chairmen and vice-chairmen, urban-metropolitan Senators have not fared as well as their House counterparts (see Tables 2D and 1D). Every Senate legislative and population index, for both urban and metropolitan Senators, started at a lower point than in the House and was still at a much lower point after reapportionment. All are now around the .50 mark.[7]

Before reapportionment, urban Senators were highly successful in obtaining leadership positions (category 3), although small numbers were involved (see Table 2E). The legislative index here was 2.12, and the position population index was 1.36. After reapportionment both indices dropped, the former by 89 points and the latter by 46 points.

Summary and Discussion

The overall picture of reapportionment and urban position-holding in the Georgia Legislature is as follows: Urban positional gains in absolute terms, and in terms of the state's population, are accompanied by losses in relation to urban members in the Legislature. In addition, most of these losses go from above to below the 1.0 mark. Also, urban positional gains in relation to the state's population still fall short of equality. Proportionate *rural* position-holding, on the other hand, has increased after reapportionment in both houses.

Half of the urban legislative indices in the Senate are lower after reapportionment than in the House, despite an additional post-reapportionment session in the former. This shows more tenacious rural position-holding in the Senate, due in part, no doubt, to the fact that the Lieutenant Governor in all post-reapportionment sessions but the last (1967) was the same rural, county unit-bred politician. His appointments, plus the alliances built up over the years, almost certainly continue to have an effect in the Senate.[8]

In short, gains in total urban membership in Georgia's General Assembly have not been matched by proportionate gains in influence positions. Quite the contrary; before reapportionment urban legislators had more than proportionate representation in relation to their numbers in the Legislature; after, they had much less than proportionate representation. Such a "before" situation, of course, qualifies a common criticism of legislatures not apportioned on a population basis. Before reapportionment, Georgia's urban legislators enjoyed much more than proportionate representation (in relation to their numbers) in influence positions.

Reapportionment in Georgia has not yet produced the positional results expected by its champions. On the contrary, influence positions are now more in rural hands in proportion to their numbers, especially in the Senate. This appears to be due in part to the seniority and greater experience of rural legislators compared with urban and metropolitan, at least in the House, and to a rural-oriented presiding officer in the Senate. Still another factor is that with reapportionment urban and metropolitan delegations have become larger and more diverse in terms of social status, race, and urban–suburban residence. Diversity is especially great where subdistricting has occurred, as in Fulton County. Large, diverse urban delegations are less unified in pressing for key committee assignments than small, homogeneous delegations. Our findings are not due, however, to partisan discrimination against the small number of Republicans, most of whom represent metropolitan districts. Republicans have enjoyed generous key committee assignments after reapportionment.

Of course, Georgia's reapportionment is a recent phenomenon: the situation with respect to influence positions may change with the passage of time. The present analysis, however, offers only conflicting evidence on that score.

On the one hand, a separate analysis of the first two post-reapportionment Senate sessions shows almost uniformly lower legislative indices than when the third session is included. This suggests a progression with the passage of time toward urban position-holding more proportionate to urban membership. On the other hand, after three sessions urban Senators remain no better represented, proportionately, in influence positions than their House counterparts— and they are much worse off in committee offices—despite one more session and the passage of more time. Thus the important question of the impact of time on the proportionate holding of influence positions is not answerable with these data. Our data do suggest, however, that reapportionment's champions may have to wait longer than expected for urban–metropolitan districts to be proportionately represented in key legislative positions.

Notes

1. Agriculture, Appropriations, Banks and Banking, Education, Highways, Judiciary, Rules, and Ways and Means. The latter has no equivalent in the Senate and is excluded from the analysis of the upper chamber.
2. Until the 1967–68 session, the Administration Floor Leader was also the majority leader—making that position even more influential. Majority leaders of the 1967 session are not included in this analysis because no "before" basis for comparison exists.
3. The Lieutenant Governor, who usually presides over the Senate, is elected by state-wide vote at the same time as the Governor. He further serves as Chairman of the Senate Rules Committee, but on the basis of his state-wide election is excluded from committee analyses.

4. Donald R. Matthews, *U. S. Senators and Their World* (N.Y.: Vintage Books, 1960).

5. The classifications are based on the urban composition of the entire legislative district—not the county of residence of the legislative position-holder. *Urban places* are those which the Bureau of the Census defines as urban—essentially communities with 2,500 inhabitants or more. The districts here designated *metropolitan* are also classified by the U.S. Census as metropolitan. They include the cities of Albany, Atlanta, Augusta, Columbus, Macon, and Savannah. Baldwin County, with an urban population of 82.3 percent, is classified as metropolitan under our criterion but excluded from the Census listing. The district demographic data were collected under the National Municipal League grant mentioned in our authors' note.

6. After reapportionment, the important Appropriations and Highways committees had urban officers, whereas before they had none. Metropolitan Representatives also gained key positions on the same two committees after reapportionment, and on Rules also, whereas before they served as officers only of Banking and Judiciary. Even so, the Chairman of the Appropriations Committee has been from a rural district in all sessions examined here.

7. It may also be of interest that in the two sessions before reapportionment, urban Senators held six of 26 possible positions, but on only four committees. Metropolitan Senators held a chairmanship or vice-chairmanship on each of two committees. After reapportionment, urban Senators held nine positions in the three sessions, with but one additional committee involved. Since reapportionment, metropolitan Senators have held seven positions involving four committees.

8. This is indicated by a fight in early 1967 between some of his supporters and those of the new Lieutenant Governor (a man with a more urban-oriented reputation) over the power to name committee officers. The former wanted to eliminate that power, but the latter won. The new man's appointments, however, still do not reflect proportionately the Senate's urban–metropolitan composition.

Suggested Readings:
Apportionment

CONGRESSIONAL QUARTERLY SERVICE. *Representation and Apportionment.* A CQ Background Report. Washington, D.C.: The Congressional Quarterly Service, 1968. A concise, lucid, highly readable account of recent events in the area of apportionment. Summary of important developments in legal history of apportionment, Supreme Court's emerging theories of representation, and politics of reapportionment, especially those events surrounding the Dirksen Amendment.

DIXON, ROBERT G., JR. *Democratic Representation: Reapportionment in Law and Politics.* New York: Oxford University Press, 1968. The most comprehensive, definitive work on the subject.

GOLDWIN, ROBERT A. (Ed.) *Representation and Misrepresentation: Legislative Reapportionment in Theory and Practice.* Rand McNally Public Affairs Series. Chicago: Rand McNally & Co., 1968. A collection of original penetrating essays concerning practical and theoretical problems of equitable representation.

HARVARD, WILLIAM C., and LOREN P. BETH. *The Politics of Misrepresentation: Rural-Urban Conflict in the Florida Legislature.* Baton Rouge: Louisiana State University Press, 1962. A slightly dated, but still insightful case study about the real day-to-day meaning in the legislative process of underrepresentation of urban areas.

LEE, CALVIN B. T. *One Man, One Vote: WMCA and the Struggle for Equal Representation.* New York: Charles Scribner's Sons, 1967. A detailed case study of one state's apportionment struggle. Representative of the complexities of reapportionment efforts.

SHARKANSKY, IRA. "Voting Behavior of Metropolitan Congressmen: Prospects for Change with Reapportionment." *Journal of Politics*, vol. 28 (November 1966), 774–793. Illustrative of the type of empirical research that attempts to show the real changes, if any, that will result from the "reapportionment revolution."

4/Metropolitan Reorganization:
Macro or Micro?

The literature of urban affairs has long been concerned with the problem of governmental fragmentation in urban areas. Simply stated, there is a general awareness of too many units of government in the large metropolitan areas for effective government. Area-wide problems are not being solved. Fragmentation has produced major problems in policy planning and implementation and a general inability to deal with that socioeconomic complex referred to as "the urban problem." The solution is to be found in some type of operational integration.

Luther Gulick, speaking of attempts to solve area-wide problems such as transportation, pollution, and water supply under the fragmented system, concluded there is "accumulating evidence of failure everywhere, in spite of many heroic efforts."[1] He continued,[2]

> Once an indivisible problem is divided nothing effective can be done about it. . . . Spreading area-wide problems cannot be handled geographic piece by geographic piece. They must be tackled in their entirety, comprehensively, and are difficult even so.

In addition, concern is developing for the increasing disparities between the financial resources of some suburbs and the money-demanding problems of other jurisdictions in the typical metropolis. "The concentrations of social need are now badly out of kilter," says Gulick.[3]

The first articles in this section give four different views of the effects of fragmentation. The vocabulary and approach differ from selection to selection, but the same general concern about governmental order in metropolitan areas exists in all the readings.

Proposed solutions to these problems of fragmentation take two broad approaches. The first is a demand for complete, or nearly complete, restructuring of the governments in a metropolitan area according to a pre-set model of the ideal metropolis. This generally means some type of metropolitan government. The proponents of this approach we have here termed "reformists."

In recent years, a new school of thought about metropolitan reorganization has emerged. These "realists" recognize certain advantages in the fragmented metropolitan system and respect the political difficulties, perhaps impossibilities, of major governmental reorganization for most metropolitan areas. The articles by Edward C. Banfield and Thomas R. Dye are examples of this approach.

The race factor is an increasingly important explanation of why voters reject proposals for a more rational governmental structure for the metropolis. Parris N. Glendening and John Wesley White examine the racial variable for reorganization referenda in Florida. Understanding of political realities, as outlined in the final three selections in Part 4, will to a large extent determine whether the future organization of metropolitan areas will evolve into some type of macro-authority or continue to operate on the basis of a fragmented micro-system.

Notes

1. Luther H. Gulick, *The Metropolitan Problem and American Ideas* (New York: Alfred A. Knopf, Inc., 1962), 23.
2. *Ibid.*, 24.
3. Luther H. Gulick, "Goals for Metropolis," *National Civic Review*, vol. 49 (1960), 592. [See also the selections in Part 5 of this book.]

The Fragmented Metropolis:
View Number One

Underlying many metropolitan problems is the failure of governmental institutions to come to grips with the growing interdependence of people and communities within metropolitan areas. As urban settlement spreads across lines of local jurisdiction, the cities and suburbs together come to comprise a single integrated area for living and working. People look for housing and employment within a broad region circumscribed more by the convenience of commuting and by personal preferences than by local government boundaries. The existence of a metropolitanwide housing and job market is, in fact, the basis for defining metropolitan areas. In the definition of the U.S. Bureau of the Budget and the Bureau of the Census, "the general concept of a metropolitan area is one of an integrated economic and social unit with a recognized large population nucleus."

The detailed criteria used in defining "standard metropolitan statistical areas" (SMSA's) provide further insight into the integrated character of these areas. Each area must contain at least one city of 50,000 inhabitants or more, or "twin cities" with a combined population of at least 50,000. The metropolitan character of the county containing the central city or cities is established by determining that the county is a place of work or residence for a concentration of nonagricultural workers. The specific conditions that must be met include a requirement that at least 75 percent of the labor force must have nonagricultural occupations, and other tests concerning population density and job concentrations. In New England, the components of metropolitan areas are cities and towns rather than counties. Outlying counties (cities and towns in New England) are considered part of the metropolitan area if they meet either of the following tests:

(1) If 15 percent of the workers living in the county work in the county where the central city is located; or
(2) If 25 percent of those working in the outlying county live in the county where the central city is located.

If the information concerning these two requirements is not conclusive, other kinds of information are considered: reports of news-

Advisory Commission on Intergovernmental Relations, *Metropolitan America: Challenge to Federalism*, Report M-31. (Washington, D.C.: U.S. Government Printing Office, 1966), pp. 5-9.

paper circulation, the extent to which residents of outlying areas maintain charge accounts in central city retail stores, official traffic counts, and other indicators of central city-suburban interaction.

Metropolitan areas are integrated in other ways, as well. Local communities share many kinds of natural resources used for urban living: water supplies, drainage basins, recreation areas. They also share many manmade facilities that cut across local boundaries, such as highway and utility systems, and many other facilities that serve large segments of the metropolitan population, such as airports and commercial centers. These forms of interaction, together with the metropolitan character of housing and employment markets, create a broad area of common interest. The optimum use of shared facilities and resources calls for a high level of cooperation and for coordinated action by interdependent communities.

The policies of any one community typically have considerable impact in other parts of the metropolitan area. If one locality fails to control air or water pollution, its neighbors suffer. This principle was illustrated recently when Nassau County, which borders New York City, demanded that New York put its mosquitoes under surveillance. The public works commissioner of Nassau County charged that swarms of mosquitoes from the city had been invading Nassau territory: "Mosquitoes have no respect for boundary lines or home rule," he complained.[1]

The effects of local action (or inaction) that spread into other communities have come to be known as "spillovers." They are very common in metropolitan affairs and often consist of indirect effects. Thus, suburban communities that succeed in excluding the poor impose considerable burdens on other communities where the poor are concentrated. Spillovers can also be beneficial to neighboring localities. Effective traffic control or public health measures benefit people outside a city or town as well as local residents. Spillovers usually imply disparities between tax and service boundaries. Thus the residents of central cities may be taxed to provide services that are important to the suburbs as well as to themselves. Or suburbanites may be taxed to clean up polluted streams that flow into neighboring territory. In all these cases, people who do not live in a particular jurisdiction nevertheless have a strong interest in its performance of government functions.

The prevalence of spillovers constitutes a strong case for cooperation in metropolitan areas. Metropolitan service needs also provide compelling arguments for joint action. In such fields as water supply and sewage disposal, the cost of service per household can be reduced dramatically in large-scale operations by joint agreement of local governments. Similarly, areawide transportation systems—highways, public transit—require joint planning if they are to provide needed service at reasonable cost.

Despite the evident and important benefits of cooperative action in metropolitan areas, many local governments continue to go it alone. The realities of functional interdependence in metropolitan areas are in conflict with concepts of home rule that predate the age of metropolitan growth. Home rule in the contemporary metropolitan setting has often led to local isolation and conflict, to the detriment of the metropolitan population at large. Each community, in pursuing its own interests, may have an adverse effect on the interests of its neighbors. A major task for government in metropolitan areas is to develop policies consistent with the integrated character of the modern metropolitan community. Federal policies are guided increasingly by an awareness of this need, as President Johnson emphasized in his message on the cities:

> The interests and needs of many of the communities which make up the modern city often seem to be in conflict. But they all have an overriding interest in improving the quality of life of their people. And they have an overriding interest in enriching the quality of American civilization. These interests will only be served by looking at the metropolitan area as a whole, and planning and working for its development.

Governmental Obstacles

The fundamental metropolitan problem is not that there are difficulties in supplying public services or ameliorating social and economic disparities. It is that governments in metropolitan areas are often unable to cope with these issues. The system of local government in the United States has many achievements to its credit, but, like any social system, it also has its disadvantages. Within metropolitan areas, many important issues of public policy can no longer be handled by local communities acting alone; their small areas of jurisdiction are inadequate for either administering areawide services or resolving areawide problems.

The close ties of people and businesses to one another in metropolitan areas have no parallel in government. While social and economic relationships have shifted to an enlarged metropolitan scale, governments and the loyalties they inspire have remained local. As Roscoe Martin has put it:

> The metropolitan area has no capital, courthouse, or city hall, no corporate existence, no body, no soul, no sense of being, indeed no being in any concrete meaning of the term. Al Smith was from the sidewalks of New York, not from the sidewalks of the New York-Northeastern New Jersey standard consolidated area.[2]

Metropolitan areas are governed not only by traditional cities, towns, and counties, but also by a wide variety of special districts that overlap other boundaries. The complexity of local government can be illustrated by listing the array of local jurisdictions responsible for Park Forest, a suburb of Chicago, as of 1956: Cook County, Will County, Cook County Forest Preserve District, village of Park Forest, Rich Township, Bloom Township, Monee Township, Suburban Tuberculosis Sanitarium District, Bloom Township Sanitary District, Non-High School District 216, Non-High School District 213, Rich Township High School District 227, Elementary School District 163, South Cook County Mosquito Abatement District.[3]

Fragmentation of this kind may appear to bring government "closer to the people," but it compounds the difficulties of achieving coordination within metropolitan areas. Political responsibility for government performance is divided to the point of obscurity. Public control of government policies tends to break down when citizens have to deal with a network of independent governments, each responsible for highly specialized activities. Even where good channels are developed for registering public concern, each government is so circumscribed in its powers and in the area of its jurisdiction that important metropolitan action is virtually impossible for local governments to undertake. If a few governments are prepared to agree on joint measures or coordinated programs, their efforts can be blocked by others that are unwilling to cooperate.

Local governments, fragmented as they are, nevertheless keep the metropolis running. They operate the schools, maintain the streets, take care of police and fire protection. But when issues of metropolitanwide importance arise—such as commuter transportation, water supply, or racial and economic segregation—people must turn to other channels for action. As Robert Wood has pointed out, an "embryonic coalition" of metropolitan leaders tends to emerge to tackle areawide problems. These leaders—politicians, editors, businessmen, labor leaders—operate informally and outside the regular structure of government, as they attempt to prod government into action. They lack the requirements for effective policymaking: an adequate institutional base, legal authority, direct relationships with the metropolitan constituency, and established processes for considering and resolving issues as they emerge.[4]

When important public issues can only be handled informally and outside government channels, it is time to review the system of government in metropolitan areas and to regard the shortcomings of this system as major problems in themselves. Norton Long has set the problems of metropolitan areas in this political context:

> The problems of the metropolis are important, but not because of flooded cellars or frustrated motorists, nor because they seriously threaten the viability of the metropolitan economy. They are important because they are symptomatic of the erosion of the com-

petence of local government. . . . The threat of the eroded central city and the crazy-quilt triviality of suburbia is the threat to destroy the potential of our maintaining and reconstructing meaningful political communities at the local level. What has been treated as a threat to our physical well-being is in reality a threat to our capacity to sustain an active local civic life.[5]

The Federal System and Metropolitan Issues

With local governments often unwilling or unable to meet metropolitan needs, the Federal and State Governments have taken on increasing responsibilities for metropolitan welfare. The State role ranges from financial aid to local governments to direct State operations in metropolitan areas, such as highway building, and State establishment of special metropolitan authorities responsible for such functions as water supply and port development. The Federal role consists mainly of financial assistance for programs administered by State or local government. The number and size of Federal-aid programs have been growing at a striking rate: there are now more than 70 Federal-aid programs that directly support urban development, as well as a number of other kinds of Federal aid available to local governments in metropolitan areas.

State and Federal programs are helping to cope with many metropolitan needs, but they also raise troublesome political and governmental issues. Federal and State participation in metropolitan affairs greatly complicates the already fragmented governmental scene. Activities of all three levels of government now function in close juxtaposition, subject to an extremely complicated web of Federal, State, and local laws and administrative regulations. In the course of supplying needed help, Federal and State programs threaten to push the confused governmental situation closer to a state of chaos. Coordination of efforts is a prime requirement for effective government action in metropolitan areas; yet the problems of coordination are compounded by the addition of higher levels of government to the fragmented local scene.

There is an implicit danger that greater reliance on Federal and State action in metropolitan areas may be a form of political abdication in which local governments wash their hands of difficult responsibilities and pass the buck to higher levels. This approach would lead to waning local influence over policies and programs that have significant local impact. Thus it is important to find ways of administering State and Federal programs within a system of democratic control in which metropolitan citizens can shape the programs that operate in their own areas.

Notes

1. "Nassau Protesting Queens Mosquitoes," *New York Times*, Sept. 12, 1965, p. 1.

2. Roscoe C. Martin, *Metropolis in Transition: Local Government Adaptation to Changing Urban Needs* (Washington: Government Printing Office, 1963), p. 141.

3. Edward C. Banfield and Morton Grodzins, *Government and Housing in Metropolitan Areas* (New York: McGraw-Hill, 1958), p. 18.

4. Robert C. Wood, *Metropolis Against Itself* (New York: Committee for Economic Development, 1959), p. 38.

5. Norton E. Long, "Citizenship or Consumership in Metropolitan Areas," *Journal of the American Institute of Planners*, XXXI (February 1965), pp. 4–5.

COMMITTEE FOR ECONOMIC DEVELOPMENT

The Fragmented Metropolis: View Number Two

*1960 Statement**

Metropolitan growth has placed heavy demands on the governmental structure to meet new and expanding local and area-wide needs. One response has been a great increase in the number of local units of government.

There are some 16,000 local jurisdictions in the 192 standard metropolitan areas of the United States. About 40 percent of them are school districts. One in six is a special district with a single function such as fire protection, drainage, soil conservation, or cemetery maintenance. The rest are municipalities, townships and counties. With the exception of school districts, the number of governmental units in metropolitan areas is growing. The Chicago area, for example, had 55 units in 1890, 109 in 1920, and 960 in 1954. One factor in this mushrooming of metropolitan governments is unrealistic tax and debt limitations. Unable to secure a desired public service within the fiscal constraints imposed on existing jurisdictions, communities have simply created new ones.

A consequence of this balkanization of metropolitan government is failure to secure maximum efficiency in public operations. For many types of functions, such as welfare administration, highway units and health agencies, a base of 20,000 to 30,000 people is con-

*Committee for Economic Development, *Guiding Metropolitan Growth* (New York: The Committee, 1960), 27–30. Reprinted by permission.

sidered necessary to achieve economies of scale. But in 1950 there were approximately 3,000 municipalities in metropolitan areas with populations of less than 20,000. In the aggregate, these small municipalities contained about 9 million people.

Area-wide needs have not been completely neglected. Transportation, water supply, parks and recreation, air and water pollution, and other area-wide services have to some extent been provided for by special-purpose institutions, area-wide or state-wide in scope. Public corporations, special authorities, state commissions, large special districts—single-function and frequently autonomous agencies —have provided some essential services. Over the years we have seen the development of many limited-function, area-wide agencies such as the Port of New York Authority, the Boston Metropolitan District Commission, the North Jersey Water Supply District, the Chicago Park District, and the New York Triborough Bridge and Tunnel Authority.

Another development is increasing reliance on a higher level of government to meet area-wide needs. State highway departments and state park commissions have not only served public needs outside the metropolitan areas, they have also provided for local or metropolitan needs in the absence of a metropolitan agency. In recent years the difficulty of meeting area needs from local resources has pushed the call for assistance to the Federal level. The Federal urban renewal program has provided both financial and technical assistance to municipalities in their effort to get blighted real estate into more productive uses. The Federal interstate highway program, passed partly as a defense measure, has actually been a major contributor to construction of metropolitan highway networks. Probably half of the Federal funds provided on 90–10 matching basis have gone for construction in urban areas. The rise in Federal and state contributions to municipal revenue, noted earlier, is a result of the need to carry problems to a higher level.

But neither the collection of municipalities and small special-service districts, nor the area-wide agencies, nor the state and Federal agencies devoted to meeting a single need are able to formulate effective governmental policy for the metropolitan area as a whole. Decisions as to area-wide priorities are made by conflict among these special purpose, region-wide, and higher-level agencies. There is no mechanism for balancing the needs of the region as a whole against its resources, nor the marginal productivity of resources devoted to one use against the marginal productivity of another use.

Inability of the limited-purpose, area-wide agencies to meet all aspects of a problem such as transportation or to allocate revenue resources in accordance with marginal social benefits inevitably forces local governmental officials to turn to higher levels of government for help. At present only the state and Federal governments can tap the economic resources of the area as a whole for necessary public purposes. Thus there is increasing pressure by localities for state and Federal assistance to deal with problems which the individual municipal government is incapable of managing or financing. With the existing framework of local governmental organization, this trend toward more and more state and Federal participation in metropolitan affairs—both in financing and in decision-making—seems irreversible.

Evaluation

On the whole, the minimum local service needs of communities in the metropolitan areas are being met. Some communities with a very favorable ratio of resources to population are providing a high level of services without strain. But many communities are scarcely able to finance an adequate minimum of services without outside help. Some area-wide needs are being met by special-purpose agencies or by a higher level of government. But there are very few cases in which a general governmental unit at the metropolitan level has been developed to provide area-wide services on a unified basis.

Two results of the present pattern of the governmental response are waste and gradual loss of local control with regard to area-wide problems.

Waste is of several origins. The multiplicity of local governmental units results in duplication, in providing services on too small a scale to be economic, and in providing inadequate services because revenue resources are not efficiently used.

A more serious form of waste arises from unplanned growth, poor location, unsightly highway strip development, and failure to anticipate public service needs.

A third source of waste is the inability to develop a comprehensive view of an area's needs and a system of priorities governing the meeting of needs. Since area-wide needs are met either by regional single-purpose agencies, or by units of a higher level of government, the development of priorities is a result of inter-agency struggle, not the result of a rational analysis or considered public judgment. Important needs may be long neglected while others of no greater importance may have a high priority at the public treasury. Not only are resources misallocated, but basic needs may go unmet until they reach a critical stage which necessitates an expensive "crash" program.

Self-government authority is sacrificed in the present methods of providing area-wide services. Most of the special-purpose area-wide authorities are subject to a minimum of public control in the performance of their functions. State and Federal agencies are still less subject to effective local control.

The net effects of our fractionated metropolitan governmental system thus are the retention of control in small local units over those public services which can be provided and paid for at the local level, the gradual loss of local control over those basic area-wide services which are essential to modern urban living, and the absence of a system for establishing priorities and allocating resources on a rational, area-wide basis.

1970 Statement*

Metropolitan areas embrace most of our greatest resources. They are centers of commerce and industry, fashion, culture, and thought. Many metropolitan areas are wealthier and more populous than most nations.

Yet metropolitan America is in trouble. In cities and suburbs alike, citizens are beset by complexities that disturb their everyday lives. They are threatened by crime in the streets, by impure air and water, by breakdowns in public transportation. They are burdened by high taxes and inflationary prices. The deprived minorities in the slums and ghettos suffer more than other citizens of metropolis, for they are more likely to be jobless or sick, badly educated or poorly housed. What is worse, they are handicapped by racial discrimination in their efforts to improve their own condition.

Vigorous leadership is essential if the plight of metropolitan Americans of all races—in cities and suburbs—is to improve. The national and state governments must develop relevant substantive programs designed to deal with a host of diverse and elusive metropolitan problems. At the same time, metropolitan areas must develop a system of government that is capable—administratively, fiscally, and politically—of translating substantive programs into action. Such a system must be geared to respond not only to problems of metropolitan-wide concern, but to those of local communities within metropolitan areas.

* * *

The structure of government in metropolitan areas has a profound impact on the daily lives of metropolitan citizens. But, as this Committee has long recognized, the present arrangement of overlapping local units is not serving the people well. Citizens in metropolitan areas are confronted by a confusing maze of many—possibly a dozen—jurisdictions, each with its own bureaucratic labyrinth. This

---

*Committee for Economic Development, *Reshaping Government in Metropolitan Areas* (New York: The Committee, 1970), 9–11. Reprinted by permission.

baffling array of local units has made it difficult for citizens—the disadvantaged particularly—to gain access to public services and to acquire a voice in decision-making.

Clearly, a fragmented system of government works better for some than for others. In gaining access to the system, citizens with greater political influence and sophistication may succeed in bypassing bureaucratic governmental procedures. Moreover, the system generally works better for suburbanites than it does for residents of the central cities. The haphazard arrangement of local governments in metropolitan areas has created great inequalities between resources and needs. In the suburbs, the combination of superior fiscal strength and fewer problems usually yields a higher quality of public service; in the central cities the situation is reversed. But it is not entirely by chance that such disparities have developed. One of the principal failings of a fragmented system of government is its inability to take an overview in matters of planning, transportation, and population dispersal. Zoning and other land-use control powers wielded by small suburban communities tend to exclude from the suburbs black citizens and other low-income minority groups.

Fragmented local governments reflect great variations in character and viewpoint. The fact that fragmentation persists indicates a determination among local communities to control their own affairs and preserve their own identities. While this attitude makes for greater local pride, it also results in failure of local communities to unite on matters of area-wide concern, such as environmental pollution and transportation congestion, which seriously undermine the quality of metropolitan life.

JOHN C. BOLLENS
HENRY J. SCHMANDT

The Fragmented Metropolis: View Number Three

Effects of Proliferation and Inadequate Coordination

The proliferation of governments and the lack of adequate coordination of public programs have many important injurious effects

"Effects of Proliferation and Inadequate Coordination" from *The Metropolis: Its People, Politics, and Economic Life* by John C. Bollens and Henry J. Schmandt, Copyright © 1965 by John C. Bollens and Henry J. Schmandt. Reprinted by permission of Harper & Row, Publishers.

on the metropolis. As various types of governments have grown numerically, the volume of personalities and issues on which the voters are expected to make intelligent judgments has also expanded. Conscientious persons have enough difficulty remaining reasonably knowledgeable about several governments—national, state, and local —but the proliferation of local units has made their total task impossible. They would have to devote countless hours to being well informed about their local governments, for the system has come to resemble a circus of many more than the usual three rings. Few individuals have time for this herculean task.

Public control and accountability

The frequent consequences are a further decrease in public interest, which even in less complex years was not at a high level, and a resulting decline in public control and accountability. In time, voter turnout becomes lower as public disinterest, cynicism, and alienation mount and as fewer candidates seek certain offices in the wide range of elective possibilities. The scattering of public authority has reached the point in some areas where various incumbent office-holders have called off scheduled elections due to the absence of any opponents filing for the positions and have declared themselves re-elected.

Even the most conscientious citizens, those somehow able to spend enough time on their formidable assignment, meet insurmountable obstacles to adequate public control and accountability. One such impediment occurs when governments are composed entirely of non-elective officials, who might appropriately be called "the untouchables." This situation prevails in those special districts, some handling functions of metropolitan-wide significance, where officials are appointed by officers of other governments. In some instances they are selected by elective officials of other local governments (sometimes these elective officials choose the appointees from their own number), a procedure that furnishes the voters some degree of control, but one that is twice removed from them and thus quite remote. In other cases the authorities of one government charged with selecting the officials of another government are elected by a constituency much larger than the metropolis, or they themselves are appointed. Popular metropolitan control and accountability obviously do not exist at all under such circumstances.

Another obstacle to public control and accountability caused by governmental proliferation and fragmentation is that voters are compartmentalized into many governmental units, customarily small in territory. As a result, their decisions on a matter of general concern —such as improving mass transit or water pollution—are therefore generally binding on only a portion of the metropolitan area. And such compartmentalization breeds political irresponsibility. For example, some nonresidents of a city who work in it exert influence on its government through participation in civic, business, and labor organizations located in the city, but their activities are not tempered by residence in the municipality and the accountability of direct action.

Metropolitan consensus

The fact that the metropolis is usually not controlled by the metropolitan public but by a host of sub-publics is related to another serious consequence of governmental proliferation: the difficulty, indeed the common impossibility, of arriving at a metropolitan consensus on area-wide matters through formal public means. The dispersion of power among a large number of governmental units makes it legally possible for each of them to reach decisions without concern for their consequences or spillover effects, which may be harmful to other governments and residents of the metropolis. Moreover, such scatteration of authority has produced an increasing number of small formal decision centers, thus generally making it extremely difficult to attain formal metropolitan-wide acceptance of vital proposals. This situation, as pointed out by Robert C. Wood, a discerning analyst of metropolitan affairs, has often led to a coalition of politicians, newspaper editors, businessmen, and labor leaders taking on leadership in area-wide problems, usually on a single-problem basis. Devoid of the elements necessary for effective policy-making—an adequate institutional base, legal authority, direct and regular relationships with the metropolitan constituency, and established processes for considering and resolving issues—this coalition, he concludes, transmits what metropolitan policy it agrees upon to the existing governments, where it receives an uncertain reception and its utilization depends upon voluntary acceptance.[1]

Conflicting programs

When each government is a king in the fragmented public environment of the urban complex, some major programs undertaken by individual local units tend to work in counteracting rather than synchronized ways and to produce fewer positive area-wide results. And in such circumstances, the state and national governments are destined to assume more active service roles in the metropolis and, as we have seen, often to do so haphazardly, even to the point where agencies of the same government carry out conflicting activities.

Services and financial disparities

Governmental proliferation also contributes to wide disparities between service needs and financial resources in different parts of the metropolis and in turn to deficiencies in local public activities.

Allowing pockets of wealth to wall themselves off largely from the total community of which they are a part (and for which many of their well-to-do residents may depend for their income) inevitably leads to the emergence of areas of poverty. Consequently, some units are wealthy and can satisfy the comparatively few public needs of their residents at a luxury level and with a low tax rate, while others are poor and have extensive needs they frequently are financially unable to meet. Ironically, the resulting service and regulatory deficiencies in the poor pockets sometimes break out of their confines and cause large-scale problems. Such deficiencies also prompt advocacy of proposals to bring about a degree of area-wide financial equalization (most often advocated in terms of school districts) and increased state and national governmental interest and participation in metropolitan areas.

Area-wide problems

A very important result of the fragmented and uncoordinated governmental operations of metropolitan areas is the existence and at times the continued growth of grave area-wide problems of service and regulation. The list of shortcomings is long or brief, according to the particular metropolis, but frequently includes clogged mass and private means of transportation (principally road and commuter rail transportation, but also sometimes involving air, truck, and port facilities), pollution of water and air, disposal of various wastes, dwindling water supplies, insufficient park and recreation areas, declining amounts of needed open spaces, growing ugliness, exploited uses of irreplaceable land, inadequate developmental plans and controls, and others. The metropolitan citizenry occasionally becomes vocal and irritated about one or a few of these area-wide problems (most often transportation, pollution, waste disposal, water, and parks and recreation), but in general its concern about them is slight until a critical condition develops.

The Governance of the Metropolis

Despite weaknesses in the organization and processes of its governmental system, the metropolis so far has been able to avoid major disasters. This feat has been accomplished by continually adjusting to keep the pressure points from reaching catastrophic levels. Ironically, by averting crisis, these *ad hoc* measures have helped to stifle or defeat most efforts at comprehensive restructuring of the governmental pattern of the metropolis. The process of governing has involved local units, which remain on center stage, other public agencies, and private organizations and individuals. The techniques utilized to sustain the system vary among metropolitan areas, but the process is generally similar.

The governmental mix

The governmental mixture usually consists of intergovernmental cooperation, a county government of rising importance, a network of small and large districts, and growing state and national programs. Contracts between local units, a formal type of cooperation, have been expanding in number. Almost invariably negotiated between two governments, they are always voluntary and usually terminable after notice. Some are mutual aid agreements, which become operative only when a fire, police, or civil defense emergency arises. Others are arrangements whereby a government, such as a county or a city, consents to provide a service to another local unit for a set period of time and a specified amount of money. The time period can be extended upon joint approval and the amount of payment then is also subject to renegotiation. In some instances, too, emergency aid or the use of a service or a facility of one government by another is based on informal understandings between administrators rather than written contracts.

By providing services and facilities through formal and informal means of cooperation with other units, intensifying levels of activity in unincorporated urban areas, and taking on more functions, many county governments have assumed larger roles in the metropolis and have prevented certain ⟩problems from becoming more serious. Moreover, a multitude of non-school special districts has been spawned, most of them concerned with small trouble spots and relatively few with individual metropolitan-wide problems.

In addition, the state and national governments have loomed larger on the metropolitan scene. Backed by diversified sources of revenue and staffed by functional specialists, they have plugged certain local and area-wide gaps in the metropolis, usually by offering financial grants that contain stipulations to be met before being awarded. Often these state and federal activities are condemned by local officials as intervention, on the assumption that a stand of this sort is good politics and popular with their constituents. Yet at the same time such efforts by "foreign" governments are widely sought and welcomed as aids in the handling of particular difficulties.

Private activities

Numerous private organizations and individuals also participate in governing the metropolis. Business and industrial interests, labor unions, political parties, private welfare agencies, civic associations, metropolitan and suburban newspapers, and television and radio stations (which now can take editorial positions) all have important stakes in keeping the metropolitan community operating as a going concern. They possess varying degrees of power and influence (but, as we will see in detail in the next chapter, none to the point of dominating or controlling the community) and they espouse a broad range of objectives. In the process they interact and negotiate with one another and with the elected politicians and professional governmental bureaucrats who make the formal decisions on public policies.

A system of public and private relationships that furnishes a vehicle for decision-making of both a positive and negative nature obviously has always existed in the metropolis; it is a basic necessity for averting crises and for parcelling out some of the rewards of metropolitan life. The system in operation further demonstrates that the proliferated and diffused formal governmental organization of most metropolitan areas is not totally the result of drift; in important part it is the product of deliberate, conscious decisions and actions by numerous governments and private organizations. The multicentered process of governance composed of public and private elements lumbers along by using the techniques of intermittent bargaining and diplomatic maneuvering. In general, the process stands as a formidable barrier to the formation of a governmental institution charged with decision-making on matters of area-wide concern and with the execution of those policies within the framework of the welfare of the total metropolitan community—one providing for appraising the goals of the multicentered forces of interest and influence in the light of the aims and well-being of the entire metropolis.

Note

1. Robert C. Wood, *Metropolis Against Itself* (New York: Committee for Economic Development, 1959), p. 38.

ROBERT C. WOOD

The Fragmented Metropolis: View Number Four

The New York Region is more than an urban area—it is a metropolitan area. It is metropolitan in the sense that its five hundred autonomous general governments and almost one thousand other

Reprinted by permission of the publishers from pp. 51–55, 60–64 of Robert C. Wood, *1400 Governments*. Cambridge, Mass.: Harvard University Press, Copyright, 1961, by Regional Plan Association, Inc.

governments with various legal and functional prerogatives share responsibility over the urban complex. Thus, though the separate forces represented by industrial property, density, and the like are inseparably intertwined in the economic and population aspects of this complex, the political and sometimes social identities within the Region are quite distinct. Political boundary lines criss-cross the entire area and interject a number of additional complications into the interaction between economic development and governmental behavior.

Thus, some jurisdictions receive a lion's share of business and industrial wealth; others accept major deposits of population. Some, situated in sparsely settled portions of the Region, face the problems of installing new community facilities and at the same time can hope for a tax windfall from a new plant in a space-hungry industry. Others are little more than clusters of neighborhoods afflicted with the liabilities of old age, and their governments are plagued with problems of blight. The political fact of separateness pulls apart the concomitance of factors which, if taken together, constitute an urban economy. Thus on top of the complications introduced by the different stages of neighborhoods represented in the Region is the further complication that these neighborhoods are something more than collections of peoples. They are municipalities or school districts or villages—legal entities—and this fact, in and of itself, bequeaths a particular identity.

Perhaps the most obvious effect of present governmental arrangements is that they are responsible for extreme variation in size among the jurisdictions—and this fact alone is of some consequence for our expenditure analysis. The size of the community has a significant bearing upon the relative scope and variety of its major public programs. Chart 10 depicts, for the sample of 64 middle-sized New Jersey municipalities, the association of size with the pattern of expenditure allocations of the municipal budget while holding constant every other environmental characteristic. With variations in these characteristics controlled, the smaller governments appear to concentrate their nonschool budgets on police protection and street maintenance, and to require a larger administrative overhead to do so. The larger ones allocate their money more evenly across the array of services and give relatively more emphasis to other programs— notably fire protection, sanitation, and social services.

By other calculations we concluded that there seems to be a critical threshold in the size of a jurisdiction—somewhere around 10,000 population—below which differences in expenditure levels appear primarily a function of the availability of revenue rather than of needs and pressures. Holding constant the value of residential and business property, we found that dwelling-unit density, which is

Chart 10. Distribution of municipal operating expenditures in two hypothetical communities differing only in size

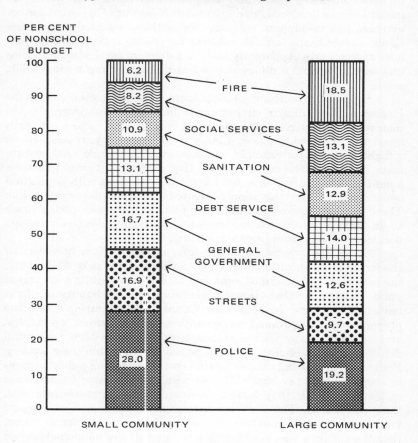

Note: Calculations are based upon the data collected for the 64 middle-sized New Jersey municipalities mapped in Chart 2. "Social services" include health, welfare, recreation, and libraries and civic services.

symbolic among the 64 middle-sized Nemw Jersey unicipalities of a particular cluster of service requirements, exerted no significant impact upon expenditure levels among the 65 smaller jurisdictions coexisting in the same counties.

The middle-sized New Jersey municipalities then are not just the small municipalities "writ large." They respond differently to a similar mix of environmental circumstances; they serve up different "packages" of public programs. The casualness of a small suburb, even when as densely populated as the Bronx, may allow its residents to avoid installing curbs and sidewalks and to rely on volunteers instead of a professional fire department. New York City, at the other extreme, has to support not only fire stations but Shakespeare festivals, public baths, official quarters for distinguished visitors, parades and concerts. Apparently there is a different level of expectations and capacities, and a different political process for registering public needs.

Beyond bequeathing an assortment of public sectors across the Region so that similar environments have different programs, the metropolitan governmental structure has another effect. It pulls apart the forces which, over a large enough territory, coexist. If, on a flight of fancy, for example, one conceived of a single local government embracing the entire Region, that government would comprehend both the demand-oriented factors that go along with population concentrations and the supply-oriented factor of industrialization. The question of government spending would boil down pretty much to an issue of how much resources the politically effective residents decided to divert from private spending.

Given the present boundary lines in the Region, however, all the forces of urbanization do not necessarily go hand in hand. Instead, the now familiar pattern of some municipalities wrestling with urgent public needs and others serenely accepting the tax bounty of "light industry" appears. In Middlesex County, for example, where the predominant occupational concentrations are craftsmen, operatives, and laborers, many municipalities have relatively high residential densities without having many industrial plants within their borders. For those governments the estimated cost of providing public services in 1958 was $600 per family. But with an average value per residence of about $15,000, they had no resources base commensurate with their obligations. The 1955 tax rate was $9 per $1,000 of assessed valuation and that valuation was set at 22 percent of market value; thus the tax levy was $297 per family—or half the municipal service cost. Without state aid or industrial windfalls, the only fiscal alternatives are deficit financing or sharply increased tax efforts. By contrast, in Greenwich, Connecticut, where exurbanites abound, the average value of a new house in 1956 was $31,250. With such a base, the town's ratio of assessed to true market value of property had fallen by 25 percent in the last seven years, and all capital improvements were being financed on a pay-as-you-go basis.

One is impressed most of all by the distorting influence of governmental structure. The longer one examines the jurisdictions' expenditure patterns at the present time, the more apparent it becomes that historical caprice, in the form of ancient boundary lines, disrupts the pattern of regularity which the forces themselves display. Thus, especially in New Jersey where the jurisdiction is small and where the county does not carry out the broad range of functions assigned to its New York counterpart, the location of a single industrial plant, the decision of a developer to build one hundred homes, the construction of one express highway—insignificant elements in the total urban complex of the Region—drastically affect the public fortunes of the jurisdiction. In any jurisdiction the character of public needs and the resources available to meet needs are almost certain to be sharply different not only from its neighbors but also from the Region's at large. It may not be too far-fetched—though it is certainly an oversimplification—to think of local governments as players at a roulette wheel, waiting to see what number will come up as a result of decisions beyond their direct control.

The larger a municipality is, of course, the more chance it may have to encompass a balanced blend of expenditure-inducing factors. Hence the less vulnerable it becomes to decisions made in the private sector—the choice of individual industrial locations or the consequences of population settlement pursued in a general search for space and status. New York City appears in command of a large enough territory to comprehend almost all the elements of urbanization. The close to $10 billion of taxable real estate in Manhattan, almost half of the entire City's valuation, provides a base from which the six million inhabitants in the other more residential boroughs may be supported. The public sectors of Westchester and Nassau Counties, by virtue of the pre-eminent role of county government, also have access to industrial and commercial valuations for many programs on a reasonably broad geographical basis.

Yet, even these larger units are likely to have a mix of forces which is quite different from that of the Region at large. Certainly, New York City and Newark have a disproportionate share of the special expenditure-inducing factors. Being the first home of immigrants and almost the only home for some minority groups, they have the largest number of hardship cases within their borders. As old cities, they are pressed more heavily by conditions of age and obsolescence. As we shall have occasion to observe again later, such conditions plus the absence of open space for future developments frequently provoke a set of public problems as serious in their financial implications as those of densely populated residential communities which lack compensating industrial resources.

Thus the existence of as many different types of public sectors as there are combinations of the components of urbanization forbids any one-shot generalization on the public financial patterns of the Region. In place of a broad interpretation which views the over-all Region's political economy as a result of a coincidence of demand and supply components, the total public sector is revealed as the sum of many small compartmentalized and quite different sectors. Within this complex, a high level of expenditures is not, by and of itself, indicative of any single component or any single combination. It may be the result of an ample supply of taxable wealth; it may arise from a reasonable supply of wealth plus a predominant civic preference for "quality" public product; it may occur through the compulsion of high density. By the same token, low levels of expenditure may not express conditions of fiscal struggling; they may be a function of the absence of many obvious needs for public service or a consciously conservative disposition on the part of the jurisdiction's inhabitants. Out of this diversity of experiences, one municipality may find itself so insulated from the pressures of urban growth that it has real choices about the level and extent of its public services. Another may be a captive of its environment—with little industrial property and with low-value residences, yet with a population which requires large expenditures simply to provide minimal services and meet the urgent needs of the moment.

Paradoxically, however, as various and haphazard as these municipal public sectors appear to be, they yield a common interpretation for the behavior of the 1400 managers, a backdrop for understanding the process of political decision-making and behavior as it relates to economic development. When we understand how different components of urbanization work in quite different ways to force up the level of public expenditures and to distribute the burdens of cost, the moves and countermoves among the factions within a local citizenry do not appear as senseless controversy, born of misunderstanding and misinformation. Rather, they emerge as the actions of highly sensible people who realize that the outcome of political battles on tax rates, assessed valuations, and budgets bestow unequal penalties and unequal benefits. Environmental circumstances combined with an established revenue system make particular strategies and particular controversies almost certain.

In the same way, when we recognize the roulette-wheel aspect of municipal finance, combined with the predominant influence of industrial wealth on expenditures and of density on tax effort, we come to understand the policies adopted by local public officials. In this context, their contentious squabbles with their neighbors, their insularity, their persistent claim to self-identity, the protective devices they employ—all these are not the products of whim or a failure to recognize reality. On the contrary, with an intuitive grasp of the political implications of urbanization, these officials shape policies adapted to the given situation. By whatever way they proceed, they are reaching toward an accommodation to the forces spawned by urbanization. The pattern of their response provides an additional explanation for the substance of the public sector today and feeds back on the process of urbanization itself.

EDWARD C. BANFIELD

The Politics of
Metropolitan Area Organization

I

That there is a critical need to integrate local government organization in the metropolitan areas has become an article of faith with
practically all who are concerned with urban affairs. In the last thirty
years eighty-eight major surveys have been made of metropolitan
organization, and at the present time in almost every metropolitan
area at least one official or unofficial body is endeavoring to bring
about a "rationalization" of government structure by annexation,
consolidation, federation, functional transfers, creation of special districts, or some combination of these.[1]

Despite all the study and talk, not much has been accomplished.
If school districts are left out of account, the number of local governments is increasing, and no metropolitan area is yet possessed of a
government able to deal with a number of functions on an area-wide
basis. Of the eighty-eight major surveys, only three were followed by
the adoption of major recommendations.

Probably one reason for this is that the metropolitan area
"problem" is to some extent spurious. That there are (for example)
1,071 independent local governments in the New York area may not
be as bad as it is made to sound. Perhaps there should be even more.
There are some real and important problems of metropolitan organization, of course, but the "one local government for one local area"
idea reflects a taste of symmetry, simplicity, and, in a special sense,
logic.[2]

To the extent that the movement for metropolitan area organization arises out of these naive biases its political failure is accounted
for. But the problem is by no means wholly illusory and so some
additional explanation for the failure of reform is needed. This article
is intended to supply it.

Reprinted from "The Politics of Metropolitan Area Organization," *Midwest Journal of Political Science*, 1.1 (1957), by Edward C. Banfield by
permission of the Wayne State University Press. Copyright 1957 by the
Wayne State University Press.

II

If we look at the facts of political arithmetic (as demography was once called), we see that profound changes are underway. The electorate, already predominantly urban, is rapidly becoming overwhelmingly so. Areas are expected to grow fast both in absolute numbers and as a proportion of the whole population. Central cities are expected to grow relatively little. The big increases will come in the fringe areas.

These population movements are changing the character of both the central cities and the suburbs. "The central cities," Woodbury has written, "will become increasingly the place of residence of new arrivals in the metropolitan areas, of nonwhites, lower income workers, younger couples, and the elderly."[3] The rate at which the Negro populations of the larger central cities are increasing is one of the most striking features of the situation. A pioneering study by Bogue suggests that in ten years the nonwhite population of Chicago may be more than 900,000 (23.4 percent of the whole) while that of the suburbs will be less than 200,000 (6.4 percent of the whole).[4] Negroes have accounted for much of the population increase in large central cities but for little of it in the suburbs.

It is not easy to generalize about the suburbs. "Dormitory" suburbs within commuting distance of the big cities are predominantly middle and upper income.[5] But many once fashionable suburbs are fast becoming slums or near-slums.[6] There are also, of course, many industrial suburbs, particularly in the northeast. The movement to the suburbs is in many places a levelling one: the high concentration of upper-income, upper-educated, upper-class people in the suburbs is being diluted by migration from the central cities and from rural places. By and large, the dilution is with respect to the suburban "ring" as a whole: each individual suburb may retain a fairly homogeneous character while the character of the ring as a whole changes. "To some extent," Lubell has remarked, "the suburban exodus appears to have revived the old patterns of segregation. Around New York City there are suburban districts which have become as heavily Jewish, or Italian, or Irish in family ancestry as were the ghettos or 'Little Italy's' or 'New Erins' of the lower East Side of twenty-five years ago. The old-law tenements of the East Side have given way to ranch houses with sylvan settings and neatly cultivated lawns. Yet the walls of discrimination and intolerance still stand."[7]

In general the large cities are heavily Democratic and the suburban rings heavily Republican. (See Table 1.)

It seems likely that the central cities will become more and more Democratic.[8] Those who are leaving them for the suburbs include a disproportionate number of Republicans and of the upward mobile people who are likely to become Republicans. Their places are taken

Table 1. Democratic vote as a percentage
of major party vote, central city and suburbs, 1954

New York City	65.9
Suburban Counties	
Rockland	40.7
Westchester	35.3
Nassau	36.1
Suffolk	30.9
Chicago	64.2
Cook County except Chicago	40.5
Philadelphia	57.7
Montgomery County	38.1
Detroit	66.9
Wayne County except Detroit	57.1
Pittsburgh	56.8
Allegheny County except Pittsburgh	54.3
St. Louis City	62.0
St. Louis County	45.0
San Francisco	49.3
Suburban Counties	
Marin	35.2
San Mateo	40.8
Cleveland	70.0
Cuyahoga County except Cleveland	51.4
Minneapolis	58.8
Hennepin County except Minneapolis	47.2
Buffalo	52.8
Erie County except Buffalo	36.9
Milwaukee	59.8
Milwaukee County except Milwaukee City	45.5
Cincinnati	43.8
Hamilton County except Cincinnati	39.2

Source: Based on data from R. M. Scammon, *America Votes*, Government
Affairs Institute, 1956. Except for St. Louis City and St. Louis County,
which were for President in 1952, the votes were for governor or senator.

almost entirely by poor whites from the South, Negroes, Puerto
Ricans and Mexicans. At least four-fifths of these are normally
Democratic.

There is, of course, a possibility that in the struggle over school
integration the Negro will lose his allegiance to the Democratic party.
In the 1956 election the Negro Democratic vote fell off dramatically
in some places, particularly in the South. In certain places in the
North, the Republicans made impressive percentage gains. These
gains do not necessarily reflect shifts in party allegiance, however.
For example, in Congressman William Dawson's district in Chicago
the Republican share of the vote increased from 26.5 percent in 1952
to 35.5 percent in 1956. But this percentage increase does not reflect
an important absolute gain to the Republicans: while Dawson's vote
dropped from 95,899 to 66,704, that for his opponent climbed only
from 34,571 to 36,847. Thousands of Negro voters, impelled by slum
clearance or other circumstances, had moved into other districts
where—presumably—they were still voting heavily Democratic.[9]

The Republicanism of the suburban rings is being diluted by the movement into them from the central cities and rural areas. "Hillbillies" and Negroes are moving into suburbs which not long ago were solidly middle-class and solidly Republican. Industrial suburbs are growing like big Disneyland mushrooms. Even in the middle and upper class "dormitory" suburbs a good many of the newcomers are Democrats. However, the dilution of the Republican suburban vote

**Table 2. Republican vote as a percentage
of major party vote, suburbs, 1948 and 1954.**

Suburban Area	1948	1954	Percent Increase or Decrease 1954 over 1948
New York Suburbs			
Rockland County	61.2	59.3	− 1.9
Westchester	64.8	64.7	− .1
Nassau	72.2	63.9	− 8.3
Suffolk	72.1	69.1	− 3.0
Cook County except Chicago	64.6	59.4	− 2.8
Montgomery County (Pennsylvania)	67.5	61.9	− 5.6
Wayne County except Detroit	44.3	42.4	− 1.9
Allegheny County except Pittsburgh	46.7	45.4	− 1.3
St. Louis County	52.6	55.0	+ 2.4
San Francisco Suburbs			
Marin County	57.2	64.8	+ 7.6
San Mateo County	56.8	59.2	+ 2.4
Cuyahoga County except Cleveland	60.6	48.6	−12.0
Hennepin County except Minneapolis	52.0	51.5	− .5
Erie County except Buffalo	55.7	62.8	− 7.1
Milwaukee County except Milwaukee City	51.9	54.3	+ 2.4
Hamilton County except Cincinnati	58.8	60.7	+ 1.9

Source: 1948 figures computed from data in *The Political Almanac*, New York: B. C. Forbes and Sons, 1952. 1954 figures computed from *America Votes*. The 1948 figures are for a Presidential vote; the others are votes for governor or senator. These are not altogether satisfactory for comparison.

does not seem to be as great as, judging from the size of the population movement, one would expect. It may be that many of the central city Democrats who move to the suburbs become Republicans as soon as they learn what is expected of them in their new surroundings.[10] At any rate, as Table 2 suggests the Republican suburban vote has in general suffered little from the increase in population.[11]

III

These facts suggest that for many years to come it will be difficult or impossible to integrate local governments where the two-party system operates. Even if the proportion of Republicans declines sharply in the suburbs, metropolitan area government north of the Mason-Dixon line would almost everywhere be Republican government. In effect, advocates of consolidation schemes are asking the Democrats to give up their control of the central cities or, at least, to place it in jeopardy.

It may be that in time Democratic politicians will become so persuaded of the necessity of metropolitan government by the propaganda of the good government movement that they will support it against their own interest and that of their party. (Certainly many politicians are convinced of the merits of the merit system, although it has gone far toward undermining the party system.) Or it may be that the Democrats will be forced to accept metropolitan government by a public opinion which will have come to share the general bias of the experts in favor of symmetry and simplicity. These eventualities are not unlikely, but it will probably be a good many years before they are realized.

Three-quarters of the metropolitan areas lie entirely within a single county. From the standpoint of administration there is much to be said for city-county consolidation: it would make sense to endow county governments with the powers of cities and to organize them to exercise those powers efficiently. Schemes like this are being worked out in Miami, Atlanta, and Nashville, but it is highly unlikely that they will be tried where there is a two-party system. If Buffalo, for example, were to be consolidated with Erie County, control over it would pass from the Democratic party to the Republican. If Chicago were consolidated with Cook County, the Democrats would have a fighting chance of capturing it. But as matters now stand control of Chicago is a sure thing for the Democrats. Why should they change?

City-county separation will be unacceptable for the same reason. If Chicago—to take a typical case—were made a county by itself, apart from the rest of Cook County, the Democrats, although their control of the city would not be jeopardized, would no longer have a chance in Cook County. That would be safely Republican.

For the same reason that they will refuse to turn all of their powers over to a Republican county government, the Democrats of the central cities will refuse to turn over some of them to special function districts. Recently Sheriff Joseph Lohman of Cook County, a good government and planning-minded Democrat (he was formerly chairman of the Washington, D.C. Planning Commission), observed that law enforcement in the Chicago metropolitan area is "hamstrung" by limited jurisdictions and resources. He proposed putting the 11,000 policemen who now serve more than two hundred governmental units within the county under nine elected commissioners and suggested that a police commissioner be elected from each of nine wedge-shaped districts extending from the center of Chicago to the county line. The plan attracted no support from either Lohman's fellow-Democrats or from the Republicans. Obviously the Democrats are not going to give the Republicans the chance—the very good chance—of controlling the police of the central city. Nor are the Republicans going to run the risk of letting control of their suburban police fall into the hands of the central city Democrats.

There will probably be some instances—Detroit and Wayne County appear to be one and Pittsburgh and Allegheny County another—where the number of suburban Republicans is too small to make much difference. Consolidation may be possible in these cases. They will be few, however.

The Republicans outside of the central cities will of course want to remain apart: they are as well satisfied with a one-party system as are the Democrats of the central cities.

It would be a mistake to suppose that the conflict lies altogether or even mainly between the two party organizations or among the professional politicians who have a stake in them. The party differences are important in themselves, but they reflect deeper and still more important differences. Metropolitan government would mean the transfer of power over the central cities from the largely lower-class Negro and Catholic elements who live in them to the largely middle-class white and Protestant elements who live in the suburbs.

It should be remembered that between the central city resident and the suburbanite there are also differences of interest which have no necessary connection with race or class. If overnight all of the people of the central cities were transformed into middle-class white Protestants, there would still be the basis for conflict between them and the suburbanites. It would still have to be decided, for example, whether thousands of central city residents should be relocated to build expressways to give suburbanites quicker access to the city as well as how taxes to pay for such improvements should be levied. In St. Louis a metropolitan transit scheme failed of adoption recently apparently because of fears that improved service for suburbanites would be paid for by the fares of central city residents. Such instances abound.[12]

The situation will not be altogether different where the city is non-partisan. The major parties are alive and watching for their chances even in non-partisan cities. But even if they were not alive, the fundamental differences of interest and of status which separate the central city and the suburban populations would nevertheless be expressed at the polls and elsewhere.

The few Republicans of the central cities and, in general, the good government forces—in short, all those who want to weaken the Democratic machines—will favor adding the suburban vote to the central city vote wherever the suburbs are predominantly middle or upper class. It is not surprising that in Kansas City, Mo., City Manager Cookingham annexed some fringe areas over their violent opposition. He knew that, bitter as they might be at forced annexation, in the long run they would have to side with him against the remains of the Pendergast machine.[13]

As the Negro tide rises in the central cities, many white Democrats will begin to think of annexation and consolidation as ways to maintain a white (but, alas, Republican!) majority.[14] Unless there is consolidation, some cities will probably have Negro mayors within the next twenty years. Negroes can be expected to oppose annexation and consolidation under these circumstances, of course, and if the issue were to be decided on the metropolitan scene they could probably prevent gerrymandering along racial lines. Rural—and therefore white—dominated legislatures will have the decisive say in these matters, however, and they will be almost immune from Negro influence.

There are fast-growing lower class, and even Negro, suburbs close to some central cities. Democratic politicians will not ordinarily have much incentive to annex these because the Democratic majorities in the central cities will be large enough without them. But where lower class suburbs are large enough to insure Democratic county government, one stumbling block in the way of city-county consolidation will not exist. There will be another in such cases, however: Republican legislatures will be reluctant to pass enabling legislation.

IV

Professor Charles E. Merriam was certainly right in declaring years ago that "the adequate organization of modern metropolitan areas is one of the great unsolved problems of modern politics."[15] The problem is not, however, as many seem to think, merely one of creating organization for effective planning and administration. It is also—and perhaps primarily—one of creating, or of maintaining, organization for the effective management of conflict, especially of conflict arising from the growing cleavages of race and class.

These needs may be incompatible to some extent: the organization which would be best for the management of conflict may not be best for area-wide planning and administration. Indeed, it may be that area-wide planning and administration would of necessity heighten conflicts by raising questions which can only be settled by bitter struggle.

Conflict is not something to be avoided at all costs. It may be well, nevertheless, to consider if there are not decisive advantages in the organizational arrangements which now exist—arrangements which, while handicapping or entirely frustrating some important undertakings, also serve to insulate opposed interests and to protect them from each other. In view of their differences, it may be well, despite the obvious disadvantages, that the peoples of the central cities and of the suburbs live largely in separate political communities.

This is not to conclude that area-wide planning and administration should not be attempted. They should be attempted through the political structures which already exist. Rather than enter upon the probably futile and possibly dangerous course of creating new bodies by consolidation or federation it would be better in those places where fundamental cleavages exist to look to the political leaders of existing jurisdictions to negotiate among themselves settlements on the basis of which action may proceed. In effect this means that the political leaders of the central cities must be expected to come to terms with the political leaders of the states. For this to occur it is not necessary that both sets of leaders be of the same party, but it is necessary that both have power. In short, the metropolitan area problem will have to be solved—insofar as it is solved at all—by strong mayors and strong governors engaged in political give and take. Where special function districts are required, their managers should be accountable to the voters, but not directly so, for this would entail the transfer of power from one electorate (and thus one party organization) to another, something which is usually not feasible even if desirable. Instead, the people who run such districts should be accountable to a committee of mayors, county supervisors, governors who have a stake in the matter or to a committee of their appropriate subordinates. In this way accountability can be secured without the necessity of changing radically the distribution of political power. On this basis it should be possible to bring together administratively areas which are growing apart politically.

Notes

1. For an account of these endeavors see the Council of State Governments, *The States and the Metropolitan Problem* (Chicago, 1956), especially pp. 130–32. See also the annual articles in the *Municipal Yearbook* and the elaborate forthcoming bibliography compiled by the Government Affairs Foundation.

2. The principle of "one local government for one local area" was recommended in the Council of State Governments, *State-Local Relations* (Chicago, 1946). In the report on housing policy referred to above, Morton Grodzins and the writer have shown that although "fragmentation" of government structure in metropolitan areas impedes improvement of the housing situation in some important respects, the effect is on the whole a good deal less serious than is commonly supposed.

3. Coleman Woodbury, "Suburbanization and Suburbia," *American Journal of Public Health*, XLV (January 1955), 9.

4. Donald J. Bogue, *An Estimate of Metropolitan Chicago's Future*

Population: 1955 to 1956, published jointly by the Chicago Community Inventory, University of Chicago, and the Scripps Foundation, Miami University (Ohio), Feb. 2, 1955.

5. For a comprehensive statistical account of these differences see O. D. Duncan and A. J. Reiss, Jr., *Social Characteristics of Urban and Rural Communities, 1950* (New York, 1956).

6. See the table on substandard dwelling units in suburban areas in Victor Jones, "Local Government Organization in Metropolitan Areas," *The Future of Cities and Urban Redevelopment,* ed., Coleman Woodbury (Chicago, 1953), p. 511.

7. Samuel Lubell, *The Revolt of the Moderates* (New York, 1956), p. 246.

8. The Democrats lost many of the central cities in 1956. Stevenson got 48.7 percent of the vote in Chicago (and only 27.7 percent in the rest of Cook County!). But in Philadelphia he got 56.9 percent.

That President Eisenhower carried the central cities signifies nothing for the future since he cannot run again and no other Republican will have his popularity. Besides, in this context the important elections are the local ones. In these the Democratic vote is more reliable.

9. In four Black Belt wards of Chicago registrations dropped 15 percent from 1952 to 1956. In 1952, 75 percent of those registered voted; in 1956 only 71 percent voted. If in three of these wards (2, 3 and 20) the smaller number of voters had divided between the parties in the same proportion as in 1952, the Democratic candidate for governor would have got 11.5 percent more votes than he actually did get. In the fourth of these wards (4) there was no net change in registration and the Democratic candidate for governor got 29 percent fewer votes than in 1952. In these wards Eisenhower ran 9 percent ahead of the Republican candidate for governor; in Chicago as a whole he ran 25 percent ahead.

In the three most heavily Negro wards of Philadelphia (30, 32 and 47) Stevenson got 79.3 percent of the vote in 1952 and 75.5 percent in 1956. The total vote in these wards was 10 percent less in 1956 than in 1952. In the Negro wards Eisenhower ran 1 percent ahead of the Republican candidate for senator; in the city as a whole he ran 2.7 percent ahead.

10. A *New York Times* story of May 31, 1956 summarized the views of suburban politicians in the New York metropolitan area on the reasons for this change of political allegiance: "One reason is a sense of property rights and a concern for tax rates that comes with the key to a suburban home and the mortgage. Another is a desire for social status and a feeling that it can be achieved by belonging to the 'right' social groups and parties. A third is a feeling that local conditions require a Republican enrollment if there is any hope of a consequent political career or political favors."

There is some reason to believe that in new suburbs many converts to Republicanism become disenchanted when schools go on three shifts, taxes rise, houses require repairs, and transit systems become overloaded.

11. 1956 returns for most places are not at hand as this is written. However, it is clear that in the Philadelphia and Chicago regions, at least, the Republicanism of the suburban rings is somewhat diluted.

In Philadelphia suburbs the Republican percentages of the vote for senator were as follows:

	1952	1956
Montgomery County	65.6	62.5
Bucks "	61.4	52.6
Delaware "	60.8	58.9

U. S. News & World Report (Dec. 1, 1956) concluded that the movement to the suburbs of Chicago has not diluted their Republicanism. As evidence, it reported Eisenhower's percentage of the majority party vote as follows:

	1952	1956
Calumet City	42.9	54.5
Chicago Heights	52.5	64.0
Elmwood Park	62.8	71.8
Evanston	75.4	76.5
Harvey	56.8	65.7
Oak Park	76.9	79.1
River Forest	84.5	85.6
Wilmette	82.6	83.7
Winnetka	79.0	80.9

The data do not bear out the conclusion, however. For one thing, in half the suburbs cited the shift was only one or two percentage points, surprisingly little in view of Eisenhower's great popularity. For another, many of those who voted for Eisenhower are still Democrats and may be expected to vote Democratic as a general rule in the future.

12. See, for example, Daniel R. Grant, "Urban and Suburban Nashville: A Case Study in Metropolitanism," *Journal of Politics*, XVII (Feb. 1955), 93–95.

13. See the account of this in the manuscript by A. Theodore Brown, "The Politics of Reform: Kansas City's Municipal Government, 1925–1950." It is interesting that the districts where Pendergast had been strong were almost decisively against annexation. Chapter X, p. 8.

14. In Nashville, Tenn., six months after the removal of the poll tax in 1951, Councilman Glenn Ragsdale argued—successfully—that an annexation was necessary to offset the growing Negro vote in his district.— Creed C. Black, "The Politics of Metropolitanism: Opposition to Annexation in Nashville, Tennessee," unpublished Master's thesis, Department of Political Science, University of Chicago, August, 1952, p. 40.

15. In his preface to Victor Jones, *Metropolitan Government* (Chicago, 1942), p. ix.

THOMAS R. DYE

Metropolitan Integration by Bargaining Among Sub-Areas

Urban ecologists have observed that a distinguishing characteristic of metropolitan areas is areal specialization, or homogeneity in spatially defined subpopulations with respect to class or status, life style and economic function. Areal specialization results not only in inter-

"Metropolitan Integration by Bargaining Among Sub-Areas," by Thomas R. Dye, is reprinted from the *American Behavioral Scientist* (May 1962) p. 11, by permission of the publisher, Sage Publications, Inc.

dependence and the need for integrating structures for the metropolitan area but also differentiation of interest and demands for autonomy. In the past, students of municipal government have focused upon service functions of local government where the demands for metropolitan integration were most clearly manifested. Studies of the divisive forces within metropolitan areas are relatively rare. The objective of our recent research was to describe the distribution of persons with different status and life style characteristics throughout the metropolitan area and to identify certain political differences associated with this distribution. Such information is employed as a basis for developing propositions about the structure of the political system of the metropolitan area, particularly with regard to the identity and impact of the forces resisting metropolitan integration.

The Dimensions of Area Specialization

Our studies have employed the social area analysis tool developed in San Francisco by Eshref Shevky and Wendell Bell (UCLA) to observe social differentiation among 48 selected communities in the Philadelphia Standard Metropolitan Area. The political variables that were found to associate with areal specialization included: variation in community voting behavior, differences in the social characteristics and recruitment of local political leadership, variation in certain attitudinal attributes of subpopulations and their leaders, variation in popular images of community decision-making, differences in community choice of policy roles for local government and differences in community response to specific issues.

Eight Functions of Specialization

Analysis revealed that there are real and persistent conflicts of interest associated with areal specialization which divide subpopulations in metropolitan areas. These divisions operate to maintain a decentralized, or "fragmented," governmental structure and to inhibit the growth of intergovernmental cooperation. Analysis suggested that a decentralized political structure was functional to the metropolitan system from the following points of view: 1) it provides a source of social identification for individuals and groups enabling them to relate themselves to the metropolitan system; 2) by reducing the scale of social experience, it curbs feelings of apathy, isolation, and anomie among individuals and aggregates; 3) it provides an institutional device whereby subpopulations may protect themselves from those whose standards and way of life they do not share; 4) it provides additional institutional settings for the release of individual and group frustration and grievance through public catharsis; 5) it offers an opportunity for a larger number of elites to exercise power; 6) it expands available opportunities for individual participation as a means of contributing to both individuals and public policy; 7) by providing additional points of access, pressure, and control, it gives additional insurance that political demands will be heard; 8) it permits minorities to avail themselves of government position and power and exert greater influence over policy.

Uniting Where Necessary

Empirical observations about the divisive forces in a metropolitan area in no way challenge the desirability of attending to inadequacies of the larger political structure. But such observations can reflect upon the strategic value of various proposals for achieving metropolitan political integration. The prospects for comprehensive institutional reorganization of government decision-making in the metropolitan area appear remote. But the classical techniques of decision-making, the hierarchal and democratic models, do not exhaust the possibilities of structuring the decision-making process. The great extent of social and political differences among communities of a metropolis suggests that a third alternative technique for policy formulation, that of bargaining among leadership groups, may be a most appropriate, if not the only feasible, technique for achieving policy integration within the metropolitan area. Bargaining is made possible by the fact that conflict, while a basic form of interaction among metropolitan communities, is not necessarily of the non-zero sum type. Competitive bargaining can result in the formation of rewarding coalitions. Strategy requires that integrative efforts be concentrated upon structuring the decision-making process in metropolitan areas to facilitate bargaining, rather than upon comprehensive "solutions" that ignore the consequences of social and political diversity.

Facilitating Bargaining

Within the context of intergovernmental relations in a metropolitan area, bargaining can be facilitated by: 1) the provision of an arena, preferably informal, where elected political heads of metropolitan municipalities will come together regularly; 2) the encouraging of information exchange among metropolitan governments at technical levels; 3) the avoidance of special-function districts, commissions, and activities which remove functions from the bargaining arena and reduce the potential for effective negotiations; 4) the administration of agreements which emerge from the bargaining process through agen-

cies directly responsible to the political heads of the governments
concerned rather than through independent or quasi-independent
boards; 5) the writing of interjurisdictional and contractual agreements between metropolitan governments in such a form so as to
facilitate renegotiation; 6) the reduction of mutual distrust and
suspicion among urban governments by insuring their political independence and renouncing proposals for centralizing the institutional
structure of the metropolitan area.

PARRIS N. GLENDENING
JOHN WESLEY WHITE

The Politics of Metropolitan Reorganization: The Black Vote

It is recognized today, in both the popular press and the literature of
social science, that American urban and metropolitan areas are facing
a time of crisis. The authors of one recent study note that "from the
highest levels of government to the blighted ghettos of our central
cities, the concept of crisis has become commonplace in our discussion
of the urban condition."[1]

The "crisis" is a complex of problems which are basically economic, sociological, and even psychological. Yet, the answers to the
urban problems cannot be given entirely in terms of economics,
sociology, or psychology. There is a very important governmental
factor. It is apparent that administrative complexities and governmental fragmentation resulting from attempts to adapt nineteenth-
century governmental machinery to the twentieth-century city must
be modified before the urban crisis problems can be overcome.

To this end, a large number of local government reorganization
proposals have been made. Almost all of these reorganization plans
have been rejected by the voters.

If it is clear that the fragmented governmental system costs
more in terms of inferior services, higher costs, and serious deficiencies in the areas of planning, pollution control, and so forth, why
do voters consistently reject proposals for a more rational organization of the metropolitan area? While the answer is complex, it is
becoming increasingly evident that race is a major explanatory variable.[2]

Adapted from Parris N. Glendening and John Wesley White, "Local
Government Reorganization Referenda in Florida: An Acceptance and a
Rejection," *The Florida State University Governmental Research Bulletin*,
vol. 5, no. 2, (Tallahassee: The Institute of Governmental Research, The
Florida State University, March 1968). Reprinted by permission.

The earlier observations of writers such as Edward C. Banfield increasingly are being borne out. His 1957 essay has even more import today:[3]

> It would be a mistake to suppose that the conflict lies altogether or even mainly between the two party organizations or among the professional politicians who have a stake in them. The party differences are important in themselves, but they reflect deeper and still more important differences. Metropolitan government would mean the transfer of power over the central cities from the largely lower-class Negro and Catholic elements who live in them to the largely middle-class white and Protestant elements who live in the suburbs. . . .
>
> As the Negro tide rises in the central cities, many white Democrats will begin to think of annexation and consolidation as ways to maintain a white (but, alas, Republican!) majority. Unless there is consolidation, some cities will probably have Negro mayors within the next twenty years. Negroes can be expected to oppose annexation and consolidation under these circumstances. . .

Similar views have been put forth in many of the case studies on specific reorganization efforts.[4]

The Referenda

On June 27, 1967, a proposal was submitted to referendum which would have changed greatly the administrative organization of Hillsborough County, Florida, and consolidated the governments of the city of Tampa and Hillsborough County. The referendum on this proposal followed the national pattern. It was defeated by a vote of 28,796 to 11,428. On August 8, 1967, the voters of Duval County, Florida, went against the national trend and accepted a major administrative reorganization and city-county consolidation plan by a vote of 52,585 to 28,875.

The obvious question is, why did the advocates of metropolitan reorganization meet "both an impressive victory and a disappointing defeat"[5] in a period of less than six weeks? This brief paper will examine some of the voting patterns on the two votes in order to provide a partial answer to the posed question; in light of the remarks by Banfield, particular attention will be paid to the race variable.

As mentioned above, almost all of the major reorganization proposals across the nation have been turned down by the electorate. Certain patterns have become clear in these defeats. The suburban voters are almost always pitted against the central city electorate. The vote of the former has repeatedly spelled the death knell for local governmental reform.

Other alignments for and against governmental reorganization are also apparent. Republican precincts generally are more anti-reform than are Democratic precincts. Similarly, black precincts usually give a larger negative vote than do white precincts.[6] Although a detailed analysis of governmental reorganization referenda has not been attempted to date, the voting behavior described in these two paragraphs has been so consistent that it can clearly be referred to as a "pattern."[7]

Table 1 shows that political party registration did not play a major role in either the Duval or the Hillsborough referendum. Both counties are unusually Democratic, even for this normally Democratic state.

Table 1. Duval and Hillsborough County
party registration by place of residence

Party	DUVAL			HILLSBOROUGH		
	City %	Suburbs %	Total %	City %	Suburbs %	Total %
Democratic	95.3	90.3	92.4	94.8	87.1	89.5
Republican	4.7	9.7	7.6	5.2	12.9	10.5

Source: *Report of the Secretary of the State of Florida, passim.*

Given the size of the majorities in the two referenda and the percentage of Republicans in both counties, it can be assumed that party registration had a minimal effect, if any, on the outcome of the referenda.

The suburb-central city conflict did not materialize in the Duval referendum (Table 2). The suburbs had only a 3.6 percent more negative vote than did the central city. However, the national pattern of strong suburban hostility toward this type of governmental reorganization was definitely followed in Hillsborough County. Only 11.4 percent of the suburban ballots supported the proposed Hillsborough charter, while 41.2 percent of the central city vote was cast in favor of the document.

This deviation from the national pattern of massive suburbanite opposition to reform on the part of the Jacksonville suburban voters

Table 2. Two-county referenda vote by place of residence

Vote	DUVAL			HILLSBOROUGH		
	City %	Suburbs %	Total %	City %	Suburbs %	Total %
For	66.8	63.2	64.5	41.2	11.4	28.4
Against	33.2	36.8	35.5	58.8	88.6	71.6

*Data for Tables 2, 3, and 4 are from the Office of the Supervisor of Elections of Duval County, Florida, and the Office of the Supervisor of Elections of Hillsborough, Florida, *Official Records, passim.*

Table 3.   Duval and Hillsborough County
registered voters by race and place of residence

Race	DUVAL			HILLSBOROUGH		
	City %	Suburbs %	Total %	City %	Suburbs %	Total %
Black	40.0	9.3	21.7	14.3	5.5	11.4
White	60.0	90.7	78.3	85.7	94.5	88.6

goes far in explanation of the unexpected Duval victory. Why did the anticipated suburban negativism fail to materialize?

Much of the explanation can be seen in terms of race. Table 3 shows that in Duval County 40 percent of the central city voters were black. Given the normal lower registration rate for blacks, it can be assumed, in the absence of precise census figures, that approximately one-half of the Jacksonville population was black. Thus, blacks had a potential for political power in, or even possible political control of, the Duval County central city. Since the Jacksonville suburbs are, for the most part, dormitory-oriented, many of the white suburbanites faced the possibility of having their major area of work and recreation under black domination within the next decade. A consolidated county-wide government would not permit this possibility. In Hillsborough County the central city electorate was less than 15 percent black. The race issue did not serve as a counterbalance for the normal suburban desire to maintain political independence and low taxes; the expected large suburban anti-reorganization vote (88.6 percent) was cast.

Table 4 indicates that the anticipated black opposition to the proposed charters did appear. Row 7 of Table 4 shows the difference between the negative vote of those precincts in which at least 95 percent of the electorate was black (Row 1) and those precincts in which at least 95 percent of the electorate was white (Row 6).

In both counties the black central city negative vote was greater than the white negative vote. The black suburban negative vote was slightly less than their white counterparts' anti-reorganization vote in both Duval County (−3.1 percent) and Hillsborough County (−.1 percent).

In light of the national voting patterns of blacks on governmental reorganization, and the fact that blacks would lose whatever potential for central city control they possessed, why was the total black vote only 3.8 percent more negative than the total white vote in Duval County? The council membership plan of the proposed charter offers a partial explanation.

The new city council is made up of nineteen members, fourteen of whom are elected by district. The council district boundaries, drawn before the referendum, assured blacks of at least a minimum

Table 4. Two-county anti-reorganization negative vote by race

Precincts by racial composition	DUVAL			HILLSBOROUGH		
	City %	Suburbs %	Total %	City %	Suburbs %	Total %
100–95% Black	41.5 (22)	35.3 (6)	40.1 (28)	89.8 (1)	89.5 (1)	89.7 (2)
94–50% Black	42.4 (6)	52.0 (1)	43.8 (7)	84.2 (10)	— (0)	84.2 (10)
49–25% Black	37.5 (5)	58.8 (4)	46.9 (9)	79.6 (6)	95.8 (4)	85.7 (10)
Average[a]	41.0 (33)	43.0 (11)	41.5 (44)	82.9 (17)	93.7 (5)	85.4 (22)
25–5% Black	42.1 (6)	41.3 (15)	41.6 (21)	71.8 (9)	91.0 (2)	75.3 (11)
White[b]	31.8 (39)	38.4 (83)	36.3 (122)	56.4 (50)	89.6 (29)	68.5 (79)
Difference Rows 1 & 6	+9.7	–3.1	+3.8	+33.4	–.1	+21.2

Note: Figures in parentheses indicate the number of precincts in each category.

[a]Average of all precincts in which blacks equalled 25 percent or more of the registered voters.

[b]Less than 5 percent black.

of political power. In addition, charter provisions for a decennial reapportionment of council districts and a charter prohibition against gerrymandering are likely to favor the rapidly expanding black population. A possibility of future black political power of undetermined strength was, apparently, traded for immediate power of limited strength in Duval County.

The Hillsborough proposal did not offer a similar immediate political gain for blacks. In that county black precincts had an 89.7 percent anti-reorganization vote, i.e., 21.2 percent more negative than the Hillsborough white precincts. Numerous descriptive and survey-based studies appear to support this conclusion. The editors of *The Negro Education Review* noted that[8]

> the expected opposition of Jacksonville Negroes to consolidation was a flop. Negroes both in and out of the city voted in the majority for consolidation. . . .
>
> If the various commentaries of analysts are to be taken to mean anything, then it seems clear that white Jacksonville and Duval County support of consolidation was for reasons entirely different from Black Jacksonville. . . .
>
> Since 40 percent of the central city votes were Negroes, it would appear that Negroes had a potential for political power . . . The few Negro political leaders who attempted to persuade others with this argument of the future Negro potential, received no support.

The black anti-consolidation leaders argued that blacks who supported the reform movement were "selling out." The leader of this group based his argument on "the simple arithmetic that within the city *all* political candidates had to court black voters, who constituted 42% of the total; whereas under consolidation blacks would be much less important as only 19% of the total vote."[9]

The pro-consolidation leaders argued that the legislature would likely annex much of suburban Duval County to Jacksonville rather than permit the city to fall under black control.[10] Further, as the most outstanding pro-consolidation black leader stated:[11]

> I argued that such a town as Jacksonville was becoming couldn't really hope to attract industry or new business, or new blood. And that if that was the case, the black man obviously had more to lose than anybody else. All of the wealth in the community was outside the corporate limits. The young folks—black and white—were pretty much outside the corporate limits. All of the innovators and the creators were moving into the suburbs. That's where the industry and business was, except for a few little stores—and Main Street was declining. Main Street was a street of black faces and store windows, shop windows. The educated were in the suburbs and not in the corporate limits. Jacksonville was being run from! It would do me no good to be mayor of such a town as Jacksonville was becoming. There would certainly be no interest on the part of the people sitting out there in the suburbs if they were fighting coming in all the while.

Sloan and French report that the most important reason for black support was that[12]

> many black leaders saw consolidation as the lesser of two evils. The need of white consolidationists to prevent a heavy negative black vote put black leaders in a position to bargain for the best deal possible. The crucial issue was the provision in the proposed charter for a council with 14 of 19 members elected by district. Three black councilmen were assured a seat by drawing district lines to create black majorities in their districts, and they also had a chance, albeit a slim one, to win one of the five at-large seats. The tacit support of white leaders of the candidacy of certain blacks for an at-large seat was also suggested. . . .

Conclusion

Normal American conservatism concerning changes of or alterations in established forms of government, active opposition of persons and groups that are likely to lose political power as a result of reorganization, and suburban fears of higher taxes combine to make the adoption of major governmental reorganization plans difficult. The active opposition of one or more major partisan or racial groups within the community leads to rejection majorities of 70 percent or more, as in the Hillsborough referendum.

The prospects for reform are further complicated by the fact that proposals or campaigns designed to gain the support of one group will often ensure the antagonism of that group's counterpart. It appears that success at the polls demands a reorganization proposal and/or campaign that will permit all major groups involved to gain, or to think that they will gain, from the change. A non-zero-sum game, or at least a perceived non-zero-sum game, must be involved. That is, political advantage gained by one group will not mean that another group must lose politically.

A non-zero-sum game was perceived in Duval County. The central city voters gained the expanded tax base and the modernized government needed for an expansion of desired services. The white suburbs gained an assurance of political control over the city in which they must work and play. The blacks gained a degree of political influence and representation. No major group perceived an important loss for itself. More than 64 percent of those voting supported the Duval charter.[13]

Notes

1. Jeffery K. Hadden, Louis H. Masotti, and Calvin J. Larson, eds., *Metropolis in Crisis: Social and Political Perspective* (Itasca, Ill.: F. E. Peacock Publishers, Inc., 1967), p. vi.

2. For an examination of some of the factors involved in such voter rejection, see: Advisory Commission on Intergovernmental Relations, *Factors Affecting Voter Reactions to Governmental Reorganization,* Report M-15 (Washington, D. C.: U. S. Government Printing Office, 1962); Edward C. Banfield, "The Politics of Metropolitan Area Organization," *Midwest Journal of Political Science,* vol. 1 (1957), pp. 77–91; John C. Bollens, and Henry J. Schmandt, *The Metropolis: Its People, Politics, and Economic Life,* (2nd edition; New York: Harper & Row, Publishers, 1970), pp. 47–70, 196–225, and 373–396; Scott Greer, *Metropolitics: A Study of Political Culture* (New York: John Wiley & Sons, Inc., 1963); Oliver P. Williams, *et. al., Suburban Differences and Metropolitan Policies* (Philadelphia: University of Pennsylvania Press, 1965); and the numerous case studies on specific reorganization campaigns.

3. Banfield, *op. cit.,* pp. 87–89.

4. See, for example, Greer, *Metropolitics, op. cit.;* Brett W. Hawkins, *Nashville Metro: The Politics of City-County Consolidation* (Nashville: Vanderbilt University Press, 1966); Richard Martin, *Consolidation: Jacksonville–Duval County* (Jacksonville: Crawford Publishing Co., 1968); and Lee Sloan and Robert M. French, "Race and Governmental Consolidation in Jacksonville," *The Negro Educational Review,* vol. 21 (April–July 1970), pp. 72–78.

5. William N. Cassella, Jr., "Jacksonville and Duval County Unite," *National Civic Review,* vol. 56 (October 1967), p. 532. For a more detailed review of these two reorganization proposals, see Parris N. Glendening and John Wesley White, "Local Government Reorganization Referenda in

Florida: An Acceptance and A Rejection," *The Florida State University Governmental Research Bulletin*, vol. 5, no. 2 (March 1968).

6. A word of caution must be added at this point. We may be observing a spurious relationship since suburbs are predominantly white and Republican. A more sophisticated analysis of the referenda is obviously needed.

7. See 2 and 4, above.

8. "Jacksonville and Its New Government: Defining the Situation," *The Negro Educational Review*, vol. 21 (April–July 1970), pp. 52–53.

9. Sloan and French, *op. cit.*, p. 73.

10. *Ibid.*, pp. 73–75; and Martin, *op. cit., passim*.

11. Quoted in Sloan and French, p. 74.

12. *Ibid.* The authors refer to this action as "benign gerrymandering."

13. It must be noted that a non-zero-sum game is not always possible. Banfield concluded his study on the politics of reorganization with the observation that the "facts suggest that for many years to come it will be difficult or impossible to integrate local governments where the two-party system operates. Even if the proportion of Republicans declines sharply in the suburbs, metropolitan area government north of the Mason-Dixon line would almost everywhere be Republican government. In effect, advocates of consolidation schemes are asking the Democrats to give up their control of the central cities or, at least, to place it in jeopardy." Banfield, *op. cit.*, p. 86. This conclusion is supported by the observation that all of the post-1945 reorganization plans for area-wide government that have been accepted by the voters have been in the one-party South where non-zero-sum games are possible.

Suggested Readings:
Metropolitan Reorganization

ADVISORY COMMISSION ON INTERGOVERNMENTAL RELATIONS. *Alternative Approaches to Governmental Reorganization in Metropolitan Areas*. Report A-11. Washington, D. C.: U. S. Government Printing Office, 1962. Also *Factors Affecting Voter Reactions to Governmental Reorganization in Metropolitan Areas*. Report M-14. Washington, D. C.: U. S. Government Printing Office, 1962. Two concise descriptive accounts of alternatives available for metropolitan reorganization and the reasons why the voters consistently reject most major reorganization alternatives.

BOLLENS, JOHN C., and HENRY J. SCHMANDT. *The Metropolis: Its People, Politics, and Economic Life*. Second Edition. New York: Harper & Row, Publishers, 1970. Extremely comprehensive discussion of the problem and results of governmental fragmentation, possible alternative systems, the politics of reorganization, and other forces, such as national government actions, that are likely to influence the structure of metropolitan America.

DYE, THOMAS R., and BRETT W. HAWKINS (eds.) *Politics in the Metropolis: A Reader in Conflict and Cooperation.* Second Edition. Columbus, Ohio: Charles E. Merrill Publishing Company, 1971. One of the best anthologies available on the topic.

MARTIN, ROSCOE C. *Metropolis in Transition: Local Government Adaptation to Changing Urban Needs.* Washington, D. C.: Housing and Home Finance Agency, 1963. Martin's taxonomy of procedural and structural adaptive devices for dealing with the fragmented metropolis is still definitive. Helpful synopsis published in *The National Civil Review*, vol. 52 (1963), pp. 302–307, 316, 363–367, 371.

SOFEN, EDWARD. *The Miami Metropolitan Experiment.* Second Edition. New York: Doubleday & Company, Inc., 1966. One of the best case studies of metropolitan reorganization available.

OSTROM, VINCENT, CHARLES M. TIEBOUT, and ROBERT WARREN. "The Organization of Government in Metropolitan Areas: A Theoretical Inquiry." *American Political Science Review*, vol. 55 (December 1961), pp. 831–842. Recognized already as a classic description of practical and theoretical advantages of the fragmented metropolis.

5/Finance:
Who Pays?

The mayor of a large city, testifying before the National
Commission on Urban Problems (the Douglas Commission),
observed "Our problems are financial ones. I have sometimes
characterized the three major problems as being money,
finances, and revenue."

In many ways the mayor's flippant statement was very
close to the truth. At the very base of such problem areas
as education, housing, and transportation is the problem
of finance. Even the race problem is largely one of finance if
one sees it as unemployment, underemployment, inadequate
housing and education, legal and social discrimination,
and inequity.

There are several major questions that must be answered
when discussing state and local finances. First, of course,
is how much money. The governments of the United States
could carry on with considerably less funds than they
currently receive *if* they were to perform considerably fewer
functions; however, we as a nation have decided the
government should intervene to ensure adequate housing,
education, transportation, and other basic services. The
answer to how much, then, is more, much more, than is
presently available to the states and localities.

Second is the question of the source of new revenues.
Are lower jurisdictions to rely increasingly on intergovermental
transfer of funds from higher jurisdictions as was discussed
in Part 2? Are more functions to be passed upward? Is
there a need, as the Douglas Commission states, for wholesale
tax reorganization at the state and local levels? The
Commission noted a particular necessity for moving away
from the major reliance on regressive, inflexible property
taxes at the local level.

Third is the increasingly serious question of how to deal with economic disparities in the political system. Ira Sharkansky discusses the disparities among regions and among states. Accommodation has been achieved in this area through the use of federal grants-in-aid, regional spending patterns, and so forth. Accommodation to the disparities between central city and suburb is not so likely to occur. As both the Advisory Commission on Intergovernmental Relations and the National Commission on Urban Problems point out, the economic disparities between central city and suburb are the major cause of financial difficulties in metropolitan America. The problem is not the lack of economic resources in most metropolitan areas; it is the distribution of these resources.

Finally, there is the question of how to ensure that state and local decision-makers maintain control of the budget, their chief instrument of public policy. As Michael R. Stone and Parris N. Glendening note, certain institutional factors severely limit the options open to these officials. Besides the obvious implications for democratic theory, one can ask how these decision-makers are to respond to rising public demands if the chief vehicle for change, the budget, becomes increasingly beyond their control. These points will surely come to mind again in the section on urban violence.

John C. Bollens analyzes the cities' problems as a combination of structure, inadequate funds, and uneven distribution of resources. He calls for a comprehensive reordering of the governmental and economic structure of metropolitan America.

The statistics so often used in these articles can distort one's perception of the reality and immediacy of the urban fiscal crisis. The Advisory Commission on Intergovernmental Relations cautions on this point: commenting on Dr. Samuel Johnson's observation, "When a man knows he is going to be hanged in a fortnight, it concentrates his mind wonderfully," the Commission wrote that[1]

> unfortunately, most of the critical problems in urban areas are more in the nature of a quiet or creeping crisis. The problems that face our urban communities are too often illustrated by long-term trend lines: the economic decline of central cities, the physical and social disintegration of slum areas, increasingly fragmented and overlapping patterns of government, urban sprawl, housing problems and school problems in all parts of the urban complex,

inadequate transportation facilities, and growing confusion and ugliness where there should be beauty. Yet, behind these statistics and population patterns, are individual personal and community tragedies.

One more point should be made. The political-legal battle of matters of state and local finance is often directed at a limited, specific type of expenditure proposal rather than at the more general questions of revenue disparities among jurisdictions or new sources of revenues. The last two selections in Part 5, which concern public support for parochial schools, illustrate this type of specific controversy.

Note

1. Advisory Commission on Intergovernmental Relations. *Metropolitan America: Challenge to Federalism*. Report M-31. (Washington, D. C.: U. S. Government Printing Office, 1966), p. vii.

IRA SHARKANSKY

The Regional Affiliation of States and Government Spending

The books and articles of V. O. Key, Frank Munger, Duane Lockard, Frank Jonas, Thomas Donnelly, and John Fenton have described at length the practices of political parties and electoral processes as they operate in the states of the South, the Middle West, the border states, New England, the Rocky Mountain area, and the Greater West.[1] Daniel Elazar has considered regional patterns in political culture and traces these patterns to the "geology" created by initial settlements and transcontinental migrations from these settlements.[2] The data of the University of Michigan Survey Research Center document regional differences in attitudes toward public affairs.[3] The work of Harvey S. Perloff testifies to regional economic patterns that produce differences in personal well-being and in the character of industry and agriculture.[4] Unfortunately for the present analysis, none of these publications deals explicitly with regional variations

Ira Sharkansky, *Spending in the American States*, American Politics Research Series (Chicago: Rand McNally & Company, 1968), 93–95, 99–105. Reprinted by permission.

in government expenditures or other aspects of public policy. Most of the work by political scientists has focused on party-electoral aspects of politics in a single region. While the Elazar and Perloff volumes have considered a variety of regions across the United States, they have not dealt systematically with the policies of state and local governments. As a result, one is left only with the impression that differences in economics, politics, and historical experiences that are common to neighboring states might leave their impact on state government expenditures.

* * *

The contemporary practices of state officials, as well as the residue of history and economics, may have an impact on regional differences in spending. There is some evidence that state administrators and legislators consciously adjust their programs and levels of spending to their perceptions of regional norms. State officials feel that neighboring states have problems and resources that resemble their own. Many officials also believe that they are competing with other states in their region for new industries. Both of these beliefs work in the direction of similar levels of taxation and spending among neighboring states.

As part of a survey among budget officers of 67 major agencies in the southern states of Florida, Georgia, Kentucky, and Mississippi,[5] an attempt was made to identify the states that served as the budgeteers' reference group. In this survey, the following question was asked:

> *Have you or any of your colleagues contacted officials in other states in an attempt to learn how they deal with a particular situation that you have encountered in your work?*

When a budget officer answered in the affirmative, he was then asked:

> *What states do you feel are the best sources of information?*

The 67 respondents made 198 nominations of states that were among the "best sources of information." Eighty-seven percent of their nominations were in the region that includes the 11 states of the Confederacy and the border states of Delaware, Maryland, Kentucky, West Virginia, and Oklahoma. Thirty-five percent of the nominations were states that bordered directly on the states of the respondents. It is conceivable that southern officials are more parochial in their references than are officials in other regions. Nevertheless, these nominations suggest that the regional identifications of administrators may help to create similarities in the expenditures of neighboring states.

* * *

There are clear regional differences in the expenditures of American states. This is made evident by the data of Table I, which expresses the average expenditures of states in each region as a percentage of the average state expenditures over the nation as a whole.

Table I. Mean expenditures per capita of states in each region as percentages of national means, by major field, 1962

		Total	Education	Highways	Public Welfare
North		.93	.82	.92	.88
New England		.99	.65	1.12	1.05
Mid-Atlantic	North	.95	.99	.75	.73
Great Lakes	and	.85	.84	.87	.81
Northeast	East	.93	.69	.95	.95
North Central		.89	.83	.98	.88
Plains		.92	.82	1.07	.92
Transmississippi		1.10	1.16	1.16	1.09
Mountains	West	1.18	1.24	1.47	1.00
Far West		1.33	1.46	1.15	1.23
Transplains		1.24	1.40	1.27	1.09
Southwest		1.08	1.33	.93	1.34
Southeast	South	.92	.98	.84	1.02
South		.96	1.03	.86	1.06

		Health and Hospitals	Natural Resources	Public Safety	General Government
North		1.25	.74	1.11	1.07
New England		1.40	.99	1.24	1.31
Mid-Atlantic	North	1.40	.58	1.15	2.86
Great Lakes	and	.91	.59	.93	.73
Northeast	East	1.35	.85	1.13	1.23
North Central		.94	.84	.88	.73
Plains		.95	1.01	.85	.75
Transmississippi		.87	1.31	1.08	1.09
Mountains	West	.84	1.76	1.07	1.25
Far West		1.00	1.71	1.71	1.59
Transplains		.85	1.63	1.30	1.40
Southwest		.64	.87	.84	1.03
Southeast	South	.89	.83	.72	.76
South		.96	.78	.81	1.19

States in northern and eastern regions (including states north of the Ohio River and as far west as the Plains) tend to score low on expenditures per capita for education, public welfare, and natural resources, but high on expenditures for health and hospitals, public safety, and general government. The low state expenditures for education may reflect the regional emphasis on local financing for that service, plus the relatively high reliance on private schools (especially Roman Catholic parochial schools). Low spending for natural resources may be a product of high population congestion in most of these regions and also the result of relatively little governmental attention given to resource development. High expenditures for public safety, especially in the New England and Mid-Atlantic states, reflect well-developed state police forces in those areas.

Western regions (Transplains, Mountain, Far West, Trans-mississippi, and Southwest) score high on most expenditures, especially in the fields of education, highways, and natural resources. The large highway budgets in relation to population may reflect the diffusion of population throughout the western states, as well as the difficult terrain that roads must traverse. The natural-resource spending of western states could reflect programs to develop water resources, forestry, and recreational opportunities. The high spending for education in the West reflects the tendency to rely heavily on state funds for the support of public elementary and secondary schools. In addition, the large educational expenditures may also be the product of the well-developed systems of public higher education.

In the fields that account for the bulk of state spending per capita, i.e., education, highways, public welfare, and health and hospitals, southern regions show no consistent deviations from national averages. However, the southern regions score consistently low on state spending for public safety. This finding is consistent with the heavy emphasis upon local control of law enforcement which is found throughout the South and which produces strong county sheriffs and extensive systems of county prisons and work camps.

Along with these regional patterns, there are, nevertheless, marked variations in the expenditures of neighboring states. Table II shows that Vermont scores in the highest quartile of total expenditures per capita, while most states of its region score low. In the South, Kentucky and Louisiana score in the highest quartile of total expenditures, while Florida scores in the lowest quartile. In the Southwest, more than $100 per capita separate the spending of the neighboring states of Texas and New Mexico. Table III indicates the degree of uniformity that exists in the expenditures of states in each region. It lists the regional coefficients of variability (i.e., the standard deviation divided by the mean of each region's expenditures). *Low coefficients indicate high uniformity in spending.*

States in the Far West have shown the greatest uniformity in expenditures during recent years. The coefficients of variability for this area are .10 to .14 for the 1957–1965 period. Among regions with more than ten states, Transplains and Southeast have shown the greatest homogeneity in spending. States of some regions show great variety in spending. Even small regional groups (*e.g.*, the five states of the Mid-Atlantic) have coefficients as high as .41.

When the coefficients of variability for each region are compared with the coefficients for the nation as a whole, they provide some support for the notion that regional norms influence the level of state spending. Throughout the 1903–1965 period, coefficients generally indicate greater uniformity of spending at the regional level than in the nation as a whole. The relative uniformity of regional spending levels suggests that budget-makers are more likely to follow the

Table II. Total expenditures per capita, by states and regions, 1962

Regions	Expenditures per Capita
NEW ENGLAND	
Maine	$163.19
New Hampshire	151.71
Vermont	255.10
Massachusetts	159.58
Rhode Island	169.71
Connecticut	182.12
MID-ATLANTIC	
New York	176.46
New Jersey	110.47
Pennsylvania	145.92
Maryland	179.28
Delaware	246.53
SOUTHEAST	
Virginia	141.56
West Virginia	180.73
North Carolina	157.52
South Carolina	141.80
Georgia	156.20
Florida	135.79
Kentucky	209.25
Tennessee	142.97
Alabama	164.19
Mississippi	168.34
Arkansas	155.14
Louisiana	251.74
GREAT LAKES	
Ohio	130.34
Indiana	144.87
Illinois	131.33
Michigan	195.87
Wisconsin	168.92
PLAINS	
Minnesota	182.76
Iowa	161.25
Missouri	140.61
North Dakota	214.29
South Dakota	186.57
Nebraska	125.49
Kansas	160.06
MOUNTAINS	
Montana	196.43
Wyoming	283.69
Colorado	192.13
Idaho	188.46
Utah	208.60
SOUTHWEST	
Oklahoma	203.64
Texas	137.21
New Mexico	238.68
Arizona	205.45
FAR WEST	
Washington	249.62
Oregon	221.18
Nevada	277.06
California	218.30

Table III. Coefficients of variability for
total state expenditures per capita, by region

		1965	1962	1957	1952	1947	1942
North		.27	.23	.25	.29	.18	.17
New England		.18	.21	.18	.05	.11	.14
Mid-Atlantic	North	.41	.29	.35	.42	.17	.24
Great Lakes	and	.18	.18	.21	.22	.24	.13
Northeast	East	.22	.23	.23	.06	.13	.13
North Central		.20	.18	.19	.21	.17	.14
Plains		.21	.18	.18	.20	.10	.15
Transmississippi		.25	.21	.24	.23	.30	.23
Mountains		.23	.19	.19	.14	.11	.08
Far West	West	.10	.11	.14	.11	.27	.15
Transplains		.17	.15	.18	.15	.20	.12
Southwest		.27	.22	.28	.25	.35	.32
Southeast	South	.16	.20	.26	.25	.19	.30
South		.25	.21	.29	.33	.22	.31
U.S.		.27	.23	.26	.28	.28	.27

		1939	1929	1924	1918	1913	1903
North		.20	.44	.25	.30	.29	.41
New England		.06	.44	.15	.22	.24	.40
Mid-Atlantic	North	.27	.45	.27	.26	.17	.16
Great Lakes	and	.26	.26	.30	.33	.38	.24
Northeast	East	.14	.41	.15	.31	.24	.41
North Central		.27	.36	.43	.32	.35	.26
Plains		.26	.38	.46	.34	.37	.29
Transmississippi		.26	.38	.43	.37	.46	.75
Mountains		.17	.34	.33	.24	.19	.21
Far West	West	.18	.46	.43	.41	.55	.38
Transplains		.17	.36	.38	.31	.41	.39
Southwest		.20	.33	.36	.52	.43	.50
Southeast	South	.34	.22	.19	.27	.33	.43
South		.39	.40	.42	.31	.44	.41
U.S.		.32	.41	.44	.43	.45	.50

spending examples of neighboring states (as perhaps other officials
in the state government follow the examples of their neighbors in
taxation and levels of public services) than they are to look toward the
activity of "national leaders." This finding complements the discovery
of regionalism in the "states of reference" nominated by the state
budget officers who are mentioned in the introduction to this chapter.
It appears that state officials judge their own performance in the light
of what their neighbors are doing. State officials often judge that their
regional partners must meet economic and social problems that are
most similar to their own. When moved by a sense of following
leadership, state officials probably view the regional leader (rather
than the national leader) as representing the target of their own
development. Regional neighbors are likely to have similar service and
spending levels; thus, following a leader is less demanding within
regions than between regions.

Table IV. Ratios of actual total spending per capita to spending estimated on basis of 48-state regression model, by region, 1962

Region		Ratios
North		.99
New England		.99
Mid-Atlantic	North	1.01
Great Lakes	and	1.00
Northeast	East	1.00
North Central		1.00
Plains		1.00
Transmississippi		1.02
Mountains		1.00
Far West	West	1.00
Transplains		1.15
Southwest		.85
Southeast	South	.98
South		.97

Regional Expenditures
and the Correlates of Expenditures

Despite differences in spending levels, the major factors relating to spending are similar in almost every region. Table IV indicates the degree to which expenditures in each region respond to items that influence state expenditures throughout the nation. The table lists the ratios between actual spending in each region and the level of spending estimated for each region by the nationwide model of the expenditure system for 1962. Twelve of the fourteen ratios in Table IV are within 3 percent of perfect correspondence between actual and estimated expenditures. In no case does the spending of a region vary by more than 15 percent from the spending estimated by the 48-state model.

Notes

*This chapter has been adapted from the author's article "Regional Patterns in the Expenditures of American States" in the December 1967 issue of *Western Political Quarterly*.

1. V. O. Key, *Southern Politics in State and Nation* (New York: Alfred A. Knopf, 1949); Duane Lockard, *New England State Politics* (Princeton, N.J.: Princeton University Press, 1959); John H. Fenton, *Midwest Politics* (New York: Holt, Rinehart & Winston, 1966); John H. Fenton, *Politics in the Border States* (New Orleans: Hauser Press, 1957); Frank Munger, ed., *American State Politics: Reading for Comparative Analysis* (New York: Thomas Y. Crowell Co., 1966); Frank H. Jonas, *Western Politics* (Salt Lake City: University of Utah Press, 1961); and Thomas R. Donnelly, *Rocky Mountain Politics* (Albuquerque: University of New Mexico Press, 1940).

2. Daniel J. Elazar, *American Federalism: A View from the States* (New York: Thomas Y. Crowell Co., 1966).

3. See V. O. Key, *Public Opinion and American Democracy* (New York: Alfred A. Knopf, 1961), especially chapt. 5; and Angus Campbell *et. al.*, *The American Voter* (New York: John Wiley & Sons, 1960), especially chapt. 16.

4. Harvey S. Perloff *et. al.*, *Regions, Resources, and Economic Growth* (Baltimore: Johns Hopkins University Press, 1960), and Lawrence A. Leonard, "State and Local Governmental Revenue Structures—A National and Regional Analysis," *National Tax Journal*, 11 (March 1958): 67–77.

5. A "major agency" was defined as one having a budget of at least $1 million during the year (1966) of the survey.

COMMISSION ON
INTERGOVERNMENTAL RELATIONS

Restoring Fiscal Balance
in the Federal System

References to "the urban fiscal crisis" are commonplace. In practically any issue of big city newspapers there are reports about critical budgetary and tax problems that face the central city and other local governments in the metropolis. One mayor, testifying before the National Commission on Urban Problems in 1967, was only half joking when he observed:

> Our problems are financial ones. I have sometimes characterized the three major problems as being money, finances, and revenue.

Yet it is nearly as commonplace that major urban areas account for most of the Nation's wealth and income. Metropolitan areas, having but two-thirds of the total population, account for:

> More than four-fifths (82 percent) of savings and loan deposits;
> Four-fifths (80 percent) all bank deposits;
> More than three-fourths (77 percent) of the value added by manufacturing:
> Three-fourths (75 percent) of all personal income in the Nation;
> More than seven-tenths (71 percent) of all retail sales; and
> Seven-tenths (70 percent) of all values officially assessed for property taxation.

Personal income per person averages half again more in metropolitan areas than elsewhere in the United States—in 1966, $3,314 compared with $2,236 per person. Earning rates for various kinds of employment

Advisory Commission on Intergovernmental Relations, *Urban America and The Federal System*. Report M-47. Washington, D.C.: U. S. Government Printing Office, October, 1969. Footnotes abridged.

are also typically higher in SMSA's—for example, by 28 percent for local government employees in 1962, and by 31 percent for manufacturing workers in 1965.

Furthermore, nearly all the Nation's recent population growth has occurred in metropolitan areas, a result of both natural increase and net in-migration.

Why a Local Fiscal Crisis?

But if it is clear—as so many measures attest—that metropolitan areas are so typically "better off," it is no less true that most of the problems besetting urban America show up most sharply in these areas. The answer to this seeming paradox is to be found in a growing fiscal imbalance within our federal system—a disorder that is most apparent among the jurisdictions in metropolitan areas in general and in the dire fiscal plight of many of the nation's central cities in particular. This intergovernmental fiscal imbalance is the product of many factors—conditions that either increase the "tilt" or prevent a restoration of balance:

- A progressive political fragmentation of the tax base of most metropolitan areas—a fiscal splintering that places powerful constraints on the ability of local jurisdictions to raise revenue and creates a radical mismatch of resources between the "have" and "have not" jurisdictions within the same metropolitan area.
- Misallocation of responsibility for financing education and public welfare programs—a factor that causes a severe tax overload for many jurisdictions. This year the local tax base will be forced to underwrite over half of the estimated $32 billion bill for public elementary and secondary education and approximately $1.5 billion for public welfare costs.
- The constant local revenue crisis caused by the fact that urban expenditure demands and especially big city demands consistently outpace both the growth in the nation's income and the "automatic" increase in local taxes.
- A lopsided Federal aid system, under which, despite its steadily growing fiscal superiority, the Federal Government has failed to develop a balanced system of support for State and local government. Heavy Federal emphasis on narrow categorical-type aid has unduly restricted State and local budgetary powers while intensive Federal use of the personal income tax has discouraged effective State use of this prime revenue source.
- Faulty State aid systems that often aggravate rather than compensate for the growing fiscal disparities among local governments within the metropolitan areas.

- A defective local property tax, the shortcomings of which (unequal assessments, regressive incidence and adverse land use effects) become increasingly apparent as local governments are forced to make more intensive use of this levy.
- Limited revenue potential to be derived from local nonproperty taxes and user charges due to the limited jurisdictional reach of local governments coupled with their extreme vulnerability to interlocal competition. These limitations, particularly in metropolitan areas, severely constrict the possibilities of any particular local government from mounting an "operation bootstrap," of which rugged individualists still like to dream.

Countervailing economic and political trends

While each of these factors has made its contribution to the general state of fiscal imbalance, two countervailing trends—one economic and the other political—merit special attention. These trends are reflected most dramatically in two fiscal facts; with each passing year the fiscal supremacy of the National Government becomes more apparent and the fiscal plight of many of America's central cities becomes more desperate. The economic trend—the growing interdependency of the nation—gives the Federal tax collector, equipped with the most productive tax and the broadest geographical reach, the best opportunity to tap the growing affluence of the national economy. The political trend—the progressive subdivision of the metropolitan area into more and still more governmental units—works in precisely the opposite direction. It both constricts the tax reach of the local jurisdictions and saddles the "have nots" (usually the central cities) with enormously disproportionate burdens.

Fiscal mismatch

To put the urban fiscal problem another way, growing economic unity is inexorably forcing upwards the "revenue cream" generated by our expanding economy. It can be tapped fairly effectively by the States but most effectively by the Federal Government. On the other hand, growing political splintering, based upon popular attachment to local home rule, forces massive and disproportionate expenditure burdens to be borne by a fragmented and defective local property tax base in general and on a severely overloaded central city base in particular.

This growing fiscal imbalance takes on an even sharper focus when given a State government dimension. The more opposition the State throws up against those who would encapsulate themselves and their taxable possessions within suburban jurisdictions and the more willingness the State demonstrates to assume responsibility for financing the high cost intergovernmental programs (such as education), the less threatening becomes the local fiscal climate.

This critical State role is reflected in the sharply contrasting fiscal conditions of two cities—desperate Newark, New Jersey, with the highest local tax rate among the nation's major cities and affluent Honolulu, Hawaii, with the lowest property tax rate. Newark's metropolitan tax base is badly sub-divided, the central city population is approximately 50 percent black, and the city's tax base is required to meet most of the cost of public education and a relatively large share of welfare costs. In contrast, there is virtually no splintering off of the Honolulu metropolitan tax base, and the State underwrites almost all the cost of public education and welfare.

Fiscal consequences

The worst features of the mismatch of needs and resources are now clearly apparent in the growing social, economic, and fiscal disparities among local jurisdictions in the great metropolitan areas of the Northeast and Midwest. At one extreme are the "big losers"—usually the central cities—"stuck" with an extremely anemic tax base and confronted with rapidly mounting expenditure demands incident to the governing, educating and "welfaring" an increasing proportion of relatively poor, black families. At the other extreme are the "big winners"—those white suburban jurisdictions wealthy enough to be able to underwrite a superior public educational system with a below average tax effort.

The political-fiscal dilemma

The ultimate cause of this radical mismatch of needs and resources is political—State and Federal policy-makers are unable to muster sufficient support necessary either to prevent this head-on collision of economic and political forces or to provide sufficient compensation for damages to the local victims. This inability to engineer consent, in turn, can be traced to a political-fiscal dilemma. A strong tradition of local home rule ordinarily blocks any attempt to bring needs and resources into better alignment via the administrative centralization approach—i.e., creation of a metro-type government of the shifting of all responsibility for certain high cost functions such as education or welfare to the State or National Government. On the other hand, popular support for a "Puritan" ethic that discourages the divorce of tax and expenditure responsibility ordinarily stands in way of a "fiscal" decentralization solution—i.e., the transfer of Federal funds to State and local government on a "no strings" basis or for State assumption of virtually all the responsibility for financing education while leaving wide policy discretion in the hands of local school boards.

Political Balkanization of the Metropolitan Area

Prior to the great post-World War II exodus of the middle and upper income families to suburbia, our system for governing urban America appeared to conform to Aristotle's view of the "most perfect" way to shield the community from the perils of political extremism.

> "In every city the people are divided into three sorts: the very rich, the very poor and those who are between them. . . . The most perfect political community must be amongst those who are in the middle rank, and those states are best instituted wherein these are a large and more respectable part, if possible, than both the other; or, if that cannot be, at least than either of them separate; so that being thrown into the balance it may prevent either scale from preponderating."[1]

Within the city's boundary were found the relatively few rich, the preponderate middle class, and the poor who often lived on "the other side of the tracks." The great cities of America, however, were more than social "melting pots." They were also balanced economically in the sense that they encompassed within their boundaries, virtually all of the urban area's residential, commercial, and industrial development.

Because they possessed social and economic unity, our municipalities were also generally characterized by fiscal balance. The municipality's "deficit" areas—the low-income residential areas—were offset by the "surplus" areas—the high tax producing districts associated with the central business area, the industrial section, and the high income residential neighborhoods.

By far the most important social function performed by the great "balanced" municipalities was political in the Aristotelian sense—that of keeping the public peace by moderating the competing demands of the various classes that comprise the urban body politic.

The rise of the lopsided communities

In many of our metropolitan areas the twin forces of urban expansion and social segregation have combined to burst the shell of the old "balanced" community and in the process have profoundly altered the social and political character of the urban municipality. Whereas the old municipality was socially and economically balanced, the new municipalities are "lopsided," i.e., the wealthy estate and industrial enclaves and the upper, middle and lower income bedroom communities. While the sprawling and subdivided metropolitan area still has a central or "core" city, typically it is becoming smaller, poorer and blacker when compared to the burgeoning economy of white suburbia.

The political leadership of the old "balanced" municipality

was under constant pressure to blur and moderate the conflicting demands of the urban rich, poor and middle class. In contrast, the leaders of the new "lopsided" municipalities are virtually forced by their narrow-gauged constituencies to sharpen and reinforce the divisive elements within our uptight urban society.

This political transformation becomes even more ominous because our highly decentralized system of government historically has relied almost entirely on the cohesive powers of the municipality to hold together the highly segregated components of our urban population. Moreover, the nation has leaned heavily on the local tax base in general and the property tax in particular for financing its domestic needs. It is ironic that the political balkanization of our urban areas occurs in the face of a growing need for social cohesion in an increasingly interdependent society.

The tendency for metropolitan areas to split politically along their income and racial seams is most apparent in the Northeast and Midwest, and least noticeable in the Southwest. More and more rare in the Northeast quadrant of the United States, is the large city that still encompasses within its boundaries most of the residential areas occupied by the white middle class let alone those of the wealthy. In striking contrast stand Houston, San Antonio, and Phoenix. Their vigorous annexation policies may be prompted by the spectacle of the older Eastern cities slowly being choked to death by the "white noose" of suburban municipalities.

Grim fiscal outlook for central cities

A few successful annexations, however, cannot mask the grim fiscal prospects for most of the nation's great cities. The findings of a recent Advisory Commission study of metropolitan fiscal disparities clearly substantiate the widespread belief that most of our major cities are now in a desperate situation.

1. The central cities, particularly those located in the industrial Northeast and Midwest, are in the throes of a deepening fiscal crisis. On the one hand, they are confronted with the need to satisfy rapidly growing expenditure requirements triggered by the rising number of "high cost" citizens. On the other hand, their tax resources are increasing at a decreasing rate (and in some cases actually declining), a reflection of the exodus of middle and high income families and of business firms from the central city to suburbia.
2. The concentration of high cost citizens in the central city is dramatically underscored by public welfare statistics. For example, 27 percent of Maryland's population is located in Baltimore, yet 72 percent of Maryland's AFDC expenditures is to be found in

that city. By the same token, Boston, with 14 percent of Massachusetts' population, accounts for 40 percent of that State's AFDC expenditure.

3. A clear disparity in tax burden is evident between central city and outside central city. Local taxes in the central cities are 7.5 percent of income; outside the central cities only 5.6 percent of income. Higher central city taxes are reinforcing the other factors that are pushing upper income families and business firms out of the central city into suburbia.

4. On the educational or "developmental" front, the central cities are falling farther behind their suburban neighbors with each passing year. In 1957 the per pupil expenditures in the 37 metropolitan areas favored the central city slightly—$312 to $303 for the suburban jurisdictions. By 1965, the suburban jurisdictions had forged far ahead—$574 to $449 for the central cities. This growing disparity between the central city and suburban school districts takes on a more ominous character in light of the fact that the central city school districts must carry a disproportionately heavy share of the educational burden—the task of educating an increasing number of "high cost" underprivileged children. Children who need education the most are receiving it the least!

5. On the municipal service or "custodial" front, the presence of "high cost" citizens, greater population density, and the need to service the needs of commuters force central cities to spend far more than most of their suburban neighbors for police and fire protection and sanitation services. The 37 largest central cities had a non-educational (municipal) outlay of $232 per capita in 1965—$100 greater than their suburban counterparts.[2]

The situation for most central cities takes on an even more dismal cast because there is little prospect for a *voluntary* solution arising from within the metropolitan area. Suburban political leaders can generally be counted upon to oppose stoutly any proposal that would call for a significant redistribution of resources such as an area-wide tax with a strong equalization twist to aid the central city. By the same token, suburban leadership can be expected to view with a jaundiced eye any major redistribution of burdens, i.e., the rezoning of suburban land to permit low income central city families to obtain public or low cost housing in suburbia.

Cracks in suburbia's picture window

Comparing the fiscal behavior of the central city with the entire suburban area, however, tends both to obscure and to distort the disparity story because it lumps together diverse suburban jurisdictions.

Anyone familiar with the fiscal landscape of suburbia is keenly aware of the fact that it does not present a uniform picture of affluence. On the contrary, suburbia fairly bristles with contrasts between rich, poor, and middle income jurisdictions.

In most metropolitan areas, the range between the most affluent and impoverished suburban jurisdiction is considerably greater than that between central city and suburbia in general. For example, elementary school districts in Cook County, Illinois, reveal a range of about 30-to-1 in their property tax base per pupil in 1964 and various studies have reported ranges of 10-to-1 or more in the per capita tax base of municipalities within various metropolitan areas.

Because they lack a diversified tax base, most of the lower to middle income residential suburbs can also expect a steady deterioration in their fiscal prospects.

> There is evidence which indicates that, as the suburban expansion grows, it is increasingly the lower middle class white collar worker and the blue collar worker who is fleeing the central city for suburbia, giving increasing rise to the demand for suburban development which caters to the economic capabilities of these groups. The composite of these trends all seems to indicate that the newly developed suburban community of the future will be developed with tax bases which fail to provide adequate fiscal capacity for the support of municipal and educational services.[3]

A few winners and many losers

Because the concept of local fiscal disparities is of necessity a relative matter, the political splintering of Urban America along income and racial lines produces its share of municipal winners as well as losers. While difficult to measure with precision, it nevertheless appears possible to detect several gradations along the disparity spectrum ranging from the big winners at one end (i.e., Scarsdale, New York, and Lake Forest, Illinois) to the big losers at the other end (Newark and East St. Louis). Most metropolitan communities can be placed in one of five categories:

1. *Highly disadvantaged*—A community that falls far short on the public service side even though it makes an extraordinary tax effort.
2. *Disadvantaged*—A community that must make an extraordinary tax effort to break even or provide an average level of public service.
3. *Balanced*—A community that can bridge the gap between resources and needs by providing an adequate level of service with an average tax effort.
4. *Advantaged*—A community that can provide a superior level of service with an average tax burden.

5. *Highly advantaged*—A community that can provide a superior level of service with a minimal tax effort.

If most or all of the communities within metropolitan areas fell in the "balanced" category there would be little cause for concern with the fiscal health of the nation's cities, or little need for State and National governments to enact fiscal equalization measures. But that is not the case. Serious widespread disparities do exist. Many of the largest central cities are in the "highly disadvantaged" category. And some of these disparities continue to grow.

Beggar thy neighbor

Ever mindful that no community within the metropolitan area "stands still" in relation to its neighbors, local policymakers are under unremitting pressure to adopt a highly aggressive policy in order to maintain or obtain a favorable competitive position. As it enters the metropolitan arena, each governmental unit has three prime weapons —the power to tax, the power to spend, and the power to determine land use.

This fiscal contest among municipalities in the same metropolitan area might be described as the local Tax and Zoning Game. In order to hold down education costs, suburban legislators are under strong temptation to use a low density approach to residential zoning. Although the one-acre suburban lots can be denounced as an example of "snob" or restrictive zoning, they are also hailed as an act of local financial prudence—the only sure way of placing a lid on school costs and property tax rates. The zoning of great stretches of suburban land for commercial and/or light industrial purposes is another example of fiscal zoning. There is always the hope that a large share of the local tax burden can be exported to neighboring communities by snagging the giant shopping center, the industrial research park or the massive public utility installation. In brief, the name of the game is cutthroat intergovernmental competition, and the object of the game is to "zone in" urban resources and to "zone out" urban problems.

Operating under a logic that goes back to the Domesday Book of William the Conquerer, each autonomous principality has the unchallenged and exclusive right to protect and to exploit all taxable resources within its domain. While this "winner take all" philosophy makes good sense in terms of the old "balanced" community, it takes on a harsh and inequitable color in a sprawling metropolitan area inhabited by aggressive and lopsided governmental units. One jurisdiction can reap all the tax benefits of an industrial location while the neighboring communities are often required to pay the costs of educating the children of the new employees.

"Staying in line":
an exquisite tax-expenditure calculus

Local policymakers competing in a metropolitan arena are keenly sensitive to inter-community tax rate differentials. There is a constant fear that an above average tax rate will act as a powerful deterrent to economic development within the local jurisdiction. While this fear may be exaggerated, the local concern for a "competitive" tax position is very real; it cannot be dismissed as foolish.

The effect of local tax differentials upon industrial location within a metropolitan area was underscored in a recent Advisory Commission report.

> The relative importance of the tax differential factor in industrial location decisions appears to increase as the location process narrows down to a particular jurisdiction within a general region. As among regions of the country, the non-tax factors such as access to markets and to labor and comparative transportation and supply costs stand out as the primary location considerations. As between neighboring States, there appears to be no direct relationship between industrial growth and tax differentials due largely to the fact that States are careful not to get "too far out of line" with their immediate neighbors. As among local governments within a State and especially within a metropolitan area, tax differentials exert discernible plant location pull—the industrial tax haven stands out as the most conspicuous example. *In almost every metropolitan area there exists wide local property tax differentials—a cost consideration that can become a "swing" factor in the final selection of a particular plant location.*[4]

Because of the desire to "stay in line," the relatively low level of taxation that is possible in the more affluent jurisdictions tends to serve as a brake on higher taxes throughout the metropolitan area. This braking action takes place despite the fact that higher taxes may be urgently needed in other jurisdictions.

Inter-community fiscal competition, however, is not restricted to the tax side of the equation. "Staying in line" with neighboring jurisdictions also forces each municipality and school district to re-examine constantly its expenditure policies. Whereas municipalities are fearful lest their tax rates become too high, they also are concerned lest their public service standards in general and their education standards in particular fall too far below those set by their neighbors. This keen concern for maintaining a competitive educational position often results in local school boards being played off against one another when it comes time to negotiate revised pay scales for teachers.

The fortunate fiscal position of the more affluent jurisdictions within the metropolitan area, therefore, creates a bitter dilemma for their less well endowed neighbors. The below average tax rates of the affluent jurisdictions provide aid and comfort to those persons advocating a tough, "hold-the-line" tax position. On the other hand, the high educational standards of the more fortunate jurisdictions provide heavy ammunition to those persons advocating larger appropriations for the schools.

Caught in this crossfire, the policymakers in the less fortunate jurisdictions must attempt to frame both a tax policy that will underwrite a "fairly decent" brand of public services and an expenditure policy that will not force taxes to "confiscatory" levels—a painfully exquisite form of political-fiscal calculus.

Too Little and Too Lopsided: The State and Federal Aid Response

In theory at least the States and the National Government—armed with superior fiscal resources—could have intervened and radically reduced local fiscal tensions. They could have responded to the challenge created by the widespread collapse of the balanced municipality and the rise of the lopsided metropolitan jurisdiction by rifling high-powered aid on the basis of need and local fiscal capacity into the coffers of the most "disadvantaged" localities and school districts.

Poor state equalization performance

In practice, there is little evidence to suggest that State and Federal aid combined has materially slowed down (let alone reversed) the forces working to increase metropolitan fiscal disparities. On the contrary, there is considerable evidence to suggest that State school aid and tax sharing polices in particular have had the effect of throwing gasoline on the fires. Federal mortgage insurance, highway and other grant-in-aid policies have had an equally incendiary effect. In addition, so-called "impact aid" to school districts often has tended to widen fiscal and social disparities in urban education.

Because of little or no explicit recognition of educational and municipal overburdens, most State aid programs increase the central city–suburban educational resources gap. By the same token, the not uncommon State practice of sharing a part of its tax receipts with local government on the basis of taxpayer residence also both promotes the cause of metropolitan political splintering and increases the gap between the "have" and "have not" communities.

One of the dramatic illustrations of this anti-equalization effect is found in Wisconsin's present system for sharing personal income tax receipts with its municipalities. In 1966, the high income residential suburbs in the Milwaukee metropolitan area received a $100.94 per capita share of the State personal income tax compared to $18.62 for the central city of Milwaukee and $18.47 per capita share for the area's low income residential suburbs. In order to provide a slim fare for its poorest jurisdictions Wisconsin has to set out a banquet for its richest municipalities!

To the extent that State and Federal aid programs have equalizing effects they are usually indirect—the by-products of a specific program designed to help poor people rather than direct results of programs designed to find and to help poor local jurisdictions *per se*. Because the poor increasingly tend to cluster together in the same municipality within a metropolitan area, any State or Federal program with a direct poverty orientation is bound to have an inter-local equalization effect, albeit of an indirect nature.

It may also be argued that any Federal program designed to prevent indigency also has a beneficial and indirect equalizing effect on local and State finances. In this case the Federal social insurance program—OASDI—must be cited as an important force working in the right direction.

Nevertheless, even after all of the State and Federal programs with the most indirect equalization effects are thrown on the scales, the fact remains that outside financial help has not come in sufficient magnitude to turn the fiscal tide for the nation's hard pressed central cities.

Financing education and public welfare: Misallocation of financial responsibility

In addition to chalking up a rather poor equalization record, most of the States have demonstrated little interest in assuming primary responsibility for the financing of education. As a result, the local property tax base will be forced this year to underwrite slightly more than one-half the cost of the nation's $32 billion elementary and secondary school program—a function that long ago lost most of its local character.

Slowly but surely the claims of public education are driving other local or municipal-type demands—i.e., police, fire—to the fiscal wall. Prior to World War II, about 33 percent of the total $4 billion tax collection went to the educators; this year more than 50 percent of estimated $31 billion property tax collection is earmarked for education. To put the issue more sharply, the school boards are pushing the municipalities and counties off the property tax preserve. In many suburban districts, the property tax has virtually become a school tax with as much as 75 cents of every property tax dollar going for education. In fact, the quality of local education is often largely determined by the accidents of local property tax geography.

In a number of States, the local property tax is still required to underwrite a considerable part of the non-Federal share of public welfare. As a result, the local tax base will produce approximately

$1.5 billion for this purpose in 1969—a most flagrant example of misallocation of financial responsibility.

If most States have fallen short on the education front, the same can be said about the National Government's role in financing public assistance programs. Despite the vastly superior fiscal resources of the National Government, and in the teeth of mounting evidence that only a truly national welfare program can distribute costs and benefits equitably across the land—despite all of this, State and local governments were required to pick up almost half of the nation's $10 billion welfare tab in 1968. The Congress which lost little time in 1965 in enacting the Medicaid program (actually it was developed and added onto Medicare with but a very few weeks for legislative consideration) has been slow indeed to admit and react to the tremendous pressures the program has placed upon State treasuries. Many State officials have with much validity termed the action of the Congress in this field the height of intergovernmental fiscal irresponsibility.

The ultimate, however, in the misallocation of financial responsibility among levels of government is to be found in the grim spectacle of a regressive and heavily overburdened local property tax (Newark's) being forced to underwrite a substantial part of the cost of its own extra heavy public welfare case load.

By forcing a limited and defective local revenue system to produce almost $18 billion for public education and welfare, the States and the Federal Government not only intensify the urban fiscal crisis with a vengeance, they also turn the logic of federalism upside down. In theory, the superior revenue system of the States and the National Government should reinforce the limited revenue capabilities of local government but in practice the opposite situation obtains. The local property tax is forced to serve as the general backstop for State and Federal programs!

Notes

1. Aristotle, *Politics*, Book IV, Chapter XI, pp. 126–127. Madison advanced essentially the same thesis in *The Federal Papers*, Number 10.

2. This analysis was conducted by Professor Seymour Sacks of Syracuse University and appears as a part of the Advisory Commission's study *Fiscal Balance in the American Federal System* (A-31; October 1967), Vol. 2.

3. James M. Banovetz, W. John Pembroke and Peter J. Fugiel, "Fiscal Disparities in the Chicago, Illinois Metropolitan Area," in *Fiscal Balance . . .*, Vol. 2, p. 243.

4. Advisory Commission on Intergovernmental Relations, *State-Local Taxation and Industrial Location* (A-30; April 1967), pp. 78 and 79. (Underscoring added).

State-Local Action
Toward Better Urban Financing

Significant steps by the Federal Government are urgently needed to help deal with the crisis of urban financing. But most of the action needed must be at the State-local level. The States have a major share of the responsibility because of their ultimate legal control over the property tax system and other local taxes and because of the close relationship between State and local government finances.

We therefore submit recommendations that mainly contemplate State and local government action toward a broader and fairer base for urban financing. Our proposals are for—

Broadening the base of State taxation by significant use of both a personal income tax and a general sales tax, including authorization for local governments to impose supplementary rates on a piggy-back basis;

A review by each State of its pattern of State-local relationships to provide a more effective and equitable means of State aid to local school financing; assumption by the State government of financial responsibility for non-Federal public welfare costs; and provision of incentives in State grant programs to improve local governmental structure;

Reexamination by State and local governments of the potentiality of user charges to finance public services;

State legislation for increased regionalization of property taxation for public schools in metropolitan areas, utilizing a countywide or multicounty taxing area, with proceeds allotted to school jurisdictions as prescribed by State laws;

Joint Federal-State-local action to establish a system of interstate metropolitan taxing areas under which, by State and local decision, a supplemental rate could be added to the Federal income tax with proceeds returned to the local governments involved; and

State legislative action to improve the property tax by eliminating unenforceable features, professionalizing the assessment function, moving to full-value assessment, ascertaining and pub-

Condensed from National Commission on Urban Problems, *Building the American City: Report of the National Commission on Urban Problems to the Congress and to the President of the United States* (Washington, D. C.: U. S. Government Printing Office, 1968), pp. 362–366.

licizing assessment ratios, and providing effective taxpayer appeals machinery.

A Broader Financing Base

Some defects of the property tax are inherent in its very nature, and can only be handled by limiting reliance upon this form of taxation to some reasonable level.

In the nation as a whole, about five-sixths of all local tax revenue in metropolitan areas is obtained from the property tax. Even when intergovernmental receipts and nontax sources are added, property taxation accounts for nearly half of all urban government revenue. Property taxation supplies nearly as much revenue as all other State and local taxes combined.

There is marked geographic variation on this score. The property tax portion ranges from less than one-fifth to more than two-thirds of State-local tax revenue in various individual States.

Relative de-escalation of the property tax will depend, above all, upon further State action toward increased tapping of other revenue sources.

Recommendation No. 1 — Move To Balanced State-Local Revenue Systems

The Commission recommends that those States which have not done so move as rapidly as possible toward a balanced State-local revenue system which, besides providing for equitable property taxation, involves significant use by the State of both a personal income tax and a general sales and use tax. We also urge that States which have not done so consider granting authority for local governments to impose limited supplementary rates of income or sales tax, to be collected and returned by the State to the taxing jurisdictions.

Thirty States now impose both personal income and general sales taxes; in 17 of these States, local sales taxes are also authorized (usually with State collection and distribution), and two States authorize local supplements to State income taxes. Thus there is widespread precedent for the main thrust of our recommendation, which takes account of two major elements of fiscal reality: (1) strongly rising needs and expectations for public services at both local and State government levels; and (2) the prospect that additional Federal Government financing, although highly desirable, cannot be expected fully to meet these growing requirements.

It would be unrealistic and irresponsible to urge expanded State participation in the financing of urban needs without recognizing also, as we do in this proposal, the question of how the necessary funds are to be obtained. Fortunately, recent action in numerous States provides a helpful guide. In particular, effective means have been devised to maintain the productivity of general sales taxes but at the same time to remove their regressive impact upon low-income people. Such arrangements, which originated in Indiana and have since spread elsewhere, involve a special crediting in State income tax laws. Either by exempting food and medicine, or by appropriate credits (under income tax formulas) for taxable purchases of such necessities, it is possible to avoid inequities that otherwise arise with general sales taxes. We commend the sales tax, with such features, as one element of a balanced tax system which would help stem excessive property tax levels.

The three types of tax referred to do not, of course, account for all of the States' financing arsenal; we have further suggestions to offer in a later chapter with regard to the taxation of land. However, these "big three" are of primary importance: 70 percent of all State-local tax revenue is obtained from property, general sales, and personal income taxes. Their respective percentages in calendar 1967 were as follows: property, 43.1; general sales, 16.7; personal income, 9.8. It is increasingly clear that *both* general sales taxes and personal income taxes must be used by State and local governments if urgent public service needs are to be met without an undesirable further increase of property tax rates in many areas. (Where property taxation is very low, balance of course would be achieved by raising the level.)

All or most of the added funds from a broader tax system would best be collected by the State governments, even though destined for distribution in large part to local governments. Related State action is therefore indicated concerning their grant-in-aid programs. Present State-local fiscal patterns are generally the result of historical problem-by-problem handling. In very few instances have State grant-in-aid systems been subjected recently to comprehensive reexamination and overhauling.

Recommendation No. 2—
Review and Revision of State-Local Fiscal Relations

The Commission urges State governments to review intensively and where appropriate to revise their existing arrangements for State-local fiscal relations so that, as a minimum:

(a) *Each State provides a generous foundation program for local school financing:*

(b) *Educational grant formulas take account of the additional costs of enriched school programs for economically and culturally deprived children;*

(c) *Each State government finances all or substantially all public welfare costs that are not covered by Federal aid; and*

(d) *Various State grant programs include appropriate incentives toward improved local government structure, including the development of major viable multipurpose governments in metropolitan areas.*

We emphasize financing requirements for education and public welfare on obvious grounds. Public schools make up by far the most costly single elements of local government, and their benefits are not limited to small local areas but have a widespread impact in our increasingly mobile society. The States' responsibility for underwriting a sizable share of public school costs thus is socially and economically justified, as well as consistent with the legal framework for public education in most States.

Provisions are widespread for State grants to underwrite certain excess costs of public schools in sparsely populated rural areas, particularly in the form of aid for pupil transportation. Various programs exist also for special State aid for educating physically handicapped children. Until recently, however, State grant systems have rarely made any allowance for the overburden involved in providing, through local public schools, enriched programs for economically and culturally deprived children. We urge specific State attention to this as one desirable component of State school-aid systems.

In about half the Nation, public welfare costs are financed nearly entirely from State and Federal sources. However, in States where such an arrangement does not apply, the locally financed portion represents a significant burden, adding materially to property tax requirements. This cost component is likely to be especially onerous because it tends to vary inversely with local fiscal capacity. Moreover, such financing arrangements commonly place a heavier burden upon major central cities, where so many poor families are located, than upon most suburban communities. We strongly urge, therefore, that those States which have not done so assume direct responsibility for substantially all public welfare costs that are not financed by the Federal Government. The same reasoning justifies generous State underwriting of other important though less costly poverty-linked services, such as those in the field of public health.

Intensive review of existing grant-in-aid programs in any particular State should take account of the relation of such grants to local government structure. As shown by experience with State aid to local school districts, fiscal aid may be deliberately used to encourage desirable structural changes, or on the other hand, may actually tend to shore up outdated institutions.

Recommendation No. 3—
Increased Local Government Use
of User Charges, Where Appropriate

The Commission urges that local governments reexamine intensively their existing practices with regard to service and benefit charges, and make adjustments needed to put appropriate services on a self-sustaining basis. We also urge the State governments to encourage and assist local governments in such efforts.

User charges already represent a significant revenue source for urban local governments. However, there is great variation: some governments use them to an important extent, while others in effect make the general taxpaying public subsidize various activities which provide selective benefits. Although user charges have little relevance to some costly services, such as education, public welfare, police and fire protection, they can be an important resource for financing of urban highways and parking facilities, water supply and sewers, waste disposal, and recreational activities.

User charges can help to hold property tax requirements within reason and to provide equity between taxpayers and specially benefited users of various services. Two other aspects of this proposal deserve particular attention: (1) User charges can help to prevent excessive or wasteful levels of user demand—illustrated by carelessness in water consumption where no metering applies, or by excessive urban street congestion in commercial sections where street parking is allowed free or at only very nominal meter rates; (2) With rising levels of urban government salaries and other expense factors, the fees or prices set for particular public services need to be periodically adjusted lest charges lag seriously behind related costs.

A word of caution should be added about balancing or choosing between user charges and taxes for particular activities. Most urban government services have an important element of general public benefit; for example, an adequate sewer system is of major concern to the community as a whole, not only to individual households. Unless such social factors are sufficiently recognized, the more attractive sound of charges than of taxes may encourage excessive use of charges, with undesirable or inequitable results. In fact, some municipalities substantially subsidize their general government needs from the revenue surpluses of their water supply or electric power utilities. This is the effective equivalent of placing a high excise tax upon the utility services involved. Such taxation may, obviously, be even more regressive or otherwise undesirable than the use of the property tax or other available means of financing. Benefit charges are also sometimes misused in a potentially discriminatory fashion—for instance by imposing fees for admission to local parks, in order to limit their use to nearby or socially desirable patrons. While reasonable charges may be justified for the use of some public recreational facilities (e.g., golf courses or marinas) that have a selective appeal, it is of major social importance that facilities which serve more basic needs be available at little or no direct cost.

Thus we are not urging the maximum possible use of benefit charges but their greater application in those instances where, in the light of careful consideration, they offer an economically and socially desirable substitute for taxation.

Regionalizing school costs

Public education involves by far the largest component of local government activity. This function typically accounts for about four-tenths of all local public expenditure in metropolitan areas, and an even higher fraction elsewhere. A sizable portion of local education expenditure is financed from State and Federal grants, and such aid should continue to grow, as we urge above. However, a major part of school spending is met from local sources, principally property taxation. The base for such financing is fractionated geographically, and in most metropolitan areas there is a considerable range in the relative fiscal capacity of school-administering governments. Basic restructuring of local government and provision of increased Federal and State aid are needed to help meet this situation, but another approach is also widely indicated.

Recommendation No. 4—
    Countywide or Multicounty
    Taxation for Public Schools

The Commission recommends that States provide that a significant proportion of all local property tax support for public schools be supplied through levies imposed by countywide or multicounty school taxing districts, with the proceeds allocated to school-administering units on a State-prescribed basis.

This proposal has limited relevance where public schools are already administered (and locally financed) through countywide units. For a number of other States also its adoption would mainly involve an expansion of existing arrangements that provide some countywide taxation for school purposes. Usually, however, such county levies are only minor, and most States lack any such device for spreading the local tax burden for education.

Local public education is a highly logical candidate for a broader local base on several grounds: because of its costliness, it makes up a sizable part of local property taxes everywhere; it permits a simpler basis for allocation of funds than could apply to many other local government services; and the benefits of public education, in our increasingly mobile society and economy, reach out far beyond individual school administering areas.

State action along this line would end part of the substantial escape from property taxation which is now enjoyed in various local tax havens. By curtailing present wide disparities of property tax rates in metropolitan areas, it would reduce incentives toward socially undesirable fiscal zoning, and, perhaps, also lessen resistance to the more basic restructuring of local government which is so urgently desirable in many areas.

The Commission is not proposing here a regionalization of education, but rather of *property taxation for educational purposes*. Neighborhood schools as service units and school systems as administering entities would not be replaced, but a larger part of their financing would come from a geographically broader base.

Interstate metropolitan taxing areas

Most of the foregoing discussion has referred to steps toward a broader and fairer base for urban government financing that can—and should—be taken by State and local governments. Effective action along the lines suggested, we are confident, would be highly productive. Moreover, we are sure that the problems of urban government must continue in the future as in the past to be handled mainly by local and State action. Not only because of the structural inheritance of our Federal system but for a host of other reasons, the role of the National Government can at best be selective and indirect, stimulative and helpful—especially in financing. The National Government is *not* suited to take on directly any sizable part of the responsibilities traditionally handled at the State and particularly at the local level. Hence the concern we have expressed for a more effective structure of local government, especially in major urban areas.

Even widespread action on all the matters discussed above, however, would not fully deal with a financial problem that is especially pertinent to metropolitan areas which cut across or are adjacent to State boundaries. In 1960, such areas had more than 41 million residents, or nearly one-fourth of the Nation's total population. For any such area, problems of local disparities in fiscal capacity and of constraints upon tax policy become interstate in nature. But no effective means is now available to deal with such problems on an areawide basis, *involving concerted action by governments on both sides of the State boundaries*. As a result, each of the States concerned is likely to encounter special difficulty in carrying through desirable actions it might otherwise undertake. For example, a vigorous effort by various means to get rid of tax havens in one State's portion of such an interstate area would face the threat of traditionally privileged businesses moving to low-tax parts of the area in the neighboring State.

Recommendation No. 5—
Supplement to Federal Income Tax in Interstate Metropolitan Areas

The Commission recommends, for consideration by Congress and the various States concerned, enactment of a system by which a supplemental rate of personal income tax could be applied within interstate metropolitan areas, to be collected directly in conjunction with the Federal income tax and with the proceeds returned to appropriate local governments.

It should be emphasized that, if such a system is developed, the supplemental tax rate would be imposed by local or State action, rather than by the Federal Government; the proposal thus contemplates a "piggyback" arrangement like that now widely used for locally imposed, State-collected supplements to State sales taxes. The plan might operate through certification by the Governors of the affected States that a favorable vote in an areawide election had favored the imposition of a supplemental rate for Federal collection and return, and with allocation of the resulting revenue to be as specified by the respective Governors in accordance with statutory provisions in their respective States. Appropriate Federal legislation should no doubt (as in the case of the States' "piggybacking" provisions) set a limit on the supplemental rate available, and on the frequency of allowable change or cancellation; at least for administrative reasons, it might even be found desirable to provide for only a single available rate of supplementation, subject to "yes-or-no" action by eligible areas.

It is obvious that the design of a workable system of this nature demands careful analysis of many factors, so that it would be presumptuous to spell out proposed features in complete detail. The suggested basic approach, however, deserves thoughtful and sympathetic consideration on several grounds:

(1) An advantage already noted would be to reduce the constraints upon otherwise desirable action concerning urban government structure and financing that apply uniquely in interstate metropolitan area;

(2) Another advantage is the opportunity it would open for increased local use, in an efficient fashion, of income taxation as a partial substitute for property taxation. A limited number of local governments (mostly sizable municipalities) already administer their own personal income taxes, but in most instances these apply

only or mainly to salaries and wages. It is generally agreed that separate taxes of this nature cannot be nearly as well administered locally as on a State or National basis. Only two States have thus far authorized local "piggybacking" on their State income taxes; while further action of this nature is probably desirable and likely (despite problems of appropriate revenue allocation where local governments are numerous) it cannot operate on an interstate basis.

MICHAEL R. STONE
PARRIS N. GLENDENING

State and Local Expenditures: Who Sets the Budget?

Budgets are political documents which contain a government's most important policy statement. State and local governments have some involvement in almost every aspect of our individual and collective life. There are few, if any, governmental activities that do not require some spending of public funds. The budgetary process is the very heart of state and local politics.

Thus, one would expect political activity to be most important when the variables which determine expenditures are discussed. However, we are becoming increasingly aware that, in fact, the determination of state and local expenditure policy is largely out of the hands of state and local politicos. This does not mean that state and local decision-makers do not have an influence on expenditures, rather that this influence must be seen in relationship to all other influences.

The first and most important variable that determines expenditures is "what was spent last year" or, in more general terms, "what has been the previous expenditure pattern?" Budgets must be seen as a part of a process that gives a high priority to stability and continuity. This stability and continuity is translated into the retention of certain goods and services on which the community places high value.

Programs and agencies are not ephemeral, existing only from one budget to the next. Education, adequate transportation, continued public order, etc. are services which we have come to take for granted. They are essential to an expected way of life and any major change in their continued provision would almost certainly be followed by a changed pattern of living.

Budgets, then, must take into account existing programs and commitments in order that there can be a continuity in provided services. This, of course, does not necessarily mean that changes in expenditure patterns cannot take place, but it does mean that changes are likely to be minimal when compared to the desire to maintain what we already have. Wildavsky, referring to the budget of the Federal government, has noted that "the budget may be conceived as an iceberg with by far the largest part below the surface, outside the control of anyone."[1]

The concept of using previous expenditures as a base for current expenditures is commonly called incrementalism. This stems from the notice that increments of change take place in confined areas and are minor additions or subtractions to what has gone before. Incrementalism reduces the complexity of budgeting; consequently, active consideration of budget proposals are generally narrowed to a few items of requested increases, or suggested decreases, over last year's base.[2]

This is particularly important when consideration is given to the fact that state and local budget-makers often lack both the experience and resources to analyze budgets as a whole. As Sharkansky points out, the high turnover of state legislators, the lack of viable seniority systems, and inadequate legislative staff support combine to prevent the emergence of real fiscal expertise in most state legislatures.[3] This is even more true of local legislative bodies.

Not unexpectedly, such legislators have little sophisticated knowledge of fiscal planning. What has been accepted in previous budgets does not have to be defended and that which does not have to be defended provides safe political ground. Further, budget decision-makers are also exposed to pressure from agencies who at a very minimum wish to maintain the status quo. How can budget-makers decide between the relative merits of agencies competing for funds? In most circumstances they do not, preferring rather to disperse public resources as done in the past and confining changes to the smallest possible area. Existing programs, agency pressures, and a lack of experience and technical resources combine to create an environment in which expenditures are never reviewed as a whole.

Incrementalism should by no means become a portrayal of an act of blind faith in the past. It is better viewed as an act of expediency that provides the base for predictability, stability, and certainty. When viewed in a broad perspective, incrementalism is highly functional to the system. However, it also limits severely expenditure opportunities and induces a conservative attitude toward policy change.

Another factor that further reduces the area of initiative for budget decision-makers is the earmarking of funds, that is, the formal designation of various revenues for specific purposes. Earmarking is distinguished from incrementalism in that the former is almost always a legal or constitutional commitment, while the latter is an administrative or political expedient.

More than 30 states have provisions for some form of major earmarking of funds. Eleven states dedicate more than one-third of their revenues to particular funds, thus placing them outside of the budget-making processes.[4] If all types of earmarking are taken into consideration, the situation becomes even more critical.[5] As one student of state finances has observed: "In some states earmarking is practiced so extensively as to make anything approaching comprehensive budgeting quite impossible."[6]

Earmarked funds range from relatively insignificant amounts, such as the practice of placing hunting and fishing license fees in a conservation fund, to the very significant amounts earmarked for such important functions as education. The most commonly earmarked revenue is that derived from highway user taxes. Earmarking is much less extensively used in the case of local governments with the exception of debt retirement funds.

Maxwell concludes that earmarking illustrates the distrust of voters in the wisdom and integrity of state legislators.[7] Even if this is no longer the case, the net effect of earmarking is very similar to incrementalism. The areas that budget-makers can effectively initiate or control are further reduced.

The third major determinant of state and local expenditures is intergovernmental transfer of funds. For practical purposes, intergovernmental revenues herein refer to federal grant-in-aid programs.

Federal grants-in-aid are payments made by federal agencies to state and local governments in order that certain programs may be carried out. In 1968 federal grants to state and local governments amounted to $17.5 billion which was equivalent to fifteen percent of all state and local revenues. The major grant-in-aid programs are education, welfare, housing and urban renewal, and highways.

The grant-in-aid program has a three-fold underpinning. They help to equalize the poor and rich states. They provide a stimulus for undertaking neglected or unpopular programs, and they often provide the funding which would be beyond the financial resources of certain states or localities. There is ample justification for the grant-in-aid program, but federal funds are not distributed without some repercussion in the State and local budget-making processes.

These funds further impinge upon the decision-making ability of state and local budget-makers. Grants-in-aid carry with them minimum standards and "guidelines." These often become determinants of policy in themselves. Further reducing the state and local real options, is the matching requirement. The match ratio, *i.e.*, those funds put up by the receiving unit of government, may vary from program to program. Whatever the ratio, states and localities taking part in federal grants-in-aid programs are committed to putting a proportion of their resources toward a project over which they cannot exercise complete control.

Participation in grants-in-aid programs is essentially voluntary and it has been argued that state and local decision-makers are free to set their own policies by determining whether they wish to participate. This is a simplistic view of what often happens. In fact a very real and intentional influence from above takes place. Mayor Jones of Big City realizes he will have ten million dollars surplus for the next budgetary period. Will he spend it on unmatched function X? Or, on function Y which is matched on a fifty-fifty basis? Or, on function Z which is matched on a 90:10 basis? Unfortunately, all too often decision-makers report that they had *no real option* and had to spend in matched areas.[8] Thus, the national government's setting of priorities limits the power of state and local budget-makers. Indications exist that many of the federal grant programs, especially those of HUD, may be influencing the very structure of local government.[9]

Finally, there is the obvious but important fact that income determines expenditure. While the national legislature may consider expenditures independent of revenues (using the borrowing power to make up any deficit), state legislatures are restricted in that expenditures may not, except for capital construction and certain bonded services, exceed revenue predictions. State and local governments with small revenue bases can only have limited expenditures.

Incrementalism, earmarking, intergovernmental funding, and the fact that revenue determines expenditure combine to greatly restrict the options open to state and local budget decision-makers. Speaking of the national budget and real decision-making, Wildavsky notes that "a rather small percentage—seldom larger than 30 percent, often smaller than 5—is within the realm of anybody's (including Congressional and Budget Bureau) discretion as a practical matter."[10] The percentages are much smaller for state and local decision-makers.

Who, then, sets the budget? Are popularly elected, politically responsive decision-makers in control, or are state and local fiscal policies largely determined by the preset institutional givens mentioned in this essay? The authors are certain that it is much more the latter than the former.

The implications of such a conclusion are obvious. If the institutional variables suggest that change will occur only over an extended period of time and the political pressures demand an immediate, major reallocation of state and local resources, systemic stress will be clear and constant.

Notes

1. Aaron Wildavsky, *The Politics of the Budgetary Process* (Boston: Little, Brown and Company, 1964), p. 13.

2. See, for example, Thomas R. Dye, *Politics in States and Communities* (Englewood Cliffs: Prentice-Hall, Inc., 1969), esp. pp. 460–467; and Ira Sharkansky, *Spending in the American States*, American Politics Research Series (Chicago: Rand McNally & Co., 1968).

3. Ira Sharkansky, *The Politics of Taxing and Spending*, The Bobbs-Merrill Policy Analysis Series (Indianapolis: The Bobbs-Merrill Co., Inc., 1969), p. 91.

4. Dye, *op. cit.*, p. 463.

5. See, for example, the analysis in James A. Maxwell, *Financing State and Local Governments* (2nd ed. revised; Washington, D. C.: The Brookings Institution, 1969), esp. pp. 212–227.

6. Clyde F. Snider, *American State and Local Government*, The Century Political Science Series (2nd ed. revised; New York: Appleton-Century-Crofts, 1965), p. 697.

7. Maxwell, *op. cit.*, p. 221.

8. Parris N. Glendening, "Revenue Sharing Versus Grants-in-Aid: Political Implications," Paper presented at the national meeting of the American Society for Public Administration, Miami, Florida, May 1969. (Mimeographed.)

9. Parris N. Glendening, "The Federal Role in Regional Planning Councils: Trends and Implications," Paper presented at the national meeting of the Southeastern Regional Science Association, New Orleans, April 1970. (Mimeographed.)

10. Wildavsky, *op. cit.*, p. 14.

JOHN C. BOLLENS

The Fiscal Dilemma

Financing the metropolis is one of the biggest problems in our nation, and fiscal difficulties are evident in both the insufficiency of the funds available to local governments and the gross unevenness in the financial resources of the various parts of the typical metropolitan area. The concentration of more and more people in urban centers has produced a demand for a constant increase in public services and facilities. Large numbers of people living in close proximity develop needs that are unknown, or of far less importance, in other environments. Moreover, metropolitan dwellers have attained higher standards of living and greater expectations of local government, both in terms of raising the levels of traditional public activities and launching forth upon new endeavors. These requirements of the metropolitan area may be met by local governments only if they possess a considerable amount of money.

John C. Bollens, "The Fiscal Dilemma," in Jim Chard and Jon York, eds., *Urban America: Crisis and Opportunity* (Belmont, Calif.: Dickenson Publishing Co., Inc., 1969), 178–181. Reprinted by permission.

Governmental Reorganization or Fiscal Reform?

Governmental finance is frequently recognized as the number one problem of the metropolis. Some contend that if adequate funds could be obtained and a fair system of distribution developed, most of the other metropolitan problems could be solved without substantial changes in the pattern of government. Others, however, while agreeing with the significance of the financial problem, maintain that the lack of adequate governmental machinery in the metropolis is the reason for many of its fiscal troubles. The latter refer to the many local governments competing for the tax dollar and other public funds, the broad disparity in fiscal capacity of local units, and the difficulty of relating taxes and benefits when activities transcend local governmental boundaries, as many of them do in a metropolitan area. Both views contain an element of truth.

Large-scale reorganization of the government of the metropolis would not guarantee a substantial improvement in services and facilities. It would make possible an eradication or lessening of the existing financial inequities and provide a formal means for appraising areawide needs in relation to areawide resources. But government would still be faced with a financial problem. On the other hand, improving the financial situation of the existing governmental system of the metropolis would alleviate some of the shortcomings in services and facilities but might also bolster certain uneconomic and inefficient units. In point of fact, then, a combination of both types of reform, structural and financial, may often be appropriate, although highly difficult to accomplish.

Over the last twenty years in particular, as tax levies have continued to rise, individuals and organizations have developed a growing tax consciousness. Some have judged their tax burdens to be oppressive and unreasonable. In various localities a mood of resistance, if not revolt, has been increasing. The general reason is not hard to determine. Governmental expenditures at all levels have jumped tremendously in recent decades. For instance, in 1942 national, state, and local expenditures totaled $45\frac{1}{2}$ billion. Twenty years later the total was in excess of $165 billion. In this period, annual expenditures for local governments alone increased about fourfold.

Several factors should be kept in mind when considering rising public expenditures. First, the public dollar, as well as the private dollar, has been subject to the continuing onslaught of inflation. Accordingly, it requires more public dollars than it did twenty years ago to furnish the identical service. Second, the population served by local and other governments, especially in metropolitan areas, is larger than in the late 1940's. Third, at the same time governmental expenditures have expanded, the general economic status of the citizenry has gone up appreciably. This third factor means that the general public now has a greater ability to pay for the expenditures of its governments.

The conflict between an increased ability to pay for government and a growing unwillingness to pay may reflect the mood of the citizenry to spend more on private wants and less on public needs, despite the conclusions of various economists that we are underspending in the field of public needs. Or it may demonstrate a conviction, not that the total governmental financial burden is excessive, but that certain types of taxes, say property taxes, are too high or that the current tax system makes an inequitable exaction from certain categories of wage earners.

Although most of the nation's wealth is located in its metropolitan areas, they are frequently in financial difficulties. This is so because of the relative allocation of financial authority to the local governmental level compared to the state and national levels and because of the wide variances in certain sections of the same metropolis between local resources and local public needs. In the former, nation and state have largely preempted the lucrative fields. In the latter, chiefly by reason of land-use development, wealthy communities with comparatively few public needs exist side by side with poor communities that have many public needs.

Overcoming Fragmented Government

The problem of vast disparities between local resources and local public needs in a metropolitan area has resulted from the fragmentation of the local governmental system. This fragmentation has divided the total local financial resources and has left some local governments with little fiscal capacity; consequently, local financial resources are spread very unevenly among the local governments of the metropolis. Contrary to what many believe, the problem is not one of a poor central city in contrast to all wealthy suburbs. In point of fact, great differences between ability and need are present more often among various suburbs than between the central city and all of suburbia.

The current system of local finance also ignores the spillover effects of the extension of public activities across the boundaries of individual local governments, which makes it practically impossible to relate taxes and benefits. The work of a high-quality police department in one community has a carryover effect on the crime rate in nearby communities; efficient sewage disposal methods by one unit benefits its downstream neighbors; and the top-rate schools of one district increase the economic potential of the entire metropolis. As demonstrated by these illustrations, each local government is sometimes the originator and sometimes the recipient, favorably or unfavorably, of these spillovers. But it is improbable that the costs and benefits are balanced for each unit.

Assuming that governmental organization in most metropolitan areas will continue to be fragmented in the immediate future, there are certain techniques that may be employed to alleviate the discrepancies between resources and needs among local units. Three techniques should be considered here: (1) superimposing new governments on the existing governmental pattern; (2) transferring responsibility or functions to units of larger territorial size; and (3) redistributing tax resources.

The first technique is represented by the establishment of metropolitan districts. Each such district, handling one or a few services on a metropolitan basis, may achieve on a smaller scale what a single government for an entire metropolis may achieve completely; that is, elimination of uneven distribution of taxable capacity and inequities resulting from spillovers. These districts are able to tap areawide resources, thereby reducing the substantial differences in wealth among parts of a metropolis. The second technique, the transferring of certain functions to a larger unit, produces the same result. In a one-county metropolis the larger unit may be the county government. In an intercounty area it will more likely be a special district or the state government. The third technique, reducing the disparity between resources and needs in a metropolis by redistribution of tax funds, can be implemented by a metropolitan taxing agency to collect and distribute funds on the basis of an equalization formula.

These three techniques offer only partial answers, and their disadvantages may be serious. For example, it may be argued that the formation of metropolitan districts makes the governing of a metropolis more complex and that redistribution of tax funds may bolster certain local units that should not continue to exist. These claims may be true, but they do not consider a compelling fact: metropolitan reform generally comes by improvisation and evolution, rather than by large-scale quick change based on rational design. Although the number and size of federal grants to local units in the metropolis are growing, the state governments remain the major decision-makers in meeting the metropolitan fiscal problems, which center on the total amount of money that is necessary and the variations between local needs and resources. The surprising element here is the slowness of the response of many of the states.

NEIL G. McCLUSKEY

Public Funds for Parochial Schools?
Yes!

The question of public support for church-related schools has been debated and discussed and argued over for generations. Over the years, most of the arguments that I have listened to about parochial schools have no direct bearing on the problem of support. These arguments rather hit another point—the very existence of such schools.

For example, all that class of argument which calls parochial school education "divisive" or "un-American" or "undemocratic" should conclude by demanding the suppression of these schools. It has nothing to do really with the question of support. If the common good of the American nation and the future of democracy depend uniquely on public schooling (as we know it now), then no competing system of schools should be tolerated. It is not the further growth of non-public schools that should be questioned but the propriety of their remaining in existence. This is the point to which critics of the growth of nonpublic schools should honestly address themselves. Either nonpublic schools have the right to exist and to multiply according to the wishes of their patrons, or they do not. If they do not have the right, the state should, at the very most, allow only a few schools of this type to operate in widely separate areas as a symbol of America's traditional tolerance—showcases, on the model of the churches left open in some Communist countries. Those who agree with a former president of Harvard University that, "The greater the proportion of our youth who attend independent schools, the greater the threat to our democratic unity," should logically insist on a quota or cut-off point, a percentage beyond which nonpublic schools become an intolerable menace.

The Basic Issue

At the beginning of the century, there were 854,523 students enrolled in Catholic primary and secondary schools in the United States. This represented 5.2 percent of the entire elementary and secondary school population of the nation. Today, the number has grown to over five million or about 14 percent of the total enrollment. The trend

Neil G. McCluskey, S. J., "Public Funds for Parochial Schools? Yes!" *Teachers College Record*, vol. 62 (October 1960), 49–55. Reprinted by permission.

shows no sign of abating. It seems to be limited only by available resources. Very many, perhaps most, of the other five million Catholic school children that are now in public schools would not be there if there were enough desks and schools to accommodate these children within the Catholic system. These figures invite reflection.

The public school, at least as presently constituted, has been judged by the American Catholic parent as incapable of providing the kind of education he desires for his child. The history of the American public school has made it painfully apparent that the American people have been caught in an unresolved ambiguity. They insist that the common school assume a certain responsibility for character education, but the 250 different religious bodies and the millions of unchurched Americans do not agree on what should comprise character education or form its basis. The people have given the common school a moral mandate, therefore, whose subject remains in dispute among the different groups served by the school. This is not to blame the school or to suggest that the school staff is derelict. Public school administrators and teachers did not create this problem; they inherited it and are helpless to cope satisfactorily with it. The central problem is the contradiction inherent in the very idea of one common school's attempting to serve a religiously pluralistic society. Correlative to this problem, of course, is the place of the independent, church-related school in the total scheme of things and, specifically, the claim this school has on appropriate public support.

I respectfully submit that it is in the best interests of the American nation that the church-related schools, which have assumed a generous share of America's educational burden, receive appropriate recognition and support. My two basic reasons are that (1) only in this way can the constitutional guarantee of freedom of religion be effectively safeguarded, and that (2) only in this way can the nation's youthful talent be fully realized.

Right of Family Choice

That freedom of choice in education is an integral part of freedom of religion requires no involved proof. The family right in education is prior to the rights of civil and ecclesiastical society because it is based on the natural relation of parents to their offspring. Common sense, a venerable tradition in Western free society, and several important U. S. Supreme Court decisions have put the priority of family right beyond dispute.

Need we do more than recall that the Supreme Court has, on several occasions, unqualifiedly reaffirmed the principle that "the child is not the mere creature of the state" (*Pierce v. Society of Sisters,* 1925); and that "the custody, care and nurture of the child reside first in the parents" (*Prince v. Massachusetts*, 1944)? Or to remind ourselves that unambiguous support for the primacy of the family right is likewise to be found in the *Universal Declaration of Human Rights*, proclaimed by the General Assembly of the United Nations (December 10, 1948): "Parents have a prior right to choose the kind of education that shall be given to their children" (Article 26, 3).

To state this truth is not to deny or diminish in any way the state's rights in education. A modern democratic state rests on the intellectual alertness and moral maturity of its citizenry. The state, accordingly, is obligated, directly or indirectly, to maintain a level of universal education sufficient to ensure its own economic, political and cultural well-being. However, this obligation can be discharged in many ways. It does not follow that the state itself must invariably set up its own quasi-monopolistic system of schools. An imposing number of countries, whose traditions and sympathies are as liberal and democratic as America's own, have long accepted—and sub-sidized—the assistance of other agencies in achieving the goal of universal education.

The American state has passed compulsory school attendance laws, and to assist parents to comply with such legislation, has established a system of free public schools, but without any provision in them for religious training. In pursuit of the common good, the state taxes all citizens alike to form a common pool for the support of education, so that it may provide for its school children the sub-stantial benefit of free education and certain auxiliary benefits related to education. But this can only take place within the type of school the state itself chooses. Catholic parents judge that in all conscience they must, if at all feasible, send their children to a Catholic school. For Catholics believe that secular education during the child's forma-tive years must be integrated with religious training. The Catholic parent looks to the public school not reproachfully but regretfully. As a policy statement issued only a few years ago by a commission of the NEA-AASA has solemnly told him, "As public institutions, the public schools of this nation must be nondenominational. They can have no part in securing acceptance of any one of the numerous systems of be-lief regarding a supernatural power and the relation of mankind thereto."[1]

A family seeking to follow simultaneously the dictates of con-science and the compulsory education law may not now, for all practical purposes, share in the state's provision for the common welfare. In the concrete, the state has set up what amounts to a religious test. If public benefits are so administered that citizens must do violence to their conscience in order to share in them, then the bene-fits are discriminatory. They are not truly public because to them is attached a religious qualification. That portion of the public which prefers to follow the dictates of conscience fails to qualify (1) in general for the basic benefit of free education and (2) in most states for the bulk of the supplementary benefits given for the sake of the school child.

It is not the American way simply to dismiss this conscience as a private affair, a Catholic idiosyncrasy, and to let it go at that. Religious liberty and the constitutional prohibition of religious qualifications mean little unless these are related to the distinctive peculiarities of each type of conscience. As Dean Robert Henle of St. Louis University has pointed out,[2]

> our courts have shown a punctilious and precise concern to protect the consciences even of minorities commonly regarded as extremists. The court simply inquires what the conscience of the individual is; it does not judge that conscience as a conscience, but takes it into account as a fact and provides for it. (p. 244)

Nor can the question be loftily waived with a statement, like that of Justice Wiley B. Rutledge in his *Everson* (1947) dissent, that, "Like St. Paul's freedom, religious liberty with a great price must be bought. And for those who exercise it most fully, by insisting on religious education for their children mixed with secular, by the terms of our Constitution the price is greater than for others." This is preposterous. The last thing our founding fathers intended to do was to put a price tag on the religious liberty protected by the First Amendment that would put it beyond the reach of some citizens. The rights and freedoms guaranteed to American citizens in the Bill of Rights were intended to be common. The equal protection guarantee, said the Supreme Court, "requires that all persons . . . shall be treated alike, under like circumstances and conditions, both in the privileges conferred and in the liabilities imposed" (*Hayes v. Missouri*, 1887).

Religious Freedom

In its simplest terms, this entire issue boils down to a question of the primacy of spiritual over temporal concerns. Maybe more of us should agree with Dr. Butts's assumption (1) that every American somehow owes a prior duty of loyalty to a "democratic" state-established school. But neither the history of Western civilization nor the tradition of our American courts offer support for this assumption.

Based upon their acknowledgement of the primacy of the spiritual order, the courts have made it clear that the government must leave parents free to send their children to schools of their choice. The corollary question is now before us: Does the First Amendment permit the government to respect that freedom further by arranging distribution of its various benefits so as to avoid discrimination against parents or students who make this choice? As far as auxiliary benefits are concerned, the courts have given an affirmative answer to this question, although they have not always applied it with consistency.

It is a matter of record that the same majority decision of the U.S. Supreme Court in the *Everson* (1947) case that declared, "no tax in any amount, large or small, can be levied to support any religious activities or institutions," also solemnly warned, "We must be careful in protecting the citizens of New Jersey against state-established churches, to be sure that we do not inadvertently prohibit New Jersey from extending its general state law benefits to all its citizens without regard to their religious belief." The high court made it clear that fear of establishment must not lead to a restriction of constitutionally guaranteed freedom:

> Other language of the First Amendment commands that New Jersey cannot hamper its citizens in the free exercise of their own religion. Consequently, it cannot exclude individual Catholics, Lutherans, Mohammedans, Baptists, Jews, Methodists, Non-believers, Presbyterians or the members of any other faith, because of their faith, or lack of it, from receiving the benefits of public welfare legislation.

The purpose of the First Amendment is frustrated in that its protection of religious freedom does not extend to citizens who wish to send their children to religiously oriented schools. At present, these citizen-parents do not enjoy full freedom to direct the education of their offspring, but are forced to pay a price to implement the theoretical right that is theirs.

The usual rejoinder here is to repeat (1) that Catholics may share equally in the basic and supplemental benefits of publicly supported education by sending their children to the public schools, where they will be welcome, and (2) that Catholics have every right to establish religious schools but they cannot expect any public support because *that* would violate the American tradition of separation of church and state. Within the somber shadow of that wall there is no place for further discussion. So the mystical wall remains high, the public conscience is soothed, and each succeeding year the Catholic community feels itself more aggrieved. And yet the men who built the American Republic proclaimed the separation of church and state only as a means to an end. Separation was never conceived as an end in itself but as something instrumental and subordinate to the great end they envisioned of religious liberty.

Cultivation of Talent

My second reason for suggesting appropriate public recognition and support for church-related schools is that only in this way can the nation's youthful talent be fully realized.

Perhaps this argument can be best appreciated by a look at Title I of the National Defense Education Act of 1958, which states the philosophy of this important public law. In summary, it holds (1) that the security of the nation requires the fullest development of the mental resources and technical skills of its young men and women and (2) that we must increase our efforts to identify and educate more of the talent of the nation. To all this, Catholic parents and educators voice a hearty amen. But let us see how these basic assumptions are interpreted in the rest of the Act.

In Title II, there is provision for the cancellation of up to one-half of any loan, plus interest, at a yearly rate of 10 percent for college students who will enter full-time teaching in a *public* elementary or secondary school. No "forgiveness" of debt is granted to interest future teachers in nonpublic schools, where the pressures and the needs are just as great, if not greater.

According to the terms of Title III, outright grants go to states for the acquisition of laboratory or other special equipment for instruction in science, mathematics, and modern foreign languages in *public* schools. Nonprofit, nonpublic schools may borrow money from the government for these same purposes. Under the same title, there is provision for a grant to states for the expansion or improvement of supervisory services in the fields of mathematics, science, and foreign languages, but exclusively in *public* elementary and secondary schools or junior colleges. But is it not conceivable that a fair proportion of the scientific "brains" the government sorely needs can be developed within Catholic schools?

Title V makes grants to assist public secondary schools in their counseling and guidance programs. But what happens to the program in Rhode Island, for instance, where 31 percent of the elementary and secondary school population is enrolled in parochial schools?

While the NDEA does not distinguish between public and private institutions of higher learning, it clearly does on the secondary and elementary school level. Thus, despite its many excellent provisions, the Act pinpoints the Catholic grievance. It is projected for the defense of the American people; it offers support for the improved training of the nation's school population. Yet simply because they are in religiously oriented schools, Catholic students and teachers are accorded second-class treatment for fear of non-Catholic protest that the benefits of the Act might incidentally accrue to Catholic institutions.

Let me read once more the assumptions underlying this Act in their *applied* meaning: First, the security of the nation requires the fullest development of the mental resources and technical skills of its young men and women *except* those had by the five million young people that are in Catholic schools. Second, we must increase our efforts to identify and educate more of the talent of the nation *except* in Milwaukee, Boston, Chicago, Philadelphia, Buffalo and New

Orleans and other places, where one-third or more of the school enrollment is in Catholic schools.

Put this way, the whole thing sounds harshly discriminatory. It is. During these years, when the nation cannot afford to leave any talent undeveloped wherever available, have not Catholics the right to expect that government supported programs in counseling, testing, and guidance will include their children in parochial schools? If the federal government, in the interests of national defense and world leadership, is going to help local communities to identify, guide, and subsidize student talent, should it not do so in a rational, comprehensive manner?

Immediate Objectives

Several times I have used the phrase "appropriate" recognition and support. In this discussion, I have been arguing for the acceptance of a principle. However, the Catholic laity and clergy of the United States are fully aware that direct basic support by the government to parochial schools is out of the question for perhaps several more generations. If for no other reason, the rancor and strife set off by organized Catholic efforts to obtain such aid would poison community relations for years to come, and Catholics themselves would be losers in the long run. But this is not an abjuration of the claim to support in principle, for this is basically a question of civil rights.

But what do Catholics want *now*? Fundamentally, they want a sympathetic hearing for their case, public recognition of their problem, and help in working out an equitable solution. There is wide consensus among clergy and laity that Catholic energies would be best spent on achieving fuller distribution of educational items immediately related to the child benefit principle, the legal dimensions of which have already been largely indicated by the courts.

Even back in 1949, Cardinal Spellman was emphasizing that the subject of the controversy over Federal aid was not basic institutional support (New York *Times*, August 6, 1949) but what the U.S. Supreme Court and the Supreme Courts of California, Kentucky, Louisiana, Massachusetts, Maryland, and New Jersey had solemnly approved. These items concerned health services, nonreligious textbooks, and bus transportation for all American school children.

An awareness is growing that the sheer dimensions of the Catholic school system make its needs and interest more than the concern of the Catholic community. Having recognized the primacy of parental choice in education, the wider American public cannot be indifferent to the consequences of the exercise of this freedom. Neither Dr. Butts nor the citizens of Pittsburgh, for instance, can turn their backs completely on 42 percent of that city's school population in

Catholic schools. The international pressures and social realities of today are different from those of yesterday. In its own time, American society will translate its appreciation of the religious school into a corresponding pattern of appropriate support. The American people have approached other delicate problems of culture and freedom with honesty, fairness, and mutual sympathy. America's more-than-a-century-old school problem will one day be resolved in the same spirit.

Notes

Adapted from a paper read at the annual convention of the American Association of School Administrators at Atlantic City, N. J., 15 February, 1960. The argument of Professor R. Freeman Butts, to which Father McCluskey's present paper is a rebuttal, is published on pp. 57–62 of the current issue of the *Teachers College Record*.

1. National Education Association, American Association of School Administrators, Educational Policies Commission, *Moral and Spiritual Value in the Public Schools*. Washington; The Commission, 1951.

2. R. Henle, "American Principles and Religious Schools," *St. Louis University Law Journal* (1955) 3, 237–251.

SHELDON ACKLEY

Public Funds, Private Religion

One of the signal accomplishments of the founders of the United States was the framing of the First Amendment, which guaranteed religious freedom—along with other freedoms of thought and action—and for the first time in history required the separation of church and state in order to defend this freedom. Where earlier secular governments in the modern world had sought either to control or to establish churches, the founders of our government sought the neutrality of government with respect to religious affairs. They were not motivated by anti-religious feelings in divorcing the two, but rather by strong convictions that religion would flower only apart from political pressures.

This novel approach to a persistent and troublesome problem was devised and introduced within a period of fifteen years between 1776 and 1791. The Continental Congress began its sessions in 1775

Sheldon Ackley, "Public Funds, Private Religion," *The Humanist*, vol. 28 (May/June, 1968), 6–10. Reprinted by permission.

with a resolution calling for prayer at the beginning of each session and designating a Church of England clergyman as its chaplain. In its deliberations there were many references to religion expressed in thoroughly Protestant terms and legislation on morality, sin, repentance, penance, public worship, chaplains, and Thanksgiving. The following year the Declaration of Independence was issued with four references to deity. At the time of the Revolution, eight of the thirteen former colonies had established religions, and four of the remaining supported religion publicly. Several religions were among these state-supported churches. In 1786 a bill was introduced in the Virginia legislature for the establishment of religion there. This was defeated, and instead, Thomas Jefferson's "Statute of Religious Liberty" was passed. This signaled a turning point. The following year the Constitutional Convention met for four months without a prayer. Benjamin Franklin, then 81, moved for the introduction of prayers at the end of the first month, but, after much embarrassment, the Constitutional Convention delegates adjourned the meeting without acting on the motion. The Constitution drafted in the Convention contains no allusion to God, and its only reference to religion is its ban on religious tests for office holders. This shift to a separatist position culminated in the adoption of the First Amendment in 1791.

This dramatic and rapid shift focused several important trends. It gave expression to the dominant Protestantism of the day—a pietism that taught that religion should be personal: "Render unto Caesar that which is Caesar's and unto God that which is God's." It was consistent at the same time with the deism of influential founding fathers—Jefferson, Paine, etc.—who were religious but regarded God's greatest handiwork to be nature with its presumed order and rationality. For them free religion and free thought were bound together. The resolution contained in the First Amendment was also politically expedient, for the religious beliefs of the Colonists were by no means unanimous. The Pilgrims were separatists, but the Puritans were theocrats. Some colonists came to the new world to free themselves of religions supported by the state, while others came to establish religious communities that would control all secular affairs. The neutrality of government proclaimed in the First Amendment is, therefore, a neutrality among competing religions as well as public neutrality with respect to religion of all kinds. For all these positions it is sensible to include religious freedom in the same amendment with free thought. Separation is seen as one aspect of religious freedom, not merely a means to another end. Government should be neutral with respect to religion, permitting all religions to function but aiding none.

The neutrality imposed upon government by the First Amendment is by no means anti-religious; it is urged out of respect for religion and follows from the conviction that religion will be genuine only if independent. This is a theme that runs through the decisions of justices who have participated in cases interpreting the First Amendment. Justice Rutledge, in his dissent in *Everson* wrote, "The great condition of religious liberty is that it be maintained free from sustenance, as also from other interferences, by the state. For when it comes to rest upon that secular foundation, it vanishes with the resting." In this passage he was paraphrasing James Madison's *Remonstrance*. Justice Douglas wrote in *Engel v. Vitale*, the 1962 prayer case, "The philosophy is that if government interferes in matters spiritual, it will be a divisive force. The First Amendment teaches that a government neutral in the field of religion better serves all religious interests." This, then, is the traditional American view of the proper relation of church and state. Separation is an essential of religious belief. It prevents the state from coercing any citizen in the support of any religion, his own or another. Such coercion is an invasion of the religious or personal beliefs of the citizen. The state cannot require anyone to pay for the support of clergy, the operation or construction of churches, the costs of religious services or instruction, the operation of programs or institutions that perform services incidental to the propagation of religion, or materials used in the maintenance, operation, or teaching of religion. The tyranny resulting from such coercion is relatively unknown in this country because separation has been our tradition for so long. This is, in one way, unfortunate, for it leaves Americans unsuspecting and vulnerable. We must recognize that this "hands off" attitude on the part of the government has permitted the flowering of many religions and has increased the options available to individuals. Dissent is established, for every citizen lives alongside and respects other citizens whose religion he refuses to accept and refuses to support. This is a pluralistic society and a far cry from the church-dominated Middle Ages. David Dudley Field, the American jurist, has gone so far as to say that the "greatest achievement ever made in the course of human progress is the total and final separation of church and state." Certainly it is one of the important and successful social experiments conducted by this country. Yet, in spite of long and favorable experience, the separation of church and state is being subjected to the heaviest attack ever. The attack is mounted in an effort to free public funds for the support of parochial schools. The arguments on each side should be clearly understood if we are to make sound judgments in this area of public policy.

The First Amendment begins quite simply with the assertion that "Congress shall make no law respecting an establishment of religion or prohibiting the free exercise thereof." This is the bulwark of religious freedom in the United States. The First Amendment makes no reference to schools or education, and this has been interpreted by some to mean that the proscription does not extend to funds in aid of parochial schools. However, public education did not exist in the early republic. With its appearance in the middle of the nineteenth century, most state legislatures passed statutes (13) or constitutional provisions (35) worded like an amendment proposed at one time by Senator James G. Blaine for the federal constitution. In the form in which it appeared in the New York State Constitution (now Art. XI, Sec. 3) originally it read:

> Neither the state nor any subdivision thereof shall use its property or credit or any public money, or authorize or permit either to be used, directly or indirectly, in aid or maintenance, other than for examination or inspection, of any school or institution of learning wholly or in part under the control or direction of any religious denomination, or in which any denominational tenet or doctrine is taught.

Such laws were written to apply the separation clause explicitly to educational institutions, thus preventing sectarian influences in the new public schools and barring public support for parochial schools. Both federal and state courts have, in general, rendered decisions upholding the principle of the separation of the church and state, although there is not anything approaching unanimity or uniformity of interpretation. In spite of this, the debate rages on.

The issue is a complex one, but opposition to the separation of church and state rests upon two arguments. The first is generally known as the *child benefit theory*, and the second may be called the *public benefit theory*. Each of these purports to justify the use of public funds for parochial schools, and, since this is the topic of much heated debate each needs to be understood.

The child benefit theory perhaps can best be understood by reviewing the *Everson* case (1946). Justice Black, writing the majority opinion in this case, formulated the principles which are today the prevailing ones in this area for the Supreme Court. Three times since they were enunciated in this opinion as the minimal meaning of the establishment clause of the First Amendment, they have been quoted approvingly in other cases, once by a unanimous court. Justice Black applied the separation clause to the question of public funds to parochial schools in the following language: "No tax in any amount, large or small, can be levied to support any religious activities or institutions, whatever they may be called, or whatever form they may adopt to teach or practice religions." This is prevailing law.

Yet in the *Everson* case the nine justices who agreed on this statement of principle split 5–4 on the decision in the case with which they were faced. This had to do with the use of tax funds to provide bus transportation for parochial students comparable to that offered to public school students. The majority held such a service did not contravene the First Amendment; their view was not unreasonable. Fire and police protection are offered to religious institutions, and medical and welfare benefits are given to parochial school students just as to public school students, often in the parochial schools. To with-hold these services and benefits would be to discriminate against one group of citizens on the basis of their religion. Black posed the dilemma in his opinion:

> New Jersey cannot consistently with the "establishment of religion" clause of the First Amendment contribute tax-raised funds to the support of an institution which teaches the tenets and faiths of any church . . . we must be careful in protecting the citizens of New Jersey against state-established churches, to be sure that we do not inadvertently prohibit New Jersey from extending its general state law benefits to all its citizens without regard to their religious belief.

The decision reached by the majority upheld the use of tax money for bus transportation on their judgment that this was a service to the children and not support for the parochial education being offered them. They concluded, with respect to the situation before them, "The state contributes no money to the schools. It does not support them. Its legislation, as applied, does no more than provide a general program to help parents get their children, regardless of their re-ligion, safely and expeditiously to and from accredited schools."

It seems clear that the Court in *Everson* was assuming that the education offered in parochial schools is religious in nature, pervaded by the religion of the sponsoring church, and an aid in indoctrinating the students in that religion. The supporters of aid to parochial schools, in noting that the courts are sympathetic to legislation that will benefit the children, but not aid the religion, have now disputed this assumption. They contend that education benefits the child and that public funds should be made available for a child's education regardless of the sponsorship of the school in which he is enrolled.

Out of this view comes a proposal that tax funds be used to give a lump sum to each child for use in a school of his own choice. This is the "tuition grant" system proposed also by racial segregationists as a means of circumventing the 1954 Supreme Court decision calling for the end of school segregation. The Supreme Court rejected the plan in a case involving Prince Edward County in Virginia, saying that it is an essential part of the concept of American freedom that each child be given the opportunity to obtain a *public* school education. It held that the tuition grant system was a clear invasion of the community's responsibility for such a public school system. It seems clear from this decision that, quite apart from First Amendment considerations, there are limits upon the uses to which public funds may be put in support of private education. When, on top of these considerations, it is seen that such tax money is used to strengthen a religion, the objection becomes overwhelming. In 1961 the Vermont high court ruled unconstitutional a statute authorizing payment of tuition grants for students attending parochial schools, and similar decisions may be expected in like circumstances elsewhere. The key fault lies in that parochial education does in fact involve inevitably and pervasively the teaching of religion. It has been argued, to the contrary, that some or many subjects covered in parochial schools are completely secular. Were this true, it could well be argued, although there is no legal precedent in which the principle is established, that public funds could be used in support of this portion of the curriculum. That this is not the case is fairly clear. One needs to refer only to the curriculum in the largest of the parochial school systems in this country. Catholic doctrine requires special treatment of many historical and scientific subjects, literary and artistic topics, and areas involving personal standards or public policy. The official policy of the Church requires that the subjects reflect the Church's point of view. As stated, for example, in the encyclical "Christian Education of Youth" issued by Pope Pius XI in 1930, it reads, "To be [a fit place for Catholic students] . . . it is necessary that all the teaching and the whole organization of the school, and its teachers, syllabus and textbooks in every branch, be regulated by the Christian spirit." Other denominations express the same interest in education permeated by religion throughout. This fact influenced the highest court of Oregon to rule in the *Dickman* case (1962) that, since religious aspects of parochial education cannot be separated from secular ones, secular textbooks cannot be loaned to parochial school students by the state. It would hardly make sense to finance separate school systems, if, in fact, the education offered were not appreciably different. Parochial schools are the product of missionary zeal; they are maintained at considerable sacrifice in order to promote a religion.

The child benefit theory has had limited success in cases that have been tested in the courts. Bus transportation has already been mentioned, and peripheral services, such as hot lunches and medical and dental programs have not been contested. Textbooks have been granted in some cases and have been withheld in others. In 1928, a Louisiana statute lending textbooks in secular subjects to parochial students was upheld (in the *Cochran* case) on the grounds of benefit to the children. Later, Mississippi courts upheld, while Maine, South Dakota, New Mexico, and Oregon courts invalidated, similar statutes. New York invalidated such a law in the *Judd* case (1938) and then upheld one in the *East Greenbush* case (1966). The argument has never successfully sustained public grants for teachers' salaries or funds for the construction of classrooms, buildings, or other facilities.

The child benefit theory has, to the extent it has permitted public funds to be used for textbooks, lowered the wall of separation, for textbooks are an essential part of any curriculum in which they are used and church funds are released for other purposes to the extent that tax monies pay for textbooks. The religious aims of the parochial school are served by public funds in such cases. At most, however, the arguments have had a very limited success.

While efforts continue to secure funds for a part of the program of parochial schools on the grounds this portion is secular and does not promote religion, a second argument is also being forwarded. This argues that parochial schools serve a public purpose and on this ground should receive public money. This I call the "public benefit theory." Its plausibility rests upon the fact—increasingly evident as our culture becomes more complex and technologically oriented—that the education of its citizens is requisite for personal effectiveness and social progress. The education of children benefits the public, whether provided by public or private schools. This is recognized in the well-established right of parents to send their children to private schools as long as these schools meet educational standards set by the state. But private schools are usually established in order to achieve other goals than those sought by the public schools. In order to achieve these private goals, the private schools often adopt practices that are not proper for public agencies. The private purposes are the motivating ones and—when the private purposes are religious—public funds are improperly used in their support.

Parochial schools are established to propagate a religion through offering education consistent in all respects with the religion. Any public benefit they provide is incidental to this primary purpose. Their practices make clear this priority of private purposes over public. Professor George LaNoue (*Public Funds for Parochial Schools?*, 34–35) states criteria by which we may judge whether a given school operates in such a fashion that it can be considered to fulfill a public purpose.

If a school truly serves a public purpose, it should be willing:

1) to admit all qualified students regardless of race, religion, or national origin;
2) to hire its staff without regard to race, religion, or national origin;
3) to allow democratically-elected public representatives to have a voice in its policies:
4) to avoid sectarian teaching or sectarian practices.

It is obvious that the operation of schools meeting these simple standards would not be worth the effort for a religion. Yet the standards are reasonable—in fact, minimal. The Supreme Court has ruled that racial segregation is impermissible in public schools; the standard must be the same with respect to religion, and so schools supported by public funds cannot select students on the basis of religion. The Constitution bars religious tests for public office holders and would certainly impose its standards upon the faculties of such schools. Public representatives should not only have a voice, but a controlling voice, in schools supported by tax funds. Standards of performance would have to be determined by the state, which would have also to determine that these standards are being met. No sectarian or religious teaching could be included in the curriculum, as this would offer the support of government to their religion. Religions do not really wish to sponsor *public* schools; they wish only to obtain public funds to pay the cost of teaching a religion in schools under their own control and using private standards of selection. They cannot have it both ways.

The public benefit theory has had some political success. It has been used to justify some appropriations in the antipoverty program and has influenced the Higher Education Facilities Act of 1963 and the Elementary and Secondary Education Act of 1965. In general these federal laws have used the *Cochran* decision as their precedent (in spite of the fact that most state courts when faced with similar statutes have declared them unconstitutional) and the public library system as a model. Congress has limited support for parochial school students to the lending of textbooks and materials that are approved for use by the State. In general, Congress has conformed to the standards suggested by Professor LaNoue and quoted above. For example, both the House and Senate Committee drafting the ESEA Act of 1965 placed explicit restrictions upon the use of funds under that Act, generally following standards summarized above. Later House Report 1814 reiterated the same standards with respect to Title II of the same Act.

In its most common form the public benefit theory argues that the grants are made to effect public purposes—train underprivileged children, offer instructions in subjects required in the public interest, underwrite research needed for national defense, etc.—and benefit religion only incidentally. This argument was explicitly rejected by the courts in Oregon in the *Dickman* case (1962). Such a public function, if actually performed by a parochial school, is apt to be a narrow one. For example, it may be in the interest of both the school and the government to train students in the Chinese language and literature. If so, grants for this particular purpose may be justified. Such appropriations are classed as project grants rather than institutional grants. They are more familiar in institutions of higher education, where religious sponsorship and aims are also often less closely related.

As is well known, however, private institutions have frequently been influenced by the availability of public funds to shape their programs so as to become eligible for such funds. To the extent a parochial school becomes dependent upon public funds, it is subjected to pressures to replace its original objectives with those of the funding agent. Thus the granting of public funds to parochial schools poses a threat to religious freedom. Either public funds are appropriated unconstitutionally or religious freedom is abridged. This is one of the serious flaws in public aid to religious institutions.

Neither the child benefit nor the public benefit theory is substantial enough to justify public support for parochial schools. The former depends upon the fallacy that some parts of the parochial school curriculum will be unaffected by the religious beliefs of its sponsors, and the latter depends upon the fallacy that the religious motivation of those who run the school will not materially influence the curriculum or management of the school. Our whole experience forces us to the contrary conclusion that parochial schools have as their primary and overriding purpose the inculcation of their religion in the students enrolled.

In spite of this, religious forces are going all out to weaken the principle of separation in this country so that public funds can be used in support of parochial schools. Two chief arenas exist at the moment. They have been chosen because the courts, both federal and state, have interpreted the First Amendment fairly restrictively in the cases it has reviewed. At the federal level, as indicated above, legislation providing support for parochial schools has been passed under the guise of aid to needy children or aid for public projects. This has been made possible by the inability of citizens to establish their right under ordinary circumstances to sue the federal government to test the constitutionality of these laws. Religious lobbyists have been successful so far in preventing the passage of legislation that would permit such tests, although a bill with this purpose has passed the Senate. The Supreme Court recently agreed to rule whether a group of organizations including the New York Civil Liberties Union, the United Parents Association, The American Jewish Congress, and the United Federation of Teachers, AFL-CIO, have standing to test the constitutionality of the Elementary and Secondary Education Act of 1965.

At the state level the most important activity has centered upon efforts in several states to call constitutional conventions in order to eliminate those provisions in state constitutions banning the use of public funds for parochial schools. The first, and in many ways the most important, of these took place during the summer of 1967 in New York State. There the Constitutional Convention recommended deletion of the appropriate section. As mentioned above, the clause in question is significant chiefly because it explicitly prohibits indirect aid in the field of education. Such legislation has prevented certain kinds of aid to parochial schools, although the most recent interpretation of it in New York is a grotesque misreading that pretty well emasculates it at least for the time being.

In proposing the change, the convention sought to substitute First Amendment language for this so-called Blaine Amendment, to insert a clause permitting a citizen to bring suit to test the constitutionality of any state legislation, and to prohibit schools receiving public funds from discriminating in the selection of its students on the basis of their religion. The constitution as it was submitted to the voters was treated by the more sophisticated constitutional delegates who worked out this "compromise" as a more perfect defense of the separation principle.

Quite apart from the niceties of legal interpretation of both the present New York State Constitution and the one proposed by the Constitutional Convention, the options confronted the voters with a referendum upon the separation principle. Feelings ran high on both sides, and the proposed constitution was defeated resoundingly. In view of the fact that most analysts found a great number of the other provisions to be improvements over the existing constitution, this issue must be considered the greatest single cause of the constitution's defeat. The outcome was a surprising one and encourages one to believe that the clamor for public funds for parochial education comes from a distinctly minority group. The campaign revealed, not unexpectedly, that this issue is a dangerously divisive one—in this respect proving once again the wisdom of separating religion from governmental attention and solicitude.

The defeat of the proposed New York State constitution was an important victory for the principle of the separation of church and state, for, should the proposed constitution have been substituted for the existing one, there would have been tremendous pressures for grants of public money in support of parochial schools. These pressures would have been felt by school board members, legislators, and even judges. And under these circumstances these officials might not have shown the same understanding and support of constitutional principles as we have come to expect from our courts in the past few decades. Nor would these pressures have been felt only in New York State. A precedent would have been established and there would undoubtedly have been great efforts to hold constitutional conventions in the 34 other states with similar constitutional provisions for the express purpose of removing them. And, of course, there may still be such efforts. The threat to religious freedom is indeed a real one, perhaps the most serious that has ever faced the country.

As never before, we need to understand and support the principle of the separation of church and state as a bulwark of religious freedom in the United States. The principle can be stated simply: The Constitution guarantees religious freedom to all Americans. This freedom requires that no American be coerced to support a belief other than his own. Tax money cannot be used to support one religion or all religions without forcing all taxpayers of other religions or no religion to support a belief other than their own. As Jefferson wrote in the preamble to the Bill for the Establishing of Religious Freedom in Virginia, "To compel a man to furnish contributions of money for the propagation of opinions which he disbelieves and abhors, is unjust and tyrannical."

The great push being made now for public support of religious institutions, especially parochial schools, seeks to make all Americans both victims of and parties to this injustice and tyranny.

Suggested Readings:
Finance

ADVISORY COMMISSION ON INTERGOVERNMENTAL RELATIONS. *State and Local Finances: Significant Features, 1967 to 1970.* Report M-50. Washington, D. C.: U. S. Government Printing Office, November 1969. Detailed tabular and graphic listing of latest trends in state and local finances. Notes perceived characteristics of a "high quality state-local tax system" and suggests model state tax and finance reform legislation.

————. *Fiscal Balance in the American Federal System.* 2 Volumes. Report A-31. Washington, D. C.: U. S. Government Printing Office, 1967. One of the comprehensive reviews of the complexities of public finances in the American federal system; with suggested reforms. Volume Two examines in detail the social and economic disparities between suburb and central city in most of metropolitan America.

DAVIES, DAVID. "Financing Urban Functions and Services." *Law and Contemporary Problems,* vol. 30 (Winter 1965), pp. 127–161. A leading economist's review of important theoretical and practical problems of financing urban services.

ECKER-RACZ, L. L. *The Politics and Economics of State and Local Finance.* Englewood Cliffs: Prentice-Hall, Inc., 1970. Best and most readable study of the political-economic interactions of state and local public policy.

FENTON, JOHN H., and DONALD W. CHAMBERLAYNE. "The Literature Dealing with the Relationships Between Political Processes, Socio-economic Conditions and Public Policies in the American States: A Bibliographical Essay." *Polity,* vol. I (Spring 1969), pp. 388–394. Comprehensive, analytical review of this very important emerging area of study.

MAXWELL, JAMES A. *Financing State and Local Government.* Revised Edition. Washington, D. C.: The Brookings Institution, 1969. Analysis of the financing of state and local governments with major attention paid to intergovernmental variables.

6/Urban Violence:

Community or Jungle?

As John Stuart Mill has noted, "the struggle between liberty and authority is the most conspicuous feature in the portions of history."[1] The very creation of the United States was part of this struggle. In a very real way, American history has been a series of new institutions designed to promote and protect individual liberties vis-à-vis needed governmental authority. In this area, we have had repeated successes.

There is, however, another struggle which recurs in history, that of violence versus order, peaceful intercourse versus forceful exchange, community versus jungle. In this sense, America has failed. As a nation, we were conceived in violent revolution, fought one of the bloodiest civil wars in history, and have been in almost constant warfare since 1942. Our political and social objectives are literally fought out in the streets: civil war draft riots, labor union struggles, race riots of the 1940s, civil rights violence of the 1950s and 1960s, attempts to decide foreign policy in the streets, even political assassination.

The violence of the 1960s and that predicted for the 1970s differs from that of the past. This is an enduring and rather constant form of violence. The articles in Part 6 stress this difference. There are few periods of the last decade that were not marked by civil strife. "The annual burning of the cities" has become a fact of life. The years ahead will be similarly marked.

Note the testimony of Dr. Kenneth B. Clark before the Kerner Commission:[2]

> I read that report . . . of the 1919 riot in Chicago, and it is as if I were reading the report of the investigating committee on the Harlem riot of '35, the report of the investigating committee on

the Harlem riot of '43, the report of the McCone Commission on the Watts riot.

I must again in candor say to you members of this Commission—it is a kind of Alice in Wonderland—with the same moving picture reshown over and over again, the same analysis, the same recommendations, and the same inaction.

Can anyone seriously doubt that if Dr. Clark were testifying today, he would include the Kerner Commission's findings and recommendations in his looking-glass world?

The readings suggest another similarity of recent riots. The violence is not, for the most part, merely an emotional, negative reaction to an immediate event. There is a certain positiveness to the disorders. Professors Boskin and Geschwender, as well as the Kerner Commission selections, emphasize the positive, directed aspects of recent violence. Geschwender refers to the 1960 strife in our cities as an extension of the civil rights movement—a social movement. It was "creative riot."

The unanswered questions suggested by the readings run rampant. What are the causes of the violence? Will it run its course, or force suppressive counterviolence? Is our government so unresponsive that we must use such means to force change? Can we reform our institutions so as to render the need for such conflict unnecessary? If so, how? If not, are we destined to live in an armed police state which is sure to destroy 200 years of gains in political liberty?

We will know the answers to most of these questions, for better or worse, by the end of the 1970s.

Notes

1. John Stuart Mill, *On Liberty,* ed. by Currin V. Shields (Indianapolis: The Bobbs-Merrill Co., Inc., 1956), p. 3.
2. *Report of the National Advisory Commission on Civil Disorders* (Washington, D.C.: U.S. Government Printing Office, 1968), p. 13.

JOSEPH BOSKIN

The Revolt
of the Urban Ghettos, 1964–1967

Alternating extremes of elation and despair have characterized black protest in the 1960's. Vacillating between the studied nonviolent and the spontaneous violent approaches to the entrapments of ghetto life, Negro behavior has mirrored the dilemma of the exploited, dark-skinned person: whether to withstand the rejection of the majority in the hope that ameliorative actions would bring rewards within the system or to lash out and destroy the hated environment, thus bringing abrupt awareness to the majority and release for oneself. Over one hundred major revolts in as many cities in the incredibly short space of three years have demonstrated that for those blacks outside of the civil rights and other allied protest movements of the mid-1950's and early 1960's, the course of protest was to be disruptive and violent. Clearly, the behavior of blacks in the large and small ghettos connoted a consensus of attitude toward their own communities, one another, and the larger society. Their actions signified the most important underclass revolt[1] in recent American history.

The Continuing Conflict of Race

The urban protest riots proved to be the pivotal black response. The riots affected the course of the civil rights movement; they coalesced the young, lower- and middle-class Negroes in the cities; they marked the growing conflict between the generations and the classes in Negro communities throughout the nation. Further, they symbolized the inability of American democracy to cope effectively with the historical-psychological problem of racism. The riots, in fact, split the nation in the 1960's and prompted the period of polarization. The clashes of the summer of 1967, however, marked an end to the spontaneous outbursts of the previous period of urban violence. A new stance was effected, as militant groups fashioned a framework of sociopolitical objectives essentially absent in the earlier period of protest.

As the incidence of riots marked the departure from the civil rights period, this new expression of protest in the 1960's can be differentiated from the more characteristic form of urban racial violence

Joseph Boskin, "The Revolt of the Urban Ghettos, 1964–1967," *The Annals of the American Academy of Political and Social Science*, 382 (March 1969), 2–14. Reprinted by permission.

which prevailed in the past. With the exception of the Harlem riots of 1935 and 1943, which seemed more clearly to be the consequence of economic and wartime conditions, the riots of the past two centuries were initiated by Caucasians and were motivated by racist attitudes.

In these racial episodes, Negroes suffered the bulk of personal and property damage, with little restitution offered from civil authorities. Between 1900 and 1949, there were thirty-three major interracial clashes. Of these, eighteen occurred during the period of World War I and its aftermath, whereas five occurred during World War II. Obviously, the majority of these occurrences reflected situations of a critical nature.

From the end of World War II until 1964, there were several large-scale urban disturbances which reflected the underlying potential for social violence. None of these conflicts expanded into major urban conflagrations. Rather, most of the clashes were manifestations of what Allen Grimshaw has called "assaults upon the accommodative structure," that is, Negro challenges to the socioeconomic structure of a community. The most intense violence occurred when minority groups attempted to change residential patterns or when a number of Caucasians defined the situation as one in which such an attempt was being made.

The volatility of these situations was constantly reflected in the years following the termination of the war. Resentment against Negroes who moved into all-white neighborhoods resulted in more than a hundred incidents: the Airport Homes violence in Chicago in November 1945; the Fernwood Project violence, also in Chicago, August 1947; the Georgia house-bombings in May 1947; and the highly publicized violence of 1951 in Cicero, Illinois. Some of the weapons employed by white assaulters—bricks, guns, sniping, Molotov cocktails—were those which were utilized by blacks in the 1960's. Racial violence also occurred when Negroes attempted to use public recreational facilities traditionally reserved for Caucasians in northern and midwestern cities. In sum, the race riots which raged in American society from the turn of the century until the mid-1960's reflected extensions of white racism. The rebellions which began in 1964 represented a major response to that racism.

The explosion of the blacks in the urban ghettos from 1964 to 1967 was presaged three decades ago in the lines of poet Langston Hughes:

> Negroes,
> Sweet and docile,
> Meek, humble, and kind:
> Beware the day
> They change their minds![2]

As late as the year of the first riots came the powerful words of Kenneth Clark, the eminent psychologist, in his work *Dark Ghetto:*

The poor are always alienated from normal society, and when the poor are Negro, as they increasingly are in the American cities, a double trauma exists—rejection on the basis of class and race is a danger to the stability of the society as a whole.[3]

And, in 1965, a shocked but largely lethargic surburban society was admonished by Mayor Robert Wagner of New York:

There are lions in the streets, angry lions, aggrieved lions, lions who have been caged until the cages crumbled. We had better do something about those lions, and when I speak of lions I do not mean individuals. I mean the spirit of the people. Those who have been neglected and oppressed and discriminated against and misunderstood and forgotten.[4]

Yet, despite a year of violent urban disruptions and countless admonitions from leaders in the Caucasian and black communities, the disturbances were ascribed to a minority of disgruntled blacks. Few were prepared—even after studies had demonstrated that a sizable proportion of Negroes were actively involved in the rebellions—to accept the fact that Negroes were indeed alienated from American society and angry enough to destroy the environments immediately surrounding them which represented the outside repressive world.

That blacks vented their antagonism on the buildings, streets, and businesses within their immediate reach and avoided these same places in exclusively white areas is crucial to an understanding of their motivations. Central to the development of the *zeitgeist* of the revolts were the attitudes of the Caucasian not only regarding the Negro—which, to understate the situation, is well understood as being antagonistic—but regarding the Negro's environment, that is, the city itself. The experience of the blacks in their mass migration into the core cities was inextricably related to the attitudes of whites toward the cities. For it is not merely the fact of high-density populations living in slum conditions which brought blacks to convulsive actions but, more importantly, the approach which predominates in relation to those enclaves which we call the city. The riot was a response to the interaction of both majority and minority in their respective attitudes toward the ghetto and the city. An essential component of its origin was the majority's rejection of the city as a viable and creative environment within which to live. Thus, an ecological malaise was one of the primary causes of the violent protest.

The City: Never the Promised Land

One of the most poignant and enduring conflicts in our national life, frequently subtle, yet constantly gnawing, has been the antagonism between rural and urban America. This has been far more than a conflict between the political and power interests of divergent human locales; it has been a conflict in the American consciousness, and is implicit in the American value system. Since the early nineteenth century, millions of Americans have yielded to a seemingly fatal attraction to make the great migration from farm and village to the city. Whatever may have been the harsh imperatives which guided them, there was a persistent tendency to look back, with a degree of nostalgia and with a sense of irreparable loss, to an idyllic rural setting. In a nation in which the forces of urbanization were unrelenting, where urban living was clearly the shape of the future, there was a deep conviction, as Walter Lippmann wrote, that the city should not be acknowledged as the American ideal. This mood was not limited merely to those who had strayed from the intended ways, but was shared by those who were born in the city environs. The city has never been conceived as being the preferred place to inhabit permanently, nor has it been romanticized in the arts and mass media. It has rarely been regarded as a focus for creative living.

The burgeoning of industry, and the expansion of the middle class, with its increased financial and physical mobility, enabled the nostalgic rural life to be transplanted into suburbia and exurbia. Thus, for this group of urban dwellers, alternatives of living were possible. The actuality of choice, however, gave rise to an ambivalence in which the best and worst of feelings conjoined: the desire for the idealized rural life-style and a strong desire to partake in the activities of the city.

The movement into the cities in the past two centuries, then, was not accomplished without the creation of a basic paradox. The economic means to achieve a fuller life, though associated with the city, was not fulfilled within the city. The compromise of the suburban community seemed to provide a solution to the uncomfortable dilemma of rural versus urban life. Seemingly, one could have the best of both styles. Several difficulties, however, prevented the suburb from becoming the American middle-class nirvana. The magnitude of the march to the suburbs necessitated mass transportation to and from the central cities. The city administrators' choice, the freeway, soon became a strangulated contact with the city, bringing it not close enough, yet too far away. Yet, many who lived in suburbia were economically dependent upon the city, so that contact with the core city was never physically far removed. Ironically, too, transportation arteries made possible the invisibility of the ghettos.

The development of a sophisticated mass communications system, in the form of television, in the early 1950's reinforced the ambivalent antagonisms towards the city. Throughout the 1950's and 1960's, television portrayed the city as a violent, unhealthy, dirty, corrupt, lonely, unseemly place for people to live, develop, and grow. Survival appeared to be the main component dramatized in series after series. With the exceptions of such productions as were bor-

rowed from earlier successful radio shows, the bulk of television per-
formances were antiurban in substance. In such medical series as
"Ben Casey," "The Young Interns," and "The Nurses," psychological maladies or life and death were constant themes. The decade
of the 1920's, depicted in such series as "The Roaring Twenties" and
"The Untouchables," consistently associated the city with gang violence. In such outstanding series as "Naked City," which dealt with
some realistic problems of life in New York, and "East Side, West
Side," a series based on the experiences of a social worker, the promise
and potential of the city were lacking. Television largely reinforced
the image of the city earlier perpetuated by literature and the movies.
As Herbert Kosower has correctly noted: "Almost all of Hollywood's
films deal with contemporary urban life on a superficial fantasy
plane."[5] Even *Street Scene, On the Waterfront, The Naked City, The
Pawnbroker*, and *A Thousand Clowns* tended to reflect the harsh
aspects of urban life.

Resistance to city living grew from several sources. The organization of the city was felt to be antagonistic to basic American values.
It bred impersonality, detachment, and unhealthy conditions. Criticism stemmed from the conception of the city as being anti-
individualistic. Groups of people were herded together in living and
working conditions which placed a premium on co-operative and
collectivistic solutions to social problems.

The city was further indicted for altering the landscape of
America, for denying its past and playing havoc with its future. As
Anselm Strauss has accurately written, the United States managed to
develop an industrial economy without developing a thoroughly urbanized citizenry. Americans, he noted, entered upon the great urbanization of the nineteenth century "protestingly, metaphorically
walking backward."[6]

The image of the city was capped in the catch phrase originally
ascribed to New York City: "It's a nice place to visit but I wouldn't
want to live there." Living was to be done in the suburbs, away from
the source of corruptions. The "Promised Land," then, was to be
sought outside the city.

Aided by affluence, millions fled from the city into the land-
scaped suburbs—leaving the core cities to the newer migrant and
immigrant groups. Negro-, Puerto Rican-, Mexican-, and Japanese-
Americans, and other smaller American minority groups with dark or
nonwhite skins, filled the central cities. By the 1960's, all major and
most smaller cities had sizable numbers of various ethnic groups in
the downtown areas, living in slum ghettos, breathing the increasingly
foul urban air, and becoming increasingly alienated. They gradually
developed an urban consciousness—a consciousness of the entrapped
underclass.

The sense of entrapment stemmed from the inability of the

ethnic groups to break out of the urban ghetto and become part of the burgeoning middle classes. Alienation grew out of the anger of betrayal, a betrayal that began when the inner-city dwellers were made the inheritors of decaying cities. That they were being deserted, that the promised land in the North and West was drying up, as Langston Hughes caustically expressed it, "like a raisin in the sun," became increasingly clear in the decades of the 1950's and 1960's. Claude Brown, in his *Manchild in the Promised Land*, an affectionate portrayal of Harlem, began his sketch with this denial of the promise:

> I want to talk about the first Northern urban generation of Negroes. I want to talk about the experiences of a misplaced generation, of a misplaced people in an extremely complex, confused society. This is a story of their searching, their dreams, their sorrows, their small and futile rebellions, and their endless battle to establish their own place in America's greatest metropolis—and in America itself.
> The characters are sons and daughters of former Southern sharecroppers. These were the poorest people of the South, who poured into New York City during the decade following the Great Depression. These migrants were told that unlimited opportunities for prosperity existed in New York and that there was no "color problem" there. They were told that Negroes lived in houses with bathrooms, electricity, running water, and indoor toilets. To them, this was the "promised land" that Mammy had been singing about in the cotton fields for many years. . . . It seems that Cousin Willie, in his lying haste, had neglected to tell the folks down home about one of the most important aspects of the promised land: it was a slum ghetto. There was a tremendous difference in the way life was lived up North. There were too many people full of hate and bitterness crowded into a dirty, stinky, uncared-for closet-size section of a great city.
> Before the soreness of the cotton fields had left Mama's back, her knees were getting sore from scrubbing "Goldberg's" floor. Nevertheless, she was better off; she had gone from the fire into the frying pan.
> The children of these disillusioned colored pioneers inherited the total lot of their parents—the disappointments, the anger. To add to their misery, they had little hope of deliverance. For where does one run to when he's already in the promised land?[7]

One runs to one's soul brother.

The significant consequences of the great migration along the hallelujah trail was the development of an urban consciousness in the ghettos of the industrial cities. Alain Locke, in his important book in the 1920's, *The New Negro*, took cognizance of the ecological forces at work in Harlem. Proscription and prejudice, he noted, had thrown dissimilar black elements into a common area of contact and interaction. Prior to the movement into Harlem, the Negro was "a race more in name than in fact, or to be exact, more in sentiment than in experience." The central experience between these groups, he continued, was that of "a common condition rather than a life in common.

In Harlem, Negro life is seizing upon its first chances for group expression and self-determination."[8] The fusing of sentiment and experience in Harlem was repeated over and again in ghettos across the country. Indeed, ghetto experience became a common denominator, its life-style and language and conditions a similarity of experiences.

Had the ghetto become a viable environment within a dynamic city existence, the level of grievance-consciousness shared by Negroes would have been muted. But the opposite occurred. Instead, the ghetto became a dead-end to those who lived in it. It became an object of loathing, a mirror of a squalid existence. Feelings of hopelessness and isolation were recurrent themes in the testimony of the slum residents, wrote the United States Commission on Civil Rights in 1967. When asked what she would do if she had sufficient income, one resident declared, "The first thing I would do myself is move out of the neighborhood. I feel the entire neighborhood is more or less a trap."[9]

Compounding these antagonisms were, of course, the intensifying antiurban attitudes of whites. "The people in Harlem," wrote James Baldwin in *Nobody Knows My Name*, two years before the first protest riot, "know they are living there because white people do not think they are good enough to live elsewhere. No amount of 'improvement' can sweeten this fact. . . . A ghetto can be improved in one way only: out of existence."[10] These resentments were further exacerbated by the obvious disparity between the Caucasian and black neighborhoods. Said a young man to Budd Schulberg in the Watts Happening Coffee House immediately after the riots:

> The contrast: the spectacular growth of central and west L. A. vs. the stagnation of Watts. . . . You've conquered it, baby. You've got it made. Some nights on the roof of our rotten falling down buildings we can actually see your lights shining in the distance. So near and yet so far. We want to reach out and grab it and punch it on the nose.[11]

The mythical urban melting pot began to simmer and finally boiled over.

The protest riots which occurred in massive profusion were thus the consequence of a myriad of historical and ecological factors which fused in the 1960's. Their outstanding feature was a collective mode of attitude, behavior, and sense of power.

The Cry: Burn, Baby, Burn

The sudden burst of rage which rent Harlem in July 1964 was the third mass outburst in that community in the twentieth century. On two previous occasions, the first time during the Great Depression and the second during World War II, blacks in one of the most highly concentrated, racially, ethnic ghettos in the nation signified their protest in spontaneous rioting. Unlike the earlier uprisings which were confined to Harlem, however, the actions in 1964 proved to be the beginning of an urban black protest throughout the country. In city after city, summer after summer, blacks took vengeance by wrecking the hated symbols within their own ghetto areas.

The violent protest in Harlem was rapidly repeated in seven other urban Negro ghettos in the next two months: Bedford-Stuyvesant (Brooklyn), Rochester, Paterson, Jersey City, Elizabeth, Philadelphia, and Dixmoor (Chicago). In 1965, eruptions occurred in five cities, the major conflagrations taking place in Chicago and especially in Los Angeles. Large-scale rioting increased in intensity in the following year, when blacks took to the streets in twenty cities, including Cleveland, Chicago, Omaha, East Oakland, and San Francisco. The year 1967 began on a volatile note as disturbances occurred in the spring in the Southern cities of Nashville, Jackson, and Houston. As the heat of the summer increased, so did the temper for violence. There were mass assaults in Roxbury (Boston), Tampa, Dayton, Atlanta, Buffalo, and Cincinnati in the month of June. Within the next two months, Negroes swarmed through the ghettos of twenty-two cities in the North, Midwest, and South, with the largest riots taking place in Toledo, Grand Rapids, Plainfield (New Jersey), Milwaukee, and especially in Newark and Detroit. By 1968 the rioting had subsided, suggesting that the anger had been channeled into aggressive community programs.

The toll of the rioting over the four-year period was devastating. Between 1964 and 1967, approximately 130 civilians, mainly Negroes, and 12 civil personnel, mainly Caucasian, were killed. Approximately 4,700 Negroes and civil personnel were injured. Over 20,000 persons were arrested during the melees; property damages mounted into the hundreds of millions of dollars; many cities resembled the hollowed remnants of war-torn cities.[12]

Despite the disparity of distance, there was a consensus of attitudes and a similarity of actions among those urban blacks who revolted and those who supported the violent protest.[13] Significantly, the riots were largely umplanned, unorganized, and unscheduled. Ray Lewis, a Cleveland youth worker, explained the origins of the outbreak in that city:

> It wasn't that people planned our riot so consciously. But take a Negro ghetto where men sit around for years saying, "we gonna get whitey," and you build up a group knowledge of what to do.[14]

Taken together, the riots were the actions of a people, poor and dispossessed and crushed in huge numbers into large slum ghettos, who rose up in wrath against a society committed to democratic ideals. Their outburst was an expression of class antagonism, resentment against racial prejudice, anger at the unreachable affluence around them, and frustration at their sociopolitical powerlessness. "What are these people riotin' about in other cities?" exclaimed Efelka Brown, of the "Sons of Watts," an organization set up to train young males in trade skills. "They want *recognition* and the only way they goin' get it is to riot. We don't want to overthrow the country— we just want what we ain't got."[15]

The sense of betrayal of expectations brought about a focus on the grievances of the past and present. The visibility of an affluent, comfortable, middle-class life, made possible by a powerful mass communications system, was in itself enough to induce dual feelings of resentment and emulation. Pronouncements by the political establishment, however, served only to increase these emotions. Thus, enticed by advertising of the leisure life, excited by legislative programs such as the Civil Rights Acts and the War on Poverty, lured by television programs depicting middle-class life, and hopeful of change in their environment, the poor anticipated an imminent improvement in their socioeconomic position. The failure of society effectively to raise the status of those trapped in the cities contributed immensely to the smoldering resentments.

The urge to retaliate, to return the hurts and the injustices, played an integral part of the protest. By itself, the riot was not "a major thing," stated James Richards to the United States Commission on Civil Rights after the Hunter's Point riot in San Francisco in 1966:

> It was just an idea to strike out at something and someone. Even if you don't do anything but break a window or a chair or something like this, you feel that you are hurting a white man or something like this because the white man is the one that is doing everything to you that causes you to have all these problems on you now.[16]

Similar expressions of deep-welled anger were heard from Puerto Ricans in Spanish Harlem. Piri Thomas, author of *Down These Mean Streets,* in testimony before the National Advisory Commission on Civil Disorders, described the origins of the explosion in that area:

> Did you ever stand on street corners and look the other way, at the world of muchos ricos and think, I ain't got a damn? Did you ever count the garbage that flowed down dirty streets, or dig in the back yards who in their glory were a garbage dumps dream? Did you ever stand on rooftops and watch night time cover the bad below? Did you ever put your hand around your throat and feel your pulse beat say, "I do belong and there's not gonna be nobody can tell me, I'm wrong?"[17]

Intense grievances vis-à-vis their inability to achieve even the basic promises of American life of work, status, and housing combined with other minor factors to make the cities highly combustible. The National Advisory Commission found in almost all the cities surveyed "the same major grievance topic among Negro communities."[18] The Commission ranked three levels of grievances among Negroes:

First Level of Intensity:
1. Police practices
2. Unemployment and underemployment
3. Inadequate housing

Second Level of Intensity:
1. Inadequate education
2. Poor recreational facilities and programs
3. Ineffectiveness of the political structure and grievance mechanisms

Third Level of Intensity:
1. Disrespectful white attitudes
2. Discriminatory administration of justice
3. Inadequacy of federal programs
4. Inadequacy of municipal services
5. Discriminatory consumer and credit practices
6. Inadequate welfare programs[19]

To strike out against the visible symbols of white society became a sign of brotherhood. In more than one instance, rock-throwing blacks placed missiles into the hands of residents of the community, saying, "You're either with us or against us, man." In the Watts riot, Mervin Dymally, a Negro assemblyman, was asked by one of the rioters to prove his loyalty by heaving an object at a police car. Dymally refused, saying, "No, man, I'm for peace." The boy quickly replied, "No, you're with the man."[20] Many residents of ghetto areas who did not participate in the actions shouted their approval to those on the streets.

That a general approval, a collective behavior, pervaded the ghettos can be borne out by analysis of the actions of blacks. The two groups singled out for attack were the police and Caucasian-owned businesses. Relations between the police and the minorities, particularly members of the dark-skinned ethnic groups, have always been volatile. As an institution, the police have reflected the attitudes of the majority. To have expected the police to act as a social agency oriented towards reform or conflict-amelioration is to misconstrue their primary function as they view it: namely, the maintenance of law and order. Thus, the police have practiced physical attacks and verbal harassment on minority-group members without interference. Though the public was generally unaware of the treatment accorded minority-ethnic-group members, a prejudicial attitude on its part sanctioned police actions. The language of the police vis-à-vis Negroes —"nigger," "monkey," "them," "boy"—were terms in general usage in American culture. For many years, blacks have attempted to bring to light the ample evidence of discriminatory beatings and humiliations. One such attempt in 1965, by furious blacks in the South-Central area of Los Angeles, compiled a listing of the discriminatory remarks of the then Los Angeles Chief of Police William H. Parker— which resulted in a fifteen-page report entitled "Police Chief William H. Parker Speaks"—and distributed it in the community.[21]

Yet, the police became a main focal point for attack not only because of their attitude toward and behavior with minority groups, but primarily because they came to symbolize the despised invisible white power structure. Of the institutional contacts with which ghetto-dwellers have intimate contact—schools, social welfare and employment agencies, medical facilities, business owners—the police embody the most crushing authority. For many blacks, the police had come to represent more than enforcement of law; they were viewed as members of an occupying army and as an oppressive force acting on behalf of those who rule their environment but who fled it for the greener pastures. "A policeman is an object of contempt," Ernie W. Chambers of Omaha bitterly stated in testimony given before the National Advisory Committee on Civil Disorders.[22] The system represented by the police has been oppressive, the method of rule has been heavy with force, and the phrase "maintain law and order" has been directed basically towards the control of Negroes. "Like why, man, should I get home?" angrily inquired a young black during the Watts riot. "These cops have been pushin' me 'round all my life. Kickin' my—— and things like that. Whitey ain't no damn good, he talks 'bout law and order, it's his law and order, it ain't mine [word deleted by the Commission]."[23]

That a collective wrath directed against the police goaded ghetto residents is evident from an analysis of the early stages of the riots. It is significant that most revolts began as a consequence of an incident in which the police were, in some manner, involved. In several instances, the initiating episode was in the line of routine activity. In the Watts situation, for instance, police stopped two men who were driving in an intoxicated condition. Nevertheless, the significance of the specific event bore no relation to the more serious undercurrent of animosity which had been previously created. In other cases, verbal and physical actions by the police were instrumental in increasing a tense situation by inflaming the ghetto people, as happened in the Newark riot of 1967, which really began when the police charged out of the station house towards a large group of demonstrating and jeering Negroes.

Equally instructive is the fact that snipers, despite their numbers, hit extremely few policemen and firemen during the three years of rioting. The low number of deaths of law officials could hardly be ascribed to poor marksmanship. By 1967, especially in Detroit, the incidence of sniper fire had increased considerably; yet, only four law officers were killed, as compared to thirty-nine civilians. Indeed, of the eighty-three persons who died in seventy-five disorders analyzed by the Permanent Sub-committee on Investigations of the Senate Committee on Government Operations in 1967, approximately ten persons were public officials, primarily law officers and firemen, whereas the remainder were civilians, primarily Negroes.[24]

White businessmen were the second most exposed group singled out for attack. Resentment against the practices of exploitation, in the form of hidden and higher interest rates, shoddy goods and lower quality, higher prices and questionable service, had likewise been building for many years. The communications system in the community had long isolated such business establishments. Consequently, the majority of stores damaged and looted were those against which ill-feelings had developed. Negro stores frequently were protected by identifying signs: "Blood Brother," "Soul Brother," "Negro-owned." Not only were black businesses generally left untouched, but so, too, were libraries, schools, hospitals, clinics, and, surprisingly, governmental agencies. There were instances of bricks and sniper fire hitting these various buildings; however, no concerted attack was conducted. Many places burned down because of the refusal of the rioters to permit fire engines into the area.

Nevertheless, retail businesses suffered a much greater proportion of the damage during the violence than public institutions, industrial properties, or private residences. In Newark in 1967, 1,029 establishments listed damage to buildings or loss of inventory or both.[25] Those businesses which were hardest hit by rioters were those which were felt to be the most exploitative in their business practices: liquor, clothing, food, and furniture stores. Indeed, in at least nine of the riots studied by the President's National Advisory Commission on Civil Disorders, the damage was, in part, the result of "deliberate attacks on white-owned businesses characterized in the Negro community as unfair or disrespectful toward Negroes."[26]

The riot brought a sense of exultation in the community. It served as a release of frustration, anger, and helplessness. Even those participants who afterwards regretted their actions admitted to the joy that they had personally experienced. In testimony before the McCone Commission, conducted after the riot in central Los Angeles, Winston Slaughter, age twenty, a junior college student, responded to the question: "Do you think the riot helped or hurt the Negro cause?"

Well, you can say regret and then you can say there are some who are glad it happened. Now, me personally, I feel that I regret it, yes. But, deep down inside I know I was feeling some joy while it was going on, simply because I am a Negro.[27]

Others felt no regret, but a sense of pride. As the riots spread to other ghetto areas, those communities which experienced no turmoil felt the need to emulate their brothers. An exchange between three young blacks after the Detroit riot indicated the fulfilling exuberance of the historical moment:

> "Those buildings goin' up was a pretty sight," a long-legged kid said. "I sat right here and watched them go. And there wasn't nothin' them honkies could do but sweat and strain to put it out."
> "Yeah, man," a pal chimed in, "it's about time those honkies started earnin' their money in this neighborhood."
> "You know," said Long Legs, "we made big news. They called this the country's worst race riot in history."
> "Yeah," said another gangly kid, straddling the railing. "My kids goin' to study about that in school, and they'll know their old man was part of it."
> "We got the record man," exulted another youth. . . . "They can forget all about Watts and Newark and Harlem. This is where the riot to end all riots was held."[28]

Further, the protest riot assumed certain features of conventional warfare. The weapons and tactics employed were those standardized in the past thirty years: Molotov cocktails, selected targets, visible enemies, harassing tactics, sniping, mobility, and a capitulation to a more powerful military force in the form of national guardsmen or federal troops. Parallels between war as a means of confronting an enemy and the protest riot could also be observed in the attitudes of ghetto residents. Although the term "riot" was used by blacks, it became clear that they meant to describe their actions in a larger sense. "We in a war," a black youth told a reporter. "Or hasn't anybody told you that?"[29]

The attitude of immediacy was heard from many persons. "Many Negroes would rather die than live under conditions as they are now," exclaimed a male at a youth symposium. "For these people, riots present the only chance of ever achieving equality."[30] An absence of fear was notable among those who actively participated in the streets. "The cops think we are scared of them because they got guns," stated a male in testimony before the McCone Commission, "but you can only die once: if I get a few of them I don't mind dying."[31] Thus, the riots were emotionally liberating. The joy in retaliating and the fun in looting reinforced the feelings of communal action. The individual acts fused with the collective act. The term "we" was used with frequency among the protesting rioters: "We put ourselves on the map." "We were whole again." During the civil violences, there was a partial suspension of conscience. "This liberation from conscience and from conscientiousness made possible for the rioters an involvement and an extreme commitment usually denied them."[32] Moreover, the pride in action played an integral role in the historical consciousness of the community. Two years after the Watts riot, black and brown high school students, selected to participate in an upward-bound educational project, were asked to complete a form which contained the question: "What kinds of civil rights activities have you participated in?" One student answered: "Watts Riot." Such statements and actions indicate a high degree of participation in the protest disturbances.

Several significant studies have pointedly noted a high degree of community participation in the violence of the small and large riots in the 1960's. The Los Angeles Riot Study (LARS), initiated immediate'y after the 1965 riot, collated the interviews of 2,070 persons living within the curfew area.[33] The group of Negroes interviewed was a random sample, stratified by age, sex, and income. Interviews were approximately two hours in length; the interview covered questions of attitude toward the riot, activity in the riot, general social and political attitudes, and background information. The LARS survey noted that the majority of Negroes had spent their childhood in the South but that over 60 percent of the sample had matured in urban areas. Significantly, about the same percentage had lived in Los Angeles ten years or longer at the time of the riot. Contrary to reports about the low educational level of the rioters, the study indicated that over half of the sample had completed high school. Contrary to popular assumptions as well, the study indicated that 72 percent of the males and 35 percent of the females were employed in August 1965.

With regard to participation in the riot, the LARS survey demonstrated that up to 15 percent of the Negro adult population, or about 22,000 persons, were active at some point during the rioting; that an additional 35 or 40 percent, or 51,000 persons, were active spectators. Support for the violence was greater among the younger persons, was greater among men than women, and was as great among relatively long-time residents of South-Central Los Angeles as it was among the more recent migrants from the South. The latter point is of particular importance, inasmuch as it undercut the notion that the riot was largely the work of the unacculturated and of the recent influx of migrants from the South.

A high percentage of the community supported the violence, in attitude if not in action. Approximately 34 percent of the sample were favorably disposed toward the actions, and 38 percent of the population in the curfew area felt that the revolt would help in their quest to improve their positions. Only 20 percent indicated that the riot hurt the community. In sum, a high proportion of persons in the riot area participated in, or gave support to, the action of fellow residents.

Studies undertaken after the LARS report substantially corroborated its conclusions. The National Advisory Commission on Civil Disorders conducted 1,200 interviews in approximately twenty cities, studied arrest records in twenty-two cities, and elicited additional reports from participants. According to the Report of the Commission, the typical rioter was an unmarried male, between the ages of fifteen and twenty-four, born in the state, and a lifelong resident of the city in which the riot occurred. His education was substantially good, having attended high school, and, economically, his position was approximately the same as his counterpart who did not actively participate in the riot. Nonetheless, he was more likely to be working in a menial or low-status job as an unskilled laborer. In special surveys taken after the Newark and Detroit revolts, interviewers noted strong feelings of racial pride, "if not racial superiority."[34] The riot experience was a definite factor in increased self- and communal pride:

> INTERVIEWER: You said you were feeling good when you followed the crowd?
> RESPONDENT: I was feeling proud, man, at the fact that I was a Negro. I felt like I was a first-class citizen. I didn't feel ashamed of my race because of what they did [Detroit, 1967].[35]

The nature of the rioting which marked the mid-1960's appeared to undergo serious change by the end of the decade. Two indications of this change were, firstly, the Detroit riot of 1967 in which a sizable proportion of Caucasians joined with the Negroes in burning and looting, thus indicating a meshing of an economic underclass; and, secondly, the development and intensity of the Black Power movement. The activists have been concerned with developing cultural, economic, and political programs within the community. These activist organizations have, on more than one occasion, prevented violent outbreaks by ghetto residents who were angered by representatives of the power structure, particularly the police. Within the broad Black Power movement, moreover, militant groups have counseled for the termination of nonviolence as a technique of bringing about necessary change. "We know that we cannot change violent people by nonviolence," read a mimeographed sheet handed out by the Black Student Union at the University of California, San Diego, immediately after the assassination of Dr. Martin Luther King in April 1968. "We must build mass armed self-defense groups. We must unite to get rid of the government and people that oppress and murder Black People." Thus, by the end of the decade, the energies of the younger blacks were oriented towards more specific, militant goals.

In sum, the revolts in the mid-1960's—more than the nonviolent movement of Dr. Martin Luther King and the extraordinarily powerful civil rights movement of the early 1960's—directed attention to the anguished plights of millions of Negroes, Puerto Ricans, and Mexican-Americans living in the urban centers of the country. The spontaneous outbursts, the collective actions, and the consensual attitudes of blacks and browns highlighted the failure of American society to recognize the problems of the racial minority groups in the cities. The events stemmed not only from the tradition of racist mentality but also from the ambiguous attitudes towards the city itself. The enormity of the failure led to one of the most intense social crises in American society in the twentieth century.

Notes

1. The terms "riot" and "revolt" are used interchangably in this study. They describe acts of assault on the status quo and its tangible legitimate authorities, in this instance, the police and business establishments.

2. Langston Hughes, "Roland Hayes Beaten," *One-Way Ticket* (New York: Alfred A. Knopf, 1949), p. 86.

3. Kenneth Clark, *Dark Ghetto* (New York: Harper and Row, 1964), p. 21.

4. Quoted in Gurston D. Goldin, "Violence: The Integration of Psychiatric and Sociological Concepts," *Notre Dame Lawyer*, Vol. XL, No. 5, 1965, p. 513.

5. Herbert Kosower, King Vidor, and Joseph Boshur, "The Arts," *Psychology Today*, Vol. II, No. 3 (August 1968), p. 16.

6. Anselm Strauss, *Images of the American City* (New York: Free Press, 1961), p. 123.

7. Claude Brown, *Manchild in the Promised Land* (New York: New American Library, 1965), pp. vii–viii.

8. Alain Locke, *The New Negro* (New York: Albert and Charles Boni, 1925), pp. 6–7.

9. U.S. Commission on Civil Rights, *A Time to Listen . . . A Time to Act* (Washington, D.C.: U.S. Government Printing Office, 1967), p. 6.

10. James Baldwin, *Nobody Knows My Name* (New York: Delta Books, 1962), p. 65.

11. "Watts—End or Beginning," *Los Angeles Times*, Calendar, May 15, 1966, p. 3, col. 2.

12. The rioting which occurred following the assassination of Dr. Martin Luther King in April 1968 is not covered in this paper. These actions were not specifically related to the origins and spread of the urban revolt.

13. For a further analysis of the 'consensus of attitudes and behavior,' see Joseph Boskin, "Violence in the Ghettos: A Consensus of Attitudes," in *Violence in Contemporary Society*, ed. Joseph Frank, *New Mexico Quarterly*, Vol. XXXVII, No. 4 (Winter 1968), pp. 317–334.

14. John Allan Long, "After the Midwest Riots," *Christian Science Monitor*, November 10, 1966, p. 11.

15. "The Hard-Core Ghetto Mood," *Newsweek*, Vol. LXX, No. 8, August 21, 1967, p. 21.

16. *A Time to Listen . . . A Time to Act*, p. 5.

17. Piri Thomas, in testimony before the National Advisory Commission on Civil Disorders, September 21, 1967.

18. U.S., Riot Commission, *Report of the National Advisory Commission on Civil Disorders* (New York: Bantam Books, 1968), p. 143.

19. *Ibid.*, pp. 143–144.

20. *Report of the Governor's Commission on the Los Angeles Riot*, Vol. II (Sacramento, 1966), pp. 88–89.

21. William H. Parker, "Police Chief William H. Parker Speaks" (Los Angeles: Community Relations Conference of Southern California, 1965).

22. Ernie W. Chambers, in testimony before the National Advisory Commission on Civil Disorders, September 23, 1967. The Commission described Chambers as a "grass-roots leader."

23. *Report of the Governor's Commission on the Los Angeles Riot*, Vol. I (Sacramento, 1966), p. 43.

24. *Report of the National Advisory Commission on Civil Disorders*, pp. 115–116.

25. *Ibid.*

26. *Ibid.*

27. *Report of Governor's Commission on the Los Angeles Riot*, Vol. XIII (Sacramento, 1966), pp. 28–29.

28. "The Hard-Core Ghetto Mood," p. 20.

29. *Ibid.*

30. California, Alameda County, Human Relations Commission, "Youth Discuss Racial Problems," *Human Relations News*, Vol. I, No. 2 (September 1967), p. 1.

31. *Report of Governor's Commission on the Los Angeles Riot*, Vol. I, p. 16.

32. Frederick J. Hacker and Aljean Harmetz, "What the McCone Commission Didn't See," *Frontier*, Vol. XVII, No. 5 (March 1966), p. 13.

33. Institute of Government and Public Affairs, University of California, Los Angeles, 1967.

34. *Report of the National Advisory Commission on Civil Disorders*, p. 133.

35. *Ibid.*

KERNER COMMISSION

Summary and Recommendations

Introduction

The summer of 1967 again brought racial disorders to American cities, and with them shock, fear, and bewilderment to the Nation.

The worst came during a 2-week period in July, first in Newark and then in Detroit. Each set off a chain reaction in neighboring communities.

On July 28, 1967, the President of the United States established this Commission and directed us to answer three basic questions:

Report of the National Advisory Commission on Civil Disorders (Washington, D.C.: U.S. Government Printing Office, 1968), pp. 1–13.

What happened?

Why did it happen?

What can be done to prevent it from happening again?

To respond to these questions, we have undertaken a broad range of studies and investigations. We have visited the riot cities; we have heard many witnesses; we have sought the counsel of experts across the country.

This is our basic conclusion: Our Nation is moving toward two societies, one black, one white—separate and unequal.

Reaction to last summer's disorders has quickened the movement and deepened the division. Discrimination and segregation have long permeated much of American life; they now threaten the future of every American.

This deepening racial division is not inevitable. The movement apart can be reversed. Choice is still possible. Our principal task is to define that choice and to press for a national resolution.

To pursue our present course will involve the continuing polarization of the American community and, ultimately, the destruction of basic democratic values.

The alternative is not blind repression or capitulation to lawlessness. It is the realization of common opportunities for all within a single society.

This alternative will require a commitment to national action—compassionate, massive, and sustained, backed by the resources of the most powerful and the richest nation on this earth. From every American it will require new attitudes, new understanding, and, above all, new will.

The vital needs of the Nation must be met; hard choices must be made, and, if necessary, new taxes enacted.

Violence cannot build a better society. Disruption and disorder nourish repression, not justice. They strike at the freedom of every citizen. The community cannot—it will not—tolerate coercion and mob rule.

Violence and destruction must be ended—in the streets of the ghetto and in the lives of people.

Segregation and poverty have created in the racial ghetto a destructive environment totally unknown to most white Americans.

What white Americans have never fully understood—but what the Negro can never forget—is that white society is deeply implicated in the ghetto. White institutions created it, white institutions maintain it, and white society condones it.

It is time now to turn with all the purpose at our command to the major unfinished business of this Nation. It is time to adopt strategies for action that will produce quick and visible progress. It is time to make good the promises of American democracy to all citizens—urban and rural, white and black, Spanish-surname, American Indian, and every minority group.

Our recommendations embrace three basic principles:

- To mount programs on a scale equal to the dimension of the problems;
- To aim these programs for high impact in the immediate future in order to close the gap between promise and performance;
- To undertake new initiatives and experiments that can change the system of failure and frustration that now dominates the ghetto and weakens our society.

These programs will require unprecedented levels of funding and performance, but they neither probe deeper nor demand more than the problems which called them forth. There can be no higher priority for national action and no higher claim on the Nation's conscience.

We issue this report now, 5 months before the date called for by the President. Much remains that can be learned. Continued study is essential.

As Commissioners we have worked together with a sense of the greatest urgency and have sought to compose whatever differences exist among us. Some differences remain. But the gravity of the problem and the pressing need for action are too clear to allow further delay in the issuance of this report.

I. What Happened?

Chapter 1. Profiles of disorder

The report contains profiles of a selection of the disorders that took place during the summer of 1967. These profiles are designed to indicate how the disorders happened, who participated in them, and how local officials, police forces, and the National Guard responded. Illustrative excerpts follow:

NEWARK

* * * It was decided to attempt to channel the energies of the people into a nonviolent protest. While Lofton promised the crowd that a full investigation would be made of the Smith incident, the other Negro leaders began urging those on the scene to form a line of march toward the city hall.

Some persons joined the line of march. Others milled about in the narrow street. From the dark grounds of the housing project came a barrage of rocks. Some of them fell among the crowd. Others hit persons in the line of march. Many smashed the windows of the police station. The rock throwing, it was believed, was the work of youngsters; approximately 2,500 children lived in the housing project.

Almost at the same time, an old car was set afire in a parking lot. The line of march began to disintegrate. The police, their heads protected by World War I-type helmets, sallied forth to disperse the crowd. A fire engine, arriving on the scene, was pelted with rocks. As police drove people away from the station, they scattered in all directions.

A few minutes later a nearby liquor store was broken into. Some persons, seeing a caravan of cabs appear at city hall to protest Smith's arrest, interpreted this as evidence that the disturbance had been organized, and generated rumors to that effect.

However, only a few stores were looted. Within a short period of time, the disorder appeared to have run its course.

* * * * *

* * * On Saturday, July 15, [Director of Police Dominick] Spina received a report of snipers in a housing project. When he arrived he saw approximately 100 National Guardsmen and police officers crouching behind vehicles, hiding in corners, and lying on the ground around the edge of the courtyard.

Since everything appeared quiet and it was broad daylight, Spina walked directly down the middle of the street. Nothing happened. As he came to the last building of the complex, he heard a shot. All around him the troopers jumped, believing themselves to be under sniper fire. A moment later a young Guardsman ran from behind a building.

The director of police went over and asked him if he had fired the shot. The soldier said "Yes," he had fired to scare a man away from a window; that his orders were to keep everyone away from windows.

Spina said he told the soldier: "Do you know what you just did? You have now created a state of hysteria. Every Guardsman up and down this street and every state policeman and every city policeman that is present thinks that somebody just fired a shot and that it is probably a sniper."

A short time later more "gunshots" were heard. Investigating, Spina came upon a Puerto Rican sitting on a wall. In reply to a question as to whether he knew "where the firing is coming from"? the man said:

"That's no firing. That's fireworks. If you look up to the fourth floor, you will see the people who are throwing down these cherry bombs."

By this time four truckloads of National Guardsmen had arrived and troopers and policemen were again crouched everywhere looking for a sniper. The director of police remained at the scene for 3 hours, and the only shot fired was the one by the Guardsman.

Nevertheless, at 6 o'clock that evening two columns of National Guardsmen and State troopers were directing mass fire at the Hayes housing project in response to what they believed were snipers. * * *

DETROIT

* * * A spirit of carefree nihilism was taking hold. To riot and destroy appeared more and more to become ends in themselves. Late Sunday afternoon it appeared to one observer that the young people were "dancing amidst the flames."

A Negro plainclothes officer was standing at an intersection when a man threw a Molotov cocktail into a business establishment at the corner. In the heat of the afternoon, fanned by the 20 to 25 miles per hour winds of both Sunday and Monday, the fire reached the home next door within minutes. As residents uselessly sprayed the flames with garden hoses, the fire jumped from roof to roof of adjacent two- and three-story buildings. Within the hour the entire block was in flames. The ninth house in the burning row belonged to the arsonist who had thrown the Molotov cocktail. * * *

* * * * *

* * * Employed as a private guard, 55-year-old Julius L. Dorsey, a Negro, was standing in front of a market when accosted by two Negro men and a woman. They demanded he permit them to loot the market. He ignored their demands. They began to berate him. He asked a neighbor to call the police. As the argument grew more heated, Dorsey fired three shots from his pistol into the air.

The police radio reported: "Looters—they have rifles." A patrol car driven by a police officer and carrying three National Guardsmen arrived. As the looters fled, the law-enforcement personnel opened fire. When the firing ceased, one person lay dead.

He was Julius L. Dorsey. * * *

* * * * *

* * * As the riot alternately waxed and waned, one area of the ghetto remained insulated. On the northeast side the residents of some 150 square blocks inhabited by 21,000 persons had, in 1966, banded together in the Positive Neighborhood Action Committee (PNAC). With professional help from the Institute of Urban Dynamics, they had organized block clubs and made plans for the improvement of the neighborhood. * * *

When the riot broke out, the residents, through the block clubs, were able to organize quickly. Youngsters, agreeing to stay in the neighborhood, participated in detouring traffic. While many persons reportedly sympathized with the idea of a rebellion against the "system" only two small fires were set—one in an empty building.

* * * * *

* * * According to Lieutenant General Throckmorton and Colonel Bolling, the city, at this time, was saturated with fear. The National Guardsmen were afraid, the citizens were afraid, and the police were afraid. Numerous persons, the majority of them Negroes, were being injured by gunshots of undetermined origin. The general and his staff felt that the major task of the troops was to reduce the fear and restore an air of normalcy.

In order to accomplish this, every effort was made to establish contact and rapport between the troops and the residents. The soldiers—20 percent of whom were Negro—began helping to clean up the streets, collect garbage, and trace persons who had disappeared in the confusion. Residents in the neighborhoods responded with soup and sandwiches for the troops. In areas where the National Guard tried to establish rapport with the citizens, there was a similar response.

NEW BRUNSWICK

* * * A short time later, elements of the crowd—an older and rougher one than the night before—appeared in front of the police station. The participants wanted to see the mayor.

Mayor [Patricia] Sheehan went out onto the steps of the station. Using a bull horn, she talked to the people and asked that she be given an opportunity to correct conditions. The crowd was boisterous. Some persons challenged the mayor. But, finally, the opinion, "She's new! Give her a chance!" prevailed.

A demand was issued by people in the crowd that all persons arrested the previous night be released. Told that this already had been done, the people were suspicious. They asked to be allowed to inspect the jail cells.

It was agreed to permit representatives of the people to look in the cells to satisfy themselves that everyone had been released.

The crowd dispersed. The New Brunswick riot had failed to materialize.

Chapter 2. Patterns of disorder

The "typical" riot did not take place. The disorders of 1967 were unusual, irregular, complex, and unpredictable social processes. Like most human events, they did not unfold in an orderly sequence. However, an analysis of our survey information leads to some conclusions about the riot process.

In general:

- The civil disorders of 1967 involved Negroes acting against local symbols of white American society, authority, and property in Negro neighborhoods—rather than against white persons.
- Of 164 disorders reported during the first nine months of 1967, eight (5 percent) were major in terms of violence and damage; 33 (20 percent) were serious but not major; 123 (75 percent) were minor and undoubtedly would not have received national attention as riots had the Nation not been sensitized by the more serious outbreaks.
- In the 75 disorders studied by a Senate subcommittee, 83 deaths were reported. Eighty-two percent of the deaths and more than half the injuries occurred in Newark and Detroit. About 10 percent of the dead and 36 percent of the injured were public employees, primarily law officers and firemen. The overwhelming majority of the persons killed or injured in all the disorders were Negro civilians.
- Initial damage estimates were greatly exaggerated. In Detroit, newspaper damage estimates at first ranged from $200 to $500 million; the highest recent estimate is $45 million. In Newark, early estimates ranged from $15 to $25 million. A month later damage was estimated at $10.2 million, 80 percent in inventory losses.

In the 24 disorders in 23 cities which we surveyed:

- The final incident before the outbreak of disorder, and the initial violence itself, generally took place in the evening or at night at a place in which it was normal for many people to be on the streets.

- Violence usually occurred almost immediately following the occurrence of the final precipitating incident, and then escalated rapidly. With but few exceptions, violence subsided during the day, and flared rapidly again at night. The night-day cycles continued through the early period of the major disorders.
- Disorder generally began with rock and bottle throwing and window breaking. Once store windows were broken, looting usually followed.
- Disorder did not erupt as a result of a single "triggering" or "precipitating" incident. Instead, it was generated out of an increasingly disturbed social atmosphere, in which typically a series of tension-heightening incidents over a period of weeks or months became linked in the minds of many in the Negro community with a reservoir of underlying grievances. At some point in the mounting tension, a further incident—in itself often routine or trivial—became the breaking point and the tension spilled over into violence.
- "Prior" incidents, which increased tensions and ultimately led to violence, were police actions in almost half the cases; police actions were "final" incidents before the outbreak of violence in 12 of the 24 surveyed disorders.
- No particular control tactic was successful in every situation. The varied effectiveness of control techniques emphasizes the need for advance training, planning, adequate intelligence systems, and knowledge of the ghetto community.
- Negotiations between Negroes—including young militants as well as older Negro leaders—and white officials concerning "terms of peace" occurred during virtually all the disorders surveyed. In many cases, these negotiations involved discussion of underlying grievances as well as the handling of the disorder by control authorities.
- The typical rioter was a teenager or young adult, a life-long resident of the city in which he rioted, a high school dropout; he was, nevertheless, somewhat better educated than his non-rioting Negro neighbor, and was usually underemployed or employed in a menial job. He was proud of his race, extremely hostile to both whites and middle-class Negroes and, although informed about politics, highly distrustful of the political system.

A Detroit survey revealed that approximately 11 percent of the total residents of two riot areas admitted participation in the rioting, 20 to 25 percent identified themselves as "bystanders," over 16 percent identified themselves as "counterrioters" who urged rioters to "cool it," and the remaining 48 to 53 percent said they were at home or elsewhere and did not participate. In a survey of Negro males between the ages of 15 and 35 residing in the disturbance area in

Newark, about 45 percent identified themselves as rioters, and about 55 percent as "noninvolved."

- Most rioters were young Negro males. Nearly 53 percent of arrestees were between 15 and 24 years of age; nearly 81 percent between 15 and 35.
- In Detroit and Newark about 74 percent of the rioters were brought up in the North. In contrast, of the noninvolved, 36 percent in Detroit and 52 percent in Newark were brought up in the North.
- What the rioters appeared to be seeking was fuller participation in the social order and the material benefits enjoyed by the majority of American citizens. Rather than rejecting the American system, they were anxious to obtain a place for themselves in it.
- Numerous Negro counterrioters walked the streets urging rioters to "cool it." The typical counterrioter was better educated and had higher income than either the rioter or the noninvolved.
- The proportion of Negroes in local government was substantially smaller than the Negro proportion of population. Only three of the 20 cities studied had more than one Negro legislator; none had ever had a Negro major or city manager. In only four cities did Negroes hold other important policy-making positions or serve as heads of municipal departments.
- Although almost all cities had some sort of formal grievance mechanism for handling citizen complaints, this typically was regarded by Negroes as ineffective and was generally ignored.
- Although specific grievances varied from city to city, at least 12 deeply held grievances can be identified and ranked into three levels of relative intensity:

  First level of intensity:
  1. Police practices.
  2. Unemployment and underemployment.
  3. Inadequate housing.

  Second level of intensity:
  4. Inadequate education.
  5. Poor recreation facilities and programs.
  6. Ineffectiveness of the political structure and grievance mechanisms.

  Third level of intensity:
  7. Disrespectful white attitudes.
  8. Discriminatory administration of justice.
  9. Inadequacy of Federal programs.
  10. Inadequacy of municipal services.
  11. Discriminatory consumer and credit practices.
  12. Inadequate welfare programs.

- The results of a three-city survey of various Federal programs— manpower, education, housing, welfare and community action— indicate that, despite substantial expenditures, the number of persons assisted constituted only a fraction of those in need.

The background of disorder is often as complex and difficult to analyze as the disorder itself. But we find that certain general conclusions can be drawn:

- Social and economic conditions in the riot cities constituted a clear pattern of severe disadvantage for Negroes compared with whites, whether the Negroes lived in the area where the riot took place or outside it. Negroes had completed fewer years of education and fewer had attended high school. Negroes were twice as likely to be unemployed and three times as likely to be in unskilled and service jobs. Negroes averaged 70 percent of the income earned by whites and were more than twice as likely to be living in poverty. Although housing cost Negroes relatively more, they had worse housing—three times as likely to be overcrowded and substandard. When compared to white suburbs, the relative disadvantage was even more pronounced.

A study of the aftermath of disorder leads to disturbing conclusions. We find that, despite the institution of some postriot programs:

- Little basic change in the conditions underlying the outbreak of disorder has taken place. Actions to ameliorate Negro grievances have been limited and sporadic; with but few exceptions, they have not significantly reduced tensions.
- In several cities, the principal official response has been to train and equip the police with more sophisticated weapons.
- In several cities, increasing polarization is evident, with continuing breakdown of interracial communication, and growth of white segregationist or black separatist groups.

Chapter 3. Organized activity

The President directed the Commission to investigate "to what extent, if any, there has been planning or organization in any of the riots."

To carry out this part of the President's charge, the Commission established a special investigative staff supplementing the field teams that made the general examination of the riots in 23 cities. The unit examined data collected by Federal agencies and congressional committees, including thousands of documents supplied by the

Federal Bureau of Investigation, gathered and evaluated information from local and state law enforcement agencies and officials, and conducted its own field investigation in selected cities.

On the basis of all the information collected, the Commission concludes that:

> The urban disorders of the summer of 1967 were not caused by, nor were they the consequence of, any organized plan or "conspiracy."

Specifically, the Commission has found no evidence that all or any of the disorders or the incidents that led to them were planned or directed by any organization or group, international, national, or local.

Militant organizations, local and national, and individual agitators, who repeatedly forecast and called for violence, were active in the spring and summer of 1967. We believe that they sought to encourage violence, and that they helped to create an atmosphere that contributed to the outbreak of disorder.

We recognize that the continuation of disorders and the polarization of the races would provide fertile ground for organized exploitation in the future.

Investigations of organized activity are continuing at all levels of government, including committees of Congress. These investigations relate not only to the disorders of 1967 but also to the actions of groups and individuals, particularly in schools and colleges, during this last fall and winter. The Commission has cooperated in these investigations. They should continue.

II.   Why Did It Happen?

Chapter 4.   The basic causes

In addressing the question "Why did it happen?" we shift our focus from the local to the national scene, from the particular events of the summer of 1967 to the factors within the society at large that created a mood of violence among many urban Negroes.

These factors are complex and interacting; they vary significantly in their effect from city to city and from year to year; and the consequences of one disorder, generating new grievances and new demands, become the causes of the next. Thus was created the "thicket of tension, conflicting evidence, and extreme opinions" cited by the President.

Despite these complexities, certain fundamental matters are clear. Of these, the most fundamental is the racial attitude and behavior of white Americans toward black Americans.

Race prejudice has shaped out history decisively; it now threatens to affect our future.

White racism is essentially responsible for the explosive mixture which has been accumulating in our cities since the end of World War II. Among the ingredients of this mixture are:

- *Pervasive discrimination and segregation* in employment, education, and housing, which have resulted in the continuing exclusion of great numbers of Negroes from the benefits of economic progress.
- *Black in-migration and white exodus,* which have produced the massive and growing concentrations of impoverished Negroes in our major cities, creating a growing crisis of deteriorating facilities and services and unmet human needs.
- *The black ghettos,* where segregation and poverty converge on the young to destroy opportunity and enforce failure. Crime, drug addiction, dependency on welfare, and bitterness and resentment against society in general and white society in particular are the result.

At the same time, most whites and some Negroes outside the ghetto have prospered to a degree unparalleled in the history of civilization. Through television and other media, this affluence has been flaunted before the eyes of the Negro poor and the jobless ghetto youth.

Yet these facts alone cannot be said to have caused the disorders. Recently, other powerful ingredients have begun to catalyze the mixture:

- *Frustrated hopes* are the residue of the unfulfilled expectations aroused by the great judicial and legislative victories of the civil rights movement and the dramatic struggle for equal rights in the South.
- *A climate that tends toward approval and encouragement of violence* as a form of protest has been created by white terrorism directed against nonviolent protest; by the open defiance of law and Federal authority by state and local officials resisting desegregation; and by some protest groups engaging in civil disobedience who turn their backs on nonviolence, go beyond the constitutionally protected rights of petition and free assembly, and resort to violence to attempt to compel alteration of laws and policies with which they disagree.
- *The frustrations of powerlessness* have led some Negroes to the conviction that there is no effective alternative to violence as a means of achieving redress of grievances, and of "moving the system." These frustrations are reflected in alienation and hostility toward the institutions of law and government and the white society which controls them, and in the reach toward racial consciousness and solidarity reflected in the slogan "Black Power."

- *A new mood* has sprung up among Negroes, particularly among the young, in which self-esteem and enhanced racial pride are replacing apathy and submission to "the system."
- *The police are not merely a "spark" factor.* To some Negroes police have come to symbolize white power, white racism, and white repression. And the fact is that many police do reflect and express these white attitudes. The atmosphere of hostility and cynicism is reinforced by a widespread belief among Negroes in the existence of police brutality and in a "double standard" of justice and protection—one for Negroes and one for whites.

To this point, we have attempted only to identify the prime components of the "explosive mixture." In the chapters that follow we seek to analyze them in the perspective of history. Their meaning, however, is clear:

In the summer of 1967, we have seen in our cities a chain reaction of racial violence. If we are heedless, none of us shall escape the consequences.

Chapter 5. Rejection and protest: an historical sketch

The causes of recent racial disorders are embedded in a tangle of issues and circumstances—social, economic, political, and psychological—which arise out of the historic pattern of Negro-white relations in America.

In this chapter we trace the pattern, identify the recurrent themes of Negro protest and, most importantly, provide a perspective on the protest activities of the present era.

We describe the Negro's experience in America and the development of slavery as an institution. We show his persistent striving for equality in the face of rigidly maintained social, economic, and educational barriers, and repeated mob violence. We portray the ebb and flow of the doctrinal tides—accommodation, separatism, and self-help—and their relationship to the current theme of Black Power. We conclude:

> The Black Power advocates of today consciously feel that they are the most militant group in the Negro protest movement. Yet they have retreated from a direct confrontation with American society on the issue of integration and, by preaching separatism, unconsciously function as an accommodation to white racism. Much of their economic program, as well as their interest in Negro history, self-help, racial solidarity and separation, is reminiscent of Booker T. Washington. The rhetoric is different, but the ideas are remarkably similar.

Chapter 6. The formation of the racial ghettos

Throughout the 20th century the Negro population of the United States has been moving steadily from rural areas to urban and from

South to North and West. In 1910, 91 percent of the Nation's 9.8 million Negroes lived in the South and only 27 percent of American Negroes lived in cities of 2,500 persons or more. Between 1910 and 1966 the total Negro population more than doubled, reaching 21.5 million, and the number living in metropolitan areas rose more than fivefold (from 2.6 million to 14.8 million). The number outside the South rose elevenfold (from 885,000 to 9.7 million).

Negro migration from the South has resulted from the expectation of thousands of new and highly paid jobs for unskilled workers in the North and the shift to mechanized farming in the South. However, the Negro migration is small when compared to earlier waves of European immigrants. Even between 1960 and 1966, there were 1.8 million immigrants from abroad compared to the 613,000 Negroes who arrived in the North and West from the South.

As a result of the growing number of Negroes in urban areas, natural increase has replaced migration as the primary source of Negro population increase in the cities. Nevertheless, Negro migration from the South will continue unless economic conditions there change dramatically.

Basic data concerning Negro urbanization trends indicate that:

- Almost all Negro population growth (98 percent from 1950 to 1966) is occurring within metropolitan areas, primarily within central cities.[2]
- The vast majority of white population growth (78 percent from 1960 to 1966) is occurring in suburban portions of metropolitan areas. Since 1960, white central-city population has declined by 1.3 million.
- As a result, central cities are becoming more heavily Negro while the suburban fringes around them remain almost entirely white.
- The 12 largest central cities now contain over two-thirds of the Negro population outside the South, and almost one-third of the Negro total in the United States.

Within the cities, Negroes have been excluded from white residential areas through discriminatory practices. Just as significant is the withdrawal of white families from, or their refusal to enter, neighborhoods where Negroes are moving or already residing. About 20 percent of the urban population of the United States changes residence every year. The refusal of whites to move into "changing" areas when vacancies occur means that most vacancies eventually are occupied by Negroes.

The result, according to a recent study, is that in 1960 the average segregation index for 207 of the largest U.S. cities was 86.2. In other words, to create an unsegregated population distribution, an average of over 86 percent of all Negroes would have to change their place of residence within the city.

Chapter 7. Unemployment, family structure, and social disorganization

Although there have been gains in Negro income nationally, and a decline in the number of Negroes below the "poverty level," the condition of Negroes in the central city remains in a state of crisis. Between 2 and 2.5 million Negroes—16 to 20 percent of the total Negro population of all central cities—live in squalor and deprivation in ghetto neighborhoods.

Employment is a key problem. It not only controls the present for the Negro American but, in a most profound way, it is creating the future as well. Yet, despite continuing economic growth and declining national unemployment rates, the unemployment rate for Negroes in 1967 was more than double that for whites.

Equally important is the undesirable nature of many jobs open to Negroes and other minorities. Negro men are more than three times as likely as white men to be in low-paying, unskilled, or service jobs. This concentration of male Negro employment at the lowest end of the occupational scale is the single most important cause of poverty among Negroes.

In one study of low-income neighborhoods, the "sub-employment rate," including both unemployment and underemployment, was about 33 percent, or 8.8 times greater than the overall unemployment rate for all U.S. workers.

Employment problems, aggravated by the constant arrival of new unemployed migrants, many of them from depressed rural areas, create persistent poverty in the ghetto. In 1966, about 11.9 percent of the Nation's whites and 40.6 percent of its nonwhites were below the poverty level defined by the Social Security Administration (in 1966, $3,335 per year for an urban family of four). Over 40 percent of the nonwhites below the poverty level live in the central cities.

Employment problems have drastic social impact in the ghetto. Men who are chronically unemployed or employed in the lowest status jobs are often unable or unwilling to remain with their families. The handicap imposed on children growing up without fathers in an atmosphere of deprivation is increased as mothers are forced to work to provide support.

The culture of poverty that results from unemployment and family breakup generates a system of ruthless, exploitative relationships within the ghetto. Prostitution, dope addiction, and crime create an environmental "jungle" characterized by personal insecurity and tension. Children growing up under such conditions are likely participants in civil disorder.

Chapter 8. Conditions of life in the racial ghetto

A striking difference in environment from that of white, middle-class Americans profoundly influences the lives of residents of the ghetto.

Crime rates, consistently higher than in other areas, create a pronounced sense of insecurity. For example, in one city one low-income Negro district had 35 times as many serious crimes against persons as a high-income white district. Unless drastic steps are taken, the crime problems in poverty areas are likely to continue to multiply as the growing youth and rapid urbanization of the population outstrip police resources.

Poor health and sanitation conditions in the ghetto result in higher mortality rates, a higher incidence of major diseases, and lower availability and utilization of medical services. The infant mortality rate for nonwhite babies under the age of 1 month is 58 percent higher than for whites; for 1 to 12 months it is almost three times as high. The level of sanitation in the ghetto is far below that in high-income areas. Garbage collection is often inadequate. Of an estimated 14,000 cases of rat bite in the United States in 1965, most were in ghetto neighborhoods.

Ghetto residents believe they are exploited by local merchants; and evidence substantiates some of these beliefs. A study conducted in one city by the Federal Trade Commission showed that higher prices were charged for goods sold in ghetto stores than in other areas.

Lack of knowledge regarding credit purchasing creates special pitfalls for the disadvantaged. In many states, garnishment practices compound these difficulties by allowing creditors to deprive individuals of their wages without hearing or trial.

Chapter 9. Comparing
the immigrant and Negro experience

In this chapter, we address ourselves to a fundamental question that many white Americans are asking: Why have so many Negroes, unlike the European immigrants, been unable to escape from the ghetto and from poverty?

We believe the following factors play a part:

- *The maturing economy*—When the European immigrants arrived, they gained an economic foothold by providing the unskilled labor needed by industry. Unlike the immigrant, the Negro migrant found little opportunity in the city. The economy, by then matured, had little use for the unskilled labor he had to offer.
- *The disability of race*—The structure of discrimination has stringently narrowed opportunities for the Negro and restricted his prospects. European immigrants suffered from discrimination, but never so pervasively.
- *Entry into the political system*—The immigrants usually settled in rapidly growing cities with powerful and expanding political machines, which traded economic advantages for political support. Ward-level grievance machinery, as well as personal representation, enabled the immigrant to make his voice heard and his power felt.

By the time the Negro arrived, these political machines were no longer so powerful or so well equipped to provide jobs or other favors, and in many cases were unwilling to share their remaining influence with Negroes.

● *Cultural factors*—Coming from societies with a low standard of living and at a time when job aspirations were low, the immigrants sensed little deprivation in being forced to take the less desirable and poorer paying jobs. Their large and cohesive families contributed to total income. Their vision of the future—one that led to a life outside of the ghetto—provided the incentive necessary to endure the present.

Although Negro men worked as hard as the immigrants, they were unable to support their families. The entrepreneurial opportunities had vanished. As a result of slavery and long periods of unemployment, the Negro family structure had become matriarchal; the males played a secondary and marginal family role—one which offered little compensation for their hard and unrewarding labor. Above all, segregation denied Negroes access to good jobs and the opportunity to leave the ghetto. For them, the future seemed to lead only to a dead end.

Today, whites tend to exaggerate how well and quickly they escaped from poverty. The fact is that immigrants who came from rural backgrounds, as many Negroes do, are only now, after three generations, finally beginning to move into the middle class.

By contrast, Negroes began concentrating in the city less than two generations ago, and under much less favorable conditions. Although some Negroes have escaped poverty, few have been able to escape the urban ghetto.

III.   What Can Be Done?

Chapter 10. The community response

Our investigation of the 1967 riot cities establishes that virtually every major episode of violence was foreshadowed by an accumulation of unresolved grievances and by widespread dissatisfaction among Negroes with the unwillingness or inability of local government to respond.

Overcoming these conditions is essential for community support of law enforcement and civil order. City governments need new and more vital channels of communication to the residents of the ghetto; they need to improve their capacity to respond effectively to community needs before they become community grievances; and they need to provide opportunity for meaningful involvement of ghetto residents in shaping policies and programs which affect the community.

The Commission recommends that local governments:

- Develop Neighborhood Action Task Forces as joint community-government efforts through which more effective communication can be achieved, and the delivery of city services to ghetto residents improved.
- Establish comprehensive grievance-response mechanisms in order to bring all public agencies under public scrutiny.
- Bring the institutions of local government closer to the people they serve by establishing neighborhood outlets for local, state, and Federal administrative and public service agencies.
- Expand opportunities for ghetto residents to participate in the formulation of public policy and the implementation of programs affecting them through improved political representation, creation of institutional channels for community action, expansion of legal services, and legislative hearings on ghetto problems.

In this effort, city governments will require State and Federal support.

The Commission recommends:

- State and Federal financial assistance for mayors and city councils to support the research, consultants, staff, and other resources needed to respond effectively to Federal program initiatives.
- State cooperation in providing municipalities with the jurisdictional tools needed to deal with their problems; a fuller measure of financial aid to urban areas; and the focusing of the interests of suburban communities on the physical, social, and cultural environment of the central city.

Chapter 11. Police and the community

The abrasive relationship between the police and minority communities has been a major—and explosive—source of grievance, tension, and disorder. The blame must be shared by the total society.

The police are faced with demands for increased protection and service in the ghetto. Yet the aggressive patrol practices thought necessary to meet these demands themselves create tension and hostility. The resulting grievances have been further aggravated by the lack of effective mechanisms for handling complaints against the police. Special programs for bettering police-community relations have been instituted, but these alone are not enough. Police administrators, with the guidance of public officials, and the support of the entire community, must take vigorous action to improve law enforcement and to decrease the potential for disorder.

The Commission recommends that city government and police authorities:

- Review police operations in the ghetto to ensure proper conduct by police officers, and eliminate abrasive practices.

- Provide more adequate police protection to ghetto residents to eliminate their high sense of insecurity and the belief in the existence of a dual standard of law enforcement.
- Establish fair and effective mechanisms for the redress of grievances against the police and other municipal employees.
- Develop and adopt policy guidelines to assist officers in making critical decisions in areas where police conduct can create tension.
- Develop and use innovative programs to insure widespread community support for law enforcement.
- Recruit more Negroes into the regular police force, and review promotion policies to insure fair promotion for Negro officers.
- Establish a "Community Service Officer" program to attract ghetto youths between the ages of 17 and 21 to police work. These junior officers would perform duties in ghetto neighborhoods, but would not have full police authority. The Federal Government should provide support equal to 90 percent of the costs of employing CSO's on the basis of one for every 10 regular officers.

Chapter 12. Control of disorder

Preserving civil peace is the first responsibility of government. Unless the rule of law prevails, our society will lack not only order but also the environment essential to social and economic progress.

The maintenance of civil order cannot be left to the police alone. The police need guidance, as well as support, from mayors and other public officials. It is the responsibility of public officials to determine proper police policies, support adequate police standards for personnel and performance, and participate in planning for the control of disorders.

To maintain control of incidents which could lead to disorders, the Commission recommends that local officials:

- Assign seasoned, well-trained policemen and supervisory officers to patrol ghetto areas, and to respond to disturbances.
- Develop plans which will quickly muster maximum police manpower and highly qualified senior commanders at the outbreak of disorders.
- Provide special training in the prevention of disorders, and prepare police for riot control and for operation in units, with adequate command and control and field communication for proper discipline and effectiveness.
- Develop guidelines governing the use of control equipment and provide alternatives to the use of lethal weapons. Federal support for research in this area is needed.
- Establish an intelligence system to provide police and other public officials with reliable information that may help to prevent the

outbreak of a disorder and to institute effective control measures in the event a riot erupts.

● Develop continuing contacts with ghetto residents to make use of the forces for order which exist within the community.

● Establish machinery for neutralizing rumors, and enabling Negro leaders and residents to obtain the facts. Create special rumor details to collect, evaluate, and dispel rumors that may lead to a civil disorder.

The Commission believes there is a grave danger that some communities may resort to the indiscriminate and excessive use of force. The harmful effects of over-reaction are incalculable. The Commission condemns moves to equip police departments with mass destruction weapons, such as automatic rifles, machine guns, and tanks. Weapons which are designed to destroy, not to control, have no place in densely populated urban communities.

The Commission recommends that the Federal Government share in the financing of programs for improvement of police forces, both in their normal law enforcement activities as well as in their response to civil disorders.

To assist government authorities in planning their response to civil disorder, this report contains a Supplement on Control of Disorder. It deals with specific problems encountered during riot control operations, and includes:

● Assessment of the present capabilities of police, National Guard and Army forces to control major riots, and recommendations for improvement.

● Recommended means by which the control operations of those forces may be coordinated with the response of other agencies, such as fire departments, and with the community at large.

● Recommendations for review and revision of Federal, state and local laws needed to provide the framework for control efforts and for the callup and interrelated action of public safety forces.

Chapter 13. The administration of justice under emergency conditions

In many of the cities which experienced disorders last summer, there were recurring breakdowns in the mechanisms for processing, prosecuting, and protecting arrested persons. These resulted mainly from longstanding structural deficiencies in criminal court systems, and from the failure of communities to anticipate and plan for the emergency demands of civil disorders.

In part, because of this, there were few successful prosecutions for serious crimes committed during the riots. In those cities where mass arrests occurred, many arrestees were deprived of basic legal rights.

The Commission recommends that the cities and states:

● Undertake reform of the lower courts so as to improve the quality of justice rendered under normal conditions.
● Plan comprehensive measures by which the criminal justice system may be supplemented during civil disorders so that its deliberative functions are protected, and the quality of justice is maintained.

Such emergency plans require broad community participation and dedicated leadership by the bench and bar. They should include:

● Laws sufficient to deter and punish riot conduct.
● Additional judges, bail and probation officers, and clerical staff.
● Arrangements for volunteer lawyers to help prosecutors and to represent riot defendants at every stage of proceedings.
● Policies to insure proper and individual bail, arraignment, pretrial, trial, and sentencing proceedings.
● Adequate emergency processing and detention facilities.

Chapter 14. Damages: repair and compensation

The Commission recommends that the Federal Government:

● Amend the Federal Disaster Act—which now applies only to natural disasters—to permit Federal emergency food and medical assistance to cities during major civil disorders, and provide long-term economic assistance afterwards.
● With the cooperation of the states, create incentives for the private insurance industry to provide more adequate property insurance coverage in inner-city areas.

The Commission endorses the report of the National Advisory Panel on Insurance in Riot-Affected Areas: "Meeting the Insurance Crisis of our Cities."

Chapter 15. The news media and the disorders

In his charge to the Commission, the President asked: "What effect do the mass media have on the riots?"

The Commission determined that the answer to the President's question did not lie solely in the performance of the press and broadcasters in reporting the riots. Our analysis had to consider also the overall treatment by the media of the Negro ghettos, community relations, racial attitudes, and poverty—day by day and month by month, year in and year out.

A wide range of interviews with Government officials, law enforcement authorities, media personnel and other citizens, including ghetto residents, as well as a quantitative analysis of riot coverage and a special conference with industry representatives, leads us to conclude that:

● Despite instances of sensationalism, inaccuracy and distortion, newspapers, radio and television tried on the whole to give a balanced, factual account of the 1967 disorders.
● Elements of the news media failed to portray accurately the scale and character of the violence that occurred last summer. The overall effect was, we believe, an exaggeration of both mood and event.
● Important segments of the media failed to report adequately on the causes and consequences of civil disorders and on the underlying problems of race relations. They have not communicated to the majority of their audience—which is white—a sense of the degradation, misery, and hopelessness of life in the ghetto.

These failings must be corrected, and the improvement must come from within the industry. Freedom of the press is not the issue. Any effort to impose governmental restrictions would be inconsistent with fundamental constitutional precepts.

We have seen evidence that the news media are becoming aware of and concerned about their performance in this field. As that concern grows, coverage will improve. But much more must be done, and it must be done soon.

The Commission recommends that the media:

● Expand coverage of the Negro community and of race problems through permanent assignment of reporters familiar with urban and racial affairs, and through establishment of more and better links with the Negro community.
● Integrate Negroes and Negro activities into all aspects of coverage and content, including newspaper articles and television programing. The news media must publish newspapers and produce programs that recognize the existence and activities of Negroes as a group within the community and as a part of the larger community.
● Recruit more Negroes into journalism and broadcasting and promote those who are qualified to positions of significant responsibility. Recruitment should begin in high schools and continue through college; where necessary, aid for training should be provided.
● Improve coordination with police in reporting riot news through advance planning, and cooperate with the police in the designation of police information officers, establishment of information centers,

and development of mutually acceptable guidelines for riot reporting and the conduct of media personnel.

- Accelerate efforts to insure accurate and responsible reporting of
riot and racial news, through adoption by all news-gathering
organizations of stringent internal staff guidelines.

- Cooperate in the establishment of a privately organized and
funded Institute of Urban Communications to train and educate
journalists in urban affairs, recruit and train more Negro journalists, develop methods for improving police-press relations, review
coverage of riots and racial issues, and support continuing research
in the urban field.

Chapter 16. The future of the cities

By 1985, the Negro population in central cities is expected to increase
by 68 percent to approximately 20.3 million. Coupled with the
continued exodus of white families to the suburbs, this growth will
produce majority Negro populations in many of the Nation's largest
cities.

The future of these cities, and of their burgeoning Negro populations, is grim. Most new employment opportunities are being created
in suburbs and outlying areas. This trend will continue unless important changes in public policy are made.

In prospect, therefore, is further deterioration of already inadequate municipal tax bases in the face of increasing demands for
public services, and continuing unemployment and poverty among
the urban Negro population.

Three choices are open to the Nation.

- We can maintain present policies, continuing both the proportion
of the Nation's resources now allocated to programs for the unemployed and the disadvantaged, and the inadequate and failing
effort to achieve an integrated society.

- We can adopt a policy of "enrichment" aimed at improving dramatically the quality of ghetto life while abandoning integration
as a goal.

- We can pursue integration by combining ghetto "enrichment"
with policies which will encourage Negro movement out of central
city areas.

The first choice, continuance of present policies, has ominous
consequences for our society. The share of the Nation's resources now
allocated to programs for the disadvantaged is insufficient to arrest
the deterioration of life in central-city ghettos. Under such conditions,
a rising proportion of Negroes may come to see in the deprivation and
segregation they experience, a justification for violent protest, or for

extending support to now isolated extremists who advocate civil disruption. Large-scale and continuing violence could result, followed by white retaliation, and, ultimately, the separation of the two communities in a garrison state.

Even if violence does not occur, the consequences are unacceptable. Development of a racially integrated society, extraordinarily difficult today, will be virtually impossible when the present black central-city population of 12.1 million has grown to almost 21 million.

To continue present policies is to make permanent the division of our country into two societies: one, largely Negro and poor, located in the central cities; the other, predominantly white and affluent, located in the suburbs and in outlying areas.

The second choice, ghetto enrichment coupled with abandonment of integration, is also unacceptable. It is another way of choosing a permanently divided country. Moreover, equality cannot be achieved under conditions of nearly complete separation. In a country where the economy, and particularly the resources of employment, are predominantly white, a policy of separation can only relegate Negroes to a permanently inferior economic status.

We believe that the only possible choice for America is the third —a policy which combines ghetto enrichment with programs designed to encourage integration of substantial numbers of Negroes into the society outside the ghetto.

Enrichment must be an important adjunct to integration, for no matter how ambitious or energetic the program, few Negroes now living in central cities can be quickly integrated. In the meantime, large-scale improvement in the quality of ghetto life is essential.

But this can be no more than an interim strategy. Programs must be developed which will permit substantial Negro movement out of the ghettos. The primary goal must be a single society, in which every citizen will be free to live and work according to his capabilities and desires, not his color.

Chapter 17. Recommendations for national action

INTRODUCTION

No American—white or black—can escape the consequences of the continuing social and economic decay of our major cities.

Only a commitment to national action on an unprecedented scale can shape a future compatible with the historic ideals of American society.

The great productivity of our economy, and a Federal revenue system which is highly responsive to economic growth, can provide the resources.

The major need is to generate new will—the will to tax ourselves to the extent necessary to meet the vital needs of the Nation.

We have set forth goals and proposed strategies to reach those goals. We discuss and recommend programs not to commit each of us to specific parts of such programs, but to illustrate the type and dimension of action needed.

The major goal is the creation of a true union—a single society and a single American identity. Toward that goal, we propose the following objectives for national action:

- Opening up opportunities to those who are restricted by racial segregation and discrimination, and eliminating all barriers to their choice of jobs, education, and housing.
- Removing the frustration of powerlessness among the disadvantaged by providing the means for them to deal with the problems that affect their own lives and by increasing the capacity of our public and private institutions to respond to these problems.
- Increasing communication across racial lines to destroy stereotypes, halt polarization, end distrust and hostility, and create common ground for efforts toward public order and social justice.

We propose these aims to fulfill our pledge of equality and to meet the fundamental needs of a democratic and civilized society— domestic peace and social justice.

EMPLOYMENT

Pervasive unemployment and underemployment are the most persistent and serious grievances in minority areas. They are inextricably linked to the problem of civil disorder.

Despite growing Federal expenditures for manpower development and training programs, and sustained general economic prosperity and increasing demands for skilled workers, about 2 million— white and nonwhite—are permanently unemployed. About 10 million are underemployed, of whom 6.5 million work full time for wages below the poverty line.

The 500,000 "hard-core" unemployed in the central cities who lack a basic education and are unable to hold a steady job are made up in large part of Negro males between the ages of 18 and 25. In the riot cities which we surveyed, Negroes were three times as likely as whites to hold unskilled jobs, which are often part time, seasonal, low paying and "dead end."

Negro males between the ages of 15 and 25 predominated among the rioters. More than 20 percent of the rioters were unemployed, and many who were employed held intermittent, low status, unskilled jobs which they regarded as below their education and ability.

The Commission recommends that the Federal Government:

- Undertake joint efforts with cities and states to consolidate existing manpower programs to avoid fragmentation and duplication.

- Take immediate action to create 2 million new jobs over the next 3 years—1 million in the public sector and 1 million in the private sector—to absorb the hard-core unemployed and materially reduce the level of underemployment for all workers, black and white. We propose 250,000 public sector and 300,000 private sector jobs in the first year.
- Provide on-the-job training by both public and private employers with reimbursement to private employers for the extra costs of training the hard-core unemployed, by contract or by tax credits.
- Provide tax and other incentives to investment in rural as well as urban poverty areas in order to offer to the rural poor an alternative to migration to urban centers.
- Take new and vigorous action to remove artificial barriers to employment and promotion, including not only racial discrimination but, in certain cases, arrest records or lack of a high school diploma. Strengthen those agencies such as the Equal Employment Opportunity Commission, charged with eliminating discriminatory practices, and provide full support for Title VI of the 1964 Civil Rights Act allowing Federal grant-in-aid funds to be withheld from activities which discriminate on grounds of color or race.

The Commission commends the recent public commitment of the National Council of the Building and Construction Trades Unions, AFL–CIO, to encourage and recruit Negro membership in apprenticeship programs. This commitment should be intensified and implemented.

EDUCATION

Education in a democratic society must equip children to develop their potential and to participate fully in American life. For the community at large, the schools have discharged this responsibility well. But for many minorities, and particularly for the children of the ghetto, the schools have failed to provide the educational experience which could overcome the effects of discrimination and deprivation.

This failure is one of the persistent sources of grievance and resentment within the Negro community. The hostility of Negro parents and students toward the school system is generating increasing conflict and causing disruption within many city school districts. But the most dramatic evidence of the relationship between educational practices and civil disorders lies in the high incidence of riot participation by ghetto youth who have not completed high school.

The bleak record of public education for ghetto children is growing worse. In the critical skills—verbal and reading ability—Negro students are falling further behind whites with each year of school completed. The high unemployment and underemployment rate for Negro youth is evidence, in part, of the growing educational crisis.

We support integration as the priority education strategy; it is essential to the future of American society. In this last summer's disorders we have seen the consequences of racial isolation at all levels, and of attitudes toward race, on both sides, produced by three centuries of myth, ignorance, and bias. It is indispensable that opportunities for interaction between the races be expanded.

We recognize that the growing dominance of pupils from disadvantaged minorities in city school populations will not soon be reversed. No matter how great the effort toward desegregation, many children of the ghetto will not, within their school careers, attend integrated schools.

If existing disadvantages are not to be perpetuated, we must drastically improve the quality of ghetto education. Equality of results with all-white schools must be the goal.

To implement these strategies, the Commission recommends:

- Sharply increased efforts to eliminate de facto segregation in our schools through substantial federal aid to school systems seeking to desegregate either within the system or in cooperation with neighboring school systems:
- Elimination of racial discrimination in Northern as well as Southern schools by vigorous application of Title VI of the Civil Rights Act of 1964.
- Extension of quality early childhood education to every disadvantaged child in the country.
- Efforts to improve dramatically schools serving disadvantaged children through substantial federal funding of year-round quality compensatory education programs, improved teaching, and expanded experimentation and research.
- Elimination of illiteracy through greater Federal support for adult basic education.
- Enlarged opportunities for parent and community participation in the public schools.
- Reoriented vocational education emphasizing work-experience training and the involvement of business and industry.
- Expanded opportunities for higher education through increased federal assistance to disadvantaged students.
- Revision of state aid formulas to assure more per student aid to districts having a high proportion of disadvantaged school age children.

THE WELFARE SYSTEM

Our present system of public welfare is designed to save money instead of people, and tragically ends up doing neither. This system has two critical deficiencies:

First, it excludes large numbers of persons who are in great need, and who, if provided a decent level of support, might be able to become more productive and self-sufficient. No Federal funds are available for millions of unemployed and underemployed men and women who are needy but neither aged, handicapped nor the parents of minor children.

Second, for those included, the system provides assistance well below the minimum necessary for a decent level of existence, and imposes restrictions that encourage continued dependency on welfare and undermine self-respect.

A welter of statutory requirements and administrative practices and regulations operate to remind recipients that they are considered untrustworthy, promiscuous, and lazy. Residence requirements prevent assistance to people in need who are newly arrived in the state. Searches of recipients' homes violate privacy. Inadequate social services compound the problems.

The Commission recommends that the Federal Government, acting with state and local governments where necessary, reform the existing welfare system to:

- Establish, for recipients in existing welfare categories, uniform national standards of assistance at least as high as the annual "poverty level" of income, now set by the Social Security Administration at $3,335 per year for an urban family of four.
- Require that all states receiving Federal welfare contributions participate in the Aid to Families with Dependent Children-Unemployed Parents Program (AFDC-UP) that permits assistance to families with both father and mother in the home, thus aiding the family while it is still intact.
- Bear a substantially greater portion of all welfare costs—at least 90 percent of total payments.
- Increase incentives for seeking employment and job training, but remove restrictions recently enacted by the Congress that would compel mothers of young children to work.
- Provide more adequate social services through neighborhood centers and family-planning program.
- Remove the freeze placed by the 1967 welfare amendments on the percentage of children in a State that can be covered by Federal assistance.
- Eliminate residence requirements.

As a long-range goal, the Commission recommends that the Federal Government seek to develop a national system of income supplementation based strictly on need with two broad and basic purposes:

- To provide, for those who can work or who do work, any necessary supplements in such a way as to develop incentives for fuller employment.

- To provide, for those who cannot work and for mothers who decide to remain with their children, a minimum standard of decent living, and to aid in saving children from the prison of poverty that has held their parents.

A broad system of supplementation would involve substantially greater Federal expenditures than anything now contemplated. The cost will range widely depending on the standard of need accepted as the "basic allowance" to individuals and families, and on the rate at which additional income above this level is taxed. Yet if the deepening cycle of poverty and dependence on welfare can be broken, if the children of the poor can be given the opportunity to scale the wall that now separates them from the rest of society, the return on this investment will be great indeed.

HOUSING

After more than three decades of fragmented and grossly underfunded Federal housing programs, nearly 6 million substandard housing units remain occupied in the United States.

The housing problem is particularly acute in the minority ghettos. Nearly two-thirds of all nonwhite families living in the central cities today live in neighborhoods marked by substandard housing and general urban blight. Two major factors are responsible:

First: Many ghetto residents simply cannot pay the rent necessary to support decent housing. In Detroit, for example, over 40 percent of the nonwhite-occupied units in 1960 required rent of over 35 percent of the tenants' income.

Second: Discrimination prevents access to many nonslum areas, particularly the suburbs, where good housing exists. In addition, by creating a "back pressure" in the racial ghettos, it makes it possible for landlords to break up apartments for denser occupancy, and keeps prices and rents of deteriorated ghetto housing higher than they would be in a truly free market.

To date, Federal programs have been able to do comparatively little to provide housing for the disadvantaged. In the 31-year history of subsidized Federal housing, only about 800,000 units have been constructed, with recent production averaging about 50,000 units a year. By comparison, over a period only 3 years longer, FHA insurance guarantees have made possible the construction of over 10 million middle and upper income units.

Two points are fundamental to the Commission's recommendations:

First: Federal housing programs must be given a new thrust aimed at overcoming the prevailing patterns of racial segregation. If this is not done, those programs will continue to concentrate the most impoverished and dependent segments of the population into the central-city ghettos where there is already a critical gap between the needs of the population and the public resources to deal with them.

Second: The private sector must be brought into the production and financing of low and moderate-rental housing to supply the capabilities and capital necessary to meet the housing needs of the Nation.

The Commission recommends that the Federal Government:

* Enact a comprehensive and enforceable Federal open-housing law to cover the sale or rental of all housing, including single-family homes.
* Reorient Federal housing programs to place more low- and moderate-income housing outside of ghetto areas.
* Bring within the reach of low- and moderate-income families within the next 5 years 6 million new and existing units of decent housing, beginning with 600,000 units in the next year.

    To reach this goal we recommend:

* Expansion and modification of the rent supplement program to permit use of supplements for existing housing, thus greatly increasing the reach of the program.
* Expansion and modification of the below-market interest rate program to enlarge the interest subsidy to all sponsors, provide interest-free loans to nonprofit sponsors to cover pre-construction costs, and permit sale of projects to nonprofit corporations, co-operatives, or condominiums.
* Creation of an ownership supplement program similar to present rent supplements, to make home ownership possible for low-income families.
* Federal writedown of interest rates on loans to private builders constructing moderate-rent housing.
* Expansion of the public housing program, with emphasis on small units on scattered sites, and leasing and "turnkey" programs.
* Expansion of the Model Cities program.
* Expansion and reorientation of the urban renewal program to give priority to projects directly assisting low-income households to obtain adequate housing.

Conclusion

One of the first witnesses to be invited to appear before this Commission was Dr. Kenneth B. Clark, a distinguished and perceptive scholar. Referring to the reports of earlier riot commissions, he said:

> I read that report * * * of the 1919 riot in Chicago, and it is as if I were reading the report of the investigating committee on the Harlem

riot of '35, the report of the investigating committee on the Harlem riot of '43, the report of the McCone Commission on the Watts riot.

I must again in candor say to you members of this Commission—it is a kind of Alice in Wonderland—with the same moving picture reshown over and over again, the same analysis, the same recommendations, and the same inaction.

These words come to our minds as we conclude this report.

We have provided an honest beginning. We have learned much. But we have uncovered no startling truths, no unique insights, no simple solutions. The destruction and the bitterness of racial disorder, the harsh polemics of black revolt and white repression have been seen and heard before in this country.

It is time now to end the destruction and the violence, not only in the streets of the ghetto but in the lives of people.

Notes

1. The term "ghetto" as used in this Report refers to an area within a city characterized by poverty and acute social disorganization and inhabited by members of a racial or ethnic group under conditions of involuntary segregation.
2. A "central city" is the largest city of a standard metropolitan statistical area, that is, a metropolitan area containing at least one city of 50,000 or more inhabitants.

JAMES A. GESCHWENDER

Civil Rights Protest and Riots: A Disappearing Distinction

The civil rights movement has dominated much of the American scene from 1954 to the present, with urban disorders pretty well taking over center stage since 1963. The liberal segment of white America has generally had a positive image of the civil rights movement but has viewed big city riots with a mixture of fear and disgust. A number of social scientists also view civil rights activities and riots as two different and contradictory types of phenomena. This paper will take the assumption of difference as a hypothesis rather than a postulate. In this discussion sociologists' conceptualizations of social

James A. Geschwender, "Civil Rights Protest and Riots: A Disappearing Distinction," *Social Science Quarterly*, 49 (December 1968), 474–484. Reprinted by permission.

movements and riots will be examined, characteristics of recent urban disorders will be evaluated, and conclusions will be drawn.

It must be emphasized that the problem to be examined is not one of mere labeling. This paper is concerned with the proper label for recent urban disorders, but only because the question has broader implications. First, there are important theoretical considerations. The nature of the concepts used, the theories invoked, and the hypotheses drawn all will be influenced by the correct classification of the disorders as riots or as parts of a developing social movement, for the problem cannot be understood accurately by using an invalid classificatory scheme. If predictions of the future are to be accurate, we must start with a valid base.

The second implication—the application of sociological principles—is closely related to the need for accurate prediction. Social scientists cannot make useful recommendations for action to politicians or segments of society unless they have a correct image of the current expressions of black unrest, a correct image of the depth and intensity of unrest, a perception of the extent to which this unrest has crystallized into a prerevolutionary movement, and some reasonably accurate predictions for the future. The types of societal changes that will ameliorate conditions producing hostile outbursts will not be sufficient to change the direction of a social movement which is developing along potentially revolutionary lines.

Hostile Outbursts and Social Movements

Neil J. Smelser has developed a highly elaborate conceptual framework for the analysis of collective behavior.[1] He uses a value-added approach in which six determinants (necessary conditions) of collective behavior combine to specify the nature and characteristics of any particular collective episode. The six determinants are structural conduciveness, structural strain, growth and spread of a generalized belief, precipitating factors, mobilization of participants for action, and the operation of social control.[2] Any particular form of collective behavior produced by these determinants may be analyzed in terms of four basic components of social action, values, norms, mobilization of motivation for organized action, and situational facilities.[3] Each component of social action is categorized into seven levels of specificity, but present purposes do not require a detailed exposition of the theory.

For Smelser, the crucial distinction between hostile outbursts (riots) and norm-oriented movements (that category of social movements which includes the civil rights movement) lies in the area of growth and spread of generalized beliefs. The value-added analysis of the development of hostile outbursts begins by examining ambiguity and anxiety. Anxiety is fused with the mobilization series to produce a generalized belief that some agent, or agents, is responsible for the anxiety-producing situation. This suspicion of agents is short-circuited to the selection of a particular kind of agent. A desire to punish, restrict, damage, or remove the agent then emerges, and wish-fulfillment beliefs of two types manifest themselves. They take the form of an exaggerated belief in the ability to punish agents of evil and to remove the evils ascribed to the agents. This belief is basically a generalized sense of omnipotence which is short-circuited to specific results.[4]

The early stages of the development of a norm-oriented movement are identical to those in the development of a hostile outburst. The norm-oriented movement, too, begins with ambiguity, anxiety, the attachment of the anxiety to some agent, and the exaggeration of the threatening nature of that agent. At this point, however, its development diverges. A belief develops that the normative control of the agent is inadequate and this belief becomes directed toward a particular set of laws or customs. Thus it comes to be accepted that the problem can be solved by changing the normative structure. This expectation becomes channeled into a decision about the particular type of normative change that would be expected to immobilize or destroy the agent, eliminating the source of the problem.[5]

The distinction between hostile outbursts and social movements focuses attention on the belief system. If the episode of collective behavior is seen as a direct attempt to attack or punish the agents of evil (in this case, police and white businessmen), then it is classed as an hostile outburst (a riot). However, if the episode of collective behavior is seen as a means of bringing about normative change to prevent the agents from working their evil, then it is termed a social movement. The presence or absence of scapegoating and/or violence does not determine the classification of a particular episode, because violence and scapegoating are elements of both hostile outbursts and norm-oriented movements. Smelser states that

> hostile outbursts are frequently adjuncts of larger-scale social movements. On certain occasions reform movements . . . may erupt into violence. Revolutionary movements . . . are frequently accompanied by violence. The primary difference among terms such as "riot," "revolt," "rebellion," "insurrection," and "revolution" all of which involve hostile outbursts—stems from the scope of their associated social movements.[6]

The task, then, is to determine whether the recent urban disorders are isolated outbursts of pent-up hostility directed against perceived oppressors, such as police and white businessmen in the black ghetto, or part of a larger movement aimed at bringing about fundamental alterations in the normative order of American society.

Probably a majority of white liberals and many social scientists have decided on the former alternative.

Characteristics of the Disorders

Research reports suggest that three aspects of the disorders contribute most to the labeling of the disorders as riots. First, the prime activity of most participants was looting. Second, the disorders were spontaneous, relatively unorganized, and leaderless. Third, the participants apparently did not attempt to seize permanent control of an area or specify political demands. These objections will be examined one at a time.

Looting. First, the existence of looting, per se, should be investigated. Oberschall makes two points with regard to looting. He suggests that many petty thieves and small-time professional crooks came into the Watts area to engage in looting but left prior to the major waves of arrests. He indicates further that looting is a frequent occurrence in all disasters, natural or otherwise.[7] Both of these points may be well taken. Fires, floods, tornadoes, and riots all represent periods of upheaval. At such times, the burden upon police and other agents of social control is greatly increased. They are not in a position to enforce all aspects of the law and many persons take this opportunity to improve their lot temporarily by acquiring a ham, a television set, furniture, or liquor. Looting during a riot may be, as Lee Rainwater describes it, "a kind of primitive attempt at an income redistribution."[8] In other words, the "have-nots" temporarily increase their possessions without seriously attacking the distributive system.

This view must be balanced with an alternative one, for theft of any sort may be considered an act of rebellion. Hobsbawm has documented the fact that banditry in peasant societies has often been a form of social protest and represents an archaic form of social movement.[9] In such a case, the bandit who followed the Robin Hood model of stealing from the privileged and redistributing a portion of his gains to the underprivileged often had the support and affection of the peasantry. American history has its counterparts. Jesse James, Pretty Boy Floyd, and Babyface Nelson are only a few of the many American bandits who have been renowned in song and legend for their fights against the propertied and their generosity toward the needy. Theft, when directed against the right targets, may be seen as a direct attack upon the exploiter and upon the whole system of exploitation.

There is evidence that looting during the recent urban disorders was so directed. Rustin indicates that in the Watts riot the victims of looting and arson were whites rather than blacks.[10] He further points out that not all whites were victims; the white-owned businesses that had reputations for fair dealing and nondiscriminatory practices were spared. In Detroit some black-owned businesses were also targets.[11] These, however, were black merchants who had the same reputation for exploitation as did many whites.[12] There is, incidentally, some indication that in Detroit a group of individuals provided leadership in looting without participating in it themselves.[13]

A more basic criticism of the Oberschall interpretation of looting must be made, however. Dynes and Quarantelli state that looting rarely occurs in natural disasters and the little that does occur differs in many significant respects from that which occurs in urban disorders.[14] They cite one example of major looting in a natural disaster (the Chicago snowstorms of January and February, 1967) but suggest that the similarity in area of incidence may mean that this looting was a continuation of the looting during the disorder of 1966.[15]

If looting is characteristic of the current urban disorders but rarely occurs in natural disasters, it cannot be explained in the same terms in both cases. It is doubtful that the Dynes-Quarantelli interpretation in terms of property redefinition is adequate.[16] Looting appears to be more than simply a protest against the prevailing definition of property rights. The selection of white and black exploiters as targets of looting and arson suggests that it is an attack upon the system of distribution of property and that it also provides an opportunity to acquire property. In short, looting constitutes an attack upon exploitation rather than upon exploiters—an act more characteristic of social movements than of hostile outbursts.

Organization. Second, the fact that the disorders were spontaneous rather than the result of conspiracy is informative. The Kerner Commission saw no evidence of conspiracy, of deliberate incitement, or of organization in the disorders.[17] This is, however, no reason to conclude that they are not part of a social movement. To make such a statement is to misunderstand the nature of a social movement.

The treatment of social movements by Lang and Lang provides instructive insights.[18] They define a social movement as a "large-scale, widespread, and continuing, elementary collective action in pursuit of an objective that affects and shapes the social order in some fundamental aspect."[19] A social movement is seen as having organized associations at its core that provide general direction and focus; but it also includes large, unorganized segments pushing in the same direction but not integrated with the core associations. Lang and Lang specifically state that "unless we are able to distinguish between the core group and a larger mass of supporters not formally joined, we are not dealing with a social movement."[20]

Not all participants in every social movement need to have identical definitions of goals, strategy, and tactics; it is only necessary that they share the same general objectives. The degree of mutual cooperation and coordination of activities is, in fact, problematic in any given social movement. Lang and Lang state:

> One group working for a cause . . . may appear to be so involved in its quarrels with another group sharing its objective that members of both groups hardly seem to be participants in the same movement. Yet, however riddled by factional disputes a movement may be, the knowledge that other groups are working toward the same ends gives each unit a sense of participation in it. They compete to see which is the purest representative of the doctrine.[21]

Thus it would seem that any definition of the civil rights movement must be broad enough to include such disparate organizations as the Urban League, National Association for the Advancement of Colored People, Southern Christian Leadership Conference, Student Nonviolent Coordinating Committee, and the Congress on Racial Equality, provided they are all working for the same general objectives, such as the furthering of the position and rights of the black American. The definition must also be broad enough to include the unorganized participants of demonstrations, boycotts, and even urban disorders, provided, again, that the participants have the same general goals.[22] The lack of organization does not, *ipso facto*, exclude looters, snipers, and arsonists from the civil rights movement. Their motives must be examined, which will be done later in this paper.

Tactics. Third, does the absence of stated political demands and/or any attempt to seize permanent control of a geographic area exclude urban disorders from the category of social movements? The answer to this question requires a comprehensive analysis of the nature and role of tactics in a social movement.

The reluctance to treat urban disorders as a segment of the civil rights movement very likely stems from the tendency to define the movement in terms of its organized core associations and to define its tactics in terms of the more respectable ones of court suits, nonviolent direct action, and voter registration drives. Killian and Grigg note, however, that each of the above tactics emerged when previous modes of behavior proved inadequate in bringing about sufficiently broad results as rapidly as desired.[23] It is plausible to assume that segments of the black community have become dissatisfied with the slow, token changes brought about by the respectable tactics and are developing more drastic ones to increase the speed and scope of change. Oberschall lends support to this interpretation when he states:

> The collective significance of these events, however, is that the civil rights gains made by the Negro movement in the last few years, which have benefitted the Southern Negro and middle-class Negroes, have not altered the situation of the lower-class urban Negroes outside of

the South and have not removed the fundamental sources of grievances of a large proportion of the Negro population in the U.S.[24]

The historical role of urban mobs in controlling ruling elites and in attempting to bring about changes is well documented. Hobsbawm states:

> Provided the ruler did his duty, the populace was prepared to defend him with enthusiasm. But if he did not, it rioted until he did. . . . The treatment of perennial rioting kept rulers ready to control prices and to distribute work or largess, or indeed to listen to their faithful commons on other matters.[25]

> Nevertheless, such a symbiosis of the "mob" and the people against whom it rioted was not necessarily the fundamental factor about its politics. The "mob" rioted, but it also sometimes made revolutions. . . . It was poor; "they" were rich; life was fundamentally unjust for the poor. These were the foundations of its attitude. . . . The implicit revolutionism of the "mob" was primitive; in its way it was the metropolitan equivalent of the stage of political consciousness represented by social banditry in the countryside.[26]

Thus, a plausible assumption is that the civil rights movement has undergone an evolution of tactics. As one tactic proves inadequate to the task it is replaced by another seen as more adequate. In the recent past, accommodation gave way to court suits. The orderly tactics gave way to the less orderly tactics of direct action, which Waskow analyzes under the concept of "creative disorder."[27] "Creative disorder" may now be giving way to "creative rioting."[28] Ghetto riots may be an attempt to use violent disorder creatively to bring about change. This does not mean that all individuals involved in the civil rights movement are now, or will be, participating in riots. There always has been a tactical division of labor: some civil rights adherents use court suits; others engage in nonviolent direct action; others, however, may have moved on to creative rioting.[29]

The stating of political demands and the attempts to permanently occupy and control a given territory are tactics which are likely to appear in a fully developed insurrection or revolution. The tactic of creative rioting represents a move in this direction developing from creative disorder. It is an intermediate tactic which does not go as far as revolution. That is, it may appear in prerevolutionary situations—situations which have the potential for developing into revolutions but which will not necessarily do so.

Oberschall may not be entirely accurate when he states that political demands are missing in the current urban disorders. The Kerner Commission report states:

> In 21 of the 24 disturbances surveyed, discussion or negotiation occurred during the disturbances. These took the form of relatively

formal meetings between government officials and Negroes during which grievances and issues were discussed and means were sought to restore order.[30]

These meetings usually were with "established leaders" but youths were involved in 13 discussions. The combination of discussion of grievances and the presence of the more militant youths indicates the presence of some sort of political demands even though no attempt to occupy territory permanently may have been made. Urban disorders, therefore, may be a new civil rights tactic which stops short of revolution.

The case for creative rioting—ghetto riots as an integral part of the civil rights movement—has not yet been fully demonstrated. The nature and pattern of looting lend more support to this interpretation than they do to the alternative interpretation of urban disorders as hostile outbursts. The lack of deliberate instigation or organization in the disorders is neutral, as it is equally consistent with either interpretation. The lack of an attempt to assume permanent control of a given territory does not prevent the current ghetto riots from being a step in the evolution of tactics within the civil rights movement just short of full-blown insurrection. Due to the inconclusive nature of the foregoing, one must analyze the characteristics of riot participants prior to drawing final conclusions. The prime source of data will be the recent surveys of riot participation conducted in Detroit and Newark.

Characteristics of Riot Participants

A number of characteristics of self-identified rioters or riot supporters correspond to those noted in the sociological literature as characterizing individuals who are prone to participate in social movements or revolutions. Both Lyford P. Edwards and Crane Brinton state that individuals who perceive their legitimate aspirations for mobility to be blocked are especially prone to engage in revolutionary behavior.[31] The Kerner Commission report notes that the self-identified rioters in Newark were significantly ($p < .05$) more likely than the self-reported noninvolved individuals to believe that their level of education entitled them to a job with more income and responsibility than the one they presently possessed.[32] The Newark rioters were also less likely than the noninvolved to perceive that there was an opportunity for them to acquire their desired job ($p < .06$) and significantly more likely ($p < .025$) to believe that discrimination was the factor preventing them from so doing. No comparable data from Detroit are available. Taken jointly, these characteristics indicate the existence of the blocked-mobility syndrome that Edwards and Brinton find typical of potential revolutionaries.

Status inconsistency also has been interpreted as a characteristic that predisposes individuals toward participation in social movements or revolutions.[33] Evidence suggests that rioters tend to be status-inconsistent. The Detroit rioters were significantly *better educated* than the noninvolved (p <.05) and the Newark rioters, too, tended to be better educated than the noninvolved (p <.06). Both Newark and Detroit rioters tended to have *lower incomes* than the noninvolved, although neither difference is statistically significant. The Newark rioters also tended to have lower job status than the noninvolved (p <.06). No data on occupational status are available from Detroit. While there is no difference between rioters and the noninvolved in terms of current rate of unemployment, the Newark rioters were significantly more likely to have been unemployed for a month or longer within the past year (p <.05). No comparable data are available from Detroit.

These data together indicate that rioters were considerably less likely to be able to bring their occupational status, income, or employment status up to a level comparable to their level of education. When this observation is combined with the fact that Negroes are more likely than whites to have their levels of occupation and income lag behind their educational level, then there can be no doubt that active rioters are status inconsistent—and inconsistent to a greater degree than the noninvolved.[34] More important, the rioters' "profiles" are inconsistent with high education–low income or high education–low occupation profiles, which are precisely the ones most likely to produce participation in extremist social movements of leftist inclinations.[35]

The fact that rioters exhibit status inconsistency and possess thwarted aspirations does not in itself demonstrate that riots are part of a social movement. One additional factor, however, lends credence to this interpretation. Ransford found that Watts Negroes who were socially isolated from whites were significantly more willing to use violence than were those with greater contact with whites.[36] This conclusion agrees with the suggestion by Marx that the isolation of an aggrieved category of persons into an interacting collectivity is likely to produce a conflict group with a high degree of group consciousness and an awareness of a common enemy.[37] The likelihood that racially isolated blacks may develop "black consciousness" and a hostility toward whites which could manifest itself in rioting as revolutionary activity gains support from data on the Detroit and Newark rioters. Both Newark and Detroit rioters were significantly more likely than the noninvolved to believe that Negroes are more dependable than whites (p < .05 and < .001, respectively) and that Negroes are "nicer" than whites (p < .025 and < .001, respectively). Newark rioters were significantly more likely than the noninvolved to describe themselves as "black" (p < .025) and were more prone to believe that all Negroes should study African history and languages (p < .06). No comparable data are available from Detroit. Newark rioters were significantly more likely than the noninvolved to believe that presently integrated civil rights groups would be more effective without whites (p < .005) and to admit that sometimes they hated whites (p < .001). While there are no data on the likelihood that Detroit rioters hated whites, they, also, were more likely than the noninvolved to say that integrated civil rights groups would be more effective without whites (p < .10).

These data strongly suggest that rioters are individuals largely isolated from whites, that they interact with blacks who share common grievances, that they develop a high level of hostility toward whites, combined with a high level of black consciousness, and that they subsequently participate in riots as a means of attacking the "system." In short, they are participating in a social movement that may or may not reach revolutionary proportions.

The suggestion presented above—that urban riots may represent an evolution of tactics from the more respectable to the more violent —gains support from the following facts. Newark rioters were significantly more likely than the noninvolved to participate in discussions of Negro rights (p < .025), to participate in activities of civil rights groups (p < .05), to identify political figures (p < .205), to be politically knowledgeable (p < .025), and to not trust the Newark government to do what is right (p < .10). While there are no directly comparable data from Detroit, the rioters there were significantly more likely than the noninvolved to feel that anger toward politicians (p < .05) and toward the police (p < .05) had much to do with causing the riots.

Conclusion

The rioters discussed above are not the normally apathetic, noninvolved individuals who participate in hostile outbursts. They tend to be politically knowledgeable and active in civil rights activities. Many of them have apparently come to the conclusion that traditional political and civil rights tactics cannot bring about desired results and thus they have shifted to newer tactics. This interpretation is supported by the desire of a large number of rioters to exclude whites from civil rights organizations. The theoretically relevant characteristics of thwarted aspirations and status inconsistency suggest, but do not demonstrate, this conclusion. The factor of racial isolation, though, pushes further in the direction indicated. Political knowledgeability, civil rights activities, black consciousness, hostility toward whites, and mistrust of government "put the icing on the cake" and make the conclusion emphatic.

The earlier discussion of looting strongly suggested that current urban disorders were a developing part of the civil rights movement. The discussions of degree of organization of riots and of tactics were consistent with the interpretation of urban disorders as either hostile outbursts or segments of a social movement. The discussion of the characteristics of rioters, however, removed remaining doubts. The present author no longer questions that the urban disorders are, in fact, creative rioting. Creative rioting falls clearly within the evolutionary pattern of the civil rights movement, a social movement which may or may not eventually become revolutionary.

This thesis should not be misconstrued; this paper does not contend that all urban disorders were creative rioting. The outbreaks of 1964 in Harlem, Rochester, Jersey City, and Philadelphia may have been simple hostile outbursts, although they did bring about a response on the community, state, and national levels. As subsequent riots continued to bring about real, if limited, results, individuals may have become aware of riots as a potentially successful tactic. This is not to say that the riots were deliberately instigated. Rather, a potential riot situation may have made some individuals aware of the utility of rioting, which in turn stimulated riot behavior. Once a riot was underway, other individuals were motivated to continue and direct it. Thus, rioting shifts from the category of a hostile outburst to that of a creative force in the civil rights movement.

Notes

1. Neil J. Smelser, *Theory of Collective Behavior* (New York: The Free Press of Glencoe, 1963).

2. *Ibid.*, pp. 14–17.

3. *Ibid.*, pp. 23–28.

4. *Ibid.*, pp. 101–103.

5. *Ibid.*, pp. 111–112.

6. *Ibid.*, p. 227.

7. Anthony Oberschall, "The Los Angeles Riot," *Social Problems*, 15 (Winter, 1968), pp. 335–338.

8. Lee Rainwater, "Open Letter on White Justice and the Riots," *Transaction*, 9 (Sept., 1967), p. 25.

9. E. J. Hobsbawm, *Primitive Rebels* (New York: W. W. Norton, 1959), esp. Ch. 2.

10. Bayard Rustin, "The Watts 'Manifesto' and the McCone Report," *Commentary*, 41 (March, 1966), pp. 29–35.

11. *Report on Civil Disorders*, p. 88.

12. Private interviews with observers of the disorder.

13. Louis E. Lomax, "Seeds of Riot Planted Here by Salesmen," *Detroit News*, August 6, 1967, pp. 1–2.

14. Russell Dynes and E. L. Quarantelli, "What Looting in Civil Disturbances Really Means," *Transaction*, 5 (May, 1968), pp. 9–14.

15. *Ibid.*, p. 12.

16. *Ibid.*, pp. 13–14.

17. *Report on Civil Disorders*, pp. 201–202.

18. Kurt Lang and Gladys Engel Lang, *Collective Dynamics* (New York: Crowell, 1961), pp. 489–544.

19. *Ibid.*, p. 490.

20. *Ibid.*, p. 497.

21. *Ibid.*, p. 496.

22. Although probably clear from the context, the term "civil rights movement" is not here used in the narrow sense of attempts to acquire legal rights and legal equality through normative means. It is used in the broader sense of all attempts to gain legal rights and legal-equality as well as those attempts to translate legal rights into actual functioning rights and equality.

23. Lewis Killian and Charles Grigg, *Racial Crisis in America* (Englewood Cliffs, N.J.: Prentice Hall, 1964), pp. 18–23.

24. Oberschall, "Los Angeles Riot," p. 341.

25. Hobsbawm, *Primitive Rebels*, p. 116.

26. *Ibid.*, p. 118.

27. Waskow, *From Race Riot to Sit-In*, pp. 225–290.

28. "Creative rioting" as used herein refers to a particular tactical type of behavior aimed at bringing about societal change. It involves the conscious and deliberate use of violent attacks against property and/or persons. The violence against property may be either of a destructive or of a confiscatory (theft) nature. Violence against persons usually is not directed randomly against persons as individuals or members of a group; rather, it is frequently directed against persons as symbols of authority or oppression. It tends to be incidental to attacks upon property or the system of exploitation.

Thus, creative rioting differs from creative disorder in that the latter is nonviolent and, while disruptive of societal processes, is not destructive of property. Creative rioting also differs from revolution in that it tends to be too short-lived, less organized, and less coordinated than required for a full-scale, violent attempt to seize control of society.

29. Similarly, there may be a division of labor within a rioting mob. Some participants may consciously use rioting as a tactic to promote change, while others simply attempt to improve their personal well-being by acquiring more possessions, and still others try to avenge real or alleged wrongs. The latter two groups are not, strictly speaking, using creative rioting, but by swelling the numbers of rioters—thereby increasing the duration and intensity of the disorders—they contribute to the overall effect of the creative rioters.

30. *Report on Civil Disorders*, pp. 126–127.

31. Lyford P. Edwards. *The National History of Revolution* (Chicago: The University of Chicago Press, 1927), p. 30; and Crane Brinton, *The Anatomy of Revolution* (New York: W. W. Norton, 1938), p. 78.

32. *Report on Civil Disorders*. Henceforth, self-reported rioters and self-reported noninvolved will be referred to, respectively, as rioters and noninvolved.

33. For a summary of such literature see James A. Geschwender, "Continuities in Theories of Status Inconsistency and Cognitive Dissonance," *Social Forces*, 46 (Dec., 1967), pp. 160–171.

34. James A. Geschwender, "Negro Education: The False Faith," *Phylon* (forthcoming); and James A. Geschwender, "Social Structure and the Negro Revolt: An Examination of Some Hypotheses," *Social Forces*, 43 (Dec., 1964), pp. 248–256.

35. Geschwender, "Continuities in Theories," pp. 169–171.

36. H. Edward Ransford, "Isolation, Powerlessness, and Violence: A Study of Attitudes and Participation in the Watts Riot," *American Journal of Sociology*, 73 (March, 1968), p. 586.

37. Reinhard Bendix and Seymour Martin Lipset, "Karl Marx' Theory of Social Classes," in Reinhard Bendix and Seymour Martin Lipset, eds., *Class, Status and Power* (New York: Free Press of Glencoe, 1953), pp. 26–35.

KERNER COMMISSION

Who Riots?

It is sometimes assumed that the rioters were criminal types, over-active social deviants, or riffraff—recent migrants, members of an uneducated underclass, alienated from responsible Negroes, and without broad social or political concerns. It is often implied that there was no effort within the Negro community to attempt to reduce the violence.

We have obtained data on participation from four different sources:

- Eyewitness accounts from more than 1,200 interviews in our staff reconnaissance survey of 20 cities;
- Interview surveys based on probability samples of riot area residents in the two major riot cities—Detroit and Newark—designed to elicit anonymous self-identification of participants as rioters, counterrioters or noninvolved;
- Arrest records from 22 cities; and
- A special study of arrestees in Detroit.

Only partial information is available on the total numbers of participants. In the Detroit survey, approximately 11 percent of the sampled residents over the age of 15 in the two disturbance areas admittedly participated in rioting; another 20 to 25 percent admitted to having been bystanders but claimed that they had not participated; approximately 16 percent claimed they had engaged in counterriot activity; and the largest proportion (48 to 53 percent) claimed they were at home or elsewhere and did not participate. However, a large proportion of the Negro community apparently believed that more

Report of the National Advisory Commission on Civil Disorders (Washington, D. C.: U. S. Government Printing Office, 1968), pp. 73–77.

was gained than lost through rioting, according to the Newark and Detroit surveys.

Greater precision is possible in describing the characteristics of those who participated. We have combined the data from the four sources to construct a profile of the typical rioter and to compare him with the counterrioter and the noninvolved.

The Profile of a Rioter

The typical rioter in the summer of 1967 was a Negro, unmarried male between the ages of 15 and 24. He was in many ways very different from the stereotype. He was not a migrant. He was born in the state and was a lifelong resident of the city in which the riot took place. Economically his position was about the same as his Negro neighbors who did not actively participate in the riot.

Although he had not, usually, graduated from high school, he was somewhat better educated than the average inner-city Negro, having at least attended high school for a time.

Nevertheless, he was more likely to be working in a menial or low status job as an unskilled laborer. If he was employed, he was not working full time and his employment was frequently interrupted by periods of unemployment.

He feels strongly that he deserves a better job and that he is barred from achieving it, not because of lack of training, ability, or ambition, but because of discrimination by employers.

He rejects the white bigot's stereotype of the Negro as ignorant and shiftless. He takes great pride in his race and believes that in some respects Negroes are superior to whites. He is extremely hostile to whites, but his hostility is more apt to be a product of social and economic class than of race; he is almost equally hostile toward middle class Negroes.

He is substantially better informed about politics than Negroes who were not involved in the riots. He is more likely to be actively engaged in civil rights efforts, but is extremely distrustful of the political system and of political leaders.

The Profile of the Counterrioter

The typical counterrioter, who risked injury and arrest to walk the streets urging rioters to "cool it," was an active supporter of existing social institutions. He was, for example, far more likely than either the rioter or the noninvolved to feel that this country is worth defending in a major war. His actions and his attitudes reflected his substantially greater stake in the social system; he was considerably better educated and more affluent than either the rioter or the non-involved. He was somewhat more likely than the rioter, but less likely than the noninvolved, to have been a migrant. In all other respects he was identical to the noninvolved.

Characteristics of Participants

Race

Of the arrestees 83 percent were Negroes; 15 percent were whites. Our interviews in 20 cities indicate that almost all rioters were Negroes.

Age

The survey data from Detroit, the arrest records, and our interviews in 20 cities, all indicate that the rioters were late teenagers or young adults. In the Detroit survey, 61.3 percent of the self-reported rioters were between the ages of 15 and 24, and 86.3 percent were between 15 and 35. The arrest data indicate that 52.5 percent of the arrestees were between 15 and 24, and 80.8 percent were between 15 and 35.

Of the noninvolved, by contrast, only 22.6 percent in the Detroit survey were between 15 and 24, and 38.3 percent were between 15 and 35.

Sex

In the Detroit survey, 61.4 percent of the self-reported rioters were male. Arrestees, however, were almost all male—89.3 percent. Our interviews in 20 cities indicate that the majority of rioters were male. The large difference in proportion between the Detroit survey data and the arrestee figures probably reflects either selectivity in the arrest process or less dramatic, less provocative riot behavior by women.

Family structure

Three sources of available information—the Newark survey, the Detroit arrest study, and arrest records from four cities—indicate a tendency for rioters to be single. The Newark survey indicates that rioters were single—56.2 percent—more often than the noninvolved—49.6 percent.

The Newark survey also indicates that rioters were more likely to have been divorced or separated—14.2 percent—than the noninvolved—6.4 percent. However, the arrest records from four cities indicate that only a very small percentage of those arrested fall into this category.

In regard to the structure of the family in which he was raised, the self-reported rioter, according to the Newark survey, was not significantly different from many of his Negro neighbors who did not actively participate in the riot. Twenty-five and five-tenths percent of the self-reported rioters and 23 percent of the noninvolved were brought up in homes where no adult male lived.

Region of upbringing

Both survey data and arrest records demonstrate unequivocally that those brought up in the region in which the riot occurred are much more likely to have participated in the riots. The percentage of self-reported rioters brought up in the North is almost identical for the Detroit survey—74.4 percent—and the Newark survey—74 percent. By contrast, of the noninvolved, 36 percent in Detroit and 52.4 percent in Newark were brought up in the region in which the disorder occurred.

Data available from five cities on the birthplace of arrestees indicate that 63 percent of the arrestees were born in the North. Although birthplace is not necessarily identical with place of upbringing, the data are sufficiently similar to provide strong support for the conclusion.

Of the self-reported counterrioters, however, 47.5 percent were born in the North, according to the Detroit survey, a figure which places them between self-reported rioters and the noninvolved. Apparently, a significant consequence of growing up in the South is the tendency toward noninvolvement in a riot situation, while involvement in a riot, either in support of or against existing social institutions, was more common among those born in the North.

Residence

Rioters are not only more likely than the noninvolved to have been born in the region in which the riot occurred, but they are also more likely to have been long-term residents of the city in which the disturbance took place. The Detroit survey data indicate that 59.4 percent of the self-reported rioters, but only 34.6 percent of the noninvolved, were born in Detroit. The comparable figures in the Newark survey are 53.5 percent and 22.5 percent.

Outsiders who temporarily entered the city during the riot might have left before the surveys were conducted and therefore may be underestimated in the survey data. However, the arrest data, which is contemporaneous with the riot, suggest that few outsiders were involved: 90 percent of those arrested resided in the riot city,

7 percent lived in the same state, and only 1 percent were from outside the state. Our interviews in 20 cities corroborate these conclusions.

Income

In the Detroit and Newark survey data, income level alone does not seem to correlate with self-reported riot participation. The figures from the two cities are not directly comparable since respondents were asked for individual income in Detroit and family income in Newark. More Detroit self-reported rioters (38.6 percent) had annual incomes under $5,000 per year than the noninvolved (30.3 percent), but even this small difference disappears when the factor of age is taken into account.

In the Newark data, in which the age distributions of self-reported rioters and the noninvolved are more similar, there is almost no difference between the rioters, 32.6 percent of whom had annual incomes under $5,000, and the noninvolved, 29.4 percent of whom had annual incomes under $5,000.

The similarity in income distribution should not, however, lead to the conclusion that more affluent Negroes are as likely to riot as poor Negroes. Both surveys were conducted in disturbance areas where incomes are considerably lower than in the city as a whole and the surrounding metropolitan area. Nevertheless, the data show that rioters are not necessarily the poorest of the poor.

While income fails to distinguish self-reported rioters from those who were not involved, it does distinguish counterrioters from rioters and the noninvolved. Less than 9 percent of both those who rioted and those not involved earned more than $10,000 annually. Yet almost 20 percent of the counterrioters earned this amount or more. In fact, there were no male self-reported counterrioters in the Detroit survey who earned less than $5,000 annually. In the Newark sample there were seven respondents who owned their own homes; none of them participated in the riot. While extreme poverty does not necessarily move a man to riot, relative affluence seems at least to inhibit him from attacking the existing social order and may motivate him to take considerable risks to protect it.

Education

Level of schooling is strongly related to participation. Those with some high school education were more likely to riot than those who had only finished grade school. In the Detroit survey, 93 percent of the self-reported rioters had gone beyond grade school, compared with 72.1 percent of the noninvolved. In the Newark survey the comparable figures are 98.1 and 85.7 percent. The majority of self-reported rioters were not, however, high school graduates.

The counterrioters were clearly the best educated of the three groups. Approximately twice as many counterrioters had attended college as had the noninvolved, and half again as many counterrioters had attended college as rioters. Considered with the information on income, the data suggest that counterrioters were probably well on their way into the middle class.

Education and income are the only factors which distinguish the counterrioter from the noninvolved. Apparently, a high level of education and income not only prevents rioting but is more likely to lead to active, responsible opposition to rioting.

Employment

The Detroit and Newark surveys, the arrest records from four cities, and the Detroit arrest study all indicate that there are no substantial differences in unemployment between the rioters and the noninvolved.

Unemployment levels among both groups were extremely high. In the Detroit survey, 29.6 percent of the self-reported rioters were unemployed; in the Newark survey, 29.7 percent; in the four-city arrest data, 33.2 percent; and in the Detroit arrest study, 21.8 percent. The unemployment rates for the noninvolved in the Detroit and Newark surveys were 31.5 and 19.0 percent.

Self-reported rioters were more likely to be only intermittently employed, however, than the noninvolved. Respondents in Newark were asked whether they had been unemployed for as long as a month or more during the last year. Sixty-one percent of the self-reported rioters, but only 43.4 percent of the noninvolved, answered, "yes."

Despite generally higher levels of education, rioters were more likely than the noninvolved to be employed in unskilled jobs. In the Newark survey, 50 percent of the self-reported rioters, but only 39.6 percent of the noninvolved, had unskilled jobs.

Attitudes about employment

The Newark survey data indicate that self-reported rioters were more likely to feel dissatisfied with their present jobs than were the non-involved.

Only 29.3 percent of the rioters, compared with 44.4 percent of the noninvolved, thought their present jobs appropriate for them in responsibility and pay. Of the self-reported rioters, 67.6 percent, compared with 56.1 percent of the noninvolved, felt that it was impossible to obtain the kind of job they wanted. Of the self-reported rioters, 69 percent, as compared with 50 percent of the noninvolved, felt that racial discrimination was the major obstacle to finding better employment. Despite this feeling, surprising numbers of rioters (76.9 percent) responded that "getting what you want out of life is a matter of ability, not being in the right place at the right time."

Racial attitudes

The Detroit and Newark surveys indicate that rioters have strong feelings of racial pride, if not racial superiority. In the Detroit survey, 48.6 percent of the self-reported rioters said that they felt Negroes were more dependable than whites. Only 22.4 percent of the noninvolved stated this. In Newark, the comparable figures were 45 and 27.8 percent. The Newark survey data indicate that rioters wanted to be called "black" rather than "Negro" or "colored" and were somewhat more likely than the noninvolved to feel that all Negroes should study African history and languages.

To what extent this racial pride antedated the riot or was produced by the riot is impossible to determine from the survey data. Certainly the riot experience seems to have been associated with increased pride in the minds of many participants. This was vividly illustrated by the statement of a Detroit rioter:

> Interviewer: You said you were feeling good when you followed the crowds?
> Respondent: I was feeling proud, man, at the fact that I was a Negro. I felt like I was a first-class citizen. I didn't feel ashamed of my race because of what they did.

Similar feelings were expressed by an 18-year-old Detroit girl who reported that she had been a looter:

> Interviewer: What is the Negro then if he's not American?
> Respondent: A Negro, he's considered a slave to the white folks. But half of them know that they're slaves and feel that they can't do nothing about it because they're just going along with it. But most of them they seem to get it in their heads now how the white folks treat them and how they've been treating them and how they've been slaves for the white folks.

Along with increased racial pride there appears to be intense hostility toward whites. Self-reported rioters in both the Detroit and Newark surveys were more likely to feel that civil rights groups with white and Negro leaders would do better without the whites. In Detroit, 36.1 percent of the self-reported rioters thought that this statement was true, while only 21.1 percent of the noninvolved thought so. In the Newark survey, 51.4 percent of the self-reported rioters agreed; 33.1 percent of the noninvolved shared this opinion.

Self-reported rioters in Newark were also more likely to agree with the statement, "Sometimes I hate white people." Of the self-reported rioters, 72.4 percent agreed; of the noninvolved, 50 percent agreed.

The intensity of the self-reported rioters' racial feelings may suggest that the recent riots represented traditional interracial hostilities. Two sources of data suggest that this interpretation is probably incorrect.

First, the Newark survey data indicate that rioters were almost as hostile to middle-class Negroes as they were to whites. Seventy-one and four-tenths percent of the self-reported rioters, but only 59.5 percent of the noninvolved, agreed with the statement, "Negroes who make a lot of money like to think they are better than other Negroes." Perhaps even more significant, particularly in light of the rioters' strong feelings of racial pride, is that 50.5 percent of the self-reported rioters agreed that "Negroes who make a lot of money are just as bad as white people." Only 35.2 percent of the noninvolved shared this opinion.

Second, the arrest data show that the great majority of those arrested during the disorders were generally charged with a crime relating to looting or curfew violations. Only 2.4 percent of the arrests were for assault and 0.1 percent were for homicide, but 31.3 percent of the arrests were for breaking and entering—crimes directed against white property rather than against individual whites.

Political attitudes and involvement

Respondents in the Newark survey were asked about relatively simple items of political information, such as the race of prominent local and national political figures. In general, the self-reported rioters were much better informed than the noninvolved. For example, self-reported rioters were more likely to know that one of the 1966 Newark mayoral candidates was a Negro. Of the rioters, 77.1 percent—but only 61.6 percent of the noninvolved—identified him correctly. The overall scores on a series of similar questions also reflect the self-reported rioters' higher levels of information.

Self-reported rioters were also more likely to be involved in activities associated with Negro rights. At the most basic level of political participation, they were more likely than the noninvolved to talk frequently about Negro rights. In the Newark survey, 53.8 percent of the self-reported rioters, but only 34.9 percent of the noninvolved, said that they talked about Negro rights nearly every day.

The self-reported rioters also were more likely to have attended a meeting or participated in civil rights activity. Of the rioters, 39.3 percent—but only 25.7 percent of the noninvolved—reported that they had engaged in such activity.

In the Newark survey, respondents were asked how much they thought they could trust the local government. Only 4.8 percent of the self-reported rioters, compared with 13.7 percent of the noninvolved, said that they felt they could trust it most of the time; 44.2 percent of the self-reported rioters and 33.9 percent of the noninvolved reported that they could almost never trust the government.

In the Detroit survey, self-reported rioters were much more likely to attribute the riot to anger about politicians and police than were the noninvolved. Of the self-reported rioters, 43.2 percent—but only 19.6 percent of the noninvolved—said anger against politicians had a great deal to do with causing the riot. Of the self-reported rioters, 70.5 percent, compared with 48.8 percent of the noninvolved, believed that anger against the police had a great deal to do with causing the riot.

Perhaps the most revealing and disturbing measure of the rioters' anger at the social and political system was their response to a question asking whether they thought "the country was worth fighting for in the event of a major world war." Of the self-reported rioters, 39.4 percent in Detroit and 52.8 percent in Newark shared a negative view. In contrast, 15.5 percent of the noninvolved in Detroit and 27.8 percent of the noninvolved in Newark shared this sentiment. Almost none of the self-reported counterrioters in Detroit—3.3 percent —agreed with the self-reported rioters.

Some comments of interviewees are worthy of note:

> Not worth fighting for—if Negroes had an equal chance it would be worth fighting for.
> Not worth fighting for—I am not a true citizen so why should I?
> Not worth fighting for—because my husband came back from Vietnam and nothing had changed.

Suggested Readings: Violence

ENDLEMAN, SHALOM (ed.) *Violence in the Streets.* Chicago: Quadrangle Books, 1968. A readable collection of essays on the origins and forms of violence, the impact of mass media on the development and spread of violence, and the role of the police in dealing with collective civil violence.

GRAY, J. GLENN. *On Understanding Violence Philosophically and Other Essays.* Harper Torchbooks. New York: Harper & Row, Publishers, 1970. Three little-known penetrating essays on the philosophical basis of violence.

NATIONAL COMMISSION ON THE CAUSES AND PREVENTION OF VIOLENCE. *Violence in America: Historical and Comparative Perspectives.* Signet Books. New York: The New American Library,

1969; Washington, D.C.: U.S. Government Printing Office, 1969. Popular publication of one of the most comprehensive collection of materials available for the study of violence in America.

NIEBURG, H. L. *Political Violence: The Behavioral Process.* New York: St. Martin's Press, Inc., 1969. Based on original research for the National Commission on the Causes and Prevention of Violence, this study attempts to create a model for the development of political violence and its impact on the social process.

SKOLNICK, JEROME H. *The Politics of Protest.* Clarion Books. New York: Simon and Schuster, Inc., 1969. One of the most readable of the task force reports submitted to the National Commission on the Causes and Prevention of Violence.

URBAN COALITION. *One Year Later: An Assessment of the Nation's Response to the Crisis Described by the National Advisory Commission on Civil Disorders.* New York: Frederick A. Praeger, 1969. An analytical critique of the nation's response that is more relevant today than when first written.

YOUNG, RICHARD P. (ed.) *Roots of Rebellion: The Evolution of Black Politics and Protest Since World War II.* New York: Harper & Row, Publishers, 1970. The best available anthology on the subject.

7/Urban Redevelopment:
Renew? Restore? Resettle?

Urban renewal is not a new idea. Modern engineers and planners improve on its technical aspects, but the construction and reconstruction of cities has been an ongoing process throughout history. Pericles rebuilt Athens; Augustus, Rome. Large portions of London, Tokyo, Berlin, and Leningrad were reconstructed after World War II. Urban renewal is constantly taking place as new structures replace old, highways are rerouted, subways built, and the skyline altered. Some of these changes are deliberate attempts to reshape the physical character of cities on a planned basis. Others are the results of an individual's action to redevelop his property.

The type of urban renewal that sparked the controversy presented in this section resulted from the Housing Act of 1949. The advent of the federal urban renewal program brought an entirely new concept into American life. There had been previous attempts to restore blighted neighborhoods, but nothing had struck at the foundations of private property as did the urban renewal program. For the first time, government took private property in slum areas on a large scale and *sold it for private redevelopment*. This revolutionary concept grew out of the need to strike a massive blow at problems affecting the older cities of the country. Large areas of central cities had deteriorated to such an extent that piecemeal restoration was inadequate. The declining economic base that resulted prevented cities from dealing effectively with problems created by overcrowding, slum housing, and dependent populations.

In its early years, the urban renewal program focused on clearing entire areas and replacing slums with new business structures and high-income residences. Not much concern was voiced for the people displaced by demolition of their homes. When public housing was built on the site, it tended to be high-rise apartments, which isolated the poor from the rest of the community.

At its outset, this program created little controversy. Business leaders welcomed the idea of revitalizing the downtown areas. Civic officials were pleased with the opportunity to get rid of slums and to bolster the tax base. Those concerned with welfare programs saw it as a chance to eliminate slum housing.

As urban renewal accelerated, however, criticism mounted. While the condemnation of private property produced immediate controversy, other objections soon developed. There was widespread censure of the wholesale destruction of viable neighborhoods which might have been redeveloped at far less expense and with more socially acceptable results. Protests mounted over the razing of homes of the poor and their replacement by upper-income housing designed to revive the economic base of the central city. In the articles which follow, Martin Anderson, one of the harshest critics of the program, condemns the urban *removal* rather than the urban *renewal* approach. Robert P. Groberg defends urban renewal actions. John H. Kain and Joseph J. Persky criticize the pouring of more money into the ghetto to upgrade standards and services. In "Alternatives to the Gilded Ghetto," they advance the proposition that it is preferable to disperse ghetto residents to other areas. The Kerner Commission contends that immediate-action development programs are necessary along with long-range dispersal. Bennett Harrison presents data indicating that dispersal is not a viable solution because movement of blacks to the suburbs does not solve the blacks' economic problems; most of those who would move in a dispersal program would be low-income blacks.

MARTIN ANDERSON

The Sophistry That Made
Urban Renewal Possible

This member of government was at first considered as the most harmless and helpless of all its organs. But it has proved that the power of declaring what the law is, *ad libitum*, by sapping and mining, slyly, and without alarm, the foundations of the Constitution, can do what open force would not dare to attempt.

—Thomas Jefferson:
Letter to Edward Livingston, 1825

For over fifteen years government agencies throughout the United States have been taking private property by eminent domain for the private use of some person other than the original owner. Why? To carry out the federal urban renewal program (FURP). How? Because such action was apparently deemed constitutional by the Supreme Court in 1954.[1]

The purpose of this article is twofold: first, to summarize briefly the record of the FURP, and second, to analyze the opinion of the Supreme Court on the 1954 *Berman v. Parker* case, which made urban renewal possible.

Passed in 1949 by Congress, the essential purpose and clear intent of the FURP was to "help" our economic system of free enterprise achieve better housing conditions for all Americans. The decision made by the Supreme Court in 1954 appeared to sanction the constitutionality of the program. Since then the FURP has grown rapidly and it has been endorsed enthusiastically by many well-known, influential people.

Today the consensus seems to be that (1) the program is absolutely necessary, and, except for a few setbacks here and there, is making significant progress, and (2) in spite of some uneasiness over the idea of taking private property by eminent domain for private use, it "must" be all right because the Supreme Court has indicated that it is constitutional.

I disagree. In my judgment the FURP is not necessary, it is not working, and it is clearly unconstitutional.

Martin Anderson, "The Sophistry That Made Urban Renewal Possible." Reprinted with permission from a symposium, "Urban Problems and Prospects," appearing in *Law and Contemporary Problems* (vol. 30, no. 1, Winter 1965), published by the Duke University School of Law, Durham, North Carolina, Copyright, 1965, by Duke University.

The Record of the
Federal Urban Renewal Program

The FURP has been a failure. Contrary to the widely publicized claims of the proponents of federally aided and directed urban renewal, the program has worsened the housing situation that it set out to help; it has not revitalized a single city; and its costs—both in dollars and personal liberty—have been great.[2] Seldom have so many people been hurt and so much money been spent with such perverse consequences. Some of the more serious consequences are these:

- From 1950 through 1960, about 126,000 housing units were destroyed in urban renewal areas. Of these, 101,000 were classified as substandard by local renewal officials; 25,000 were sound homes in good condition—some of them in excellent condition. Only about 28,000 housing units were built; 25,000 of them are privately owned, the rest are public housing units. Thus about four times as many homes were destroyed as were built. Those destroyed were predominantly low-rent homes, those built were predominantly high-rent homes.
- As of March 31, 1963, about 609,000 people had been evicted from their homes. I estimate that one million will have been evicted by the end of 1965. And, according to the Commissioner of Urban Renewal Administration, around four million will be displaced by 1972—or one out of every fifty persons living in the United States.
- The FURP has strong racial overtones and is sometimes referred to as the "Negro Removal Program." About two-thirds of those forced to move are Negroes and Puerto Ricans.
- The process is taking a very long time. An average-size urban renewal project can easily run ten to twelve years from the start of planning to the completion of the new construction.
- FURP is very expensive. Many billions have already been spent, and the plans call for vastly increased spending.
- On an overall basis there are strong indications that the program is causing a net decrease in cities' tax revenues.

But in spite of the failures of urban renewal and its negative effects, housing quality in the United States has increased enormously. The economic system of free enterprise has moved powerfully and swiftly toward achieving better housing conditions for all Americans. From 1950 to 1960, over 18 million standard homes were added to the housing supply. The total number of standard homes increased from 29.1 million to 47.7 million, an overall increase of sixty-four percent.[3]

And these gains were possible to all Americans. For example, the nonwhite population of the United States enjoyed a substantial increase in the quality of its housing. From 1950 to 1960 there was an increase of 1,813,000 standard units occupied by nonwhites, accompanied by a decrease of 537,000 substandard units.[4]

Virtually all of this was accomplished by private construction, rehabilitation, and demolition efforts financed by massive amounts of private funds. These activities were in no way connected with the FURP.

Thus, facts tell us that the economic system of free enterprise has made enormous gains, while FURP—which was supposed to aid and complement private means—has actually made the housing situation worse, particularly for low-income families and individuals, and has done so at a high cost. The FURP is acting as a brake on the economic system of free enterprise.

Is the FURP Constitutional?

The rest of this article deals basically with one simple, clear issue— the issue of whether or not any government agency in the United States should have the right to take private property by eminent domain for private use.

The basic idea of forcibly seizing the private property of one man, compensating him for it at the appraised value, and then conveying this property to someone else is, I am convinced, considered illegal and immoral by the great majority of the people in the United States—particularly when this abstract principle becomes concrete and people are faced with the prospect of having their own homes seized.

In 1954 the constitutionality of the FURP was challenged. At this time the nine men who were then the Justices of the Supreme Court had the opportunity to stop this program in its infancy before it had a chance to grow into the firmly entrenched giant that it is today, reaching into over 750 cities and embracing over 1500 projects.

But they did not; instead they released the FURP to interfere with the property rights and lives of millions of city dwellers in the United States. The opinion was written by Justice Douglas and concurred in by the rest of the Court. Since then, the composition of the Court has changed significantly—only four of the Justices remain who participated in this decision. They include Justice Douglas, the author, Chief Justice Warren, and Justices Black and Clark. The five present Justices who did not participate in *Berman v. Parker* are Harlan, Brennan, Stewart, White, and Goldberg.

It is my contention that the opinion handed down in 1954 is illogical and contains sophistic reasoning. On a quick, superficial reading it may appear plausible, but a careful, detailed reading will reveal basic errors. Following is the complete text of the opinion handed down by the Court in 1954 in the case of *Berman v. Parker*.[5]

Interspersed through it are my comments on what I consider to be the crucial elements of the opinion.

> This is an appeal (28 U.S.C. § 1253) from the judgment of a three-judge District Court which dismissed a complaint seeking to enjoin the condemnation of appellants' property under the District of Columbia Redevelopment Act of 1945, 60 Stat. 790, D.C. Code 1951, §§ 5-701-5-719. The challenge was to the constitutionality of the Act, particularly as applied to the taking of appellants' property. The District Court sustained the constitutionality of the Act. 117 F. Supp. 705.

Here the Court clearly identifies the main issue to be decided upon—"the constitutionality of the Act, particularly as applied to the taking of the appellants' property."

> By § 2 of the Act, Congress made a "legislative determination" that "owing to technological and sociological changes, obsolete layout, and other factors, conditions existing in the District of Columbia with respect to substandard housing and blighted areas, including the use of buildings in alleys as dwellings for human habitation, are injurious to the public health, safety, morals, and welfare, and it is hereby declared to be the policy of the United States to protect and promote the welfare of the inhabitants of the seat of the Government by eliminating all such injurious conditions by employing all means necessary and appropriate for the purpose."[1]
>
> Section 2 goes on to delcare that acquisition of property is necessary to eliminate these housing conditions.
>
> Congress further finds in § 2 that these ends cannot be attained "by the ordinary operations of private enterprise alone without public participation"; that "the sound replanning and redevelopment of an obsolescent or obsolescing portion" of the District "cannot be accomplished unless it be done in the light of comprehensive and coordinated planning of the whole of the territory of the District of Columbia and its environs"; and "that the acquisition and the assembly of real property and the leasing or sale thereof for redevelopment pursuant to a project area redevelopment plan . . . is hereby declared to be a public use."

The main issue is clarified further here. Congress declares that it must use "all means necessary" and then goes on to declare "that acquisition of property is necessary" and further that this is a "public

---

[1]The Act does not define either "slums" or "blighted areas." Sec. 3(r), however, states: " 'Substandard housing conditions' means the conditions obtaining in connection with the existence of any dwelling, or dwellings, or housing accommodations for human beings, which because of lack of sanitary facilities, ventilation, or light, or because of dilapidation, overcrowding, faulty interior arrangement, or any combinations of these factors, is in the opinion of the Commissioners detrimental to the safety, health, morals, or welfare of the inhabitants of the District of Columbia." [Footnote, *Berman v. Parker*, 348 U.S. 26 (1954)].

use." Because Congress declares something to be a "public use" does not necessarily mean that it is, in fact, a public use. Approximately seventy percent of all new construction in federal urban renewal areas is privately owned—and this is clearly a private use as anyone may easily verify by attempting to use these homes or places of business as he would use a public park or a highway.

> Section 4 creates the District of Columbia Redevelopment Land Agency (hereinafter called the Agency), composed of five members, which is granted power by § 5(a) to acquire and assemble, by eminent domain and otherwise, real property for "the redevelopment of blighted territory in the District of Columbia and the prevention, reduction, or elimination of blighting factors or causes of blight."
> Section 6(a) of the Act directs the National Capital Planning Commission (hereinafter called the Planning Commission) to make and develop "a comprehensive or general plan" of the District, including "a land-use plan" which designates land for use for "housing, business, industry, recreation, education, public buildings, public reservations, and other general categories of public and private uses of the land." Section 6(b) authorizes the Planning Commission to adopt redevelopment plans for specific project areas. These plans are subject to the approval of the District Commissioners after a public hearing; and they prescribe the various public and private land uses for the respective areas, the "standards of population density and building intensity," and "the amount or character or class of any low-rent housing."

This section clearly shows that there is a contradiction in the Act itself. Earlier the process of federal urban renewal was "declared to be a public use." Here they clearly specify (twice) that there will be both "public *and private* uses of the land." Unless one attempts to maintain the intellectually indefensible position that a private use can be construed to be a public use (this is a contradiction in terms), then the only conclusion one can draw is that the wording of the Act itself is illogical and contradictory.

> Once the Planning Commission adopts a plan and that plan is approved by the Commissioners, the Planning Commission certifies it to the Agency. § 6(d). At that point, the Agency is authorized to acquire and assemble the real property in the area. *Ibid.*
> After the real estate has been assembled, the Agency is authorized to transfer to public agencies the land to be devoted to such public purposes as streets, utilities, recreational facilities, and schools, § 7(a), and to lease or sell the remainder as an entirety or in parts to a redevelopment company, individual, or partnership. § 7(b), (f). The leases or sales must provide that the lessees or purchasers will carry out the redevelopment plan and that "no use shall be made of any land or real property included in the lease or sale nor any building or structure erected thereon" which does not conform to the plan. §§ 7(d), 11. Preference is to be given to private enterprise over public agencies in executing the redevelopment plan. § 7(g).

This brief description of how the process of federal urban renewal will work implies that private use is involved. For example, it is stated that land can be sold or leased to an *individual*. By no distortion of the thinking process can this be construed to be a public use.

The first project undertaken under the Act relates to Project Area B in Southwest Washington, D.C. In 1950 the Planning Commission prepared and published a comprehensive plan for the District. Surveys revealed that in Area B, 64.3% of the dwellings were beyond repair, 18.4% needed major repairs, only 17.3% were satisfactory; 57.8% of the dwellings had outside toilets, 60.3% had no baths, 29.3% lacked electricity, 82.2% had no wash basins or laundry tubs, 83.8% lacked central heating. In the judgment of the District's Director of Health it was necessary to redevelop Area B in the interests of public health. The population of Area B amounted to 5,012 persons, of whom 97.5% were Negroes.

The plan for Area B specifies the boundaries and allocates the use of the land for various purposes. It makes detailed provisions for types of dwelling units and provides that at least one-third of them are to be low-rent housing with a maximum rental of $17 per room per month.

After a public hearing, the Commissioners approved the plan and the Planning Commission certified it to the Agency for execution. The Agency undertook the preliminary steps for redevelopment of the area when this suit was brought.

Appellants own property in Area B at 712 Fourth Street, S.W. It is not used as a dwelling or place of habitation. A department store is located on it. Appellants object to the appropriation of this property for the purposes of the project. They claim that their property may not be taken constitutionally for this project. It is commercial, not residential property; it is not slum housing; it will be put into the project under the management of a private, not a public, agency and redeveloped for private, not public, use. That is the argument; and the contention is that appellants' private property is being taken contrary to two mandates of the Fifth Amendment— (1) "No person shall . . . be deprived of . . . property, without due process of law"; (2) "nor shall private property be taken for public use, without just compensation." To take for the purpose of ridding the area of slums is one thing; it is quite another, the argument goes, to take a man's property merely to develop a better balanced, more attractive community. The District Court, while agreeing in general with the argument, saved the Act by construing it to mean that the Agency could condemn property only for the reasonable necessities of slum clearance and prevention, its concept of "slum" being the existence of conditions "injurious to the public health, safety, morals and welfare." 117 F. Supp. 705, 724–725.

The power of Congress over the District of Columbia includes all the legislative powers which a state may exercise over its affairs. See *District of Columbia v. John R. Thompson Co.*, 346 U.S. 100, 108.

This summarizes the situation that was presented to the Justices of the Supreme Court. Now Justice Douglas begins with the analysis and the conclusion derived therefrom, in which the rest of the Justices concurred.

We deal, in other words, with what traditionally has been known as the police power. An attempt to define its reach or trace its outer limits is fruitless, for each case must turn on its own facts. The definition is essentially the product of legislative determinations addressed to the purposes of government, purposes neither abstractly nor historically capable of complete definition. Subject to specific constitutional limitations, when the legislature has spoken, the public interest has been declared in terms well-nigh conclusive.

But the main point here is *"subject to specific constitutional limitations"*—and no matter what the *purpose* of the legislature, no matter how well-meaning, no matter how plausible the reasons, it is the responsibility of the Supreme Court to analyze logically the totality of the law—not only to see if the primary purposes of the law are unconstitutional, but also to see if anything incidental, but necessary, to the law is also unconstitutional.

For example, if Congress passed a law whose purpose was to eliminate slums, but which contained a proviso stating that the government could conscript labor for the actual physical work, the mere fact that the *good* of eliminating slums is desirable would not therefore ustify the re-institution of slavery.

The fact that an action necessary to implement a law is incidental to the main purpose of the law does not mean that the "incidental" action is immune from scrutiny as to its constitutionality.

In such cases the legislature, not the judiciary, is the main guardian of the public needs to be served by social legislation, whether it be Congress legislating concerning the District of Columbia (see *Block v. Hirsh*, 256 U.S. 135), or the States legislating concerning local affairs. See *Olsen v. State of Nebraska*, 313 U.S. 236; *Lincoln Union v. Northwestern Co.*, 335 U.S. 525; *California State Ass'n v. Maloney*, 341 U.S. 105.

Of course, the legislature, and not the Supreme Court, is the governmental body that drafts and enacts laws. No one ever suggested the possibility that perhaps the Supreme Court was some sort of "Guardian." The role of the Supreme Court is to ascertain whether or not this legislation drafted by Congress is constitutional.

This principle admits of no exception merely because the power of eminent domain is involved. The role of the judiciary in determining whether that power is being exercised for a public purpose is an extremely narrow one. See *Old Dominion Land Co. v. United States*, 269 U.S. 55, 66; *United States* ex rel. *TVA v. Welch*, 327 U.S. 546, 552.

The Court states that its role "in determining whether that power is being exercised for a public purpose is an extremely narrow one." The critical word here is *"purpose."* But the issue is not whether eminent domain is being used for a public purpose, but rather whether the use of the land seized will be *public* or *private.*

The appellants claim—in the Court's own words—that their property, after it has been taken, "will be put into the project under the management of a private, not a public, agency and redeveloped for private, not public, use." The critical word here is *"use."*

According to the *American College Dictionary* the legal definition of "use" is "the enjoyment of property, as by the employment, occupation, or exercise of it." "Purpose," on the other hand, is "the object for which anything exists or is done, made, *used,* etc."

Use refers to the actual employment of material objects—to their occupation or to their exercise. *Purpose* refers to the object or goal *for which* any particular material object is used. Purpose and use do not mean the same thing.

The elementary point that should be decided by the Court is whether or not private property is being taken for *public* use or for *private* use. The question of whether or not it is for a public *purpose* is irrelevant here.

The word "public" pertains to the people as a whole—and thus the concept embraces every single individual within the community, state or nation that the context of its use implies. The word "private" means belonging to some *particular* person or persons.

To illustrate, the maintenance of an army would constitute a public purpose (in a national sense) because its function is to protect *all* the citizens of the nation. The maintenance of a police force by a community or city constitutes a public purpose (in a community sense) because it is used to protect *all* the citizens of the community or city. On the other hand, the maintenance of a police force for a privately owned housing development constitutes a private purpose, since it concerns only the particular individuals living in the housing development.

It appears that early in its analysis the Court has made a serious error. They have construed their role as one of determining whether the police power is being used for a public purpose. This is not the crucial issue. The crucial issue is whether or not private property can be taken for private *use* if the legislature decrees this taking to be for a public purpose. Whether or not the taking is for a public purpose is irrelevant to the question of whether or not the means employed to achieve this purpose result in an action that is clearly unconstitutional.

> Public safety, public health, morality, peace and quiet, law and order—these are some of the more conspicuous examples of the traditional application of the police power to municipal affairs. Yet they merely illustrate the scope of the power and do not delimit it. See *Noble State Bank v. Haskell,* 219 U.S. 104, 111.

It may be true that the traditional application of the police power to municipal affairs only illustrates the scope of its power and does not delimit it, but it does not follow from this that Supreme Court Justices have a carte blanche for deciding the desirable limits. The Court has no right to condone the extension of police power if this extension involves actions that are unconstitutional.

> Miserable and disreputable housing conditions may do more than spread disease and crime and immorality. They may also suffocate the spirit by reducing the people who live there to the status of cattle. They may indeed make living an almost insufferable burden. They may also be an ugly sore, a blight on the community which robs it of charm, which makes it a place from which men turn. The misery of housing may despoil a community as an open sewer may ruin a river.

This highly emotional statement, while dealing with an important problem, does not pertain to the main point of constitutionality at issue here.

> We do not sit to determine whether a particular housing project is or is not desirable. The concept of the public welfare is broad and inclusive. See *Day-Brite Lighting, Inc. v. Missouri*, 342 U.S. 421, 424. The values it represents are spiritual as well as physical, aesthetic as well as monetary. It is within the power of the legislature to determine that the community should be beautiful as well as healthy, spacious as well as clean, well-balanced as well as carefully patrolled. In the present case, the Congress and its authorized agencies have made determinations that take into account a wide variety of values. It is not for us to reappraise them. If those who govern the District of Columbia decide that the Nation's Capital should be beautiful as well as sanitary, there is nothing in the Fifth Amendment that stands in the way.

The clear statement that it is within the power of the legislature to determine that the community should be beautiful, spacious and well-balanced has far reaching implications. In effect they are saying that Congress may dictate to the individual citizens of the United States what style of architecture they may build (because what is beautiful to one may not be to another), how much space should be between buildings, and what they must do to make the community "well-balanced." "Well-balanced" puzzles me. Do they mean it should be racially balanced, and, if so, what ratio? Do they mean that it should be culturally balanced, and, if so, to what cultural activities are they referring?

> Once the object is within the authority of Congress, the right to realize it through the exercise of eminent domain is clear. For the power of eminent domain is merely the means to the end. See *Luxton*

v. North River Bridge Co., 153 U.S. 525, 529–530; *United States v. Gettysburg Electric R. Co.*, 160 U.S. 668, 679. Once the object is within the authority of Congress, the means by which it will be attained is also for Congress to determine.

In simple terms, this says that *the end justifies the means*. This is an appalling philosophy to be upheld by any court, let alone the Supreme Court. Here the Court has clearly stated that if the Court agrees that the object of a law passed by Congress is within its authority, then it has no concern about the means used to acquire this object.

This is an illogical and immoral position. Clearly the means by which the legislature attempts to gain its ends must be moral and just—and when legislation is challenged, it is the responsibility of the Court to see to it that the means are constitutional, not to dismiss the issue.

What if Congress were to pass a law which had as its goal the elimination of poverty (clearly within the terms of "public welfare" as defined by the Court) and had as its means gas chambers to liquidate the poor who after all may be "a blight on the community which robs it of charm"? Would the Court declare that, "Once the object is within the authority of Congress, the means by which it will be attained is also for Congress to determine"? Of course not. The reasoning used by the Court here is illogical. The result of this error is to lead the Court into the untenable position where it implicitly adopts the principle that the means are irrelevant if the end is "good."

> Here one of the means chosen is the use of private enterprise for redevelopment of the area. Appellants argue that this makes the project a taking from one businessman for the benefit of another businessman.

Taking from one businessman by force for the benefit of another businessman is *not* private enterprise. Private enterprise is based solely on *voluntary* trade—the use of physical force is prohibited. This is clearly government action with private individuals and firms engaged to carry out the task.

> But the means of executing the project are for Congress and Congress alone to determine, once the public purpose has been established. See *Luxton v. North River Bridge Co., supra;* cf. *Highland v. Russell Car Co.*, 279 U.S. 253. The public end may be as well or better served through an agency of private enterprise than through a department of government—or so the Congress might conclude. We cannot say that public ownership is the sole method of promoting the public purposes of community redevelopment projects. What we have said also disposes of any contention concerning the fact that certain property owners in the area may be permitted to repurchase their properties for redevelopment in harmony with the overall plan.

That, too, is a legitimate means which Congress and its agencies may adopt, if they choose.

This clinches their position—the end justifies the means.

> In the present case, Congress and its authorized agencies attack the problem of the blighted parts of the community on an area rather than on a structure-by-structure basis. That, too, is opposed by appellants. They maintain that since their building does not imperil health or safety nor contribute to the making of a slum or a blighted area, it cannot be swept into a redevelopment plan by the mere dictum of the Planning Commission or the Commissioners. The particular uses to be made of the land in the project were determined with regard to the needs of the particular community.

This last sentence is not quite accurate. It should read: "The particular uses to be made of the land in the project were determined with regard to the needs of particular people in the community." What happened to the "needs" of those living in the community whose property is to be seized? Why do the "needs" of some take precedence over the "needs" of others?

> The experts concluded that if the community were to be healthy, if it were not to revert again to a blighted or slum area, as though possessed of a congenital disease, the area must be planned as a whole. It was not enough, they believed, to remove existing buildings that were insanitary or unsightly. It was important to redesign the whole area so as to eliminate the conditions that cause slums—the overcrowding of dwellings, the lack of parks, the lack of adequate streets and alleys, the absence of recreational areas, the lack of light and air, the presence of outmoded street patterns. It was believed that the piecemeal approach, the removal of individual structures that were offensive, would be only a palliative. The entire area needed redesigning so that a balanced, integrated plan could be developed for the region, including not only new homes but also schools, churches, parks, streets, and shopping centers. In this way it was hoped that the cycle of decay of the area could be controlled and the birth of future slums prevented. Cf. *Gohld Realty Co. v. Hartford*, 141 Conn. 135, 141–144, 104 A.2d 365, 368–370; *Hunter v. Redevelopment Authority*, 195 Va. 326, 338–339, 78 S.E.2d 893, 900–901. Such diversification in future use is plainly relevant to the maintenance of the desired housing standards and therefore within congressional power.

The implication of this whole section is that if the "experts" say it is so, it *is* so, and therefore is desirable, lawful and just. I find it quite incredible that Justices of the Supreme Court could ascribe such knowledge and wisdom to city planning experts. The profession of city planning is in its intellectual infancy—and there are few generally accepted standards or criteria by which these people operate.

The District Court below suggested that, if such a broad scope were intended for the statute, the standards contained in the Act would not be sufficiently definite to sustain the delegation of authority. 117 F. Supp. 705, 721. We do not agree. We think the standards prescribed were adequate for executing the plan to eliminate not only slums as narrowly defined by the District Court but also the blighted areas that tend to produce slums.

At this point I can only refer to the footnote that the Court itself appended to its opinion. In the footnote the Court states, "The Act does not define either 'slums' or 'blighted area,' " and now, a few pages later in the same opinion, they say, "We think the standards prescribed were adequate. . . ." The logic here is impeccably false. Standards that do not exist cannot be adequate.

Property may of course be taken for this redevelopment which, standing by itself, is innocuous and unoffending. But we have said enough to indicate that it is the need of the area as a whole which Congress and its agencies are evaluating. If owner after owner were permitted to resist these redevelopment programs on the ground that his particular property was not being used against the public interest, integrated plans for redevelopment would suffer greatly. The argument pressed on us is, indeed, a plea to substitute the landowner's standard of the public need for the standard prescribed by Congress. But as we have already stated, community redevelopment programs need not, by force of the Constitution, be on a piecemeal basis—lot by lot, building by building.

It is not for the courts to oversee the choice of the boundary line nor to sit in review on the size of a particular project area. Once the question of the public purpose has been decided, the amount and character of land to be taken for the project and the need for a particular tract to complete the integrated plan rests in the discretion of the legislative branch. See *Shoemaker v. United States*, 147 U.S. 282; *United States* ex rel. *TVA v. Welch, supra*, 327 U.S. at 554; *United States v. Carmack*, 329 U.S. 230, 247.

For the third time—the end justifies the means.

The District Court indicated grave doubts concerning the Agency's right to take full title to the land as distinguished from the objectionable buildings located on it. 117 F. Supp. 705, 715–719. We do not share those doubts. If the Agency considers it necessary in carrying out the redevelopment project to take full title to the real property involved, it may do so. It is not for the courts to determine whether it is necessary for successful consummation of the project that unsafe, unsightly, or insanitary building alone be taken or whether title to the land be included, any more than it is the function of the courts to sort and choose among the various parcels selected for condemnation.

The Supreme Court Justices do not seem to share anyone's doubts with regard to any areas concerning this case. Now they say that "if the Agency (not the legislature) considers it necessary . . . to take full title to the real property, it may do so." Does this also imply that the Court would support anything the "Agency" wished to do as long as the "Agency" considered it necessary?

> The rights of these property owners are satisfied when they receive that just compensation which the Fifth Amendment exacts as the price of the taking.

There are many property owners and others that do not agree that their rights are satisfied simply by receiving what someone else thinks their seized property is worth.

> The judgment of the District Court, as modified by this opinion, is *affirmed*.

Conclusion

In essence the Supreme Court was presented with the established fact that a law had been passed by Congress which involved, as part of the means of implementation, the taking of private property by eminent domain for private use. This is proven by the fact that approximately seventy percent of the new construction in urban renewal areas is privately owned, and also by the intent and wording of the act itself.

The Constitution is unequivocal on this question. A specific reference clearly states, "nor shall private property be taken for public use, without just compensation." And "for public use" is *not* the same as "for public purpose."

Faced with this problem the Justices appear to have found themselves in something of a dilemma. They had three alternatives: (1) If they decided that the Constitution meant what it said, it would mean the end of the FURP. If they found this alternative unpalatable, they had two other possibilities. (2) They could declare that private property could be taken by eminent domain for private use, or (3) they could somehow attempt to evade the issue and simply declare that the FURP was constitutional because it was "within the power of the legislature to determine that the community should be beautiful as well as healthy, spacious as well as clean, well-balanced as well as beautiful" and then go on to say that "the power of eminent domain is merely the means to the end."

By not taking the first alternative, which, in my judgment, is the only logical conclusion, they were left with two untenable choices. To accept the second alternative would put them clearly on record in favor of allowing private property to be seized by eminent domain for private use. The enormous implications of a clear, unqualified acceptance of this principle probably deterred them from this course. Thus they were left with only one alternative: to somehow allow eminent domain to be used as a tool in the FURP, and to evade any clear endorsement of the principle involved.

This is the course they followed by concurring in the opinion drafted by Justice Douglas. If we take this opinion literally, the Court has upheld the general principle that the end can justify the means, and that once the legislature has determined the end, the means are incidental to it, thus clearly implying that the crucial issue of whether or not a law is constitutional is irrelevant when the law deals only with the means employed to gain some particular end.

But it is obvious that the means of any legislation must clearly lie within the specific limitations of the Constitution. To declare otherwise is to revert in history to the rule of men, and to abandon the rule of law and the concept of human rights. An evasive decision of this type simply allows government seizure of private property by eminent domain for private use without openly endorsing it.

On the other hand, it might be that the Court simply did not address itself to the main issue raised in *Berman v. Parker:* Is it constitutional to seize private property by eminent domain for private use? The Justices are human, and thus fallible, and it is certainly reasonable to expect some errors in the decisions they make, particularly when one considers the tremendous time pressures under which they operate.

If this is the case, then they should rule on this crucial issue at some time in the future, and steer clear of expounding on what they feel is in the best interests of the community. When, and if, they do face this issue squarely, they will have to choose between the following alternatives:

1. Rule that private property *cannot* be taken by eminent domain for private use, and thus eliminate the FURP.
2. Rule that private property *can* be taken by eminent domain for private use, and thus cause the FURP to continue. Of course, the adoption of this principle has far-reaching implications. It means that no man's property would be absolutely safe from seizure by a government official, if that government official maintained that the seizure was for a "public purpose" and could show this to the satisfaction of the Court.

In my judgment, the first alternative is the only logical and moral course to follow.

Notes

1. *Berman v. Parker*, 348 U.S. 26 (1954).
2. MARTIN ANDERSON, THE FEDERAL BULLDOZER (1964).

3. U.S. DEP'T OF COMMERCE, CENSUS OF HOUSING: 1960, FINAL REPORT HC (I)-I, UNITED STATES SUMMARY Table O, p. xxxvi.
4. HOUSING AND HOME FINANCE AGENCY, OFFICE OF THE ADMINISTRATOR, OUR NONWHITE POPULATION AND ITS HOUSING: THE CHANGES BETWEEN 1950 AND 1960 (May 1963).
5. *Supra* note I.

ROBERT P. GROBERG

Urban Renewal Realistically Reappraised

Recent—and often misguided—critical outpourings against urban renewal justify an effort to determine realistically the actual and potential contribution of government to the solution of urban problems. Broadly defined, urban renewal can encompass all public and private efforts to improve city form and life. Realism requires recognition at the outset that there are no panaceas for every problem a city may possess and that some "solutions" create or emphasize other problems. Equally, realism requires careful consideration of the genesis and purposes of government programs with limited objectives so that criticism of them relates to their efforts and not to the broader notion of urban renewal goals. One recent attempt at major analysis[1] has gone astray partly because its author failed to see clearly the historical perspective and the limits of federal aid for slum clearance and redevelopment authorized by Congress under the Housing Act of 1949 and its amendments.[2]

The author of *The Federal Bulldozer* views this urban redevelopment assistance as though it had been expected by the Congress to solve *all* national housing problems. He cites the 1949 Declaration of National Housing Policy, preface to a comprehensive housing act with six separate titles, as though that declaration pertained only to title I. He then proceeds to condemn urban renewal for not achieving the aims of titles II, III, IV, V, VI, and other national housing efforts. *The Federal Bulldozer* is based on the assumption that federal assistance for local slum clearance and redevelopment projects was meant to achieve the housing aims of such other programs as low-rent public

Robert P. Groberg, "Urban Renewal Realistically Reappraised." Reprinted with permission from a symposium, "Urban Problems and Prospects," appearing in *Law and Contemporary Problems* (vol. 30, no. 1, Winter 1965), published by the Duke University School of Law, Durham, North Carolina, Copyright, 1965, by Duke University.

housing and FHA mortgage insurance. By incorporating these and other myths in his analysis, he began with unrealistic expectations for urban renewal efforts undertaken with federal assistance.

I. Urban Renewal Is a Local Program

Another myth incorporated into *The Federal Bulldozer* is that there is a separate, monolithic "federal urban renewal program" run from Washington by decree. The author completely misunderstands that urban renewal is a local program. He makes it appear that the power to plan, acquire, and prepare project sites for redevelopment or rehabilitation is vested in the federal government and based on an opinion of the United States Supreme Court. He does not recognize that the federal government cannot initiate any project. He does not mention that there can be no urban renewal project anywhere unless:

—a state legislature has first adopted an enabling law to give cities the governmental power for urban renewal, and some forty-eight states have;

—an elected city council has first organized an operating local renewal agency, and some 800 cities have;

—the same city council has first approved the project, and some 1600 projects have been so approved;

—the local government has first authorized local public expenditures to supplement federal funds, and more than one billion dollars in local public funds have been so approved to back the program;

—local citizens are participating in the urban renewal process, as required by law, and citizens everywhere are so doing.

By ignoring these facts, he never explains that the program depends completely on active local political support, given through the established system of representative government. The author does not state that the federal government neither operates any bulldozer, nor acquires any property for any urban renewal project. Instead, he alleges that "the federal urban renewal program is a firmly entrenched giant, reaching into virtually every important city in the United States . . ."[3] and falsely claims that "the federal government . . . will forcibly displace . . . American citizens . . ."[4] and that "the Urban Renewal Administration reported . . . that . . . businesses had already been acquired by them [*i.e.*, the URA] in urban renewal projects throughout the United States. . . ."[5] The federal government cannot select a project area, cannot prepare a plan, cannot acquire property, cannot demolish dilapidated structures, cannot sell the land or install the public improvements. Yet these are the critical steps in urban renewal projects. This misleading emphasis on the "federal" role in urban renewal programs all but obscures the fact that the powers to carry out urban renewal derive from state enabling legislation.[6]

In fact, some twenty-five states had slum clearance and redevelopment legislation of some kind prior to the Housing Act of 1949. New York state, for example, passed a constitutional amendment in 1938 and enacted legislation in 1942 authorizing slum clearance and redevelopment projects. State enabling acts have withstood constitutional attacks based on state and federal constitutional provisions beginning in 1947 in Pennsylvania.[7] By 1954 (when the U.S. Supreme Court upheld redevelopment legislation for the District of Columbia),[8] the courts in twenty-one states had reviewed such legislation, and in all but two states had upheld the constitutionality of urban redevelopment. At present urban renewal legislation has been tested and upheld in the highest courts of thirty-three states. Only in South Carolina, Georgia, and Florida has such legislation successfully been assailed. In Georgia a later constitutional amendment authorized the undertaking of urban renewal, while in Florida the position originally taken has been modified substantially by the state's highest court. In short, the author of *The Federal Bulldozer* seems to have been quite unaware, as are many opponents of urban renewal, that if his suggestion for "repeal" of the "federal" urban renewal program were adopted (cf. chapter fourteen), the program's authority would not be impaired at all because, with constitutional powers derived from the states, it is locally run.

II. The Use of the Power of Eminent Domain in Urban Renewal Rests on a Long Tradition of State Court Decisions

At this late date complaints concerning the constitutional basis of urban renewal would seem ill-timed.[9] They may arise from those who ignore or misread the historical basis for government action to solve the problems of society. Foes of urban renewal have attempted to create a mythology with respect to the "inviolate" right of private property in support of their contention that government should not have the power to act in removing slums, and they have focused their attacks on the Supreme Court of the United States: "The federal urban renewal program has drastically altered the traditional concept of eminent domain; it is doubtful if any of the founding fathers could recognize it in its present form."[10] Instead of citing "the founding fathers," they cite Pitt and Blackstone, the latter in a classic example of tearing statements from context: "Regard of the law for private property is so great that it will not authorize the least violation of it, not even for the general good of the whole community; for it would be dangerous to allow any private man, or even any public tribunal, to be the judge of this common good. . . ." The preceding lines are the full text of a quote from *The Federal Bulldozer.*[11] The identical passage is also cited in a book published in 1962.[12] Both books ignored what came before and what followed in Blackstone's *Commentaries.* The quoted passage is preceded in Blackstone by the phrase "save only by the laws of the land" and is followed by: "In this and similar cases the legislature alone can, and indeed frequently does, interpose, and compel the individual to acquiesce . . . by giving him a full indemnification and equivalent for the injury thereby sustained."[13] Thus, while Blackstone recognized the importance of private property, he also acknowledged that the legislature could authorize the taking of property for proper purposes upon payment of just compensation to the owner. This view was incorporated in the fifth amendment to the United States Constitution: ". . . nor shall private property be taken for public use without just compensation." It was written into some, but not all state constitutions.[14] But its incorporation in the federal and state constitutions still left to the legislatures the determination of what were proper purposes for the use of eminent domain.

In some states from the very start it was clear that private uses served public purposes. For instance, Idaho's constitution of 1890, cited by Professor Haar:[15]

> The necessary use of lands for the construction of reservoirs or storage basins, for the purpose of irrigation, or for rights of way for the construction of canals, ditches . . . or for the drainage of mines . . . or any other use necessary to the complete development of the material resources of the state, or the preservation of the health of its inhabitants, is hereby declared to be a public use and subject to the regulation and control of the state.

Such state constitutional provisions or amendments were adopted over a period from 1780 (Massachusetts) to 1938 (New York).

The courts of most states have ruled that "public use," as it appears in state constitutional provisions authorizing takings of private property by eminent domain, is equivalent to "public benefit." As one leading text puts it:[16]

> Anything that tends to enlarge the resources, increase the industrial advantages and promote the productive power of any considerable number of the inhabitants of a section of a state, or which leads to the growth of towns and the creation of new resources for the employment of capital prosperity of the whole community and, giving the constitution a broad and comprehensive interpretation, constitutes a public use. Under this view it has been held that the scope of eminent domain has been made as broad as the powers under the police and tax provisions of the constitution.

In accord with this view innumerable state legislatures and courts have authorized eminent domain proceedings in behalf of mills, railroads, power companies, private universities, and for other private concerns whose operations were considered to involve "public benefit." In these instances the property was taken by a *private* enterprise through a judicial proceeding which assured the payment of just compensation to the property owner; the title was not acquired by a public body or agency.

On the other hand, in urban renewal programs the property is acquired by a local *public* agency pursuant to the provisions and safeguards of an urban renewal plan adopted by a city council or other local governing body, after public hearings. Although most courts consider the elimination of the slum to be the public purpose for which the power of eminent domain may be employed, they also recognize that the prevention of future slums is a related public purpose. The existence of an official urban renewal plan is considered by these courts to be necessary to assure that this public purpose is served.

Thus, there is a tradition of broad interpretation of the term "public use" which would justify the use of eminent domain for urban redevelopment despite the fact that the property might eventually end up in private ownership. But in line with the finding that slum clearance and prevention are the public purposes which justify the employment of eminent domain in urban renewal, most courts have held that the disposition of the land is *incidental*, and the fact that it may be sold to private parties for private use does not vitiate the public purpose of slum clearance.

There is a minority view which holds in South Carolina where the sale of such land must be to public bodies. The foes of urban renewal hold fast to this narrow position, and they interpret the language of the fifth amendment of the United States Constitution literally. Not only does this fly in the face of the tradition described above, it flies in the face of what is now thoroughly understood to constitute the general well-being of society in the twentieth century. The following quote from a California court opinion which upheld an urban renewal project on predominantly vacant land sums it up:[17]

> It might be pointed out that as our community life becomes more complex, our cities grow and become overcrowded, and the need to use for the benefit of the public areas which are not adapted to the pressing needs of the public becomes more imperative, a broader concept of what is a public use is necessitated. Fifty years ago no court would have interpreted, under the eminent domain statutes, slum clearance even for public housing as a public use, and yet, it is now so recognized. To hold that clearance of blighted areas as characterized by the [California] act and as shown in this case and the redevelopment of such areas as contemplated here are not public uses, is to view present day conditions under the myopic eyes of years now gone.

Notes

1. MARTIN ANDERSON, THE FEDERAL BULLDOZER (1964) [hereinafter cited as ANDERSON].

2. Note that the 1949 Act authorized federal loans and grants for what was defined as "slum clearance and redevelopment" and is now often cited as "urban redevelopment." The term "urban renewal" did not come into use until the Housing Act of 1954 amended and broadened the 1949 program to encompass a city-wide program—including renewal of commercial and industrial areas—rather than individual projects. With new emphasis on code enforcement, structural rehabilitation and neighborhood conservation, the objectives were extended to slum prevention as well as slum clearance. Amendments since then have sought to improve the assistance and provide better tools to achieve the program's goals.

3. ANDERSON 33.

4. *Id.* at 55.

5. *Id.* at 68.

6. For a summary and citations to state enabling acts, see HOUSING AND HOME FINANCE AGENCY, LIST OF CITATIONS TO STATUTES, CONSTITUTIONAL PROVISIONS, AND COURT DECISIONS (1962).

7. Belovsky v. Redevelopment Authority of the City of Philadelphia, 357 Pa. 329, 54 A.2d 277 (1947).

8. Berman v. Parker, 358 U.S. 269 (1954).

9. For a well-reasoned discussion of these issues, see COLEMAN WOODBURY (ED.), URBAN REDEVELOPMENT: PROBLEMS AND PRACTICES, pt. IV, "Eminent Domain in Acquiring Subdivision and Open Land in Redevelopment Programs: A Question of Public Use" (1953).

10. ANDERSON 188.

11. *Id.* at 185.

12. THOMAS F. JOHNSON, JAMES R. MORRIS & JOSEPH G. BUTTS, RENEWING AMERICA'S CITIES ch. III, at 46 (The Institute for Social Science Research, 1962).

13. 1 WILLIAM BLACKSTONE, COMMENTARIES ON THE LAWS OF ENGLAND 138 (Sharswood ed. 1895).

14. Professor Charles M. Haar of the Harvard Law School observes that: "The constitutions of most of the thirteen original states did not require compensation upon the condemnation of land. . . . But with the establishment of roads, limitations began to appear. . . ." CHARLES M. HAAR, LAND USE PLANNING 470 (1959).

15. *Id.* at 411.

16. PHILIP NICHOLS, THE LAW OF EMINENT DOMAIN § 7.2 (Sackman & Van Brunt, 3d ed. rev., 1963).

JOHN F. KAIN
JOSEPH J. PERSKY

Alternatives to the Gilded Ghetto

We are faced today with a spate of proposals and programs for improving the ghetto through economic development, renewal, and reconstruction. The intellectual basis of many of these proposals stems from a false analogy of the ghetto to an underdeveloped country in need of economic development. This oversimplified and misleading view ignores the strong linkages that tie the ghetto to the remainder of the metropolis and to the nation. When the nature of these linkages and the complex relationship between the ghetto and metropolitan development is understood, the potential destructiveness of these proposals becomes apparent. In this article we attempt to describe these interrelationships and the ghetto's consequent culpability for an expanded list of urban problems.

The Ghetto and the Metropolis

If we begin with the usual list of "ghetto problems"—unemployment, low income, poor schools, and poor housing—it is easy to see the appeal of proposals aimed at making the ghetto livable. Moreover, casual observation of the slow pace of school desegregation, residential integration, and fair employment practices would indicate that the promise of integration and the gains achievable from the process are to be made only at an obscure point in the future. Thus, in the short run, the argument for ghetto improvement would have us view the ghetto as something of a community unto itself, a community that could substantially benefit from economic development and especially heavy investments of physical capital.

The weakness of this argument, however, is attested to by a growing body of evidence that indicates that (1) the above list of ghetto problems is much too short, because it ignores the serious implications of the growing ghetto for the metropolis as a whole and that (2) the ghetto itself is responsible for, or seriously aggravates, many of the most visible problems of urban Negroes.

The central Negro ghetto has produced a significant distortion of metropolitan development, which has added substantially to prob-

John F. Kain and Joseph J. Persky, "Alternatives to the Gilded Ghetto," *The Public Interest*, no. 14 (Winter 1969), 74–87. Copyright © National Affairs, Inc., 1969. Reprinted by permission of National Affairs, Inc.

lems in central city finance, metropolitan transportation, housing, and urban renewal. The decline of central cities has been hastened by a conviction in the white community, both individual and corporate, that the ghetto would continue its rapid expansion, carrying along its associated problems of concentrated poverty and social disorganization.

Although historically lower income groups have tended to live in central cities, this residential pattern was the result of a highly centralized employment structure. Low income households, constrained by limited housing and transportation budgets, clustered tightly around the work places in the densest accommodations available. High income households, by contrast, with more disposable income and preferences for less congested living conditions, found it expedient to commute to suburban areas where land costs were lower. These lower housing costs in suburban locations more than compensated them for the time, inconvenience, and out-of-pocket costs of commuting. Today, it still remains true that low income households cluster more closely around their work places than do high income households. However, with the accelerating pace of suburbanization of industry and jobs—itself no doubt due partly to the ghetto's expansion—these jobs are found less frequently in cities. Thus the poor are found less frequently in the central city; it is mainly the Negro poor who are found there. The inference is inescapable; *central cities are poor largely because they are black, and not the converse.*

The residential locations of whites in similar income groups support this contention. This is clearly shown in Table 1, which gives the proportion of low income whites and Negroes living in the suburban rings of the ten largest metropolitan areas (Table 1 also includes data for all whites and Negroes). For example, 45 percent of Detroit's poor white families live in suburbs, but only 11 percent of its poor Negro families do so. These figures belie the argument that Negroes are concentrated in central cities because they are poor. This finding is consistent with the work of numerous researchers who have concluded that little of the existing pattern of Negro residential segregation can be explained by income or other socioeconomic characteristics. One of the authors of this article has elsewhere estimated that, on the basis of Negro employment locations and of low income white residential choice patterns, as many as 40,000 Detroit Negro workers and 112,000 Chicago Negro workers would move out of central ghettos in the absence of racial segregation.[1]

This residential pattern imposed on the Negro has led to an unduly large proportion of poverty-linked services being demanded of central cities. At the same time, the expansion of the ghetto has encouraged the exodus of middle income whites. The result has been rapid increases in local government expenditures and a severe constraint on the ability of central cities to raise revenues. Hence, the

Table 1. Percent of white and Negro families (total and poor) living in the suburban ring of the ten largest urbanization areas*

		White		Negro	
		All Families	Families with Incomes $3,000	All Families	Families with Incomes $3,000
1	New York	27.8%	16.3%	9.4%	8.2%
2	Los Angeles	65.2	61.6	27.3	23.3
3	Chicago	47.6	37.2	7.7	5.9
4	Philadelphia	50.8	37.4	15.7	14.2
5	Detroit	58.9	44.9	12.1	11.3
6	San Francisco-Oakland	57.8	48.8	29.2	25.8
7	Boston	74.3	64.0	19.2	13.9
8	Washington	75.7	59.6	9.8	10.4
9	Pittsburgh	70.5	63.3	29.4	27.1
10	Cleveland	59.2	39.3	3.1	2.4

*For New York and Chicago the suburban ring is the difference between the SMSA and central city. For all other cities it is the difference between the urbanized area and central city. Both San Francisco and Oakland are counted as central cities.

current crisis in city finances. Although the problem can be handled in the short run by various schemes of redistributing governmental revenues, a preferable long-run solution would involve a major dispersal of the low income population, in particular the Negro. Central cities will continue to have a high proportion of the poor as long as they contain a large proportion of metropolitan jobs. However, there is no rationale for exaggerating this tendency with artificial restraints.

Housing, Transportation, Schools

Housing segregation has also frustrated efforts to renew the city. At first sight the logic of renewal is strong. By offering federal subsidies to higher income whites locating within their boundaries, central cities have hoped to improve their tax base. The same logic underlies community efforts to woo industry. However, to the extent that these groups consider the city an inferior location, because of the existence of the ghetto, such subsidies will continue to fail. As long as the ghetto exists, most of white America will write off the central city. Spot renewal, even on the scale envisioned in the Model Cities program, cannot alter this basic fact.

In this context, even the small victories of central cities are often of a pyrrhic nature. So long as the central business district (CBD) manages to remain a major employment location, the city is faced with serious transportation problems, problems that would be substantially reduced if more of the centrally employed whites were willing to reside in the city. To a great extent, the CBD stakes its existence on an ability to transport people rapidly over long distances. Pressures for more expressways and high-speed rail transit are understandable—and yet both encourage the migration to the suburbs. The city must lose either way, so long as the ghetto is a growing mass that dominates the environment of its core and the development of its metropolitan area.

From the above argument, it is clear that the impact of the ghetto on the processes of metropolitan development has created or aggravated many of our most critical urban problems. These costs are borne by Negroes and whites alike. However, the same interaction between the ghetto and metropolis has produced other important distortions whose costs fall almost exclusively on the Negro community. The ghetto has isolated the Negro economically as well as socially. In the first place, the Negro has inadequate access to the job market. For him, informal methods of job search, common to low skilled employment, are largely limited to the ghetto. Jobs may be plentiful outside of the ghetto, yet he will know little or nothing of these opportunities. Moreover, the time and cost necessary to reach many suburban jobs, frequently compounded by the radial character of public transit services, often will discourage Negroes from taking or even seeking such jobs. Granted that the ghetto generates a limited number of service jobs, this effect is more than offset by the discriminatory practices of nonghetto employers. Research on the distribution of Negro employment in Northern metropolitan areas indicates the importance of these factors, by demonstrating that the proportion of Negroes in an area's work force is dependent on that area's distance from the ghetto and the racial composition of the surrounding residential neighborhoods. These distributional characteristics also affect the level of Negro employment. Estimates indicate that as many as 24,000 jobs in Chicago and 9,000 in Detroit may be lost to the Negro community because of housing segregation.[2] These figures are based on 1956 and 1952 data and may well underestimate the current situation. The continuing trend of job decentralization also may have aggravated the situation.

De facto school segregation is another widely recognized limitation of Negro opportunities resulting from housing market segregation. A large body of evidence indicates that students in ghetto schools receive an education much inferior to that offered elsewhere. Low levels of student achievement are the result of a complex of factors including poorly trained, overworked, and under-motivated teachers, low levels of per student expenditures, inadequate capital plants, and the generally low level of students' motivation and aspiration. This last factor is, of course, related to the ghetto's poverty and social disorganization.

The continued rapid growth of central city ghettos has seriously expanded the realm of *de facto* segregation and limited the range of possible corrective actions. For example, in 1952, 57 percent of Cleveland's Negro students went to schools with more than 90 percent Negro enrollment. In 1962, 82 percent went to such schools. By 1965, Chicago, Detroit, and Philadelphia all had more than 70 percent of their Negro students in these completely segregated schools.[3]

In addition to sharply curtailing Negro economic and educational opportunity, the ghetto is an important disorganizing force. It represents the power of the outside community and the frustration of the Negro. The sources of nourishment for many of the psychological and sociological problems too common to Negro Americans can be found here. Drug addiction, violent crime, and family disorganization all gain a high degree of acceptance, creating a set of norms that often brings the individual into conflict with the larger society. Kenneth Clark puts the case well: "The dark ghetto is institutionalized pathology; it is chronic, self-perpetuating pathology . . . " Although this pathology is difficult to quantify, it may well be the ghetto's most serious consequence.

In reviewing our expanded list of problems, it may seem that we have made the ghetto too much the villain. Physical segregation may have only been the not-so-subtle way to avoid discriminatory practices that might otherwise be rampant. Many ghetto problems might still exist in some other guise. Nevertheless, the problems as structured *now* must continue as long as the metropolis harbors this "peculiar institution."

Nothing less than a complete change in the structure of the metropolis will solve the problem of the ghetto. It is therefore ironic that current programs which ostensibly are concerned with the welfare of urban Negroes are willing to accept, and are even based on, the permanence of central ghettos. Thus, under every heading of social welfare legislation—education, income transfer, employment, and housing—we find programs that can only serve to strengthen the ghetto and the serious problems that it generates. In particular, these programs concentrate on beautifying the fundamentally ugly structure of the current metropolis and not on providing individuals with the tools necessary to break out of that structure. The shame of the situation is that viable alternatives *do* exist.

Thus, in approaching the problems of Negro employment, first steps could be an improved information system at the disposal of Negro job seekers, strong training programs linked to job placement in industry, and improved transit access between central ghettos and outlying employment areas. Besides the direct effects of such programs on unemployment and incomes, they have the added advantage of encouraging the dispersion of the ghetto and not its further concentration. For example, Negroes employed in suburban areas distant from the ghetto have strong incentives to reduce the time and cost of commuting by seeking out residences near their work places. Frequent, informal contact with white co-workers will both increase their information about housing in predominantly white residential areas and help to break down the mutual distrust that is usually associated with the process of integration.

Prospects of housing desegregation would be much enhanced by major changes in urban renewal and housing programs. Current schemes accept and reinforce some of the worst aspects of the housing market. Thus, even the best urban renewal projects involve the government in drastically reducing the supply (and thereby increasing the cost) of low income housing—all this at great expense to the taxpayer. At best there is an implicit acceptance of the alleged desire of the poor to remain in central city slums. At worst, current programs could be viewed as a concerted effort to maintain the ghetto. The same observation can be made about public housing programs.[4] The Commission on Civil Rights in its report on school segregation concluded that government policies for low cost housing were "further reinforcing the trend toward racial and economic separation in metropolitan areas."

An alternative approach would aim at drastically expanding the supply of low income housing *outside* the ghetto. Given the high costs of reclaiming land in central areas, subsidies equivalent to existing urban renewal expenditures for use anywhere in the metropolitan area would lead to the construction of many more units. The new mix by type and location would be likely to favor small, single-family homes and garden apartments on the urban periphery. Some over-building would be desirable, the object being the creation of a glut in the low income suburban housing market. It is hard to imagine a situation that would make developers and renters less sensitive to skin color.

These measures would be greatly reinforced by programs that increase the effective demand of Negroes for housing. Rent subsidies to individuals are highly desirable, because they represent the transfer of purchasing power that can be used anywhere in the metropolitan area. Other income transfer programs not specifically tied to housing would have similar advantages in improving the prospects of ghetto dispersal. Vigorous enforcement of open housing statutes would aid the performance of the "impersonal" market, perhaps most importantly by providing developers, lenders, and realtors with an excuse to act in their own self interest.

Suburbanization of the Negro

Even in the face of continuing practices of residential segregation, the suburbanization of the Negro can still continue apace. It is important to realize that the presence of Negroes in the suburbs does not necessarily imply Negro integration into white residential neighborhoods. Suburbanization of the Negro and housing integration are not synonymous. Many of the disadvantages of massive, central ghettos would be overcome if they were replaced or even augmented by smaller, dispersed Negro *communities*. Such a pattern would remove the limitations on Negro employment opportunities attributable to the geography of the ghetto. Similarly, the reduced pressure on central city housing markets would improve the prospects for the renewal of middle-income neighborhoods through the operations of the private market. Once the peripheral growth of central city ghettos is checked, the demands for costly investment in specialized, long-distance transport facilities serving central employment areas would be reduced. In addition programs designed to reduce *de facto* school segregation by means of redistributing, busing, and similar measures would be much more feasible.

Although such a segregated pattern does not represent the authors' idea of a more open society, it could still prove a valuable first step toward that goal. Most groups attempting to integrate suburban neighborhoods have placed great stress on achieving and maintaining some preconceived interracial balance. Because integration is the goal, they feel the need to proceed slowly, and make elaborate precautions to avoid "tipping" the neighborhood. The result has been a small, black trickle into all-white suburbs. But if the immediate goal is seen as destroying the ghetto, different strategies should be employed. "Tipping," rather than something to be carefully avoided, might be viewed as a tactic for opening large amounts of suburban housing. If enough suburban neighborhoods are "tipped," the danger of any one of them becoming a massive ghetto would be small.

Education is still another tool that can be used to weaken the ties of the ghetto. Formal schooling plays a particularly important role in preparing individuals to participate in the complex urban society of today. It greatly enhances their ability to compete in the job market with the promise of higher incomes. As a result, large scale programs of compensatory education can make important contributions to a strategy of weakening and eventually abolishing the Negro ghetto. Nevertheless, the important gains of such compensatory programs must be continually weighed against the more general advantages of school desegregation. Where real alternatives exist in the sho: t run, programs consistent with this latter objective should always be chosen. It is important to note that truly effective programs of compensatory education are likely to be extremely expensive and that strategies involving significant amounts of desegregation may achieve the same educational objectives at much lower costs.

Busing of Negro students may be such a program. Like better access to suburban employment for ghetto job seekers, busing would weaken the geographic dominance of the ghetto. Just as the informal experience of integration on the job is an important element in changing racial attitudes, integration in the classroom is a powerful learning experience. Insofar as the resistance of suburban communities to accepting low income residents and students is the result of a narrow cost-minimization calculus that attempts to avoid providing public services and in particular education, substantial state and federal subsidies for the education of low income students can prove an effective carrot. Title I programs of the Elementary and Secondary Education Act of 1965 and grants to areas containing large federal installations are precedents. Subsidies should be large enough to cover more than the marginal cost of educating students from low income families, and should make it *profitable* for communities and school districts to accept such students. The experience of the METCO program in Boston strongly suggests that suburban communities can be induced to accept ghetto school children if external sources of financing are available.

Because the above proposals would still leave unanswered some immediate needs of ghetto residents, a strong argument can be made for direct income transfers. Although certain constraints on the use of funds, for example rent supplements, might be maintained, the emphasis should be on providing resources to individuals and not on freezing them into geographic areas. The extent to which welfare schemes are currently tied to particular neighborhoods or communities should be determined, and these programs should be altered so as to remove such limitations on mobility. Keeping in mind the crucial links between the ghetto and the rural South, it is essential that the Southern Negro share in these income transfers.

The Ghetto and the Nation

Although there are major benefits to be gained by both the Negro community and the metropolis at large through a dispersal of the central ghetto, these benefits cannot be realized and are likely to be hindered by programs aimed at making the ghetto a more livable place. In addition to the important objections discussed so far there is the very real possibility that such programs will run afoul of major migration links with the Negro population of the South. A striking example of this problem can be seen in the issue of ghetto job creation, one of the most popular proposals to improve the ghetto.

Although ghetto job creation, like other "gilding" programs, might initially reduce Negro unemployment, it must eventually affect the system that binds the Northern ghetto to the rural and urban areas of the South. This system will react to any sudden changes in employment and income opportunities in Northern ghettos. If there are no offsetting improvements in the South, the result will be increased rates of migration into still restricted ghetto areas. While we need to know much more than we now do about the elasticity of migration to various economic improvements, the direction of the effect is clear. Indeed it is possible that more than one migrant would appear in the ghetto for every job created.[5] Even at lower levels of sensitivity, a strong wave of in-migration could prove extremely harmful to many other programs. The South in 1960 still accounted for about 60 percent of the country's Negro population, more than half of which lived in nonmetropolitan areas. In particular, the number of *potential* migrants from the rural South has not declined greatly in recent years. The effect of guaranteed incomes or jobs available in the metropolitan ghetto can be inferred from an analysis of the patterns of migration from the South.

Historically, the underdeveloped nature of the Southern region has proven a spur to the migration of *both* whites and Negroes. What recent progress has been achieved is overwhelmingly "whites only." The 1950's were the first decade in this century in which there was net white in-migration to the Southern region as a whole. This change is very likely the result of the expansion of industrial activity throughout the South and particularly its border areas. White male agricultural employment losses of about 1 million were more than offset by strong gains in manufacturing, wholesale and retail trade, and professional and related services. By way of contrast, Negroes concentrated in the slowest-growing and most discriminatory states of the Deep South showed no major gains to offset the almost 400 thousand jobs lost in agriculture. Thus, despite rapid contraction of the agricultural sector, 1960 still found 21 percent of all Southern Negro males employed in agriculture as compared to 11 percent of Southern whites. It is not surprising, in terms of this background, that nearly 1.5 million Negroes (net) left the South in the 1950's.

The major result of the massive migrations of the 1940's and 1950's was to make the metropolitan areas of the North and West great centers of Negro population. In 1940 these areas accounted for only 20 percent of all Negroes in the country, whereas in 1960 37 percent of all Negroes lived in these same areas. Moreover, statistics on the migration of Negroes born in Southern states indicate a definite preference for the largest metropolitan areas of the country over smaller cities.

Developing the South

Some appreciation for migration's contribution to the growth of Northern ghettos is provided by a comparison of the components of Negro population increase. Fifty-four percent of the 2.7 million increase in Northern Negro populations from 1950 to 1960 was accounted for by net in-migration of Southern Negroes. Although the data on more recent population changes are scanty, the best estimates suggest that Negro net migration from the South has been averaging about 100,000 per year for the period 1960 to 1966. It therefore appears that the contribution of Southern migration to the growth of Northern ghettos, even though it may now be on the decline, remains substantial.

The pattern of Negro migration is in sharp contrast with the pattern of white out-migration from the same areas of the South. Thus, there are about 2.5 million Southern born whites and 2.5 million Southern born Negroes in non-Southern metropolitan areas greater than a million, but 1.42 million whites and 4.2 million Negroes in non-Southern cities of 250,000 to a million. Cities greater than 250,000 account for 89 percent of Negroes who have left the South, but only 60 percent of whites. The framework of opportunities presented to the individual Negro migrant is such as to increase the desirability of a move out of the South and to stress the comparative desirability of large cities as against rural areas and medium-sized cities.

Although the differential in white and Negro migration is clearly related to differential economic opportunity the over-all level of Southern out-migration must be ascribed to the underdeveloped nature of the region. A more rapid pace of Southern economic development could change these historic patterns of Negro migration. Tentative research findings indicate that both manufacturing growth and urbanization in the South reduce Negro out-migration. Although the holding effect of these changes is not so strong for Negroes as for whites, the difference between the two responses can be substantially narrowed. If development took place at a higher rate, the job market would tighten and thus encourage Negroes to stay. Moreover, the *quid pro quo* for large scale subsidies for Southern development might be strong commitments to hire Negro applicants. A serious program of Southern development is worthwhile in its own right as a cure to a century of imbalance in the distribution of economic activity in the nation. From the narrow viewpoint of the North, however, the economic development of the South can play a crucial role in providing leverage in the handling of metropolitan problems.

Belated recognition of the problems created for Northern metropolitan areas by these large-scale streams of rural migration have led in recent months to a large number of proposals to encourage development in rural areas. Not surprisingly the Department of Agriculture has been quick to seize the opportunities provided. A "rural renaissance" has been its response. Full-page advertisements headed, "To save our cities, We must have rural-urban balance," have appeared in a large number of magazines under the aegis of the National Rural Electric Cooperative Association. These proposals invariably fail to recognize that Negro migration from the rural South differs in important respects from rural-urban migration and has different consequences. Failing as they do to distinguish between beneficial and potentially disruptive migration, these proposals for large-scale programs to keep people on the farms, everywhere, are likely to lead to great waste and inefficiency, while failing to come to grips with the problem that motivated the original concern.

Improving Skills

A second important approach to easing the pressure on the ghetto is to improve the educational and skill level of incoming migrants. An investment in the under-utilized human resource represented by the Southern white and Negro will pay off in either an expanded Southern economy or a Northern metropolitan job market. Indeed, it is just this flexibility that makes programs oriented to individuals so attractive in comparison to programs oriented to geography. To the extent that a potential migrant can gain skills in demand, his integration into the metropolis, North or South, is that much eased. In light of these benefits, progress in Southern schools has been pitifully slow. Southern Negro achievement levels are the lowest for any group in the country. Southern states with small tax bases and high fertility rates have found it expedient in the past to spend as little as possible on Negro education. Much of the rationalization for this policy is based on the fact that a large proportion of Southern Negroes will migrate and thus deprive the area of whatever educational investment is made in them. This fact undoubtedly has led to some underinvestment in the education of Southern whites as well, but the brunt has been borne by the Negro community.

Clearly it is to the advantage of those areas that are likely to receive these migrants to guarantee their ability to cope with an urban environment. This would be in sharp contrast to migrants who move to the ghetto dependent on the social services of the community and unable to venture into the larger world of the metropolis. Nor are the impacts of inadequate Southern education limited to the first generation of Negro migrants. Parents ill-equipped to adjust to complex urban patterns are unlikely to provide the support necessary for preparing children to cope with a hostile environment. The pattern can be clearly seen in the second generation's reaction to life in the ghetto. It is the children of migrants and not the migrants themselves who seem most prone to riot in the city.

Thus, education of potential migrants is of great importance to both the North and South. The value of the investment is compounded by the extent to which the over-all level of Negro opportunity is expanded. In the North, this is dependent on a weakening of the constricting ties of the ghetto. In the South it depends on economic development per se.

Concluding Thoughts

This article has considered alternative strategies for the urban ghetto in light of the strong economic and social link of that community to the metropolis in which it is imbedded and to the nation as a whole. In particular the analysis has centered on the likely repercussions of "gilding programs."

Included prominently among these programs are a variety of proposals designed to attract industry to metropolitan ghettos. There have also been numerous proposals for massive expenditures on compensatory education, housing, welfare, and the like. Model cities programs must be included under this rubric. All such proposals aim at raising the employment, incomes, and well-being of ghetto residents, *within* the existing framework of racial discrimination.

Much of the political appeal of these programs lies in their ability to attract support from a wide spectrum ranging from white separatists, to liberals, to advocates of black power. However, there is an overriding objection to this approach. "Gilding" programs must accept as given a continued growth of Negro ghettos, ghettos which are directly or indirectly responsible for the failure of urban renewal, the crisis in central city finance, urban transportation problems, Negro unemployment, and the inadequacy of metropolitan school systems. Ghetto gilding programs, apart from being objectionable on moral grounds, accept a very large cost in terms of economic inefficiency, while making the solution of many social problems inordinately difficult.

A final objection is that such programs may not work at all, if pursued in isolation. The ultimate result of efforts to increase Negro incomes or reduce Negro unemployment in central city ghettos may be simply to induce a much higher rate of migration of Negroes from Southern rural areas. This will accelerate the already rapid growth of black ghettos, complicating the already impressive list of urban problems.

Recognition of the migration link between Northern ghettos and Southern rural areas has led in recent months to proposals to subsidize economic development, educational opportunities, and living standards in rural areas. It is important to clarify the valuable, but limited, contributions well-designed programs of this kind can make to the problems of the metropolitan ghetto. Anti-migration and migrant improvement programs cannot in themselves improve conditions in Northern ghettos. They cannot overcome the prejudice, discrimination, low incomes, and lack of education that are the underlying "causes" of ghetto unrest. At best they are complementary to programs intended to deal directly with ghetto problems. Their greatest value would be in permitting an aggressive assault on the problems of the ghetto—their role is that of a counterweight which permits meaningful and large scale programs within *metropolitan* areas.

What form should this larger effort take? It would seem that ghetto dispersal is the only strategy that promises a long-run solution. In support of this contention we have identified three important arguments:

1. None of the other programs will reduce the distortions of metropolitan growth and loss of efficiency that result from the continued rapid expansion of "massive" Negro ghettos in metropolitan areas.
2. Ghetto dispersal programs would generally lower the costs of achieving many objectives that are posited by ghetto improvement or gilding schemes.
3. As between ghetto gilding and ghetto dispersal strategies, only the latter is consistent with stated goals of American society.

The conclusion is straightforward. Where alternatives exist, and it has been a major effort of this article to show that they do exist, considerable weight must be placed on their differential impact on the ghetto. Programs that tend to strengthen this segregated pattern should generally be rejected in favor of programs that achieve the same objectives while weakening the ghetto. Such a strategy is not only consistent with the nation's long-run goals, but will often be substantially cheaper in the short run.

Notes

1. John R. Theyer, John F. Kain, and Martin Wohl, *The Urban Transportation Problem* (Cambridge, Mass.: Harvard University Press, 1965), pp. 164–165.
2. John F. Kain, "Housing Segregation, Negro Employment, and Metropolitan Decentralization," *Quarterly Journal of Economics*, LXXXII, No. 2 (May 1968), 175–197.
3. U.S. Commission on Civil Rights, *Racial Isolation in the Public Schools* (Washington, D.C.: U.S. Government Printing Office, 1967), Vol. 1, p. 13.
4. Of the one-quarter million public housing units constructed by all city authorities, only 76, and these in only one metropolitan area, have been built outside central cities. U.S. Commission on Civil Rights, *op. cit.*, p. 24.
5. Casual empirical evidence on this point is provided in a recent article in the *Washington Post* (February 16, 1968): "Job Scheme Backfires in Detroit." In response to a job creation program for the hardcore unemployed, the Detroit Urban League reported out-of-city job seekers using their employment facilities were up 9 to 12 percent over 1966.

The Future of the Cities

Introduction

We believe action of the kind outlined in preceding pages can contribute substantially to control of disorders in the near future. But there should be no mistake about the long run. The underlying forces continue to gain momentum.

The most basic of these is the accelerating segregation of low-income, disadvantaged Negroes within the ghettos of the largest American cities.

By 1985, the 12.1 million Negroes segregated within central cities today will have grown to approximately 20.3 million—an increase of 68 percent.

Prospects for domestic peace and for the quality of American life are linked directly to the future of these cities.

Two critical questions must be confronted: Where do present trends now lead? What choices are open to us?

The Key Trends

Negro population growth

The size of the Negro population in central cities is closely related to total national Negro population growth. In the past 16 years, about 98 percent of this growth has occurred within metropolitan areas, and 86 percent in the central cities of those areas.

A conservative projection of national Negro population growth indicates continued rapid increases. For the period 1966 to 1985, it will rise to a total of 30.7 million, gaining an average of 484,000 a year, or 7.6 percent more than the increase in each year from 1960 to 1966.

Central Cities.—Further Negro population growth in central cities depends upon two key factors: inmigration from outside metropolitan areas, and patterns of Negro settlement within metropolitan areas.

From 1960 to 1966, the Negro population of all central cities rose 2.4 million, 88.9 percent of total national Negro population growth.

Report of the National Advisory Commission on Civil Disorders, Chapter 16, "The Future of the Cities" (Washington, D.C.: U.S. Government Printing Office, 1968), pp. 215–225. Footnotes abridged.

We estimate that natural growth accounted for 1.4 million, or 58 percent of this increase, and in-migration accounted for one million, or 42 percent.

As of 1966, the Negro population in all central cities totaled 12.1 million. By 1985, we have estimated that it will rise 68 percent to 20.3 million. We believe that natural growth will account for 5.2 million of this increase and in-migration for 3.0 million.

Without significant Negro out-migration, then, the combined Negro populations of central cities will continue to grow by an average of 274,000 a year through 1985, even if no further in-migration occurs.

Growth projected on the basis of natural increase and in-migration would raise the proportion of Negroes to whites in central cities by 1985 from the present 20.7 percent to between an estimated 31 and 34.7 percent.

Largest Central Cities.—These, however, are national figures. Much faster increases will occur in the largest central cities where Negro growth has been concentrated in the past two decades. Washington, D.C., Gary, and Newark are already over half Negro. A continuation of recent trends would cause the following 10 major cities to become over 50 percent Negro by the indicated dates:

New Orleans	1971	St. Louis	1978
Richmond	1971	Detroit	1979
Baltimore	1972	Philadelphia	1981
Jacksonville	1972	Oakland	1983
Cleveland	1975	Chicago	1984

These cities, plus Washington, D.C. (now over 66 percent Negro) and Newark, contained 12.6 million people in 1960, or 22 percent of the total population of all 224 American central cities. All 13 cities undoubtedly will have Negro majorities by 1985, and the suburbs ringing them will remain all white, unless there are major changes in Negro fertility rates, in-migration, settlement patterns, or public policy.

Experience indicates that Negro school enrollment in these and other cities will exceed 50 percent long before the total population reaches that mark. In fact, Negro students already comprise more than a majority in the public elementary schools of 12 of the 13 cities mentioned above. This occurs because the Negro population in central cities is much younger and because a much higher proportion of white children attend private schools. For example, St. Louis' population was about 36 percent Negro in 1965; its public elementary school enrollment was 63 percent Negro. If present trends continue, many cities in addition to those listed above will have Negro school majorities by 1985, probably including:

Dallas	Louisville
Pittsburgh	Indianapolis
Buffalo	Kansas City, Mo.
Cincinnati	Hartford
Harrisburg	New Haven

Thus, continued concentration of future Negro population growth in large central cities will produce significant changes in those cities over the next 20 years. Unless there are sharp changes in the factors influencing Negro settlement patterns within metropolitan areas, there is little doubt that the trend toward Negro majorities will continue. Even a complete cessation of net Negro in-migration to central cities would merely postpone this result for a few years.

Growth of the young Negro population

We estimate that the Nation's white population will grow 16.6 million, or 9.6 percent, from 1966 to 1975, and the Negro population 3.8 million, or 17.7 percent, in the same period. The Negro age group from 15 to 24 years of age, however, will grow much faster than either the Negro population as a whole, or the white population in the same age group.

From 1966 to 1975, the total number of Negroes in this age group nationally will rise 1.6 million, or 40.1 percent. The white population aged 15 to 24 will rise 6.6 million, or 23.5 percent.

This rapid increase in the young Negro population has important implications for the country. This group has the highest unemployment rate in the Nation, commits a relatively high proportion of all crimes and plays the most significant role in civil disorders. By the same token, it is a great reservoir of underused human resources which are vital to the Nation.

The location of new jobs

Most new employment opportunities do not occur in central cities, near all-Negro neighborhoods. They are being created in suburbs and outlying areas—and this trend is likely to continue indefinitely. New office buildings have risen in the downtowns of large cities, often near all-Negro areas. But the out-flow of manufacturing and retailing facilities normally offsets this addition significantly—and in many cases has caused a net loss of jobs in central cities while the new white collar jobs are often not available to ghetto residents.

Providing employment for the swelling Negro ghetto population will require society to link these potential workers more closely with job locations. This can be done in three ways: By developing incentives to industry to create new employment centers near Negro residential areas; by opening suburban residential areas to Negroes and encouraging them to move closer to industrial centers; or by creating better transportation between ghetto neighborhoods and new job locations.

All three involve large public outlays.

The first method—creating new industries in or near the ghetto

—is not likely to occur without Government subsidies on a scale which convinces private firms that it will pay them to face the problems involved.

The second method—opening up suburban areas to Negro occupancy—obviously requires effective fair housing laws. It will also require an extensive program of federally aided, low-cost housing in many suburban areas.

The third approach—improved transportation linking ghettos and suburbs—has received little attention from city planners and municipal officials. A few demonstration projects show promise, but carrying them out on a large scale will be very costly.

Although a high proportion of new jobs will be located in suburbs, there are still millions of jobs in central cities. Turnover in those jobs alone can open up a great many potential positions for Negro central-city residents—if employers cease racial discrimination in their hiring and promotion practices.

Nevertheless, as the total number of Negro central-city job-seekers continues to rise, the need to link them with emerging new employment in the suburbs will become increasingly urgent. . . .

Choices for the Future

The complexity of American society offers many choices for the future of relations between central cities and suburbs and patterns of white and Negro settlement in metropolitan areas. For practical purposes, however, we see two fundamental questions:

- Should future Negro population growth be concentrated in central cities, as in the past 20 years, thereby forcing Negro and white populations to become even more residentially segregated?
- Should society provide greatly increased special assistance to Negroes and other relatively disadvantaged population groups?

For purposes of analysis, the Commission has defined three basic choices for the future embodying specific answers to these questions:

The present policies choice

Under this course, the Nation would maintain approximately the share of resources now being allocated to programs of assistance for the poor, unemployed and disadvantaged. These programs are likely to grow, given continuing economic growth and rising Federal revenues, but they will not grow fast enough to stop, let alone reverse, the already deteriorating quality of life in central-city ghettos.

This choice carries the highest ultimate price, as we will point out.

The enrichment choice

Under this course, the Nation would seek to offset the effects of continued Negro segregation and deprivation in large city ghettos. The enrichment choice would aim at creating dramatic improvements in the quality of life in disadvantaged central-city neighborhoods—both white and Negro. It would require marked increases in Federal spending for education, housing, employment, job training, and social services.

The enrichment choice would seek to lift poor Negroes and whites above poverty status and thereby give them the capacity to enter the mainstream of American life. But it would not, at least for many years, appreciably affect either the increasing concentration of Negroes in the ghetto or racial segregation in residential areas outside the ghetto.

The integration choice

This choice would be aimed at reversing the movement of the country toward two societies, separate and unequal.

The integration choice—like the enrichment choice—would call for large-scale improvement in the quality of ghetto life. But it would also involve both creating strong incentives for Negro movement out of central-city ghettos and enlarging freedom of choice concerning housing, employment, and schools.

The result would fall considerably short of full integration. The experience of other ethnic groups indicates that some Negro households would be scattered in largely white residential areas. Others— probably a larger number—would voluntarily cluster together in largely Negro neighborhoods. The integration choice would thus produce both integration and segregation. But the segregation would be voluntary.

Articulating these three choices plainly oversimplifies the possibilities open to the country. We believe, however, that they encompass the basic issues—issues which the American public must face if it is serious in its concern not only about civil disorder, but the future of our democratic society.

The Present Policies Choice

Powerful forces of social and political inertia are moving the country steadily along the course of existing policies toward a divided country.

This course may well involve changes in many social and economic programs—but not enough to produce fundamental alterations in the key factors of Negro concentration, racial segregation, and the lack of sufficient enrichment to arrest the decay of deprived neighborhoods.

Some movement toward enrichment can be found in efforts to encourage industries to locate plants in central cities, in increased Federal expenditures for education, in the important concepts embodied in the "War on Poverty," and in the Model Cities Program. But Congressional appropriations for even present Federal programs have been so small that they fall short of effective enrichment.

As for challenging concentration and segregation, a national commitment to this purpose has yet to develop.

Of the three future courses we have defined, the present policies choice—the choice we are now making—is the course with the most ominous consequences for our society.

The probability of future civil disorders

We believe that the present policies choice would lead to a larger number of violent incidents of the kind that have stimulated recent major disorders.

First, it does nothing to raise the hopes, absorb the energies, or constructively challenge the talents of the rapidly growing number of young Negro men in central cities. The proportion of unemployed or underemployed among them will remain very high. These young men have contributed disproportionately to crime and violence in cities in the past, and there is danger, obviously, that they will continue to do so.

Second, under these conditions, a rising proportion of Negroes in disadvantaged city areas might come to look upon the deprivation and segregation they suffer as proper justification for violent protest or for extending support to now isolated extremists who advocate civil disruption by guerrilla tactics.

More incidents would not necessarily mean more or worse riots. For the near future, there is substantial likelihood that even an increased number of incidents could be controlled before becoming major disorders, if society undertakes to improve police and National Guard forces so that they can respond to potential disorders with more prompt and disciplined use of force.

In fact, the likelihood of incidents mushrooming into major disorders would be only slightly higher in the near future under the present policies choice than under the other two possible choices. For no new policies or programs could possibly alter basic ghetto conditions immediately. And the announcement of new programs under the other choices would immediately generate new expectations. Expectations inevitably increase faster than performance. In the short run, they might even increase the level of frustration.

In the long run, however, the present policies choice risks a seriously greater probability of major disorders, worse, possibly, than those already experienced.

If the Negro population as a whole developed even stronger feelings of being wrongly "penned in" and discriminated against, many of its members might come to support not only riots, but the rebellion now being preached by only a handful. Large-scale violence, followed by white retaliation could follow. This spiral could quite conceivably lead to a kind of urban *apartheid* with semimartial law in many major cities, enforced residence of Negroes in segregated areas, and a drastic reduction in personal freedom for all Americans, particularly Negroes.

The same distinction is applicable to the cost of the present policies choice. In the short run, its costs—at least its direct cash outlays—would be far less than for the other choices.

Social and economic programs likely to have significant lasting effect would require very substantial annual appropriations for many years. Their cost would far exceed the direct losses sustained in recent civil disorders. Property damage in all the disorders we investigated, including Detroit and Newark, totaled less than $100 million.

But it would be a tragic mistake to view the present policies choice as cheap. Damage figures measure only a small part of the costs of civil disorder. They cannot measure the costs in terms of the lives lost, injuries suffered, minds and attitudes closed and frozen in prejudice, or the hidden costs of the profound disruption of entire cities.

Ultimately, moreover, the economic and social costs of the present policies choice will far surpass the cost of the alternatives. The rising concentration of impoverished Negroes and other minorities within the urban ghettos will constantly expand public expenditures for welfare, law enforcement, unemployment, and other existing programs without arresting the decay of older city neighborhoods and the breeding of frustration and discontent. But the most significant item on the balance of accounts will remain largely invisible and incalculable—the toll in human values taken by continued poverty, segregation, and inequality of opportunity.

Polarization

Another and equally serious consequence is the fact that this course would lead to the permanent establishment of two societies: one predominantly white and located in the suburbs, in smaller cities, and in outlying areas, and one largely Negro located in central cities.

We are well on the way to just such a divided nation.

This division is veiled by the fact that Negroes do not now dominate many central cities. But they soon will, as we have shown, and the new Negro mayors will be facing even more difficult conditions than now exist.

As Negroes succeed whites in our largest cities, the proportion of low-income residents in those cities will probably increase. This is likely even if both white and Negro incomes continue to rise at recent rates, since Negroes have much lower incomes than whites. Moreover, many of the ills of large central cities spring from their age, their location, and their obsolete physical structures. The deterioration and economic decay stemming from these factors have been proceeding for decades and will continue to plague older cities regardless of who resides in them.

These facts underlie the fourfold dilemma of the American city:

● Fewer tax dollars come in, as large numbers of middle-income taxpayers move out of central cities and property values and business decline;

● More tax dollars are required to provide essential public services and facilities, and to meet the needs of expanding lower income groups;

● Each tax dollar buys less, because of increasing costs;

● Citizen dissatisfaction with municipal services grows as needs, expectations and standards of living increase throughout the community.

These are the conditions that would greet the Negro-dominated municipal governments that will gradually come to power in many of our major cities. The Negro electorates in those cities probably would demand basic changes in present policies. Like the present white electorates there, they would have to look for assistance to two basic sources: the private sector and the Federal Government.

With respect to the private sector, major private capital investment in those cities might have ceased almost altogether if white-dominated firms and industries decided the risks and costs were too great. The withdrawal of private capital is already far advanced in most all-Negro areas of our large cities.

Even if private investment continued, it alone would not suffice. Big cities containing high proportions of low-income Negroes and block after block of deteriorating older property need very substantial assistance from the Federal Government to meet the demands of their electorates for improved services and living conditions.

It is probable, however, that Congress will be more heavily influenced by representatives of the suburban and outlying city electorate. These areas will comprise 40 percent of our total population by 1985, compared with 31 percent in 1960; and central cities will decline from 32 percent to 27 percent.

Since even the suburbs will be feeling the squeeze of higher local government costs, Congress might resist providing the extensive assistance which central cities will desperately need.

Thus the present policies choice, if pursued for any length of time, might force simultaneous political and economic polarization in many of our largest metropolitan areas. Such polarization would involve large central cities—mainly Negro, with many poor, and nearly bankrupt—on the one hand and most suburbs—mainly white, generally affluent, but heavily taxed—on the other hand.

Some areas might avoid political confrontation by shifting to some form of metropolitan government designed to offer regional solutions for pressing urban problems such as property taxation, air and water pollution, refuse disposal, and commuter transport. Yet this would hardly eliminate the basic segregation and relative poverty of the urban Negro population. It might even increase the Negro's sense of frustration and alienation if it operated to prevent Negro political control of central cities.

The acquisition of power by Negro-dominated governments in central cities is surely a legitimate and desirable exercise of political power by a minority group. It is in an American political tradition exemplified by the achievements of the Irish in New York and Boston.

But such Negro political development would also involve virtually complete racial segregation and virtually complete spatial separation. By 1985, the separate Negro society in our central cities would contain almost 21 million citizens. That is almost 68 percent larger than the present Negro population of central cities. It is also larger than the current population of every Negro nation in Africa except Nigeria.

If developing a racially integrated society is extraordinarily difficult today when 12.1 million Negroes live in central cities, then it is quite clearly going to be virtually impossible in 1985 when almost 21 million Negroes—still much poorer and less educated than most whites—will be living there.

Can present policies avoid extreme polarization?

There are at least two possible developments under the present policies choice which might avert such polarization. The first is a faster increase of incomes among Negroes than has occurred in the recent past. This might prevent central cities from becoming even deeper "poverty traps" than they now are. It suggests the importance of effective job programs and higher levels of welfare payments for dependent families.

The second possible development is migration of a growing Negro middle class out of the central city. This would not prevent competition for Federal funds between central cities and outlying areas, but it might diminish the racial undertones of that competition.

There is, however, no evidence that a continuation of present policies would be accompanied by any such movement. There is already a significant Negro middle class. It grew rapidly from 1960 to 1966. Yet in these years, 88.9 percent of the total national growth of Negro population was concentrated in central cities—the highest in history. Indeed, from 1960 to 1966, there was actually a net total in-migration of Negroes from the urban fringes of metropolitan areas into central cities.[1] The Commission believes it unlikely that this trend will suddenly reverse itself without significant changes in private attitudes and public policies.

The Enrichment Choice

The present policies choice plainly would involve continuation of efforts like Model Cities, manpower programs, and the War on Poverty. These are in fact enrichment programs, designed to improve the quality of life in the ghetto.

Because of their limited scope and funds, however, they constitute only very modest steps toward enrichment—and would continue to do so even if these programs were somewhat enlarged or supplemented.

The premise of the enrichment choice is performance. To adopt this choice would require a substantially greater share of national resources—sufficient to make a dramatic, visible impact on life in the urban Negro ghetto.

The effect of enrichment on civil disorders

Effective enrichment policies probably would have three immediate effects on civil disorders.

First, announcement of specific large-scale programs and the demonstration of a strong intent to carry them out might persuade ghetto residents that genuine remedies for their problems were forthcoming, thereby allaying tensions.

Second, such announcements would strongly stimulate the aspirations and hopes of members of these communities—possibly well beyond the capabilities of society to deliver and to do so promptly. This might increase frustration and discontent, to some extent canceling the first effect.

Third, if there could be immediate action on meaningful job training and the creation of productive jobs for large numbers of unemployed young people, they would become much less likely to engage in civil disorders.

Such action is difficult now, when there are about 585,000 young Negro men aged 14 to 24 in the civilian labor force in central cities— of whom 81,000 or 13.8 percent, are unemployed and probably two or three times as many are underemployed. It will not become easier in the future. By 1975, this age group will have grown to approximately 700,000.

Given the size of the present problem, plus the large growth of this age group, creation of sufficient meaningful jobs will require extensive programs, begun rapidly. Even if the Nation is willing to embark on such programs, there is no certainty that they can be made effective soon enough.

Consequently, there is no certainty that the enrichment choice would do much more in the near future to diminish violent incidents in central cities than would the present policies choice. However, if enrichment programs can succeed in meeting the needs of residents of disadvantaged areas for jobs, education, housing, and city services, then over the years this choice is almost certain to reduce both the level and frequency of urban disorder.

The Negro middle class

One objective of the enrichment choice would be to help as many disadvantaged Americans as possible—of all races—to enter the mainstream of American prosperity, to progress toward what is often called middle-class status. If the enrichment choice were adopted, it could certainly attain this objective to a far greater degree than would the present policies choice. This could significantly change the quality of life in many central-city areas.

It can be argued that a rapidly enlarging Negro middle class would also promote Negro out-migration, and that the enrichment choice would thus open up an escape hatch from the ghetto. This argument, however, has two weaknesses.

The first is experience. Central cities already have sizable and growing numbers of middle-class Negro families. Yet only a few have migrated from the central city. The past pattern of white ethnic groups gradually moving out of central-city areas to middle-class suburbs has not applied to Negroes. Effective open-housing laws will help make this possible, but it is probable that other more extensive changes in policies and attitudes will be required—and these would extend beyond the enrichment choice.

The second weakness in the argument is time. Even if enlargement of the Negro middle class succeeded in encouraging movement out of the central city, it could not do so fast enough to offset the rapid growth of the ghetto. To offset even *half* the growth estimated for the ghetto by 1975 an out-migration from central cities of 217,000 persons a year would be required. This is eight times the annual increase in suburban Negro population—including natural increase—that occurred from 1960 to 1966. Even the most effective enrichment program is not likely to accomplish this.

A corollary problem derives from the continuing migration of poor Negroes from the Southern to Northern and Western cities. Adoption of the enrichment choice would require large-scale efforts to improve conditions in the South sufficiently to remove the pressure to migrate. Under present conditions, slightly over a third of the estimated increase in Negro central-city population by 1985 will result from in-migration—3.0 million out of total increase of 8.2 million.

Negro self-development

The enrichment choice is in line with some of the currents of Negro protest thought that fall under the label of "Black Power." We do not refer to versions of Black-Power ideology which promote violence, generate racial hatred, or advocate total separation of the races. Rather, we mean the view which asserts that the American Negro population can assume its proper role in society and overcome its feelings of powerlessness and lack of self-respect only by exerting power over decisions which directly affect its own members. A fully integrated society is not thought possible until the Negro minority within the ghetto has developed political strength—a strong bargaining position in dealing with the rest of society.

In short, this argument would regard predominantly Negro central cities and predominantly white outlying areas not as harmful, but as an advantageous future.

Proponents of these views also focus on the need for the Negro to organize economically as well as politically, thus tapping new energies and resources for self-development. One of the hardest tasks in improving disadvantaged areas is to discover how deeply deprived residents can develop their own capabilities by participating more fully in decisions and activities which affect them. Such learning-by-doing efforts are a vital part of the process of bringing deprived people into the social mainstream.

Separate but equal societies?

The enrichment choice by no means seeks to perpetuate racial segregation. In the end, however, its premise is that disadvantaged Negroes can achieve equality of opportunity with whites while continuing in conditions of nearly complete separation.

This premise has been vigorously advocated by Black-Power proponents. While most Negroes originally desired racial integration, many are losing hope of ever achieving it because of seemingly implacable white resistance. Yet they cannot bring themselves to accept the conclusion that most of the millions of Negroes who are forced to live racially segregated lives must therefore be condemned to inferior lives—to inferior educations, or inferior housing, or inferior status.

Rather, they reason, there must be some way to make the quality of life in the ghetto areas just as good—or better—than elsewhere. It is not surprising that some Black-Power advocates are denouncing integration and claiming that, given the hypocrisy and racism that pervade white society, life in a black society is, in fact, morally superior. This argument is understandable, but there is a great deal of evidence that it is unrealistic.

The economy of the United States and particularly the sources of employment are preponderantly white. In this circumstance, a policy of separate but equal employment could only relegate Negroes permanently to inferior incomes and economic status.

The best evidence regarding education is contained in recent reports of the Office of Education and Civil Rights Commission which suggest that both racial and economic integration are essential to educational equality for Negroes. Yet critics point out that certainly until integration is achieved, various types of enrichment programs must be tested, and that dramatically different results may be possible from intensive educational enrichment—such as far smaller classes, or greatly expanded preschool programs, or changes in the home environment of Negro children resulting from steady jobs for fathers.

Still others advocate shifting control over ghetto schools from professional administrators to local residents. This, they say, would improve curricula, give students a greater sense of their own value, and thus raise their morale and educational achievement. These approaches have not yet been tested sufficiently. One conclusion, however, does seem reasonable: Any real improvement in the quality of education in low-income, all-Negro areas will cost a great deal more money than is now being spent there—and perhaps more than is being spent per pupil anywhere. Racial and social class integration of schools may produce equal improvement in achievement at less total cost.

Whether or not enrichment in ghetto areas will really work is not yet known, but the enrichment choice is based on the yet-unproven premise that it will. Certainly, enrichment programs could significantly improve existing ghetto schools if they impelled major innovations. But "separate but equal" ghetto education cannot meet the long-run fundamental educational needs of the central-city Negro population.

The three basic educational choices are: Providing Negro children with quality education in integrated schools; providing them with quality education by enriching ghetto schools; or continuing to provide many Negro children with inferior education in racially segregated school systems, severely limiting their lifetime opportunities.

Consciously or not, it is the third choice that the Nation is now making, and this choice the Commission rejects totally.

In the field of housing, it is obvious that "separate but equal" does not mean really equal. The enrichment choice could greatly improve the quantity, variety, and environment of decent housing available to the ghetto population. It could not provide Negroes with the same freedom and range of choice as whites with equal incomes. Smaller cities and suburban areas together with the central city provide a far greater variety of housing and environmental settings than the central city alone. Programs to provide housing outside central cities however, extend beyond the bounds of the enrichment choice.

In the end, whatever its benefits, the enrichment choice might well invite a prospect similar to that of the present policies choice: separate white and black societies.

If enrichment programs were effective, they could greatly narrow the gap in income, education, housing, jobs, and other qualities of life between the ghetto and the mainstream. Hence the chances of harsh polarization—or of disorder—in the next 20 years would be greatly reduced.

Whether they would be reduced far enough depends on the scope of the programs. Even if the gap were narrowed from the present, it still could remain as a strong source of tension. History teaches that men are not necessarily placated even by great absolute progress. The controlling factor is relative progress—whether they still perceive a significant gap between themselves and others whom they regard as no more deserving. Widespread perception of such a gap—and consequent resentment—might well be precisely the situation 20 years from now under the enrichment choice, for it is essentially another way of choosing a permanently divided country.

The Integration Choice

The third and last course open to the Nation combines enrichment with programs designed to encourage integration of substantial numbers of Negroes into the society outside the ghetto.

Enrichment must be an important adjunct to any integration course. No matter how ambitious or energetic such a program may be, relatively few Negroes now living in central-city ghettos would be quickly integrated. In the meantime, significant improvement in their present environment is essential.

The enrichment aspect of this third choice should, however, be recognized as interim action, during which time expanded and new programs can work to improve education and earning power. The length of the interim period surely would vary. For some it may be long. But in any event, what should be clearly recognized is that enrichment is only a means toward the goal; it is not the goal.

The goal must be achieving freedom for every citizen to live and work according to his capacities and desires, not his color.

We believe there are four important reasons why American society must give this course the most serious consideration. First, future jobs are being created primarily in the suburbs, while the chronically unemployed population is increasingly concentrated in the ghetto. This separation will make it more and more difficult for Negroes to achieve anything like full employment in decent jobs. But if, over time, these residents began to find housing outside central cities, they would be exposed to more knowledge of job opportunities, would have much shorter trips to reach jobs, and would have a far better chance of securing employment on a self-sustaining basis.

Second, in the judgment of this Commission, racial and social-class integration is the most effective way of improving the education of ghetto children.

Third, developing an adequate housing supply for low-income and middle-income families and true freedom of choice in housing for Negroes of all income levels will require substantial out-movement. We do not believe that such an out-movement will occur spontaneously merely as a result of increasing prosperity among Negroes in central cities. A national fair housing law is essential to begin such movement. In many suburban areas, a program combining positive incentives with the building of new housing will be necessary to carry it out.

Fourth, and by far the most important, integration is the only course which explicitly seeks to achieve a single nation rather than accepting the present movement toward a dual society. This choice would enable us at least to begin reversing the profoundly divisive trend already so evident in our metropolitan areas—before it becomes irreversible.

Conclusions

The future of our cities is neither something which will just happen nor something which will be imposed upon us by an inevitable destiny. That future will be shaped to an important degree by choices we make now.

We have attempted to set forth the major choices because we believe it is vital for Americans to understand the consequences of our present drift:

Three critical conclusions emerge from this analysis:

1. The nation is rapidly moving toward two increasingly separate Americas.

Within two decades, this division could be so deep that it would be almost impossible to unite:

- a white society principally located in suburbs, in smaller central cities, and in the peripheral parts of large central cities; and
- a Negro society largely concentrated within large central cities.

The Negro society will be permanently relegated to its current status, possibly even if we expend great amounts of money and effort in trying to "gild" the ghetto.

2. In the long run, continuation and expansion of such a permanent division threatens us with two perils.

The first is the danger of sustained violence in our cities. The timing, scale, nature, and repercussions of such violence cannot be foreseen. But if it occurred, it would further destroy our ability to achieve the basic American promises of liberty, justice, and equality.

The second is the danger of a conclusive repudiation of the traditional American ideals of individual dignity, freedom, and equality of opportunity. We will not be able to espouse these ideals meaningfully to the rest of the world, to ourselves, to our children. They may still recite the Pledge of Allegiance and say "one nation . . . indivisible." But they will be learning cynicism, not patriotism.

3. We cannot escape responsibility for choosing the future of our metropolitan areas and the human relations which develop within them. It is a responsibility so critical that even an unconscious choice to continue present policies has the gravest implications.

That we have delayed in choosing or, by delaying, may be making the wrong choice, does not sentence us either to separatism or despair. But we must choose. We will choose. Indeed, we are now choosing.

Note

1. Although Negro population on the urban fringe of metropolitan areas did increase slightly (0.2 million) from 1960 to 1966, it is safe to assume an actual net in-migration to central cities from these areas based upon the rate of natural increase of the Negro population.

BENNETT HARRISON

Suburbanization and Ghetto Dispersal: A Critique of the Conventional Wisdom

A theme which dominates much of the recent literature in urban economics concerns the progressive decentralization of jobs from the late nineteenth century to the present (with a brief interruption during

Bennett Harrison, "Suburbanization and Ghetto Dispersal: A Critique of the Conventional Wisdom," adapted from *Education, Training and the Urban Ghetto* (Department of Economics, University of Pennsylvania, 1970), Unpublished Ph.D. dissertation, by permission.

the 1930s). This trend has allegedly made suburban residence the optimal location in terms of maximizing access to urban employment opportunities. Since nonwhites tend to be concentrated in the oldest neighborhoods of the central city, it is this growing distance between place of residence and place of potential employment that is the principal cause of continued urban poverty.

Reverse Commuting

Short of actually relocating inner-city minorities to the suburbs, the conventional wisdom recommends a policy of investment in "reverse commuting." The objective here is to transport workers from the urban core out to the suburban fringe where an increasingly larger number of the allegedly "decent" jobs are located. Many specific proposals have been made, including the reservation of parking or breakdown lanes for the unobstructed use of special buses, extensions of the subway system (where such a system already exists), and the subsidization of car pools.

Even as a short-term expedient, reverse commuting experiments have not met with much success in the municipalities where they have been tried—Boston, Detroit, Washington, and elsewhere. In the nation's capitol, in fact, there is evidence that special buses running in both directions carry more suburbanites *into* the city than nonwhite ghetto dwellers *out* of the city.

To be sure, intra-metropolitan transportation should be sufficiently well developed to permit efficient journeys-to-work for all residents of the area. Much further research on the costs of traveling from home to job is needed. To some extent, as Oscar Ornati has shown, antiquated mass transit routes may well contribute to the "effective isolation" of the ghetto.

But the question of greatest priority is whether or not, *given* access to suburban jobs (however achieved), nonwhite economic opportunity is in fact increased. Before bringing my own research results to bear on this question, I should like to first examine the more ambitious policy proposal known as "ghetto dispersal."

Ghetto Dispersal:
Programmed Nonwhite Suburbanization

The full-scale strategy of moving ghetto workers into the wider private metropolitan job market is popularly referred to as "ghetto dispersal." Its most persuasive advocate within the economics profession is Professor John F. Kain of Harvard University. The dispersal strategists propose a number of interrelated public policies: relocation of ghetto residents to areas in the suburbs which are closer to blue-collar industrial complexes, open housing and income or rent subsidies, and large-scale investment in Southern economic development in order to reduce the migration pressure on those "Northern" cities where "ghetto dispersal" has not been completed.

For Kain, the suburbanization of the kinds of jobs for which minorities are "best suited"—and the suburban residential segregation which prevents these minorities from relocating—constitute the principal agenda of the "urban crisis."

> Low-income white workers adapt their residential choices to their job locations and to available transit services. When their jobs are in suburban areas, an increasing trend, they invariably live in suburban areas. When Negro jobs are located in suburban areas, they must either be foregone or they represent difficult, costly, and time-consuming trips from [the central ghetto out] to suburban workplaces.[1]

Kain estimates that there were at least 9,000 jobs in suburban Detroit in 1952 and 30,000 jobs in suburban Chicago in 1956 which blacks might have had "for the asking," *if* they had been able to find residences in the suburbs.

Moreover, the high and growing concentration of blacks inside the central city exacerbates the problem by stimulating the intransigence of newly "suburbanized" whites who are afraid that their former neighbors in the city will try to follow them out. Some have proposed that it would be better—if not politically easier—to promote minority economic development within the central city than to challenge this intransigence of suburban whites. Kain writes:

> Recognition of high rates of Negro unemployment, low incomes and other undesirable conditions found in central city ghettos have led to widespread demands for corrective action. A majority of practical men [he may be referring here to the late Robert F. Kennedy in particular] seem to have concluded that residential integration is either impossible or will take too long. They contend the problems of the urban Negro are current and real and that while residential integration might be desirable as a short-range goal, such a course for the immediate future is uncertain, difficult, and politically dangerous. . . .
> Proposals to patch up [or "gild"] the ghetto and make it a better place to live and to create jobs there are heard with increasing frequency.[2]

Kain, however, opposes "ghetto-gilding." For one thing, such programs would "reduce pressure for residential integration and would tend to perpetuate existing patterns and practices of racial segregation." For another, the capital absorption capacity of the ghetto is far too small to permit sufficient internal job development to make up the entire deficit, particularly if the amelioration of underemployment as well as outright unemployment is the goal. Another and

> most telling objection is that such policies might well [aggravate the situation]. There are strong links between Northern ghettos and the still vast pools of rural, Southern Negroes. Ghetto improvement and particularly job-creation programs might well have as their principal result increased migration of Southern Negroes to Northern metropolitan areas. Growth rates of Northern ghettos might increase severalfold, greatly aggravating the problems . . . the distortions of metropolitan growth would be magnified, and the goal of assimilating and integrating the Negro into urban society would be made far more difficult.[3]

Instead, Kain asserts that "there is no alternative but vastly increased *suburbanization* of Negro populations, if we are to avoid unnecessary economic waste and growing social and political conflict." Public policy "should emphasize the strengthening of the Negro's ability to break out of the ghetto [by] (education and job training) and the expansion of suburban housing opportunities."

I perceive at least six different assumptions underlying Kain's position. First, the jobs which blacks are most capable of performing are believed to be suburbanizing most rapidly. This "mis-match hypothesis" is in itself of questionable validity. Charlotte Fremon of the Urban Institute found, in eight different SMSA's, that semiskilled and unskilled jobs were expanding almost as rapidly in 1965–67 in the central city as in the suburbs. The openings were being filled by suburban commuters—"while, we should add, manpower training programs [for central city workers] were expanding."[4] In any case, Kain himself has admitted that his results may be biased; "the census data presented in . . . this paper may be providing a misleading picture of employment changes by focusing on those employment categories that are decentralizing most rapidly."[5] One sector in particular is omitted in all of Kain's tables: state and local government. According to the Department of Labor, employment in this sector will grow by 42 percent between 1968 and 1980—faster than any other sector of the American economy. And most of this growth will take place inside central cities. Between 1958 and 1967, for example, "local governments provided nearly 100,000 new jobs for New York City's workers. This was nearly twice the number generated by the next 'best' sector, business services." [6]

Second, there is in Kain's argument the implicit assumption that those nonwhites who are able to "suburbanize" will in fact be hired, and that this suburban employment will improve their economic status. I shall return to this point.

Third, Kain predicts an increase in Northern migration of Southern blacks in response to a ghetto job development program. This "negative feedback effect" will swamp any ghetto renewal effort.

There are several responses one can make to this prediction. One is to indicate that there are other urban economists who disagree even with the premise. Anthony Pascal of RAND suggests, for example, that "a good deal of data now becoming available seem to indicate that migration behavior for the low-skilled and disadvantaged segments of the population is significantly motivated by factors other than employment opportunities."[7] Even if the premise is correct, however —even if Southern blacks are responsive to Northern urban jobs programs—Kain's analysis of its implications is too static. It ignores the improvements in ghetto and city-wide political organization over time: changes in the "technology" of social organization which permit communities to absorb new immigrants, to find a place for them in the neighborhood social structure. It is these dynamic "self-help" institutions—from the Cooper Unions and Workmen's Circles of the Jews to the ghetto development corporations and the community action agencies of the blacks—which prevent immigration from necessarily constituting a "negative feedback."[8]

Fourth, Kain argues that it would be impossible to "create" nearly enough jobs within the ghetto to meet any meaningful employment target. This is quite true, but Professor Kain attacks a straw man here, for no advocate of ghetto development has ever seriously suggested that such a program would be feasible. On the contrary, it is Kain who takes the more extreme position, arguing as he does that "inside" and "outside" development are mutually exclusive alternatives. There is *no* alternative to dispersal, he writes. Surely, the appropriate attitude of an economist should be to ask: "What is the optimal mix?" rather than to assert the existence of a corner solution.

Fifth, Kain asserts that investments in education and training for ghetto dwellers will "strengthen the Negro's ability to break out," *i.e.* to "suburbanize." Recent research efforts by young economists such as Stephan Michelson and Randall Weiss of Harvard indicate that investments in the human capital of minority workers have not contributed significantly to the elimination of poverty. My own contributions to this literature have focused on the residents of eighteen central city ghettos across the country. Racial discrimination pervades even the poorest of these neighborhoods. In 1965–66, high school had three times as high a marginal earnings payoff for ghetto whites as for ghetto nonwhites. For the latter, the discounted present lifetime value of a high school diploma was estimated to be no more than $6,000, an income well below the returns available in any number of illicit "street activities" in the slums. Whatever their educational attainment (up to and including college), the predominantly nonwhite workers living in the ten very poorest innercity neighborhoods could not expect to earn more than a maximum of $2/hour, in any occupation or industry. And while the white high school graduate from the ghetto could expect to be unemployed nearly 4 percent less often than the white ghetto dweller who never entered high school at all, I was able to find no appreciable difference between the expected incremental unemployment rates of high school and grammar school nonwhites.[9] It is therefore unlikely that many ghetto blacks will (at least under present institutional arrangements) be able to finance a "house in the country" out of the net returns to increased schooling. Ample evidence exists for drawing a similar conclusion with respect to job training.

Sixth, and perhaps most important of all, Kain assumes that there is at least a significant public (if not a private) commitment to integrating the suburbs.

However, whatever the contributory factors, it is now clear that residential segregation in American cities is actually increasing. After a decade of improvement in some neighborhoods during the 1950s, the last decade witnessed both absolute and relative increases in segregation. Proportions of blacks living in tracts which were predominantly white in 1960 fell. Indeed the proportion of blacks residing in the suburban rings of our metropolitan areas has actually been falling steadily since at least 1900, although some very modest gains were scored in some areas during the 1960s.

The social and political costs of challenging these powerful vested interests and traditional prejudices may reasonably be assumed to be substantial. While this does *not* mean that such a challenge ought not to be one element in a larger urban anti-poverty program, it does suggest that exclusive reliance on such a strategy would be foolish.

Empirical findings on the insensitivity of nonwhite employment opportunity to intrametropolitan residential location

Studies of the spatial distributions of white and nonwhite earnings, unemployment, and occupational status in twelve SMSA's in 1965–66 indicate that minority employment opportunities are highly insensitive to where in the metropolis the worker happens to live.[10] In particular, while white economic opportunity was found to be substantially expanded by suburbanization of residence, average nonwhite economic welfare actually falls slightly with the "move" from central city to suburb! Nor are the marginal returns to nonwhite education significantly greater in the suburbs than in the ghetto.

In general, for whites and nonwhites, education is associated with increased mobility into what are nationally considered to be higher-status occupations. For whites, this promise is realized; as education increases, whites move into new occupations where they receive higher earnings and face lower expectations of unemployment.

Moreover, these improvements in white employment status are greater in the non-poverty neighborhoods of the central city than in the ghetto, and still greater in the suburbs.

For nonwhites, however, the promise is not realized. As their education increases, nonwhites move into new occupations, but their earnings are hardly affected at all by anything short of a college degree, and there is virtually no effect whatever on their chances of finding themselves without a job over the course of the year. Moreover, the effects are no greater outside the ghetto than inside. The economic opportunities of individual suburban nonwhites are as severely constrained as is the case for nonwhites in the urban ghetto.

Conclusion

Even without considering the positive arguments for "ghetto development,"[11] the "ghetto dispersal" strategy must be rejected as an exclusive approach to combatting urban poverty. In *no* part of the American city does the labor market "work" for minorities. Only through a direct transformation of the demand for his labor can the ghetto dweller's economic situation be improved. Attempts to change the worker himself—whether to remedy his personal "defects" or to relocate him to a "better" environment—have not worked in the past, and there is no evidence that they will work in the future.

Notes

1. John F. Kain, "The Big Cities' Big Problem," *Challenge*, September-October, 1966; reprinted in Louis A. Ferman, *et al.* (eds.), *Negroes and Jobs* (Ann Arbor: University of Michigan Press, 1968), p. 238.

2. *Ibid.*, p. 242.

3. *Ibid.*, pp. 242–43.

4. Charlotte Fremon, "The Occupational Patterns in Urban Employment Change: 1965–67," Urban Institute Working Paper, 1970.

5. John F. Kain, "The Distribution and Movement of Jobs and Industry," in James Q. Wilson (ed.), *The Metropolitan Enigma* (Cambridge: Harvard University Press, 1968), p. 30.

6. Bennett Harrison, "Public Service Jobs for Urban Ghetto Residents," *Good Government*, Fall, 1969, p. 2; reprinted in U.S. Senate, Subcommittee on Manpower, Employment and Poverty, *Hearings*, 91st Congress, 2nd Session (April 1, 1970), pp. 1422–1449.

7. Anthony H. Pascal, "Manpower Training and Jobs," in Pascal (ed.), *Cities in Trouble: An Agenda for Urban Research* (Santa Monica: The RAND Corporation, August, 1968), RM-5603-RC, p. 71.

8. Thomas Vietorisz and Bennett Harrison, *The Economic Development of Harlem* (New York: Praeger Publishers, 1970), ch. 2.

9. Bennett Harrison, "Education and Underemployment in the Urban Ghetto," in David M. Gordon (ed.), *Problems in Political Economy: An Urban Perspective* (Lexington, Mass.: D. C. Heath, 1971).

10. For a detailed review, see Harrison, *Education, Training, and the Urban Ghetto*, ch. 4.

11. For a review of some of the positive arguments, see Matthew Edel, "Development or Dispersal: Approaches to Urban Poverty," in Jerome Rothenberg and Matthew Edel (eds.), *Urban Economics: Text and Readings* (New York: Macmillan, forthcoming); and Vietorisz and Harrison, *op. cit.*

Suggested Readings:
Urban Redevelopment

ANDERSON, MARTIN. *The Federal Bulldozer.* New York: McGraw-Hill Book Company, 1967. Probably the most forceful attack on the urban renewal program.

BELLUSH, JEWEL, and MURRAY HAUSKNECHT (eds.) *Urban Renewal: People, Politics, and Planning.* Garden City: Doubleday & Company, Inc., Anchor Books Edition, 1967. A reader with many fine selections concerning the political controversies and social realities of revitalizing the American city.

GREER, SCOTT. *Urban Renewal and American Cities: The Dilemma of Democratic Intervention.* Indianapolis: The Bobbs-Merrill Co., Inc., 1965. Advocates evaluation of what urban renewal has accomplished.

JACOBS, JANE. *The Death and Life of Great American Cities.* New York: Random House, Inc., Vintage Books, 1963. Presents the thesis that neighborhood preservation is vital to urban life.

WEAVER, ROBERT C. *The Urban Complex: Human Values in Urban Life.* Garden City: Doubleday & Company, Inc., 1964. The first Secretary of Housing and Urban Development evaluates urban renewal.

8/Responsive Government:
Does the Government Hear?

The administrative activities of state and local governments
pervade almost every aspect of our daily lives. From issuance
of birth certificates to recording of deaths, their regulations
and requirements are always with us.

It is under the police power—the power to interfere with
an individual's freedom of action or free use of his property
in order to preserve public health, safety, morals, good order,
or convenience of the community—that most state and local
regulation comes. State and local authorities vaccinate us,
license us to drive and arrest us if we do it poorly, prohibit
us from using narcotics freely, and zone our property. They
require licenses to marry, to practice law, medicine, barbering,
or engineering, and to operate bars, hotels, and other
businesses. We must have government permits to construct
buildings or to tear them down. Our dairies are inspected,
our teachers certified. Hardly anything we do escapes attention.
All these things, and many more provide opportunity for the
abuse of administrative discretion.

The complexities of modern life make it impossible for
legislatures to enact laws covering every possible situation.
As a consequence, rule-making authority and discretion within
the law are delegated to administrative officials. Discretion
may turn into discrimination or partiality. An arbitrary,
careless, tired, or indifferent civil servant can make decisions
with grave consequences for a citizen, decisions which may
deprive him of his property or his livelihood.

Law enforcement officials are sometimes careless of
citizens' rights, especially in ghetto areas. Zoning boards may
be inclined to listen to developers and highway interests
rather than to the less affluent citizen about to lose his home

or see its value destroyed. Public decisions cannot please everyone, but in a democratic system everyone should have a right to be heard, a chance to have his pleas against arbitrary action considered and, when possible, remedied.

What recourse has the citizen against arbitrary government action? How can he make the government hear and respond to his complaints? Many remedies have been tried. One innovative effort to protect the citizen is the ombudsman, or citizens' representative, as practiced in Scandinavian countries. In the first article in this section, Ralph Nader advocates importing this idea on the state government level. Frank Zeidler assesses the possibility of an ombudsman for cities and concludes that a great number of people, in paid and voluntary capacities, are fulfilling many of his functions. He asserts that an ombudsman could have little effect in a large city because of the enormous problems; and in small cities he would not be effective because of elite power groups.

Daniel Bell and Virginia Held turn their attention to the accelerating demands for citizen participation in government decisions. More and more groups are clamoring for a voice in the distribution of community resources and in other decisions affecting their interests. And in almost every major social service area, federal legislation now provides for community participation. In some communities it has spread to other fields. Irving Kristol discusses local control of public schools and points out the confusion between the practice of democracy and the expression of dissent. What will be the effect of demands for citizen control? Will government hear and become more responsive to citizen needs, or will it become so hampered by requirements for citizen participation that it will be unable to act?

Government responsiveness is put to the test in relations with its own employees. The enormous growth in public employment since World War II was accompanied by a commensurate expansion of public employee unions. Strikes by public employees, once a novelty, are no longer unusual. Policemen, firemen, teachers, sanitation workers, and others in communities across the country practice "slow-downs" or leave their jobs. The so-called "blue flu," or the concurrent use of sick leave by large numbers of firemen and policemen, is becoming commonplace. Bitter controversy has developed over the right to strike of essential public servants, whose conscientious devotion to duty is vital to public safety. Should police and firemen be allowed to strike? If so, who is to protect citizens during this period? If not, how do we deal with grievances and demands of these groups? Roger N. Baldwin and H. Eliot Kaplan debate an issue that promises to be one of the most controversial of this decade: Do public employees have the right to strike?

The readings in Part 8 touch only a few issues of government responsiveness. They embroider on the question: Can the government hear?

RALPH NADER

Ombudsmen for State Governments

Under the American federal system the fifty states encompass a broad variety of governing processes within similar constitutional frameworks. Also, sizable differences in their population, geography, economy and political traditions pattern different results from comparable structures. While it is well to recognize such heterogeneity, there is sufficient, common ground for generalizing about the governmental context at this level for Ombudsman institutions.

For a generation, observers and practitioners alike have been bemoaning the loss of power and prestige of the states to the federal government. The reality of this loss notwithstanding, no other governmental unit pervades the lives of more citizens more regularly than does the state. All states have undergone in recent decades an enormous growth of regulatory, service and fiscal operations which have increased sharply the interactions of citizen and administration. At the same time this growth is posing serious obstacles to practical remedies for the citizen against administrative abuses. The bureaucratic apparatus of all state governments share similar traits which do violence to equal protection for citizens in their variety of dealings with the administration.

Ralph Nader, "Ombudsmen for State Governments," in *The Ombudsman: Citizen's Defender*, ed. Donald C. Rowat (London: George Allen & Unwin Ltd.; Toronto: University of Toronto Press; Sweden: P. A. Norstedt & Soner, 1968), pp. 240–246. Reprinted by permission. © Donald C. Rowat, 1965, 1968.

State constitutions, with their neat separation of government into legislative, executive and judicial branches allegedly balancing and checking one another, make no provision for the rise of a vast state bureaucracy now employing over a million and a half people and having expenditures exceeding $30 billion in 1963. The operating realities of this bureaucracy have forged above and beyond the formal structures and assumptions of state governments to create a towering imbalance between the executive and legislative branches of government.

The vast administrative framework necessary to perform state functions can be shown by taking a representative state such as Kentucky. This state has 33 constitutional and statutory departments. Within these departments there are some 150 subordinate boards, divisions and bureaus. There are approximately 80 independent agencies and 9 inter-state agencies. All 272 of these administrative units have the express or implied authority to promulgate rules and regulations. The output of new regulations annually in Kentucky is proceeding at an approximate rate of four times the volume of 15 years ago.[1] Along with this prolific exercise of basically legislative power, many state agencies adjudicate cases and thus combine all three of the 'separate powers' under single administrative units. This truly stupendous upsurge in state administrative activity has come about primarily in the last three decades. Sizable federal grants, totalling $8 billion in 1963, have helped expand several of these activities.

The development of the administrative state has undermined deeply the effectiveness of the old institutions of check embodied in the principle of separate powers. The legislatures, in creating new agencies and expanding existing ones, have delegated broad policy making powers affecting intimately the lives of most citizens. These agencies have acquired vested interests in ways of doing things that have long gone unchallenged. State legislative oversight of the administrative agencies is non-existent in many cases, highly sporadic and superficial in others.

In sharp departure from the period up to about 1915 when the legislature reigned supreme, the executive is now by far the most active branch in the government; it is the chief proposing power in legislative formulation and it has strong powers of persuasion stemming from party discipline, expertise with the subject matter of legislation, and association with pressure groups having similar objectives. Conflicts of interest within the legislature, such as that affecting subtly or overtly many lawyer legislators having an active practice before state regulatory agencies, tend to compromise the independence of the legislature further.

Moreover, constitutional restrictions seriously impede legislatures from asserting a stronger role in the initiation of legislative policy and the process of representing the electorate generally. Only

18 state legislatures meet annually and often are constitutionally limited to 60 or 90 day sessions. The remaining 32 states have biennial sessions many of whose length is similarly curtailed. Legislators work under great time pressure and are grossly underpaid in most states, compelling many of them to consider their legislative duties as part time employment subsidiary to their regular job. This offers increased opportunities for representatives of special interests, who descend upon the legislature and, together with seasoned spokesmen of state agencies, are largely responsible for rendering perfunctory most hearings and formal debates on pending legislation.

Lack of an assertive role in law making and in oversight of administrative agencies by legislatures has profound significance for the quality of justice which many citizens receive from these agencies. Vague policy standards in the delegating acts and inadequate procedural safeguards pave the way for uncontrolled discretionary authority by the agencies to enforce, adjudicate and promulgate rules. Discretionary authority too often turns into partiality, which sees some infractions and overlooks others. When coupled with detailed but little enforced regulations, such as sanitary rules for barbershops, such authority can be used arbitrarily to intimidate any barber who does not give unqualified assent to the mandates of the barber licensing and supervisory commission, which is controlled by the barber association. The proliferation of such licensing boards for occupations ranging from architects to undertakers and from cosmeticians to tree surgeons, largely through the efforts of the occupational associations themselves, is part of the widespread process of legislating group privileges under the guise of regulation. They are 'little governments' characterized by many of the trappings of tyranny.

This differential treatment of organized interests and individual claimants extends throughout state administration. Teachers, organized labor, utilities, insurance companies, agriculture, shipping, motor transport and mining interests are all part of a functional or group representation via a large number of agencies. Administrators are likely to come to their position from a former position in the industry or group they are to regulate. Many take well placed jobs in the industry after finishing their term of office. Advisory bodies composed of members representing the regulated group maintain close consultation, familiarity and understanding with the particular agency which they are appointed by law to advise. The few administrators who try to resist forfeiture of the 'public interest' in this environment find that the statutory independence of their agency within the executive branch actually increases the likelihood of capitulation to group demands. This overwhelming dominance of group government in a polity dedicated to the safeguarding and respect of individual rights has obvious strains for the lone claimant.

The decentralization of power and responsibility in the executive is so widespread as to amount to a particular kind of administrative lawlessness without adequate sanctions. In many instances, Governors do not have control or co-ordinated responsibility over departments and agencies. In many states, a number of the principal administrative officers are directly elected. Heads of other important state departments may be appointed to a term exceeding that of the Governor who appointed them. As a consequence, in state after state, Governors have been able to stand aloof and emerge unscathed from the exposure and prosecution of major scandals affecting the agencies.

The corruption or laxity uncovered when a scandal breaks usually reveals that hundreds or even thousands of people in or close to the agency involved knew about the situation but the facts remained effectively insulated from the larger public audience. Such revelations spotlight how large and important a part of the governmental process is hidden from public scrutiny.

The public information policies of agencies border on the disgraceful. Less than a third of the states have adopted explicit administrative procedures governing their agencies. Attorneys for claimants regularly find themselves unable to locate the rules of state agencies, prevented from seeing the factual basis for agency determination, and thwarted by influences channelled through ex parte communications by agency administrators and hearing examiners. In cases possessing little monetary value, these difficulties easily discourage citizens from retaining counsel and counsel from accepting such cases. The fact that the system is flexible enough to allow redress for important personages through personal contacts, favors and the like from counsel or a local politico, only encourages the perpetuation of the evils of the system.

The difficulty in obtaining information about how the agencies are carrying on their responsibilities—a kind of access that is basic to democratic politics—is seriously impeding the most elemental type of scholarly analysis of state administration. William J. Pierce, Professor of Law at Michigan, phrased the problem well:

> At the present time it is extremely difficult in many situations to uncover any information concerning the policies, objectives, and procedures of administrative agencies even when it is obvious that their operations have a tremendous impact upon a substantial segment of the populace. . . . The mere availability of the knowledge will make it possible for society's leaders to come to grips with some of the basic policy problems that will inevitably demand re-evaluation. This in turn will lead to improvements in the law and public confidence in our democratic institutions and the rule of law.[2]

The courts, as presently constituted and under the well-established judicial acceptance of a limited reviewing function over administrative behavior, cannot be considered as a practical source of remedies for complainants except in the more egregiously abusive acts. Moreover, many of the controversies between citizen and agency are not justiciable in nature and are heavily larded with political considerations avoided by a court of law. Judicial delays and appeals contribute to the rarity of recourse to the courts.

Awareness of the need to establish channels for publicly exposing misconduct by public officials goes back many years. For neither the ballot nor the press—the two traditional checks on governmental malfeasance toward citizens—were considered adequate even in the last century and they are even less so today if for no other reason than the exponential growth and complexity of state activity. Many states long have allowed their grand juries to make investigations and presentments about inefficient, incompetent public officials or agencies, along with the power to indict for criminal behavior. But the grand jury does not often show an initiative greater than the public prosecutor who guides it. Its probing into bureaucratic abuses is mostly reserved for the most serious aberrations from proper administrative conduct.

More recently, particularly since 1945, many states have established Legislative Councils which, besides researching on legislative proposals, are often commissioned by statute to examine the effects of previously enacted laws, recommend amendments, search out waste and engage in other administrative oversight. However, this function has rarely been pursued vigorously and has never been backed up with sufficient authority even if the will was present. The Council staff has been fully occupied with being the research arm of the legislature. Those legislators who make up the Council's bipartisan membership are careful to minimize the investigative role lest they arouse the enmity of other legislators over trying to create a 'little legislature' under their domination.

The growing number of state laws on conflicts of interest will often empower the Attorney General to make periodic inspection of state agencies and investigate situations which come to his attention relating to suspected conflict of interest situations. Political complexions which inevitably attach to the Attorney General's Office are not conducive to thorough pursuance of such duties except for flagrant situations teetering on the brink of public exposure. More often than not, the Attorney General will take his cue to investigate from his Governor, rather than act on his own initiative in an area having possibly severe political consequences for the incumbent party.

Another check on administrative waywardness has been attempted by a few incoming Governors usually flush from victory at the polls. This has taken the form of opening their office a few hours a a week or month to any citizen who wants to come in and express a complaint, want or suggestion. These 'citizen sessions' rarely last more than a few months. One reason is that the agencies resent them and furthermore the possibility of a Pandora's box of abuses being inadvertently uncovered by an innocent gubernatorial probe for a complainant is not relished by the Governor himself as his incumbency matures.

Finally, professional politicians holding public positions through patronage make representations informally to agencies whose acts may have aggrieved a party faithful or even an ordinary citizen, as a significant method of solidifying party loyalty or their political image.

From the foregoing, it can be seen that an Ombudsman attached to the legislature and empowered to directly receive and investigate citizens' complaints against the administration as well as to initiate inquiries and make inspections unilaterally, would start his work in a considerably hostile and suspicious political environment dominated by party professionals, state administrators and representatives of organized pressure groups. Quite expectedly, the Ombudsman institution would be viewed as a threat to these groups. For any intrusions into the informal pattern of relationships between them will incur their opposition. Connecticut's brief experience with an Ombudsman proposal introduced into the General Assembly in 1963 revealed this opposition.

Thus both the authority of the Ombudsman and his initial effectiveness will depend to a large extent on three factors: (1) the kind of support for and the circumstances preceding enactment of an Ombudsman bill, (2) the level of administrative and political integrity and competence of the particular state, and (3) the stature and skill of the person holding the new office. These factors will vary with each state.

While a model Ombudsman Act may give the officeholder authority to present the case of a complainant in court under certain conditions, limit the requests to investigate that are made by legislators in order to maintain his non-political position, eliminate any filing fee for complaints, eliminate the requirement for a complainant to have 'standing' (a sufficient personal interest in the subject matter of the complaint)—all these may have to be omitted or compromised, as they were in the Connecticut Bill, to increase the chance of being enacted. In every state, advocates of such legislation may have to decide whether no Ombudsman is preferable to one shackled by severe restrictions on his authority.

However, while the Ombudsman will have to be given certain minimum authority, such as the subpoena power, as the *sine qua non* of his mission, his power and influence should increase out of the judicious handling of his duties at a measured pace. The zeal he must express to draw the confidence and support of the public and legislature must be tempered by restraint in his investigations of administrative terrain long accustomed to little external scrutiny and having considerable political strength. Such seems to be the experience of the Danish Ombudsman now in his tenth year of office.

The sensitivity of the areas to be probed can be illustrated by a sample of abuses which would be the concern of the proposed Connecticut Ombudsman: preferential treatment and influence peddling, inadequate or unpublished regulations, wrongful detention, state police overzealousness or laxity, unjust procedures in agency hearings, arbitrary censorship or secrecy, agency reluctance or refusal to give explicit reasons for decisions, patronage excesses, inefficiencies and delays by state personnel, undesirable conditions in prisons and mental institutions, payoffs and kickbacks in state contracts, and discriminatory enforcement or flagrant non-enforcement of state laws.

Perhaps the best way to conceive of the role of an Ombudsman on the state governmental level is to compare the office to a continuous, non partisan linchpin for initiatives working toward administrative justice. As an example, the press may not dig out abuses on its own accord, but it is quite likely to report and possibly follow up an Ombudsman's findings of such abuses. The legislatures may have neither the time, skill nor inclination to oversee administrative methods, standards, manners and corruption, but the findings by its Ombudsman, flush before the public, together with his reasoned recommendations, may prod it into action. The head of an agency may be lax in supervising his subordinates, but knowing that an Ombudsman having the confidence of the legislature is nearby may stimulate him to greater attentiveness. For the Ombudsman would be obtaining, from the feedback of citizens, information on administrative behavior in specific cases which is now mostly unknown outside the agency concerned. In addition, if it is of little avail to complain, or if to do so might incur retaliations by agency personnel, complaints will very often not be made. Affording an outlet for complaints will result in data of very considerable importance, under a skilled Ombudsman, for varied improvements of the public administration.

Thus a chief impact of the office would be preventive, as has been the case in Sweden and Denmark. Here the existence of power is more important than its exercise. Although too much can be expected of an Ombudsman, to underestimate the catalytic impact of a wisely operated office, quite apart from the direct handling of complaints, would be to err in the other direction.

Notes

1. Commonwealth of Kentucky, Legislative Research Commission, *Administrative Procedures Law in Kentucky* (Frankfort, Kentucky, Research Report No. 12, 1962), 5–6.

2. 'The Act as Viewed by an Academician' in 'Symposium on the Model State Administrative Procedure Act,' *Administrative Law Review* 16 (Fall 1963), 53.

FRANK P. ZEIDLER

An Ombudsman for Cities?

The current growth in bureaucracy in government, the result of the large-scale social and political problems that have emerged in United States society and culture, has brought about a new interest in the function of the Ombudsman, the independent appointee of a government who acts as the people's investigator, defender, pleader, and guide in the struggle against the authority of an unchecked or insensitive bureaucracy.

The concept seems best suited to the struggle of the citizen against the federal bureaucracy, but there appears to be some appeal in the idea for those interested in improving the quality of urban or metropolitan life.

A general review of urban conditions reveals that the idea has merit and is indeed being practiced in some manner in many aspects of urban life; but the urban ills of America exceed the Ombudsman's capacity to solve, and require fundamentally new efforts at political action.

Types of Urban Complaints

Urban people have certain kinds of complaints against local government. If an attempt were made to tabulate the frequency of such complaints, no doubt, complaints about taxes, licenses, fees, and other collections of local government for supporting itself would be important, but they would probably be exceeded by complaints about garbage and rubbish collections and the failure of the public works agencies to perform their functions. A large number of complaints are concerned with the amount of welfare assistance and relief payments. Also, complaints about local nuisances, dogs, taverns, unsightly buildings, neighbors, and the failure of the bureaucracy to remove abandoned automobiles effectively, come to the city officials.

A large number of complaints certainly arise from administrative decrees issued by health departments, building-inspection departments, zoning offices, fire-safety inspectors, and other code enforcement officers. People in urban areas also have grievances against ur-

Frank P. Zeidler, "An Ombudsman for Cities?" *The Annals of the American Academy*, 377 (May 1968), 123–127. Reprinted by permission.

ban development departments, highway departments, public housing agencies, and other public agencies which exercise the right of urban domain and which evict them from their houses and neighborhoods. Planners also trouble people; any plan produced for some supposed urban improvement is bound to conflict with someone's deeply felt interest.

Complaints about transportation service, parking, and traffic bottlenecks also are a fruitful source of trouble for the urban bureaucrat, and now the airport and its unhappy side-effects on local residents constitute a new source of grievance.

All of these types of complaints can be serious. Even more serious are citizens' complaints against the police departments, though for seemingly contradictory reasons. Either the police are not protecting the people on the streets, or the police are brutal with people. These complaints may not be so contradictory as it would seem at first glance; they reflect urban ills much deeper than the surface anger expressed at the police.

Complaints About Racial Problems

Most critical of all the complaints now, and those which dwarf all the others, are the complaints of the races about each other, something which I predicted would worsen in the United States, and which I described in this publication in 1957.[1] If a bureaucracy is controlled by one race, no matter what it does, it is likely to be suspect to some people of another race.

One would not want to live in an environment without some challenge and struggle, because a cultural climate or environment without some stress would be deadly; but it is likely that in United States cities today, in many places, the stress of multiracial division has become so severe that the mental strain on people will cause them to turn against and destroy their physical environment and even themselves.

Existing Types of "Ombudsmen"

The stresses in United States urban life have become so severe that many kinds of groups and people have merged as types of Ombudsmen or pleaders for the people against the bureaucracy. The unexpected direction of the poverty program is an example. When that portion of the Economic Opportunity Act which called for participation by the poor in decisions affecting them was interpreted as a war on the mayors, the power structure, and city hall, the mayors understandably were quite surprised. They had not realized that there were enough social workers around who felt that they could organize the poor so as to force the social workers' way into the select circle of city decision-makers. An even later example is the rise of Black Power militants, who see in the public unhappiness with city bureaucracy and elected officials a chance to practice the teachings of guerrilla warfare.

These latter types have similarities to the followers of Saul D. Alinsky. Alinsky's teachings of getting power for the powerless through community organization and deliberate conflict with city hall have won disciples among hundreds of urban clergymen and religious women, social workers, and other people who feel deeply about the distress of the urban poor, but who are not yet so politically sophisticated as are Black Power proponents.

The more moderate types of the American variety of Ombudsmen have been around a long time. These types include the clergyman who acts as a case worker for distressed families and people in his church in their brush with some arm of government. Private social welfare workers have also acted as pleaders, although one may be inclined now to regard many private social-worker professionals as part of the interlocking top bureaucracy of accepted public and private agencies. County agents in urban counties now often act as Ombudsmen for people who do not know how to cope with problems of urban living.

Settlement workers and adult education and recreation workers, even though part of the government, often act as guides, pleaders, and defenders of people against other branches of the bureaucracy. Community organizations and block clubs often produce spontaneously a volunteer type of individual who acts as leader, pleader, and defender of his group's interest. Bridging the gap between these volunteers and the official bureaucracy are some of the official community workers in special community liaison departments of city government now being created.

For the middle class and those who have funds, there are attorneys and lobbyists. The ethnic and national groups have long had their own leaders.

For everyone, there is the political party unit and the local political leader who knows how to intervene on behalf of the party workers or the friends of the party workers.

One must not forget the local press, whether daily or weekly, which considers itself the tribune of the people. More recently, radio and television editorialists sometimes act in the general public interest, despite the economic biases of their networks' owners.

All in all, there are many people in the metropolitan areas who function in some ways as an Ombudsman, expert in dealing with the ways of administrative bureaucracy.

It might be desirable for some urban community in America to experiment with creating the position of Ombudsman, just as Representative Henry S. Ruess is now doing in his congressional district, the Fifth Wisconsin Congressional District. He has created such a post for his constituents.

However, it does not seem that the office of Ombudsman can be particularly effective at this stage in the evolution of United States urban society, because there are serious obstacles to the effective functioning of the Ombudsman both in small and in large cities.

Magnitude of Urban Problems

The current problems of urban and metropolitan areas in the bigger cities seem too enormous to permit their solution through the efforts of the office of Ombudsman, and in the smaller communities, under the social and political systems that frequently prevail, the Ombudsman is not likely to be effective because of the control of power by one person or by a very small group.

In the smaller communities of the United States, it frequently happens that the political system is dominated by some small economic group, or even by one individual. Appeal against a governmental action by the dominant local group is often difficult. An attempt at an appeal may result in loss of employment in areas where there is a surplus of labor. Appeals for relief or public assistance or against the decision of welfare agencies in such areas are also quite difficult. Usually, appeals are effective only when they are directed through a chain of friends, with the appeal finally reaching a person of influence.

The problems of the larger communities are of a different order. The current problems of housing, race relations, crime, traffic, pollution, and employment opportunities in some of the communities are so great as to constitute mass phenomena which cannot be solved by Ombudsmen or even by an office of administrative counsel. Such offices could only deal with a small portion of the main problem. The solution of many urban problems requires fundamental changes in people's attitudes, in their education, in economic relationships, in governmental powers and structure, and indeed in the philosophy and direction of society. The most important effort must be directed toward effecting the fundamental changes first.

The difficulties under which an Ombudsman might have to function, when the total milieu functions to prevent a solution of the problem, could completely negate his work. An aggrieved welfare client could complain that the public case worker is depriving him of an adequate budget to keep alive and is applying the rules unjustly. This indeed might be the case, but in many cities with large welfare loads, the fact is that not enough money can be raised from all sources to meet the full welfare needs of all clients, and, as a result, stringent budgets are put into effect. Some additional assistance may be obtained for one person, but the major problem is practically untouched.

Similarly, a complaint against a housing authority may provide some relief for one family, but what about the numerous other families who do not have proper accommodation? The city had better address itself to the solution of the underlying and fundamental problems; this is the best way to employ its human and financial resources. When these problems are solved, it can then direct its attention to refinements of the administrative process by providing for some kind of administrative appeal for people entrapped in administrative regulations.

Rewards to City Spoilers

One of the most frustrating things about American urban society is that, at the present time, it seems to reward those people and forces busily trying to break it down, either consciously or unconsciously. The racial extremists often triumph at the elections. The polluters of land, water, and air are so politically influential that they cannot be prevented from carrying on their unethical practices. The slum landlords can hire attorneys to frustrate the city ordinances. The vice lords and the gambling syndicates seem to have partial control of many city governments. The social snobbery of an upper-middle income group prevents the solution of the problem of the racial ghetto in housing. The private motorist, who refuses to allow himself to be properly taxed to meet municipal government costs that arise from his vehicle use, is the dominant factor in municipal voting. The mass transit rider has little political power; and the pedestrian, almost none at all.

The people who make their fortunes in the downtowns of the inner city of the metropolitan area reside elsewhere, and their taxes often go to strengthening the community of their residence against the place where they earn their income. The older central cities of the United States metropolitan areas, with their numerous and relatively poorly educated constituents, are dominated by suburban people who control the press, the media of communication, business and industry, better income opportunities, and also the elections of the inner city.

Against the large-scale human problems that result from such an environment, physical and social, an Ombudsman, or a group of Ombudsmen in an office of administrative counsel, would have little effect. Only when these fundamental conditions are changed, and when government and society, on the whole, function so that the productive and useful activities of men are rewarded in urban society, might the work of the Ombudsmen have a good effect in coping with the problems that inevitably arise when people and a bureaucracy deal with each other.

The Urban Struggle for Democracy

If the struggle to preserve a democratic society in urban places does not succeed, it does not seem possible that there can be a role for the office of Ombudsman at any level of government in American society. The reason for this is that the struggle in the cities is now essentially a struggle to establish a caste system of society and to defeat and reject the democratic method of solving political and social problems. The Negro and white champions of racial separatism are seemingly in a struggle with each other over the control of power in society; but, actually, both groups are fighting against those who hold the concept of an integrated society. The question of race, which in so many metropolitan areas is now the overwhelming issue, is not really a difference between the separatists of different color, but between those separatists, of whatever color, who want social secession from American society and those people, of whatever color, who want no social secession or withdrawal of any group or caste. If the secessionists succeed, and they are succeeding at the polls in many places, the decisions of society will be made on the basis of caste and between races. No Ombudsman, then, intervening for a person of the wrong caste, will be able to advance his cause on the basis of some abstract principle of equal justice for all. The decisions will be made on the basis of castes and what the castes demand of each other.

For people who have the strength and energy to work on the problems of American government today, it would seem that, at this stage, their energy could best be spent in political organization and education to fight for and keep secure the democratic processes by electing and keeping in office public officials committed to an integrated democracy, and not to racial separatism. This is where the big challenge in society is today; it is not in an irresistible movement of the bureaucracy against the individual. In many instances, the bureaucracy will as readily lend itself to the demands of a totalitarian as to those of a democratically inclined official. At present, the bureaucracy is subordinate to the authority of the elected official. Once the principle of democratic participation in government is again preserved (one might even say, rescued) in American city government, then the development of the office of Ombudsman would have more importance and significance.

Note

1. Frank P. Zeidler, "Urbanism and Government, 1957–1977," THE ANNALS, Vol. 314 (November 1957), pp. 74 ff.

DANIEL BELL
VIRGINIA HELD

The Community Revolution

> . . . *Two neighbors may agree to drain a meadow, which they possess*
> *in common: because it is easy for them to know each other's mind; and*
> *each must perceive, that the immediate consequence of his failing in his*
> *part, is the abandoning the whole project. But it is very difficult, and in-*
> *deed impossible, that a thousand persons should agree in any such action;*
> *it being difficult for them to concert so complicated a design, and still*
> *more difficult for them to execute it; while each seeks a pretext to free*
> *himself of the trouble and expense, and would lay the whole burden on*
> *others. Political society easily remedies both these inconveniences. . . .*
> *Thus, bridges are built, harbours opened, ramparts raised, canals formed,*
> *fleets equipped, and armies disciplined, everywhere, by the care of gov-*
> *ernment, which, though composed of men subject to all human infirmi-*
> *ties, becomes, by one of the finest and most subtle inventions imaginable,*
> *a composition which is in some measure exempted from all these in-*
> *firmities.*
>
> —David Hume, *A Treatise of Human Nature*

One cliché of contemporary political discourse is that "the people
have no real voice—or, less and less of a voice—in their political affairs," a view reinforced by a ponderous academic sociology that
asserts "a decline or eclipse of the local community" and a change
wherein "all groupings based on traditional criteria such as shared
ethnic descent and inheritance of status are undermined. . . ."

We believe both assertions to be quite wrong. In fact, the opposite may be true—that there is more participation than ever before
in American society, particularly in the large urban centers such as
New York, and more opportunity for the active and interested person to express his political and social concerns. That very state of
affairs leads to a paradox because it is the increase in participation
which creates a sense of powerlessness and consequent frustration.

A person who is socially conscious wants results, paticularly *his*
results, and he wants them immediately. But the very fact that there
is an increase in the number of claimants leads, inevitably, to lengthier
consultation and mediation, and more importantly, to a situation
wherein thousands of different organizations, each wanting diverse
and contradictory things, simply check each other in their demands.
As a Mrs. Gladys Gonzales, vice-president of the Parents Teachers

Daniel Bell and Virginia Held, "The Community Revolution," *The Public
Interest*, no. 16 (Summer 1969), 142–177. Copyright © 1969 by National
Affairs, Inc. Reprinted by permission of National Affairs, Inc.

Association of Junior High School 71, is reported as saying at the public hearings of the Board of Education on the school decentralization plan, "You graciously allow us to say what is on our mind and then turn around and do what you want to do anyway." But this is precisely what *every* speaker, whatever his point of view, feels and says at such a meeting; and the result is rancor and a sense of frustration.

Forty years ago, a Tammany political boss could give an order to a mayor. Today, no such simple action is possible. On each political issue—decentralization or community control, the mix of low income and middle income housing, the proportion of blacks in the city colleges, the location of a cross-Manhattan or cross-Brooklyn expressway, etc.—there are dozens of active, vocal, and conflicting organized opinions. The difficulty in governing New York—and many other cities as well—is not the "lack of voice" of individuals in city affairs, or the "eclipse of local community," but the babel of voices and the multiplication of claimants in the widened political arena. In this new participatory democracy the need is for the creation of new political mechanisms that will allow for the establishment of priorities in the city, and for some effective bargaining and tradeoffs between groups; without that the city may end in a shambles.

The Multifarious Associations

Writing on his trip to the United States in 1904, Max Weber could comment, after Tocqueville, "In the past and up to the present, it has been a characteristic precisely of the specifically American democracy that it did *not* constitute a formless sandheap of individuals, but rather a buzzing complex of strictly exclusive, yet voluntary associations."

No count has ever been made of the number of voluntary associations in the United States or in any major American city. In New York, the *Directory of Social and Health Agencies of New York City* lists 1200 welfare organizations, voluntary and public, excluding civic, educational, and religious organizations. Ten years ago, Sayre and Kaufman in *Governing New York City* remarked, "No careful census of these nongovernmental groups in the city has ever been made, but the number seems to run at least to *tens of thousands*. This estimate comprises only those groups sufficiently well organized to have letterheads, telephones, and/or to appear in some published directory." (our italics)

Whatever the total ten years ago, the number of groups, particularly local block associations, tenants organizations, welfare councils—name the issue and a dozen groups spring into being—have since multiplied spectacularly. The chief reason has been the revolution in the political structure of urban life that was initiated by the Kennedy-Johnson administrations, a development obscured and to some extent distorted by the Vietnam war. Just as the Wagner Act of 1935 facilitated—indeed, shaped—the organization of the economic workplace by trade unions, so the community action provisions of the Poverty Act of 1964 established the basis for neighborhood organization by community groups. In so doing, it has created a potential for political bargaining on urban community issues just as there is economic bargaining on issues in the workplace.

There are substantial differences of course. The Wagner Act created a rule-making institution in the National Labor Relations Board with well-defined contestants, specific issues, and real pay-offs. The structure of political bargaining in the community is still inchoate. Whether it will function is moot. The system has been quickly repudiated, in part, by the Johnson and Nixon administrations; the militants, who initially sought to take advantage of the system to gain a place in society, have turned to more radical and direct action tactics; and the established political machines have fought the community action programs and in many places have taken them over. Yet the potential remains, particularly in New York City, for disadvantaged groups—or more specifically their indigenous leaders—to get "a share of the action" or at a minimum to act as veto groups in the system. The full thrust of community organization may have been blunted in these last couple of years, but it would be foolish to ignore what may yet be one of the great structural changes in the political system of American urban society.

The Patterns of Communal Life

Going back sixty years or more—there has been an extensive network of participation by different kinds of groups in the communal life of New York City, and these have tied into the political system in different ways. For purposes of analysis, one can identify three different kinds of communal systems in the city life.

The first might be called the *civic associations*. These are the old, established, predominantly upper middle class, business, and "good government" organizations. They include such groups as the Citizens Union (established in 1897 growing out of the City Reform Club whose members included Theodore Roosevelt and elected reform mayor William L. Strong), the Citizens Budget Commission (business-supported), the Citizens' Committee for Children (primarily wealthy, liberal Jewish women), the Men's and Women's City Clubs, the Civil Service Reform Association, the Public Education Association, the Citizens Housing and Planning Council, the Commerce and Industry Association, the League of Women Voters, etc.

These are all politically-minded, politically active, "clean government," reform movements.

The second is the more numerous and more diffuse *fraternal and service organizations* built, traditionally, around the religious and ethnic groups. These consist of the Protestant Council, the Catholic Charities, the Federation of Jewish Philanthropies, the hospitals, family service centers, old age homes, child care centers, parochial schools, and the like. They are represented in the large, coordinating, research and information agencies, such as the Community Council of Greater New York, and in major service groups, such as the Community Service Society of New York. These agencies, plus the many "old country" associations, particularly among the Jews and the Irish, have provided the means whereby the poor immigrants of an earlier era were helped to settle in New York. These organizations have been the backbone of the communal, self-help structures of New York.

And third, there has been the large network of *neighborhood organizations:* settlement houses, parent-teachers associations, block associations, tenants associations, local churches and synagogues. The center of these activities was often the local political club. City aldermen, state assemblymen, and state senators kept in touch with these organizations which meant grievances or needs were funneled through the elected representatives.

In the past, almost all of these three "communal systems" were private and voluntary. They were sustained by the monies and time of individuals who gained status, political visibility, or simple personal satisfaction through these activities. They were maintained by professional staffs who provided the day-to-day services, as well as structural continuity through time, and who often "recruited" new leaders for these organizations in order to sustain the monies and activities.

In addition, the political system itself was the main "brokerage" agency for patronage, reward, wealth, status, and power. New immigrants could get jobs through "pull" at city hall or through the large number of business concerns whose existence depended in part on political favor; for example, Consolidated Edison, pier stevedore concerns, construction companies, and truckers. The quid pro quo was jobs for votes. The political clubs serviced the new and unorganized poor (on the lower east side before World War I, it was not uncommon for a person who had an appendicitis attack, to go to his precinct captain, because he often didn't know where the hospital was, and he certainly did not have a telephone). They told city hall what was needed in the neighborhoods. In the current jargon, the political clubs were the chief modes of communication and control.

Over the past decades, the political machines that were the structure of government in New York have broken down. Under the New Deal, the locus of power and attention shifted to Washington, and the major jobs and finances of the society came under federal control. The rise of middle class liberal reformers within the Democratic Party—reform, previously, had always operated outside the party, usually in some "fusion" slate—cracked the singular power of the old bosses because the reform clubs were oriented more to issues than to jobs. The extension of the merit system in the 1960's, "upward, outward and downward," reduced the role of patronage. More and more frequently, administrators of the top agencies came from career ranks and party background almost became a mark of disqualification. As Theodore Lowi observed, "The triumph of Reform really ends in paradox: *Cities like New York become well-run but ungoverned.*"[1]

In the past thirty years, the influx of Negro and Puerto Rican migrants brought a double problem. They lacked the resources and often the will to build voluntary community structures. They arrived on the scene at a time when the older political mechanisms were in disarray. The blacks did achieve some political power, with the votes of Harlem as a base. When Hulan Jack became borough president in Manhattan in 1953, it became clear that for the foreseeable future this post would be a black prerogative. (And so it has been with his successors, Constance Motley and Percy Sutton.) But the other rewards —political contracts, the protection of rackets, the patronage to the lawyers and professionals—that had gone in the past to the ethnic minorities did not follow this political power: in part, because such rewards were no longer available and, in part, because there were few blacks able to claim them. The chief point here is that the blacks lacked the communal network that could interact with the political base, and thus provide the basis for the kind of advancement that had been made by earlier ethnic groups.[2]

It has always been the case in modern society, that the three fundamental hierarchies are power, wealth, and status. In the past, wealth commanded power or power commandeered wealth. But for the ethnic groups in the United States, these two were reinforced through the *communal* structures, which provided status and prestige for the wealthy and powerful, and which also provided a cohesion for the group coming into the society. The communal structures set up a network of full-time professionals who would advance the interests of the ethnic groups and their activities furthered and reinforced the contacts and social ties which aided the lawyer, the businessman, the financier in their business and professional careers.

The problem for the blacks, thus, was that at the time they were coming into urban life the political base was restricted and their communal structures were weak. In time, the two weaknesses would doubtless have been corrected. It is only in the last decade, after all, that the blacks have become primarily urban and concentrated in the north. But time is no longer available. What took the Irish three generations, the Italian two, and the Jews one to achieve—the security of middle class status—is something the blacks want immediately. They have been here the longest, and have been held down the most. They no longer want to wait. What they are asking for is power and resources; these have to come through the community.

The Redemption of the Cities

To this political and sociological crisis is added another crucial fact: the multiplication of social problems arising from the demographic transformation of the country. The population of the country is being concentrated in metropolitan areas, the older sections of the cities are dilapidated, the transportation systems are choked and swollen, and services are lagging. It is easy, and deceptive, to blame this simply on "capitalism," or, more ambiguously on "the system." But this crisis derives in the first instance from one of the most fundamental facts about modern society: *the increase in number and movement of persons, and the increased demand for a level of services and amenities for all which has been hitherto unknown in the society.* Sixty-five years ago, a million persons a year could pour into the country in a steady stream for a decade, and jam together in crowded ghettoes, with little direct impact on the settled middle class lives of the older inhabitants, but that is no longer possible today. Each person wants full access to education and to services; and today each middle class person, sitting in his car, among 80 million others, wants a free and unobstructed highway.

These demands for services underscore what has been evident for a long time: that the administrative structure of the cities, organized as they are in a crazy-quilt pattern of counties, townships, and districts, are out of whack with the times. The United States may have the most modern economy and technology in the world, but its administrative structure, as Samuel Huntington has observed, is a Tudor polity. This is particularly evident in New York. The population of New York *City* (not of the metropolitan region) is *twice* the population of Norway, and is greater than the population of Austria or Sweden. But the city's political structure is wholly incongruent with the social realities. The mayor almost has to keep in touch with every birth, briss, confirmation, wedding, national day, death, and memorial service of the multifarious nationality groups in the city in his ceremonial duties; but in his administrative role, the mayor is unable to be in control of the day-to-day functions of the city or to determine its long-range planning requirements.

In 1947, the Citizens Union proposed the division of New York

City into districts "for more orderly planning and decentralization of municipal services and community development." The report recommended the grouping of city services in one location in each district, and proposed that each district would develop its own plan in cooperation with the City Planning Commission. In 1950, the City Planning Commission took up the idea and proposed 66 districts as "logical units for the planning of schools, housing, hospitals, libraries, playgrounds, local street systems and other public facilities as well as for consideration of land use and zoning patterns." As Borough President of Manhattan in 1951, Robert Wagner set up a Community Planning Council, consisting of 15 to 20 members, for each of the 12 Manhattan districts suggested by the City Planning Commission. In part, Wagner did this, because the local political clubs that had been the source of information and mediation between the districts and the city had largely ceased to function, and the administrative agencies increasingly were being overwhelmed by the local groups who took their claims and grievances directly to the city heads. Through these Local Planning Boards, Wagner sought to set up a mediating mechanism against the anarchic onslaught of the multiple organizations in the city.

Thus, the idea of decentralization and local community organizations as the basis of new administrative and political functions was underway, slowly, haltingly, and confusedly, in the 1950's.

To this the Kennedy administration added a new ideology, the ideology of "participation." The upsurge of the blacks, the discovery of the poor, the argument that these groups could not help themselves because they were powerless, all led to the conception that in programs fostered by government one should encourage the creation of new communities. In this way, new structures could be built that could provide help and training for the poor through institutions under their control or influence. In these communities, new, indigenous leaderships would emerge who would lead their constituents "into" the society. Thus the groundwork was laid for a change in the structure of American urban life, a transformation fostered by and financed by the federal government. It is a story unique in American history.

The Ideology of Participation

The heart of the participation ideology was the Poverty Program, and the section entitled the Community Action Programs (CAP) which provide for participation by the poor in the programs that will affect their lives. The key phrase in the section was "maximum feasible participation," a phrase which for some was rhetoric, for some ideology, and for some an instrumental means whereby the poor would gain a sense of political identity. As Daniel P. Moynihan observes,

"Community action with citizen participation was a coherent and powerful idea working its way into national policy, albeit little noticed or understood at the time."

One of the earliest pamphlets produced by CAP, entitled "A Hometown Fight," sets forth this idea in its instructions to communities on how to apply for community-action grants:

> Local community action programs are central to the war on poverty. . . . The individual community decides how best to attack poverty in its midst. Initiative and direction must come from the community itself. . . . In a community with limited resources, local leaders can begin a community action program in stages. For example, with the 'building block' approach a community might start a child development program including health services. . . . The major goal of community action programs is to help individuals help themselves.

The assumptions behind these propositions were quite clear. As John G. Wofford indicates, "There was to be no federal blueprint, no magic formula worked out in Washington that would be imposed on local problems. . . . Problems of decaying mining towns in Kentucky, of Indian reservations, of rural Mississippi, and of urban slums were seen as too different to permit meaningful detailed federal direction." There was also a more important reason, as Mr. Wofford details it:

> Planning itself was seen as a form of action. The very process of getting communities to think about their problems was viewed as an essential means of mobilizing local resources most of which had been either unused or diffused in the past. In communities throughout the country, at the time of the enactment of the anti-poverty legislation, most programs dealing with local poverty were 'single-tracked.' School boards, city halls, departments of welfare, juvenile courts, settlement houses, were going their separate ways without significant contact with each other. The person who suffered programmatic insularity was, of course, the poor person himself; his problems were segmented into traditional molds, and he was rarely, if ever, viewed as one human being with connected crises, needs and styles of life. Thus 'linkage' of programs at the local level became an important goal, and the local planning needed to develop these linkages was conceived as the first and one of the most important forms of community action.[3]

While the rationale and intentions of the "participation" idea are clear, the political history of its emergence and realization is still somewhat of a mystery. The Wagner Act had behind it a large social movement, a long history of agitation, and a political ideology. The Community Action Program had none of these. It was initiated almost completely from the "top," by professionals, rather than by the poor, and on the basis of a mystique of participation.[4]

Much of the original push in this direction came from the Ford Foundation through the proddings of its public affairs director, Paul Ylvisaker, a former philosophy professor at Swarthmore. In the 1950's, American communities had little awareness of the huge problems ahead. Urban renewal, which had been initiated by the Housing Act of 1949, had brought physical change to the center of the cities, but the social changes, particularly the displacement of the poor, were largely ignored. Through Ylvisaker, the Ford Foundation "Gray Areas" programs gave substantial grants to cities to set up community agencies in such fields as youth employment, education, and community services. Ylvisaker had no specific program for social reform—the very idea went against his grain—but he believed in the method of self-help through which communities could bring forth programs suitable to their needs.

A very different source of the participation ideology was a group that had gathered around Robert Kennedy when he was Attorney-General. Kennedy had become concerned with the growing extent of youth crime and he had set up a President's Committee on Juvenile Delinquency and Youth Crime, actually an interagency team from the departments of Labor, Justice, and Health, Education and Welfare, directed by David Hackett, a close friend. This committee accepted a theory of delinquency that had been advanced by two sociologists from the Columbia University School of Social Work, Richard Cloward and Lloyd Ohlin, a theory derived from Robert Merton's hypothesis of the relation between "social structure and *anomie*." Delinquency, they argued, is not an individual pathology, to be "cured" by psychiatric or social work therapies. Lower class youths, they said, do have conventional goals (e.g., success), but face a disparity between what "they are led to want and what is actually available to them." Delinquency then, is an illegitimate means of achieving what the society prescribes. In the formal language of the two sociologists, "delinquency is not . . . a property of individuals . . . it is a property of social systems in which these individuals and groups are enmeshed." The major task, therefore, for those who wish to eliminate delinquency must be to reorganize the slums and to create new "functional substitutes for traditional structures." In short, one must provide the slum youngsters with realistic opportunities for social mobility, and to do this one has to create, not just jobs, but a whole new way of life, a new community.

This theory was translated into practice in Mobilization for Youth, a project on the lower east side of New York. By 1963, to cite Sundquist, "the work of the President's Committee on Juvenile Delinquency and Youth Crime had become 'a $30 million test of Ohlin's opportunity theory.' " The MFY demonstration included employment programs, work preparation, evaluation and guidance, skills training, antidiscrimination activities, remedial education, home visits, and neighborhood service centers. More importantly, the Cloward and Ohlin theories about community action, and Ylvisaker's faith in the efficacy of experiment as the means whereby community goals would emerge out of experience and self-organization (a quixotic fusion of John Dewey and Quaker philosophy), became the ideology of the Kennedy-Johnson antipoverty program and the basis of a putative "participation revolution" in American politics.

The Intention To Change

There is no legislative history as to the meaning and intent of Congress in providing for maximum feasible involvement of the poor in the Economic Opportunity Act's definition of "community action." Adam Yarmolinsky, one of the legislative drafters of the act, recalls that, "the requirement of 'maximum feasible participation' was incorporated into the language of the bill from its very first draft; but it was thought of simply as the process of encouraging the residents of poverty areas to take part in the work of community action programs and to perform a number of jobs that might otherwise be performed by professional social workers. . . . The possibility of major conflict between the organized poor and the politicians in city hall was simply not one that anybody worried about during this period, although Shriver and his associates did see the possibility of conflicts between city hall and the poverty community on the one side and the organized social work hierarchy on the other side."[5]

But this vague intention did contain an implicit commitment. As Wofford puts it, the "key—and often unstated—objective of the Community Action Program [was] institutional change." And, as Leonard Chazen, in a study of the act (in the *Yale Law Journal*, March 1966) writes: "section 202 (a) (3) . . . has been commonly interpreted as a mandate for federal assistance in the effort to create political organizations for the poor."

None of this was "planned" by social scientists. It was implicit in the intention of the Great Society to include the poor and the blacks into the society, just as the New Deal had included labor and the farmers. As James L. Sundquist writes, in summing up the American Academy of Arts and Sciences Project: "The decision to set the new and revolutionary institution in the midst of every American community, all at once, was made not by social theorists but by politicians—or, more precisely, their speech writers. The key word that ordained all that followed was neither 'maximum,' 'feasible,' nor 'participation,' but 'unconditional' from President Johnson's declaration of 'unconditional war on poverty.' That set the tone from which there could be no retreat. That this would mean the organization of the poor for a frontal assault on the power structure in city after city—merging inevitably into racial conflict—was not planned by those who wrote the language of the Economic Opportunity Act any more than it was foreseen by those who accepted and enacted it."

What some of the social scientists only dimly sensed quickly became a reality: that for the indigenous leaders of the poor, particularly the militant blacks, the movement for "participation" became a drive for "power." This challenge was aimed at the local political machines, and was correctly understood as such by the local politicos. In San Francisco, black leaders succeeded early in 1965 in taking over control of the Poverty Program, and they sought to use the program to build a political base for black control. Plans were laid to have a part-time community organizer for almost every block and a full-time organizer for every eight blocks. Little of the monies went into services for the residents. In the political struggle within the black community, and between it and city hall, the original black leaders lost out. In Philadelphia, a program dominated by independent blacks was pulled back to city hall influence, though not with total city hall control. In New York City, the situation was reversed. The Poverty Program was used by the Lindsay administration to build a new political base by putting the black militants on the community action payrolls, tying them in with the Urban Action Task Forces, and using them as a battering ram against the older political machines.

Whatever the political outcome, the fact remains that a new institutional structure began to be built into the American political system. The question whether local community groups will *control* particular programs—schools, health, housing—is still being fought out. But the *participation* of the community is no longer in doubt. The Johnson administration felt that the Poverty Program had gone too far; but in setting up the Model Cities program it realized that little could be done without community participation, and that act stipulates that local community groups have to be consulted in the drawing up of new neighborhood plans. (Mindful of the experience of the Poverty Program, it provides that the control and final decisions over the plans are to be lodged in the mayor's office and in city hall.) The Nixon administration has chosen to expand the Model Cities program, rather than the Poverty Program, as its instrument for the basis of a coherent urban policy, and the participation of the local community will be further institutionalized under that scheme. How far and how effective the "community revolution" will be in American political life remains to be seen. In the remainder of this essay we shall explore the extent of that change, as it has become manifest in New York City, and raise some questions about the meanings and extent of "community participation" for the political structure of the society.

The Community Revolution in New York

The "community revolution" has been more extensive—and, one might say, explosive—in New York than in any other city in the United States. The reasons for this lie largely in the inchoate nature of the political system of the city.

First, as we have noted earlier, there was a receptivity to the idea of decentralization, and this had led to the establishment of local planning boards in Manhattan and the demarcation of planning districts in other boroughs.

Second, there was strong ideological support for the creation of local community structures, both from the reform elements and from the liberal establishment in the city, particularly the foundations. Depending on the ideological position one holds, one can describe these efforts as either helping the blacks to full citizenship, or as "cooling" a tense and heated situation (particularly after the rioting in Watts and Newark), as (as the SDS puts it) a "counter-insurgency" tactic by McGeorge Bundy to blunt a revolutionary upsurge by the exploited. However one depicts the motive, the fact is that a number of the "activist" foundations (Ford, Taconic, New World) financed a significant number of community demonstration projects in different parts of the city. The two most contentious were the Ocean Hill-Brownsville school districts and the I.S. 201 complex in Harlem. These two educational efforts were given a high degree of autonomy by the Board of Education and, until the teachers strikes, had come under considerable "community control."

A third, and somewhat different, impetus were the decisions by Kennedy and Lindsay to cultivate the blacks and the poor in order to create a new political base as against the older dilapidated machines. Kennedy, aided by wealthy Wall Street friends, such as André Meyer of Lazard Frères, set up a corporation in Brooklyn's Bedford-Stuyvesant district to help rehabilitate the neighborhood and he brought in a former Justice Department assistant, John Doar, to head up this effort. Through the Poverty Program and the Urban Action Task Forces, Lindsay built an extensive network of contacts in the ghettos, and put a large number of street leaders on the Human Resources Administration payroll.

Encouraged by these attentions, but in greater measure arising out of the new upsurge of black militancy, a large number of new, indigenous leaders emerged in the neighborhoods to play a role as community activists. What they quickly discovered is that their ability to "holler" and to threaten violence would give them, if not control, then at least a veto over government projects in their neighborhoods. Thus, the rise of CORE in Harlem, or the Afro-American Teachers Association, or the dozens of other new organizations, became a fourth dimension in the community revolution.

But behind all this there is the simple fact that in every major area which touches on the lives of people, especially in social services, the prevailing federal legislation now calls for community participation, and in New York, because of the political climate and official encouragement, the community movement has spilled over into more areas than in any other city in the country.

Nine Community Systems

Despite the importance and proliferation of the community efforts, the extraordinary fact is that nowhere in the city administration is there a single office which keeps track of all the community and neighborhood programs, coordinates the information about (let alone the overlapping jurisdictions of) these programs, or maintains a register of community leaders in each neighborhood and in each program, in order to assess the representativeness of the participation.

From what we have been able to piece together, there are nine different "community systems" in the city—nine areas, each comprising a number of different programs in which "the community" is supposed to have a voice. The nine are: Planning . . . Community Development . . . Health . . . Housing and Urban Renewal . . . Model Cities . . . Police . . . Youth Services . . . Urban Action Task Force . . . Schools.

In all these areas, as we said, "the community" is supposed to be involved. But what does this mean? We can try to gauge what participation means, in practice, by considering two programs, Poverty and the Model Cities.

The Poverty Program

Although the idea of community participation may have been launched in the Poverty Program somewhat inadvertently, its career is by now quite deliberately molded. A significant number of persons have acquired a stake in its future and do their best to swell its tide. A significant number of others fear the consequences of the escalation of demands upon the political system, to which community participation contributes, and would like to curb its rise. By now, the latter intent is probably futile and possibly dangerous. As Jeremy Bentham noted long ago, it is psychologically harder to lose than simply not to gain, and as the urban poor have almost acquired the status of having something to lose, they are not about to give it away quietly.

The question is no longer *whether* but *how* to involve "the community" in the processes of decision; and officials, planners, reformers, and politicians now vie with one another in claiming that their programs and methods achieve the most and the best of that elusive attribute, participation. There is widespread recognition that once the original phases of dramatic chaos and exciting turmoil have been outgrown, the militant young hotheads often do not participate in the developed processes of participation—the meetings between community groups and government officials, the public hearings, the elections for local boards, the consultations and deliberations. But there is also a growing recognition that, in providing the possibilities for meaningful participation, the supports on which the militants erect their rhetoric are weakened. "The difference between us and them," said a well-dressed, hard-working black poverty program official in his thirties, "is ten years. We used to think, too, that the only thing to do was to tear it down, but now we're trying to change the system from the inside, and sometimes we think there's a chance."

The Poverty Program's claim to have developed a significant degree of participation by the inhabitants of the ghetto in the planning and operation of services designed to help them is a fair one. In some ways New York City has gone further than most other cities; 25 of the 51-member city-wide Council Against Poverty (set up in September 1966) are representatives of the poor who are selected by the 25 communities designated by the city as poverty areas. On the Council Against Poverty are also 17 public officials, including the Mayor, Borough Presidents, the Superintendent of Schools and the Administrator of the Housing and Development Administration. Nine seats represent labor, business, religious, racial, and civic groups designated by the mayor as eligible to send a representative. Council Against Poverty sets priorities among antipoverty efforts, gives final approval to program grants using both city and federal funds, and supervises the setting up of what are called—one does not yet know whether the term is unfortunate or instructive—local "Community Corporations." In New York City, one-third of the members of Community Corporation boards must be directly elected by the poor; two-thirds of the members must be residents of the area; and, in most plans, one-third of the members must be, in the literal sense, poor—that is, have incomes below the poverty line. The Community Corporations screen and recommended program requests and operate programs or subcontract for them with "delegate agencies" at an even more local level. Twenty-five Community Corporations have now been formed.

The numbers of poor people who have taken part in the elections for these boards are not large, and are sometimes cited as percentages of the total inhabitants of an area to discredit the reality of participation: 5,276 voters out of a total Bedford-Stuyvesant population of 250,000, and 3,991 out of 190,000 residents of East Harlem, are not high percentages, although the numbers of eligible voters who take part in these elections sometimes run as high as 10 percent. The more significant issue is how these levels of participation compare with whatever participation existed before, and here the picture is more impressive. Participation in the Poverty Program has involved much more than mere reshuffling—the reorganization of people already caught up in the block associations and parent organizations into new groups. It has drawn in many new members, and propelled them through its processes to a point where a sanitation worker from Bedford-Stuyvesant chairs a Council Against Poverty committee on which some of the highest officials of the city government sit.

What has not always been anticipated is that the more the community is drawn into the process of consultation, participation, and advocacy of its own interests, the closer it may come to demanding that it be the final authority as well as a source *for* its own programs, able to summon outside funds and expert advice, but maintaining the most prized and constantly sought power—the final say. When one set of persons moves closer to power, however, another set is displaced; and the Poverty Program's early efforts to achieve the specified "maximum feasible participation" by organizing the poor to pressure the politicians has led to an inevitable reluctance on the part of those in the established structures to be shouted at or bypassed. The result has been a compromise. In 1967 Congress amended the original Economic Opportunity Act to require that one-third of the membership of bodies allocating Poverty funds consist of public officials.

Model Cities

The road to participation is, of course, not as straight as some advocates of the war on poverty have presented it. Because community participation threatened to develop into a drive for community control, a different mode was devised within the Model Cities program. There it is emphasized that participation does *not* mean control, and when a New York City Model Cities Neighborhood Director is pressed to discuss how the line is drawn for the Model Cities program, he repeats his most carefully chosen words, "It is the *Mayor's* program."

The federal Demonstration Cities and Metropolitan Development Act was passed in 1966. In New York City an executive order by the mayor in 1967 set up a Model Cities Committee composed of the Director of City Planning as chairman, the Director of the Budget, and four other persons including the HRA administrator and the acting chairman of the Council Against Poverty. Mrs. Eugenia Flatow, a former co-leader of the reform Riverside Democrat Club, became executive secretary.

Three areas in the city, populated by some 900,000 residents, have been designated as Model Cities Neighborhoods and have received planning grants from the federal government's Housing and Urban Development agency. These are Central Brooklyn (including Bedford-Stuyvesant, Brownsville, and East New York), Harlem-East Harlem, and South Bronx (including parts of Mott Haven, Morrisania, and Hunts Point). Sixty-five million dollars were set aside for these three areas, $28.8 million of it for Central Brooklyn. Plans for the expenditure of the total $65 million were approved by HUD in June 1969, and HEW has made another $5 million available.

Although the Nixon administration has decided to spread the effort more evenly and more thinly, the Model Cities approach in New York has been to concentrate its efforts on a multiplicity of ills in a few selected areas. Planning proceeds under the rubrics of physical development, education, economic development, sanitation and safety, and multiservices. As Mrs. Flatow explains the guidelines under which the Model Cities program operates, existing city agencies are given "first crack" at getting accomplished what needs to be done—whether it be rehabilitating houses or improving police-community relations. But where an existing agency "cannot or will not" operate a needed program, Model Cities can and will develop and carry out alternative means.

Spelling this out in greater detail, staff members explain that if local residents want, more than anything else, to get the garbage service improved, the Model Cities staff will seek to circumvent the contract provisions whereby the city's sanitation workers refuse to go beyond the building line in front of which all garbage is to be placed—which leaves yards and alleys and vacant lots untouched. And if the local residents want the paying jobs involved, instead of hiring outsiders, Model Cities planners will try to devise a way to hire trucks and give the local people jobs as sanitation "assistants"— so that the sanitation "workers" will not call a city-wide strike to protest this threat to their job waiting lists and their prestige. Again, if the poor in Brooklyn express their opposition to outside builders from Queens constructing their projects, arrangements will be made to put aside the usual bidding requirements, demanded by the Comptroller's Office, in order to favor possibly less efficient local contractors, who will give jobs to local blacks and Puerto Ricans, many of whom will have tried, unsuccessfully, to join building and construction trades unions.

On balance, what are the gains and what are the losses of participation? There is some dispute as to whether or not it actually lengthens the time required for action to be accomplished. Major

Owens, head of the Community Development Agency, and an ardent advocate of participation, estimates that the benefits are worth the effort even though it "at least doubles the amount of time required to accomplish any task in the areas of planning, budgeting, and evaluation." Donald Elliott, Chairman of the City Planning Commission, claims that, in the long run, working with community groups shortens the time needed for planning urban renewal projects before construction can begin. To go ahead without participation, and then to meet strong opposition, causes the most serious delays. "Obviously," he says, "if the city is going to give community groups the responsibility to determine their own destiny, it has to allow them to resolve their own internal struggles. We have found that the community, when given the actual responsibility of having to resolve problems by themselves, solves them better without interference from the city administration."

One seasoned black participant admits with some sadness his conclusion that "leaders don't grow on trees," but he remains convinced that if efforts are to be more than temporary handouts, they must contribute to the organizing of the poor to assert themselves.

Some of the political problems that have arisen have been serious. There have been ugly battles over who truly represents whom, racial differences among the poor have been exacerbated, racial hatreds towards those with jobs and power have been inflamed, and the whole question of the effectiveness and wisdom of inciting the poor to pressure the politicians has been questioned by knowledgeable students of American society and by friends of the poor.

At a theoretical level, one might wish to assert that, if there were no costs involved in arriving at decisions, everyone should participate in every decision, even to the extent of yielding nothing involuntarily. James Buchanan and Gordon Tullock, in their book *The Calculus of Consent*, have written that "if the costs of organizing decisions voluntarily should be zero, *all* externalities [i.e., disadvantages to persons] would be eliminated by voluntary private behavior of individuals. . . . There would, in this case, be no rational basis for state or collective action. . . . The choice between voluntary action, individual or cooperative, and political action, which must be collective, rests on the relative costs of organizing decisions, on the relative costs of social interdependence."

But in the real world the costs in time, energy, delay, and wasted funds, of decisions in which individuals talk out their differences and voluntarily arrive at agreement, can be very high. And the more numerous the individuals participating in the deliberations, the higher such costs become. The less justifiable these costs for a given kind of issue appear to be, the more attractive becomes the alternative of imposing a decision from above, by a federal or city bureaucracy. But there the costs are hidden by administrative procedures and by the seeming "efficiency" of issuing decrees or plans by fiat. Such procedures do not gain consent, and the virtues of a participatory scheme—despite the rancors and irrationalities it may engender—are that the final product is the work of those whose lives are affected by the decisions that are made.

The commitment to participation, it seems to us, is inescapable in the kind of multigroup society in which we live. The real sociological problem—and this is the set of issues to which we finally turn—is the definition of the participating unit itself—the neighborhood or community—and its relations with the other political and sociological entities in the society.

The Boundaries of Community

To sum up: two problems have emerged for city government in recent years, that of the decentralization of functions because of the unwieldy administrative structures, and the claims of community decision (particularly in the black areas) over these functions. The two are not necessarily the same. Decentralization, in most instances, as in government or corporate enterprise, means giving a high degree of autonomy to subordinate administrative *officials* within a centralized policy structure. Community decisions represents a political shift in the locus of control. In recent years, the two modes have become fused. Decentralization has come to mean community decisions and, as in the campaign program of Norman Mailer, the cry has even become "*all* power to the local neighborhoods." The difficulty with this slogan, so redolent of an earlier revolutionary time, is in the complication of defining a neighborhood both in communal and administrative terms.

A neighborhood becomes a community when there is a shared life and purpose built around local institutions. In New York, one can identify, historically, six overlapping types of neighborhoods. Traditionally, there are the neighborhoods built around kin and church, family life and synagogues. Religious buildings are the oldest symbol of community, and within a strange area they are the first marks of identification. Thus, there are the Catholic, Protestant and Jewish neighborhoods.

There are, second, the ethnic clusters, such as Polish, Irish, Italian, who even though all Catholic, still congregate among their own; as do, of course, German, Ukranian, Jewish, Chinese, etc. The distinctive food stores and specialty shops make these sections visible.

There are, third, subethnic clusters of a highly defined kind— the Hassidic Jews in Williamsburg, the Sephardic Jews in Bensonhurst, the West Indian Negroes in Harlem—who cling to each other even more tenaciously than do the larger ethnic groups of which they are a part, intermarry more frequently, engage in specialized crafts and occupations (diamonds for the Hassidim, embroidery for the Bensonhurst Sephardi) and maintain a high clannishness among themselves in distinct geographic districts.

There is, fourth, the segregation by income and class, as in the upper east side along Central Park, or in Brooklyn Heights or Riverdale.

Fifth, there is the neighborhood defined by function, such as the university enclave around Morningside Heights.

And, finally, there are the *quartiers* marked off by a distinct style of life, such as Greenwich Village or East Village, or, more numerous, yet less well known, the neighborhoods of rooted middle class home ownership such as in Bay Ridge, east Flatbush, north Bronx or Staten Island, which, too, have a distinctive style of life.

Most of the "natural" neighborhoods of the city are in Brooklyn, north Bronx and the older sections of Queens and Staten Island. These are "natural" clusters, self-defined by individuals in relation to each other. The continual shifting about which takes place because of upward social mobility, or changes in the life cycle (i.e., having small children, or children leaving home), tends to redefine neighborhoods, such as the departure of the Italians out of east Harlem into home ownership in the north Bronx, or the movement of the Germans out of Yorkville, the Irish from the west side, etc. But in the last twenty years this process has been distorted by a number of rigidities. Rent control has frozen movements which would have taken place under normal circumstances, such as keeping elderly persons and small families in large apartments along West End Avenue and Riverside Drive. More importantly, deliberate social policy, by the federal government and the city, has sought to mix income classes and neighborhoods by placing low income projects in high land-cost areas, or by mixing low income and middle income housing projects. The very act of beginning slum clearance during a tight housing shortage shortly after World War II, and locating these new projects in dense and high land-cost acquisition areas, wreaked further havoc. At that time, Nathan Straus, then housing administrator, proposed that any new low-cost housing be located in Staten Island, Queens, the north Bronx, and the outlying sections of the city. There, low rise, garden type developments could be built cheaply. But he was shouted down by political leaders in Harlem who feared the dispersion of their voting base, and attacked by liberal reformers for proposing that low income persons be forced to travel a considerable distance to work. The result was that, as the city began to remake the faces of east Harlem and the East River drive with project housing, the displaced inhabitants were dumped onto the west side, where landlords began cutting up the large apartments into small rabbit warrens, and the pattern of neighborhoods became a shambles.

The large influx of Negroes and Puerto Ricans in the postwar

years, amidst the upheaval in social mobility, created a further problem of definition of community. Once jammed largely into Harlem,
the blacks (and Puerto Ricans) have spilled over into south Bronx
(Hunts Point and Morrisania), east Harlem, the lower east side,
Brownsville and Bedford-Stuyvesant in Brooklyn, and pockets of the
west side in Manhattan—taking over, largely, the areas vacated by
Italians, the Irish, and the Jews. Here are concentrated the dilapidated and slum housing, the oldest school buildings, and antiquated
hospitals and clinics.

But even Harlem, as a once settled area, has suffered the fate
of the other ethnic sections of New York. From the 1920's to the
1940's, Harlem had its own "Society"—the Negro doctors, lawyers,
ministers and entertainers who lived in Hamilton Grange, Sugar Hill,
Edgecombe Avenue—the sections in north Harlem and the rocky
heights fronting the Harlem River facing the Bronx. These persons
gave a coherence to the area. Today, while many may still work there,
the Negro middle and upper class lives in Hastings, New Rochelle,
Amityville, and other suburbs in Westchester or Long Island. Dances
once held in the Savoy Ballroom are now held in the Americana Hotel.
What is left is the street gangs and the jungle.

There is no single Harlem "community," a veteran observer of
black life has remarked. There are different groups of activists, each
of whom has staked out a claim on an issue. If you want to open a
business in Harlem—a branch say, of a brokerage house or a bank—
you go to the Harlem Chamber of Commerce, or to Roy Innis of
CORE, and clear it with them. If you want to appoint a principal of
a school, you go to another group. The Harlem Architects Committee
(ARCH), which led the fight against Columbia's intention to build
a gymnasium in Morningside Park, has no constituency, but it has
the ability, as do many of the multifarious groups in Harlem, to put
any "outsider" on the spot. What unites all of Harlem is essentially
an anger at "The Man," and groups compete in utilizing and exacer-
bating this anger. The new activists, thus, have no authority, but
they do have power: the power to interfere, to raise hell, to shut
things down.

This process has been accelerated to a considerable extent by
the Lindsay administration which, in seeking to make contacts in the
ghettoes, has provided recognition, some status, and some patronage
for the militants. As one of the heads of the Urban Action Task Force
explained: "When you have to go in and cool the ghetto, the older,
established church groups or political clubs don't count; you have to
find the local 'influential.' " As anthropological lore, or for political
firefighting, all of this is very true and highly relevant. But what the
Lindsay administration has also sought to do is to use this indigenous
leadership as the base for its own political machine and to bypass the
established groups who, traditionally, have been allied to the Demo-

cratic Clubs. In short, what the Poverty Program and the Lindsay administration have tended to do is to "place their bets" on the militants and activists as the source of new community leadership. What may be effective for local political base building is not, however, functional for institution-building and strengthening of community ties.

The Decentralized Crazy-Quilt

If it is difficult, sociologically, to define neighborhood communities in New York, then, administratively, there is a worse mess. There are, as we have pointed out, at least 9 community systems now operative in the city, plus other services which have local offices: 62 Planning Districts, 25 Community Corporations, 35 Urban Renewal areas, 3 Model Cities projects, 30 Health Districts, 76 Police Precincts, 30 School Districts, 22 Urban Action Task Forces, 5 Neighborhood City Halls, 58 Sanitation districts, 15 Fire Department divisions, 42 welfare centers, 14 offices of the Bureau of Emergency Repair Services, etc.

The Citizens Union, when it proposed dividing New York City into districts "for more orderly planning and decentralization of services," recommended, it may be recalled, that all city services in each district be grouped in one location so that each district could develop its own plan in cooperation with the City Planning Commission. But the startling fact is that almost *none* of the present community boundaries, as it turns out, correlate with divisions of police, school, planning, etc. Neither is there much relation between the community planning districts and the political boundaries of districts, especially the councilmanic. If the city councilman is supposed to be the local representative in city hall, as the state assemblyman or state senator is in Albany, then the major political lines should have some determinate relation to the service and administrative boundaries; but they do not.

The City Planning Commission, which most recently had to wrestle with the problem of defining communities, had no real guide. The 1961 City Charter, which mandated community planning boards, stated: "Such districts shall coincide, so far as is feasible, with the historic communities from which the city has developed and shall be suitable as districts to be used for the planning of community life within the city." But there is not in the charter, perhaps prudently, any definition of what is meant by "historic communities" and no elaboration about the orbit of concerns which are to be encompassed in "the planning of community life" within the city. The commission, in setting down the boundary lines, sought to use "old names," but its chief criteria for districts was the identification of certain "cores" (e.g., Morningside Heights, Greenwich Village, Bay Ridge, Ridgewood) and to look for "communication barriers" such as waste land or major highways as the boundary lines. As the commission noted, in its own defense: "Stable and continuous areas containing persons with the same culture, have not been characteristic of New York. From its earliest beginnings, as an outpost of the Dutch West India Company, the city has consisted of a thrashing diversity of peoples, tongues, customs, national backgrounds and beliefs existing in proximity of each other."

The Accommodation of Conflict

A number of extraordinary changes are taking place in American life and, in conclusion, we can deal only schematically with these changes and the problems they pose.

There is, first, the increasing "politicalization" of society, particularly in urban affairs. Activities which were once allocated through the market are now subject to political decisions or political controls. Previously the question of who was to be housed where, would be settled through a "rationing by purse." Today, the decisions as to where housing is to be sited, what tax abatements are to be given, what proportion is to be reserved for low income or for municipal housing, etc. are made politically. And this carries over into many other areas as well. The sociological question is whether a society, this society, can carry such an increasing burden. The classical effects of politicalization are clear: the decision points are visible, rather than dispersed. The consequences are plain, for people know "whose ox will be gored." There is an overconcentration on law and legislation, and an increasing burden on administration. All of this, inevitably, increases the potential for group conflict. One of the chief reasons why in the last twenty years New York has been deemed to be "ungovernable" is the increasing politicalization of decision-making.

Second, a group of "new men" have come into the political system, specifically among the blacks. They are angry and they feel deprived. Their goal, in many instances, is not integration or the sharing of power but the control of their "own" institutions and enclaves. Yet two things are remarkable about this movement. The projects in which a large number of the new leaders are employed are federally-funded. And second, other than schools and a few local services such as health and the like, there is little possibility that the blacks will achieve control of major economic or political resources, for the locus of these resources are not in the neighborhood or community. To this extent, a whole series of unrealistic expectations are being generated in the black communities which may boomerang badly. What the black leadership may be able to achieve is a significant bargaining power, or even a veto in many instances, of city policies, but the talk of the ultramilitants about gaining control of the "major" institutions of society is unreal. The outcome will either be some accommodation or an increase in senseless rage. Despite the ultramilitant talk, the likelihood, still, is of accommodation.

Finally, we have seen the emergence, in a formal way, of the idea of "group rights" as the means whereby disadvantaged groups, particularly the blacks, can establish their claims in the system. The focal point here is education and it lies in the demands of the blacks for control of the schools in black districts, and for a quota or some preferential system in the colleges. This demand has brought the militant blacks squarely into conflict with the teachers union, which has felt its position threatened by the demand. It has raised the ugly spectre of anti-Semitism because a number of the blacks, particularly those in the leadership of the Afro-American Teachers Association, have deliberately made anti-Semitic statements in order to frighten away Jewish teachers and particularly Jewish principals from schools in the ghetto.

Three issues are involved in the argument for group rights. One is that of merit: the question whether a person should or should not achieve a position on the basis of his demonstrated ability, or whether a proportion of posts should be allotted on the basis of group membership. The second, allied to it, is that of common culture. The argument, made by Rhody McCoy at Ocean Hill, for example, was that any principal from the civil service list would be white, but that a white principal could not understand or guide a black child. Such an argument strikes at the traditional understanding of a common education and raises the question whether, in the future, all education in the major American cities may not be parochial or segmented by class or race. Third is the question of representation. Should there be majority rule or proportional representation; and if the latter, by geography or by group? When the New York State legislature proposed the election of a city Board of Education by boroughs, the Rev. Milton A. Galamison cried that the bill "deprives the blacks and Puerto Rican people of representation . . . Whenever we get into this nose-counting business, it's to the disadvantage of blacks and Puerto Ricans." And the administrator of Harlem's IS 201 district, Charles Wilson, agreed, saying: "The notion that the elected board will democratize the system is not so." What are the appropriate answers?

These divisive questions of political rights and political philosophy conjoin with a different set of problems that arise out of the nature of the size of the polis in a modern society. In a brilliant essay in the *American Political Science Review*, for December 1967, "The City in the Future of Democracy," Robert A. Dahl raised the question, "which is no longer a subject of discussion among political scientists," of what "is the optimum size for a city." And, he remarks, "the evidence seems to me . . . that the all-round optimum size for a contemporary American city is probably somewhere between 50,000 and 200,000 which, even taking the larger figure, may be within the threshold for wide civic participation."

Not only has there been little discussion on the optimum size of a city or a "quarter" of a large city, but there has been little thought as to what is the appropriate size and scope of the appropriate social unit to handle what problems: i.e., what services and functions can be left to a neighborhood or community, what has to be handled on a borough or city level, what has to be conducted in a region, and what has to be federalized? All that we have are shibboleths. We have the traditional decentralizers such as Paul Goodman, or the regionalists, or the federalizers. But nowhere is there a detailed examination of what functions of government are best handled at what levels of government.

A few suggestions may be hazarded, but they must be tentative. They involve ways of separating kinds of decisions in such a way that some are best decided at the periphery by participatory discussion and voluntary agreement, and some are best decided at more central levels, not only in order to arrive at such decisions with dispatch, but also to be able to bring local interests into line with wider, more regional considerations. An example of such a division of decision-making power is the way the Human Resources Administration divides antipoverty funds between the various poverty areas according to impartial, mathematical calculations of the areas' poverty index. But then, once the amounts have thus been centrally fixed on the basis of such formulas, decisions on how to spend these funds are allowed to reflect the ebbs and flows of local sentiment and preference. Another example is the way the central Council Against Poverty decided this year, also on the basis of general and quantifiable criteria, to establish priorities to which all Community Corporations would be expected to allocate 70 percent of their funds. These priorities are "Education Action, Manpower Action, Economic Development and Consumer Education, and Housing." Within the bounds of these general requirements, the localities can then pursue these objectives in ways that satisfy the particular moods, tastes, and nonquantifiable enthusiasms of their members. In the field of housing, central and long-range decisions on appropriate relative proportions of low and middle-income housing units can be recommended, within which communities can develop the housing projects that seem to them most humane and habitable. And central decisions on the allocation of funds for education according to fairly abstract principles of justice can still make possible neighborhood determination of the particular ways to spend such funds.

Behind the notion of optimum level is not just the question of administrative efficiency. There is the larger question, which is the theme of this essay, of participation. One virtue of participation is a simple one. It not only creates a basis of community, by allowing people to share in decisions that affect their lives, it is also a deeply conservatizing institution for, like property, it gives people a stake in the decision which becomes binding on all.

Participation, however, is not the end of politics, as it seems to be in some of the rhetoric of the new left. It is the beginning, for politics arises in the first instance when one realizes that there is no such thing as *the* people—that no single decision can please all people. There are only *peoples*, with contradictory and conflicting ideas and interests. Suggest a jetport near some builtup area and a committee will arise to save 'our' community; locate an airport on a swamp, and there will be a committee to protect the wildlife; suggest a floating airport and a group will form to keep our lakes and waters clear of pollution.

A rational politics, to the extent there can be one, is bounded by economics, that is the recognition of the principle of relative scarcity and the necessity, therefore, of bargaining as a means of allocation and adjudication within some principle of justice. If in a multigroup society, within which there is to be effective participation, social conflict is to be regulated within bounds, then, just as mechanisms for economic bargaining were worked out in the 1940's and 1950's which brought the trade unions in the society, so mechanisms for political bargaining have to be established which allow for a tradeoff of objectives between groups. This means a more formal recognition of political groups, just as there was recognition of trade unions, and the establishment of rules of the game, within boundaries of defined communities within which the bargaining can take place.

But if economics deals with relative scarcity, politics includes the effort to gain relative advantage; and this is a never-ending process in human affairs. The political problem is to make sure that the process takes place within bounds and does not tear the society apart. And this possibility can only be realized if one strengthens that most fragile of social relations—the trust that each person has in the other that the rules of the game will be observed and that each will have his chance to participate.

Notes

1. Theodore Lowi, "Machine Politics—Old and New," *The Public Interest*, No. 9 (Fall 1967).
2. In Chicago, the political structure is still sufficiently strong to serve as an integrative mechanism. Negroes coming into Bronzeville (the long central strip on the south side in which blacks are congregated) are met by the local precinct captain who provides services, information and

job leads, in exchange for votes. For in Chicago, the political machines are still operative. (To reverse the Lowi paradox, Chicago is governed, but not well-run.) The rackets, and the revenues derived from them, are still intertwined with the machines, and unlike Harlem, the major black political organization in Chicago has a monopoly on the rackets in the black areas.

3. "The Politics of Local Responsibility," in James Sundquist, ed., *On Fighting Poverty* (New York: Basic Books, 1969).

4. Daniel P. Moynihan, "The Professionalization of Reform," *The Public Interest*, No. 1 (Fall 1965).

5. "The Beginnings of O.E.O.," in the Sundquist volume, *op. cit.*

IRVING KRISTOL

Decentralization for What?

The major story on page 1 of *The New York Times* for November 17, 1967, reported that the Model Cities Program was getting under way:

> "The Administration made public today a list of 63 cities . . . that will take part in the first phase of the model cities program . . .
>
> ". . . The winners will share $11-million in planning money appropriated by Congress last year. The exact amount of each grant will be worked out in negotiations between federal and local officials.
>
> "After the cities have drawn up detailed plans and submitted them to Washington, they will become eligible for $300-million appropriated last month to carry out the rebuilding process."

At first glance, this looks all too familiar—a recipe for bureaucratic nightmare, after the fashion of the older urban renewal program, now generally thought to be something less than a success. You will have a small group of experts in the sixty-three cities—men who will, for the occasion, be presumed to be highly knowledgeable about slum life, slum people, slum buildings, slum real estate, etc.—trying to come up with a blueprint they can sell to their local constituencies and to their Washington overseers. You will have a smaller group of presumed experts in Washington, working desperately to make sense of the detailed plans submitted to them, hoping against hope that the plans will actually be carried out as intended, worrying endlessly (and legitimately) about whether the reports they are receiving "from the field" have any connection with what is really happening. Very few of the experts will, of course, be expert enough to avoid

Irving Kristol, "Decentralization for What?" *The Public Interest*, no. 11 (Spring 1968), 17–25. Copyright © 1969 by National Affairs, Inc. Reprinted by permission of National Affairs, Inc.

major miscalculations. And even if they were, there would still be the delays imposed by bureaucratic red tape to throw their calculations into disarray. In short: a typical social welfare program that threatens to metamorphose into one controversial shambles after another.

Only, in this case, there is something new. The men who devised the Model Cities program were alert to the problems of bureaucratic mismanagement. They therefore wrote into the law a provision for "popular participation" in this bold new venture into city planning. To get its allotted funds, each of these sixty-three cities has to demonstrate to Washington's satisfaction that citizens' governing boards in the affected neighborhoods "participated actively in planning and carrying out" the program. These boards are now being formed via popular election. In Atlanta, a white neighborhood has elected a couple of Ku Klux Klansmen. In Detroit, in a half-Negro, half-white neighborhood, the board is all-Negro. Officials in Washington are reported to be very upset at the ways things are going.

Which leads one to contemplate the possibility that there is more than one kind of bureaucratic nightmare—and that the worst kind may yet turn out to be of the "anti-bureaucratic" variety.

The Right Problem at the Wrong Time

Americans have never taken questions of public administration too seriously. To do so is to suggest that there may be inherent limitations on the execution of the popular will (and our democratic ideology discourages such a notion) or that the natural capacities of the average American may be inadequate to the detailed tasks of government (a national heresy since the days of Andrew Jackson). But the experience of liberals during the Kennedy Administration was a critical one. Whereas they had previously scoffed at criticisms of "bureaucracy"—by conservatives in general, and businessmen in particular—they soon discovered that there really was such a thing and that its power to thwart or distort social programs was never to be underestimated. Just as most intellectuals only get interested in education when their children start going to school, so the liberal intellectuals around John F. Kennedy suddenly found themselves getting interested in public administration when they discovered that their good ideas and fine intentions got mangled on the way to achieving reality.

The simple fact, they learned, is that the number of programs the political and sociological imagination is capable of inventing always exceeds the number of available people who can realize these programs *as intended*. You always end up with programs being carried out by a bureaucratic hierarchy that understands them only imperfectly and possibly may not even be much interested in them at all.

So it became proper for liberals to talk about the problems of "bureaucracy" and of "centralization," and many started doing so. As a matter of fact "decentralization" has in general become a very fashionable idea. Thus, where political scientists used to argue that municipal government was incapable of coping with the problems of the city and that larger, more comprehensive metropolitan governments were needed, this argument has suddenly been reversed. In his recent presidential address to the American Political Science Association, Robert Dahl pointed out that the population of New York City is about the same as that of Sweden, and that New York is "badly in need of being broken up into smaller units for purposes of local government." Indeed, Professor Dahl took a dim view of any unit of local government that encompasses more than 200,000 souls.

So far, so good. We have become keenly aware—and it's about time, too—of the deficiencies of overly centralized planning and overly centralized government. We are all decentralists now. But, unfortunately, liberal intellectuals do seem to have an uncanny knack for focusing on the right problem at the wrong time, and in the wrong way. They have opted for decentralization with the same kind of enthusiastic abstractness they once brought to centralization. They have slighted, when they have not entirely ignored, the supreme political consideration—circumstance. For, as Edmund Burke long ago observed, "Circumstances . . . give in reality to every political principle its distinguishing colour and discriminating effect. The circumstances are what render every civil and political scheme beneficial or noxious. . . ."

I shall have something to say later about the most significant "circumstance" that today affects (or should affect) our efforts at decentralization. But, first of all, it is worth taking a look at the way the *idea* of decentralization became the *ideology* of decentralization.

Populism and Neo-Populism

We have, during this past decade, witnessed a mounting anxiety about the fate of democracy in a mass, industrialized society. We have simultaneously witnessed a sharp upsurge of populism in American feeling—both on the left and (to a somewhat lesser extent) on the right. A "credibility gap" has emerged which separates the citizen, not merely from any particular administration, but from government itself. As a result, the need for "visible government" (in Mayor Lindsay's phrase) and the importance of "participation" (in just about everyone's phrase) has become widely accepted among social critics and social reformers. The vision of the American people regaining a lost political heritage through a revival of "the town meeting" within our large urban centers has become exceedingly attractive. And, since there is no blinking the fact that ours is a complex and interdependent society, the constituency for such "town meetings" is frequently redefined along "functional" lines, so as to transcend mere locality and encompass all those involved with one governmental program or another. Has not Sargeant Shriver roundly announced that "welfare without representation is tyranny"?

At about the same time, various sociologists, psychologists, anthropologists, and social theorists came to the conclusion that conventional populism was not enough. The people had not merely to be "involved" or "consulted" so as to gain their active consent. The people had to "participate" in their democracy in a very special way— i.e., through "social conflict." What these social critics had in mind was no reconstituted New England town meeting of any kind: *that* was a vehicle for consensus. Rather, they entertained images of mass picketing, rent strikes, organized boycotts of local merchants, harassment of all official bureaucracies, etc. Activities such as these, it was insisted, were necessary to the mental health and spiritual uplift of the people, and especially the poor and dispossessed among them.

Just where this particular ideology came from, and how it achieved its popularity, is an interesting question but, for our purposes, an irrelevant one. (Obviously, it had more to do with an initial animus against the status quo than with any ripe sagacity about the difficulties of public administration in a large democracy.) In any event, it came to be accepted by many eminent authorities and respectable institutions. The Ford Foundation has been a leader in stimulating this novel version of populism. A group of scholars at the Columbia School of Social Work has also played a notable role in sponsoring a neo-populist rebellion against "the welfare establishment." The New Left has made it clear that, in its eyes, "participatory democracy" was essentially connected with the class struggle. And black nationalism in the ghettos has learned to insist that true democracy is essentially connected with race conflict, and indeed is quite simply Black Power.

The whole business has by now become a thoroughly confusing tragi-comedy of errors. And no group has been more confused than our governing authorities. Congressmen who voted for Community Action Programs and all sorts of "maximum participation" clauses, thinking they were striking a blow against "bureaucrats" and in favor of "the grass roots," are beginning to wonder what they have wrought. In desperation, they resort to the only kind of defensive action they can think of: indiscriminately cutting the budget for social services.

The Schools of New York

Meanwhile, the impulse to decentralization, oblivious to its own ideological muddle and blind to circumstance, gathers momentum.

The most sensational venture of the "new decentralization" is the Ford Foundation's program for turning over New York's public schools to locally elected school boards. This is not the occasion to go into a detailed critique of the Ford plan. Suffice it to say that in my opinion—and it is not mine alone—Ford's plan will drive white parents out of integrated (i.e., mixed) neighborhoods, white children out of public schools, and white teachers out of the city altogether. It will have the same effect on many middle-class Negroes. In addition, it will certainly result in inferior education for Negro children in the central city, as experienced white teachers move (or are moved) elsewhere. All this will be accomplished in the name of "decentralization" and "neighborhood self-government"—which, in reality, will mean school boards that polarize and intensify all latent racial political conflicts in any particular section of the city.

It is conceivable—let us even say it is probable—that, had the Ford program been introduced fifteen or twenty years ago, it would have represented an improvement. At that time, the politics of the Negro community centered around the demand for "integration," and Negro leaders would have had considerable latitude in negotiating with whites over the manner and matter of education. This is no longer true. The dominant political ethos of the Negro community is now black nationalism.[1] So far as one can see, this ethos will become stronger rather than weaker in the troubled years that lie immediately ahead. This being the case, the popularly elected school boards are going to be forums for conflict and hostility rather than cooperation and communality. They are going to be weak and turbulent authorities, not strong and resolute centers of direction. (Indeed, where such school boards already exist, on an advisory basis, this is precisely what is happening.) And if, after the initial turmoil and chaos, they should become strong and resolute, they are very likely to behave in a thoroughly racist way.

Decentralization Confused with Democracy

To criticisms of this kind, which have been directed against its plan for reorganizing public education in New York, the Ford Foundation has only one strong rejoinder: the present system doesn't work. It would be more accurate and more candid to say that the system "works" no less well than it ever did, but that it has not been able to cope with lower-class Negroes as it previously coped with, say, lower-class Italians. (Essentially the same thing can be said about our welfare system.) Still, it is clear enough that New York's public education system, even when and where it works, is very efficient in enforcing petty regulations, extremely inefficient in coping with new problems or new opportunities. There is indeed, then, *in the abstract*, a valid case for decentralization. But, even in the abstract, what kind of decentralization?

It is always a good idea, when reforming an institution or a program, to take guidance, not only from general principles or preconceived opinions, but from comparable institutions and programs that do seem to work. Now, not all of education in New York City is out of popular favor. The affluent private schools, on the whole, are well regarded by parents, students, and teachers. So are the anything-but-affluent parochial schools, which the majority of Negro parents would be delighted to send their children to, were there room for them. What is it that makes these schools acceptable at the least, desirable at the best?

The answer has nothing to do with these schools being run on principles of local democracy which they are not. It has everything to do with these schools being run on principles of *delegated authority*. Specifically, the reason these schools "work" better is that they are governed by headmasters who have considerable managerial power, managerial discretion, managerial immunity to outside pressures (*including* parental pressures). From what I have seen of public school principals in New York City, they compare favorably enough to private school headmasters. What they lack is any kind of real power to do a good job.

I am not unaware of the difficulties involved in conceding to them this power. Indeed, the difficulties are just about identical with those the Ford Foundation program is likely to encounter, but with the tumult swirling around the choice of principal instead of the school board. In any case, I am not here interested in arguing the case for one particular kind of educational reform as against another. I wish only to stress a significant, and frequently misconceived, point: decentralization is one thing, democracy is another. The government of Sweden is far more decentralized than the government of New York City, but it is not thereby more democratic. Indeed, the Swedish government is probably *less* democratic than is New York's—and better governed.

Or, to put it another way: *decentralization, if it is to work, must create stronger local authorities, not weaker ones. Effective decentralization does not diffuse authority; it takes the power that is diffused throughout a large bureaucracy and concentrates it into new nuclei of authority.* Before we commit ourselves to any scheme of decentralization, we ought to make certain that this particular reconstitution of authority is what we really want. And I find it instructive to note that many of those who favor radical decentralization of education in our Northern urban regions are simultaneously demanding the extension of federal bureaucratic controls over education in the South.

The Most Important Circumstance

In the United States today, the key "circumstance" that ought to affect one's attitude toward decentralization is the relationship between black and white—the present racial tensions we dare not ignore, the future integration we dare not despair of. Every reforming enterprise must, first of all and above all, take its bearings from this circumstance. It is always useful to inquire to what extent we can decentralize our cumbersome service bureaucracies (in education, welfare, housing, perhaps even policing.) But it is even more useful to inquire to what extent we can decentralize our services *without fractioning our heterogeneous political community*. I am not saying that, under present circumstances, such decentralization is always undesirable. I am saying simply that we must always ask *whether* it is, in the light of these circumstances.

Indeed, were it not for the racial heterogeneity of this nation, the organization of our social services would be a relatively superficial problem. Politicians, of course, might kick up a big fuss about one thing or another. But whichever way the issue were resolved, it wouldn't make all that amount of difference. Take education, for instance. To begin with, were it not for the race issue, it might not be widely regarded as a "problem" at all. (In the all-white neighborhoods of Brooklyn, Queens, and Staten Island there isn't even as much dissatisfaction with the New York public school system as, in my opinion, there ought to be.) Second, if one wished to experiment with various forms of "decentralization," one easily could—whatever controversies they engendered would not be more damaging than, say, present controversies in smaller communities over local school board issues. (In these controversies, feelings run high—but only temporarily.) Third, one could even contemplate experimenting with quite radical reforms that go beyond "decentralization"—such as extending "consumer sovereignty" to the educational sector by abolishing "free" schools and distributing educational expenditures (in either cash or vouchers) to parents, who could then shop for schools as they please. The important thing is that, whatever was tried or not tried, whatever worked or didn't work, would not seriously affect the shape of the American republic or its ultimate destiny.

But we *are* a racially heterogeneous nation. And we *are* committed to creating a racially integrated society.[2] This fact and this commitment are—and ought to be—dominant in our minds. It is therefore of great importance that the major impulses toward "decentralization" now come from the white segregationists in the South and the black nationalists (together with their white, radical allies) in the North. Should these impulses prevail, the task of molding this country into one nation will be made infinitely more difficult, and perhaps impossible. The statesman's responsibility is to resist these impulses where he can, to "contain" them where he cannot resist. "Decentralization," in practice, has come too often to mean the hasty "appeasement" of these tendencies.

The School as Scapegoat

There are two further—and not unimportant points—to be made:

1. "Decentralization" is not likely to solve any of the problems of education in our Northern ghettos.

The sociological evidence seems to be conclusive that the schools themselves have only a partial—maybe only marginal—impact on broad educational achievements. What we glibly call the "problem of education in the ghetto" is probably little more than an aspect of the problem of poverty. Though a devoted, imaginative, and inspiring teacher can always make a difference, in any school, any time, there's not much point in asserting that what the ghetto needs is masses of such teachers: they just don't exist in the mass. Nor is there any evidence that changes in the curriculum matter much; or new school buildings as against old; or even smaller classes as against larger ones. What does count is the environment, as established by home and community. The basic fact is that middle-class Negroes, living in middle-class neighborhoods (whether integrated or not), do *not* have a "crisis in education." Centering one's attention on the schools is an effective way of distracting one's attention from the far more important realities of poverty and discrimination.

One can understand why residents of the slums should be tempted to make the schools scapegoats for all of their frustrations. One can even understand—though with less tolerance—why government officials should join in this witch hunt, denouncing the schools for failing to achieve what no schools can achieve. But it is less easy to understand why social scientists in general should wish to participate in this demagogic campaign. Perhaps they do so for the same reason right-wing groups also tend to make the school a center of controversy: they feel impotent to engender controversy about anything else.

2. It is an accidental fact, but an important one, that *our large and cumbersome bureaucracies, in such fields as education, welfare, and in the civil service generally, happen to play a crucial role in integrating large numbers of middle-class Negroes into American society.* These bureaucracies are, in truth, the best-integrated sectors of American society. To this end, they "work" exceedingly well. Decentralization of these bureaucracies will almost certainly mean disintegrating them. We shall end up with only Negro teachers in Negro schools, only Negro police in Negro neighborhoods, only Negro social workers handling Negro clients, etc. That, in my view, would be a major step backward. And I take it as a terrible irony that the idea of "separate

but equal" should, fourteen years after the Supreme Court's *Brown* decision, become so dear to the progressive heart and mind.

Even among the various racial and ethnic minorities themselves, decentralization is already furthering conflict. In New York City, the anti-poverty program is pitting Negroes against Puerto Ricans in open hostility, with each side claiming that the results of local elections to the governing boards of various agencies are "unrepresentative." And, indeed, since so few people take part in these elections, the consequences are bound to be haphazard. The city is trying to cope with this problem by issuing directives that set "correct" numerical ratios, according to race, creed, and color. Since neighborhoods are always changing their ethnic complexion, these directives are subject to constant, and mathematically refined, revisions.

Nor is that all. If this kind of apportionment is to continue, someone will have to decide *who* is black, white, or in-between. This is less simple than would appear at first sight. A group of Negro employees of New York's Community Development Agency have opposed a Negro candidate for the post of commissioner on the grounds he is "not really black." The group informed both the city authorities and the press that it reserved the right to define blackness.

I began this essay by suggesting that, at this time and this place, bureaucratic nightmares might not be the worst imaginable nightmares. I also believe that, if by some miracle these bureaucracies did not now exist, we should have to invent them, as an indispensable mechanism of racial integration. Come to think of it, if we *did* invent them, and gave them a fancy over-all title (Office for Professional Equality?), we should flatter ourselves on having taken a great stride forward to the Great Society.

Decentralizing these bureaucracies remains a valid and important long-term objective. But in these times, under these circumstances, it is precisely the wrong objective.

Notes

1. I am not saying that the majority of Negroes are, or ever will be, black nationalists—except perhaps in a highly attentuated and rather passive way. But it seems clear that no Negro group will be able to *oppose* black nationalism without committing political suicide. The anti-nationalists are already in the process of being transformed into "moderate" nationalists.

2. One of the arguments of those who propose decentralization along racial lines is that "integration" is turning out to be a will-o'-the-wisp, anyway. I think these people have an erroneous and highly utopian notion of integration. Yes, of course the proportion of all-Negro or predominantly Negro schools is increasing in our central cities, as the Negro population of these cities grows. That is inevitable. But I would argue that this is a stage in the process of integration, rather than some kind of contrary tendency. The Irish, the Italians, and the Jews also flooded their local schools, in

their time. Integration doesn't mean instant assimilation. It doesn't mean—has never meant in America—that a new ethnic group is going to be warmly welcomed into the bosom of the old. It means, to begin with, the establishment of a checkerboard pattern of ethnic neighborhoods—and many Negro "neighborhoods" are now emerging in different sections of New York City, for instance. (We mindlessly persist in calling them all "ghettos," but many people who live there don't think of them as such. After all, even in Bedford-Stuyvesant some 15 percent of the residents are homeowners.) Every day, and in almost every way, New York City is becoming much more "mixed up" racially than it used to be. Decentralization can freeze the pattern and reconvert neighborhoods back into ghettos.

ROGER N. BALDWIN

Have Public Employees the Right To Strike?—Yes

The distinctions commonly made between the right of workers in private industry and those in the public service to strike will not stand up under examination. They are based on no solid considerations of either the public welfare or of civil liberties. They arise from an unthinking hostility to "strikes against the government" as if all strikes of public employees are somehow or other political in motive. Along with that prejudice runs the substantial practical objection to strikes in certain essential services whose cessation would be catastrophic to the whole community—notably the firemen and police. The spectacle of this catastrophe is made to justify denial of the right to strike in the entire public service.

When the right to strike is thus denied, the argument is commonly extended against all trade unionism in the public service. It is alleged that because government does not function for private profit public employees are not exploited. It is maintained that since civil service employees enjoy pay, tenure, and pensions fixed by law, and not available to private employees, they need no other protection. Even when it is conceded that the conditions of civil service employees can be improved, the remedy is held to lie not in trade union organization but in pressure on legislative and administrative agencies.

The whole conception appears to be without substantial merit. Let us take the latter arguments first, since they can be most readily met.

Roger N. Baldwin, "Have Public Employees the Right to Strike? Yes," *National Municipal Review*, vol. 30 (September 1941), 515–517. Reprinted by permission.

While government does not function for profit the pressure for economy often produces precisely the same effects in low wages. Arbitrary authority in the hands of politicians and administrative officials bears down with the same results on public employees as on private. Protection by trade union organization is the only practicable method for counteracting such pressures.

While it is true that civil service employees enjoy advantages not commonly shared by workers in private industries, these advantages are far from meeting all needs. Practical experience with unions in the public service demonstrates their usefulness in adjusting and reforming scores of practices not covered by civil service law or regulations. Anyone with any experience in administration knows that no employer or administrator is capable of sensing from on top the needs of an army of employees. Only those who actually compose the rank and file of employees appreciate fully their own problems and are capable of speaking for themselves.

It follows that when remedies are sought from legislative bodies unions of employees are of great assistance in formulating grievances and demands. The voice of organized labor is frequently the only effective means of directing the attention of both the legislature and the public to injustices in the public service. This has been so long apparent in the relation of teachers to the school system and the community that it only needs to be stated to make the argument conclusive.

Strikes Not Political

As to the more dramatic aspect of trade unionism involved in the right of public employees to strike, we should dismiss at once the notion that such strikes are in any way aimed at the function of government itself. The Columbia University study of over one thousand strikes in the public services shows that not a single one of them had political motivation. They were aimed at particular politicians or administrators, not against the government as such. They are in that respect exactly like strikes in private industry.

The more substantial argument against strikes in the public service rests upon the fear that the essential functions of governments may be paralyzed, and that the government therefore has the right to insist that its services be not interrupted.

Let us at once exclude from consideration the case, so commonly cited, of policemen and firemen, for they perform a unique service in which it is not unreasonable to require that the right to strike shall be surrendered. In the comparatively few cities with unions of policemen and firemen they have commonly waived the right to strike, recognizing the exceptional character of their occupations. In a very few cities the right is denied by law. The basis for distinguishing policemen and firemen from other employees necessarily rests on the catastrophic consequences to the community of a strike, since substitutes cannot be recruited nor any emergency provision made for replacing their function.

We are met with the rejoinder that if this is true, the distinction applies equally to employees of public water works, electric light plants, hospitals, buses, street railways, subways, and a host of other services. But in all these services either emergency crews can be substituted sufficient to carry on essential functions, or, as in many strikes, the unions themselves provide for their continuance by a skeleton force to meet emergency needs.

Identical services in many communities are not in the hands of public agencies, but private utilities. Nobody, I think, argues that strikes in privately-owned utilities should be prohibited; yet the considerations of public inconvenience and danger are precisely the same. It therefore seems a reasonable distinction to place in one category, where the right to strike may be denied, those essential services which are by their nature operated exclusively by public employees—firemen and police—and to accord the right to strike in services which are variously performed by either public or private agencies.

The arguments against the right to strike in the public service tend to lose sight of one persuasive fact. That fact is the sense of community loyalty which most public employees so deeply feel. To them, as to others, a strike is a weapon of last resort. It is never lightly entered into at the behest of leaders or Communist intriguers, as is so often charged. In the public service, as the record shows, the tendency to strike to redress wrongs is far less than in private industry. Not only is this true because of the attitude of public employees to their work, but because they have channels for the settlement of grievances not open to private employees. Public attention can be aroused and support enlisted, as it cannot be for private employees.

The arguments against strikes in the public service fall a bit flat when the actual dangers are so fanciful. The Columbia University study showed only sixty-six in police and fire departments, navy yards, arsenals, and armories. Excluding the navy yards, arsenals, and armories in peacetime—where a strike could hardly be regarded as catastrophic—the dangers so commonly visualized were obviously trifling.

It remains only to note one false issue which has confused the discussion—the closed shop in government employment. It has been raised not by the unions but by public officials fearful that unions might demand it. No union whose members come under the civil service has done so. It should be clear that the closed shop is wholly incompatible with requirements that appointments be made by competitive examination and with the provisions for tenure and promotion under the merit system. Union membership in government agencies under civil service must obviously be entirely voluntary.

The controversy over the rights of government employees to organize, bargain collectively, and strike is only a phase of the larger trade union conflict rapidly nearing a stable solution. The long resistance of private employers to trade unions is being conclusively broken. Congress has refused so far to curtail the right to strike even in defense industries, recognizing the very practical consideration that the country cannot get production by coercion. Slowly we as a nation are coming around to the concept that voluntary measures alone will settle the conflicting interests of capital and labor, employers and employees. The practice of genuine industrial democracy with free trade unions and honest collective bargaining will go a long way to avoid the desperate resort to strikes.

In the public service, as in private, unions and collective bargaining should be encouraged as essential to industrial democracy. Our democracy is incomplete so long as it is confined to the arena of politics. The public service should lead the way in model practices, adding to the guarantee of the civil service system the protection afforded only by independent organizations of employees dealing freely with their superiors.

H. ELIOT KAPLAN

Have Public Employees the Right To Strike?—No

Expansion of government in fields viewed heretofore as within the exclusive province of private enterprise prompts the suggestion that the relationship between government and civil employees needs to be considered anew. Where employees in private industry are brought into the civil service it is not surprising that they carry over earlier precedents and customs, and with them ideas which may prove to be inimical to government administration and impractical of application in the public service.

Two major factors have tended to persuade some people toward new concepts of the relationship between government and its em-

H. Eliot Kaplan, "Have Public Employees the Right to Strike? No," *National Municipal Review*, vol. 30 (September 1941), 518–523. Reprinted by permission.

ployees: (1) the National Labor Relations Act, which significantly excepts government service from its application, and (2) extension of governmental activities—the transition from a policing and regulatory government to a servicing government.

At the outset it should be made clear that the right of public employees to organize for their mutual welfare as they see fit must not be denied. The only issues that need concern us are, first, to what degree should public employees be permitted to affiliate with outside labor unions or organizations, and second, to what extent should the rights and privileges accorded to private employee unions and organizations be extended to similar associations of public employees.

Many civil service employee organizations have long been affiliated with public employee organizations of other jurisdictions. Many of them have been affiliated with labor unions—local, state, and national. Both the A.F. of L. and the C.I.O. have been vying with each other in persuading civil employees to join their ranks.

The people are generally aware of their responsibility for the economic welfare of their own employees. They are also aware that public employees owe a certain responsibility to the people.

The issue is not solely whether the public employee should be devoted exclusively to the people's interest but rather whether he should be responsible only to the people and not to a political boss, a demagogue, or a labor leader. Fundamentally, that is the crux of the problem. If we miss this concept of public employee responsibility to the people alone, under our democratic system, we are bound to misunderstand the proper relationships in public employment.

Just how far public employees should be permitted to join with outside labor unions must depend on what the purposes of such affiliation may be and the obligations assumed by public employees under such outside affiliation. Political machines and arrogant administrators have, of course, thrown many a monkey wrench into attempts of civil service employees to organize. They have sought to control employee organizations for their own political or administrative purposes—a practice which closely resembles a "company union" idea. In attempting to meet this occasional difficulty we must be careful not to permit other abuses or practices equally detrimental to the people's interests to take its place.

Purposes of Affiliation

The public may view with suspicion any affiliation between public employee organizations and outside labor unions unless there is some patently direct interest which they both share. One can well understand a community of interest between carpenters in civil service positions and carpenters in private employment, for instance, or between machinists or motormen in their respective fields. But what desirable purpose can there be in affiliation of a union of municipally employed clerks, patrolmen, gas inspectors, or engineers with a C.I.O. or A.F. of L. union of hodcarriers, instrument-makers, or garment workers, other than the selfish purpose of overawing a city or state administration or a department head, by a show of solidarity, into making unwarranted concessions which cannot be justified on their merits and which may be against the public interest? One would have to be naive indeed to assume that administrative officials can exercise their judgment untrammeled by a combined, highly organized pressure group, particularly if the labor or employee leadership falls into unscrupulous hands.

It is one thing for civil employees in a local jurisdiction to affiliate with other civil employees in a state or national organization for their mutual welfare in educating public opinion as to their common needs and seeking to persuade the people toward certain policies affecting them. It is another thing, however, for civil employees to affiliate with outside labor unions primarily for the purpose of using their combined strength to coerce action that may be utterly inimical to the people's interests and to employ methods which run counter to orderly governmental and democratic procedure. The people must not tolerate the use of the civil service by irresponsible labor leaders for purposes that could place the people at the mercy of their very own employees, such as a sympathetic strike wherein civil employees are dragged into a situation in which they themselves have no direct interest. It is conceivable that they can be used in some cases actually to overcome the will of the majority in a community, particularly when the tactics employed to coerce action in private industry are injected to coerce administrative action.

If this seems fantastic, let us weigh the implications of the civil employees' strike recently called in Racine, Wisconsin. There the employees of the city, aided by affiliated labor unions, brought pressure on the mayor and city council to meet their demands for salary increases. The city officials felt that the demands were unwarranted and resisted them. The city employees went out on strike. Other labor unions, it is alleged, threatened to join them in a sympathy strike. A hurried meeting of the city officials was called and, to prevent tie-up of the city's business and safeguard the people, officials yielded to the demands of the city employees.

The People Paramount

We must appreciate that it is for the people alone to decide what rights or privileges may or may not be granted to public employees by the people's representatives. Public officials act for the people, not for themselves—even if administrators seem to forget that elementary principle occasionally. The right to strike against themselves—the people—can be granted to public employees in given cases and under such circumstances as the people may choose. It is analogous to the privilege granted individuals by the people to sue the state. Regardless of private injury or loss, an individual may sue the state—the people— only to the extent granted by the people. In other words, not until the people recognize by law the right of public employees to refuse to obey their superior officers under specified circumstances and strike against the actions of public officials, is there any "right" of public employees to strike. No employee has the right to interfere with the orderly conduct of public affairs or to interrupt public services for the people without the people's consent. That is the difference between private and public employment.

It would be foolish to suppose that existing relationships between administrative officials and public employees are ideal even under the best administered merit system of today. Public employees should be granted the privilege to negotiate with public officials on matters of concern both to employees and the people whom they serve, such as the fixing of wages, hours, and conditions of employment, sick leave privileges, etc., or to adjust and remedy grievances. Unfortunately this privilege is too often denied them. Arrogant administrative "bosses" can be as tyrannical as the worst despot in private enterprise. But even so the civil employees may not take it in their own hands to interfere with the orderly functioning of government by striking against such a public tyrant. Do they strike against him or against the people? True, the majority of the people directly or indirectly are responsible for that arrogant administrator. But we cannot sanction the right of public employees to resort to a strike to force the people to oust the recalcitrant administrator who may have been elected or appointed for a fixed term. That is a right which the people reserve to themselves.

Who is to determine whether the particular administrator (representing the people) is right or wrong, the civil service employees? Suppose the administrator is trying to protect the public from concerted selfish action on the part of the people's employees, as in the case of an unreasonable wage demand far beyond the ability of the taxpayers to meet. Ought we permit employees to quit work and so attempt to coerce the administrator into granting their demand? Suppose an employee organization or a labor union affiliate disapproves of the dismissal of one of its number and all the employees walk out on the people in protest? This has actually occurred in more than one jurisdiction. Where does one draw the line as to just how far employees may go in attempting to coerce administrative action against the public interest? These are questions that need be given thought in any appraisal of the relationships in public employment.

Morale Important

It is, of course, decidedly in the public interest that those serving the people be a satisfied and contented group. Morale of their employees is a matter of vital importance to the people. The kind of service the people will get from their public servants will depend in large measure upon the treatment the public employees get from the people.

It is essential to the people's interest, however, that conditions of employment in the civil service be remedied in more or less the same general manner and orderly means as is to be expected of any other change of public policy. Civil employees have as great, and in many respects greater, opportunities to educate public opinion toward their view of problems as has any other class of citizens. If the people do not yet see it their way, it is up to the employees to crystalize public sentiment in their direction. If the method at their disposal is too slow for them, then they may properly agitate for a change in methods and machinery for more effectively and speedily meeting their problems.

Of course, public employees have the right to strike—if by that we mean that any individual has the right to quit his job. There is no general statutory prohibition outlawing strikes of public employees. Whether or not they have the right, however, is beside the point. Unwillingness of public employees by concerted action to serve the public can hardly be condoned. There is no inherent right of public employees collectively to refuse to serve the people and still retain the privilege of continuing in the service of the people. We would not recognize the right of motorists to refuse to pay their automobile license fees but still insist upon the privilege of running their autos on the public highways merely because they did not like the gasoline tax. It is no less offensive to the public interest for an employee because of a strike to decline to run the elevators in a public office building than for a hospital nurse to leave a dying patient and join a strike parade. A motor bus operator of a city-owned transit line may no more abandon his bus full of passengers to join in a "sympathy strike," than may a fireman leave a burning building to answer a strike call.

Many mental gymnastics have been indulged in by those who should know better in attempting to distinguish between the rights and privileges of public employees in one and another type of government service. It is easy for them to postulate that a policeman or fireman or health officer should not have the right to strike because that would rob society of an imperative protection. They would distinguish the "usual" governmental function from services they consider proprietary. They seize upon the classic case of a public utility taken over by a municipality and see no reason why the employee relationship should change merely because the city operates the utility in place of the private company.

Those who argue thus forget that the people have not chosen to take over a public utility until public necessity required it. A utility or function assumed by a city becomes a service for the people. Simultaneously the relationship of employees to the people must perforce change. Many municipal functions and services of a proprietary nature have heretofore been accepted in the same light of "usual" government service as have the police, fire, and health agencies. Water supply services, collection of garbage, and similar services have been long performed by municipalities. What was not a public need yesterday may become one tomorrow. The rights and privileges of individual employees under private ownership must yield to the public interest. The people become the new "boss" and the employees the people's public servants. Attempts to distinguish between one kind of public function wherein employees may continue to have the rights accorded them as private employees, and another kind wherein such rights are denied, just begs the question.

Collective Bargaining

Equally cogent issues beside the right to strike need to be weighed. Collective bargaining is one. There is no point in stressing the fact that agreements sought to be made by public officials and their employees are not legally binding on the people in the absence of express authority to make any such "contracts." Unless we have a general distrust of our public officials there seems to be no real purpose in encouraging, or rather insisting upon, formalized "contracts" of this nature. What may be informally agreed upon between administrators and employee representatives can be incorporated in a declaration of policies or rules or regulations promulgated by the agency after informal negotiation with employee representatives. Closer cooperation and better understanding between management and employees and a mutual appreciation of the problems on each side should be encouraged. This, however, is far from a system of collective bargaining such as operates in private industry, wherein negotiation may be had solely with an exclusive union or organization of employees which might bring in to represent it an outside organization or union in no wise directly concerned in the negotiations.

Discussion as to whether the closed or only the union shop is feasible or desirable in the people's service is also beside the point. The issue is not whether we should accept the principle of the closed shop as distinguished from the union shop, but whether it is desirable to have either system in the civil service. Advocates of the closed shop principle, while recognizing the closed shop as incompatible with an open competitive system of selection for public positions, urge the union shop principle in the civil service. The distinction is really only one of degree rather than of principle. Nor is it simply a question of whether the closed shop or union shop interferes with the competitive selection system.

The fear that lack of a union shop in the civil service would tend to break down the union shop system in private employment is unwarranted. Labor unions are well able to protect the closed shop or union shop system in private employment. They need not worry about encroachment by the civil service. The basic conditions that prompt necessity for a closed or union shop in private employment are generally absent in the public service. The purposes sought by a closed shop or a union shop in private employment are not suited for the people's service.

No "Super-Agency"

In private enterprise the relationship between employers and employees can always be subjected to government regulation, supervision, or even control. There is no "super-agency" that can step in to control, regulate, or supervise disputes between public employees and the people except the people themselves, through their representatives. Public employees, like any other class of citizens, have an equal right through orderly processes under our democratic form of government to petition the legislature and public officials for redress of grievances, adjustment of claims, and acceptance of their views. To encourage any class of citizens to ignore, or abandon in defiance of authority, such orderly procedure to gain its ends, no matter how justified its action may appear to be, would defeat our democratic process.

The public must guard against a potential danger that may be as formidable and uncontrollable as our dubious political organization machines—a self-perpetuating labor dictatorship, which could conceivably overcome the will of the people through control of governmental machinery manned by public employees. This is not a possibility to be dismissed as too fantastic. Situations have already arisen in some jurisdictions which should warn us to apply the brakes immediately.

If the two cogent issues referred to early in this article have not been adequately met and answered here it is because the relationship of public employees during this period of transition from a "policing" government to a "servicing" government is still in a state of flux, and we have yet to see and learn in just what direction it is best and safest to go. We may be reasonably sure, however, that the concepts of labor relations common to private enterprise and the practices indulged in by capital and labor are not practicable or desirable in the civil service.

Suggested Readings:
Responsive Government

ANDERSON, STANLEY V. (ed.) *Ombudsman for American Government.* Englewood Cliffs: Published for the American Assembly by Prentice-Hall, Inc., 1968. A thorough examination of the concept of the ombudsman and its possible use in the United States.

BACHRACH, PETER, and NORTON S. BARATZ. *Power and Poverty: Theory and Practice.* New York: Oxford University Press, 1970. Presents the thesis that participation in decision-making often means no decisions are made.

CRAIN, ROBERT L., ELIHU KATZ, and DONALD B. ROSENTHAL. *The Politics of Community Conflict: The Fluoridation Decision.* Indianapolis: The Bobbs-Merrill Co., Inc., 1968. Treats one of the most controversial subjects of the past two decades and examines its political implications.

FANTINI, MARIO, MARILYN GETTELL, and RICHARD MAGAT. *Community Control and the Urban School.* New York: Praeger Publishers, Inc., 1970. This comprehensive study of the participation issue in urban politics argues for community control.

GELHORN, WALTER. *When Americans Complain: Government Grievance Procedures.* Cambridge: Harvard University Press, 1966. An in-depth analysis of the methods used to deal with citizen's complaints against the government.

———. *Ombudsmen and Others: Citizen's Protectors in Nine Countries.* Cambridge: Harvard University Press, 1966. The most exhaustive treatment of the subject of protecting citizens from arbitrary governmental action.

9/The Future?

As one reviews the prior chapters on the controversies facing
state and local systems, it becomes clear that these governments face a time of increasing change and turmoil, both in
the tasks they undertake and in the way they perform those
tasks. Direct comment on the future course of the substantive
activities reviewed in this book, such as urban renewal and
law enforcement, will not be undertaken; it is sufficient to
note that these areas have been the focus of controversy in
the past and will continue to be so in the future.

However, the editors feel it is incumbent upon them
to comment on the procedural and structural changes debated
herein. The last essay, "The Future of State and Local
Government and American Federalism," discusses major
procedural and structural defects that are perceived to be
facing state and local systems, proposed corrections of these
defects, and the likelihood of major change occurring in the
near future.

Public perception of performance ability will determine
the type of change demanded; commitment to change will
ensure acceptance or rejection of suggested reforms. If a
perception of both low or inadequate performance ability *and*
a low or nonexistent commitment to change exists, the result
will be a decade even more marked by dissatisfaction,
alienation, turmoil, and violence than was the "violent '60s."
This is the theme of the concluding essay.

PARRIS N. GLENDENING
MAVIS MANN REEVES

The Future of State & Local
Government & American Federalism

All federal systems are unstable. This instability, produced by a universal dynamism that constantly moves the system, can be ranked on a continuum ranging from complete centralization (unitary government) to complete decentralization (dissolution of the federal structure).

What causes this motion? There appear to be universal pushes in both directions. Even if we have a federal system in which all major groups are satisfied with the degree of centralization (or decentralization), there would still be dynamic forces at work moving that system in the direction of a highly centralized federation, or, perhaps, even a unitary government. These forces include complex technology, defense needs, taxation systems, the need to regulate complex economies, and so forth. At the same time, major variables, such as a decentralized political power base and regional racial, religious, social, or economic differences, push in the direction of dissolution.[1]

What, then, permits a system to overcome the forces and remain effectively federal? A variety of explanations has been advanced. One of the more widely accepted theses is that of William H. Riker. He maintains that

> the federal relationship is centralized according to the degree to which the parties organized to operate the central government control the parties organized to operate the constituent governments. This amounts to the assertion that the proximate cause of variations in the degree of centralization (or peripheralization) in the constitutional structure of a federalism is the variation in degree of party centralization.[2]

He further observes that

> whatever general social conditions, if any, that sustain the federal bargain, there is one institutional condition that controls the nature of the bargain in all the instances . . . examined and in all others with which I am familiar. This is the structure of the party system, which may be regarded as the main variable intervening between the background social conditions and the specific nature of the federal bargain.[3]

Other comprehensive explanations have been advanced.[4]

The authors contend, however, that there is no single institutional or structural variable that by itself or in some ordered pattern with other variables will explain the outcome of the centralization-decentralization tensions. Rather, the future of a federal system will be determined by the viability of the various units making up that system.

Viability means the ability to perform functions assigned to the unit. Neither the citizens nor the decision-makers of a political system will permit the continued, long-term assignment of functions to a level of government unable to perform those functions. Thus, *performance ability* determines the amount of centralization or decentralization a federal system will realize. In fact, performance ability will be the major determinant in the continued existence of a federal system.

Long ago, the United States chose effective decentralization of political power. Further, this country chose to preserve maximal policy alternatives by maintaining a number of separate decision-making centers. In other words, the nation made a strong value decision in favor of an effective federal system.

Despite this decision, the tremendous international and military demands of the twentieth century, the requirements of economic regulation, the need to ensure a minimum standard of living for all citizens, and other pressures converged to push the system toward increasing centralization. Only the continued viability of state and local governments can prevent total centralization in the United States. States and localities must be able to meet demands placed on them or realize the transfer of those demands to the national government. The ability of state and local governments to perform effectively will determine the future of American federalism.[5] State and local performance effectiveness hangs on the threads of fiscal adequacy and structural change.

Fiscal Federalism

Since World War II, combined state and local expenditures have grown much more rapidly than federal domestic expenditures. Today, states and localities together spend more than twice as much as the federal government on civilian services.[6] One could, perhaps, then predict a sound fiscal future for those units of government.

Such a prediction cannot be made. The publicity-making financial difficulties of cities such as New York, Newark, Philadelphia, and Cleveland are being repeated in nearly every major city of the United States, as well as in many of the medium-size and smaller cities. The very real projection is that atypical events, such as the early closing of schools in Philadelphia and Youngstown, will become typical. The *Washington Post*, reporting on financial difficulties of cities, noted that St. Louis

> needs 600 more policemen to meet a soaring crime rate. It can't afford them. It needs a fire boat to protect its revitalized river front. It can't pay for one. Its maintenance programs for public roads and

buildings have been pared way back. Instead of repaving 50 miles of roads a year, it had been paving 22. Now, the city has cut back to 13 miles.[7]

Such reports are increasingly commonplace. The cities will not collapse overnight; they will go by degrees. As St. Louis' Mayor Cervantes states:

> Pretty soon people can see the trash piling up. And soon the potholes get deeper and the trees in the park don't get trimmed, and at the city hospital, people find they're waiting longer than they ever did before.[8]

The states, too, find themselves slowly sinking in a financial quagmire. While it is true that demands for government services always exceed available resources, the states are barely able to keep up with natural growth—population increases, inflation, technological demands. Each year more unmet needs and demands are "deferred for the next session."

What, then, of the future? Will the states and localities continue to defer needed expenditures until systemic tensions become so great the system breaks down? Will major functions increasingly be performed inadequately or not performed at all?

Unfortunately, the immediate projection must be one of guarded despair. Major segments of society can anticipate that most of their needs will be unmet because of the paucity of public resources at these levels of government. Alienation of urban poor will still be a source of crime and violence. Rural poor will still experience malnutrition, hunger, and an almost complete lack of social services. Education at all levels will continue in a manner that ensures inadequate performance. The transportation, public assistance, and public safety systems can expect recurring paralysis.

True, this dark picture is not universally valid for all states and municipalities all the time. And, as Robert C. Wood has noted,

> despite our predictions, disaster has not struck; urban government has continued to function, not well perhaps, but at least well enough to forestall catastrophe. Traffic continues to circulate; streets and sewers are built; water is provided; schools keep their doors open; and law and order generally prevail.[9]

Wood concluded, nevertheless, that while "we may not face catastrophe . . . this is no reason for countenancing one-hour commuting schedules, for permitting blight, for condoning the repellent sprawl of cheap commercial developments, inadequate parks, congested schools, mediocre administration, traffic jams, smog, pollution, and the hundred and one irritations which surround us."[10]

If we are to avoid such irritations, what is the solution to the financial bind of states and local governments? The traditional answer has two dimensions: (1) reforming and restructuring the existing state and local· revenue system, and (2) greater use of the adaptive devices of fiscal federalism.

The first approach places great reliance on (1) legislative reform of assessment and taxation laws; (2) improvement of technical abilities to locate, collect, and manage revenues; (3) creation of a more flexible revenue base; and (4) a more rational approach to the division of state and local revenues. The second approach looks for a greater and more "rational" use of the resources of the national government through a myriad of devices, including direct federal expenditures and assumption of functions—notably the politically unpopular and expensive function of welfare—grants-in-aid, revenue sharing, and possibly even a tax credit system. Literature on both the reform and restructuring of the state and local revenue system and on fiscal federalism is massive and need not be reviewed here.

How effective will these approaches be in meeting the fiscal crisis of state and local governments? The first approach will require great political effort; many people currently enjoy advantages under existing tax processes and structures. Massive resistance to change will continue to be mobilized effectively. More important, this approach gives very little additional revenue. At best, it creates a more equitable and flexible revenue base; and if greater reliance on income and user taxes is achieved, it helps to reduce some disparities in available resources between the central city and the suburbs.

The current grant-in-aid system has had, according to most observers, a major impact on state and local policy-making. This is most obviously true with reference to the state and local budgetary process. Budgets were influenced with regard to both level of expenditures and relative functional allocation. One 1965 study indicated that as much as 39 percent of the variations in state and local expenditures can be explained by the amount of federal aid received.[11] Most observers view this development with misgivings.

With regard to total state and local revenues, the national grant-in-aid policy obviously stimulates new demands.[12] The political implications of such new demands are evident. Less evident, but perhaps more important, is the pressure to pick and choose among areas of expenditure according to the availability of federal funds, rather than according to a more ideal democratic process. Increasingly, state and local officials express fears that decisions made without real alternatives are not decisions, but delusions of decisions. One student of fiscal federalism, elaborating on this theme, noted that

> . . . grants set conditions in which federal administrative officials may substantially restrict the policy action and discretion of elected state and local officials. Given the financial inducements and conditions attached to grants, the states and their local units are all but required to adjust their behavior to fit specified nationally-prescribed constraints.

> Federal grants bring about a direct confrontation between conflicting national and state (or local) policy preferences. National decision-making criteria and institutional forces have an entirely different constituency base from that to which state or local officials respond. Federal statutory and administrative requirements, for example, interject policy objectives that may conflict sharply with state and local views of what is desirable or necessary in a given program area.[13]

Any increase in the present federal grant-in-aid programs will reduce policy choices available to state and local officials. Since allocation of resources is the very heart of political power, this gives cause for careful thought.

Even more ominous to state officials is the increase in federal revenues given directly to local governments. This type of aid, confusingly referred to as "direct federalism," increased substantially in recent years. Resource allocation here becomes largely a matter of national choice, rather than local decision-making; state control becomes minimal.

Recognition of this loss of policy-making power is one factor leading to increased demands for consolidated or "bloc" grants-in-aid, that is, general grants for functionally related areas, rather than narrowly defined program grants. Since this adaptive device has been used in only a limited way to date—although it promises to be a major tool of fiscal federalism for the 1970s—we have little basis for analysis. Certain tentative observations can be made.

First, more alternatives will be available to state and local policy-makers. Yet choices will be still largely restricted. Major areas of expenditures will be determined by choices made in Washington, not in the state house or city hall.

In addition, while state and local officials may gain under this proposal, much of the original purpose of earlier grant programs will be lost. That is, bloc grants will not provide stimulus for particular types of functions. For example, if Congress decided a stimulus is needed for function X, under the present system it merely funds attractive matching grants for the performance of X. If, on the other hand, bloc grants-in-aid were used, and if X were a subset of functional grouping W, X, Y, and Z, the recipient government could spend all received funds on W, Y, and Z and entirely ignore function X. Any attempt to impose conditions on the expenditure distribution within the functional grouping would, in fact, be a return to the narrower grant-in-aid system.

Increased attention is being focused on alternatives to grants-in-aid, whether limited-purpose or bloc grants. This is the idea of revenue sharing. A minor revenue sharing plan, such as the provision of $5 billion currently being considered, would offer very slight relief when divided among fifty states and their local governments, no matter what the distribution formula. The impact of a major revenue sharing plan is uncertain. Therein is the basis of concern and caution. Such a plan is potentially one of the most radical changes our federal system has ever experienced.

Advocacy of a major revenue sharing plan is very much in vogue and has become politically very attractive.[14] Few notes of caution have been voiced. William Anderson, a recognized authority on fiscal federalism, hit hard at those who would adopt a revenue sharing plan without first carefully considering its impact on the viability of state and local governments. He noted that

> Walter Heller and some other economists look only at the dollars, the billions of dollars they want to give away. The effects of such a distribution of federal money as they propose on the long run self-government and responsibility of the states in the federal system is something they overlook or don't consider important. They propose a pork barrel to out-pork-barrel anything ever proposed. And of course the barrel will never be large enough to satisfy the appetites of the state spenders. It looks like "easy money" but easy come can also be easy go—or else Uncle Sam will have to control the states' expenditures as never before.
>
> This "tax sharing" proposal is not just a fiscal matter. Its ramifications are beyond calculation and prediction. I think the Heller proposal is as bad for the states as it is for the income tax payers.[15]

If such little relief is given through reform and restructuring of the state and local tax system, and if there are major dangers and misgivings in heavy reliance on grants-in-aid or a major revenue sharing plan, what alternatives are open for dealing with the state and local fiscal crisis? The authors see several that avoid many limitations and pitfalls mentioned above.

First is the possibility of major reductions in federal taxes, thereby permitting corresponding increases in state and local taxes. Such reductions may mean an overall reduction in federal activities, or there could be selective reductions.

Second, and closely related, is a tax credit system. A federal income taxpayer would be given a credit—a set percentage of his combined state and local taxes—subtracted directly from what he would normally pay in federal taxes. The credit could, of course, go as high as 100 percent. The use of tax credits has a long history of restricted application, such as federal credits for state inheritance taxes.

Advantages of this approach are clear. States and localities would be encouraged to increase their tax efforts without suffering immediate political backlash, since much of the increase would be deducted from federal taxes. Such a credit would draw heavily on federal resources; Congress would have to decide whether the loss could be offset by increased federal taxes or major appropriation cutbacks. The former approach offsets the rationale for a tax credit plan; the latter brings in the same type of political difficulties as federal tax reduction.

A major revenue sharing plan offers a third alternative. To be acceptable, however, it must be based on appropriate research into its impact on the federal system and its effect on the continued autonomy and viability of state and local governments. The distribution formula, administrative controls, and political guidelines must ensure that the prophecies of William Anderson and others are not realized.

Such a plan would overcome one major weakness of the first two alternatives. Namely, the distribution formula could work as an equalization device to ensure a greater proportion of funds to certain states. Added benefits could go to the poorer states, the states making the greatest tax efforts, or perhaps even those states deemed worthy of additional support because of their role in a national population redistribution policy.

By a major plan we mean one that offers a minimum of $15 billion a year to states and local governments. Ideally, this would be as much as $25 billion a year. Of course, the "gut" question is where will the money come from?

A fourth alternative is to transfer the most expensive functions upward to a more fiscally viable level of government. This has an inherent danger of considerable power loss by the transferring unit, but the loss may be offset by the gain in resources released for other functions. Other considerations, such as equalization in the areas of welfare and education, give merit to this approach. As in the case of revenue sharing, transfers should be made only after experimentation into the real effects of such changes.

Lastly is the obvious, but seldom debated, alternative of major tax increase at all levels of government. The "taxpayers' revolt" is a political revolt, not an economic one. With few exceptions, the present tax burden is not oppressive or disincentive to individual, group, or corporate taxpayers. Indeed, the combined taxes paid by the American taxpayer are still far less than those of his counterpart in most of the industrialized world.

These alternatives require either a significant increase in taxes, a reordering of public priorities, or a reduction or elimination of certain expensive "sacred cows," such as the space program or the agricultural support program. Are such changes politically possible? This question will be addressed again following examination of state and local government structure.

Structure of State and Local Government

Various forces press for change in state and local government. There is occasional mention of doing away with the states, but constitutional and political realities and normative justifications, such as decentralization of power, provision of "laboratories" for experimentation, and the maintenance of a pluralistic system, ensure that states are here to stay.

Within these parameters, the history of state government in the twentieth century is one of almost constant structural change and reform. An historical review of state governments since the 1909 Peoples' Power League of Oregon's initial thrust at twentieth century reform demonstrates continued change.

Chief among the changes are modernizing and streamlining of constitutions; substantial increases in the powers of governors; judicial reform; and greater representativeness, increased professionalization, and lessened constitutional restraints for the legislature. Other areas of change in state government are strengthened electoral institutions and greatly extended opportunities for popular sovereignty through adoption of the initiative, referendum, and recall.

Most urban states have substantially reordered relations with their local governments through legislative and constitutional home rule and by enacting enabling legislation for interlocal agreements, service contracts, voluntary associations of local governments, and participation in regional organizations.

The last major change that can be noted here concerns the scope of state government activities. Not many years ago it was commonplace to describe state governments as negative, regulatory, and reactive. This is no longer true. Most state governments today are positive agencies of social intervention. One only need look at the new state departments of community affairs, consumer affairs, and environmental protection to appreciate this trend.

Some of the major changes occurred not by the states' own volition, but because of external pressure of the federal courts. Federal court action was needed to reform the areas of apportionment, civil rights, and voting rights. Indeed, one hesitates to think of the possible action of some states if federal pressure lessened in these areas. Besides court action, some administrative reorganization and reform was required for federal assistance.

Not all states have made all the changes discussed. Regional patterns can be observed. Many states have repeatedly demonstrated an unreceptiveness to the types of innovation mentioned here. Walker's analysis of "diffusion of innovation" among the American states shows Mississippi, Nevada, Wyoming, South Carolina, and Texas to be least receptive, while New York, Massachusetts, California, New Jersey, and Michigan were most receptive.[16]

Many of the changes are symbolic, not real. Whether it be an administrative change required for federal aid, establishment of a human relations council to meet commitments made during a period of racial strife, or the creation of a community affairs department to fulfill a campaign pledge, the student of state government is faced with changes that in reality sometimes mask continuation of the status quo. Real change demands political and financial backing that is not always forthcoming.[17]

A final caution against unrestrained optimism emerges from lack of knowledge about the real, long-range impact of many of these changes. The reapportionment struggle offers an example. Prior to *Baker* vs. *Carr*, a glorious future was proclaimed for states and urban areas *if only there were fair representation* in the state houses and Congress. Under federal impetus, most states reapportioned on the basis of a "one man, one vote" formula. But where was the expected revolution in public policy? Things appeared to be just as they were before *Baker* vs. *Carr*. Urban problems were clearly growing more acute, not less. In a massive outpouring of research, political scientists and economists suddenly discovered that not much was likely to change.[18] Variables which ensured public policy would continue much the same as in the past included the incremental nature of the budgetary process, fiscal conservatism of the suburbanites—the biggest gainers under the 1962 decision—and the political astuteness of long-term rural legislators vis-à-vis their generally newly elected urban counterparts. Similar disappointments and misgivings are encountered in other reform areas.

In sum, the states appear to be making continuous, substantial improvements that better enable them to handle the problems facing them. The impetus for change can be questioned. In many cases, the sincerity and "realness" of the change appear dubious. The unevenness of progress among the states can be criticized. Yet a basic fact remains: On balance, the states are better prepared for the future than they have been at any time since the turn of the century, except in the financial area as discussed above.

Local governments realized parallel progress. Changes in urban administration, particularly adoption of the council-manager system in our suburban and medium-size counties and cities and adoption of the chief administrative officer (CAO) and other professional managers in our largest cities, are the most important post-1945 structural developments in the local political systems.

Despite improvements, a very real problem remains, that of governmental fragmentation in metropolitan areas. Simply stated, there are too many units of government in the metropolitan areas for effective government.[19] Area-wide problems are not being solved. The solution is in some type of integration, a basic belief of students of urban affairs since the 1942 publication of Victor Jones' *Metropolitan Government*.[20]

In addition to the political problems of policy planning and implementation in an urban area with many governments, there is the major problem of uneven resource distribution. The condemnation of the unevenness of resources and need is not of recent development but has been a basic reason for urging integration for years. What is new is the observation of an acceleration in the flow of wealth to suburbs and away from the problem-laden core cities.[21] The suburbs are not paying their share. Recognition of this increasing gap between resources and need has produced a new sense of urgency and crisis in demands for integration.

There have been numerous taxonomies of proposed methods for dealing with the problems of fragmentation. Roscoe C. Martin, for example, identified sixteen proposals and divided them into two categories. *Procedural adaption* includes informal cooperation, the service contract, parallel action, the conference approach, the compact, transfer of functions, extra-territorial jurisdiction, and incorporation. *Structural adaption* includes annexation, city-county separation, geographical consolidation, functional consolidation, the special district, the authority, metropolitan government, and the regional agency.[22]

With few exceptions, proposals to pull the metropolis together through major structural changes have failed. This is not entirely the result of voter ignorance of the problem. Factors such as traditional support for small local governments, voter conservatism toward major or radical reorganization proposals, racial and partisan divisions between central city and suburb, fear of high taxes, and an increasing need for areas of individual identification and participation combine to repeat the validity of Joseph F. Zimmerman's observation that "it is next to impossible to achieve a major governmental reorganization in a metropolitan area in the United States."[23] The few real successes, such as Miami-Dade County, Nashville-Davidson County, and Jacksonville-Duval County, are much in evidence because they are exceptions to the rule.

Even as these metropolitan government reorganizations are being turned down, the procedural methods of adaptation are coming under increasing attack. Some criticism focuses on the claims that these lesser devices of adaptation are too slow; ineffective in meeting recurring urban crises; unresponsive and undemocratic since many devices are "hidden" from the voters; actually complicating the fragmented structure further, since they often mean additional units of government; and unable to deal adequately with the problem of financial disparities. In other words, Martin's taxonomy is viewed along two continuums, that of effectiveness and that of political feasibilities (Diagram 1).

What is politically acceptable is seen as too ineffective, too slow, and so forth. What is perceived as effective is simply not acceptable to the voters.

This frustration paves the way for a "push from above"—the strong encouragement, perhaps even coercion, from the federal government, and to a lesser extent from the states, for substantial adaptation to deal with problems of local government fragmentation.

For the most part, initial federal activity was designed to stimulate regional planning efforts. The single most important tool used by the federal government to encourage regional planning has been to

Diagram 1.
Effectiveness

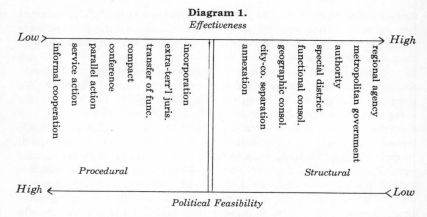

Low ⟶ ⟶ *High*

informal cooperation
service action
parallel action
conference
compact
transfer of func.
extra-terr'l juris.
incorporation

annexation
city-co. separation
geographic consol.
functional consol.
special district
authority
metropolitan government
regional agency

Procedural   *Structural*

High ⟵ ⟵ *Low*

Political Feasibility

require that applications for federal funds for most urban programs
be reviewed by an area-wide planning agency. This led to the accelerated creation of regional planning agencies, and today all the nation's
metropolitan areas have some type of multi-jurisdictional planning or
review agency. The review requirement has also been extended to
rural areas.[24]

The most controversial point about the development of these
review agencies is whether we are unintentionally and perhaps haphazardly evolving some type of metropolitan government. While
most people directly involved with the federal government and with
the review agencies would vehemently deny this possibility, statements that such a process is possible come from both practitioners
and academicians.[25]

These developments produce major concerns: Are we transferring major responsibility for determining local government structure to Washington? Will the combined impact of federal grant-in-aid
programs and regional councils' review powers further limit resource
allocation options of local administrators? If the planning agencies do
emerge as metropolitan governments or some similar authority, has
not the will of the people been circumvented? Regardless of the need
for metropolitan government, people have repeatedly voted: "No
Metro!"

Does not every restriction on the local policy-making process
place a direct obstacle in the path of responsive government? If the
review process, combined with availability of federal funds, becomes
a deciding factor in policy choices, is not responsible local government
much weaker? In particular, we refer to James Q. Wilson's comments
on the split between the audience and the constituency that is
emerging in many large cities, as well as our earlier stated concern
about local policy in a federal system.[26]

If metropolitan or regional government is politically unacceptable, if other means of adaptation are found wanting on several

accounts, and if there are major reservations about the national government's recent efforts to deal with the problem of local fragmentation, what is the future of local government in urban America? Daring new approaches must be considered. Conventional ad hoc, disjointed adaptations cannot be tolerated in face of crises that threaten the very existence of our social and physical system. We must in this area, even more than in the area of finance, begin to think the unthinkable. A few suggestions can be offered.

First, abolish referenda on governmental reorganization proposals in metropolitan areas. New governmental forms can be created by *fait accompli* of state legislatures. In regard to violence to popular sovereignty, remember that the state legislature is a representative and responsive body, accountable to the whole state polity, not just the voters of some minor suburb. Such an approach is used regularly in other democracies. The Toronto and London reorganizations are notable results of this method.

Second, consider cutting off all federal and state funds to municipalities and other metropolitan governments that are below a certain population level. Current financial assistance programs support the continuance of many of these governments. Consideration should also be given to eliminating funds for many existing limited-purpose governments. Alternatively, the state could impose a two-tier "local federalism" on the metropolitan areas, delegating responsibility for area-wide functions to an area-wide authority. Federal and state fiscal support would then be allocated on a rational, functional approach. In a few areas this has been done with reasonable success, for example, Miami-Dade County; however, its rarity suggests, again, the need for state legislative action rather than local referenda.

Some small states could become classical city-states. The state would assume responsibility for all functions, or at least all area-wide functions. Several small, but increasingly urbanized states, such as Rhode Island and Hawaii, lend themselves to this solution.

Another suggestion is that the federal government issue some type of federal charter to the many interstate metropolitan areas. This charter would grant certain legislative and financial powers as well as permit area-wide functions across state boundaries.

These proposals may seem radical. However, the destruction of our physical environment, the mounting and almost uncontrollable rate of crime and violence, and the continued deterioration of vital service capabilities *are* radical. Unconventional solutions are needed. Further, perceived radicalism pales in face of the demands by much of the New Left for total destruction of the system.

The Future?

This returns us to a question posed earlier: Are the suggestions for financing state and local governments and for the restructuring of the metropolitan areas politically feasible? At this time, the answer must be an unqualified "No!"

The American political system is basically conservative and incremental. Past experience shows that we only modify and change slightly the existing arrangements rather than seek new structures. Instead of major new approaches to financing state and local governments, we try to oil the "squeak points" of fiscal federalism, to use Grodzins's term.[27] Instead of creating a metropolitan general-purpose government to deal with area problems, we try to get along with councils of governments and other voluntary cooperative devices that give the appearance of area-wide capability but lack any real power.

The American system works on the basis of a biological stimulus-response activation. Without real stimulus for change, commitment to change will not occur; without the requisite commitment for change, the status quo will prevail.

How is this commitment produced? It is doubtful that it can be artificially manufactured. Rather, such a commitment appears to be a collective response to a crisis situation. Our perception of the American system's process of change is shown in Diagram 2.

Diagram 2.
Stimulus-Response Model of the American Political System

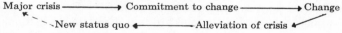

Major crisis ⟶ Commitment to change ⟶ Change
⟵ New status quo ⟵ Alleviation of crisis ⟵

What type of crisis is needed? History indicates it must be of major proportions. The economic shock and threat to individual security of the Great Depression changed our political system from a basically *laissez-faire* one to a positive, socially and economically intervening welfare system. The attack on Pearl Harbor turned us from a peace-demanding isolationist country to the military giant of World War II. The Soviet threat produced an American foreign policy and world posture unlike any experienced before in our history. The cultural shock of Selma, Alabama, and other civil rights activities of the early 1960s created a commitment to change the political and legal status of black Americans, although the shock was apparently not strong enough to change the blacks' social and economic plight.

As a nation, we have not experienced a stimulus great enough to produce a national urban policy nor the basic fiscal and structural adjustments needed to implement that policy. Why have urban riots of the 1960s not stimulated a commitment? While the answer is uncertain, there are increasing indications that they were perceived as *black* outbursts of violence, in some way a continuation of earlier racial disturbances. The riots were not viewed as a symptom of an urban crisis affecting the whole society. By the time the truth became apparent, much of the American public, numbed by a decade of violence, was unresponsive to the crisis stimulus.

What type of stimulus is needed to produce the commitment to change that will make some of the above suggestions politically feasible? This is impossible to answer, of course, but certain macabre possibilities suggest themselves: total violent destruction of one of our great cities; a race or race-class war; a "black fog" like that of London, where the neglected environment kills thousands; or the total collapse of services in some large cities. Hopefully, we will react to far less tragic events, such as the economic collapse of some large cities or states, or the repeated breakdown of certain services.

It should be noted that the authors' explanation of how the system operates is not a condemnation. Indeed, such a model ensures the generally beneficial aspects of day-to-day order and predictability. A political system that did not ensure order and permitted rather continuous deep and basic changes would destroy its parallel social and economic systems.[28]

Additionally, it must be explicitly noted that attention paid to infrastructural and institutional problems of state and local systems does not minimize the importance of such problems as racism, housing shortages, welfare inadequacies and inequities, transportation breakdowns. Rather, we maintain that solution of such problems is increasingly difficult, if not impossible, without prior solution of the infrastructural problems.

What, then, of the future of state and local government and American federalism? In sum, in certain areas, particularly in the renewed viability of state governments, the past few decades brought changes that give cause for increased optimism. Certain defects in the system, however, especially the fiscal structure of American federalism and the governmental structure of metropolitan areas, makes solution of many problems increasingly difficult.

Without a major stimulus to correct these defects, only partial solutions will be offered. These solutions may prevent total breakdown of the system, but the spectre of increasing crime, threatened riots, dangerous destruction of our environment, and unacceptable housing, education, welfare, and transportation will continue to face us well into the foreseeable future. To return to Wood's observation, "We may not face catastrophe, but this is no reason for countenancing . . . the hundred and one irritations which surround us."[29]

Notes

1. The literature of the forces of centralization is profuse and need not be mentioned here. Two excellent studies of the forces of decentralization are Thomas M. Franck (ed.), *Why Federations Fail: An Inquiry into*

484   *The Future*

the Requisites for Successful Federalism (New York: New York University
Press, 1968); and William H. Riker, *Federalism: Origin, Operation, Significance* (Boston: Little, Brown and Company, 1964).

2. Riker, *Federalism, op. cit.*, p. 129.

3. *Ibid.*, p. 136. See also, Arthur N. Holcombe, "The Coercion of
States in a Federal System," in Arthur W. Macmahon (ed.), *Federalism:
Mature and Emergent* (New York: Doubleday & Company, Inc., 1955),
pp. 115–136. One author advances the interesting proposal that it is not
the structure of the party system per se that acts as a decentralizer;
rather, it is the difference between the "in" party (Democrats) acting, for
obvious reasons, as centralizers, and the "out" party (Republicans) acting
as decentralizers. See William Buchanan, "Politics and Federalism: Party
or Anti-Party?" *The Annals of the American Academy of Political and Social
Science*, vol. 350 (May 1965), pp. 107–115.

4. For a general review of this part of the literature on federalism
see, A. H. Birch, "Approaches to the Study of Federalism," *Political
Studies*, vol. 14 (February 1966), pp. 15–33; and Carl J. Friedrich, *Man
and His Government* (New York: McGraw-Hill Book Company, 1963), pp.
585–609.

5. The correlative statement is, of course, also true: namely, that
the ability of the national government to meet demands placed on it
will determine the existence of our whole form of government as we now
know it.

6. For analysis of these trends, see James E. Maxwell, *Financing
State and Local Governments* (Revised edition; Washington, D.C.: The
Brookings Institution, 1969); and Frederick C. Mosher and Orville F.
Poland, *The Costs of American Governments: Facts, Trends, Myths* (New
York: Dodd, Mead & Co., 1964).

7. Ken Hartnett, "Lacking Funds, Larger Cities Cut Services,"
The Washington Post, August 7, 1969, sec. F, p. 2.

8. Quoted in *ibid.*

9. Robert C. Wood, "The Metropolitan Government, 1975: An
Extrapolation of Trends," *The American Political Science Review*, vol. 52
(1958), p. 112.

10. *Ibid.*, p. 119.

11. Roy W. Bahl, Jr., and Robert J. Saunders, "Determinants of
Changes in State and Local Expenditures," *National Tax Journal*, vol. 18
(1965), p. 52. For a more recent analysis, see Thomas F. Pogue and L. G.
Sgontz, "The Effect of Grants-in-Aid on State-Local Spending," *National
Tax Journal*, vol. 21 (1968), pp. 190–199.

12. See, for example, Alan K. Campbell, "National-State-Local Systems of Government and Intergovernmental Aid," *The Annals of the
American Academy of Political and Social Science*, vol. 359 (May 1965),
pp. 94–106; and articles mentioned in footnote 11, above. These studies,
of course, only show correlations, not causality.

13. Deil Wright, *Federal Grants-in-Aid: Perspectives and Alternatives*
(Washington, D.C.: American Enterprise Institute for Public Policy Research, 1968), p. 49.

14. For a summary of recent revenue sharing bills introduced to
Congress, see Advisory Commission on Intergovernmental Relations, *Fiscal
Balance*, vol. 1 (Washington, D.C.: U.S. Government Printing Office,
1967).

15. Personal letter from William Anderson to John Rouse of October 28, 1969 (authors' files); see also, William Anderson, "The Myths of
Tax Sharing," *Public Administration Review*, vol. 28 (February 1968),
pp. 10–14.

16. Jack L. Walker, "The Diffusion of Innovations Among the

American States," *American Political Science Review*, vol. 63 (September 1969), pp. 880–899.

17. For an elaboration on this theme, see Murray Edelman, *The Symbolic Uses of Politics* (Urbana: University of Illinois Press, 1964).

18. See, for example, David Brady and Douglas Edmonds, "One Man, One Vote: So What?" *Trans-action*, March 1967, pp. 41–46; Thomas R. Dye, *Politics, Economics, and the Public: Policy Outcomes in the American States* (Chicago: Rand McNally & Co., 1966); Herbert Jacob, "The Consequences of Malapportionment: A Note of Caution," *Social Forces*, vol. 43 (December 1964), pp. 260–266; and Ira Sharkansky, "Voting Behavior of Metropolitan Congressmen: Prospects for Change with Reapportionment," *Journal of Politics*, vol. 28 (November 1966), pp. 774–793.

19. See U.S. Department of Commerce, Bureau of the Census, *Census of Governments 1967* (Washington, D.C.: U.S. Government Printing Office, 1968), *passim*.

20. Victor Jones, *Metropolitan Government* (Chicago: University of Chicago Press, 1942).

21. See, for example, Advisory Commission on Intergovernmental Relations, *Fiscal Balance*, *op. cit.*, vol. 2; and Robert C. Wood and Vladimir Almendinger, *1400 Governments: The Political Economy of the New York Metropolitan Region* (Cambridge: Harvard University Press, 1961).

22. Roscoe C. Martin, *Metropolis in Transition: Local Government Adaptation to Changing Urban Needs*, a report prepared for the Housing and Home Finance Agency under the Urban Studies and Housing Research Program (Washington, D.C.: U.S. Government Printing Office, 1963). Martin's study is now out of print. The reader may wish to consult a summary of his 1963 report in Roscoe C. Martin, "Action in Metropolis—I," *National Civic Review*, vol. 52 (1963), pp. 302–307; and *ibid.*, Part II, pp. 363–367, 371. For a slightly different taxonomy, see Advisory Commission on Intergovernmental Relations, *Alternate Approaches to Governmental Reorganization in Metropolitan Areas*, Report A-11 (Washington, D.C.: U.S. Government Printing Office, 1962).

23. Joseph F. Zimmerman, "Metropolitan Ecumenism: The Road to the Promised Land," *Journal of Urban Law*, vol. 44 (Spring 1967), p. 437.

24. *Ibid.*, p. 441. For a summary of federal activities in this area, see John C. Bollens and Henry J. Schmandt, *The Metropolis* (2nd edition, revised; New York: Harper & Row, Publishers, 1970), pp. 226–250; and Parris N. Glendening, "The Federal Role in Regional Planning Councils: Trends and Implications," paper delivered at the 1970 annual meeting of the Southeastern Regional Science Association, New Orleans, 1970 (mimeographed).

25. See, for example, the statement of Executive Director of the North Texas Council of Governments, William Pitstick, "From Manager to COG Director: Journey to the Unknown," *Public Management*, vol. 5 (January 1969), p. 9; and Bollens and Schmandt, *The Metropolis*, *op. cit.*, p. 443.

26. James Q. Wilson, "The Mayors vs. the Cities," *The Public Interest*, no. 16 (Summer 1969), pp. 25–37; and Parris N. Glendening, "Revenue Sharing versus Grants-in-Aid: Political Implications," paper delivered at the 1969 annual meeting of the American Society for Public Administration, Miami, 1969 (mimeographed).

27. Morton Grodzins, "The Federal System," in The American Assembly, *Goals for Americans* (Englewood Cliffs: Prentice-Hall, Inc., 1960), pp. 265–282.

28. The reader should recognize that this is a preliminary statement of the model. Further clarification and testing is clearly needed.

29. Wood, "Metropolitan Government," *op. cit.*, p. 119.